PEACE TREATIES AND INTERNATIONAL LAW IN EUROPEAN HISTORY

In the formation of the modern law of nations, peace treaties played a pivotal role. Many basic principles and rules that governed and still govern the relations between states were introduced and elaborated in the great peace treaties from the Renaissance onwards. Nevertheless, until recently few scholars have studied these primary sources of the law of nations from a juridical perspective. In this edited collection, specialists from all over Europe, including legal and diplomatic historians, international lawyers and an International Relations theorist, analyse peace treaty practice from the late fifteenth century to the Peace of Versailles of 1919. Important emphasis is given to the doctrinal debate about peace treaties and the influence of older, Roman and medieval concepts on modern practices. This book goes back further in time beyond the epochal Peace Treaties of Westphalia of 1648, and this broader perspective allows for a reassessment of the role of the sovereign state in the modern international legal order.

RANDALL LESAFFER is Professor of Legal History at Tilburg University. He also teaches Cultural History at the University of Leuven Law Faculty, and International Law at the Royal Higher Defence Academy of the Belgian Army. He has published on the history of international law and international relations of the early modern era and the twentieth century, as well as more specifically on treaty law and the laws of war.

PEACE TREATIES AND INTERNATIONAL LAW IN EUROPEAN HISTORY

From the Late Middle Ages to World War One

Edited by

RANDALL LESAFFER

CAMBRIDGE
UNIVERSITY PRESS

CAMBRIDGE UNIVERSITY PRESS
Cambridge, New York, Melbourne, Madrid, Cape Town, Singapore, São Paulo

Cambridge University Press
The Edinburgh Building, Cambridge CB2 8RU, UK

Published in the United States of America by Cambridge University Press, New York

www.cambridge.org
Information on this title: www.cambridge.org/9780521827249

© Cambridge University Press 2004

This publication is in copyright. Subject to statutory exception
and to the provisions of relevant collective licensing agreements,
no reproduction of any part may take place without the written
permission of Cambridge University Press.

First published 2004

A catalogue record for this publication is available from the British Library

Library of Congress Cataloguing in Publication data
Peace treaties and international law in European history: from the late Middle Ages to
World War One / edited by Randall Lesaffer.
p. cm.
Includes bibliographical references and index.
ISBN 0 521 82724 8 (hardback)
1. Peace treaties – History.   2. Europe – Foreign relations – Treaties.   3. International law –
Europe – History.   I. Lesaffer, Randall.
KZ184.5.P43   2004
341.6´6´09 – dc22   2003061319

ISBN 978-0-521-82724-9 hardback

Transferred to digital printing 2007

CONTENTS

List of contributors   *page* viii
Acknowledgements   xi
Table of treaties   xii
List of abbreviations   xxi

1 Introduction   1
   Randall Lesaffer

PART I **Peace treaties and international law from Lodi to Versailles (1454–1920)**

2 Peace treaties from Lodi to Westphalia   9
   Randall Lesaffer

3 Peace treaties from Westphalia to the Revolutionary Era   45
   Heinz Duchhardt

4 Peace treaties from Paris to Versailles   59
   Heinhard Steiger

PART II **Thinking peace: voices from the past**

5 *Vestigia pacis.* The Roman peace treaty: structure or event?   103
   Christian Baldus

6 The influence of medieval Roman law on peace treaties   147
   Karl-Heinz Ziegler

7   The kiss of peace   162
    Hanna Vollrath

8   Martinus Garatus Laudensis on treaties   184
    Alain Wijffels

9   The importance of medieval canon law and the scholastic tradition for the emergence of the early modern international legal order   198
    Dominique Bauer

10 The Peace Treaties of Westphalia as an instance of the reception of Roman law   222
    Laurens Winkel

PART III   **Thinking peace: towards a better future**

11 Peace treaties, *bonne foi* and European civility in the Enlightenment   241
    Marc Bélissa

12 Peace, security and international organisations: the German international lawyers and the Hague Conferences   254
    Ingo Hueck

13 Consent and caution: Lassa Oppenheim and his reaction to World War I   270
    Mathias Schmoeckel

14 Talking peace: social science, peace negotiations and the structure of politics   289
    Andreas Osiander

PART IV   **Making peace: aspects of treaty practice**

15 The *ius foederis* re-examined: the Peace of Westphalia and the constitution of the Holy Roman Empire   319
    Ronald G. Asch

16 The peace treaties of the Ottoman Empire with European Christian powers   338
    Karl-Heinz Ziegler

17 Peace and prosperity: commercial aspects of
    peacemaking   365
    Stephen Neff

18 The 1871 Peace Treaty between France and Germany and the
    1919 Peace Treaty of Versailles   382
    Christian Tomuschat

PART V **Conclusion**

19 Conclusion   399
    Randall Lesaffer

    Appendix
    Tractatus de confederatione, pace, & conventionibus
    Principum   412
    Martinus Garatus Laudensis, ed. Alain Wijffels

    Index   448

CONTRIBUTORS

RONALD ASCH is Professor of Modern History at the University of Freiburg.

CHRISTIAN BALDUS is Professor of Roman Law at the University of Cologne and currently also at the University of Heidelberg.

DOMINIQUE BAUER is a post-doctoral research fellow at the Catholic University of Leuven.

MARC BÉLISSA is Professor of Modern History at the Sorbonne University in Paris.

HEINZ DUCHHARDT is Professor of Modern History at the University of Mainz. He is also Director of the Institute for European History, Department of Universal History.

INGO HUECK is Associate Professor of History of International Law at the Humboldt University in Berlin and Permanent Research Advisor of the Hertie Institute for Public Management of the European School of Management and Technology in Munich and Berlin.

RANDALL LESAFFER is Professor of Legal History at Tilburg University. He also teaches Cultural History at the Leuven Law Faculty and International Law at the Royal High Defence Institute of the Belgian Armed Forces.

STEPHEN NEFF is a Lecturer in International Law at the University of Edinburgh.

ANDREAS OSIANDER is a post-doctoral research fellow at the Department of Jurisprudence and Legal History of Tilburg University.

MATHIAS SCHMOECKEL is Professor of Legal History at the University of Bonn.

HEINHARD STEIGER, now retired, was Professor of International Law at the University of Giessen.

CHRISTIAN TOMUSCHAT is Professor of International Law at the Humboldt University of Berlin.

HANNA VOLLRATH is Professor of Medieval History at the University of Bochum.

ALAIN WIJFFELS is Professor of Legal History at the Catholic University of Louvain-la-Neuve.

LAURENS WINKEL is Professor of Legal History at the Erasmus University of Rotterdam.

KARL-HEINZ ZIEGLER, now retired, was Professor of Roman Law at the University of Hamburg.

ACKNOWLEDGEMENTS

This book is the result of a joint effort, not only by the contributors, but also by the many persons who had a hand in the complex and difficult process of the editing and publication. In the first place, I want to thank the Department of Jurisprudence and Legal History of the Tilburg Law Faculty, which endorsed this project by lending its facilities and personnel, as well as the Schoordijk Institute of the same Faculty. In particular, I want to extend my gratitude to Marjolijn Verhoeven, of the Schoordijk Institute, who organised the March 2001 Tilburg colloquium. Without Hildegard Penn, one of our Faculty's English editors, this project would have proven too much. I also want to thank the Department of Jurisprudence and Legal History's secretary Marianne Stolp, as well as our research assistants Aziza Azizi, Eelkje van der Kuilen-Stap, Laetitia Laman, Luigi Corrias and Tomas Roosenschoon who lent their support. I am also grateful for the help of Jo Alaerts of the Leuven Department for Roman Law and Legal History. Finally, the efforts of the staff of Cambridge University Press, in particular Finola O'Sullivan, Nikki Burton, Jackie Warren and Frances Brown as well as the support of James Crawford, Whewell Professor of International Law at the University of Cambridge, cannot go unmentioned.

TABLE OF TREATIES

BC

509, Rome–Carthage (2 SA 16) 121
321 (?), *Pax Caudina* (3 SA 27) 134
306, Philinus (3 SA 53) 130
241, Lutatius (3 SA 173) 130
226/225, Ebro Treaty (3 SA 201) 130, 131
202/201, Rome–Carthage (3 SA 291) 127

AD

562, Rome–Persia (Blockley 70) 148
587, Burgundy–Austrasia 149
1164, Alliance Emperor–England 176
1177, Lombardic League (MGH-C I, 360 no. 259) 152
1177, Venice (MGH-D X-3, 202 no. 687) 152
1183, Constance (MGH-D X-4, 68 no. 848) 151, 155–6, 158–9, 188, 189, 196
1199, Péronne, Flanders–France (CUD I-1, 125; CIGD 1 – date 1099 wrong there) 152
1199, Dinant, Flanders–Bar (CUD I-1, 125; MCIGD II, 194) 152, 159
31 May 1325, Paris (CUD I-2, 78; CIGD 109) 158, 159
8 May 1360, Brétigny (CUD II-1, 7; CIGD 208) 149
19 August 1374 (CUD II-1, 96; CGD II, 1270) 159
21 September 1435, Arras (CUD II-2, 304) 22
1435, Brest (CUD III-1, 13) 149–50, 158–159
1446, Ottoman Empire–Venice (*Orientalia Christiana Periodica* 15 (1949), 225) 340
9 April 1454, Lodi (CUD III-1, 202) 4, 18, 41
30 August 1454, Venice (CUD III-1, 221) 28, 30, 35
5 October 1465, Conflans (CUD III-1, 335) 15–17, 39
10 September 1468, Ancenis (CUD III-1, 392) 16, 24–25
14 October 1468, Péronne (CUD III-1, 394) 16, 19, 39
8 August 1470, Naples (CUD III-1, 408) 30, 35
16 February 1471, London (CUD III-1, 601) 38
25 July 1474, Westminster 1 (CUD III-1, 485) 18, 21, 36

25 July 1474, Westminster 2 (CUD III-1, 486) 36
25 July 1474, Westminster 3 (CUD III-1, 487) 36
25 July 1474, Westminster 4 (CUD III-1, 488) 36
25 July 1474, Westminster 5 (CUD III-1, 489) 36
29 August 1475, Amiens 1 (CUD III-1, 501) 28, 17–18
29 August 1475, Amiens 3 (CUD III-1, 504) 40–41
13 September 1475, Soleuvre (CUD III-1, 505) 38
13 February 1478, London (CUD III-2, 19) 38
25 January 1479, Constantinople (ADGMA III, 295)
12 January 1482, Adrianople (ADGMA III) 341
23 December 1482, Arras (CUD III-2, 100) 17–19, 23, 25, 39, 40, 41, 42
7 August 1484, Bagnolo (CUD III-2, 128) 28, 30, 31
20 August 1488, Sablé (CUD III-2, 209) 16, 40
3 November 1492, Etaples (CUD III-2, 291; CIGD 456) 21, 34–35, 41, 42, 151
19 January 1493, Barcelona (CUD III-2, 297; CIGD 463) 23, 28, 30, 39, 150, 158–159
23 May 1493, Senlis (CUD III-2, 303) 25, 35, 40, 42
1 January 1495, Rome (CUD III-2, 318) 28
14 December 1502 (ADGMA III, 344) 341
22 September 1504, Blois 1 (TIE III-1, 52) 23, 25
10 December 1508, Cambrai 1 (TIE III-1, 175) 23–25, 41, 19, 29, 27, 30
10 December 1508, Cambrai 2 (TIE III-1, 202) 19, 24–25
7 August 1514, London (CUD IV-1, 183) 19, 30–31, 35, 41–42
24 March 1515, Paris (TIE III-2, 3) 25, 29, 34, 342
13 August 1516, Noyon (TIE III-2, 73) 23, 25, 28, 34
11 March 1517, Cambrai (TIE III-2, 181) 25–26
2 October 1518, London (text of ratification by Charles V of 1519, TIE III-2, 217–35) 12, 35, 27, 30–31
6 June 1520, Guines 1 (CUD IV-1, 312) 22
6 June 1520, Guines 2 (Rymer VI-1, 187) 22
14 January 1526, Madrid (TIE III-3, 122) 17–19, 21, 23, 25–26, 28, 29, 30, 31, 32, 35, 39, 41, 42
29 June 1529, Barcelona (CUD IV-2, 1) 28, 31
5 August 1529, Cambrai 1 (CUD IV-2, 7) 23, 25, 28, 29, 31, 32, 41, 26
5 August 1529, Cambrai 2 (CUD IV-2, 42) 31, 32, 41, 42
February 1535, Ottoman Empire–France (RAI I, 83 in French; FHIG II, 71) 342
20 October 1540, Ottoman Empire–Venice (CUD IV-2, 197) 345
18 September 1544, Crépy (CUD IV-2, 279) 25, 26, 27, 30, 32, 33, 35, 38, 232–233, 237, 19, 21, 23
2 April 1559, Câteau-Cambrésis 1 (CUD V-1, 29) 23, 28, 30, 38, 19, 21, 32–33, 41
2 April 1559, Câteau-Cambrésis 2 (CUD V-1, 31) 32, 41, 42, 33
3 April 1559, Câteau-Cambrésis 1 (CUD V-1, 34) 41, 42
24 June 1564, Ottoman Empire–Venice (CUD V-1, 140)

18 October 1569, Constantinople (RAI I, 88) 342
26 May 1571, Rome (CUD V-1, 203) 30
31 October 1596, The Hague (CUD V-1, 531) 33
2 May 1598, Vervins (CUD V-1, 561) 17, 18, 23, 27, 28, 30, 33–35, 41, 42
17 January 1601, Susa (CUD V-2, 10) 33, 39
20 May 1604, Constantinople (RAI I, 93) 343
18 August 1604, London (CUD V-2, 32) 33, 35, 41, 42, 30–31
11 November 1606, Zstivatorok (RAI I, 103) 345, 346, 351
9 April 1609, Antwerp (CUD V-2, 99) 38
1612, Ottoman Empire–Republic (CUD V-2, 20) 344
21 June 1615, Asti (CUD V-2, 271) 39
1 July 1615, Vienna (CUD V-2, 264) 346
1 May 1616, Vienna (RAI I, 113; CUD V-2, 280) 346
9 October 1621, Khotin/Dnestr (CUD V-2, 371, French abridged text) 347
12 May 1629, Lübeck (CUD V-2, 584) 21
15 November 1630, Madrid (CUD V-2, 619) 21, 23, 27, 41, 368
November 1634, Pirna (II BA NF X, 4, no. 569) 329
30 May 1635, Prague (CUD V-2, 88; II BA NF X, 4, no. 554A) 39, 323, 327–332
13 August 1645, Bromsebrö (CUD VI-1, 314) 41
30 January 1648, Münster (1 CTS 1) 3, 6, 13, 14, 41, 222, 224, 229, 230–231, 237
24 October 1648, Münster (APW III B, I-1, 1–49) 3, 6, 9, 10, 13, 14, 20, 35, 36, 43, 44, 45, 46, 48, 49, 51, 56, 55, 52, 70, 74, 82, 85, 92, 157, 222, 224, 229, 237, 241, 242, 251, 319, 389, 404
24 October 1648, Osnabrück (APW III B, I-1, 95–170) 3, 6, 9, 10, 13, 14, 20, 35, 36, 43, 44, 45, 46, 48, 49, 51, 56, 55, 52, 70, 74, 82, 85, 92, 157, 222, 224, 229, 236, 237, 241, 242, 251, 319, 389, 404
5 April 1654, Westminster (3 CTS 225) 310
7 November 1659, Pyrenees (5 CTS 325) 27, 368
10 August 1664, Vasvar (CUD VI-3, 23 in Latin; 8 CTS VIII 167 in Latin and French; RAI I, 121 in French) 351
31 July 1667, Breda (10 CTS 231) 234–235, 369, 370
17 February 1668, Breda FCN (10 CTS X 441) 369
5 September 1669, Candia (CUD VII-1, 119 Latin abridged text; 11 CTS 209 in Latin and French; RAI I, 132 in French) 351–352
18 October 1672, Buczacz (CUD VII-1, 212; 12 CTS 393) 352
5 June 1673, Ottoman Empire–France (RAI I, 136; CUD VII-1, 231; 12 CTS 463) 347
19 February 1674, Westminster (13 CTS 123) 369
10 December 1674, FCN (13 CTS 255) 368, 369, 370
1675, Ottoman Empire–England (RAI I, 146 in French; CUD VII-1, 297; 13 CTS 429) 348
16 October 1676, Zoravno (CUD VII-1, 325; 14 CTS 131) 352
10 August 1678, Nijmegen (14 CTS 365) 27, 369

10 August 1678, Nijmegen FCN (14 CTS 399) 27, 369
17 August 1678, Nijmegen (14 CTS 425) 27, 369
19 August 1678, Nijmegen (14 CTS 431) 27, 369
17 September 1678, Nijmegen (14 CTS 441) 27, 369
12 September 1679, Constantinople (CUD VII-1, 435; 15 CTS 235) 352
15 September 1680, Ottoman Empire–Republic (RAI I, 169; CUD VII-2, 4; 15 CTS 471) 349
5 March 1684, Linz (CUD VII-2, 71; 17 CTS 1; FHIG II, 350 in Latin) 352
20 September 1697, Ryswick, France–Republic (21 CTS 347) 369
20 September 1697, Ryswick, FCN France–Republic (21 CTS 371) 369
20 September 1697, Ryswick, France–England (21 CTS 409) 369
20 September 1697, Ryswick, France–Spain (21 CTS 453) 369
26 January 1699, Karlowitz, Ottoman Empire–Roman Emperor (RAI I, 182; CUD VII-2, 448 in Latin; 22 CTS 219) 50
26 January 1699, Karlowitz, Ottoman Empire–Poland (CUD VII-2, 451; 22 CTS XXII 247) 347
26 January 1699, Ottoman Empire–Venice (CUD VII-2, 453; 22 CTS 265) 353
13 June 1700, Constantinople (RAI I, 197; 23 CTS 25) 353–354
1 April (?) 1710, Constantinople (CUD suppl. II-2, 78; 26 CTS 457) 354, 355
16 April 1712, Ottoman Empire–Russia (CUD VIII-1, 297; 27 CTS 231) 397, 354, 355
11 April 1713, Utrecht, France–Britain (27 CTS 475) 48, 53, 56, 242, 315, 369
11 April 1713, Utrecht FCN, France–Britain (28 CTS 1) 48, 53, 242, 315, 369–370
11 April 1713, Utrecht, France–Republic (28 CTS 37) 48, 53, 57, 242, 315, 369
11 April 1713, Utrecht FCN, France–Republic (28 CTS 83) 48, 53, 57, 246, 315, 369
11 April 1713, Utrecht, France–Savoy (28 CTS 123) 48, 53, 242, 315, 369
11 April 1713, Utrecht, France–Prussia (28 CTS 141) 48, 53, 242, 315, 369
11 April 1713, Utrecht, France–Portugal (28 CTS 169) 48, 55, 53, 57, 242, 315, 369
5 July (?) 1713, Adrianople, Ottoman Empire–Russia (CUD suppl. II-2, 110; 28 CTS 251; RAI I, 203) 53, 354, 355
13 July 1713, Utrecht, Spain–Savoy (28 CTS 269) 53, 315
13 July 1713, Utrecht, Britain–Spain (28 CTS 295) 53, 315, 370
9 December 1713, Utrecht FCN, Britain–Spain (28 CTS 429) 53, 315
6 February 1715, Utrecht, Portugal–Spain (29 CTS 201) 55, 315
21 July 1718, Pessarowicz, Ottoman Empire–Roman Emperor (RAI I, 208 in Latin; 30 CTS 341) 347, 354
21 July 1718, Pessarowicz, Ottoman Empire–Venice (CUD VIII-1, 524; 30 CTS 371) 235–236, 347, 354–355
27 July 1718, Pessarowicz (CUD VIII-1, 528 in Latin; 30 CTS 395; RAI I, 220 in French) 347, 354–355
5/16 November 1720, Constantinople (RAI I, 227; 31 CTS 271) 355
24 January 1724, Cambrai (31 CTS 455) 45
15 May 1736, Vienna, France–Emperor–Russia (34 CTS 373) 52

15 May 1736, Vienna, France–Emperor–Poland (34 CTS 381) 52
18 September 1739, Belgrade, Ottoman Empire–Roman Emperor (35 CTS 381; RAI I, 243) 347
18 September 1739, Belgrade, Ottoman Empire–Russia (35 CTS 425; RAI I, 258 in French) 347, 356
7 April 1740, Constantinople (RAI I, 270; 36 CTS 9) 349, 350
28 May 1740, Constantinople (RAI I, 271; 36 CTS 41) 349, 350
18 October 1748, Aix-la-Chapelle (38 CTS 297) 48–49, 52–53
23 March 1761, Constantinople (RAI I, 315; 42 CTS 69) 350, 351
12 February 1763, Paris (42 CTS 279) 53
15 February 1763, Hubertusburg (42 CTS 347) 52
21 July 1774, Kücük Kainarci (45 CTS 349; RAI I, 319) 357–359, 361
13 May 1779, Teschen (47 CTS 153) 52
14 September 1782, Ottoman Empire–Spain (RAI I, 344; 48 CTS 123) 351
3 September 1783, Paris (48 CTS 437) 369
20 May 1784, Paris (49 CTS 65) 258
26 September 1786, Paris FCN (50 CTS 71) 369
4 August 1791, Sistova (RAI II, 6; 51 CTS 211) 347, 358
9 January 1792, Jassy (RAI II, 16; 51 CTS 279) 358–359
19 November 1794, Washington, Jay Treaty (52 CTS 249)
15 June 1802, Paris (RAI II, 51; 56 CTS 375) 359
5 January 1809, Dardenelles (RAI II, 81 in French; 60 CTS 323) 359
28 May 1812, Bucharest (RAI II, 86; 62 CTS 25) 360
30 May 1814, Paris (Strupp I) 59, 60, 72, 73, 74, 79, 80, 82, 86, 87, 91
20 July 1814, Paris (63 CTS 297) 59, 60, 73, 74, 87, 373
14 August 1814, London (63 CTS 331) 60, 373
25 August 1814, Berlin (63 CTS 345) 60, 373
24 December 1814, Ghent (63 CTS 421) 60, 369
8 June 1815, Federation Act (Strupp I) 88
9 June 1815, Vienna Congress Act (Strupp I, 163) 60, 74, 79, 86, 88, 92, 93, 260
3 July 1815, Algiers (65 CTS 33) 374
3 July 1815, Ghent FCN (65 CTS 41) 369
20 November 1815, Paris (Strupp I) 85, 87, 91
3 April 1816, Algiers, Algiers–Sardinia (65 CTS 471) 374
3 April 1816, Algiers, Algiers–Sicily (65 CTS 479) 374
4 July 1823, Buenos Aires–Spain (68 CTS 261) 374
18 April 1825, Bogota FCN (75 CTS 195) 372
14 September 1829, Adrianople (RAI II, 166; 80 CTS 83) 360, 361, 373
22 September 1829, Colombia–Peru (80 CTS 97) 375
29 October 1834, London FCN (84 CTS 433) 372
9 March 1839, Vera Cruz (88 CTS 345) 374
29 October 1840, Buenos Aires (91 CTS 111) 374

13 July 1841, Straits Convention (92 CTS) 361
29 August 1842, Nanking (93 CTS 465) 83, 85, 95
9 March 1846, Lahore (NRG IX, 80) 83
26 March 1846, Spain–Uruguay (NRG IX, 92) 91
2 July 1850, Berlin (II NRG XV, 340) 73, 78, 80, 81
8 May 1852, Santo Domingo (NRG XVII-2, 313) 79
14/26 January 1855, Simoda (NRG XVI-2, 454) 83
30 March 1856, Paris (II NRG XV, 770; RAI III, 70; 114 CTS 409; FHIG III-1, 19) 73, 74, 87, 89, 93, 94, 361, 362
15 April 1856, Paris (RAI III, 88; 114 CTS 497) 87, 89, 94, 362
4 March 1857, Paris (NRG XVI-2, 114; 116 CTS 319) 83
10 November 1859, Zurich Conference Protocols (121 CTS 163) 88, 372–373
10 November 1859, Zurich, Austria–France (NRG XVI-2, 516; 121 CTS 145) 72, 80, 88, 372–374
10 November 1859, Zurich, Austria–France–Sardinia (NRG XVI-2, 531) 88
11 July 1859, Villafranca (NRG, XVI-2, 516) 72
25 January 1860, Guayaquil (121 CTS 309) 374
8 June 1862, Saigon (NRG XVII, 169) 95
1 January 1864, Colombia–Ecuador (129 CTS 31) 373
22 August 1864, Geneva Convention for the Amelioration of the Treatment of Wounded in the Field (129 CTS 361) 263
17 January 1865, Peru–Spain (130 CTS 405) 93, 375
26 July 1866, Nikolsburg (Preliminary Peace, NRG XVIII, 316) 72, 75, 85
26 July 1866, Nikolsburg (Armistice, NRG XVIII, 319) 71, 72, 75
13 August 1866, Berlin (NRG XVIII, 331; 133 CTS 21) 75, 80, 85, 87, 89
17 August 1866, Berlin (NRG XVIII, 333; 133 CTS 29) 75, 80, 81, 85, 87, 96
18 August 1866, Berlin, North German Federation Treaty (Huber II, 268; 133 CTS 39) 75, 80, 85, 87, 89
22 August 1866, Berlin (NRG XVIII, 336; 133 CTS 53) 75, 80, 85, 87, 96
23 August 1866, Prague (NRG XVIII, 344; 133 CTS 71) 75, 80, 82, 85, 87, 89
3 October 1866, Vienna (NRG XVIII, 405; 133 CTS 209) 75, 79
8 December 1870 (Huber II, 351) 89
28 January 1871 (143 CTS 5) 382
26 February 1871, Versailles (NRG XIX, 653) 6, 72, 73, 85, 88, 389, 391, 392
10 May 1871, Frankfurt (NRG XIX;143 CTS 163) 75, 78, 81, 85, 88, 94, 96, 372, 374, 382, 391–392, 387–388, 395
24 August 1873, Gandemian (146 CTS 345) 374
17 May 1865/22 July 1875, International Telegraph Convention (148 CTS 319)
3 March 1878, San Stefano (II NRG III, 246; RAI III, 509; 152 CTS 395) 72, 73, 87, 89, 362, 363
1 June 1878, Universal Postal Union (152 CTS 106)

13 July 1878, Berlin Congress Act (II NRG III, 449; RAI IV, 175; 153 CTS 171; partly in FHIG III-1, 38) 72, 74, 89–90, 362
26 May 1879, Sandornak (II NRG IV, 536) 83
14 August 1879, Paris (155 CTS 167) 374
12 June 1883, Lima (162 CTS 185) 372
20 October 1883, Lima (162 CTS 453) 373
26 February 1885, Congo Act (II NRG X, 414) 67, 79, 90–91
9 June 1885, FCN, France–China (167 CTS 431) 372, 374
13 January 1886, Amapala (167 CTS 295) 372–373
1890, Convention on Transport of Goods by Rail (173 CTS 75) 258
17 April 1895, Shimonoseki (Strupp II, 239; 181 CTS 217) 91
26 October 1896, Addis Ababa (II NRG XXV, 59; 183 CTS 423) 79, 375
6/18 September 1897, Constantinople (II NRG XXVIII, 715; 186 CTS 10) 72, 363
22 November/4 December 1897, Constantinople (II NRG XXVIII, 630; 186 CTS 89) 86, 94, 374–375
1899, Hague Convention on the Peaceful Settlement of Disputes (187 CTS 410) 70, 76, 258
13 February 1903, Washington, Britain–Venezuela Exchange of notes (192 CTS 413) 372
13 February 1903, Washington, Britain–Venezuela Treaty (192 CTS 414) 372
13 February 1903, Washington, Italy–Venezuela (192 CTS 418) 373
12 April 1903, Athens FCN (193 CTS 97) 375
23 August/5 September 1905, Portsmouth (Strupp II, 253) 91
18 October 1907, Hague Convention I for the Pacific Settlement of Disputes (205 CTS) 70, 76, 258
18 October 1907, Hague Convention II for the Limitation of the Employment of Force for the Recovery of Contract Debts (205 CTS 250) 70, 76, 258
18 October 1907, Hague Convention III Relating to Opening Hostilities (205 CTS 263) 70, 76, 258
18 October 1907, Hague Convention IV Respecting the Laws and Customs of War on Land (205 CTS 277) 70, 76, 258
18 October 1907, Hague Convention V Respecting the Rights and Duties of Neutral Powers and Persons in Case of War on Land (205 CTS 299) 70, 76, 258
18 October 1907, Hague Convention VI Relating to the Statute of Enemy Merchant Ships (205 CTS 305) 70, 76, 258
18 October 1907, Hague Convention VII Relating to the Conversion of Merchant Ships into Warships (205 CTS 319) 70, 76, 258
18 October 1907, Hague Convention VIII Relative to the Laying of Automatic Submarine Contact Mines (205 CTS 331) 70, 76, 258
18 October 1907, Hague Convention IX Concerning Bombardment by Naval Forces in Time of War (205 CTS 345) 70, 76, 258

18 October 1907, Hague Convention X for the Adaptation of Principles of
   the Geneva Convention to Maritime Warfare (205 CTS 359) 70, 76, 258
18 October 1907, Hague Convention XI Relative to Certain Restrictions with Regard
   to the Exercise of the Rights of Capture in Naval War (205 CTS 367) 70, 76, 258
18 October 1907, Hague Convention XII for the Establishment of an International
   Prize Court (205 CTS 381) 70, 76, 258
18 October 1907, Hague Convention XIII Concerning the Rights and Duties of
   Neutral Powers in Naval War (205 CTS 395) 70, 76, 258
11 October 1909, Automobile Circulation Convention (209 CTS 361) 258
18 October 1912, Lausanne Ouchy (217 CTS 160) 363, 372
30 May 1913, London (218 CTS) 363
28 July/10 August 1913, Bucharest (III NRG VIII, 61; Strupp II) 75, 82, 83, 96
29 September 1913, Turkey–Bulgaria (218 CTS 375) 373
1/14 March 1914, Constantinople (III NRG VIII, 643; 219 CTS 310)
9 February 1918, Brest-Litovsk (Strupp III, 79) 83, 86, 90
3 March 1918, Brest-Litovsk (Strupp III, 96) 83, 90
7 March 1918, Germany Finland (Strupp III, 125) 90
27 March 1918, Washington (Strupp III, 125; 223 CTS 172)
27 August 1918, Berlin (224 CTS 66) 90
11 November 1918, Compiègne (Strupp III, 229; 224 CTS 286) 71, 77, 382
28 June 1919, Versailles (Strupp IV, 140; 225 CTS 288) 4, 4, 6, 59, 60, 64, 73, 75, 77, 80,
   81, 83, 85, 87, 90, 92, 93, 95, 96, 98, 99, 271, 274, 275, 375, 376, 399, 401, 410
10 September 1919, Saint-Germain (Strupp IV, 1006; 226 CTS 8) 4, 59, 60, 64, 73, 75,
   77, 80, 81, 83, 85, 87, 90, 92, 93, 95, 96, 98, 99, 271, 274, 376, 399, 401
27 November 1919, Neuilly (Strupp V, 23; 226 CTS 332) 4, 59, 60, 64, 73, 75, 77, 80, 81,
   83, 85, 87, 92, 93, 95, 96, 98, 99, 271, 274, 376, 399, 401
4 June 1920, Trianon (Strupp V, 44) 4, 59, 60, 64, 73, 75, 77, 80, 81, 83, 85, 87, 90, 92,
   93, 95, 96, 98, 99, 271, 274, 399, 401
10 August 1920, Sèvres (Strupp V, 62; partly in FHIG III-2, 711 with German and
   English translations) 4, 59, 60, 64, 73, 75, 77, 80, 81, 83, 85, 87, 90, 92, 93, 95, 96,
   98, 99, 271, 274, 363, 399, 401
24 June 1923, Lausanne (28 UNTS 11, partly in FHIG III-2, 719 with German and
   English translations) 364, 376
17 August 1928, Paris, Briand–Kellogg Pact (94 LNTS 57) 256, 382, 410
26 June 1945, Charter of the United Nations (1 UNTS xvi) 87, 385, 410
10 February 1947, Paris, Peace with Bulgaria (41 UNTS 21) 377
10 February 1947, Paris, Peace with Hungary (41 UNTS 135) 377
10 February 1947, Paris, Peace with Italy (42 UNTS 3) 377
10 February 1947, Paris, Peace with Romania (42 UNTS 31) 377
10 February 1947, Paris, Peace with Finland (48 UNTS 203) 377
24 February 1949, Egypt-Israel (42 UNTS 251) 378–379
23 March 1949, Israel-Lebanon (42 UNTS 287) 378–379

3 April 1949, Israel-Jordan (42 UNTS 303) 378–379
20 July 1949, Israel-Syria (42 UNTS 327) 378–379
8 September 1951, Los Angeles (136 UNTS 45) 377
5 November 1954, Burma-Japan (251 UNTS 215) 377
19 October 1956, Soviet Union–Japan Joint Declaration (263 UNTS 99) 377
8 February 1957, Japan-Poland (318 UNTS 251) 377
19 October 1956, Soviet Union–Japan Trade Protocol (263 UNTS 119) 377
6 December 1957, Soviet Union–Japan (325 UNTS 35) 377
26 April 1958, Japan-Poland FCN (340 UNTS 291) 377
23 May 1969, Vienna Convention on Law of Treaties (8 ILM 679) 133, 163, 384
27 January 1973, Paris (935 UNTS 52) 378–379
30 May 1974, Israel-Syria 378–379
26 March 1979, Egypt-Israel (1136 UNTS 101) 380
26 October 1994, Arava (34 ILM 46) 380, 433

ABBREVIATIONS

ADGMA III   Franz Miklosich and Joseph Müller (eds.), *Acta et diplomata Graeca Medii Aevi*, vol. III: *Acta et diplomata res Graecas Italasque illustrantia* (Vienna, 1865, reprint 1968)
APW   Konrad Repgen (ed.), *Acta Pacis Westphalicae* (Münster, since 1962)
APW III, B, I-1   Antje Oschmann (ed.), *Die Friedensverträge mit Frankreich und Schweden. Urkunden* (Konrad Repgen (ed.), *Acta Pacis Westphalicae* III, B, I-1; Münster, 1998)
BA NF   *Briefe und Akten zur Geschichte der Driessigjährigen Krieges*, Neue Folge (Munich and Vienna, 1982)
Blockley   R.C. Blockley, *The History of Menander the Guardsman* (Liverpool, 1985)
CGD   Johann Christian Lünig, *Codex Germaniae diplomaticus* (Frankfurt and Leipzig, 1733)
CIGD   W.G. Leibniz, *Codex iuris gentium diplomaticus* (Hanover, 1693)
Cod.   Codex of Justinian
CTS   Clive Parry (ed.), *The Consolidated Treaty Series* (Dobbs Ferry, 1969–81)
CUD   Jean Dumont, *Corps universel diplomatique du droit des gens* (Amsterdam and The Hague, 1726–31; supplements ed. Jean Rousset de Missy, Amsterdam and The Hague, 1739)
Dig.   Digest of Justinian
FCN   Treaties of Friendship, Commerce and Navigation
FHIG   Wilhelm G. Grewe (ed.), *Fontes historiae iuris gentium* (Berlin and New York, 1988–95)
Huber   Ernst Rudolf Huber, *Dokumente zur deutschen Verfassungsgeschichte* (3rd edn, Stuttgart, 1986)

ILM	*International Legal Materials* (since 1962)
Inst.	Institutes
IPM	Peace Treaty of Münster of 24 October 1648
IPO	Peace Treaty of Osnabrück of 24 October 1648
L.F.	*Libri feodorum*
LNTS	*League of Nations Treaty Series* (920–40)
MBS	Munich, Bayerische Staatsbibliotheek
MCIGD	W. G. Leibniz, *Mantissa codicis iuris gentium diplomatici* (Hanover, 1700)
MGH-C	*Monumenta Germaniae Historica, Constitutiones* (since 1893)
MGH-D	*Monumenta Germaniae Historica, Diplomata* (since 1872)
NRG	Georg Friedrich von Martens *et al.*, *Nouveau Recueil général de traités* (Göttingen and Leipzig, 1817–1969: [I] Göttingen, 1840–75; II Göttingen, 1876–1908; III Leipzig, 1909–69)
PBN	Paris, Bibliothèque Nationale
RAI	Gabriel Noradounghian, *Recueil d'actes internationaux de l'Empire ottoman* (Paris, 1897, reprint 1978)
RGB	*Reichsgezetsbuch*
Rymer	Thomas Rymer, *Foedera, conventiones, literae . . .* (The Hague, 1739–45)
SA	Herman Bengtson (ed.), *Die Staatsverträge des Altertums* (Munich, 1969–75)
Strupp	Karl Strupp (ed.), *Documents pour servir à l'histoire du droit des gens* (2nd edn, Berlin, 1923)
TIE	P. Marino (ed.), *Tratados internacionales de España: periodo de la preponderancia española* (Madrid, 1978–86)
TUB	Tübingen, Universitätisbibliothek
UNTS	*United Nations Treaty Series* (since 1946)
X	Liber Extra of Decretals of Pope Gregory IX

1

Introduction

RANDALL LESAFFER

Since the 1960s and more particularly since the end of the Cold War, interest in the history of international law has greatly increased among international lawyers and legal historians alike.[1] Nevertheless, as an academic discipline, it is still lagging behind compared to most other branches of legal history. Recent efforts cannot be expected to make up for the neglect the field has suffered during most of the past two centuries.

The causes of the traditional neglect of the history of international law are many and much debated.[2] Paramount among them is – or was? – the dominance of national states and national law. This caused lawyers and legal historians to concentrate on internal legal developments. Moreover, in the heyday of state sovereignty, the binding character of public international law came to be disputed or even denied, which surely caused legal historians to turn away from its study.

Notwithstanding the efforts of many scholars from all over the world during recent decades, the study of international law is still lagging behind the field. Fundamental methodological questions have not been answered or even seriously debated.[3] Most of the sources – even the most important ones like treaties – still await modern, critical editions. The vast majority of recent scholarship still tends to concentrate, as it has been the case before, on doctrine and not on legal practice. And above all, most of the endeavours of recent years have been individual. There have hardly been any sustained, coordinated efforts, nor is the field organised.

Two initiatives – which saw the light of day in the late 1990s – have brought some change in that last respect. At the Max Planck Institute for

---

[1] Ingo Hueck, 'The Discipline of the History of International Law', *Journal of the History of International Law* 3 (2001), 194–217.
[2] See on the causes of this neglect: Johan W. Verzijl, 'Research into the History of the Law of Nations' in *International Law in Historical Perspective* (Leiden, 1968), vol. I, pp. 400–34.
[3] Wolfgang Preiser, *Völkerrechtsgeschichte: ihre Aufgaben und Methoden* (Wiesbaden, 1964); Heinhard Steiger, 'Probleme der Völkerrechtsgeschichte', *Der Staat* 26 (1987), 103–26.

European Legal History in Frankfurt a research project was set up under the leadership of Ingo Hueck on the German contribution to international legal doctrine in the nineteenth and twentieth centuries. In 1999, thanks to the endeavours of R. St. J. Macdonald (Dalhousie Law School), the first issue of *The Journal of the History of International Law* was published.

International coordination of research in the history of international law is of the utmost importance. Not only is it expedient to join forces for practical reasons and to allow scholars to enter into discussions with their colleagues, but it is also necessary to protect this young and not fully grown field from the 'slings and arrows of outrageous fortune'. After all, the resurgence of interest in the history of international law is not unique. Even today, it is still not safe to submit that present interest is more fundamental than it is fashionable. We are living in an era of great change in current international law. As before, it is just that which causes historical reflection on international law to be more popular. The periods of World War I and, somewhat less, World War II were also marked by a brief and limited increase in popularity of historical discourse among international lawyers and, though to a lesser extent, legal historians.

This book is the result of an attempt to bring together those European scholars from different backgrounds who over the last decades have worked on historical peace treaties. Among the contributors to this volume are legal historians, Roman lawyers, international lawyers, diplomatic historians and an International Relations theorist. Though all present were acquainted with one another's work, for many of them the meeting at Tilburg University on 30 and 31 March 2001 where they presented and discussed their ideas was the first occasion to meet colleagues in the flesh. It was physical proof of the necessity to combine efforts and coordinate work.

Peace Treaties and International Law in European History delves into the history of peace treaties as legal instruments in early modern Europe (late fifteenth century to 1920). However, the book by no means exhausts the subject. It draws from the most recent research, by both the contributors and others, but at the same time indicates the many lacunae that still exist there. In many respects, the book seeks to open debate and not to end it.

The scope of the book is twofold. Both the law which governs peace treaties – peace treaty law – and the law as it emerged from peace treaties are under scrutiny. The book goes beyond the analysis of treaties as legal instruments to the analysis of peace treaties as sources of the law of nations. Even the term 'source' is to be understood in both senses: treaties as historical sources for the existing rules of substantive international law and treaties as *traités lois* constitutive for new rules of material international law. In short, it is felt by the authors that the study of peace treaties is an appropriate way to start systematic and coordinated research into the history of international legal practice. As one of the main instruments used among the primary subjects and authors of the law of nations, peace treaties are a microcosm of that law. Moreover, while the book is an attempt to break through the traditional concentration on doctrine and turn to legal practice as well, the historical discourse of scholars is not overlooked.

There are two important limitations to the scope of the book. First, there is a geographical one. This is a history of European peace treaty practice. For the most part, treaties between and with non-European powers are excluded, and the whole problem of European expansion and colonialism is largely overlooked. Certainly this last limitation is an important one. Nowadays, more and more scholars accept that the confrontation of Europe from the 1500s onwards with the world beyond Europe was of the utmost importance for the formation of modern international law. Though the authors of this book do not deny this, it is felt that its impact only came to change the fundamental structure of international law from the nineteenth century onwards. Heinhard Steiger, who covers this period in this volume, therefore includes this issue in his chapter.[4]

Second, there is a limitation as regards the period covered. The book concentrates on the early modern era and the nineteenth century. While the Peace Treaties of Westphalia of 1648 have for a long time been held to be the very birth certificates of the modern European states system and its law of nations, the book goes farther back beyond this epochal date. While it cannot be denied that Westphalia is a benchmark in the history of the law of nations, the Peace Treaties of Westphalia as well as later treaties drew on a tradition of peace treaties and law that was older. Since the beginning of the twentieth century, it has become quite common to push back the beginnings of the modern law of nations to the sixteenth century and to the writings of the Spanish neo-scholastics, Francisco de Vitoria (*c.* 1480–1546) being first and foremost among them. While the early sixteenth century is indicated because of developments in doctrine, there are also events in general and political history such as the rise of the great dynastic states and the Reformation, which had an important impact on peace treaty practice. These considerations force us to take the

---

[4] See also Heinhard Steiger, 'From the International Law of Christianity to the International Law of the World Citizen', *Journal of the History of International Law* 3 (2001), 180–93.

whole sixteenth century and even the late fifteenth century into account. It is surely rewarding to include the practices of the Italian states of the late fifteenth century, as Italy is often considered to be a laboratory for later European diplomatic practices.[5]

The choice of the Peace Treaties of Paris (1919/20), which ended the Great War, as *terminus ad quem* is a more obvious one. These treaties, and particularly the Peace Treaty of Versailles between the Allied victors of the Great War and Germany, marked a fundamental turning point in the history of international law. Not only was it the first punitive peace between sovereigns since at least the late Middle Ages, thus dealing a serious blow to state sovereignty, but it also was the starting point for the era of international organisations.[6] Moreover, during the twentieth century, peace treaties gradually lost their monopoly in the field of peace settlement. After World War II, many wars did not end with the conclusion of a peace treaty. One of the most important recent wars, the Second Gulf War (1991) was ended by means of a UN Security Council Resolution. Many wars only led to armistices, while others just died out and peace was restored without an explicit juridical settlement.

The book is subdivided into four parts. In Part I, chapters 2 to 4 offer a chronological survey of the legal history of peace treaties and their contributions to international law from the Peace of Lodi (1454) to the Treaties of Paris (1919/20). The authors Randall Lesaffer, Heinz Duchhardt and Heinhard Steiger summarise the findings of recent research. As there is much more accessible secondary literature on the era between 1648 and 1815, and as many features of peace treaty practice of that era are common knowledge, Duchhardt can concentrate on some less well-known aspects.

Part II, 'Thinking peace: voices from a distant past', takes us back in time, beyond the early modern era. One of the central assumptions underlying this book is that early modern peace treaty law drew on a long tradition of thought and practice, which was rooted in the late Middle Ages, which in its turn, like all medieval scholarship, referred back to Antiquity. Christian Baldus, a specialist in Roman treaty practice, discusses the legal dimension of Roman peace treaty practice. Karl-Heinz Ziegler, another specialist

---

[5] See also Randall Lesaffer, 'The Grotian Tradition Revisited: Change and Continuity in the History of International Law', *British Year Book of International Law* 73 (2002), 103–139.

[6] Wilhelm G. Grewe, 'Was ist klassisches, was ist modernes Völkerrecht?' in Alexander Böhm, Klaus Lüdersen and Karl-Heinz Ziegler (eds.), *Idee und Realität des Rechts in der Entwicklung internationaler Beziehungen: Festgabe für Wolfgang Preiser* (Baden Baden, 1983), pp. 111–31.

in Roman treaty law, assesses the impact of Roman law on medieval doctrine and practice. Hanna Vollrath and Alain Wijffels address two important issues of canon law influence on the medieval 'law of peace'. Vollrath's exposition of the role of ritual, and more particularly the kiss, in the process of peacemaking illustrates the emergence of canon law as the primary source of the medieval *ius gentium*. Alain Wijffels's chapter is the very first in-depth analysis of the most comprehensive autonomous treatise on peace treaty law from the learned tradition of medieval *ius commune*, a work by the fifteenth-century Italian canon lawyer Martinus Garatus Laudensis. An edition of this treatise by Wijffels forms an appendix to this volume. With these four chapters, the authors aspire to offer insights into the ideas and practices of the Middle Ages that, partly through the prestige the learned *ius commune* continued to enjoy, are felt to have thoroughly influenced the modern law of nations in its formative period, until deep into the seventeenth century. To assess the exact impact of medieval and classical ideas on modern peace treaties and the modern law of nations would take many decades of systematic research. However, Dominique Bauer and Laurens Winkel – the former as regards canon law, the latter as regards Roman law – try to disperse some of the clouds by highlighting some examples.

While the doctrine of the seventeenth century was overshadowed by its dialectical debate with medieval scholarship, rationalism and the Enlightenment caused the eighteenth- and nineteenth-century scholars to look ahead. The third part, 'Thinking peace: towards a better future', highlights three aspects of eighteenth- and nineteenth-century thinking about peace. Marc Bélissa illustrates the contribution of the French eighteenth-century *philosophe* Mably. Ingo Hueck and Mathias Schmoeckel turn to the decades before and after 1900 when from different angles the existing sovereign state system was challenged and the idea of securing peace through international organisations won ground. Hueck offers a synthesis of recent research on German scholarship and its role in the Hague Peace Conferences of 1899 and 1907, while Schmoeckel in discussing the ideas of Lassa Oppenheim gives a better insight into the impact of the Paris Peace Treaties of 1919/20 on international law. Andreas Osiander's chapter holds a somewhat peculiar place, as he does not address historical thought, but approaches the subject from the perspective of social science, and more specifically International Relations theory. In fact, he claims that the political discourse surrounding peace negotiations often sheds more light on the structural and legal context within which a treaty has to be considered than contemporary doctrine.

The last part, 'Making peace: aspects of treaty practice', concentrates on four fundamental aspects of early modern European treaty practice on which somewhat more research has already been done. Ronald Asch and Christian Tomuschat turn to two of the most epochal peace settlements of the era discussed, Westphalia and Versailles. Over the last few years, in the context of the 350th anniversary of the Westphalia Peace Treaties, a vast amount of literature on these Treaties saw the light of day, and Asch has selected an aspect which has received surprisingly little attention, the right of the imperial estates to make alliances with other estates and with foreign powers. In addressing this issue, Asch clarifies some of the difficulties of interpretation historians have met in dealing with the Peace Treaties of Wespthalia because of their hybrid nature as both international peace treaties and constitutional instruments. Tomuschat sheds light on the importance of Versailles through a comparison with the peace settlement that ended the Franco-German war of 1870/71. Karl-Heinz Ziegler contributed a second chapter, this time on the peace treaties between Christian powers and the Turkish Empire. Even in a book on peace treaties between European – read Christian – powers, the continuous relations with the major non-Christian European power of the early modern era could not be neglected. Finally, Stephen Neff goes into the problem of restoring commercial relations between former enemies which, during the era discussed, was often done in separate treaties.

PART I

Peace treaties and international law from
Lodi to Versailles (1454–1920)

2

Peace treaties from Lodi to Westphalia

RANDALL LESAFFER

The myth of Westphalia

Historians and international lawyers alike have for a long time been quite unanimous in calling the Peace Treaties of Westphalia of 1648 the very birth certificates of the modern European states system and the modern law of nations. In the context of the 350th anniversary of these treaties, scholars from various countries and disciplines have gone a long way to challenging this Westphalian myth.[1]

Traditionally, it was alleged that the Westphalian Treaties laid down the basic principles of the modern law of nations, such as sovereignty, equality, religious neutrality and the balance of power. However, this cannot be sustained after a careful analysis of the treaties themselves and a comparison with older peace treaties. These principles are to be found in none of the three main Westphalian Peace Treaties, at least not as principles of international law.[2] In fact, references about the sovereignty and equality of religions can only be found in the treaties when they concern the constitutional arrangement for the Holy Roman Empire. Moreover,

[1] Derek Croxton, 'The Peace of Westphalia of 1648 and the Origins of Sovereignty', *International History Review* 21 (1999), 569–91; Randall Lesaffer, 'The Westphalia Peace Treaties and the Development of the Tradition of Great European Peace Settlements prior to 1648', *Grotiana* NS 18 (1997), 71–95; Meinhard Schröder, 'Der westfälische Friede – eine Epochengrenze in der Völkerrechtsentwicklung?' in Meinhard Schröder (ed.), *350 Jahre westfälischer Friede: Verfassungsgeschichte, Staatskirchenrecht, Völkerrechtsgeschichte* (Schriften zur europäischen Rechts- und Verfassungsgeschichte 30, Berlin, 1999), pp. 119–37; Heinhard Steiger, 'Der westfälischen Frieden – Grundgesetz für Europa?' in Heinz Duchhardt (ed.), *Der westfälische Friede: Diplomatie, politische Zäsur, kulturelles Umfeld, Rezeptionsgeschichte* (Munich, 1998), pp. 33–80; Karl-Heinz Ziegler, 'Die Bedeutung des westfälischen Friedens von 1648 für das europäische Völkerrecht', *Archiv des Völkerrechts* 37 (1999), 129–51; Ziegler, 'Der westfälischen Frieden von 1648 in der Geschichte des Völkerrechts' in Schröder, *350 Jahre westfälischer Friede*, pp. 99–117.
[2] Treaty of Münster of 30 January 1648 between Spain and the United Provinces; Treaty of Münster of 24 October 1648 between the Empire and France; Treaty of Osnabrück of 24 October 1648 between the Empire and Sweden.

these reminiscences are not new or innovative. It was only some decades after 1648 that diplomats and jurists started to see these clauses as reflecting upon international relations. This transposition of what are in fact internal constitutional arrangements to the domain of the international, or better European, legal order can be explained by the hybrid character of the Treaty of Osnabrück of 24 October 1648, between the Empire and Sweden, and of the Treaty of Münster of the same date, between the Empire and France. Those two treaties are both international peace treaties between the Empire, its estates and a foreign power and an internal, constitutional-religious settlement for the Holy Roman Empire. The clauses that lay down international peace are far from original and do not allow an assessment of the Westphalia Peace Treaties as constituting a caesura in the technical-juridical development of peace treaty practice and law.

Nevertheless, the period of the Westphalia Peace and the decade that followed does constitute an important caesura in the development of the European legal order as a whole. The Westphalia Peace Treaties put an end to the last long and bitter religious war in Europe. They also succeeded in more or less pacifying the Holy Roman Empire and thereby giving more stability to Central Europe. Moreover, the 1640s and 1650s saw the last important rebellions and civil wars within the most important European powers such as France, Spain and England. These decades also marked the end of a century of religious strife among and religious and civil turmoil within the most powerful European countries, which had wrecked the old European legal order. In short, the Westphalia Peace Treaties did not lay down the basic principles of the modern law of nations; they did, however, lay down the political and religious conditions for allowing the European powers to start building a new international legal order.[3]

The crisis of the European legal order

Since the beginning of the twentieth century, international legal historians have come to modify the traditional view that the modern doctrine of the law of nations stems from the seventeenth century. While the impact of the Dutch humanist Hugo Grotius (1583–1645) on modern doctrine is still considered to be enormous, most historians now accept that Grotius and his successors largely drew from the writings of their sixteenth-century

---

[3] See the references in n. 1 as well as Randall Lesaffer, 'La dimensión internacional de los Tratados de Paz de Westfalia. Un enfoque juridico' in *350 años de la Paz de Westfalia: del antagonismo a la integración en Europa* (Madrid, 1999), pp. 32–53.

predecessors. At present, it is common to stress the continuity between the different writers on international problems of the sixteenth century and the modern international lawyers of the seventeenth and eighteenth centuries.[4]

More in general, the period from around 1450 until the Westphalia Peace Treaties has been crucial for the development of the modern European states system and its international law. These two centuries, and more specifically the first half of the sixteenth century, saw the final breakdown of the medieval European legal order, and marked an important step in the emergence of what was to become the modern sovereign state.

Medieval and Renaissance Europe defined itself as a religious, cultural and, to a certain extent, political and juridical unity, often referred to as the *respublica christiana*.[5] Although there were many more or less autonomous political entities in the Latin world, ranging from large dynastic monarchies to small fiefs and free cities, they were all considered to take part in a greater hierarchical and juridical *continuum* under the supreme, if theoretical, leadership of the pope and the emperor.[6] The learned *ius commune* – Roman and canon law – as well as the general rules and principles of feudal law provided a framework of juridical concepts and political ideals that was common to the whole of the Latin West, in which the legal organisation of international relations could be vested.[7]

---

[4] James Brown Scott was among the first and foremost to re-evaluate the Spanish neo-scholastics such as Francisco de Vitoria (*c.* 1480–1546) and Francisco Suarez (1548–1617); James Brown Scott, *The Spanish Origin of International Law: Lectures on Francisco de Vitoria (1480–1546) and Francisco Suarez (1548–1617)* (Washington, 1928); Scott, *The Spanish Conception of International Law and Sanctions* (Washington, 1934); Scott, *The Catholic Conception of International Law: Francisco de Vitoria, Founder of the Modern Law of Nations. Francisco Suarez, Founder of the Modern Philosophy of Law in General* (Washington, 1934); Scott, *The Spanish Origin of International Law: Francisco de Vitoria and His Law of Nations* (Oxford, 1934). Vitoria even jeopardised Grotius' acclaimed fatherhood of the modern law of nations, see Wilhelm G. Grewe, 'Hugo Grotius – Vater des Völkerrechts?', *Der Staat* 23 (1984), 161–78. Defended, however, by Karl-Heinz Ziegler, 'Hugo Grotius als "Vater des Völkerrechts"' in Peter Selmer and Ingo von Munch (eds.), *Gedächtnisschrift für Wolfgang Martens* (Berlin, 1987), pp. 851–8, and 'Die Bedeutung von Hugo Grotius für das Völkerrecht – Versuch einer Bilanz', *Zeitschrift für Historische Forschung* 13 (1996), 354–71.

[5] The term *respublica christiana* was already in use in the late Middle Ages, but became more common from the Renaissance (1450–1530) onwards. Even after the collapse of the medieval system the term survived for another two centuries.

[6] Wilhelm G. Grewe, *The Epochs of International Law* (trans. Michael Byers, Berlin, 2000), pp. 37–74; Karl-Heinz Ziegler, *Völkerrechtsgeschichte* (Munich, 1994), pp. 97, 107–11, 120–7 and 133–7.

[7] On the importance of canon law in international relations: James Muldoon, 'The Contribution of the Medieval Canon Lawyers to the Formation of International Law', *Traditio* 28 (1972), 483–97; Muldoon, 'Medieval Canon Law and the Formation of International Law',

By the mid-thirteenth century, the imperial claims to secular overlordship in Europe had been shattered. Nevertheless, the relative juridical integration and the ideal of political unity – or at least pacification – had not disappeared. Moreover, the pope still held some claims to spiritual leadership, which extended to the political domain at the beginning of the sixteenth century. The 1520s to 1540s, however, saw the final undoing of the old system. In the years after 1516, the spectacular conquest by the Ottoman Turks in the eastern Mediterranean and the Balkans had led to a steep revival of the old ideal of the *respublica christiana*. This revival centred on two ideas: internal peace within the Christian world and the launching of a joint crusade against the Turks. While various half-hearted attempts were made by the pope and some Christian princes,[8] these ideals could not seduce the two most powerful princes of the West, Emperor Charles V (1519–58) and King Francis I of France (1515–47), to give up their struggle for hegemony in Italy, and thereby in Europe. To put it somewhat cynically, the ideal of Christian unity in the face of the Turks was shattered by the fight over who was going to lead Christianity against the Turks.

Next to the struggle between the Valois and the Habsburgs over the hegemony in Europe, the Reformation was the second main factor in the collapse of the old European order. The split in the Church put an end to the spiritual leadership of the pope within the Christian world. Canon law, which for centuries had offered the hard core of the body of rules governing the relations between the most important princes and republics of Christianity, was no longer accepted as universally applicable law.

The discovery and conquest of new important territories that were previously not or hardly known around 1500 posed another challenge to the medieval international legal system. As was recognised by the main

---

Zeitschrift der Savigny-Stiftung für Rechtsgeschichte, Kanonistische Abteilung 81 (1995), 64–82. On the importance of Roman law: Hersch Lauterpacht, *Private Law Sources and Analogies of International Law* (London, 1927), pp. 8–37; Karl-Heinz Ziegler, 'Die römische Grundlagen des europäischen Völkerrechts', *Ius Commune* 4 (1972), 1–27.

[8] After the collapse of the Mameluke Empire in Syria and Egypt in 1517, Pope Leo X (1513–21) unilaterally proclaimed a general truce between all Christian powers, by papal bull of 6 March 1517; Eugène Charrière (ed.), *Négociations de la France dans le Levant ou Correspondance, Mémoires et Actes diplomatiques* (Collection des documents inédits sur l'histoire de France, Paris, 1840), vol. I, pp. 63–8. On 2 October 1518, the French and English kings signed the Treaty of London, aiming at implementing the papal goals of peace within the Christian world and of common warfare against the infidels. Charles adhered to the treaty on 19 January 1519, and thus a general peace among the leading powers was reached.

Spanish neo-scholastic thinkers – Francisco de Vitoria (c. 1480–1546) being the foremost among them – the European *ius gentium* or law of nations based on Roman and canon law was not applicable to the relations with the indigenous people of the newly discovered territories such as the Americas. These peoples had no relations whatsoever with either the Roman or the Christian past and traditions.[9]

By 1550, the old European order had collapsed and no new international system was in place yet. While princes and rulers continued to accept that they were all part of the greater whole known and referred to as the *respublica christiana*, the old legal system that governed the international relations between those princes and rulers had crumbled away. The *respublica christiana* was felt to be in crisis. The religious strife and the wars that ensued among the main European countries wrecked the normal dialogue of diplomacy and international law between the states. The internal religious wars that wrecked important territories like the Empire, France and the Netherlands prevented them for some decades from playing a constructive role on the international chessboard. The crisis of the international system was to continue until the Westphalia Peace Treaties.[10]

The emergence of the sovereign state

Another reason why it took more than a hundred years after the collapse of the old, medieval system before the new system of sovereign states could start to take form was that before the second half of the seventeenth century the sovereign state as such did not exist. The emergence of the sovereign state was a very gradual and far from rectilinear process, which started in the twelfth and thirteenth centuries. For our purposes, it is relevant to distinguish internal sovereignty from external sovereignty.

Internal sovereignty implies that the central ruler within a certain territory is the sole power enjoying the autonomous legitimisation of power. It also means that all other territorial powers – the nobility, clergy and

---

[9] See, on the impact of the discoveries on the theory and practice of the law of nations, Antony Anghie, 'Francisco de Vitoria and the Colonial Origins of International Law', *Social and Legal Studies* 3 (1996), 321–36; Jörg Fisch, *Die europäische Expansion und das Völkerrecht* (Stuttgart, 1984) and references there.

[10] Randall Lesaffer, 'Het moderne volkenrecht (1450–1750)', *Onze Alma Mater* 52 (1998), 426–51 at pp. 435–7; Lesaffer, 'War, Peace, Interstate Friendship and the Emergence of the *ius publicum Europaeum*' in Ronald Asch, Martin Wrede and Wulf E. Voss (eds.), *Krieg und Frieden in der frühen Neuzeit: die europäische Staatenordnung und die aussereuropäische Welt* (Munich, 2001), pp. 88–113.

towns – are subject in more or less the same way and through a similar sovereign authority to the central power. In so far as it reflects upon international relations and law, internal sovereignty implies that only the sovereign is subject to international law and enjoys the monopoly of acting on the international scene. Therefore, the ruler must act on the international field as the representative of the state, not in his own name. Internal sovereignty goes hand in hand with an abstract or depersonalised notion of the state. All this is a precondition to the dualism between the international and internal legal orders that became central to the modern law of nations.

External sovereignty simply comes down to the absence of any higher political authority than the sovereign ruler or state. In the modern doctrines of international law, it implies that the state is the highest law-making and law-enforcing power in the international legal order. The formation of international law is voluntaristic: sovereign rulers or powers are only subject to rules they accept themselves. No power can juridically limit their right to enforce their claims. For all practical purposes, there are no limits to the states' discretion to wage war or not. Internal and external sovereignty led to what the British School of International Relations Theory called the 'Hobbesian concept of international society'.[11] Since the later Middle Ages, the great princes of Europe and even the important city-republics of Italy have considered themselves to be, *de facto* if not *de jure*, *superiorem non recognoscentes*. This means that they did not accept the secular authority of the emperor, though it does not mean that they rejected the authority of the pope or the juridical unity of the *respublica christiana*.[12] Therefore, and because in historic reality sovereignty is also a relative concept, I do not hesitate to refer to the princes of Europe of the late fifteenth and the early sixteenth centuries, when the old system was still in existence, as sovereign princes.

The scope of this chapter is to analyse peace treaty practice from around 1450 up to the Westphalia Peace Treaties. Both the aspect of formal treaty

---

[11] Hedley Bull, 'The Grotian Conception of International Society' in Herbert Butterfield and Martin Wight (eds.), *Diplomatic Investigations* (London, 1966), pp. 51–73; Bull, *The Anarchical Society: A Study of Order in World Politics* (2nd edn, New York, 1995), pp. 23–4; Bull, 'The Importance of Grotius in the Study of International Relations' in Hedley Bull, Benedict Kingsbury and Adam Roberts (eds.), *Grotius and International Relations* (Oxford, 1990), pp. 65–93 at pp. 71–2; Benedict Kingsbury and Adam Roberts, 'Grotian Thought in International Relations' in Bull, Kingsbury and Roberts (eds.), *Grotius*, pp. 1–64.

[12] Joseph Canning, *The Political Thought of Baldus de Ubaldis* (Cambridge, 1987), pp. 64–8, 93–158 and 209–21; Kenneth Pennington, *The Prince and the Law, 1200–1600: Sovereignty and Rights in the Western Legal Tradition* (Berkeley, 1993), pp. 33–7 and 90.

law – such as the binding power of treaties, the ratification and the guaranteeing of treaties – and the aspect of material law, arising from the contents of the treaties themselves, will be studied. The central question in this analysis is if, and if so how, the collapse of the medieval concept of the European order and the emergence of the sovereign state are reflected in the treaties.[13]

In his monumental study on peace treaties throughout the history of mankind, Jörg Fisch asserts that early modern treaty practice was to a large extent determined and influenced by the tradition of the great peace treaties between France and England at the end of the Middle Ages.[14] He suggested that in the sixteenth and early seventeenth centuries, before 1648 and before the great peace treaties of the later seventeenth and eighteenth centuries, different traditions – or what I prefer to call 'families' of peace treaties – depending on the powers involved, could be discerned. Even a superficial analysis of different groups of bilateral treaties of the later fifteenth and sixteenth centuries ascertains this as being true. However, for the purposes of this chapter I shall not go into this. It will be sufficient to point out that this dissimilarity of treaties is an indication of the absence of a truly European or general law of nations after the collapse of the old international system and the emergence of the modern states system. Once the universally accepted role of canon law had come to an end, the powers of Europe were thrown back upon their own resources and the agreements they made with one another to organise legal relations among themselves.

Suzerains and vassals

First of all, the study of the fifteenth- (and sixteenth-) century peace treaties shows that the central rulers of the different European powers did not enjoy the monopoly of representing their territories or even of entering peace treaties. From the fifteenth and early sixteenth centuries, several important examples can be quoted of peace settlements between suzerain princes and their vassals. The Treaty of Conflans of 1465 and

---

[13] The chapter is based on the research I did for my doctoral thesis and subsequent, more detailed research into sixteenth-century treaty practice. For the period discussed here, I analysed over a hundred peace treaties, as well as a similar number of alliance treaties. The thesis was published as: Randall Lesaffer, *Europa: een zoektocht naar vrede? (1454–1763 en 1945–1997)* (Leuven, 1999).

[14] Jörg Fisch, *Krieg und Frieden im Friedensvertrag: eine universalgeschichtliche Studie über Grundlagen und Formelemente des Friedensschlusses* (Stuttgart, 1979), pp. 536–7.

the Treaty of Péronne of 1468 between King Louis XI of France and his rebellious vassals of the *Ligue du bien public* led by Charles the Bold (1467–77) of Burgundy offer the prime examples thereof.[15] These treaties do not indicate that the making of a treaty between a suzerain and his vassals was considered to be exceptional or was substantially different from the treaties between two sovereign princes or suzerains. Whether one considers such treaties to be true treaties under international law or not is immaterial. What is important is that no clear distinction existed yet between internal and international treaty practice. It is a first indication that an autonomous, international law regarding treaties did not exist at the beginning of the period studied here.

However, it is striking that in this kind of treaty quite a lot of attention was devoted to the legitimisation of the rebellion or civil war the treaty ended.[16] This should be seen within the context of the discussion on the *ius resistendi*, which in the sixteenth century would be more in the foreground in a reaction to the attempts of the rulers of various European powers to centralise power and to neutralise other powers within their territories.[17] Anyhow, these quite extensive justifications show that, whereas the *ius contrahendi* of the vassals was as yet not put in jeopardy halfway through the fifteenth century, their right to wage war upon their suzerains or their *ius ad bellum* was less evident.

The relative position of the parties involved and the right expressly or silently attributed to the rebellious vassals differed according to the political situation and positions. At the negotiations of Conflans and even more Péronne, the vassals held the upper hand.[18] The Treaty of Sablé of 20 August 1488 between the king of France and the duke of Brittany ended a war in which the king had been victorious. In the Preamble to the Treaty, the agreement is presented as a peace one-sidedly granted to the duke. At the end of the Preamble and in the Articles, however, it becomes clear once again that this is a true reciprocal agreement, not a privilege

---

[15] Treaty of Conflans of 5 October 1465; Treaty of Péronne of 14 October 1468.
[16] E.g. Treaty of Péronne.
[17] Robert M. Kingdom, 'Calvinism and Resistance Theory, 1550–1580' in J. H. Burns (ed.), *The Cambridge History of Political Thought 1450–1700* (Cambridge, 1991), pp. 194–218; J. H. M. Salmon, 'Catholic Resistance Theory, Ultramontanism, and the Royalist Response, 1580–1620' in Burns, *Cambridge History of Political Thought*, pp. 219–53; Quentin Skinner, *The Foundations of Modern Political Thought* (Cambridge, 1978), vol. II, pp. 302–48.
[18] On the political context of the Treaty of Péronne see Jean-Marie Cauchies, *Louis XI et Charles le Hardi: de Péronne à Nancy (1468–1477): le conflit* (Brussels, 1996), pp. 15–33.

or an edict enunciated by the king for the benefit or detriment of the duke.[19]

By the second half of the sixteenth century, this had changed in France. Between 1563 and 1598, several religious civil wars wrecked the kingdom. On other occasions, pacification was reached between the warring religions and the king. In substance these settlements were agreements reached after lengthy negotiations, but they were formally enunciated as Royal Edicts stipulating the conditions of the peace.[20] While, of course, the wars between the kings of the later fifteenth century and some of their vassals are not the same as the religious wars, this is nevertheless an indication that internal sovereignty as a concept had won much ground in France.

The ruler as treaty party

Peace treaties, just like other treaties between sovereign princes, were, from a juridical point of view, agreements between princes, not between political entities. From a strictly formal point of view, in signing the treaties, the sovereign princes did not act as a representative institution of an abstract political body; they acted in their own name. Only indirectly, through their internal power and authority, did they oblige their territories and subjects to the treaty.[21]

Peace treaties were formally not very different from private contracts. By consequence, the general rules of contract law as they emerged from canon, Roman and feudal law applied to treaties; an autonomous treaty law did not exist. It was not before the seventeenth century that an autonomous doctrine of treaty law was elaborated.[22]

The preambles and the main articles of the peace treaties of the period gave the rulers, not the territories or countries they ruled, as treaty partners. Mostly, these rulers were referred to by their names, and only in the second instance by their titles. Although there were some earlier exceptions, this custom survived into the eighteenth century.[23]

---

[19] '... avons finalement été contens de faire cesser nôtredite Armée, et d'accorder à nôtredit Cousin cette Paix'.

[20] See the Edicts of 17 January 1562, Preamble, CUD V-1, 90; 30 September 1577, Preamble, CUD V-1, 302; 2 May 1598, Preamble, CUD V-1, 545.

[21] Grewe, *Epochs*, pp. 196 and 360–2.

[22] Randall Lesaffer, 'The Medieval Canon Law of Contract and Early Modern Treaty Law', *Journal of the History of International Law* 2 (2000), 178–98 at 185–6.

[23] Grewe, *Epochs*, p. 361; Jean Ray, 'La communauté internationale d'après les traités du XVIe siècle à nos jours', *Annales Sociologiques* C 3 (1938), 14–49 at p. 19.

The preambles and the main articles of the treaties in which it was stipulated that hostilities would end, and that henceforth peace would reign between the parties, often encompassed a double reference. Normally, it was stated that the peace was agreed between the rulers, but that it would apply between the rulers, their territories, vassals, subjects, allies and adherents.[24] Until the end of the fifteenth century, the preambles to some treaties even mentioned that the princes signed the treaty for themselves and their vassals and subjects.[25] After 1500, this disappeared from the preambles. This may indicate that it was now more readily accepted that the personal obligation of the prince implied the allegiance of his vassals and subjects to the treaty obligations. Anyhow, all these formulas clearly indicated that it was the rulers who entered the treaties and that only they were directly bound to the treaty. Only through their mediation, their territories, vassals and subjects were bound to the treaties.

It is central to understand that the rulers did not act as representatives or mandatories of the polities they ruled. They did not negotiate and sign the treaty on the basis of a mandate from their states; they acted in

---

[24] 'In primi, li prefati Illustrissimi Signori de Venezia per se, soi Colligati, Adherenti, Confederati, complici, sequaci, Racomendati, Subditi, & Soldati, beni mobili, & stabili, rasione, Jurisditione, & actione, honori, & preheminienti, per una parte', Treaty of Lodi of 9 April 1454, Art. 1; 'In primis, quod bonae, sincerae, firmae & perfectae sint & inviolabiliter habeantur Treugae, Guerrarum Abstinentiae, Ligae & Confederationes inter dictos potentissimos Franciae & Angliae Principes, Provincias & Dominia omnia quaecunque, Haeredes, Successores, Vassallos & Subditos praesentes & futuros, Alligatos & Confoederatos utriusque eorum', Treaty of Amiens I of 29 August 1475, Art. 1; 'Paix finale . . . entre le Roy, Monseigneur le Dauphin, le Royaume, leur Pays, Seigneuries, & Sujets, d'une part', Treaty of Arras of 23 December 1482, Art. 1; 'Primeramente ha sido tractado e conçertado entre los sobredichos . . . que de aquí adelante entre les dichos Señores Emperador e Rey Christianíssimo e sus heredes e suçessores e sus rreynos e tierras y señoríos, vassallos e súbditos', Treaty of Madrid of 14 January 1526, Art. 1; 'entre lesdits Sieurs Rois, leurs Enfans nais & à naître, Hoirs, Successeurs & Heritiers, leurs Roiaumes, Païs & Sujets, y aura bonne . . . Paix', Treaty of Vervins of 2 May 1598, Art. 1.

[25] E.g. 'inter Illustrissimum Principem & Excellentissimum Dominum Franciscum Foscari Ducem & Inclytum Dominum Venetiarum, & c., pro se, suisque Subditis, Vassallis, Complicibus, Adherentibus, Recommendatis, & Confederatis ex una parte, & Illustrissimum Principem, & Excellentissimum Dominum Franciscum Sfortiam Vicecomitem Ducem Mediolani & c. . . . pro se, suisque filiis, & haeredibus, ac Colligatis, Adherentibus, Recommandatis, & Subditis ut infra ex altera parte', Treaty of Lodi of 2 April 1454, Preamble; 'pro se, suis Haeredibus, Successoribus, Patriis, Dominiis, Vassallis', First Treaty of Westminster of 25 July 1474, Preamble. In treaties involving republics such as Venice and other Italian city-states, the republics as treaty partners were referred to in a way as similar as possible as in treaties only involving princes. In the preambles and main articles, the highest functionaries or institutions were mentioned as treaty partners, before the republic itself, if it was referred to at all.

their own names. In fact, one could say that the treaties consisted of two different sets of obligation: (1) a contractual obligation between the actual signatory parties, the ruling princes, and (2) a set of promises made by them to use their internal authority to have the treaty applied and executed by their vassals and subjects. This construction remains far different from the modern law of treaty, where the sovereign power within the state or its delegate directly binds the state, acting as mandatories for the state and not in their own name.

In treaties from the fourteenth till the early sixteenth century, this process was made quite evident through what can be described as co-ratification. In many important peace agreements it was stipulated that the signatory princes would have some of their most important nobles, prelates and towns ratify the treaty. Sometimes, they promised to call a meeting of the three estates and have them ratify the treaty.[26] Thereby, these internal powers not only became guarantors to the treaty, having to support the victim of a breach of treaty, but were bound in a more direct way and in their own name to the treaty as well.[27] These clauses confirm the personal character of the treaty entered by the prince. The treaty partners admitted that their main vassals, subjects and towns were subjects of law in the international field and could act autonomously.

From the end of the fifteenth century onwards, treaties involving France or the Habsburg powers often stipulated that the treaty would be registered by the main courts and the exchequers of the kingdoms or territories involved.[28] Just like ratification by the three estates, this should

---

[26] Treaty of Péronne of 1468 *in fine*; Treaty of Arras of 1482, Art. 89; Treaty of Sablé of 1488, Art. 5; Treaty of Senlis of 23 May 1493, Art. 39; Treaty of London of 7 August 1514, Arts. 33–4; Treaty of Crépy of 18 September 1544, Art. 26.

[27] Klaus Neitmann does not agree with this. According to him, co-ratification only amounts to an extra guarantee. While it is true that this is expressly stressed in many treaties, it does not change the fact that, through personal ratification, the co-ratifying subjects became more directly bound to the treaty. Nevertheless, the attachment of the co-ratifying powers to the treaties proves that this personal character became problematic in the later Middle Ages. From a modern perspective, co-ratification is proof of the absence of internal sovereignty and an abstract concept of state; from the perspective of the high Middle Ages, it is a first step towards the state. Klaus Neitmann, *Die Staatsverträge des deutschen Ordens in Preussen 1230–1449: Studien zur Diplomatie eines spätmittelalterlichen deutschen Territorialstaates* (Neue Forschungen zur brandenburg-preussischen Geschichte 6, Cologne and Vienna, 1986), pp. 276–81.

[28] Treaty of Arras of 1482, Art. 88; Treaty of Senlis of 1493, Art. 40; First Treaty of Cambrai of 1508, Art. 21; Treaty of Madrid of 1526, Art. 4; Treaty of Crépy of 18 September 1544, Art. 26; First Treaty of Câteau-Cambrésis, 3 April 1559, Art. 47; Treaty of Vervins of 1598, *in fine*.

not be considered similar to the ratification of treaties by the legislative power as it is customary in most countries since the nineteenth century. Though, of course, this method of co-ratification was much less personalised and more institutionalised than the co-ratification by several individual nobles, clerics or towns, it was certainly not similar to the modern ratification by parliament. Through parliamentary ratification, the treaty is accepted under national law and is accepted by the state. When interpreting the early modern clauses on co-ratification by the estates and on registration, one has to take into account that there was no such thing as an abstract concept of the state. These institutional 'co-ratifications' by the estates are a consequence of the dualist concept of government within most kingdoms of Europe, whereby the princes ruled in accordance with the estates. Just like the personal co-ratification, institutional co-ratification led to a more direct bonding of the main powers within the territories ruled by the prince to the treaty – be they the estates or the main juridical and financial institutions of the prince – and not to binding the as yet non-existent state. In short, whereas the ratification through parliament in modern law is a matter of constitutional law, all these co-ratifications were a matter of treaty law. Nevertheless, this institutionalisation of co-ratification is a step in the gradual evolution from treaties as merely personal agreements to agreements between states. Of course, with the benefit of hindsight we can say that institutional co-ratification is a step in the evolution towards parliamentary ratification.

By the second half of the sixteenth century, the co-ratification by individual nobles, clerics and towns as well as by the estates had almost disappeared.[29] The clauses stipulating registration by courts and other institutions remained, in any case in the treaties involving France and Spain. The disappearance of personal co-ratification and of the co-ratification by the estates indicates the growing monopoly of the sovereign ruler over international relations. The fact that the registration clauses were largely restricted to France or Spain is an indication that these clauses started to reflect the constitutional law of the kingdoms more than they were part of the international law of treaties.

Another problem that is related to the personal character of early modern treaties is the question if, and if so how, they bound the heirs and successors to the princes who entered the treaties. There can be no doubt

---

[29] This was not the case in the Holy Roman Empire. On the presence of the Estates of the Empire in the Westphalia Peace Treaties of 24 October 1648, see Steiger, 'Der westfälische Frieden', pp. 40–4.

that there was no undisputed general rule stating that heirs and successors were automatically bound by the treaty. Such a rule would only be put forward and accepted in doctrine around 1600.[30]

As contracts ruled by the general private law of contract, treaties between princes were personal agreements. It was debated whether the successors of the princes were bound and whether the treaty expired with the death of one of the signatory parties.

Most of the peace treaties of the period studied expressly stated that the signatory parties entered the treaties for themselves as well as their heirs and successors.[31] These clauses show that, on the one hand, the binding of successors was not self-evident, and that, on the other hand, the princes could bind their successors. Some treaties contained more specific clauses. First, several peace treaties demanded that the successor to the throne would co-ratify the treaty at once. Normally, this was restricted to treaties involving the cession of territories or rights. Through his ratification, the heir to the throne accepted the diminution of his inheritance.[32] By consequence, these clauses do not force us to re-evaluate our position. Second, in some peace treaties it was provided that the treaty would stay valid over a certain period after the death of one or both of the signatory parties. During that period – more often than not one year – the new ruler could choose to ratify or not.[33] These clauses refute our presumption that princes could bind their successors to the treaties. However, these clauses disappeared by the 1530s. Afterwards, it seems at least to be no longer disputed that a prince could bind himself, his successors and his and their subjects perpetually. In this, another example of the gradual emergence of sovereignty and of the depersonalisation of treaty law can be read. However, even in seventeenth- (and eighteenth-) century treaties, the main articles of peace treaties still mentioned the heirs and successors as

---

[30] Balthasar de Ayala, *De jure et officiis bellicis et disciplina militari libri tres* 1, 7, 10 (Classics of International Law 2, Oxford, 1912), vol. I, pp. 83–4; Petrus Gudelinus, *De jure pacis commentarius* 12, 2–3 (in *Opera omnia*, Antwerp, 1685), pp. 563–4 (written before 1620).

[31] First Treaty of Westminster of 1474, Preamble; Treaty of Etaples of 3 November 1492, Preamble; Treaty of London of 1518, Art. 1; Treaty of Madrid of 1526, Art. 1; Treaty of Crépy of 1544, Art. 1; Treaty of Lübeck of 12 May 1629, Art. 1; Treaty of Madrid of 15 November 1630, Art. 1.

[32] One of the most famous examples is the Treaty of Madrid of 1526, whereby Francis I of France had to accept the restitution of the Duchy of Burgundy to Charles V: Art. 44. See also the First Treaty of Cambrai, 5 August 1529, Art. 47 and the First Treaty of Câteau-Cambrésis, 3 April 1559, Art. 47.

[33] '... et per annum integrum post obitum ultimo ipsorum morientis': Treaty of Etaples of 1492, Art. 1; 'duratura ad vitam utriusque ipsorum ... et per unum annum post': First Treaty of Cambrai of 1508, Art. 1.

one of the categories that would benefit from the peace. Though by then these had become standardised formulas, they indicated that the binding of successors was still not self-evident, though it was widely accepted and defended.

The ratification and safeguarding of peace treaties

During the later Middle Ages, two different techniques of negotiating and signing treaties were developed. The German scholar Walter Heinemeyer distinguished the *unmittelbare Vertragsschliessungsverfahren* from the *zusammengesetzte Vertragsschliessungsverfahren*. Under the *unmittelbare Vertragsschliessungsverfahren*, the parties to the treaty, the rulers, exchanged the identical documents they had signed and thus directly expressed their agreement on the text they or their ambassadors had negotiated. This method was predominantly used during the Middle Ages, but gradually disappeared from the late fifteenth century onwards. During the early modern period, it was only used when the rulers themselves were present, if even then. By the eighteenth century, it had disappeared altogether. The *zusammengesetzte Vertragsschliessungsverfahren* had become the standard method by 1500.[34] Here the role of the ambassadors or plenipotentiaries acting on behalf of the rulers was central. The method implied three consecutive phases: the granting of full powers to the negotiators by the rulers, the agreeing on a treaty text by the negotiators and the ratification of that text by the rulers themselves. For all these phases, documents were drawn up and exchanged.[35]

Since the Middle Ages, the confirmation by oath had been the main constitutive act in the process of ratification. Mostly, the oath was sworn during a religious ceremony in church and surrounded with material

---

[34] Sometimes, it was even applied when both rulers were present; see the Treaties of Guines of 6 June 1520, at the famous meeting between Francis I (1515–47) and Henry VIII (1509–47) at the Field of the Cloth of Gold. See on this meeting Joyceleyne G. Dickinson, *The Field of Cloth of Gold: Men and Manners in 1520* (London, 1969). In some treaties of the later sixteenth century, one of the rulers was present and signed and ratified the treaty directly, while the ambassadors of the other ruler signed a document as well. In such a case, one could say that both methods were applied at the same time; Treaty of Arras of 21 September 1435, *in fine*; Treaty of Senlis of 1493, *in fine*.

[35] Ludwig Bittner, *Die Lehre von den völkerrechtlichen Vertragsurkunden* (Berlin and Leipzig, 1944), pp. 5–8; Walter Heinemeyer, 'Studien zur Diplomatik mittelalterlicher Verträge vornehmlich des 13. Jahrhunderts', *Archiv für Urkundenforschung* 14 (1936), 357–400; Neitmann, *Staatsverträge*, pp. 137–50; Heinrich Mitteis, 'Politische Verträge des Mittelalters' in *Die Rechtsidee in der Geschichte: Gesammelte Abhandlungen und Vorträge von Heinrich Mitteis* (Weimar, 1957), pp. 567–612 at p. 579.

formalities, such as the touching of the Gospels or the Holy Cross. In principle, the ceremony was attended by the representatives of the other treaty partner. The acceptance of the treaty text by the princes was also confirmed through signed and sealed documents. During the Middle Ages, these documents mentioned and described the taking of the oath. Until the twelfth century, these only had instrumental value as evidence of the actual oath taking. From the twelfth or thirteenth century onwards these documents also obtained constitutive value.[36] Next to attesting the oath, they now constituted written contracts under signature and seal. As such, these documents were of a mixed or hybrid character.[37] The oath taking for a long time remained the most important part of the ratification process.[38]

Almost all peace treaties concluded between 1454 and 1648 were confirmed by oath, regardless of the negotiation method. In the treaties concluded through the *zusammengesetzte Vertragsschliessungsverfahren*, the confirmation by oath was stipulated in one of the last articles of the treaties themselves.[39] In the treaties up to around 1540, it was commonly stated that the parties submitted themselves to ecclesiastical jurisdiction,

---

[36] Bittner, *Die Lehre von den völkerrechtlichen Vertragsurkunden*, p. 4.

[37] Arthur Nussbaum, 'Forms and Observance of Treaties in the Middle Ages and the Early Sixteenth Century' in George A. Lipsky (ed.), *Law and Politics in the World Community: Essays on Hans Kelsen's Pure Theory and Related Problems in International Law* (Berkeley and Los Angeles, 1953), pp. 191–8 at p. 191. See, for an example, where the ratification documents still held instrumental value too: Treaty of Barcelona of 19 January 1493, ratification by the Catholic Kings: 'In quorum omnium & singulorum fidem & Testimonium praesentes Litteras manibus nostris signavimus, Siggilorumque nostrorum in nostra Civitate Barchinonae', just after the oath formulas.

[38] Heinhard Steiger, 'Bemerkungen zum Friedensvertrag von Crépy en Laonnais vom 18. September 1544 zwischen Karl V. und Franz I.' in Ulrich Beyerlin, Michael Bothe, Rainer Hofmann and Ernst-Ulrich Petersmann (eds.), *Recht zwischen Umbruch und Bewahrung: Völkerrecht – Europarecht – Staatsrecht. Festschrift für Rudolf Bernhardt* (2nd edn, Berlin, 1995), vol. II, pp. 249–65 at p. 256.

[39] 'Que encore le Roy & mondit Seigneur le Dauphin, authorisé & dispensé de son jeune âge, en la presence des Ambassadeurs & Commis de mondit Sieur le Duc ... jureront solennellement sur le precieux Corps de nostre Seigneur, sur le fust de la vraie Croix, Canon de la Messe, ou Saincts Evangiles', Treaty of Arras of 1482, Art. 87; Treaty of Etaples of 1492, Art. 17; Treaty of Barcelona of 1493, *in fine*; First Treaty of Blois of 22 September 1504, *in fine*; 'quod ... Imperator ... Rex Franciae ... teneantur ... eaque omnia propriis juramentis super Sancta Cruce & Sacris Evangeliis firmare', First Treaty of Cambrai of 1508, Art. 20; Treaty of Noyon of 13 August 1516, *in fine*; Treaty of Madrid of 1526, Art. 45; First Treaty of Cambrai of 5 August 1529, Art. 46; 'jurera solennellement sur la Croix, Saints Evangiles de Dieu, & Canon de la Messe, & sur Son Honneur', Treaty of Crépy of 1544, *in fine*; First Treaty of Câteau-Cambrésis of 3 April 1559, *in fine*; Treaty of Vervins of 1598, *in fine*; Treaty of Madrid of 1630, Art. 35.

and more specifically that of the pope and the papal courts. They would suffer all ecclesiastical punishments in the case that they broke the treaty, and thereby their oaths. In some treaties, they also expressly renounced all existing and future dispensations from the ecclesiastical authority.

The custom of ratifying or confirming treaties by oath brought the whole problem of the binding force and the enforcement of treaties within the sphere of ecclesiastical jurisdiction and of canon law. As soon as a treaty was sworn upon, canon law became applicable. The breaking of an oath was a sin, perjury, and its curbing was a concern of the Church. Perjury could be punished by excommunication as well as interdicts.[40]

As the submission to the ecclesiastical authority was automatic as soon as an oath was sworn, the express submission in the treaties was largely redundant. It only had extra juridical consequences in so far as the parties agreed to turn only to the pope and the papal courts, and not to other ecclesiastical courts such as the episcopal courts. By that, the treaty partners could not deny the *ex officio* authority of those courts. On the other hand, the pope and the Roman courts were the most neutral and independent – at least in theory – of all the ecclesiastical courts vis-à-vis the great princes of Europe. Moreover, these express submissions indicated that the princes of Europe recognised the special role the pope played as the spiritual head of the *respublica christiana*, and accepted the universal application of canon law to regulate their relations.

The custom to have treaties confirmed by oath surprisingly did not end with the Reformation. Up to the end of the seventeenth century, treaties were still sworn upon, even when rulers from different Christian churches were involved. During the second half of the sixteenth century, the confirmation by oath was, however, transformed. The canon law dimension was gradually watered down. After 1540, all express references to the canonical jurisdiction or sanctions disappeared from the treaties, first in treaties involving Protestant princes and later even among Catholic powers. The Protestant princes rejected the authority of the pope as well as the universal application of canon law. As the papal sanctioning of treaties and the application of canon law ceased to be an instrument for safeguarding agreements over the whole of Christianity, it gradually lost all meaning for the Catholic world as well.

---

[40] Marcel David, 'Parjure et mensonge dans le Décret de Gratien', 3 *Studia Gratiana* 3 (1955), 117–41; Jean Gaudemet, 'Le serment dans le droit canonique médiéval' in Raymond Verdier (ed.), *Le Serment* (Paris, 1991), vol. II, pp. 66–9; Allan Z. Hertz, 'Medieval Treaty Obligation', *Connecticut Journal of International Law* 6 (1991), 425–43 at p. 431; Nussbaum, 'Forms and Observance', pp. 191–6.

Next to swearing a religious oath, the princes often also pledged their 'princely' or 'royal' word. This implied that they made a promise upon their honour as the king and as the supreme knight of the realm. It provided an extra guarantee for the treaty under the knightly code of honour and under the feudal tradition.[41]

Finally, some words should be said about the relation between the confirmation by oath and the written ratification through documents under seal. In his 1995 article on the Peace Treaty of Crépy of 1544, Heinhard Steiger pointed out that at least from around 1500 onwards a distinction was made between written ratification and confirmation by oath. According to Steiger, the Treaty of Crépy was ratified through sealed documents and thereby became binding under the rules of *Völkerrecht*, while the swearing of an oath amounted to an additional personal obligation and led to the submission of the parties to ecclesiastical jurisdiction. An analysis of the Treaties of Senlis of 1493, of Madrid of 1526 and of Cambrai I of 1529 shows that the distinction between written ratification and confirmation by oath was already made from around 1500.[42] Steiger's view is corroborated by the fact that for some early sixteenth-century treaties two kinds of ratification documents were made: a written ratification and a document evidencing the taking of the oath.[43] Steiger is correct in asserting that written ratification and the taking of an oath were two distinct acts in the early sixteenth century. As I have mentioned before, the distinction goes back as far as the thirteenth or even twelfth century.

[41] '... en bonne foy & parole de Prince', Treaty of Ancenis of 10 September 1468, *in fine*; 'en parole de Roy', Treaty of Arras of 1482, Art. 85; 'Et insuper promittimus et juramus ad dominum Deum nostrum et eius sanctam crucem et sancta quattuor evangelia, manibus nostris corporaliter tact, bona fide et sub verbo regio et sub censuris apostolicis', Ratification of the First Treaty of Blois of 1504, by Emperor Maximilian I (1493–1519), TIE III-1, 63; 'Promittentes bona fide & in verbo Regio': Full Powers for the Treaty of London of 1514, by Louis XII of France (1498–1515) on 29 July 1514, CUD IV-1, 188; 'en parolle de Roy sur nostre honneur': Ratification of the First Treaty of Cambrai of 5 August 1529 by Francis I, CUD IV-2, 20.

[42] See on this: Steiger, 'Crépy', pp. 256–60.

[43] E.g. distinct documents of ratification under seal: Treaty of Noyon of 1516, Ratification by Charles V on 9 October 1516, TIE III-2, 124–6; Treaty of Cambrai of 11 March 1517, Ratification by Maximilian and Charles on 14 May 1517, TIE III-2, 200–4; Charles' oath to the Noyon Treaty, TIE III-2, 121–4 and Charles' and Maximilian's oath of 14 May 1517 to the Cambrai Treaty, TIE III-2, 204. The swearing of the treaty was referred upon in the first documents as well. See also: oath of Francis of 1 April 1515 on the Treaty of Paris of 24 March 1515, TIE III-2, 30–7; Ratification by the same on 23 April 1515, TIE III-2, 42–4; Ratification by Charles on 1 June 1515, TIE III-2, 51–4; Ratification by Francis of the Noyon Treaty on 29 September 1516, TIE III-2, 107–9; Ratification of the Cambrai Treaty by Francis on 10 July 1517, TIE III-2, 213–14.

Steiger concluded, at least for the Peace of Crépy, that the written ratification was the constitutive act under the law of nations, while the oath was an accessory guarantee under canon law. Inasmuch as Steiger does not distinguish the Peace of Crépy from the Treaties of Senlis, Madrid and Cambrai, one has to be very careful with this assessment. While it may be close to the truth for the Treaty of Crépy and later treaties, it is not for the first three decades of the sixteenth century.

Although in the early sixteenth century the written ratification was distinguished from the taking of an oath, it can hardly be completely separated from it. Until deep in the seventeenth century, almost all important political treaties were confirmed by oath. I agree with Steiger that the juridical consequences of these two ways of 'ratification' were different, but it is too far reaching to state that the written ratification was considered sufficient to make the treaty binding under the law of nations, or *Völkerrecht*, which suggests that the oath was only additional. The written ratification made the treaty binding upon the rulers under general principles of contract as they emerged from Roman law, feudal law and customary law systems.[44] The taking of an oath made it truly binding under canon law and made it enforceable before the ecclesiastical courts. In view of the enormous impact of canon law on treaties in particular and contracts in general, an important treaty without canonical sanction would as yet not be considered to be sufficiently corroborated. Canon law was at that time not only a substantial, but also an inextricable part of what now would be considered the 'law of nations'. So being bound under canon law was an important part of or even condition to have an obligation under the 'law of nations', or historically more correct, the law in general. In my view, both kinds of obligations were crucial for a treaty to be truly binding upon princes under early sixteenth-century treaty practice. In other words, while I agree with Steiger on the facts of contemporary ratification, we differ on what we consider to be *Völkerrecht* in the early sixteenth century. While he distinguishes canon law from the law of nations, I consider them to be intertwined. An autonomous law of nations was still inconceivable.[45]

---

[44] And not under *Völkerrecht* as Steiger states. As a written pact, it became binding under general rules of Roman and customary law. The general doctrines of contract were largely dominated by Roman, feudal and, again, canon law arguments.

[45] 'Durch diese Unterwerfung unter die Jurisdiktion des Papstes erhält die völkerrechtliche Verpflichtung eine rechtliche Sanktion, die allerdings im kanonischen Recht und nicht im Völkerrecht selbst angelegt ist', Steiger, 'Crépy', p. 259. See also Hertz, 'Medieval Treaty Obligation'; Lesaffer, 'Medieval Canon Law'; Nussbaum, 'Forms and Observance'.

Steiger was, however, only concerned with the Crépy treaty. By 1544, the political, religious and juridical circumstances had greatly changed as compared to the 1510s and even 1520s. The Reformation had made an end to the religious unity of Europe, to the universal application of canon law and the universal recognition of ecclesiastical or papal jurisdiction. What had been the cornerstone of what we now call the 'law of nations' then divided Christianity. By 1544, in canon law and ecclesiastical courts the process of decanonisation of 'international law' had started. While, till the end of the seventeenth century, treaties were still confirmed by oath, even when partners with different religions were involved, references to papal or ecclesiastical jurisdiction all of a sudden disappeared after 1540. This was true even for treaties such as those of Crépy and Vervins (1598), between Catholic powers.[46] Of course the treaty partners were not able to put an end to the authority of the ecclesiastical courts. But it was no longer relevant to them as an effective or even theoretical means of safeguarding their agreements. As far as the period in which the Reformation started to determine international relations is concerned, of which the Treaty of Crépy is the very first important international peace treaty, Steiger is right to state that the oath now was no more than an accessory means of binding the parties to the treaty, separate from 'the law of nations'. I would, however, hesitate to qualify the written ratification as part of the law of nations. The absence of a universally applicable, autonomous body of rules regulating international relations after the collapse of the old *respublica christiana* is exactly what I conceive as the crisis of the international society.

As canon law was no longer part of 'international law', what was left was the written ratification. This at least guaranteed that the treaty was binding under secular contract law, as much in Roman and feudal as in customary law. Once the law of nations became an autonomous body of rules in the seventeenth century, the rules of ratification would be based on the existing practice of written ratification. The swearing of an oath, which remained customary during most of the seventeenth century, became accessory.[47]

In the ratification clauses and formulas, princes often pledged all their goods and possessions. Of course, in reality this guarantee did not amount to anything, but it would give the victim of a breach of treaty a just cause

---

[46] Lesaffer, *Europa*, p. 159; Steiger, 'Crépy', pp. 256–7.
[47] Treaty of Madrid of 15 November 1630, Art. 35; Treaty of the Pyrenees of 7 November 1659, Art. 124; Treaty of Nijmegen of 17 September 1678, Art. 32.

to wage war: the seeking of compensation for the damages suffered by the breach of treaty.[48] Of course, the clauses underlined the personal character of the treaties. More substantial was the bailing of a certain amount of money to safeguard the treaty, or, more often than not, a specific clause.[49] Often, this security was offered through the designation of some merchants, subjects of the prince, who lived or held possessions in the territories of the treaty partner. These stipulations have to be understood in the context of the law of particular reprisals, which allowed the subject of one prince to seize the property of any subject of another prince to compensate for the unpaid debts of another subject of that same prince. As such, subjects living in foreign countries were always liable for the debts and deeds of their sovereigns. In fact, these clauses limited this general right of reprisal to certain merchants and a certain amount of money.[50]

Another method of safeguarding the peace treaty or certain clauses therein was the handing over of hostages. Hostages were often handed over or exchanged to guarantee the cession of territories, towns or fortresses or the retreat of troops.[51] More often than not, the exchange of hostages was meant to guarantee purely military clauses, and as such the custom was clearly part of the medieval laws of war and the code of chivalry.[52] Where a treaty was signed with a prince who had been taken prisoner himself, his abiding to the treaty was commonly guaranteed with important

---

[48] '. . . & Hipoteca omnium bonorum nostrorum praesentium & futurorum', Treaty of Barcelona of 1493, in fine; Treaty of Noyon of 1516, Art. 7; 'sub obligatione, & hypotheca quorumcumque bonorum dictorum Constituentium, tam praesentium, quam futurorum': Treaty of Barcelona of 29 June 1529, in fine.

[49] Treaty of Venice of 30 August 1454, in fine; '& ultra cio sotto pena de Ducati cento millia doro oror dessere pagati per la Parte, che non observerà, a la Parte observante': Treaty of Bagnolo, 7 August 1484, in fine.

[50] This was often done to guarantee the payment of the dowry in the context of a marriage agreement: Treaty of Noyon of 1516, Art. 7; Treaty of Madrid of 1526, Art. 10; First Treaty of Cambrai of 5 August 1529, Art. 3. For the whole treaty, see First Treaty of Câteau-Cambrésis of 2 April 1559, Art. 9. On the particular reprisal, see Grewe, Epochs, pp. 201–3; Maurice H. Keen, The Law of War in the Late Middle Ages (London, 1965), pp. 218–38; Ernest Nys, Le Droit de la guerre et les précurseurs de Grotius (Brussels, 1882), pp. 37–54; Nys, Les Origines du droit international (Brussels, 1894), pp. 62–77.

[51] First Treaty of Amiens of 29 August 1475, Art. 3; Treaty of Rome of 1 January 1495, Art. 6; First Treaty of Cambrai of 1529, Art. 24; First Treaty of Câteau-Cambrésis of 3 April 1559, Art. 45; Treaty of Vervins of 1598, Art. 18. See on the extradition of hostages, Johan H. W. Verzijl, International Law in Historical Perspective (Leiden, 1973), vol. VI, pp. 293–5.

[52] Theodor Meron, Henry's Wars and Shakespeare's Laws: Perspectives on the Law of War in the Later Middle Ages (Oxford, 1993), pp. 81–5. On this code, see Robert C. Stacey, 'The Age of Chivalry' in Michael Howard, George J. Andreopoulos and Mark R. Shulman (eds.), The Law of War: Constraints on Warfare in the Western World (New Haven, 1994), pp. 27–39.

hostages upon his release. This custom also reflects the code of chivalry. The exchange of hostages has to be interpreted as an extraordinary guarantee for the payment of ransom for an important prince taken prisoner in battle.[53] During the seventeenth century, both the bailing of money on merchants and the extradition of hostages became less frequent. This evolution indicates the waning of the code of chivalry as the basis for conduct in war.

The *respublica christiana* in peace treaties

It remains an interesting question whether the signatory partners to the peace treaties of the period from 1454 till 1648 referred to Europe as *respublica christiana*. In the preambles and the ratification documents of the main peace treaties of the sixteenth and early seventeenth centuries, peace was generally said to be made not only for the benefit of the subjects of the princes involved, but for the benefit of the whole of Christianity. Thus, references to the Latin West as a community of princes and estates were very common. *Respublica christiana, Christianitas, orbis christiana* or *regni et principes christiani* were the most frequent names used for the Latin West.

The preambles often stated that peace was made to put an end to the devastation of Christianity and the shedding of the blood of fellow Christians. Moreover, internal peace within Christianity was considered to be essential for the advancement of the faith and the Church. It was often mentioned that, by making peace, the princes abided by the papal exhortations.[54] Similar statements can already be found in the main peace

---

[53] The most famous example is to be found in the Treaty of Madrid of 1526, Art. 4. On the law of ransom, see Philippe Contamine, 'Un contrôle étatique croissant. Les usages de la guerre du XIVe au XVIIIe siècle: rançons et butins', in Philippe Contamine (ed.), *Guerre et concurrence entre les états européens du XIVe au XVIIIe siècle* (Paris, 1998), pp. 199–236 at pp. 201–11; Keen, *Laws of War*, pp. 156–85; Stacey, 'Age of Chivalry', pp. 36–8.

[54] 'Tamen Respublica Christiana, quantum jacturae & damni ex Principum suorum intestinis odiis, discordiis, & bellis ex multo nunc tempore sit perplexa, vel hoc unum ab omnibus fidelibus est gravissimè indolendum, quod Christiani nominis hostes immanissimi Turci, aliisque infideles hinc occassionem capientes in dies eorum vires accrescendi', First Treaty of Cambrai of 1508, Preamble to the ratification by Maximilian I on 26 December 1508, CUD IV-1, 109; 'au bien et augmentacion de toute la chose publique chrestienne et exaltacion de la saincte foy catholicque', Treaty of Paris of 1515, Preamble; 'para evitar el derramamiento de la sangre christiana, dar medio para una paz universal, para poder convertir e boluer las armas de todos los reyes, prínçipes y potentados de la Christianidad a dar rruyna e destruyçíon de los dichos ynfieles, e para desarraygar los errores de la secta lutherana', Treaty of Madrid of 1526, Preamble.

treaties between the major Italian powers of the later fifteenth century. Here, the higher interest referred to is the pacification and unity of Italy, not of Christianity as a whole.[55]

Three additional remarks are appropriate here. First, in general, peace was said to be desirable so that the Christian princes would be able to unite their forces in the war against the infidels. Most of all, this concerned the launching of a new crusade against the Turks or other Islamic powers such as the pirate kingdoms in north-west Africa. From the Reformation onwards, other Christian religions were meant as well. As such, peace was a necessary precondition to a crusade. By consequence, some major peace treaties of the early sixteenth century encompassed a treaty of Holy Alliance against the infidels. References to a crusade against the Turks were the most frequent in treaties between the leading European princes, the kings of Spain and France.[56] In these treaties, the pope and all other Christian powers were invited to adhere. The pope was often granted special status as head of the Holy League. This was not an express submission to a kind of overlordship by the pope, but it showed the recognition of the fact that the pope was the spiritual leader of Christianity. In this capacity, the pope was more acceptable than another secular ruler as titular head of the alliance to the princes of Europe. Furthermore, the defence of the pope, the Holy See and the Papal States were often stated to constitute the first obligation of the treaty partners.[57] During the second half of the sixteenth century, Holy Alliances in which the pope was granted a special position became less frequent. In the League of Rome of 26 May 1571, which led to the battle of Lepanto, the pope was still appointed as arbiter within the League. The pope's military obligations were stipulated in a way similar to those of the secular powers, Spain and Venice. This was already remarkable, as in former leagues the pope was most of all expected to use his spiritual powers to aid his allies. Here, he was treated as just

---

[55] '... ad laudam & gloriam Omnipotentis Dei, ejusque Gloriosae Virginis Matris Mariae, totiusque Curiae Triumphantis ad felicitatem & Pacem Italiae, tranquillitatem & quietem partium praedictorum', Treaty of Venice of 1454, Preamble.

[56] Fisch, *Krieg und Frieden*, p. 442. Treaty of Barcelona of 1493, Preamble; First Treaty of Cambrai of 1508, Preamble; 'ne lupus ille rapax Turcus immanissimus Christiani nominis hostis, continue quaerens quem devoret', Treaty of London of 1508, Preamble; Treaty of Madrid of 1526, Preamble; Treaty of Crépy of 1544, Preamble; First Treaty of Câteau-Cambrésis of 3 April 1559, Preamble; Treaty of Vervins of 1598, Preamble.

[57] Treaty of Venice of 1454, Art. 2; Treaty of Naples of 1470, Art. 3; Treaty of Bagnolo of 1484, Art. 7; Second Treaty of Cambrai of 1508, Art. 16; Treaty of London of 1518, Art. 2; Treaty of Barcelona of 1529, Art. 2.

another worldly ruler. Moreover, these obligations were waived, though not in view of his special position, but in view of the improbability of the pope fulfilling them.[58]

The recognition of the emperor or another secular ruler as head of the alliance and leader of a future crusade was very exceptional in the period studied. In fact, only one serious attempt at establishing a *monarchia universalis* can be detected in early modern peace practice: by Charles V (1519–58) after the battle of Pavia (1525), in which his troops captured the French king, Francis I. This attempt was heavily promoted by the young emperor's chancellor and most influential adviser, Mercurino Arborio di Gattinara (1480–1530). The dream of a universal monarchy should be seen in the context of the extraordinary accumulation of territories under the young Habsburg, his election as emperor in 1519 and the extreme challenges the Latin West was confronted with, from the outside as well as from the inside. Gattinara's idea of the emperor as *dominus mundi* or *monarcha universalis* reflected the Dantesque and Romanist traditions of the early fourteenth century.[59] It implied the recognition of the emperor as the true successor of the Roman Caesars. As secular leader of Christianity he was the supreme defender of the faith and the protector of the Church. By consequence, the emperor was the natural military leader of a common crusade, against both the external and the internal enemies of the faith.[60] However reluctantly Charles V may have followed Gattinara in these ambitions, they were to a limited extent accomplished in the Peace Treaties of Madrid of 1526 and Cambrai of 1529 with Francis I, and of Barcelona of 1529 with the pope. In the Madrid Peace Treaty, Francis I not only called the emperor the head of Christianity, but also agreed to participate as junior partner in a crusade lead by the emperor.[61] In the Treaty of Bologna with the pope, Charles was also referred to as the head of Christianity. The treaty sealed the hegemony

---

[58] Arts. 7 and 8.
[59] Most influential on the subject are the works of Franz Bosbach, *Monarchia Universalis: ein politische Leitbegriff der frühen Neuzeit* (Göttingen, 1986); Frances Yates, *Astraea: The Imperial Theme in the Sixteenth Century* (Cambridge, 1975). More recently: James Muldoon, *Empire and Order: The Concept of Empire, 800–1800* (Basingstoke, 1999); Anthony Pagden, *Lords of All the World: Ideologies of Empire in Spain, Britain and France c. 1500–c. 1800* (New Haven and London, 1995).
[60] John M. Headley, *The Emperor and His Chancellor: A Study of the Imperial Chancellery under Gattinara* (Cambridge, 1983).
[61] '... como cabeça de los prínçipes seglares de la christianidad', Treaty of Madrid of 1526, Art. 26; see also Preamble and Art. 23.

of the emperor over Italy.⁶² Charles V may have been the last emperor to be able to aspire to secular supremacy over the other 'sovereign' princes. His attempts, which came close to success in the 1520s, in the end utterly failed. After Charles' reign, no such examples of the recognition of the supremacy within the context of Christianity, however ephemeral such a thing might be, can be found in important peace treaties. In treaty practice, the ideal of *monarchia universalis* did not stand a chance any longer.⁶³

Second, the references to the Christian republic in the preambles to the peace treaties indicate that the sovereign princes considered themselves to be responsible for the commonwealth not only of their own territories and subjects, but of the whole of Christianity. In many treaties, these two responsibilities were clearly considered equally important. This concern for the *bonum commune* of the whole of Christianity was reflected in the writings of the Spanish black friar Francisco de Vitoria on the enforcement of the *ius gentium*. According to Vitoria, the sovereign princes were the highest secular authority within what he called the *totus orbis*.⁶⁴ By consequence, they were expected not only to enforce their own interests and rights under the *ius gentium*, but also to enforce the law of nations within the *totus orbis* in general. In the preambles to the peace treaties,

---

⁶² 'Sacrae Romanae Ecclesiae, Apostolicaeque Sedis, Protector, & Defensor, & Christianae Reipublicae caput', Art. 3.

⁶³ To the Treaty of Crépy of 1544 a secret Treaty was added in which Francis I had to repeat some of the relevant clauses of the Madrid and Cambrai Treaties. As in 1526, Charles V was then in a very strong position thanks to his victory over the Protestant princes of the Empire. The relevant clauses were however secret. See on that: Paul Van Petegem, 'Internationale verdragen gesloten tussen Karel V en Frans I. Onderzook haar structurele veranderingen in de christenheid en de wereld' in Randall Lesaffer and Georges Macours (ed.), *Sovereignty and the Law of Nations (16th to 18th centuries)* (Iuris Scripta Historiae, Brussels, 2005).

⁶⁴ On the international law doctrine of Vitoria, esp. on the *jus ad bellum*, see C. Barcia Trelles, 'Francisco de Vitoria et l'école moderne du droit international', *Recueils des Cours de l'Académie de Droit International* 17 (1927), 242–3; J. Eppstein, *The Catholic Tradition of the Law of Nations* (London, 1935), pp. 97–123; José Antonio Fernandez-Santamaria, *The State, War and Peace: Spanish Political Thought in the Renaissance, 1516–1559* (Cambridge, 1977), pp. 131–44; Peter Haggenmacher, *Grotius et la doctrine de la guerre juste* (Paris, 1983), pp. 170–3; Heinz Kipp, *Moderne Probleme des Kriegsrechts in der Spätscholastik: eine rechtsphilosophische Studie über die Vorassetzungen des Rechtes zum Krieg bei Vitoria und Suarez* (Paderborn, 1935), pp. 39–98; Scott, *The Spanish Origin*, pp. 142–50 and 192–238; Antonio Truyol y Serra, 'La conception de la paix chez Vitoria et les classiques espagnols du droit des gens', *Recueils de la Société Jean Bodin pour l'Histoire Comparative des Institutions* 15 (1961), 241–74; Joe Verhoeven, 'Vitoria ou la matrice du droit international' in Antonio Truyol y Serra (ed.), *Actualité de la pensée juridique de Francisco de Vitoria* (Brussels, 1988), pp. 97–128 at pp. 112–17.

the princes declared themselves to be responsible for the highest goals of Christianity as a whole.

Third, some reflections have to be made on the impact of the Reformation. Of course, during the times of the wars of religion, in some treaties the adherents of another Christian religion were taken to be enemies of the faith. Such references were more common among Catholic powers than among Protestants. In some treaties, the Protestants were regarded in a similar way as the Turks. It is, however, striking that the references to the internal peace within the Christian republic and to the common effort against the Turks did not disappear from the preambles of peace treaties during the period of the wars of religion. In treaties among Catholics, the references did not change much after the Reformation. References to the war against the infidels and to the defence of the 'faith' were hardly different from before.[65] In the preambles to treaties between princes from other religions, the references to the defence of the faith and the wars against the infidels, even the Turks, disappeared altogether halfway through the sixteenth century. The ideal of internal peace within the *respublica christiana* was expressly defended as before. Christianity, divided as it might be after the Reformation and juridically disorganised as it might be in reality after the collapse of the medieval system, was still seen as a community, which was valued or at least aspired to.[66]

Sixteenth-century treaty practice reflected the collapse of the old ideal of the *respublica christiana*. On the one hand, during the whole pre-Westphalian period, and even afterwards, Christian Europe continued to be considered as an integrated whole. Even after the Reformation had made itself felt at the international level, some time around 1540, the princes of Europe, while claiming external sovereignty, still accepted to be part of a greater whole. They accepted the existence of a greater interest – mostly understood as internal peace within the Christian world – for the defence of which they were all responsible.

On the other hand, the 1540s mark a caesura. Before 1550, the idea of a common crusade against the Turks and the definition of the common good of Christianity in terms of defending the faith were still very frequent. After 1550 they disappeared. Before 1550, the pope's position as the leader of the one Church still assured him the universal recognition of his spiritual

---

[65] Treaty of Crépy of 1544, Preamble; First Treaty of Câteau-Cambrésis of 3 April 1559, Preamble; Treaty of Vervins of 1598, Preamble; Treaty of Lyons of 17 January 1601, Preamble.
[66] Second Treaty of Câteau-Cambrésis of 2 April 1559, Preamble; Alliance Treaty of the Hague of 31 October 1596, Preamble; Treaty of London of 1604, Preamble.

leadership of the Latin West. After 1550, this spiritual leadership was no longer recognised by about half of the Christian princes, and quite soon and spectacularly lost all meaning within the Catholic world.

This decline of papal authority was reflected in the decanonisation of the oath, as it was discussed above. Furthermore, the falling into disuse of another kind of clause also highlights the demise of the old system. In some of the peace and alliance treaties of the early sixteenth century, many of them including a marriage agreement, the pope was nominated as the principal *conservator* of the treaty. This implied that he guaranteed the execution of the treaty. He thereby promised to side with the treaty partner that suffered from a breach of treaty by his partner.[67] After the 1540s, these mentions of third powers as guarantors became very rare. When they re-emerged after 1648, the pope had lost his preferential place as the first guarantor. Of course, before 1540 the pope as supreme judge within the Church could be called upon anyhow to sanction any breach of a treaty that had been confirmed by oath. After 1540, this was still possible, but papal authority was no longer accepted as an effective method of law enforcement in the context of international relations.

These changes from treaty practice indeed reflect the sudden breakdown halfway through the sixteenth century of the old medieval system. The supranational authority of the pope was rejected and the binding character of the *ius gentium* as part of Roman and canon law was challenged. While Europe continued to perceive itself as a unity, it had no general law of nations any more. Before a new generally accepted legal system could be formed, the 'law of nations' first disintegrated into a set of different laws of nations.

The inclusion of third parties in treaties

During the fifteenth century, it became quite common to include third powers in the peace treaties. This was also done in alliance treaties.[68]

---

[67] 'Les conservateurs de ce present traicté seront nostre Sainct Père, le Sainct Siège Apostolicque, le Saint Empire, électeurs et princes d'icellui, qui pourront et seront tenuz assister de leurs povoirs la partie qui entretiendra ce present traicté à l'encontre de celle qui ne le vouldra entretenir ne observer', Alliance Treaty of Paris of 1515, Art. 12; similar clause in Art. 16 of the Noyon Peace Treaty of 1516.

[68] Randall Lesaffer, 'Tussen *respublica christiana* en *ius publicum europaeum*. De ontwikkeling van de Europese rechtsordening in alliantieverdragen van de vroege Nieuwe Tijd (1450–1600)' in Beatrix Jacobs (ed.), *De rechtspraktijk in beeld: van Justinianus tot de Duitse bezetting. Handelingen van het XIV de Belgisch-Nederlands Rechtshistorisch Congres* (Tilburg, 1997), pp. 95–127 at pp. 110–18.

The third parties were said to be the allies and friends of the principal treaty partners. In some treaties, these allies and friends were mentioned expressly. Gradually, it became practice to allow each partner to name the allies and friends it wanted included within a certain time. Sometimes it was stipulated that all treaty partners had to agree on the inclusion of a third partner, and sometimes it was provided that they would propose the third partners jointly. In any case, the third power had to confirm that it wanted to be included in the treaty.[69]

It is hard to assess the exact consequences of these inclusions. According to the Dutch specialist of the history of international law, Verzijl, inclusion amounted to a true accession whereby the acceding party became full partner to the treaty.[70] This does not seem to be correct. First, most peace treaties contained specific clauses which would be irrelevant or practically impossible to apply to third powers without further negotiations. In the vast majority of the cases, no such negotiations took place. At the most, inclusion could mean that, by accepting the inclusion, the third power accepted the new juridical relations between the original treaty partners laid down in these clauses. Second, during the sixteenth century it became practice to nominate almost all European powers for inclusion. If inclusion meant the same as full accession, this would have made these treaties pan-European peace treaties, which they certainly were not.

What then was the meaning of these inclusions? The inclusion clauses in peace treaties predominantly had a political function. By including their allies and friends, the original treaty partners at least wanted to assure their allies that the peace treaty was not to their detriment. In case a third party had been supporting one of the belligerents or was a belligerent itself, it amounted to more. Then the inclusion was the guarantee for the included power that it would not have to continue the war by itself. However, often third powers were included that did not participate in the war, or that were supportive of both sides.

---

[69] Some examples of these inclusion clauses are Treaty of Venice of 1454, Art. 9; Treaty of Naples of 1470, Art. 13; Treaty of Etaples of 1492, Art. 12; Treaty of Senlis of 1493, Art. 17, CUD; Treaty of London of 1514, Art. 23; Treaty of London of 1518, Art. 10; Treaty of Madrid of 1526, Art. 43; Treaty of Crépy of 1544, Art. 14; First Treaty of Câteau-Cambrésis of 3 April 1559, Art. 46; Treaty of Vervins of 1598, *in fine*; Treaty of London of 1604, Arts. 34–5; Treaty of Münster of 24 October 1648, Para. 127; and Treaty of Osnabrück of 24 October 1648, Art. 17 (8). See on the practice of inclusion in the Italian treaties of the fifteenth century, Nicolai Rubinstein, 'Das politischen System Italiens in der zweite Hälfte des 15. Jahrhunderts', *Zeitschrift für Historische Forschung*, Beihefte, 5 (1988), 105–19 at pp. 108–10; Giovanni Soranzo, 'Colligati, raccomandati, aderenti negli Stati italiano dei secoli XIV e XV', *Archivio Storico Italiano* 99 (1941), 3–35.

[70] Verzijl, *International Law in Historical Perspective*, vol. VI, p. 203.

But what were the juridical consequences of being included in a peace treaty? In general, the inclusion meant that there would be peace between the original treaty partner who did not nominate the included third power and the latter. In the case that there had been no direct war this was quite meaningless. In the case that there had been, it was mostly deemed to be insufficient and extra negotiations were in order to make a proper peace. In at least one case, as it was brought forward by Steiger, the inclusion of a third power to a peace treaty as important as the Westphalia Treaties did not even end its war with one of the main treaty partners.[71] Nevertheless, in my view the inclusion normally amounted to something more than just peace: the inclusion vested or affirmed a juridical relationship known as *amicitia*.

Amicitia as a juridical concept referring to interstate relations was already known in Antiquity and, under other names, is still important in present-day state practice.[72] It generally comes down to the willingness to sustain peaceful relations, based on the rule of law. Thereby, the mutual – at least silent – recognition of the existence of *amicitia* is the necessary precondition to the elaboration of further legal and peaceful relations between totally independent political entities. More specifically, *amicitia* in the early modern period included the application of the rule of law to each other's subjects as well as the promise not to render help to each other's enemies.[73] From the beginning of the fifteenth century onwards, references to *amicitia* became frequent in the preambles and main articles of treaties between Italian powers. During the first decades of the sixteenth century, the references suddenly became commonplace

---

[71] Steiger, 'Der westfälischen Frieden', pp. 45–8.
[72] For a divergent opinion, see Bruno Paradisi, 'L'amitié internationale. Les phases critiques de son ancienne histoire', *Recueil des Cours de l'Académie de Droit International* 77 (1951), 329–78 at pp. 329–30. On interstate *amicitia* in Antiquity and the Middle Ages, see Maria Rosa Cimma, *Reges socii et amici populi romani* (Milan, 1976); Francesco de Martino, *Storia della costituzione romana* (Naples, 1973), vol. II, pp. 16–35; Alfred Heuss, 'Die völkerrechtlichen Grundlagen der römischen Aussenpolitik in republikanischer Zeit', *Klio* 13 (1933), Beihefte 1–59; Paradisi, 'L'amitié internationale'; Paradisi, 'L'amicitia internazionale nella storia antica' in Bruno Paradisi, *Civitas maxima: studi di storia del diritto internazionale* (Florence, 1974), vol. II, pp. 296–338; Paradisi, 'L'amicitia nell'alto medio evo' in *Civitas maxima*, vol. II, pp. 339–97; Karl-Heinz Ziegler, 'Der Freundschaftsvertrag im Völkerrecht der römische Antike' in *Pensamiento juridica y sociedad internacional: estudio Antonio Truyol y Serra* (Madrid, 1986), vol. II, pp. 1263–71.
[73] This is made quite evident from the analysis of the various Treaties of Westminster of 25 July 1474 between King Edward IV of England (1461–83) and Duke Charles the Bold of Burgundy (1467–77). See especially the First Treaty.

throughout the Latin West. During the seventeenth and eighteenth centuries, they became standardised and deteriorated to quite meaningless commonplaces.

Nevertheless, the frequency of both the references and the inclusion clauses is an indication of the growing crisis in the international system. These different kinds of establishing or confirming *amicitia* can only be explained as expressions of the need that was felt continuously to repeat the willingness to have peaceful relations based on the rule of law. This shows that such relations were no longer considered to be present. These frequent affirmations, both within and outside the context of inclusion, are therefore illustrative of the collapse of the old system and the subsequent crisis. It is striking that during the later seventeenth and early eighteenth centuries, when the new system emerged, they were less accentuated and lost much of their substance.

The observation that the inclusion clauses aimed at vesting or affirming a relationship known as *amicitia* between the third powers and the original treaty partners is only true in general. Inclusion clauses could encompass more or, as Steiger proved, sometimes even less. In some treaties more substance was given to the inclusion. But to have a more precise view, it would be necessary to study diplomatic history in order to see what kinds of rights powers actually claimed, if they did so at all, on the basis of inclusion in peace treaties.

The duration of peace

Under modern international law, peace treaties are meant to last perpetually. So far, they are distinct from truces. During the fifteenth and sixteenth centuries, the distinction seems to have been somewhat more complex. Peace treaties and truces not only differ as far as their duration is concerned. While peace treaties are intended to settle once and for all the conflicts that caused the war by determining the rights of each party involved, truces – *treugae* or *indutiae* – tend to preserve the rights and claims of parties. To be able to speak of a peace treaty, the main criterion is that a peace implies that the signatory powers accept the settlement of disputes present in the treaty as being final.[74] Thereby, the promise is made not to resort to violence in the future over the conflicts or disputes fought over during the war and dealt with in the treaty. As very few peace treaties have proved to stand the test of time, this implication of 'eternal'

[74] Fisch, *Krieg und Frieden*, pp. 355–61.

or 'perpetual' peace, as peace was often called in the treaties, is far more relevant and less naive than a mere temporal concept of timelessness.

This is all the more relevant to early modern treaty practice inasmuch as it was customary, particularly between France and England, to make truces over a very long period of time, settling quite important disputes between the parties. These treaties are both in form (duration) and substance (reservation of the right to wage war after the expiration of the truce) truces, but from a practical perspective they are closer to real peace treaties than to those frequent truces that contained only military measures and lasted some months or even weeks. Such truces did not exhaust the right of the belligerent to go to war over the same disputes, but they exhausted it over a certain time. As this period could be five, ten or even a hundred years, for all practical reasons they were similar to 'eternal' or 'perpetual' peace treaties.[75]

The law of war and peace in peace treaties

Finally, we need to analyse the way in which rules of war and peace emerged from the contents of peace treaties. As it is impossible to go into the details of the various peace treaties, some general categories of clauses can be discerned. A *summa divisio* can be made between clauses that concerned the past and clauses that concerned the future relations between the parties. The first kinds of stipulations of course dealt with the consequences of the hostilities themselves. In that respect, they also shed some light on the laws of war.

As Jörg Fisch has already lavishly established, the vast majority of early modern peace treaties contained a clause of amnesty.[76] In this clause, the signatories excused each other and each other's subjects, vassals, soldiers, allies and adherents for all sufferings, injuries and damage caused in consequence of the war. These clauses not only implied that the parties would not seek revenge or allow their subjects and allies to do so, they also meant that no judicial actions would be permitted to restore one's rights injured during the war.

---

[75] For five years, the Treaty of London of 16 February 1471, Art. 1; for nine years, the Treaty of Soleuvre, 13 September 1475, Art. 1; for a hundred years after the death of the first of the princes involved to die in the Treaty of London of 13 February 1478, Art. 1; for twelve years the Treaty of Antwerp of 9 April 1609, Art. 2.

[76] Fisch, *Krieg und Frieden*, pp. 92–117.

Such clauses were already present in the major peace treaties of the later fifteenth century as well as in treaties from before that period.[77] But from the sixteenth century onwards, they became more frequent. By the seventeenth century, they can be found in almost all peace treaties. These amnesty clauses were in clear contradiction to the medieval doctrine of the just war as theologians and canon and Roman lawyers had developed it. This doctrine implied a discriminatory concept of war and peace. According to the doctrine, in each war there was a just and an unjust belligerent. The unjust belligerent was in fact denied the right to wage war.[78] In a subsequent peace treaty, the responsibility for the war should be attributed to one of the treaty partners and a punishment should be imposed upon the unjust belligerent. This doctrine was still upheld, or at least paid lip service to, in the justifications of wars to be found in alliance agreements.[79] In the context of the emergence of the sovereign principalities and the collapse of the old legal and religious order of the West, this doctrine became totally incompatible with the realities of international politics. The emergence of the amnesty clauses during the early modern period was, therefore, in accordance with the emergence of sovereign princes.

Only minor evolutions through the early modern period can be noted. First, while during the fifteenth and (most of) the sixteenth centuries state subjects who had fought on the side of their sovereign's opponent were frequently included in the amnesty,[80] from the end of the sixteenth century onwards they were often excluded.[81] This change indicated the gradual monopolisation of warfare by the sovereign and the growing dualism between the national and the international legal order. Second, the clauses of amnesty were increasingly standardised, and from the second half of

---

[77] Fisch, *Krieg und Frieden*, pp. 79–81; Neitmann, *Staatsverträge*, pp. 381–96.
[78] On the just war doctrine in the Middle Ages and early modern times, see Haggemacher, *Grotius et la doctrine de la guerre juste*, pp. 74–126 and 154–70; Keen, *Laws of War*, pp. 63–81; Frederick H. Russell, *The Just War in the Middle Ages* (London, 1975); J. von Elbe, 'The Evolution of the Concept of Just War in International Law', *American Journal of International Law* 33 (1939), 665–88.
[79] Lesaffer, 'War, Peace, Interstate Friendship', pp. 96–101.
[80] Treaty of Conflans of 1465, Arts. 4 and 6; Treaty of Péronne of 1468; Treaty of Arras of 1482, Art. 42; Treaty of Senlis of 1493, Art. 23; Treaty of Madrid of 1526, Art. 30; Treaty of Crépy of 1544, Art. 18; First Treaty of Câteau-Cambrésis of 3 April 1559, Arts. 7, 23, 25, 27 and 40; Treaty of Susa of 1601, Art. 18; Treaty of Asti of 21 June 1615, Art. 8.
[81] E.g. Treaty of Prague of 30 May 1635, Art. 21.

the seventeenth century onwards became less elaborate. This does not imply that the clauses lost importance. Quite to the contrary, the process of standardisation and the subsequent reduction in clauses proves them to be generally accepted. Moreover, by the beginning of the seventeenth century it was held by doctrine that amnesty was inherent to peace and thus silently implied in each peace settlement.[82]

In none of the peace treaties analysed for the period between 1454 and 1648 can a clause be found in which the responsibility for the war is assigned to a single belligerent party, at least in so far as it concerns treaties between sovereigns. In some treaties between sovereigns and their rebellious vassals, the loser had to take the responsibility for the war. This indicates that the war, or better the rebellion, needed more justification than a normal war between two sovereigns. However, in none of these treaties was the accused party sanctioned for the act of rebellion or the warfare itself. This is most clear in the Treaty of Sablé of 20 August 1488, between the French king and the duke of Brittany. The duke was accused of being solely responsible for the war. The duke's acts had forced the king to take up arms. While the king had just cause, the duke had not. While the duke should be liable for all the costs and damages of the war, the king would not hold him to that.[83]

Closely related to the amnesty clauses are the restitution clauses, dealing with the restitution of private property occupied, looted or confiscated during the war. In general, these clauses stipulated the restitution of real property to the pre-war owners, while no amends were made for the interest and rents, and no restitution of moveables was expected. Through this distinction between easily identifiable real property on the one hand and moveables on the other, the clauses were aimed at limiting the discussions and conflicts arising from the war and at returning as speedily as possible to a stable and peaceful situation. Judgements on the rights and wrongs of particular cases of wartime looting and confiscations were considered immaterial. Some treaties also included stipulations about the payments of debts among the subjects of the former belligerents.[84]

Furthermore, many peace treaties stipulated that all wartime impediments and extraordinary measures concerning trade would be abolished

---

[82] Grotius, *De jure belli ac pacis* 3, 20, 15 (Paris, 1625; Classics of International Law 3, Oxford, 1913); Gudelinus, *De jure pacis* 3, 4, p. 554; Emmerich de Vattel, *Le Droit des gens ou principes de la loi naturelle* 4, 2, 20 (London, 1758; Leyden, 1758, Classics of International Law 4, Washington, 1916).

[83] Preamble and Art. 8.

[84] Treaty of Arras of 1482, Arts. 44–5; Treaty of Senlis of 1493, Arts. 24–5 and 28.

and that old privileges were restored.[85] Finally, some peace treaties contained a clause concerning prisoners of war. Under the medieval laws of war, prisoners of war were considered to be the personal prisoners of the knight who had taken them prisoner on the battlefield. The captor held a personal right to the payment of a ransom. The very presence of the clause concerning prisoners of war indicates the growing monopolisation of warfare by the sovereign. Such clauses can only be found in Italy during the fifteenth century and gradually appear outside Italy during the sixteenth century. Normally it was stated that all prisoners would be released. Ransom was only to be paid if an agreement had already been made on the ransom with the captor. The prisoner was liable, however, for the prisoner's keeping during captivity. During the seventeenth century, references to ransom and thereby the personal rights of the captors over their prisoners would disappear.[86]

In addition to these ways of limiting the consequences of the wars and restoring the pre-war situation, peace treaties also contained several clauses that aimed at stabilising the peace and preventing the outbreak of a new war. In most peace treaties, one of the main articles distinctly mentioned that the parties would not cause any damage to one another or allow or help their allies and subjects to do so. These stipulations were related to the concept of *amicitia*.[87]

Many peace treaties also held clauses concerning trade. Generally, it was stipulated that the parties agreed not to place special restrictions or taxes on the subjects of the other treaty partner when coming to or trading with their own territories. No discriminations were allowed. The subjects of one partner to the treaty would enjoy access to the same courts and procedures as the other treaty partner's subjects did. The rule of law would apply to them.[88] Thus, these clauses were again a confirmation of *amicitia*.

---

[85] Treaty of Lodi of 1454, Art. 3; Third Treaty of Amiens of 1475, Art. 3; Treaty of Madrid of 1526, Art. 31; Treaty of Madrid of 1630, Art. 24.

[86] Contamine, 'Un contrôle étatique croissant', pp. 199–236. Treaty of Lodi of 1454, Arts. 24–5; Treaty of Etaples of 1492, Art. 7; First Treaty of Cambrai of 1529, Art. 1; Treaty of Vervins of 1598, Art. 20; Treaty of London of 18 August 1604, Art. 30; Treaty of Bromsebrö of 13 August 1645, Art. 31; Treaty of Münster of 30 January 1648, Art. 63.

[87] Third Treaty of Amiens of 1475, Art. 2; Treaty of Etaples of 1492, Art. 6; First Treaty of Cambrai of 1529, Art. 1; Second Treaty of Cambrai of 5 August 1529, Art. 2; Second Treaty of Câteau-Cambrésis of 2 April 1559, Arts. 2–3; First Treaty of Câteau-Cambrésis of 3 April 1559, Art. 1; Treaty of Vervins of 1598, Art. 2; Treaty of London of 1604, Art. 3; Treaty of Madrid of 1630, Arts. 3 and 5; Treaty of Bromsebrö of 1645, Art. 35.

[88] Third Treaty of Amiens of 1475, Art. 2; Treaty of Arras of 1482, Art. 19; Treaty of Etaples of 1492, Art. 3; Treaty of Madrid of 1526, Art. 2; Second Treaty of Cambrai of 1529, Art. 1; First Treaty of Câteau-Cambrésis of 3 April 1559, Art. 4; Treaty of Vervins of 1598, Art. 2.

Often, these stipulations were accompanied by a prohibition to resort to particular reprisals in the future and by the annulment of all existing *lettres de marques et de contremarques* that allowed reprisals. However, reprisal could still be allowed in the case of a manifest denial of justice.[89] The exclusion of reprisal would become absolute in the eighteenth century. Particular reprisals were very resistant to the monopolisation of warfare by the sovereign.

In many peace treaties, the ambition to prevent future resort to violence was expressed by the agreement not to consider the peace treaty broken by an infringement by a private person, subject of one of the treaty partners. Often it was stipulated that only the guilty subjects would be punished and that the damage would be compensated for. Reprisals against innocent people were prohibited. By the sixteenth century, this clause was largely standardised.[90]

Conclusion

The peace treaties of the early sixteenth century show the quite sudden collapse of the medieval system of European legal order. The Reformation was the main factor directly causing this breakdown. By 1550, the last remains of the universal authority or supremacy of the pope had disappeared. It was, however, far worse that canon law lost its universal validity. These sudden changes can, above all, be detected in the shifting position of the oath and the changes in the methods of ratification.

The collapse of the medieval legal system in Europe did not only imply that by 1550 the sovereign princes of Europe had fully attained external sovereignty. It also implied that the old *ius gentium*, which was dependent on the *ius commune* both for its contents and for its validity, lost its authority. As the canon law was not only the most important, but also an inextricable part of this amalgam, the end of the religious unity of the

---

[89] '... nisi super & contra principales delinquentes, & eorum Bona, eorumve fautores, vel in casu manifestae denegationis Justitiae, de quâ per Litteras summationis aut requisitionis & prout de Jure requiritur sufficienter constabit', Treaty of Etaples of 1492, Art. 10; Treaty of London of 1514, Art. 10; Treaty of Madrid of 1526, Art. 2; Second Treaty of Cambrai of 1529, Art. 6; First Treaty of Câteau-Cambrésis of 3 April 1559, Art. 5; Treaty of Vervins of 1598, Art. 4; Treaty of London of 1604, Art. 6.

[90] Treaty of Arras of 1482, Arts. 80–1; Treaty of Etaples of 1492, Art. 11; Treaty of Senlis of 1493, Art. 38; Second Treaty of Câteau-Cambrésis of 2 April 1559, Art. 4; Treaty of London of 1604, Arts. 2 and 29; Treaty of Münster of 30 January 1648, Art. 60.

West could not but bring the end of its international law system based on that unity. On the other hand, the collapse of the old system did make way for the development of an autonomous doctrine of the law of nations in general, and of treaty law in particular.

The collapse of the old system left a vacuum. Owing to the ongoing religious wars, both internationally and internally, it took more than a century before a new system could be constructed. The *respublica christiana* was felt to be in crisis. The all too frequent affirmations of the basic relation of *amicitia* prove that this crisis was more than a historian's construction.

The modern system of international law that emerged after 1648 was based on the principle of state sovereignty. The analysis of pre-Westphalian peace treaties indicates that the sixteenth century was a crucial period in the emergence of that sovereign state. While, from the perspective of modern international law, it is customary to judge the period in terms of the results of that process, for a correct assessment of the treaty law of the period itself it is instrumental to look at the process itself. Such an approach highlights the conclusion that by the end of the sixteenth century the sovereign state – as an abstract institution and as an internally sovereign power – still was not in place. That, of course, is another explanation for the fact that it took more than a hundred years for the modern European state system to emerge.

Nevertheless, a close analysis of the contents of the peace treaties allows us to discover signs of the gradual emergence of the sovereign state. The now complete rejection of the discriminatory aspects of the just-war doctrine is, of course, crucial in this light. The growing control of the sovereigns over warfare is reflected in the increasing reluctance to make regular peace treaties with vassals and subjects as well as in the inroads on the medieval rights of reprisal and ransom. Therein a stricter distinction between the international and the internal legal spheres, known as dualism, lurks. The disappearance of co-ratification and the changing position on the binding force of treaties on the successors of the original signatories marked the beginning of the identification of the prince with the state as an abstract body.

The Peace of Westphalia of 1648 brought enough stability for the main powers of Europe to allow the construction of a new international legal order. While this makes it licit to call the Peace of Westphalia an important caesura, it cannot excuse the traditional neglect, if not contempt, of international legal historians for pre-Westphalian treaty practice. The process of the emergence of the sovereign state that reached its end during the century and a half after Westphalia was the continuation of a process which gained some momentum in the sixteenth century. Many of the rules and concepts, both of formal and of material treaty law, that were developed after 1648 can be traced back to pre-Westphalian treaty practice.

3

Peace treaties from Westphalia to the Revolutionary Era

HEINZ DUCHHARDT

Introduction

In 1980, I covered the problem of peace congresses in the century following the Peace Treaties of Westphalia (1648) for the first time.[1] At that time, the main interest was in formal questions, especially the institution of mediation, whose changing substance and practice I then sketched. Central to the argument was the question why and when the pre-modern age tackled the problem of peacekeeping by developing mechanisms to prevent the outbreak of conflicts instead of merely putting an end to wars, and how successful these efforts, which culminated in the congresses of Cambrai and Soissons in the 1720s, were.

After twenty years, one approaches a question quite differently, according to changing paradigms of research. In this chapter, more emphasis is put on the internal logic and the internal mechanisms of peacemaking, and also on the categories which were used in order to situate the material results of the negotiations in a particular conception of the world. But the chapter also takes into account that the interests of research have considerably moved towards historical semantics, the changing use and meaning of notions and key words, and in general the direction of the language used in the treaties.

Westphalia as a turning point?

First of all, there is a need to reflect on the specifics of the period and on the fundamental changes which took place in the character of the interstate

[1] Heinz Duchhardt, 'Friedenskongresse im Zeitalter des Absolutismus – Gestaltung und Strukturen' in *XVe Congrès International des Sciences Historiques, Rapports* (Bucharest, 1980), vol. I, pp. 204–8. The complete version of this paper was published in Konrad Repgen (ed.), *Forschungen und Quellen zur Geschichte des Dreißigjährigen Krieges* (Münster, 1981), pp. 226–39.

45

relations and the treaties in comparison with the preceding period. In this respect, one has to start with the decisive moment of the Peace of Westphalia (1648), which is used as a matter of course in standard works such as Wilhelm Grewe's.[2] This author – an international lawyer and former diplomat who died recently (2001) – brings together two periods in the Peace of Westphalia, a 'Spanish' one and a 'French' one. The fact that the Peace of Westphalia is generally viewed as a sharp turning point can be related to the high esteem it holds among international lawyers, who for a long time have been eager for the construct of a 'Westphalian order', which they think to have just come to an end in the last years of the twentieth century, as the nation-state came to be seen in relative terms owing to rivalling global or continental governmental or non-governmental organisations.

Historians are rather sceptical as far as the construct of the 'Westphalian order' is concerned,[3] and in the perspective of international law and foreign politics they rather tend to reduce the turning point quality of the Peace of Westphalia, above all as they become conscious that no durable political order of continental dimension was achieved in 1648, but only a peace order which was limited to the centre of the continent and, moreover, actually collapsed relatively quickly.[4] But historians can embrace the tendencies that led to the emergence of a new international law in the middle of the seventeenth century, which distinguishes itself more or less from the one of the previous period. In this respect, there are indeed considerable arguments in favour of having a central collection of sources such as the *Consolidated Treaty Series* start with the Peace of Westphalia.

Whether one sees the European order of law of the sixteenth and early seventeenth centuries as being in crisis or not,[5] many of its structural elements did change in any case – if not abruptly, at least noticeably. The Peace of Westphalia certainly was not the last international treaty in the preambles of which the partners called in the legitimising figure of *christianitas*, i.e. the *respublica christiana*, whose integrity had to be

---

[2] Wilhelm G. Grewe, *Epochs of International Law* (Berlin etc., 2000).
[3] Heinz Duchhardt, '"Westphalian System". Zur Problematik einer Denkfigur', *Historische Zeitschrift* 269 (1999), 305–15.
[4] Instead of mentioning many essays from the extended anniversary literature, let me just point to one of them: Heinz Duchhardt, 'Zur "Verortung" des Westfälischen Friedens in der Geschichte der internationalen Beziehungen in der Vormoderne' in Klaus Malettke (ed.), *Frankreich und Hessen-Kassel zur Zeit des Dreißigjährigen Krieges und des Westfälischen Friedens* (Marburg, 1999), pp. 11–18.
[5] Cf. the previous chapter by Randall Lesaffer.

protected, which had to be defended or brought together against external enemies. This legitimising and justifying figure goes back to the Middle Ages, and had to convey above all one thing: the unity of a political world which nobody could withdraw from, even though this did no longer go along with unrestricted approval of the pope's – or the emperor's! – leading function. But in the face of the undeniably growing policy of interests in the European states, which did not leave the pope or the emperor any room for leading functions, the formula of *christianitas* had to lose some of its substance. In the middle of the seventeenth century, one could at least notice that other legitimising figures and legal constructs were needed in order to prevent the continent from sinking into chaos and antagonisms *à tout prix*. We have to come back to this development.

A second change which could be perceived by the middle of the seventeenth century, and which resulted from the reflections of the Spanish scholastics and Jean Bodin (1530–96),[6] was that the right of concluding treaties and alliances reduced itself to the holders of 'sovereignty', i.e. the princes or the governing councils of republics. This correlated, by the way, with the *ius legationis*, which, in an exceptional case, was still observed by representatives of regional estates in the Peace Congress of Westphalia,[7] but which came more and more into the sole control of the sovereignty holders. They – i.e. as a rule the princes – in principle always concluded the treaties in their own names, not as the mandatories of the territories they ruled on. But it would definitely be wrong to assume that the princes only concluded treaties for the duration of their lives. Such limitation of the duration of treaties, as Jörg Fisch conclusively analysed in his fundamental study,[8] became exceptional during the seventeenth century; the standard peace treaty of the late seventeenth and the eighteenth centuries was an unlimited treaty, which therefore also bound the rulers' successor(s).

That the regional or national estates or – in the case of France – the Parisian Parliament were excluded from international relations in the quality of signatories of international treaties did not, by the way, mean that they disappeared completely from the treaties' texts. In particular, the Spanish *Cortes* and the Parisian Parliament were again and again called

---

[6] Heinz Duchhardt, 'La guerre et le droit des gens dans l'Europe du XVIe au XVIIIe siècles' in Philippe Contamine (ed.), *Guerre et concurrence entre les états européens du XVIe au XVIIIe siècle* (Paris, 1998), pp. 339–64.
[7] Herbert Langer, 'Die pommerschen Landstände und der westfälische Friedenskongreß' in Heinz Duchhardt (ed.), *Der Westfälische Friede* (Munich, 1998), pp. 485–99.
[8] Jörg Fisch, *Krieg und Frieden im Friedensvertrag: eine universalgeschichtliche Studie über Grundlagen und Formelemente des Friedensschlusses* (Stuttgart, 1979).

in as bodies having to ratify bilateral treaties (apart from the respective monarchs). Not to mention domestic policy: on the international stage, the supposedly 'absolutistic' French and Spanish kings could not impose their very sole authority, but had to accept the co-ratification of the respective intermediate bodies. It should, nevertheless, be admitted that this co-ratification was not provided for in the treaties, e.g. not in those concluded in Utrecht in 1713.[9]

The restriction of the active part in international law to the sovereignty holders is also mirrored in the fact that (for a long time 'international') alliances of cities such as the Hanseatic League in the middle of the seventeenth century gradually disappeared from the international scene. This first of all had to do with the fact that the League itself did no longer function and that in 1629 it handed over the authorisation to act on behalf of the whole association to the three northern German 'Hanseatic' towns. But it had primarily to do with the fact that the Hansa simply no longer fitted into a system of sovereign states and could no longer justify its existence as a league with a specific purpose, aiming at nothing else than optimising and securing its trade, within a system of sovereign states.[10]

A third field in which an era came to an end and new developments took place was that of the treaties' guarantee. At the beginning of the modern era, the widespread method to let the validity of a treaty be in force beyond the time it took the ink to dry was the personal oaths of the contracting parties and the producing of hostages: hostages were to guarantee that territories really went into the hands of the victor, that the drawing of the new borders was taken seriously, and that the payments agreed on were effected. This practice, which was accepted and approved of by Hugo Grotius (1583–1645) as a matter of fact, disappeared more or less silently from the treaty practice. The Peace of Westphalia did not provide for the producing of hostages, although many matters were unsettled and, as is well known, an executive congress in Nuremberg was necessary to resolve the open questions.[11] But also, the important peace treaties of the Ludovician time did not contain the demand for producing of hostages; the Peace of Aix-la-Chapelle of 18 October 1748 was a latecomer

---

[9] Henri Vast (ed.), *Les Grands Traités du règne de Louis XIV* (Paris, 1899), vol. III.
[10] Heinz Duchhardt, 'Die Hanse und das europäische Mächtesystem des frühen 17. Jahrhunderts' in Antjekathrin Grassmann (ed.), *Niedergang oder Übergang? Zur Spätzeit der Hanse im 17. Jahrhundert* (Cologne, Weimar and Vienna, 1998), pp. 11–24.
[11] Antje Oschmann, *Der Nürnberger Exekutionstag 1649–1650: das Ende des Dreißigjährigen Krieges in Deutschland* (Münster, 1991).

in this respect.[12] The relationships between the states became somewhat depersonalised and rationalised as the implementation of the treaties' conditions was no longer assured through people but through political pressure with or without additional guaranteeing powers.

This leads to a fourth observation, the problem of the implementation of a treaty in legal practice. Parchment or paper are patient, and even if the ratifications by the sovereigns or the estates were exchanged after the 'normal' period of three or four weeks, or fifty days,[13] one remained very far away from a one-to-one transposition. If I do not overlook anything, the decisive progress took place in the eighteenth century, as one no longer counted on the goodwill of the contracting parties but created a sort of objective supervising body: mixed commissions, to which both sides sent representatives, which carried out the detailed work on the spot and indirectly saw to it that differences of opinion about the points needing interpretation did not lead to new conflicts. The mixed French and British commissions, which were called in and did their work after the Peace of Aix-la-Chapelle, have been particularly well studied.[14]

This detail points to the philosophy of the peace treaties after the Peace of Westphalia: we never have to do with a treaty trying to humiliate one side, and that is why one never demanded reparations or declared a single party guilty, but fell back upon the clause of oblivion, i.e. permanent forgetting. There was always a fair, but definitive final stroke, symbolised by the 'eternity' of peace treaties, which superseded the limitation of international treaties to five, nine, twelve or one hundred years, very familiar still in late fifteenth-century Europe.[15] To the architects of the peace treaties, it was perfectly clear that the current treaty would not remain in force 'for ever', but they always aimed at the creation of a stable basis for a future co-existence. After some disputes had been purposely settled ambiguously or had been left in a grey area in the Peace of Westphalia, and the imperial side had had to pay a bitter bill in the form of reunions and other French annexations, one generally dispensed with imprecise formulations and abstained from trusting that the future might open up a possibility to interpret a questionable article in a sense favourable to oneself. When mediators were involved in the preparation of a peace treaty, they of course

---

[12] Art. 9. [13] These were the common periods for ratification in the 1713 Utrecht Treaties.
[14] Armin Reese, 'Den Krieg verschieben – verkürzen – ersetzen? Die französisch-englischen "gemeinsamen Kommissionen" vor dem Siebenjährigen Krieg' in Heinz Duchhardt (ed.), *Zwischenstaatliche Friedenswahrung in Mittelalter und früher Neuzeit* (Cologne and Vienna, 1991), pp. 245–60.
[15] Cf. chapter 2.

also had to see to it that no imprecise or ambiguous formulations were drawn up.

What has been said about the 'everlasting' character of early modern peace treaties and some other characteristics is only partly valid as far as the Christian–Ottoman treaties are concerned. The situation was by no means such that the Christian and non-Christian worlds were completely separated from one another. Both sides were, first of all for commercial reasons, interested in having a minimum of international relations, which were, however, always skating on thin ice as Islamic law, on principle, excluded any relations on terms of equality with non-Muslims.[16] This meant, among other things, that for a long time the Porte refused to conclude unlimited treaties with Christian rulers, and during the whole seventeenth century did not recognise the principle that its own empire's borders were fixed. Only the numerous, nearly perpetual military defeats of the Ottoman Empire in the fifteen years following the Viennese battle of Kahlenberg made it change its views and come closer to 'European' standards. From the Peace of Karlowitz in 1699 onwards, the Ottoman Empire has taken over the (unwritten) rules of the European international law of treaties step by step, and then turned relatively quickly into a quite 'normal' European power – even though its permanent diplomatic presence remained underdeveloped until the Revolutionary Age.[17]

The practices of peacemaking

These fragmentary remarks about the specificity of the peace treaties in the period after 1648, which came to an end with the French Revolution – because at least in the treaties involving France and its satellites new forms of international *cohabitation* came into use – will be completed by some observations concerning the practice of concluding peace treaties in the period in question. It was the time in which the conclusion of peace treaties became quite an art – an art which very often, as in Westphalia, as in Nijmegen, took up many years. And it was the period in which for the first time – on the basis of texts made available in the form of collections like Leibniz' or Dumont's[18] – a kind of theory of interstate relations came

---

[16] Some remarks and hints in my book *Balance of Power und Pentarchie: internationale Beziehungen 1700–1785* (Paderborn, 1997), p. 80 and *passim*.
[17] See chapter 16 by Karl-Heinz Ziegler.
[18] Gottfried Wilhelm Leibniz, *Codex Juris Gentium Diplomaticus* (Hanover, 1693); Jean Dumont, *Corps universel diplomatique du droit des gens* (13 vols., Amsterdam, 1726–39).

into being, and a corresponding subject established itself at the *studia generalia*, if not yet under this name.[19]

The styles of negotiations

The relative importance of the Peace of Westphalia,[20] bearing in mind the lines tracing back to the sixteenth and even fifteenth centuries,[21] is based on the fact that a certain style of negotiations was found in the two north-west German bishops' towns which marked the future – through bilateral dialogues partly with, partly without mediators – and that one generally came to accept the procedure that no sovereign who might in any way be affected and showed interest should be excluded from the congress: a congress which on the other hand never came into being as a general assembly of all representatives. The face-to-face principle and the way to pursue claims, counterclaims, protest, etc. in written form in a procedure similar to that of the High Courts until a convergence or a result were achieved, represented the decisive progress in comparison to the previous situation. As it became an unwritten rule in Westphalia that a delegation should be composed of several persons – the nobleman who, owing to his social position, was in a situation to represent his prince, and the actual experts, as a rule graduated jurists – the mode which was to mark the future was set here, notwithstanding the fact that we meet this manner in earlier times. The sovereigns no longer negotiated directly with each other, but high-ranking representatives and experts did it for them, which did not change the traditional way to conclude

---

[19] Heinz Duchhardt, 'Die Formationsphase der Wissenschaft von den internationalen Beziehungen: Christian Gottfried Hoffmanns "Entwurff einer Einleitung zu dem Erkänntniß des gegenwärtigen Zustandes von Europa" von 1720' in *Formen internationaler Beziehungen in der frühen Neuzeit: Festschrift für Klaus Malettke zum 65. Geburtstag* (Berlin, 2001), pp. 37–42.

[20] Owing to the commemoration in 1998, the literature on the Peace of Westphalia has grown considerably, if not abundantly. I refer to three conference proceedings and the essay volume of the catalogue of the central exhibition in Münster/Osnabrück: Heinz Duchhardt (ed.), *Der Westfälische Friede: Diplomatie – politische Zäsur – kulturelles Umfeld – Rezeptionsgeschichte* (Munich, 1998); Roland G. Asch, Wulf Eckart Voss and Martin Wrede (eds.), *Frieden und Krieg in der frühen Neuzeit: die europäische Staatenordnung und die außereuropäische Welt* (Munich, 2001); Lucien Bély (ed.), *L'Europe des traités de Westphalie: esprit de la diplomatie et diplomatie de l'esprit* (Paris, 2000); Klaus Bussmann and Heinz Schilling (eds.), *1648: Krieg und Frieden in Europa, Textband* (Munich, 1998).

[21] Cf. especially Randall Lesaffer, 'The Westphalian Peace Treaties and the Development of the Tradition of Great European Peace Settlements prior to 1648', *Grotiana* NS 18 (1997), 71–95.

treaties in the names of the princes, not in the name of the country. Thus, professionalism supplanted the summit meetings. In contrast to Charles V (1519–58), who met Francis I (1515–47) several times for pacification reasons,[22] Louis XIV (1643–1715) was no longer to meet any of his fellow kings.

Different types of peace congresses

Münster/Osnabrück represents the basic type of a peace congress of the pre-revolutionary period with the following criteria: (1) all war parties were present in one place – in that case one virtual place; (2) mediators of states with functions such as *bons offices* were involved; and (3) others than the war parties were admitted. To this model correspond, if one disregards mere bilateral peace conferences, the congresses of Nijmegen,[23] Ryswick,[24] and Aix-la-Chapelle (1748).[25]

A different type is shown in the Treaty of Utrecht:[26] (1) the material results were already agreed upon by secret diplomacy before the congress; (2) mediators were no longer considered necessary; and (3) there was only conditional openness to others than the war parties, in order to achieve quick results. To this model correspond especially Paris (1763) and Hubertusburg (1763), but also Vienna in 1736 and Paris in 1783.[27] A slightly differing type is represented by Teschen (1779),[28] where mediators were present and, in this case, even took over the guarantee of the peace concluded.

The peace congresses, which were always summoned in the course of continual war actions and as a rule did not benefit from a cease-fire, covered a structurally extended time span. This did not have to be four years like in Münster/Osnabrück, but in Nijmegen, Ryswick and Aix-la-Chapelle (1748) the congresses also stretched over a period rather to be counted in years or at least many months: mainly because it took time

---

[22] E.g. in January 1526; cf. Ernst Schulin, Kaiser *Karl V.: Geschichte eines übergroßen Wirkungsbereichs* (Stuttgart, 1999), p. 146.

[23] *The Peace of Nijmegen – 1676–1678/79 – La Paix de Nimègue* (Amsterdam, 1980).

[24] Heinz Duchhardt (ed.), *Der Friede von Rijswijk 1697* (Mainz, 1998).

[25] Thomas R. Kraus, '*Europa sieht den Tag leuchten...*': *der Aachener Friede von 1748* (Aachen, 1998).

[26] Fundamental: Lucien Bély, *Espions et ambassadeurs au temps de Louix XIV* (Paris, 1990).

[27] There are no modern monographs on these three peace treaties. As for older research, cf. Derek McKay and H. M. Scott, *The Rise of the Great Powers 1648–1815* (London and New York, 1983); Duchhardt, *Balance of Power und Pentarchie*.

[28] There is no modern monograph on the Peace of Teschen.

to organise the logistics and the transfer of information, which played a crucial role between functionaries dependent on instructions and the sovereign, who had to decide in the last instance, but also because all sides were always full of hopes – which as a rule were disappointed – of a glamorous military victory which would at once change the whole situation completely. In the pre-modern age, hardly a peace was attained by a single military event.

Peace congresses and the formation of the ius publicum Europaeum

But the considerable duration of the peace congresses also resulted from the fact that here fundamental decisions in international law were taken and written down. European international law, the *ius publicum Europaeum*, was at that time still in its formative phase, and the uncertainties as well as the need for regulation were correspondingly great. Fundamental decisions were taken which concerned, like in Nijmegen, the question of the rank of the German princes under the conditions of international law, that is, their admission or non-admission as fully legitimated members, or, like in Utrecht with respect to the Spanish succession, the repeal of dynastic law by a new law, by an international agreement. But these could also concern the precision of borders, which until the eighteenth century had the character of frontier zones rather than that of lines. On the other hand, one has to consider that some developments in international law – such as the establishment of sea borders, i.e. a state's sovereignty over a certain distance, two or three miles, into the sea – were achieved outside peace congresses. This example is, by the way, a noticeable case of interaction between the theory and the practice of international law; theorists had discussed the question right from the beginning of the eighteenth century before it was definitely decided in the 1770s.

Peace congresses and the world beyond Europe

Finally, the duration of the congresses can also be explained – as far as one did not, like in Utrecht 1713 or Paris 1763, come to a bilateral agreement before – by the fact that they took a global dimension, involving also the world beyond the seas. It was not compelling, and was not taken for granted either, that all European conflicts should continue overseas with the same constellations, but the transfer of a European conflict to America or to the Asian realm became a rule in the last quarter of the seventeenth century. This had the consequence not only that colonial and commercial pressure groups increasingly appeared at the peace conferences, but also that more time was needed because of the intricacy of the matters.[29] Incidentally, it became a sort of rule that overseas problems should be dealt with in separate treaties, mostly in the context of trade and navigation agreements.

Informed diplomats?

The increasing complexity of the peace negotiations also made it necessary that diplomats were provided with the essentials, i.e. standard works on international law such as Grotius' *De iure belli ac pacis* (1625) or descriptions of former congresses – which in the cases of Nijmegen, Ryswick and Utrecht were soon put on the market[30] – and also increasingly with maps. In his book about Utrecht, Lucien Bély compiled quotations from the sources concerning problems with maps,[31] but it is evident that there is still a big research gap. Nevertheless, it is characteristic that the French Court acquired a complete specialised library in 1711 – the Cabinet de Gaignières. Furthermore, for obvious reasons, a 'classic' such as Rousset's book on the claims of the European states advanced soon after its publication to the standard equipment of a diplomat.[32] If one considers that such a diplomat of course also collected all juridical deductions and all pamphlets which appeared during the congress he was sent to, he must as a rule have started his journey home with an immense luggage of printed matter.

Ongoing negotiations

Hardly any congress ever succeeded in dealing with its entire agenda. On the one hand, at a certain moment one wanted – either because of military exhaustion, for financial reasons or, in the case of the Netherlands

---

[29] Many good insights, as far as the eighteenth century is concerned, are in Armin Reese, *Europäische Hegemonie und France d'outre-mer: koloniale Fragen in der französischen Außenpolitik 1700–1763* (Stuttgart, 1988).

[30] *Actes et mémoires des négociations de la Paix de Nimègue* (4 vols., Amsterdam, 1679/80); *Actes et mémoires des négociations de la Paix de Ryswick* (2nd edn, 4 vols., The Hague, 1725); *Actes, mémoires et autres pièces authentiques concernant la Paix d'Utrecht* (6 vols., Utrecht, 1714/15). The first two editions were reprinted in the 1970s.

[31] Bély, *Espions et ambassadeurs*, pp. 461–2.

[32] Jean Rousset de Missy, *Mémoires sur le rang et la préséance entre les souverains de l'Europe* (Amsterdam, 1746). Cf. in general on literature of this kind: M. S. Anderson, *The Rise of Modern Diplomacy 1450–1919* (London and New York, 1993).

and Great Britain, because of the pressure of public opinion – to come to an end politically and delegated some matters to another mechanism of regulation, e.g. arbitration proceedings. To illustrate this with just one example: in 1713, Louis XIV and Victor Amadeus of Savoy (1675–1720) entrusted a mixed commission of specialists with the exact delimitation of the new borders, a commission which had to start its work within four months after the date of the signing of the contract. This was very typical and in a way a point of no return. The precise implementation of fundamental decisions from now on regularly required the collaboration of specialists, so that there was no alternative but to entrust the delimitation of the borders of the Ottoman Empire or of the colonies to commissions of specialists, which often were still busy with the matter years after the end of the congress. On the whole, it seems that after the negative experiences since 1648 with the adjournment of decisions through ambiguous or blurred formulations, one now tended towards laying down the results as precisely as possible.[33]

Guarantees

It became increasingly out of practice to submit the totality of a peace, like in Münster and Osnabrück,[34] to the guarantee of third states. Instead, the guarantee, which disappeared by no means completely from the treaties and from international law, was limited to particularly controversial points. It seems that there still were overall guarantees when the partners' political weight differed considerably; for instance, the peace between France and Portugal in 1713 was guaranteed by the English Crown, as was the simultaneous peace between France and Prussia. The same is true of the Peace of 1715 between Spain and Portugal, which also – and this seems quite exceptional – accepted guarantees of other powers, as far as they were effected in a time span of six months.

The inclusion of third parties

A special study is required to analyse the criteria according to which third states were involved in the peace treaties. It had been a custom since the fifteenth century that each contracting party nominated its allies and *amici*

---

[33] Another example: Reese, 'Den Krieg verschieben – verkürzen – ersetzen?'.
[34] Guarantee powers of the Peace of Westphalia were, besides the emperor, France and Sweden.

with their consent to be included into the treaty. Although questions were involved with this practice as to whether the non-belligerent allies became full partners to the treaty or not, the custom never died out. In the two *Instrumenta Pacis* of 1648, almost the whole of Europe was drawn, as was desired by the signatory powers.[35] But why were only Sweden, Toscana, Genoa and Parma involved in the French–English Peace Treaty of 1713, i.e. by far not all the allies of both sides? Had the allies not included rejected the offer to be integrated? And why was the Hanseatic League involved in eighteenth-century treaties, although as a corporation it had disappeared from the scene since the early 1670s?[36] The interpretation that the inclusion of third parties had the function to assure them that the treaty was not to their detriment seems convincing, but further research is needed.

The semantics of peace treaties

Maximum precision regarding the material provisions was, however, no reason why one should do without certain metaphors and fit all the single regulations into a particular conception of the world. While, in the sixteenth and seventeenth centuries, one used classical metaphors for the requirement re-establishment of peace, such as the shedding of Christian blood which ought to be stopped, and – most widely used even after the Reformation – the restoration of harmony in Christianity, because otherwise God's ire would be excessive, and other similar ones, in the seventeenth century a drastic change took place, because now two new determining factors came to the fore: the balance of power, which had to be restored, and Europe's security and tranquillity.

The absent balance of power

Although the writings of publicists and political thinkers in Europe after the end of the seventeenth century are full of the metaphor of the balance of power, in international law and its treaties this notion did not meet with the overwhelming and far-reaching response one would have expected. It is true that the big alliances concluded round 1690 were achieved under this slogan, which could easily be used against the pejorative image of the menacing universal monarchy of the *Roi-Soleil*, but in the main peace treaties of the eighteenth century it found astonishingly little expression

---

[35] IPO Art. 18 (10–11); IPM Par. 119.   [36] Duchhardt, 'Die Hanse'.

and echo, and when it did, it was only in the context of the fear of a union of the Bourbon states after Spain had gone over to a Bourbon king.[37] It was only this danger, considered fundamental for the co-existence of the European family of states, that caused the diplomats to fall back upon the metaphor of the balance of power. The slogan, which dominated interstate life as mirrored by the publicists,[38] in no way became a dominating reference in international law.

The security and tranquillity of Europe

A much more decisive factor for the development of interstate relations since the 1690s was the formula of Europe: the security and tranquillity of Europe as a heading. Since 1722, the British government had even used the formula of Europe – although in connection with the motif of balance – in front of the Parliament as an intrastate context of explanation in order to get through its yearly military financial laws, the so-called Mutiny Acts. It seems that the formula of Europe was no longer specific to a single political context or a limited group of states, although for some time it still ranked beside the formula of the tranquillity of Christianity. Louis XIV and João V of Portugal (1706–50) concluded peace on 11 April 1713 with the purpose of 'contribuer au repos de l'Europe', and on the same day Louis XIV and the Protestant Estates-General emphasised in their treaty of friendship the efforts of the (mediating) English queen towards 'le rétablissement de la tranquillité de l'Europe'. One gets the impression that, from the second decade of the eighteenth century on, the formula of Europe imposes itself as a legitimating formula along a wide front – by the great powers and by smaller ones, by neighbours and by non-neighbours, by parties of the same or of different confession – and that, as a tendency, one only did without it when princes of the Empire were involved or when the two contracting parties also or even primarily had the colonies in mind.

Conclusion

The main message of this chapter is that much research still has to be done as far as the formulas and the legitimising notions in the peace

---

[37] Heinz Duchhardt, 'The Missing Balance,' *Journal of the History of International Law* 2 (2000), 67–72.
[38] Cf., e.g., Arno Strohmeyer, *Theorie der Interaktion: das europäische Gleichgewicht der Kräfte in der frühen Neuzeit* (Vienna, Cologne and Weimar, 1994).

treaties are concerned, and that we need more studies on how the texts of the treaties were compiled. In most cases we do not know at all which of the belligerents made the first whole or part draft of a peace treaty. What we need, above all, are critical editions with the best texts including ratifications, which would enable historians and jurists to ask and to answer many more questions than until now on the basis of Parry's edition.

4

Peace treaties from Paris to Versailles

HEINHARD STEIGER

Introduction

Central to this chapter are the European peace treaties from the First Treaty of Paris of 30 May 1814 at the end of the Napoleonic wars to the Peace Treaties of 1919/20 signed in various Parisian suburbs at the end of World War I.[1] Some American and Asian treaties will also be discussed.

These one hundred years cover an era that saw stormy change and development in the area of politics, economics, culture and international law. Peace treaties as legal instruments played an important, although greatly varying role in these developments and changes, according to the circumstances and the then existing relationships between the partners, which themselves could differ greatly from one another. Treaties were instrumental in the judicial organisation of political constellations, which were in no way comparable with one another, either in content or in structure. They were used for bringing to an end classical European wars; for the ordination of the general political and judicial relationships in Europe as well as in other parts of the world; for the subjection of Asian powers to European dominance; for a comprehensive regulation of the fundamentals of economic cohesion, the position of the citizens, etc.; for the regulation of general problems in international law regarding war and peace, etc.

General developments

General political developments in Europe

The century was marked by an evolution from a European policy towards a world policy.[2] While in 1814 the Paris Peace Treaty concerned the

[1] I thank Ms Ulrike Schöne for her co-operation.
[2] Theodor Schieder, *Staatensystem als Vormacht der Welt. 1848–1918* (Propyläen Geschichte Europas 5, 2nd edn, Berlin, 1980, reprint 1998); Hagen Schulze, *Phoenix Europa: die Moderne, von 1740 bis heute* (Berlin, 1998); Theodor Schieder (ed.), *Handbuch der*

restoration of peace and the re-establishment of legal order in Europe, the Peace Conferences in Paris in 1919/20 had to find rules to establish world peace, albeit that the rearrangement of Europe was central. In 1814, only European powers were involved in the peace process, while in 1919/20 the USA, other American powers and some Asian powers participated. However, this evolution was by no means a process fixed from the outset; it was a continuation of an older and gradually developing extension of political activities going beyond Europe by some of the European nations, indeed by the most powerful among them. Their driving force, interests, and ideological and cultural bases do not have to be discussed here. One usually speaks of the Age of Imperialism.[3] European states, and also the USA, extended their domination over countries outside Europe – in Africa, Asia and the Pacific – and subjected them to their rule or at least tried to achieve a dominant influence. It was the second wave of European expansion, a continuation of what had already occurred in the fifteenth to eighteenth centuries.[4] For Europe the rest of the world became a terrain where political domination was sought. This led on the one hand to quarrels, including wars, between European powers and Asian or African rulers; on the other hand to quarrels, including wars, among European powers themselves wanting to establish their domination over these countries.

The political and legal order in Europe changed fundamentally during these one hundred years. At the beginning of this era, the European order had been set down in detail in the First Paris Treaty and the Act of the Vienna Congress of 1815, principally on the basis of the changes which had occurred during the Napoleonic period. The Holy Roman Empire was not restored. Although the German states – which were exclusively secular, some of them being significantly extended through the incorporation of smaller states by bigger states and through the exchange of territory – had

---

europäischen Geschichte (Stuttgart, 1965), vols. V and VI; Gordon Craig, *Europe since 1815* (New York, 1974); Winfried Baumgart, *Europäisches Konzert und nationale Bewegung, Internationale Beziehungen 1830–1878* (Heinz Duchhardt (ed.), *Handbuch der Geschichte der internationalen Beziehungen* vol. VI (Paderborn, 1999).

[3] Georg Schöllgen, *Das Zeitalter des Imperialismus* (3rd edn, Munich, 1994); Hans-Ulrich Wehler (ed.), *Imperialismus* (3rd edn, Cologne, 1976); Richard Koebner and Helmut Dan Schmidt, *Imperialism* (Cambridge, 1965); Wolfgang J. Mommsen, *Der europäische Imperialismus* (Göttingen, 1979); Eric J. Hobsbawm, *The Age of Empire 1875–1914* (London, 1987).

[4] See Wolfgang Reinhard, *Geschichte der europäischen Expansion* (Stuttgart, 1983–90), vol. III: *Die Alte Welt seit 1818* (Stuttgart, 1988); vol. IV: *Dritte Welt Afrika* (Stuttgart, 1990); Jörg Fisch, *Die europäische Expansion und das Völkerrecht* (Stuttgart, 1984).

joined in the *Deutsche Bund* (German Confederation), they maintained their sovereignty, at least to the outside world. In Italy some of the former states had been re-established, others had not and came under Austrian domination, such as Venice and Milan. However, contrary to what was the case in Germany, there was no overall legal unity of the single states. Since, therefore, in both countries the widespread aspirations for unity to become a nation-state were not met, these aspirations continued to influence the political developments in Europe during the first fifty-five years after the Congress of Vienna, until 1870/71 when both achieved their objective of becoming unified states. As a result, many of the sovereign states, which had been confirmed by the Vienna Congress in 1814 and subsequently recognised as participants in Europe's peacetime order, disappeared. Even Prussia, which in 1814 was one of the five Great Powers, lost its sovereignty and became only a member state of the newly founded German Empire.

In other cases, the pursuit of the nation-state contributed to the fragmentation of states consisting of several nationalities. Belgium and Luxemburg had been united in 1815 with the Netherlands into a United Kingdom. After 1830 both wanted and, in the end, achieved their independent status. In the Balkans under Turkish domination, the non-Turkish populations attempted to achieve independence through the creation of their own states, free from Turkish domination. This process was both openly and secretly encouraged by some of the European Great Powers. It only came to its end shortly before World War I. Within the multi-ethnic states of Russia and Austria-Hungary, pressure grew in favour of independence and the separation of particular nations. But only the Italian regions belonging to Austria were to a large extent incorporated in the kingdom of Italy already during the nineteenth century. For the rest, Russia, as well as Austria, succeeded in averting further disintegration until World War I.

For a long time, as far as these developments could not be stopped, all European powers tried to solve disputes through political management, primarily through European Conferences, and if possible without a major war. Wars were thereby averted, although throughout the nineteenth century several smaller regional wars took place in the Balkans, but also in Central and Western Europe. The peace treaties which put an end to these wars not only dealt with issues concerning the combatants, but also had significance for the whole European order.

Nevertheless, in the end it came to a general war, which was also fought over the independence of several European nations. When the war was over, the political map of Europe was thoroughly redrawn. Austria-Hungary disappeared and several new states were separated from Russia.

General political developments in America

Through the Declaration of Independence in 1776 by thirteen English colonies and the creation of the USA, the first sovereign state on the American continent was born. During the first half of the period here discussed, most Spanish colonies and Brazil achieved their independence. All of them became part of the international legal system and some of them, to a greater or lesser extent, took part in the global political system. This was particularly the case for the USA, which despite the Monroe doctrine was politically active in Asia and later also in Europe. At the end of the period under discussion here, the USA had become the new global Great Power.

General political developments in Asia

The political circumstances in Asia were more complicated than in America or even in Europe. The countries can be divided into two groups. First, there were the independent countries: Persia, Siam, China and Japan. Although they had numerous dealings with European powers, they took no part in the general global political system at the beginning of the period under consideration. However, from the middle of the nineteenth century onwards, and especially by the end of that century, they increasingly became part of this system. They participated in legal and political conferences, and in the end they even took part in World War I and the Paris post-war conferences. This was in particular the case for Japan, which had abandoned its seventeenth-century policy of isolation, especially as regards the European powers, in the 1890s.[5]

Second, large parts of Asia were under European domination. Europeans had already set foot in Asia at the end of the fifteenth century. At first they controlled only a few border zones. But during the seventeenth and eighteenth centuries larger parts of Asia had come under European domination, particularly India and Indonesia. Although these countries had their own political and legal organisation and had long since developed their own political powers, they gradually lost their independence

---

[5] See Baumgart, *Konzert*, p. 454; Reinhard, *Geschichte*, vol. III, p. 79 with more bibliography; Wilhelm G. Grewe, *The Epochs of International Law* (Berlin etc., 2000), p. 463.

and political autonomy. In the nineteenth century, conflicts regarding the opening of China to European and American influence became important. They resulted in numerous peace treaties between China and these powers, which in general were disadvantageous to China, which nevertheless remained as a sovereign player.

General political developments in Africa

In Africa the European powers had taken up even stronger positions than in Asia. There were only two independent states: ancient Ethiopia and Liberia, a state of recent date. The Arabs in the north were dependent on Turkey. Before the nineteenth century, several states had achieved a greater or lesser degree of independence: Morocco, Algeria, Tunisia, Tripoli and Egypt. Over the nineteenth century, they became increasingly dependent on European powers. Some became protectorates while others were integrated into the colonising state. This was even more the case for Black Africa, especially south of the Sahara. Almost the whole continent became dependent on Europe. It was divided into separate colonies, which not only had no external self-rule, but also in many cases lacked even internal self-rule and independence. This submission was often achieved by military intervention but was frequently, though not always, confirmed with a treaty laying down the peace – a peace of submission. The European powers disputed among one another over North Africa as well as over Black Africa. More than once, the danger of the outbreak of a war between the colonising powers threatened the peace between them. Important diplomatic efforts were needed. Again conference diplomacy was required in order to keep the peace and to ensure that the conquest of the land went along the lines of peace, consent and legal rules.

From a European to a global system of proceedings

At the end of the period considered here, a global system of political proceedings arose as a result, on the one hand, of the new and reinforced activities of Europe outside its own continent, and, on the other hand, of the stronger development of political activities by the American states and by some Asian states. It by no means resulted in uniform structures but was constructed in a much more diverse fashion. At first Europe remained the active centre, with its globally active powers. However, in the nineteenth century the USA had already become active in this system of proceedings, and, with an increasing influence during World War I, it achieved a dominant position by the war's end. The other American states remained on the sidelines. The same was true for the Asian countries, with the exception of Japan, which became a centre of activities, at least for Asia. For the rest, important parts of Asia and nearly the whole of Africa were not subjects but merely objects in this system, and only had a passive role.

When looking beyond specific peace provisions, we discern two kinds of attempts to establish a general system that would secure peace. War itself was thereby not abolished but it was intended to establish control over its declaration as well as its conduct. At the same time, ways had to be found to avoid wars. Subsequently, this led to the Peace Conferences in The Hague from 1899 onwards, which were supposed to be repeated every seven years. They produced a series of general treaties for maintaining peace, still in force today, including the formation of an Arbitration Tribunal. But only one further conference took place, in 1907.

The next Conference, of 1914, was never convened. World War I broke out. The first approach seemed to have met with failure. Nevertheless the powers went a step further with the Paris Treaties of 1919/20, ending World War I. They made a second start with the foundation of the League of Nations as an institution of reciprocal security supposed to organise peace. The League had to be an organisation on a global scale. The new order in Europe was now only a part of this global order, albeit for a short period it remained the core and centre of it.

Economic developments

Economic development during this period is characterised by an important expansion from national to regional economy, and from there to the first phase of world economy. This was supported by the first industrial and technical revolution with its innovative inventions such as railway, steamship and telegraph, followed by the motorcar and finally the aeroplane. The increase in scientific inventions, resulting in industrial products, advanced the development of mankind. But fundamental political and legal transformations paved the way for economic development: human rights, with the liberation from traditional dependence; the assurance of individual freedom of movement and of private ownership; the shift from an economy structured by the state to a societal economy orientated towards a free market, with free trade also between the various states and with preferential treatment, etc. These developments in particular needed regulation by treaty between states, with respect to the principle of sovereignty. These were the so-called Treaties of Peace, Friendship, Commerce and Navigation. Most of those included an explicit peace clause. Peace was considered something more than the absence of war; it was a state of friendship, exchange and diverse mutual relations, as it had been in the Middle Ages.

It was, however, the economic interests of European states that resulted in military conflicts between them, as had been the case during the struggles for access to the other continents from the late sixteenth century onwards. Access to raw materials, communication by sea, and markets and trade with Europe were disputed and fought for. As a result of the necessities of an era of industrial and capitalist development – in the first place within Europe, but also in the USA – these interests, closely linked to political power and domination, increasingly determined the relations between powers. Most bigger states developed from agricultural to industrial states, some earlier – in particular Great Britain – others somewhat later: amongst them the German states, later to become the German Empire. They all sought the extension of their power and of their economic relations beyond Europe. Indeed, economic activities were still mainly founded on national bases, but nevertheless extended over the whole world.

Here the split of the world into two parts occurred as well: the community of civilised nations on the one hand, and the dependent populations on the other. Indeed, it was 'as well', if not initially created by the economic system. The dependent regions were first and foremost suppliers of raw materials for industry and for the consumption of the rapidly growing population in Europe. In international law this had the negative consequences of disparity and inequality, primarily in favour of the European industrial states, which divided the dependent world and its resources between themselves by agreements to permit peaceful repartition.

Intellectual and cultural developments

Intellectual and cultural developments were numerous during this period. The politically relevant ones in this respect were the development of the national conscience of the different European nations; the confirmation of state authority in constitutions, together with the continuing aim towards democracy within the organised state; the development of a wide-ranging liberalism; the founding of socialism; the growth of secularisation; and the rise of an organised peace movement. However, there were also other currents – conservative, imperialist, nationalist, even racist – which showed themselves to a large extent having more power and ability to force public opinion, while in general they disposed of state power or had a decisive influence on it. All these were primarily international, European movements and currents.

Some of these currents assigned a central significance to the question of peace. For the first time, the problems of war and peace in relation to both general and particular conflicts were, contrary to earlier peace claims and works of individual writers and poets, publicly discussed and often vehemently pursued by publicly operating movements with moral purposes, in discourses, in discussions in parliaments, by the press, in pamphlets and in appeals. War was no longer accepted without questioning it and peace had to become the general state of affairs. The Conferences in The Hague of 1899 and 1907 were also influenced by the public discourse. Eventually, the social and political pacifist movements did not succeed in averting the catastrophe of World War I. In general, peace was declared an essential benefit of the political and legal order, made obligatory by reason and ethics. In practice, however, the moral issue had ambivalent effects. So, for the first time, the question of responsibility for the war was raised. This profoundly altered the conditions for reaching peace agreements. The re-establishment of peace after a war by a peace treaty no longer meant only ending military hostilities of the opponents in the war together with the establishment of friendly relations and exchanges, but also that those responsible for the war would be blamed and possibly be punished or have sanctions imposed upon them. This was applicable to the states as well as to their rulers. The idea was that because of the war the law was broken and justice had to be restored by the peace treaty. This could, however, lead to offending the people concerned and give reasons for new wars. The elements of these new peace concepts were not without internal contradictions.

The frame of international law

International law of civilised nations

The period of international law between 1815 and 1919/20 has been characterised by Grewe as the 'English era'.[6] I prefer to call it 'the international

---

[6] Grewe, *Epochs*, pp. 429–44; also Karl-Heinz Ziegler, *Völkerrechtsgeschichte* (Munich, 1994), pp. 210–39; critical Heinhard Steiger, 'Probleme der Völkerrechtsgeschichte', *Der Staat* 26 (1987), 103–26 at pp. 116–23; also Hans Ulrich Scupin, 'History of the Law of Nations 1815 to World War I' in Rudolf Bernhardt (ed.), *Encyclopedia of Public International Law* (2nd edn, Amsterdam, 1995), vol. II, pp. 767–93.

law of the civilised nations'.[7] Grewe focuses on the dominating power. I propose to explain the typical legal structure of international law in that period as the division into two legal areas, in accordance with the world divided into two parts on the ground of politics and domination. The first legal area is that of the community of sovereign states with equal rights and mutual recognition, which are linked to each other with a law, developed in mutual agreement, giving them the same rights and obligations. The second legal area developed from the relationship of these states to other people. They wished to submit to their power populations, political entities, to whom they denied 'recognition' as equal independent states on the ground that they were not civilised enough to guarantee adequate moral, legal and political standards. One can make the distinction between them as either the area of 'international law' or the area of 'colonial law'. Both were part of the 'international law of the civilised nations'. But both were exclusively formulated, codified, organised and developed by the participants to the former legal area, the members of the 'community of civilised states'. But whereas 'international law' was formulated by these states by mutual consensus or consent, the members of the so-called non-civilised world were excluded from the formulation of 'colonial law'; this was imposed upon them mostly without their real free and equal agreement, in order to bring them, gradually or not, into the dependence of the members of the former legal area. The culmination of this conduct was no doubt the Congo Act of 26 February 1885.

As a matter of fact, this dichotomy has been in existence from the beginning of the European expansion at the end of the sixteenth century to the nineteenth century.[8] In America during the period of colonisation until the end of the eighteenth century, only the norms established by the European powers were applied to the legitimacy of the colonisation and the relations with the Indians. This was even the case for the so-called natural law of nations, which was supposed to be universal, but was in fact developed by European thinkers. In Asia the legal foundation was more diverse. Here the Europeans encountered old, thoroughly organised, powerful societies, often superior or at least equivalent to their own and therefore in the position to make their own legal system equally

---

[7] Heinhard Steiger, 'From the International Law of Christianity to the International Law of the World Citizen – Reflections on the Formation of the Epochs of the History of International Law,' *Journal of the History of International Law 2001* 3 (2001), 180–93 at pp. 187–90.

[8] Fisch, *Expansion*; Reinhard, *Geschichte*, vol. I: *Die Alte Welt bis 1818* (Stuttgart, 1983) and vol. II: *Die Neue Welt* (Stuttgart, 1985).

valid.⁹ But gradually, during the seventeenth and eighteenth centuries the Netherlands, Great Britain and, to a lesser extent, France did succeed in overcoming larger parts of Asia and imposing their own legal systems. And, to that end, they always made use of treaties, including peace treaties. The quality of the legal capacity – albeit limited – of the subjugated political entities was not always denied, and not to the same extent for all. Often the legal relationship of the protectorate was used, instead of organising a dominating administration. On the basis of their supremacy, the European powers and the USA were in a position where they could take their own law as the measure to be imposed on all. Yet, in Africa treaties were agreed with native rulers, but these were only treaties of submission, which did not therefore lead to a re-establishment of normal relations under international law.¹⁰

Moreover, the belief in one's own civilising superiority from a rational as well as a scientific, technical and moral viewpoint was rooted in the European and American states. The irony expressed by Samuel Pufendorf (1632–94) about similar opinions of the Europeans in the seventeenth century was forgotten; if it had ever been taken into account.¹¹ Also, the basic principles of the natural law of nations as outlined by Francisco de Vitoria (c. 1480–1546) regarding the overall and principal legal capacity of every person, whatever his race, creed or civilised standard,¹² were no longer respected. Whereas these principles had been generally maintained during the expansion in Asia,¹³ and the rights of ownership and legal authority in particular had been recognised towards the Indians and the Asians and their peoples up to the seventeenth century, they were no

---

⁹ Charles Henry Alexandrowicz, *An Introduction to the History of the Law of Nations in the East Indies (Sixteenth, Seventeenth and Eighteenth Centuries)* (Oxford, 1967); Alexandrowicz, 'Treaty and diplomatic relations between European and South Asian powers in the seventeenth and eighteenth centuries,' *Recueil de l'Académie de Droit International* 100 (1961), 203–321; Heinhard Steiger, 'Recht zwischen Europa und Asien im 16. und 17. Jahrhundert?' in Klaus Bussmann and Elke Anna Werner (eds.), *Europa: Mythos, Bilder und Konzepte* (Stuttgart, 2003, forthcoming).

¹⁰ Charles Henry Alexandrowicz, *The European–African Confrontation: A Study in Treaty Making* (Leiden, 1973), pp. 29–105.

¹¹ Samuel Pufendorf, *De jure naturae et gentium libri octo* 3, 3, 7 (1688, Classics of International Law 17, Oxford, 1934).

¹² Francisco de Vitoria, 'Relectiones de Indis' (1557) in Francisco de Vitoria, *Vorlesungen II (Relectiones): Völkerrecht, Politik, Kirche* (ed. Ulrich Horst et al., Stuttgart, 1997), vol. II, pp. 370–541, at pp. 383–40.

¹³ Hugo Grotius, *Mare liberum sive Dissertatio de jure, quod Batavis competit ad Indicana commercia* (Leiden, 1609, reprint and English translation Oxford, 1916), pp. 13–14; Seraphim de Freitas, *Ueber die rechtmaessige Herrschaft der Portugiesen in Asien* (1625, German translation, Kiel, 1976), p. 95.

longer granted to the 'savages' in Africa and the Pacific. The opinion was largely spread that these savages were no good at political organisation, that their countries had no rulers and therefore their occupation and appropriation by the Europeans was free.

The concept of 'civilised states' or 'nations' was a replacement of the concept of 'Christianity'. It indicated an improved standard of ethics and justice, certainly the recognition of the law as a standard for political conduct.[14] So much for the positive side. The negative side was the abandonment of the 'savages' and their political culture of authority, which was at odds with the European model of law and state. As a result of the European and American 'international law of civilised nations', it was acceptable to bring or to maintain large parts of the world under direct dependence and control of the civilised states, which claimed a sort of 'right of precedence over the world'. According to this view, Africa, in particular, was a region 'without rulers' and became the new, imperialistic colonial area for nineteenth-century Europe.

The members of the international law community

Only the group of 'civilised states' was in a full political and legal sense part of the community of international law. Only they had full legal capacity under international law. But this group enlarged during that period. At first the group was limited to the European states and the USA. Next the Latin American states joined when they became independent. The same happened with the new states in the Balkans. They were all Christian states. In 1856 Turkey was explicitly accepted. Of course, this state had already maintained relations regulated by the law of nations with the other European states under the *ancien régime*. The earlier Christian reservations towards the Islamic Sublime Porte had already disappeared during the eighteenth century. Furthermore, four Asian powers belonged to the group: Persia, Siam, China and, from the 1870s onwards, Japan. Already during the sixteenth to eighteenth centuries, they had not been dominated by Europe, but had been more or less on equal terms with the European powers, sometimes even acting with superiority or cutting themselves off from contacts with them. In Africa only ancient Ethiopia, again a Christian community, and Liberia, established by the USA, were accepted

---

[14] See, as a contemporary author, e.g. Johann Caspar Bluntschli, *Das moderne Völkerrecht der civilisierten Staaten als Rechtsbuch dargestellt* (Nördlingen, 1868), esp. pp. 165–6. It was used in positive law in the anti-slavery treaties and by the Hague Peace Conferences of 1899 and 1907: Grewe, *Epochs*, pp. 446–58.

as partners of the 'civilised states'. They participated in the Peace Conference in The Hague in 1907, the last important World Conference before 1914, and some of them were also present at the Paris Peace Conferences in 1919/20. But also, then and again, dispositions were taken over large parts of Africa and Asia, without their participation.

Peace treaties

As juridical instruments re-establishing the legal situation of peace and ending the legal situation of war, peace treaties go back far. In the course of centuries peace treaties had a precise structure, even if it was not always strictly respected. This was particularly true for the European treaties, which from the Treaties of Münster and Osnabrück of 1648 onwards almost always had an identical structure.

The treaties were *grosso modo* arranged as follows: *invocatio trinitatis* or *dei*; preamble; clauses of peace and friendship; amnesty clause; operational provisions for the settlement of conflicts and problems that had led to the war and whose solution was a precondition for the restoration of peace; concluding clauses with various contents such as the settlement of consequences of the war; guarantee clauses; ratification of the text, if required with confirmation on oath by the partners to the treaty. This structure will be used as the basis for the analysis of the peace treaties from 1814 until 1919/20. It will thereby be shown that the same structure largely remained in use at the beginning of the period discussed. However, already from the beginning some important variations occurred, whilst during the second half of the period some significant basic changes took place. Besides the peace treaties ending wars, there were also other categories of treaties during the period considered, which, although not intended to end a war and to re-establish peace, can nevertheless be considered 'peace treaties'. Amongst these are peace, friendship and maritime treaties already mentioned, and also the multilateral Hague Treaties of 1899/1907. The first group of treaties played a crucial role in the material development of peaceful relations between partners. They included all kinds of stipulations about mutual rights of the partners and in particular those of their citizens. As a rule they started with the general clauses of peace and friendship. We cannot assess them in detail here, as they certainly require a separate thorough study.[15] These treaties were concluded both between

[15] They are covered in chapter 17 by Stephen Neff.

members of the first legal area as well as between them and members of the second legal area. Significant differences in content occurred, most of all in respect to reciprocity. The second group, the Hague Treaties, helped in avoiding wars and in 'harmonising' the *ius in bello*. This was also of significance for peace. However, we will not elaborate on this aspect here.[16]

Peace treaties were concluded both between so-called 'civilised states', meaning the members of the community of international law, and between them and other entities, as mentioned above. The latter look very much as if they were made according to the same structure; e.g. they contained a clause of peace and friendship. Closer analysis, however, of the form and in particular of the content shows that there were significant variations, as a result of the countries' dependence on, or the dominance by, the European power. We will only give a few examples of such peace treaties.

The conclusion of peace treaties to end a war, especially in Europe

Armistice and preliminary peace

The actual peace treaties were frequently preceded by armistices and/or preliminary peace agreements. These were only two out of more ways to work gradually to a final peace treaty. Treaties of armistice provided for the cessation of hostilities and transitional measures.[17] However, the treaties of armistice of 1918 between the Allies and the powers of Central Europe, the German *Reich* and the Austro-Hungarian Empire, included important pre-decisions regarding material measures, partly anticipating the peace arrangements.[18] Generally, these treaties were concluded between military commanders and did not require ratification. But the Armistice between the Allies and the Germans of 11 November 1918 was signed by the Commander in Chief of the Allied Forces, Maréchal Foch (1851–1929), and by the German Secretary of State without Portfolio, Matthias Erzberger (1875–1921), that is by the German government.

---

[16] Grewe, *Epochs*, pp. 512–15.
[17] E.g. the Armistice of 26 July 1866 between Prussia and Austria.
[18] In particular Alsace-Lorraine, which had to be evacuated by German forces and handed over to the Allies, Armistice of 11 November 1918, Art. 2. Rules were also set out for handing over war materials to the Allies, so that Germany would not be in a position of resuming the war (Art. 4).

During the second half of the nineteenth century, preliminary peace treaties were concluded in several cases.[19] When no armistice preceded, these treaties also served the purpose of ceasing the hostilities.[20] The writers of international law were widely of the opinion that these agreements established the binding outlines on which the mutual bases for the final peace rested and from which they could only depart by mutual consent.[21] Therefore, these preliminary treaties, contrary to the treaties of armistice, had to be ratified.[22] Their content dealt first of all with the bases for peace. The preliminary treaty did not re-establish the final peace situation. The Preamble to the Treaty of Nikolsburg of 26 July 1866 mentions the 'später abzuschließenden Friedensvertrag'. The Preamble to the Preliminary Treaty of Versailles of 26 February 1871 states 'pour servir de base préliminaire à la paix définitive à conclure ultérieurement'. The preliminary treaties may, for example, deal with territorial regulations,[23] damage settlements,[24] but also with measures for the liquidation of the war situation.[25] Particularly significant was the acceptance by Austria-Hungary of the dissolution of the *Deutsche Bund* and also the reorganisation of northern Germany by Prussia with the Nikolsburg Preliminary Treaty.[26]

There was also another form of phasing of the peacemaking process. On 30 May 1814, the Paris Peace Treaty was concluded, dealing only with particular territorial arrangements – including subsequent measures for the population – and with the navigation on the Rhine and a number of general principles regarding the reorganisation of Germany, leaving the

---

[19] Treaty of Villafranca between Austria and France of 11 July 1859; Treaty of Nikolsburg between Prussia and Austria of 26 July 1866; Treaty of Versailles between the German Empire and France of 26 February 1871; Treaty of Constantinople between Turkey and Greece of 6/18 September 1897.

[20] In Nikolsburg the same day an Armistice was concluded.

[21] Franz von Liszt, *Das Völkerrecht* (9th edn, Berlin, 1913), p. 295; E. von Ullmann, *Völkerrecht* (2nd edn, Tübingen, 1908), pp. 541–2; Théophile Funck-Brentano and Albert Sorel, *Précis du Droit des Gens* (Paris, 1877), pp. 313–14.

[22] Preliminary Treaty of Versailles of 1871, Art. 10: Ratification by the German emperor and the French National Assembly.

[23] The Preliminary Treaty of Versailles of 1871 contained the cession of Alsace-Lorraine by France to Germany, Art. 2; the Preliminary Treaty of Villafranca of 1859 contained the cession of Lombardy by Austria-Hungary to France and the cession by the latter to Sardinia, Art. 2.

[24] Preliminary Treaty of Versailles of 1871, Art. 2.

[25] Preliminary Treaty of Versailles of 1871, Arts. 2–3: evacuation of occupied territories; Art. 6: liberation of prisoners of war.

[26] Preliminary Treaty of Nikolsburg of 1866, Art. 2.

really important provision for the reorganisation of Europe to the general Congress in Vienna.[27] So this was a peace process in two steps.

The same practice was followed in 1878. After the Peace Treaty of San Stefano of 3 March 1878 between Russia and Turkey, the Berlin Congress decided on 13 July 1878 on the final order in the Balkans for all parties involved.[28]

Treaty partners

As a rule, peace treaties were negotiated and concluded on behalf of the belligerents by their plenipotentiaries. Sometimes there were also mediators.[29] When several allied states were involved on one side, either several bilateral treaties were concluded,[30] or one[31] or more[32] multilateral treaties. These treaties were, however, very closely interlinked, even largely identical in their wording, as was the case for the treaties of the First Paris Peace Treaties in 1814, or at least identical in their structure, like the Paris Treaties of 1919/20. By doing so, the actual unity of the peace agreement was clearly emphasised, while at the same time the legal difference and autonomy of each Peace Treaty was secured. Particularly, after World War I the alliance of the victors was continued as such, and even confirmed for the future by the establishment of the League of Nations, whereas the alliance of the Central European powers was stripped of its political and legal existence. The victorious allied powers acted as a community for themselves, but split the defeated coalition into its constituent states and concluded separate treaties with each of them; they did not even include the former allies of the defeated partners, contrary, for example, to the

---

[27] Paris Peace Treaty of 1814, Art. 32 (1).
[28] The situation of the Peace Treaty of San Stefano of 3 March 1878 is unclear. It was not intended as a preliminary treaty, but was later considered as such in the Berlin Congress Act of 13 July 1878, where it is also referred to as such in the Preamble; see Grewe, *Epochs*, p. 439.
[29] In the Peace Treaty between Prussia/German Confederation and Denmark of 2 July 1850, Great Britain mediated.
[30] Also the First Paris Treaties of 1814: France–Prussia. France–Great Britain, France–Austria, France–Russia; similarly in 1866 Prussia with Austria–Hungary, Bavaria, Württemberg, Baden; see below n. 37.
[31] Paris Peace Treaty of 30 March 1856.
[32] The Western Allies concluded separate treaties with the various defeated states in 1919/20: the Treaty of Versailles of 28 June 1919 with Germany; the Treaty of Saint-Germain of 10 September 1919 with Austria; the Treaty of Neuilly 27 November 1919 with Bulgaria; the Treaty of Trianon of 4 June 1920 with Hungary; the Treaty of Sèvres of 10 August 1920 with Turkey.

case of the Peace Treaties of Münster and Osnabrück of 24 October 1648, in the peace formed by the respective treaties. The separation of the members of the defeated coalition by the victorious coalition in 1919/20 was a means of strengthening their dominance.

In some cases non-belligerent third parties were also involved as partners in the peace treaty, as was the case for the Paris Peace Treaty of 30 March 1856 following the Crimean War, when Austria and Prussia, which did not participate in the war, also acted as parties, because the treaty, dealing mainly with settlements for the Balkans, was of general importance to the European order.[33] The same occurred in 1878 after the war between Russia and Turkey, with the Berlin Congress Acts, which changed the order established in the Balkans in 1856. Basically, both treaties followed the procedures established at the beginning of the period under consideration, by the Acts of the Vienna Congress of 9 June 1815, whereby a general multilateral treaty met the problems affecting the whole of Europe and the legal creation of its order. Based on the above-mentioned agreement of the Paris Peace Treaty of 1814, the then unsolved problems and questions were thoroughly settled in Vienna. Although technically not a war-ending peace treaty, the Congress Act nevertheless fulfilled the functions of a peace treaty in as far as, by its provisions, the definitive order of peace in Europe after the revolutionary and Napoleonic wars from 1792 onwards was established, especially regarding territorial matters as well as several special relationships between states, in particular between the German states with the founding of the German Confederation (*Deutsche Bund*).[34] However, in Vienna not only the five parties of the Paris Peace Treaty of 1814 were present, but also Spain, Portugal and Sweden. While peace had already been achieved, all powers, including France, participated on an equal basis. Other countries were invited to join.[35] The inclusion of a third party within the treaty by its partners, as had been the case with the peace treaties before 1792, no longer occurred.

---

[33] In Art. 7 of the Treaty the Christian European powers declared the admission of Turkey 'aux avantages du droit public et du concert Européen'.

[34] The Preamble states explicitly, 'Les Puissances qui ont signé le Traité conclu à Paris le 30 Mai 1814, s'étant réunies à Vienne, en conformité de l'art. XXXII de cet acte, avec les Princes et états de Leurs Alliées, pour compléter les dispositions dudit Traité, et pour y ajouter les arrangements rendus nécessaires par l'état dans lequel l'Europe était restée à la suite de la dernière guerre.'

[35] Art. 119. The conditions were participation in the Congress and signing of the acts additional to the general treaty, particularly the Act on the German Confederation. All German states and free cities were invited to join, Art. 118.

Designation of the partners

Under the *ancien régime*, the period of the classical law of nations of the early modern era, the monarchs acted as treaty partners. This remained the case, and not only at the beginning of the period considered here. The princes' plenipotentiaries acted in the name of their monarchs. The peace treaties of 1866, after the war between Germany and Austria, were concluded by the king of Prussia and the respective royal heads of state of the then partners, also for 'their heirs and successors, their states and subjects'.[36] Later on, the old formula was still used in some treaties, e.g. in the Peace Treaty between Romania, Greece, Montenegro, Serbia und Bulgaria of 28 July/10 August 1913.[37] For the first time, on 10 May 1871 in the Peace Treaty in Frankfurt am Main concluded between the German *Reich* and the French Republic, states were mentioned as such.[38] As for the Paris Treaties of 1919/20, their Preambles did not even use the official names of the participating states, but only general references.[39]

These references by no means meant that the monarchs were the actual partners to the treaties. The partners to the treaties always were the states, not the monarchs as individuals. This evolution from an exclusive personal bond between the monarchs to a bond between states went back to earlier periods, the late Middle Ages and the early modern era.[40] However, a complete separation between the monarch and the state still had not taken place. Also, in a constitutional monarchy, the monarch was not only an organ as head of state, but also the sole holder of state authority. The state was personified in him for the outside world. From the beginning, external authority belonged rightfully to him as sovereign.[41] In this perspective, the monarch was primarily 'a person according to international law'.[42] World War I was also in this respect a definitive caesura. The constitutional

---

[36] Treaty between Prussia and Württemberg of 13 August 1866, Art. 1; Treaty between Prussia and Baden of 17 August 1866, Art. 1; Treaty between Prussia and Bavaria of 22 August 1866, Art. 1; Treaty between Prussia and Austria of 23 August 1866, Art. 1.
[37] Art. 1.
[38] Ratification protocol of 20 May 1871, NRG XIX, 700.
[39] Preamble to the Versailles Treaty of 1919: 'the United States of America, the British Empire, France, Italy and Japan . . . Belgium, Bolivia . . . of the one part; and Germany and Austria on the other part'.
[40] Grewe, *Epochs*, pp. 196–7 and 360–2.
[41] See the classical separation of powers by John Locke, *Two Treatises of Government* 2, 145–8 (1689, ed. Peter Laslett, 2nd edn, Cambridge, 1991); Charles Louis de Secondat de Montesquieu, *De l'esprit des lois* 11, 6 (1748, ed. Robert Derathé, 2 vols., Paris, 1973).
[42] August Wilhelm Heffter, *Das europäische Völkerrecht der Gegenwart auf den bisherigen Grundlagen* (5th edn, Berlin, 1867), pp. 96 and 100–5.

monarchy was on the decrease, not only because many more states became republics, but also in those states which formally retained their previous character. During the nineteenth century, the sovereign became more and more an organ of the state, the head of state, representing the state to the external world.[43]

Treaty negotiations

As had become customary in previous centuries, treaties were negotiated by the authorised plenipotentiaries of the heads of state in bilateral or multilateral negotiations. Especially with the more important peace treaties affecting the national and political order for the whole of Europe, the negotiating process took place at large multilateral congresses: Vienna 1815, Paris 1856, Berlin 1878, Paris 1919/20.[44] In the nineteenth century, at least all of the European great powers were represented on these occasions: Prussia or the German Empire, Russia, Austria or Austria-Hungary, France, Great Britain, Sardinia-Piemont or Italy, and in Vienna in 1815 other states as well. From 1856 onwards also the Sublime Porte participated in the general European congresses. These conferences gave expression to the interest and responsibility of all great powers at the time in a general European order and peace, and their responsibility for such an order and peace, and at the same time showed the interdependence of all European nations. However, a congress was not convened every time the European order had to be modified. Neither Italian (from 1859 onwards) nor German (from 1866 onwards) unification brought about such a congress, although in both instances the European order as agreed and guaranteed in Vienna 1815 by all European states was fundamentally changed. In the case of Germany, Bismarck (1815–98) succeeded in precluding a congress, a desire expressed by Russia.

A significant change took place in the composition of congresses when, from 1885 and especially from 1899 onwards, non-European powers also began to participate.[45] Although neither of the peace conferences at The Hague in fact discussed the European or world order, they dealt with international law, which was a decisive factor for that order. This had to

---

[43] E.g. von Liszt, *Völkerrecht*, pp. 112–15. By all means formulations are often still unclear. E.g. Ullmann, *Völkerrecht*, p. 154.

[44] On the function of Congresses: Charles de Martens, *Manuel diplomatique ou Précis des droits et des fonctions des agens diplomatiques* (Paris etc., 1822), pp. 121–6; Heffter, *Völkerrecht*, pp. 415–16; Bluntschli, *Völkerrecht*, pp. 102–5.

[45] As well as Japan, China, Siam and Persia took part as equal signing powers to the Hague Peace Conferences of 1899/1907, II NRG XXVI, 920.

be drawn up not only by the Europeans, but also by the other 'civilised states'.

Then, in 1919/20, American, African and Asian powers, all non-European, directly influenced the political and legal order in Europe after World War I, both as participants in the conferences and as partners to the treaties.[46] The USA even had a very active and formative role in shaping the provisions and conditions of the treaties, although, in the end, it did not ratify the Treaty of Versailles. The difference between the Vienna Congress in 1815 and the Paris Peace Treaties of 1919/20 could not have been greater. The political development appeared most clearly in the nature and form of the countries' participation in the Congress and the way in which the results were agreed upon. This clearly marked the end of the era of the 'European law of nations' or the *droit public de l'Europe*. The road was paved towards a universal international law. Europe lost its power of self-regulation, and it seems doubtful whether it has regained it since in its full sense.

Also, fundamental changes occurred in the style of negotiation. At the bilateral peace negotiations as well as at the multilateral peace congresses of the nineteenth century, equality, reciprocity, treatment on equal terms, etc. were, at least on the formal level, generally observed. All the parties involved, defeated as well as victorious, took part in the negotiations with equal rights. These were real negotiations, albeit that the defeated were no doubt in a less favourable political position. But they were nevertheless respected. In 1919/20 the victorious allies and their associates drafted and negotiated among themselves the texts of the peace treaty, without the participation of the defeated Central European powers. Thus it was done with the Treaty of Versailles with regard to the German Empire. Only after the texts had been completed was the German delegation invited and were the papers handed over. The Germans were given a fortnight to respond in writing. The allies replied to them only with a written declaration detailing their position and rejecting the German proposals almost entirely, ordering them to sign within five days. So, there were no negotiations. As a result the treaty was subsequently referred to in Germany as the *Diktat von Versailles*. Thus, a fundamental evolution was already evident in the way the Versailles Peace Treaty came into being, regarding the view about the laws of war and peace and the responsibility of the states in these matters.

---

[46] USA, Bolivia, Brazil, Cuba, Ecuador, Guatemala, Haiti, Honduras, Nicaragua, Panama, Peru, China, Japan, Siam, Liberia: Preamble to the Versailles Peace Treaty of 1919.

As regards mediation, which repeatedly occurred in the seventeenth century and especially in the eighteenth century, I found only the one example already mentioned.[47]

Ratification

The different sorts of peace treaties had to be ratified to become permanently effective. In international law only the lawfully competent representative was qualified to do this, and generally this was the head of state. The German–French Peace Treaty of Frankfurt am Main of 1871 was ratified on the French side 'par l'Assemblée nationale et par le Chef du Pouvoir exécutif de la République française'.[48] If and to what extent the ratification of an international treaty was tied to an official act by other institutions or organs within each state, in particular by parliaments, depended on the constitutions in existence. It was only relevant with respect to international law if they limited the authority of international representation itself.[49] If this was the case, the matter had to be examined each time and for each state separately. For international agreements, the President of the USA was bound by the approval of the Senate.[50] In the German Empire before 1918, in France after 1871, in Great Britain, approval only had relevance for the internal, constitutional order but did not reflect on the state being bound internationally.[51] The German law of 10 February 1919 on the temporary authority of the German Empire, valid at the time of the Versailles Peace Treaty, required a national law for the conclusion of peace.[52] But this alone did not bring about a peaceful conclusion under international law. It needed ratification by the President of the *Reich*. Later, with the Constitution of the Weimar Republic, the representative power of the President of the *Reich* was also bound to a national law both for the declaration of war and regarding the conclusion of peace.[53]

During the period considered here, and in contrast to the Middle Ages and the early modern era, ratification was no longer considered to be an

---

[47] Peace Treaty of Berlin of 2 July 1850 between Prussia and Denmark.
[48] Peace Treaty of Frankfurt of 10 May 1871, Art. 18; von Liszt, *Völkerrecht*, p. 167, refers to the 'special situation' of 1871.
[49] Von Liszt, *Völkerrecht*, p. 166.
[50] Art. 2 (2) of the Constitution of the United States of America.
[51] Von Liszt, *Völkerrecht*, p. 167. Art. 11 of the Constitution of the Reich of 1871.
[52] Art. 6, 1919 RGBl. I, 169; agreement by law of the National Assembly in Weimar of 16 July 1919, 1919 RGBl. I, 687.
[53] Art. 45 (2) of the Constitution of the German Empire of 11 August 1919. See Gerhard Anschütz, *Die Verfassung des deutschen Reiches vom 19. August 1919, Kommentar* (14th edn, Berlin, 1933, reprint Darmstadt, 1965), pp. 260–1.

obligation and refusal to be an unfriendly act. The reason was that the plenipotentiaries were no longer sent out with elaborate, detailed, often mutually agreed mandates, in which the structures of the treaty to be drafted were already given. To be sure, the plenipotentiaries had received instructions, but these were only 'for internal use'. Therefore, they often had a wider margin to reach an agreement with the opposite partners. This made negotiations more flexible, but, on the other hand, they no longer committed the head of state.[54] Second, the often and more and more constitutionally prescribed participation of parliaments in the internal process of ratification made it impossible for the plenipotentiaries to give binding promises of the external ratification by the head of state.

The internal structure of treaties

Invocatio dei

Some treaties involving Christian powers still opened with the *invocatio trinitatis*. The First Paris Treaty and the Acts of the Vienna Congress were among them.[55] The custom, however, faded away in the course of time. In Europe the last time it was used was for the Austrian–Italian Peace Treaty of Vienna of 3 October 1866. Outside Europe, it was used for the very last time, so it seems, in the Italian–Ethiopian Treaty of 26 October 1896. In other treaties, especially those with Islamic powers, an *invocatio dei* was sometimes used. This remained customary in the nineteenth century, until the Congo Act of 1885.

With the disappearance of the *invocationes*, the last remnants of the Christian or religious embedding of international law, total secularisation was reached. At the same time an essential step was made towards its generalisation as a universal law of nations. This secularisation of the treaties did not exclude the regulation of questions of religion, especially of the freedom of worship in the text of the treaties.

Preamble

The preamble followed the *invocatio*, so, when the *invocatio* was relinquished, the treaties opened with the preamble.[56] Compared with the

---

[54] In 1867, Heffter, *Völkerrecht*, p. 166, hesitated but finally was of the opinion that only a moral, not a legal obligation for ratification is given even if the plenipotentiary stayed within his powers. In 1877, Funck-Brentano and Sorel, *Précis*, p. 162, were pleading for a complete freedom of the parties and based their opinion on the principle of sovereignty.
[55] E.g. Treaty on Danish succession to the throne of 8 May 1852.
[56] On preambles in treaties, see Ludwig Bittner, *Die Lehre von den völkerrechtlichen Vertragsurkunden* (Stuttgart, 1924), pp. 198–9.

'Great Treaties' of 1648 until 1713, the texts and material statements of the preambles had already been reduced in the course of the eighteenth century and their content had become impoverished. Generally, during the period considered here, it contained in the first place the identification of the partners to the treaty, which meant, following the rules mentioned above, the names of the heads of state, later of the states themselves. This was called the *intitulatio* of the legal subjects of the treaty.[57]

In many treaties the motives and purposes of the partners to the treaty (the *arenga*) followed. In it, the desire to achieve an end to the war, to re-establish peace, to resume good relations, etc., was expressed. However, the exposition of motives could also be omitted.[58] The motives give a summary of the attitude of the partners towards each other and of their common goals. As a rule, they express the common intention of achieving peace.[59] The motivation in the preamble of the Paris treaties of 1919/20 was completely different. The desire to have peace was only attributed to the allied and associated powers. Furthermore, Austria-Hungary and Germany were blamed and held responsible for the opening of the hostilities by their declarations of war, which, in the opinion of the allied and associated powers, had brought about their own involvement in the war.[60] Whereas in the First Paris Treaty of 1814 – also a treaty with a totally vanquished opponent who had held Europe in a bloody war for years – the desire for peace and the effort towards peace were said to be shared by all, the preamble of the Versailles Peace Treaty did not contain a single word in this respect.

After the enumeration of motives, the common intention of the partners regarding the conclusion of peace was confirmed. This is an important confirmation from a legal point of view and is a constitutive element of the conclusion of a treaty between partners.[61] It is, therefore, not without interest that in the Preamble of the Versailles Treaty of 1919 the

---

[57] Bittner, *Lehre*, p. 199.   [58] E.g. Peace Treaty of Frankfurt of 10 May 1871.
[59] Preamble to the Paris Peace Treaty of 1814: 'étant animés d'un égal désir de mettre fin aux longues agitations de l'Europe et aux malheurs des peuples par une paix solide, fondée sur une juste répartition des forces entre les Puissances, et partout dans ses stipulations la garantie de sa durée'; see also the Preamble of the Peace Treaties of Berlin of 2 July 1850; between France and Austria of Zurich of 10 November 1859, and of the Treaties between Prussia with Austria and the Southern German States of August 1866.
[60] 'The Allied and Associated Powers being equally desirous that the war in which they were successively involved directly or indirectly and which originated in the declaration of war by Austria-Hungary ... the declaration of war by Germany ... and in the invasion of Belgium'; Preamble to the Versailles Treaty of 1919.
[61] Bittner, *Lehre*, p. 208.

consideration of the concordant mutual consensus between the parties to conclude peace is completely absent.

After that, the plenipotentiaries of the parties, who were to conclude the peace in the name of the parties in the Treaty, were named. Their mandates were produced and mutually assessed. In the case of mediation, the plenipotentiaries of the mediator were named.[62]

The preamble ended with the assessment that the plenipotentiaries had reached agreement upon the 'following articles'. This formula is also to be found in the Versailles Treaty of 1919. This has a close connection with the last clause of the treaty, in which the signing of the whole treaty by the plenipotentiaries is laid down 'for authentication of the document' or 'en foi de quoi'. The two clauses together at the beginning and at the end make up the authoritative record of the texts in a legal charter delivered by the plenipotentiaries. Thus, in several respects the preamble formed a constitutive element for the character of the treaty as a charter.

The number of official copies of the treaty that were delivered and signed varies. The Versailles Peace Treaty of 1919 was made in one single original which was laid down at Paris. The partners received authenticated copies.[63] The Berlin Treaty of 17 August 1866 between Prussia and Baden was laid down in two copies, one for each party.[64]

Peace clauses

The operational part of the peace treaty always began, before 1792, with the clause of peace. This was also the case during the period considered here, with the grave exceptions of the German–French Treaty of 1871 and the Paris Treaties of 1919/20.

This clause had a long tradition.[65] The clause gave expression to the agreement between the partners named in the preamble, of concluding, restoring and keeping a lasting, honest, real and secure peace. The formulations varied. In the Middle Ages and in the sixteenth and seventeenth centuries, they were detailed in a luxurious and redundant language.

---

[62] Treaty of Berlin of 2 July 1850, Preamble.
[63] Treaty of Versailles of 1919, Art. 440. [64] Art. 11.
[65] Heinhard Steiger, 'Friedensschluß und Amnestie in den Verträgen von Münster und Osnabrück' in Heinz Duchhardt (ed.), *Krieg und Frieden im Übergang vom Mittelalter zur Neuzeit: Theorie – Praxis – Bilder = Guerre et paix du moyen age aux temps modernes* (Mainz, 2000), pp. 207–45; Jörg Fisch, *Krieg und Frieden im Friedensvertrag* (Stuttgart, 1979); Randall Lesaffer, *Europa: een zoektocht naar vrede (1453–1763/1945–1997)* (Louvain, 1999); Lesaffer, 'The Westphalia Peace Treaties and the Development of the Tradition of Great European Peace Settlements prior to 1648,' *Grotiana* NS 18 (1997), 71–95.

However, in the eighteenth century they were revised and more concisely formulated. The central content always remained, before all, the entanglement of peace and friendship, 'pax et amicitia', 'paix et amitié'. This goes back at least to the early Middle Ages.[66] *Amicitia* was taken from Roman law, but with an altered meaning. It was neither, as Carl Schmitt understood, an existential relationship nor an ontological reality.[67] It meant that in future the partners wanted to keep and maintain peaceful relations and exchanges, and would possibly also give assistance, though not in the sense of an alliance.[68] The concept, mainly, qualified peace and gave it a material element. It added something to peace as the mere absence of war.

The clauses of peace in the treaties of the era considered here have this double content. Article 1 of the Paris Peace Treaty of 1814 stipulated: 'Il y aura, à compter de ce jour, paix et amitié.' Similarly, the peace clauses in the 1866 Treaty between Prussia and its war enemies read as follows: 'Zwischen ... soll fortan Friede und Freundschaft auf ewige Zeiten bestehen ... '.[69] In Article 1 of the Paris Peace Treaty of 1856 ending the Crimean War, the partners agreed that, 'à dater du jour de l'échange des ratifications du présent Traité, paix et amitié entre ... '.[70]

The moment that peace began could vary. As a rule it was at the exchange of ratification. For multilateral peace treaties the question was whether all parties had to ratify before the treaty became effective, like for the Treaty of 1856, or whether it became immediately effective upon those parties which had completed their ratification. It also depended on whether the instruments of ratification were exchanged, as mentioned in Article 34 of the 1856 Treaty, or were entrusted to a depository, as mentioned in Article 440 of the Versailles Peace Treaty of 1919. In this article, it was stipulated that

[66] See Bruno Paradisi, 'L'"amicitia" internazionale nella storia antica' in Bruno Paradisi, *Civitas maxima: studi di storia del diritto internazionale* (Florence, 1974), vol. I, pp. 296–338; Paradisi, 'L'"amicitia" internazionale nell'alto medio evo' in Paradisi, *Civitas maxima*, pp. 339–97; Gerd Althoff, *Amicitia und pacta: Bündnis, Einung, Politik und Gebetsgedenken im beginnenden 10. Jahrhundert* (Hanover, 1992); Randall Lesaffer, 'Amicitia in Renaissance Peace and Alliance Treaties (1450–1530),' *Journal of the History of International Law* 4 (2002), 77–99.
[67] Carl Schmitt, *Der Begriff des Politischen: Text von 1932 mit einem Vorwort und drei Corollarien* (Berlin, 1963), pp. 28–37.
[68] In the old peace clauses, the principles *unio, foedus*, etc. were maintained, also when no real alliance was founded. They had already disappeared in the seventeenth century, as with the Treaties of Münster and Osnabrück of 1648.
[69] Treaty of Berlin of 23 August 1866, Art. 1.
[70] Also the formula used in the Peace Treaty of Bucharest of 1913, Art. 1.

Germany and three of the great allied and associated powers had to ratify the Treaty before it came into force and thereby the state of peace would be achieved. For the others, the state of peace came into force with the deposition of the instrument of ratification in the hands of France as the depository.

For the conclusion of peace between European powers and powers outside Europe similar clauses were used. Article 1 of the Nanking Peace Treaty between China and Great Britain of 29 August 1842 stated that: 'Il y aura désormais paix et amitié entre . . .'.[71] The Treaty of Simoda between Russia and Japan of 14–26 January 1855 stipulated in Article 1: 'Es soll fortan Friede und aufrichtige Freundschaft zwischen . . . bestehen.' For treaties between Britain and India this formula was also used, although generally they were treaties of submission.[72] The peace formula was also used by American and Asian powers for treaties between them.

The peace clause was still in use at the end of World War I in the treaties between the Central European powers and the East European states, at least in a toned-down form. Article 1 of the Peace Treaty of Brest-Litovsk of 3 March 1918 first declared that the state of war between the treaty partners was 'finished' and ran on: 'Sie sind entschlossen, fortan in Frieden und Freundschaft miteinander zu leben.'[73]

The Paris Treaties of 1919/20, however, had no peace clauses. They only declared the end of the state of war. Next: 'From that moment . . . official relations with Germany, and with any of the German States will be resumed by the Allied and Associated Powers.' Not only was the reference to the conclusion of 'Peace and Friendship' absent, the formulation also was one-sided. No reciprocal relations were restored or taken on and they were in addition characterised as of an 'official' character only and did not, so it seems, include relations between the people. This means that not only with respect to the procedure, but also with respect to the content regarding the central purpose of a Peace Treaty, a fundamental fracture occurred with the peace treaties concluded before World War I and with the centuries old practice of peacemaking and its underlying conceptions. The defeated party was no longer treated on equal terms. The treaty did not – at least not yet – reinstate a complete state of peace.

---

[71] Also Treaty of 4 March 1857 between Great Britain and Persia, Art. 1.
[72] E.g. the Treaty of Lahore of 9 March 1846 between the British government and the Maharajah; the Treaty of Sandornak of 26 May 1879 between Great Britain and Afghanistan.
[73] Art. 1; so already the Treaty of 9 February 1919 between the Central European powers and Ukraine, Art. 1.

Amnesty clauses

The same was obvious in another respect. This concerned an element of the treaty that was closely connected to the conclusion of peace: amnesty.[74] Emer de Vattel (1714–67) and Immanuel Kant (1724–1804) had argued that amnesty was a necessary element in a peace agreement.[75] The classical amnesty was linked with general oblivion.[76] It dealt with damages, additional losses, etc., during the war, whoever the perpetrators were, the army or others, for whom the parties were responsible. This meant that, once the peace was agreed upon, there would be no further consequences drawn, no claims introduced, no legal actions taken and, foremost, no new war started in reaction to anything that had occurred before or during the war. Peace came down to a new beginning. Old debts should not burden peace. Criminal proceedings were also excluded. Initially, this also meant reciprocal forgiveness. However, this aspect became obsolete as references to the question of responsibility for the war or for what happened during the war disappeared. During the early modern era, attempts to put the blame on the other party were dismissed between equal partners, that is, between sovereign states.[77] Also with respect to amnesty it was clear that by 'peace' a material state on the basis of reciprocity, equality, esteem and orientation to the future were meant. Peace, friendship and amnesty in their mutual relation were the three essential points of all classical peace agreements.

In addition to the general amnesty for damages, etc., resulting from military operations, there was personal amnesty, in the first place for collaborators who had worked with the enemy during the occupation of their own national territory and for inhabitants of regions which changed hands.

In the period considered here, the general amnesty clauses disappeared from European peace treaties. However, they were said now to be automatically implied in the peace treaty. Contemporary literature confirms this.[78] Presumably the regulation of the laws of war made the express

---

[74] See Fisch, *Krieg*, pp. 35–56; and Steiger, 'Friedensschluß', pp. 226–41.
[75] Steiger, 'Friedensschluss, pp. 244–5 and also Fisch, *Krieg*, pp. 104–5, for the eighteenth century.
[76] Fisch, *Krieg*, pp. 92–6.
[77] On the Peace of Westphalia see Steiger, 'Friedensschluß', pp. 242–5. The citations in Fisch, *Krieg*, pp. 98–102 refer to the relations of superior and subject in feudal law, etc.
[78] Fisch, *Krieg*, pp. 112–13; e.g. Heffter, *Völkerrecht*, p. 324; Ullmann, *Völkerrecht*, p. 544; von Liszt, *Völkerrecht*, p. 296; Henry Wheaton, *Eléments du droit international* (Leipzig etc., 1848), vol. II, pp. 209–10; dismissive, however, Funck-Brentano and Sorel, *Précis*, p. 316.

amnesty superfluous, since acts of war in conformity with these laws were legal acts. This has to be further examined. Nevertheless, it appears that some variations occurred. From the Paris Peace Treaty of 20 November 1815 on, increasingly reparations for war costs were imposed upon the defeated parties.[79] In 1815 the 'indemnité' amounted to 700 million francs in favour of the Allies; but the German–French Peace Agreement of 1871 imposed the huge sum of 5 billion francs. This sum was already mentioned in the Preliminary Peace Treaty of Versailles of 1871 and was confirmed in the Frankfurt Peace Treaty.[80] Payment was associated with the retreat of the occupying forces and thus secured.[81]

This way of compensation for the costs of the war was not entirely new. At the peace negotiations of Osnabrück between 1645 and 1648, the Swedes had claimed financial satisfaction in addition to territorial cessions, as payment for the war expenses of their army, and had obtained 5 million *Reichstaler*.[82] The Swedish argued that they had fought for German liberty and for the defence of the Protestant religion, and therefore in the German interest. Furthermore, the reparation was not at the expense of the emperor or the Empire as a whole, but at the expense of the *Reichsstände* of seven provinces of the Empire.[83] In the end a second treaty, the Nuremberg Peace Agreement of 1650, was needed in order to settle a number of details.[84] For the rest, this course of action remained exceptional until 1792. From 1815 onwards the imposition of the war expenses of the victorious party upon the defeated seems to have gone as a matter of course and smoothly. In 1815 the payment was explicitly called an 'indemnité'. The Treaty of 23 August 1866 between Prussia and Austria clearly mentioned the compensation of part of the 'war expenses of Prussia'.[85] This was, however, not yet a proper reparation for costs resulting from damages, nor a reparation for unjustly inflicted damage.

---

[79] Peace Treaty of Paris of 20 November 1815, Art. 4 (2); Preliminary Peace Treaty of Nikolsburg of 1866, Art. 4; Peace Treaty of Berlin of 13 August 1866, Art. 2; Peace Treaty of 17 August 1866, Art. 2; Peace Treaty of Berlin of 22 August 1866, Art. 2; Preliminary Treaty of Versailles of 1871, Art. 3; the list could go on, also with European–Asian peace treaties: e.g. Peace Treaty of Nanking of 1842.
[80] Preliminary Treaty of Versailles of 1871, Art. 2; Treaty of Frankfurt of 1871, Art. 7.
[81] Versailles Preliminary Treaty, Art. 3; Frankfurt Treaty, Art. 7.
[82] Treaty of Osnabrück of 24 October 1648, Art. 16 (8–12).
[83] About the negotiations see Fritz Dickmann, *Der westfälische Frieden* (7th edn, revised by Konrad Repgen, Münster, 1998), pp. 421–4 and 470–7.
[84] Antje Oschmann, *Der nürnberger Exekutionstag 1649–1650: das Ende des Dreißigjährigen Krieges in Deutschland* (Münster, 1991).
[85] Art. 4; also in the treaties between the States of Southern Germany of August 1866.

Such reparations were demanded for the first time at the Paris Treaties of 1919/20 at the expense of the defeated powers. Whilst at the Treaty of Brest-Litovsk the reciprocal renunciation of war damages was expressly agreed,[86] Article 231 of the Versailles Treaty stipulated that Germany was the originator of all losses and damages and was therefore responsible for them. This led to the obligation of restoring all damages inflicted upon the civil population.[87] The amount of the reparations to be paid at first was not calculated. This was again a new evolution, contrary to the tradition in international law regarding peace treaties.

The same departure from custom before 1914 also occurred with respect to personal amnesty. Article 16 of the Paris Peace Treaty of 1814 stipulated an extensive interdiction of prosecuting individual collaborators, more in particular within returned or ceded territories. Equivalent clauses were to be found in a number of European peace treaties from before World War I.[88] They applied to political activities as well as to military operations. Also in this matter, the Paris Treaties of 1919/20 brought a fundamental change. Article 227 of the Versailles Treaty stipulated that the German emperor, Wilhelm II (1888–1919, d. 1941), would be brought before a special international tribunal 'for a supreme offence against international morality and the sanctity of treaties'. And further on: 'In its decision the tribunal will be guided by the highest motives of international policy, with a view to vindicating the solemn obligations of international undertakings and the validity of international morality'. Because the Netherlands did not extradite the former emperor, it did not come to a trial. Not only was there, for the first time, an attempt to prosecute a head of state – be it a former head of state – who until then had remained sacrosanct and immune from any prosecution; also, a new and hitherto completely unknown criterion or standard was introduced, namely that of 'international morality'. Legal criteria for this did not exist. With this clause the above-mentioned change in content, visible throughout the whole treaty, was made abundantly clear. New moral principles were

---

[86] Art. 9, III, also the Treaty of 9 February 1918, Art. 5.
[87] Art. 232. The following articles deal with particularities, mostly of 'How'.
[88] The Vienna Congress Act of 1815 contained several provisions concerning each of the territories changing its state affiliation: Art. 12 (22). Also the Treaty of Zurich I of 10 November 1859 between Austria and France, Art. 21; the Treaty Zurich II of 10 November 1859 between France, Austria and Sardinia, Art. 22; Treaty of 23 August 1866, Art. 10 regarding Schleswig-Holstein; the Treaty of Frankfurt of 1871, Art. 2. The Treaty of Constantinople of 1/14 March 1914 between Serbia, Turkey and France, Art. 3 once more uses the concept 'amnestie pleine et entière' for all persons having been involved in war activities.

adopted instead of the current international law and its traditional praxis. Besides this, Article 228 of the Versailles Treaty provides for indictment of persons before allied military tribunals for having committed acts in violation of the laws and customs of war. Some of these trials actually took place, but before German courts. An additional problem was that the purposes of these indictments against the former emperor, as well as for those against these people, were completely new, surprising and, above all, one-sided. Indictment of persons on the Allied side was not anticipated.

Is it possible to decide how peace is better served: through amnesty or through prosecution? Nowadays, and with good grounds, the understanding goes in the latter direction, at least in so far as violations of international law, and especially the laws of war or international humanitarian law, are concerned. But the main problem consists in deciding whether a war is legal or not, e.g. whether it falls under Article 53 of the UN Charter. Of course this needs an objective and impartial procedure before the competent courts, and more secure, ratified, clear legal principles, as they have been developed since World War II. Perhaps for some cases it may be wiser to turn back to amnesty.

Territorial settlements

Peace treaties have to deal with the conflicts and problems which led to war in the first place or occurred during the war, and of which the settlement or solution is a prerequisite for obtaining peace. Of course these problems are different for each and every treaty, but primarily all peace treaties have to do with territorial settlements, that is, with the repartition and reallocation of territories between the partners. The conflicts concerning the repartition of territorial sovereignty and their regulation, in other words the establishment of the *Nomos der Erde*, determine the relationships between states.[89] Most wars are primarily caused by conflicts over territory. Therefore, the territorial conflicts that led to a war have to be settled in the peace treaty, albeit often only partially and temporarily, notwithstanding the claim of perpetuity expressed in the treaty itself. The extent and scope of territorial agreements are, of course, largely different. The Peace Agreements of 1814/15, 1856, 1866, 1878 and 1919/20 were very extensive territorial settlements and concerned large parts of Europe, which were given a completely new configuration. Other peace treaties

---

[89] Carl Schmitt, *Der Nomos der Erde im Völkerrecht des Jus Publicum Europaeum* (4th edn, Berlin, 1997).

affected only particular regions between two or three states, such as those of 1859 and 1871. Of course, they also influenced the general order in Europe, but not in a radical way.

At first, following the wars from 1792, until 1814, there was the general political new order shaped by the Paris Peace Treaty of 1814 and by the Acts of the Vienna Congress, by which the map of Europe was thoroughly shaken up and changed. With the Paris Peace Treaty of 1814, France had been brought back to its borders of 1792, and by the Second Paris Treaty of 1815 even to those of 1790. The organisation of states set up by Napoleon disappeared. The new order decided by the 1815 Acts of the Vienna Congress embraced the whole of Europe.[90] Poland was not reconstituted as an independent state, its partition between the three Eastern powers being only rearranged. In Germany, the new order was based on the situation that had come into being from 1803 on. The changes of 1803 and thereafter had permanently reshuffled significant parts of the former Empire. In particular, France had annexed important regions: not only the entire part to the west of the Rhine, but in the end almost the whole of north-west Germany up to the Baltic, including Bremen and Hamburg. Several German states, for example the Kingdom of Saxony, had stuck to the second *Rheinbund* or Rhine Federation of 1806, almost until the end of Napoleon's regime. The Napoleonic creations of new states, particularly the Kingdom of Westphalia, had caused territorial shifts between the regions. A new state of affairs was needed. The greater German states in principle kept the status they had reached in 1803, but with extensively modified territories. Prussia and other states recovered regions which they had obtained in 1803 by way of restitution. All German states subsequently joined together in the *Deutsche Bund* or German Confederation,[91] which Article 6(2) of the Paris Peace Treaty of 1814 had made provision for.

Belgium and Luxemburg were united with the Netherlands as one country under the House of Orange. In Italy the former states were in part reconstituted. Almost the whole of northern Italy, however, from Milan to Venice, came under Austrian sovereignty. But as explained above, these settlements did not meet the expectations and movements of European people and nations who, to a large extent, had no state of their own. The

---

[90] Part I Poland; Part II Germany; Part III Netherlands, Luxemburg, Belgium; Part IV Switzerland; Part V Italy; Part VI Portugal.
[91] Arts. 53 and following of the Vienna Congress Act of 1815 and the Federation Act of 8 June 1815.

subsequent years, until the end of the century, would have to deal with their expectations.

The years 1866 to 1870 saw the establishment of a new order in Germany, where, first, the *Deutsche Bund* was dissolved and, second, two separate political entities were created: *Kleindeutschland*, as the *Norddeutscher Bund* or the North German Confederation, expanding into the German Empire, and the now completely independent Empire of Austria-Hungary. The agreements were laid down in the Peace Treaties of 1866,[92] 1866/67[93] and 1870,[94] but one-sided legal Acts were also used, such as the annexations of Hanover, Hessen-Kassel, Hessen-Nassau and Frankfurt am Main by Prussia.[95] Despite the fact that most of the European states were partners to the Vienna Congress Acts, only some of them took part in all these Acts mentioned.

From 1859 on, the new order of Italy was on the agenda. Here, not all the Congress powers of 1815 participated either and no new Congress was convened. Important treaties for the unification of Italy were primarily the Peace Treaties of Zurich of 1859 and of Vienna of 1866, whereby Austria-Hungary had to cede its Italian territories, with the exception of South Tyrol, to France, which then ceded them to Italy. In addition, other means of unification, including plebiscites and annexations by Italy, were used. Without any form of treaty or agreement the Papal States, Naples, Parma, Tuscany, Modena and other states were incorporated by pure annexation.

And so gradually, without a general war and without a general Congress, the territorial repartition as it was decided in Vienna and the political and legal order of Europe were rearranged in major parts. Numerous states disappeared in the process, including one of the oldest, the Papal States.

The whole period was also marked by the struggle of the peoples of the Balkans against the Turks, as they wanted their independence and their own states. Illustrative of this were the Treaties of Paris of 1856, of San Stefano and Berlin of 1878, along with several treaties of Balkan states amongst each other and with Turkey, regulating the creation of new states in the Balkans on the basic principle of nation-states. Turkey lost

---

[92] Treaty of 23 August 1866.
[93] Termination of the North German Confederation by Treaty of 18 August 1866; Constitution of the *Norddeutschen Bund* of 16 April 1867, Huber II, 272.
[94] Entrance of the Southern States into the North German Confederation, Treaty of 8 December 1870.
[95] Huber II, 252–5.

the major part of its European territories in the process: partly by the foundation of new states, partly by annexation of its territories by Russia and Austria. Thus five new states emerged in the Balkans.

With all this, aspirations towards the creation of new nation-states did not come to an end. Within the bigger multinational states such as Austria-Hungary and Russia, many nationalities aspired to their own state. This led to a significant reshuffle of Europe after World War I, on the basis of the newly accepted principle of the right to self-determination for all nations.[96] The Versailles Treaty with Germany resulted in the handing over of Alsace-Lorraine to France, of North Schleswig to Denmark and of important eastern territories to the recently recreated Poland.[97] The Treaties of Saint-Germain and Trianon confirmed the separation of Austria and Hungary, the formation of Czechoslovakia out of parts of the former Double Monarchy and also the handing over of more territories to Poland and to Italy, and a newly created southern Slavonic state Serbia-Croatia-Slovenia.[98] Russia had to face, as a consequence of the process of decline from 1917 and its treaties with the Central European powers, the independence of Finland, Ukraine and the Baltic states as well as the later cession of territories to Poland.[99] As a result, Central, Eastern and South-Eastern Europe were again completely reorganised. It was hoped that through this a just and lasting peace would be established, whereby the claims of nation-states would be satisfied. In the process, a basically new principle was introduced.

Subsequently, the new territorial order established by the Paris Treaties of 1919/20 spread from Europe to the Middle East, Asia and Africa, where the colonies of Germany in these regions were reallocated[100] and the territories of Turkey in the Arab world were transformed into new states, albeit initially as mandated territories.[101]

The organisation of political power and dominance was also an item in peace treaties between European and Asian states as well as in

---

[96] First taken as principle in the Fourteen Points of the American President Woodrow Wilson on 8 January 1918 and in further discourses; Strupp III, 207. This led on the one hand to the formation of new states, on the other hand to plebiscites in some regions of Germany and Austria where changes were proposed: in Silesia, Carinthia, etc.
[97] Parts II and III of the Versailles Treaty of 1919.
[98] Parts II and III of the Saint-Germain Treaty of 1919; Parts II and III of the Trianon Treaty of 1920.
[99] Treaties of Brest-Litovsk of 9 February 1919 with the Ukraine, and of 27 August 1918 with Russia; Peace Treaty of 7 March 1918 between Germany and Finland.
[100] Part IV of the Versailles Treaty of 1919.
[101] Parts II and III of the Sèvres Treaty of 1920.

inter-Asian peace treaties.[102] Principally, however, Europe took the initiative in regulating, by means of treaties between European states, the political repartition of the territories 'without a ruler', that is, territories which were not organised as a state. This especially was the case with the Congo Act of 1885, which did not end a war but prevented one.

Of course, the treaties contained provisions regarding the consequences of territorial changes, in particular for their inhabitants. Their religious rights as well as their right to remain in the country or to leave were normally dealt with. Further, the treaties contained stipulations as regards economic and financial questions, private and public property, and moveable and immoveable goods, and administrative and legal problems.[103]

Guaranteeing the peace

Reciprocal guarantees of treaties completely vanished, in particular guarantees given by great powers, as they had appeared regularly in the later seventeenth and eighteenth centuries. But a new one-sided guarantee was introduced to assure the payment of reparation by the defeated party: the temporary occupation of some of its territory. Under this new system, troops were gradually withdrawn as payments were made. These means were also used as a safeguard against new acts of war on the part of the defeated power. The Paris Peace Treaty of 1815 provided that the eastern parts of France would be occupied for five years, whereas in the Versailles Treaty of 1919 fifteen years of occupation of western parts of Germany were stipulated, in both cases with the possibility of reducing the term.[104] Furthermore, demilitarised zones were imposed. This was completed with provisions regarding surrendering war equipment and weapons, fixation of the strength of armed forces, etc.

There were no provisions either for the peaceful settlement of disputes or about the execution of the treaties.[105] In this matter, the treaties fell

---

[102] Peace Treaty of Portsmouth of 23 August/5 September 1905 between Japan and China; Peace Treaty of Shimonoseki of 17 April 1895 between Japan and China.
[103] E.g. Treaty of Paris of 1814, Arts. 17 and following; Treaty of Zurich of 1859 between Austria and France, Arts. 7 and following; Treaty of Frankfurt of 187, Art. 2; Treaty of Versailles of 1919, e.g. Arts. 36 and 53 and following.
[104] Treaty of Paris of 1815, Art. 5 (2); Treaty of Versailles of 1919, Arts. 428 and following.
[105] Independence and Peace Treaty of 26 March 1846 between Spain and Uruguay, Art. 19, providing in a 'charge' before deciding to go to war.

back on the Treaties of Münster and Osnabrück, where this was indeed anticipated.[106]

General stipulations

Some of the peace treaties, however, also made provision for institutional changes, separate from the territorial settlements. This was not completely new. The Peace of Osnabrück had laid down important stipulations to be followed by the Holy Roman Empire of the German Nation. By being an international treaty, these became an integral part of the European legal order. Following that example, the Paris Peace Treaty of 1814 announced that the German states would be united by a 'lien fédératif'.[107]

Essentially, the foundation of the German Confederation and its Constitution were central to the Vienna Congress Acts.[108] Thus, this Constitution became a part of the European order under international law and the Federation was, as the Empire had already been in 1648, according to international law, anchored at the centre of the European order. As shown above, this had its consequences when the Germans wanted to make some changes, as the other powers were implicated by this under international law. The Constitution of the *Deutsche Bund* distinguished two legal orders. The German states remained sovereign for their external affairs towards all other countries that did not belong to the Federation, and were in these matters bound by international law. But in their relations with each other, the common law of the Federation was in force, with the international law having only a subsidiary validity. The peace, as far as relations within the Federation were concerned, had therefore been more closely determined and with more far-reaching consequences. War between the members of the Federation was forbidden, as it had been in the old Empire. Their disputes had to be settled through arbitration. In particular, there were common bodies acting for the Federation as a whole, the Assembly of the Federation (*Bundesversammlung*) with a more reduced membership, and a general assembly (*Vollversammlung*).

On the basis of general cooperation between states, the Paris Treaties of 1919/20 put into place a comprehensive institutional order: the League

---

[106] Treaty of Osnabrück of 24 October 1648, Art. 17 (6) and Treaty of Münster of 24 October 1648, Para. 115.
[107] Treaty of Paris of 1814, Art. 6 (1).
[108] Art. 53 of the Vienna Congress Act and the joined Federation Act of 1815, whose decisions, according to Art. 64, 'auront la même force et valeur que s'ils étoient textuellement insérés ici'.

of Nations. Its founding charter formed the first part of these treaties. The defeated parties were initially excluded from membership. The prevailing principle in these treaties of inequality and discrimination also appeared here in their exclusion from the group of full members of the family of nations. Nevertheless, the League of Nations marked an important step towards guaranteeing the peace. Although war itself was not yet forbidden, at least a procedure was created allowing the Council of the League of Nations to intervene in the settlement of disputes, and thereby a forum was created and organised, giving better possibilities for the peaceful settlement of disputes.[109] In fact, this first attempt at guaranteeing peace in an institutional way failed in the 1930s.

But also more modest, specialised institutions were established by peace treaties. In the first place, these included several Waterway Commissions. The regulation of navigation for transport and traffic upon international waterways, considered of the utmost urgency, went by the principle of free navigation, unhindered by regulations of the riparian states, in view of the growing economic intertwining and development of commerce. Free trade was often considered as a means of stabilising and consolidating peace.[110] For that, institutionalised co-operation was needed, especially while the watercourses had to be developed and maintained. The Vienna Congress Act instituted the Rhine Commission,[111] the Paris Treaty of 1856 the Danube Commission[112] and the Versailles Treaty the Commissions for Elbe and Oder.[113]

The Paris Treaties of 1919/20 also founded the International Labour Organisation for cooperation in improving the situation of the labour forces, in particular with respect to terms of employment.[114] In our time therefore the first initiatives were taken, followed by more far-reaching steps, towards an internationally institutionalised organisation that could guarantee peace.[115]

---

[109] Arts. 122 and following of the Charter of the League of Nations.
[110] Treaty of Paris of 1814, Art. 5 (2) gives as the aim of free navigation 'pour faciliter les communications entre les peuples et les rendre toujours moins étrangers les uns aux autres'.
[111] Art. 117 and Art. 10 of Annex C of the Vienna Congress Act of 1815.
[112] Treaty of Paris of 1856, Arts. 16 and following.
[113] Treaty of Versailles of 1919, Arts. 340 and following.
[114] Part XIII of the Treaty of Versailles of 1919.
[115] Apart from peace treaties, other international organisations were founded, such as the Universal Postal Union Treaty of 1 June 1878 and the International Telegraph Convention of 17 May 1865/22 July 1875.

Economic and commercial relations

As war normally interrupted all commercial, economic and cultural relations,[116] peace treaties had to restore the economic relations and make peaceful and undisturbed commerce possible again. The classical treaties generally did this with a clause re-establishing relations as they existed before the war. We have already mentioned regulations for navigation on rivers. There were also agreements to be reached regarding commerce, customs, railway transport, and later on post, telegraph and air transport. Overseas possessions were included in these agreements.[117] For the German states, the Customs Union of 1865 was continued in 1866, even after the German Confederation no longer existed.[118] The Peace Treaty between Germany and France of 1871 re-established all treaties with the various states, which had been annulled by the state of war. They were re-established by the reciprocal acceptance of the most-favoured nation clause.[119] Supplementary articles dealt with the railways. The agreements were not always to be found within the Peace Treaty itself; in some cases it was agreed to deal with them in a separate treaty.[120]

Further stipulations on economy and commerce were to be found in the treaties with Turkey and Asian countries. In the Paris Peace Treaty of 1856, besides the free navigation upon the Danube, the Black Sea was made neutral and free commercial navigation was opened to all. At the same time, commerce was re-established to its pre-war status on the basis of a reciprocal most-favoured nation clause.[121] The Peace Treaty between Greece and Turkey of 1897 provided for the resumption of the interrupted post and telegraph communications and for their regulation in due time by a separate treaty.[122] The economic relations between the European powers and Turkey, in spite of the admission of the Sublime Porte into the concert of European nations in 1856, were riddled with inequalities through the capitulation regime enforced upon Turkey. This country understandably tried to cut these down. In Article 6 of the Lausanne Peace Treaty between Italy and Turkey of 18 October 1912, Italy promised to conclude a commercial Treaty 'sur la base du droit public européen, c'est-à-dire qu'elle consent à laisser à la Turquie toute son indépendance économique et le

---

[116] E.g. the Treaty of Frankfurt of 1871, Art. 11.
[117] In the Treaty of Paris of 1815, Art. 12 (2), the British king granted the subjects of the French king the most-favoured clause for India.
[118] Treaties between Prussia and Württemberg, Baden, Bavaria of August 1866, Art. 7.
[119] Treaty of Frankfurt of 1871, Art. 11.   [120] Thus in Art. 8 of the Treaties of August 1866.
[121] Treaty of Paris of 1856, Art. 11 and Art. 32.
[122] Peace Treaty of 22 November/4 December 1897 between Turkey and Greece, Arts. 12–13.

droit d'agir en matière commerciale et douanière à l'instar de toutes les Puissances européennes et sans être liée par les capitulations et d'autres actes à ce jour'. The precondition was that similar commercial treaties would have to be agreed with the other European powers.[123] The reference to the 'droit public européen', respectively the 'droit international', indicates that, although this was accepted as a general standard for legal relations, it was by no means realised as regards all non European powers.

In Asia, the European powers could only slowly achieve their aim of free trade. The Peace Treaty between Britain and China of Nanking of 1842 opened only certain cities to British trade.[124] At the same time, following this treaty Hong Kong was handed over to Great Britain. For the rest, the treaty gave detailed regulations for the trade in the agreed cities, which were laid down in an additional regulation.

Other treaties between European and Asian powers agreed on reciprocal rights, e.g. the Saigon Peace Treaty of France and Spain with Annam of 5 June 1862. Tradesmen from both sides would have free entry to the ports of the other party.[125] The commercial agreements in Asia depended very much upon the political situation of the day.

The agreements on economic and other relations between the Allies and their associates, on the one hand, and the Central European powers, on the other, assumed unusual importance in the Paris Treaties of 1919/20, in particular in the Versailles Peace Treaty with Germany.[126] They dealt with economic relations in general, and with air traffic, use of ports, navigation ways and railways in particular. We have not yet elaborated on these here.[127] Generally, these agreements were not made on the basis of equality and reciprocity, as they loaded Germany unilaterally with obligations whereas the partners were granted rights. The basic principle of the treaty, of not integrating Germany as a full member with equal rights into the international community – which had the same Peace Treaty as its basis – but keeping the *Reich* in a special status for moral and political considerations, was also visible here and had an essential influence on this part.

---

[123] Art. 8 proposed a general conference for the abolition of the system of capitulation 'en le remplaçant par le régime du droit international'. This was, however, not achieved before World War I.
[124] Art. 2: Canton, Quemoy, Fuzhou, Ningbo and Shanghai. Partly these were already the agreed commercial places in the seventeenth century.
[125] Art. 5.
[126] Parts X–XII, Treaty of Versailles of 1919 with numerous additions.
[127] See Christian Tomuschat's chapter 18 in this volume.

Other stipulations and final provisions

Depending on the situation or the type of conflict, a whole range of other matters could be dealt with. Most of these were consequential to extensive territorial changes. These aspects deserve further research.

The final provisions contained agreements on the liquidation of the war situation, in particular regarding the return of prisoners of war,[128] the retreat of troops, the restitution of archives, documents and sometimes even objects of art, etc., various transitional measures, etc. Ratification specially was stipulated, generally within a fixed and mostly short time limit.[129] These further provisions were again extensive in the Paris Treaties of 1919/20, in particular in the Versailles Treaty.

Certain changes occurred in the ratification procedure. It was, in the later part of the period, linked to the constitutional requirements of the parties by the treaties themselves. The oath had disappeared during the seventeenth century.

Conclusion

First, the basis of the important changes in peace treaty practice outlined does not lie, as postulated in our introduction, within the international law, but is the result of development of social, political and economic attitudes, also of changes in mentality, and also the generalised mind-set as regards war, peace, power and law. I will only elaborate on some of these aspects.

Second, the pursuit of the nation-state mentioned and the connected pursuit of freedom and democracy caused the unification wars in Germany and Italy and the wars of independence in the Balkans. This was, in addition to other reasons, one of the main reasons for World War I in Central, Eastern and Southern Europe. The peace treaties had to take these aspirations of the people and their movements towards statehood into account and endeavour to integrate them into the shaping or even reshaping of the European order, because otherwise peace was not

---

[128] E.g. the Treaty of Bucharest of 1913 between Greece, Montenegro, Serbia and Bulgaria, Art. 9.

[129] The Treaty of 17 August 1866 between Prussia and Baden, Art. 11 set a time limit until 21 August; the Treaty of 22 August 1866 between Prussia and Bavaria, Art. 18 gave twelve days; the Treaty of Frankfurt of 1871 between Germany and France, Art. 18 gave ten days. The Treaty of Versailles of 1919 stipulated that the ratification should follow 'as soon as possible'.

attainable and the order achieved would have to be reshuffled time and again.

These principles, however, were not in the first place legal principles, not even political principles; they gradually became ethical principles, ultimately during World War I. This led not only to far-reaching changes of the political European order as it had been established in 1815, but also to the dismantling of centuries-old political-legal associations under one sovereign or state through territorial shifts and through the foundation of new states. States and monarchies that had shaped Europe's history for centuries disappeared, amongst them the Papal States and the Habsburg Empire.

Third, imperialism was the second political driving force of the era. While it was still of minor importance at the beginning of the nineteenth century, it steadily came to the foreground and produced a new rivalry between the European powers. This rivalry extended beyond the confines of Europe. The dispute over Alsace-Lorraine is in this perspective anachronistic and only explicable on historical grounds.

Fourth, it is perhaps also due to the shift in the field of rivalries that the alterations to the political structures in Germany and Italy during the second half of the nineteenth century were achieved without a general European congress. For the Balkans, and above all for the African conquest and for the regulation of the laws of war, congresses were still organised, in 1878 and 1885, and in 1899 and 1907, respectively. Nevertheless, the concept of the European Concert, of the *corps politique de l'Europe*, became visibly weaker. During the second half of the nineteenth century, it lapsed widely into bilateral treaty agreements and, subsequently, into hostile alliances. This burst out in a new important war, this time a world war because imperialism covered the whole world.

Fifth, until 1914 peace treaties were European, American or Asian. The Versailles Treaties affected the whole world: by its partners from Europe, America and Asia, by the insertion into the Treaty of the League of Nations, conceived on a scale embracing the whole planet, by the agreements on territorial questions in Europe, Asia and Africa and by other material agreements. With this a remarkable change came about: for the first time, American and Asian powers negotiated, allocated and decided together with European powers concerning the political order in Europe. Europe thus changed from being 'ruler' of the world to becoming just a part of it. This brought about the end of an international law created mainly by European powers and, in its core, concentrated on the ordering of the relations between these powers both in Europe and throughout the world, and marked the first steps of the beginning of the universal law of nations, shaped also by other nations and including more and more people and states.

Sixth, and most fundamentaly, the rupture between the 1919/20 treaties and the previous treaties is striking. Some elements can be traced to their roots in 1815: war damages and compensation, military occupation. This, however, not only was surpassed in 1919 but also was newly qualified. In particular the reciprocity in the agreements had generally disappeared. Certainly, the defeated parties had always had to accept one-sided burdens like the loss of territories or the payment for war costs. However, the basic reciprocity, above all the reciprocal esteem, had always remained. There lay the basis for the formula 'Peace and Friendship'. In the Paris Treaties of 1919/20, the formulations were consistently one-sided. I have not found any decision which would have committed the Allies and their associates in any way to something really substantial towards the Central European powers.

I have already pointed out the fundamental change in the concept of war. This was in the attitude of the allied and associated powers in 1919, especially towards Germany. Even more explicitly than in the treaty itself, this was expressed in the reply note of 16 June 1919 to the position taken by the German delegation at the Peace Conference. It stated: 'Dans l'opinion des Puissances alliées, et associées la guerre qui a éclaté le 1er août 1914 a été le plus grand crime contre l'humanité et la liberté des peuples qu'ait jamais commis consciemment une nation se prétendant civilisée.' Furthermore, Germany was responsible 'pour la manière sauvage et inhumaine dont elle [la guerre] a été conduite'.[130] This shift in the conception of war required punishment, taming and control of the culprits. Thereupon rested the exclusion of the Central European powers from the League of Nations. This was a sudden, unforeseen and above all one-sided political shift, not created by consent and not transformed into consent either. It was therefore not surprising that this revolution and, most of all, its implementation were not immediately and generally accepted. This return to the concept of a just war has often been criticised as the 'turn to a discriminating concept of war'.[131]

Seventh, out of the same impetus the League of Nations was created, as a system of reciprocal security, intended to foresee future wars, and if

---

[130] Strupp IV, 83.
[131] Carl Schmitt, *Die Wendung zum diskriminierenden Kriegsbegriff* (2nd edn, Berlin, 1988).

possible to prevent them. This was already an old idea, the most popular proposition having been that of Immanuel Kant, for a 'League of Nations' which would achieve more or less an 'eternal peace'.[132] We cannot go further into this here. However, the interconnection of peace and justice, as it was newly defined by the Paris Treaties of 1919/20, has to be considered independently of the question whether they succeeded in 1919 or not, within a centuries-old European tradition. Justice can only become a reality when there is peace, and arms are silenced. Peace can only last when there is justice. When this reciprocal connection works, there is no longer a place or function for war in between. To achieve this was the purpose of international law in 1919, and it still is today, in spite of all disappointments. This makes it necessary that, in addition to developing material law on matters such as human rights, international law further develops its legal doctrine towards neutral and impartial procedures and, above all, closes its open flank by compulsory jurisdiction.[133] A treaty on this matter would add a new quality to peace treaties, which not only end a particular war but lay the foundations for a lawful and institutionalised peace, as was proposed, for example by Kant in his treatise *Zum ewigen Frieden* (1795).

---

[132] Immanuel Kant, *Zum ewigen Frieden: ein philosophischer Entwurf* (Königsberg, 1795, enlarged 2nd edn, 1796).

[133] Heinhard Steiger, 'Plaidoyer pour une juridiction internationale obligatoire' in Jerzy Makarczyk (ed.), *Theory of International Law at the Threshold of the 21st Century: Essays in Honour of Krysztof Skubiszewski* (The Hague, 1996).

PART II

Thinking peace:
voices from the past

5

Vestigia pacis. The Roman peace treaty:
structure or event?

CHRISTIAN BALDUS

Introduction[1]

The problems related to the subject of peace treaties in Roman law are abundant.[2] Not only does the thin evidence of the sources make it difficult to gather a *status quaestionis*. What do we know about the content and function of peace treaties which have been passed down to us from history? What remains to be discovered? What questions of principle do we have to ask when it comes to the appropriate methods we should employ? 'New' sources, *nova reperta* so to speak, are only seldom found.[3] Thus, we have to resort to reinterpreting the rather limited amount of well-known sources and to reviewing the older secondary literature to see to what extent it is

---

[1] This chapter is based on two papers presented at the Conference 'Peace Treaties and International Law in History' at Tilburg University on 29 March 2001, and at the University of Pavia on 13 March 2001. I want to thank Katja Stoppenbrink for the English translation, bibliographical research and helpful comments on earlier drafts of this text.

[2] For details and more quotations before 1998, the reader is referred to Karl-Heinz Ziegler, *Völkerrechtsgeschichte* (Munich, 1994) and my own published doctoral thesis, *Regelhafte Vertragsauslegung nach Parteirollen im klassischen römischen Recht und in der modernen Völkerrechtswissenschaft* (Frankfurt am Main etc., 1998), esp. pp. 189–488, upon which the theses here expressed are based. (Reviews so far by Felice Mercogliano, *Index* 26 (1998), 590; Alain Wijffels, *Ius Commune* 27 (2000), 433–8; Karl-Heinz Ziegler, *Labeo* 46 (2000), 275–82. The latest historical introduction to international law can be found in Otto Kimminich and Stephan Hobe, *Einführung in das Völkerrecht* (7th edn, Tübingen and Basel, 2000), pp. 29–70 (Antiquity: pp. 31–4). Cf. furthermore Andreas Zack, *Studien zum 'Römischen Völkerrecht'* (Göttingen, 2001) and David J. Bederman, *International Law in Antiquity* (Cambridge, 2001; reviewed by Christian Baldus, *Klio* 85 (2003), 482–3. Apart from these, there are only bibliographical references to works not accessible through the aforementioned monographs (some including their reviews in common classical journals in order to facilitate interdisciplinary access). Recent works by the author himself are quoted mainly with regard to further references.

[3] An exception of relevance to the history of international law is the *deditio* form of the *Tabula de Alcántara* and, in great detail, Dieter Nörr, *Aspekte des römischen Völkerrechts: Die Bronzetafel von Alcántara* (Munich, 1989).

possible to make the texts speak to us – rather than being obscured by the interpretations of their own age.[4]

Taking a classical *vexata quaestio* as our starting point, we will take an overall view of the problems, first of substance and then of method, caused by the peace treaty. From this methodological discussion, we will finally return to our initial question. Even the concept of *pax* raises the problem whether *pax* is a legal act or a factual state of being. For our overall view, we first have to ask what can be said about the 'classical'[5] international law of ancient Rome as a 'system' and especially about the function of the peace treaty within such a system. The relevant questions are whether and in what sense we can suppose the existence of international law; to what extent we can trace the formation of a theoretical system,[6] which might facilitate our legal comprehension from an *ex post* perspective; to what

---

[4] Above all, this tendency is due to the respective dominant approaches in legal theory, which affect the interpretation of historical sources. We cannot evade this fundamental problem, not even by trying to work 'purely historically'. The legal historian is not able to do this; his specific domain is the effect of norms, his specific limit his dependency on historical research. All we can do is to take good notice of any possible paradigmatic change in legal theory. Thus we become less prone to ideological influences.

[5] Of course we do not claim the theory of international law to have known a classical period in the sense of a theoretical and political heyday such as Roman private law. We will presently seek the reasons why such an epoch is missing. Over some centuries, however, there had been relatively stable organisation of the structures of foreign legal relations by Rome in contrast to early republican times, which are only dimly reflected in the sources, as well as from the political and terminological confusion of the late imperial period. This last-mentioned point has to be stressed: the late imperial period now receives greater attention again. This is welcome especially for the history of international law, for there was an open political situation (see the argument in the main text) and therefore numerous treaty relations. Cf. recently in great detail above all Raimund Schulz, *Die Entwicklung des römischen Völkerrechts im vierten und fünften Jahrhundert n. Chr.* (Stuttgart, 1993); with some reservations, this work met with approval by Peter Kehne, *Historische Zeitschrift* 260 (1995), 187, and almost unreservedly by Karl-Heinz Ziegler, *Göttingische Gelehrte Anzeigen* 247 (1995), 63–76, and by Barbara Scardigli, *Gnomon* 71 (1999), 45–9. On methodical aspects, cf. Christian Baldus, Review of Dorothee Kohlhas-Müller, *Untersuchungen zur Rechtsstellung Theoderichs des Großen* (Frankfurt am Main etc., 1995), *Zeitschrift der Savigny-Stiftung für Rechtsgeschichte, Romanistische Abteilung* 117 (2000), 611–24.

[6] Obviously, we do not have to look for a 'system' in the sense of what the great codifications aspired to (and remains to be aspired to, at least on the European continent), i.e. a coherent legal penetration of all conceivable and legally controllable extra-legal phenomena in order to cope with them in an equitable way. In private law Roman lawyers strove for coherence in their own way, but the historical line of development going from Greece through Humanism and the Enlightenment to the Pandects of the nineteenth century essentially runs via Rome. Certainly, this does not mean that there could not have been such aspiration for coherence *ab initio*. Roman ideology of power aimed at educated foreign elites, and it is well conceivable that these were politically receptive to a systematic legitimation of the *pax Romana*. As to theoretical elements of a system, see for an extremely sceptical point of view Francisco

extent this law can be regarded as a sociologically functioning system; and what after all can be said about individual examples of peace treaties.

These have to be examined as to the typical function of such treaties. The treaties show their respective functions most distinctly in a situation of conflict. There is conflict about the terms of a treaty when one party to the treaty contends that the other party does not keep to the agreement. This, however, is often the case when new controversy, new grounds or even a pretext for another war are looked for. Therefore, the sources depict with particular attention the history preceding wars – which is particularly susceptible to manipulation. Finally, we will have to ask to what extent the results of our survey facilitate our comprehension of former times and of the present day: where there are still unknown spots on our map of the legal landscape and how expeditions to get there might be organised in the future.

An emblematic problem: on the legal nature of *pax*

Pax is a pivotal concept of Roman foreign policy,[7] and it is also in manifold usage in legal contexts. It has in particular been discussed whether *pax* was only a state of peace or the peace treaty as well. This question becomes relevant for instance with regard to the *postliminium in pace* (which, however, will not be dealt with here). When a Roman had been enslaved abroad outside of war and was released later on, what rules had to apply to the restoration to his original legal position? The same rules that apply to captivity in times of war? And is it of any importance whether a formal peace treaty had been concluded?[8]

Since in Rome no formation of a rigorous legal system based on formally coordinated categories was observed, we can understand Roman peace treaties without disposing of a clear-cut basic concept. However, it is characteristic that up until today we do not know the precise legal meaning of the term *pax* for the ancient belligerents themselves. There are no unambiguous findings; the sources do not allow any definite conclusion. The background of this debate is a theoretical question which until today

---

Cuena Boy, *Sistema jurídico y Derecho Romano* (Santander, 1998); cf. the review by Christian Baldus, 'Sistema giuridico europeo storicamente fondato?', *Labeo* 47 (2001), 122–34.

[7] Parallel questions are raised by the Greek *eirene*; here, however, it is easier to justify that the word primarily refers to the state of peace.

[8] For references regarding the *postliminium*, see below, n. 35; as to the concept of *pax* in this context, see Ferdinando Bona, 'Postliminium in pace', *Studia et Documenta Historiae et Iuris* 21 (1955), 249–75 at p. 259.

has not been resolved either: Was war the rule and peace the exception, which therefore required a special foundation by treaty? Was there 'natural hostility'? This was taught above all by some authorities of the nineteenth century. Nowadays this doctrine is less adhered to. To what extent do we have to explain this change by the shift in the theories of present international law, i.e. from national and nationalistic thinking to an international law of cooperation?[9] Could it be that the interpretation of a – if not the – central concept relating to the peace treaty is entirely subject to the legal historians' preconception? Does this mean that, after all, the history of international law legitimises positive law instead of critically rethinking it? And is there any possibility of approaching such questions without either repeating battles which have long been fought out or accepting digressions at the meta-level?

If, on the one hand, we stick to the meagre sources and argue with the nineteenth-century masters about philology, we get to a *non liquet* which does not allow us to draw any noteworthy conclusions for the present. Theoretical sublimation, on the other hand, leads us so far away from the sources that the results would seem to be up to the interpreter. The legal historian, however, is necessarily a 'historicist' in the sense that his reflections on the conditions of scientific findings must not become an end in themselves, otherwise he loses every link to the law in force and thus his professional identity; in the worst case he would be an amateur historian instead of contributing his specific view of the sources, a view being trained in the examination of positive law.

In the background to the following remarks there will therefore be a distinction which has become sufficiently clear in prolonged discussion among historians: the distinction between structure and event.[10] As lawyers, legal historians like to start with the individual events but aim at insights about the underlying structure. They do this in their profession

---

[9] About this, see Kimminich and Hobe, *Einführung*, e.g. p. 308; Baldus, *Regelhafte Vertragsauslegung*, pp. 74 and 738–41.

[10] Among the structuralistically influenced currents of recent historical research, we have to cite the *Annales* in the first place. However, it belongs to the changes which this School has undergone that structure and event are no longer seen in exaggerated contrast. Cf., for instance, Georges Duby, *Der Sonntag von Bouvines. 27. Juli 1214* (Paris, 1973; German translation Berlin, 1988). As secondary literature see for example – critical and with further references – Hervé Coutau-Bégarie, *Le Phénomène Nouvelle Histoire: Grandeur et décadence de l'école des Annales* (2nd edn, Paris, 1989). A balanced and very readable presentation with references to literary studies is Peter Burke, 'History of Events and the Revival of Narrative' in Burke (ed.), *New Perspectives on Historical Writing* (Cambridge, 1991), pp. 233–48. See further n. 112 below.

as lawyers as well – since normative findings are wanted. The structure looked for by the legal historian, e.g. a rule of the law of treaties, can only be identified indirectly. It has to be deduced from its expression in concrete episodes – albeit these be as selectively and tendentiously reported as seems to be the case with peace treaties.

Hence, from the point of view of legal history it is to be welcomed when historiographic theory tries to reunite structure and event. Maybe the determination of these categories with regard to the peace treaty makes it easier to categorise the concept of *pax* too. To what extent does an analysis of individual events mentioned by the sources contribute to our actual object of interest, a theory of the Roman peace treaty? And might it be useful to this end to take a comparative look at the contract under private law, which is far better represented in the sources?

The existence and peculiarities of ancient international law

Obstacles to historical research: anachronistic projections and 'tendentious' sources

The scholars of the late nineteenth century to whom we owe fundamental research in our topic were confronted with a typical dilemma of the time. The objective was to find a system in the law, but in the event could Roman international law be called 'law'? Contemporary theory widely followed the positivist conception defining as law what could be enforced by coercion.[11] Even in contemporary international law this led to problems, but all the more this was the case with ancient law, since no instance sufficiently authorised to enforce the law could be found. Thus, some of the authors denied the existence of any ancient international law. If today we would like to get a step further we first have to overcome these positivist obstacles. It is important to see what use the Romans themselves and their adversaries made of the treaty; especially the peace treaty, and the way they distinguished between the different constituent elements. Here we come across a problem hardly to be overcome by a lawyer on his own: the typically pro-Roman apologetic tendentiousness of the sources.

This tendentiousness is not just the same as propaganda. The ancient writers follow (to various extents) a historiographic understanding according to which 'objectivity' can also be aspired to by – simply

---

[11] Cf. for the latest presentation of legal positivism, Bernd Rüthers, *Rechtstheorie* (Munich, 1999), pp. 269–86 at p. 280.

speaking – telling how it may or should have been. Here we can profit from the fact that in this area research in the Classics has undergone rapid development over recent years.[12] Among the Augustan sources,[13] Livy is

[12] In this respect, only a small selection of references can be listed here; recently published collections of essays by individual scholars and several commentaries are not included. An introduction in the German language is Dieter Flach, *Einführung in die römische Geschichtsschreibung* (Darmstadt, 1998); international references: Christina Shuttlewood Kraus and Anthony John Woodman, *Latin Historians* (Oxford, 1997; reviewed by Rhiannon Ash, *Classical Review* 49 (1999), 72); John Marincola, *Authority and Tradition in Ancient Historiography* (Cambridge, 1997; of general interest for the questions which will be discussed here, mainly pp. 1–127; reviews by Emilio Gabba, *Athenaeum* 87 (1999), 321; Thomas Harrison, *Classical Review* 49 (1999), 420; Jean-Claude Richard, *Latomus* 58 (1999), 685; Gordon Shrimpton, *Phoenix* 53 (1999), 350; Donald Lateiner, *American Journal of Philology* 120 (1999), 303–7); Ronald Mellor, *The Historians of Ancient Rome* (New York and London, 1998) and his *The Roman Historians* (New York and London, 1999), both reviewed by Matthew Fox, *Classical Review* 50 (2000), 89 and J. M. Alonso-Nunez, *Journal of Roman Studies* 90 (2000), 216. Early non-Roman authors are dealt with by Dominique Briquel, *Le Regard des autres: les origines de Rome vues par ses ennemis...* (Besançon, 1997; review by Jacques Poucet, *Latomus* 59 (2000), 955).

[13] On the relationship between Augustus and the literature and culture of his time in general see Karl Galinsky, *Augustan Culture* (Princeton, 1996; reviewed by Antonio La Penna, *Athenaeum* 87 (1999), 340; Philip Hardie, *Gnomon* 72 (2000), 49–53); on the relationship of politics to literature and religion, in particular chapters V and VI, summarising on pp. 244 and 294–312; beyond Ovid, cf. Philip Hardie, 'Ovid's Metamorphoses and Augustan Cultural Thematics' in Philip Hardie *et al.* (eds.), *Ovidian Transformations: Essays on the Metamorphoses and Its Reception* (Cambridge, 1999), pp. 103–11; Thomas Habinek and Alessandro Schiesaro (eds.), *The Roman Cultural Revolution* (Cambridge, 1997; reviews by Karl Galinsky, *Classical Review* 49 (1999), 195; David Meban, *Phoenix* 53 (1999), 346–50); Francesco Guizzi, *Augusto: la politica della memoria* (Rome, 1999; review by Italo Lana, *Rivista di Filologia ed Istruzione Classica* 127 (1999), 99–102); John Scheid, 'Auguste et le grand pontificat', *Revue Historique du Droit Français et Etranger* 77 (1999), 1–19; in the German language now Jochen Bleicken, *Augustus: eine Biographie* (Berlin, 1999), esp. pp. 518–35; Antonie Wlosok, 'Freiheit und Gebundenheit der augusteischen Dichter', *Rheinisches Museum für Philologie* 143 (2000), 75–88. Even with respect to the history of international law, the comparison to Caesar is worthwhile; Caesar's *mise en scène* of himself can essentially be attributed to his own writings, the reliability of which is still questionable. If we can trust classical critics, the two latest monographs on the *Bellum Gallicum* have not brought about any substantial progress: cf. the review of Gerold Walser, *Bellum Helveticum* (Stuttgart, 1998) by Bernhard Kremer, *Gymnasium* 107 (2000), 350 and the review of G. Lieberg, *Caesars Politik in Gallien* (Bochum, 1998) by Niklas Holzberg, *Gymnasium* 107 (2000), 361. Both monographs are reviewed by Lindsay Hall, *Classical Review* 50 (2000), 78–81. Admittedly, the annotation and illustration of important passages, including the reproduction of modern interpretations by Walser, is of advantage to the non-expert reader. Apart from the authors referred to by Baldus, *Regelhafte Vertragsauslegung*, p. 403, see now the miscellany edited by Kathryn Welch and Anton Powell, *Julius Caesar as Artful Reporter: The War Commentaries as Political Instruments* (London, 1998; reviewed by Neville Morley, *Classical Review* 49 (1999), 406 and John G. Nordling, *Journal of Roman Studies* 89 (1999), 230) as well as Bryan James, 'Speech, Authority, and Experience in Caesar, Bellum Gallicum 1.39–41', *Hermes* 128 (2000), 54–64.

of special importance,[14] but the works of other authors in their respective contexts are also read with new perspectives today.[15] These pieces of research do not specifically focus on questions of international law. Thus, it remains to be clarified to what extent their approach can be applied to these issues.

On the existence of ancient international law from a modern perspective

The majority of present-day researchers assume the existence of ancient international law. They argue, however, about the grounds for their assumption. Two theories are important: the first one is primarily orientated towards the history of religion (above all Pierangelo Catalano and Alan Watson);[16] the other places emphasis on the (more political) functions of international law which are not limited to a particular age (in Germany, above all Wolfgang Preiser and Karl-Heinz Ziegler, and related approaches by Dieter Nörr and Heinhard Steiger). Should we thus rather

---

[14] On Livy: Gary B. Miles, *Livy Reconstructing Early Rome* (New York, 1995); A. Johner, *La Violence chez Tite-Live: mythographie et historiographie* (Strasbourg, 1996; review by Christina S. Kraus, *Classical Review* 49 (1999), 409); Andrew Feldherr, 'Livy's Revolution: Civic Identity and the Creation of the *Res Publica*' in Habinek and Schiesaro (eds.), *Roman Cultural Revolution*, pp. 136–57; Feldherr, *Spectacle and Society in Livy's History* (Berkeley, 1998; reviews: Timothy J. Moore, *American Journal of Philology* 121 (2000), 487–90; Rhiannon Ash, *Classical Review* 50 (2000), 453; Jane D. Chaplin, *Classical Journal* 96 (2000), 102–5; James T. Chlup, *Journal of Roman Studies* 90 (2000), 237); Mary Jaeger, *Livy's Written Rome* (Ann Arbor, 1997; reviews: Jane D. Chaplin, *Journal of Roman Studies* 89 (1999), 237; Uwe Walter, *Gymnasium* 107 (2000), 338).

[15] Literary scholars have taken a special interest in Ovid, perhaps because the debate essentially concerns the Augustan period. In these authors, however, there are only scattered passages of interest to the legal historian. Of immediate importance to the history of international law is Polybius, if only for the verification of Livy's depiction. For a monograph on Polybius see Arthur M. Eckstein, *Moral Vision in the Histories of Polybius* (Berkeley etc., 1995), not on the historiographer's image of himself in the first place but on the assessment of the actions of the depicted persons. A glance at the index reveals, however, that quite a few issues are dealt with which are of relevance to the history of international law. For criticism from a classical scholar see the review by Michel Dubuisson, *Latomus* 58 (1999), 689. Few but important passages can be found in Valerius Maximus; about him see Jean-Michel David (ed.), *Valeurs et mémoire à Rome: Valère Maxime ou la vertu recomposée* (Paris, 1998; reviewed by Ella Hermon, *Phoenix* 53 (1999), 160); further, D. Wardle, 'Valerius Maximus on the domus Augusta, Augustus, and Tiberius', *Classical Quarterly* 50 (2000), 479–93.

[16] In his review of Alan Watson, *International Law in Archaic Rome* (Baltimore and London, 1983), Adalberto Giovannini, *Gnomon* 72 (2000), 45–8, is more critical than Baldus, *Regelhafte Vertragsauslegung*, pp. 204–5: according to him, there was no Roman international law at all.

focus on the power of sacral traditions or on the rationally calculated interests of politicians? At least the argument of political realism is in favour of the latter opinion, since Roman religion is characterised by pragmatism and proximity to politics.[17] This manifests itself especially in those questions that are of special interest to us: the importance of the religious oath[18] and the idea of a quasi-contractual exchange deal between humans and deities (both are important with respect to the *foedus*);[19] the ritualised interpretation of signs revealing the gods' will;[20] the documentation of all these occurrences

---

[17] Cf. on Roman religion the excellent syntheses by Mary Beard and John Scheid in Fritz Graf (ed.), *Einleitung in die lateinische Philologie* (Stuttgart and Leipzig, 1997), pp. 469–91 (Scheid on the Republic) and 492–519 (Beard on the imperial period). Recently, in more detail and very instructive in particular on the interrelation of politics and religion, see John A. North, *Roman Religion* (Oxford, 2000); also Mary Beard, John North and Simon Price, *Religions of Rome* (Cambridge, 1998; reviews by David Noy, *Classical Review* 49 (1999), 445; John Scheid, *Journal of Roman Studies* 90 (2000), 207; Meret Strothmann, *Gymnasium* 108 (2001), 137); Scheid, *Auguste*; Hubert Cancik and Jörg Rüpke (eds.), *Römische Reichsreligion und Provinzialreligion* (Tübingen, 1997; reviews by John Vanderspoel, *Classical Review* 49 (1999), 589 and Dieter Schmitz, *Gymnasium* 106 (1999), 455–8; as indicated by the title, this work primarily deals with the interrelations of centre and periphery). Comments on the history of science and further literature can be found in the miscellany of reviews (among others, of Beard, North and Price, *Religions*) by James B. Rives, 'Roman Religion Revived', *Phoenix* 52 (1998), 345–65. About Denis Feeney, *Literature and Religion at Rome: Cultures, Contexts, and Beliefs* (Cambridge, 1998; *non vidi*), it is said that the role of the priesthood – which is of special importance for international law – is dealt with rather briefly (see the review by James Zetzel, *Phoenix* 53 (1999), 171; cf. furthermore the reviews by Annie Dubourdieu, *Latomus* 59 (2000), 477, and J. B. Rives, *Classical Review* 50 (2000), 106).

[18] Most recent: Antonello Calore, *Per Iovem lapidem alle origini del giuramento: sulla presenza del sacro nell'esperienza giuridica romana* (Milan, 2000); Ferdinando Zuccotti, *Il giuramento nel mondo giuridico e religioso antico* (Milan, 2000). Zuccotti's points of view cannot be discussed here.

[19] Advance 'payment' or 'service' of the deities at the vow; 'right' of the ritually correct 'prayer' to find a hearing. The resulting problems, for instance, with mutually exclusive wishes can be retraced in literature, hence the educated public was aware of them. Cf. Joachim Dingel, 'Non petit inpossibile. Gebete und ihr Erfolg in der Aeneis', *Gymnasium* 107 (2000), 281–93. As to cultural backgrounds, cf. moreover Christopher Gill, Norman Postlethwaite and Richard Seaford (eds.), *Reciprocity in Ancient Greece* (Oxford, 1998; review by Daniel Ogden, *Classical Review* 49 (1999), 508).

[20] See Veit Rosenberger, *Gezähmte Götter: das Prodigienwesen der römischen Republik* (Stuttgart, 1998; esp. pp. 71–8 on the function, possibilities and limits of the control of divine sign; reviews by G. J. Szemler, *Classical Review* 49 (1999), 447; Joachim Lehnen, *Gymnasium* 108 (2001), 35; critical: Tatjana Moor-Freber, *Klio* 82 (2000), 530). Further into anthropology we are led by the figure of the warrior acting in disrespect of the norms; Frédéric Blaive, *Impius Bellator* (Arras, 1996; review by Marcel Meulder, *Latomus* 58 (1999), 235). Moreover, if because of his misbehaviour a man is handed over to the enemy

in the archives of the priests.²¹ In this light, the idea that especially in matters of survival such as war and peace the Roman treaty practice always primarily followed archaic sacral forms is hardly convincing.

The setting: on the political impediments to the development of Roman international law

The peace treaty and its conceivable functions have to be seen in the light of ancient international law as a whole, just as has been expressed by Preiser:

> We can speak of an international legal order, when independent states having cultural, economic and political relations recognise each other as autonomous subjects of law of equal rank and [when these states] conclude and execute their intergovernmental agreements and comply with the practice of international relations while being governed by the conviction that they are legally obliged to keep the (express or tacit) agreement and that this obligation is immutable.²²

Thus, the different definitional elements are (1) independent political units, (2) having relations with each other, (3) recognising each other as autonomous subjects of law of equal rank and (4) accepting the rules governing their contact as immutable rules of law.

---

but is not accepted by the latter, he will become *sacer* (at unrest, unatoned, unexpiated); cf. Roberto Fiori, *Homo sacer* (Naples, 1996; review by Bernadette Liou-Gille, *Latomus* 58 (1999), 208–11).

[21] This aspect is central to a realistic assessment of the contemporary state of information and the political relevance of the priests' actions. Apart from the authors referred to by Baldus, *Regelhafte Vertragsauslegung*, pp. 415–17 (esp. the works by John Scheid), cf. Karl-Ernst Petzold, 'Annales maximi und Annalen' in K. Herbers *et al.* (eds.), *Ex ipsis rerum documentis: Festschrift für Harald Zimmermann* (Sigmaringen, 1991), pp. 3–16, and Petzold, 'Zur Geschichte der römischen Annalistik' in W. Schuller (ed.), *Livius* (Constance, 1993), pp. 151–88; both are quoted here according to Petzold, *Geschichtsdenken und Geschichtsschreibung: kleine Schriften zur griechischen und römischen Geschichte* (Stuttgart, 1999), pp. 184–221 ('Zur Geschichte...') and 252–65 ('Annales maximi...'). On the controversy about whether the priests' documentations or the historical works of the early annalists were written first and about how they influenced each other, see most recently the reconciliatory views of Uwe Walter, *Gymnasium* 107 (2000), 468–71, at p. 469, in his review of Petzold, *Geschichtsschreibung*.

[22] Wolfgang Preiser, 'Die Epochen der antiken Völkerrechtsgeschichte', *Juristenzeitung* 11 (1956), 737–44, at p. 744; and Preiser in Klaus Lüderssen and Karl-Heinz Ziegler, *Macht und Norm in der Völkerrechtsgeschichte* (Baden-Baden, 1978), pp. 105–27, at p. 105.

Part of Roman international relations – as far as 'national' and 'international' can be distinguished here – do not meet these requirements.[23] As far as hegemony reaches, the hegemonic power does not recognise the subordinate polity as being of equal rank. For Rome this means that, after the military conquest of Macedonia (Pydna, 168 BC),[24] there was no power left apart from Persia, which on the one hand Rome would have been in contact with, but which it would not have controlled, on the other.

Hence we have come to our first central problem. The existence of international law was politically impossible with respect to Rome when the theoretical instruments were to a large extent missing even in private law, i.e. at the time of the Early and High Republic and then in late Antiquity. In the Early Republic, the law only just emancipated itself from the sacral formalism to which it owed the first steps of its development. In late Antiquity the economic and political circumstances as well as the declining legal culture did not allow the Classical heritage to progress with its earlier brilliance.[25]

During the Classical period of private law – which approximately coincides with the Principate – Rome did not have any serious adversaries in the Mediterranean area. Terminology and theory of international law lagged behind the development of private law even at the time of the Republic. The growing Roman community was interested in the emergence of an independent and homogeneous order of private law – on the inside and in the form of the *ius gentium* as well as on the outside. The very opposite is the case with the emergence of an international legal order which would not have been completely under political control. Such an order could have harmed Rome's interests in this delicate period. Furthermore, there was the principle of indirect control. What we call 'foreign affairs' wavered between – in modern terms – international, constitutional and administrative law. During the Principate, we can find a highly developed theory of private law, the protagonists of which were clearly orientated towards the *princeps*;[26] the variety of the institutions of law in

---

[23] Less obvious than in modern times, clearer than in the medieval feudal polity: through Antiquity to some extent a territorial conception of 'state' increasingly emerges; for Rome, however, personal interconnection with (above all) the elites of subordinate polities is symptomatic.

[24] For chronological details, which are not of interest here, see O. P. Dany, 'Livy and the Chronology of the Years 168–167', *Classical Quarterly* 50 (2000), 432–9.

[25] Cf. note 5.

[26] Most recently on this: Javier Paricio, *Los juristas y el poder político en la antigua Roma* (Granada, 1999); Paricio, *Valor de las opiniones jurisprudenciales en la Roma clásica* (Madrid, 2001).

which Rome organised its interests increased while the force of traditional concepts and their meaning diminished.

We must add to this that in all epochs the Mediterranean has been a multilingual area. The Roman lawyers from time to time discussed Greek concepts in private law in order to be able to solve their cases more precisely. However, this was done rather by way of a cultural recourse to the Greek legal heritage than by taking up Greek legal theory. For this the ancient Greek private law was not efficient enough.[27] In international law, however, the nuances between for example *amicitia* and *philía*, *societas* and *symmachia* were not clarified in this way, probably because such terminological work would only have been of importance for an independent decision-making body. The rich Greek experience with treaties, arbitration agreements and alliances was – so it seems – deliberately not exploited.[28] We will return to this point but limit our terminological analysis mostly to the Latin terms.

In short a forceful theory of international law was either intellectually or politically impossible. Ancient international law was to a large extent law without a (contemporary) theoretical foundation. This fundamental deficit did have consequences – for instance, there is virtually no theory of interpretation in Roman international law.

Consequences

Against the background of these findings, the perspective of our examination of legal history becomes much narrower. We are used to studying the treaty in all its details as a technical means to achieve a reconciliation of interests (or their domination). It is not surprising that the preserved texts appear strangely standardised – even for Antiquity. The development of private law is spurred by the practice of legal counsel, using new and varied formulas – but here there will be advisers on both sides and the *praetor* will not accept anything which would lead to utterly one-sided results. The formulas included by Rome into the old *foedera* – which at best we know of only indirectly[29] – are not supposed to bring about a

---

[27] For background information, see Okko Behrends and Wolfgang Sellert (eds.), *Nomos und Gesetz. Ursprünge und Wirkungen des griechischen Gesetzesdenkens* (Göttingen, 1995; reviews by Lene Rubinstein, *Classical Review* 49 (1999), 455, and Wolfgang Waldstein, *Zeitschrift der Savigny-Stiftung für Rechtsgeschichte, Romanistische Abteilung* 116 (1999), 473–84).

[28] The consequences of this omission for the reception of ancient international law do not have to be clarified here. Cf. for the Greek law of treaties note 52 below.

[29] See of course once again note 3.

reconciliation of interests but are intended to set a politically controlled legal framework. These agreements do not lack legal relevance. They are agreements in which the other party indeed shows an interest of its own – but their logic is not that of an elaborate private law.

It is questionable whether the *cliché* of international law as 'primitive private law' is better suited here than elsewhere. Imbalance of strength between the parties occurs under private law too. And for a long time it has in fact been regarded as progress merely to have laid down rights in writing. The most famous example is the Twelve Tables by means of which the Roman *interpretatio* soon made amazing achievements.

In international law, however, the fact must be borne in mind that the persons involved were almost exclusively judged by themselves – a phenomenon which is not unknown even in modern times. The discourse before and with the decision-making body tends to become trivial when it is a soliloquy.

'Classical' Roman international law as a categorical system

Contemporary systematisations?

Two sources in particular, a literary and a legal source, at first sight seem to contain systematising passages: Livy 34, 57, 7 *et seq.* and Pomp. Dig. 49, 15, 5, 2. There actually appear to be different types of treaties and expressions of order.

> (7) Esse autem tria genera foederum quibus inter se paciscerentur amicitias civitates regesque: unum, cum bello victis dicerentur leges; ubi enim omnia ei qui armis plus posset dedita essent, quae ex iis habere victos quibus multari eos velit, ipsius ius atque arbitrium esse;
> (8) alterum, cum pares bello aequo foedere in pacem atque amicitiam venirent; tunc enim repeti reddique per conventionem res et, si quarum turbata bello possessio sit, eas aut ex formula iuris antiqui aut ex partis utriusque commodo componi;
> (9) tertium esse genus cum qui numquam hostes fuerint, ad amicitiam sociali foedere inter se iungendam coeant eos neque dicere nec accipere leges; id enim victoris et victi esse.[30]
>
> (7) There were three kinds of treaties, he said, by which states and kings concluded friendships: one, when in time of war terms were imposed upon the conquered; for when everything was surrendered to him who was the

---

[30] Livy 34, 57, 7–9.

more powerful in arms, it is the victor's right and privilege to decide what of the conquered's property he wishes to confiscate;

(8) the second, when states that are equally matched in war conclude peace and friendship on terms of equality; under these conditions demands for restitution are made and are granted by mutual agreement, and if the ownership of any property has been rendered uncertain by the war, these questions are settled according to the rules of traditional law or the convenience of each party;

(9) the third exists when states that have never been at war come together to pledge mutual friendship in a treaty of alliance; neither party gives or accepts conditions; for that happens when a conquering and a conquered party meet.[31]

The above is said by an envoy of King Antiochus, and he continues that Antiochus aspires to an alliance with the Romans of the last-mentioned type, which is why Rome must not set any terms of the treaty.

The other apparently systematic passage is:

In pace quoque postliminium datum est: nam si cum gente aliqua neque amicitiam neque hospitium neque foedus amicitiae causa factum habemus, hi hostes quidem non sunt . . .[32]

Postliminium is also granted in peacetime; for if we have neither friendship nor hospitium with a particular people, nor a treaty made for the purpose of friendship, they are not precisely enemies . . .[33]

At first sight, Livy uses *foedus* as a generic term. He forms a sub-group of three, the first two elements of which represent specific agreements to end the war: the dictated treaty with the defeated; the treaty by means of which, after an open ending of the war *aequo foedere*, a 'binomial' legal consequence, is brought about: *pax atque amicitia* so that *per conventionem* goods lost as a result of the war can be given back; finally, *foedus sociale* for an agreement which is neither war-related nor terminating a war. Three times *amicitia* is mentioned. The question is whether a treaty or the description of a situation is meant. Livy does not try to express a typical definition, even though he evokes this by the term *genera*. He does not reduce a generic term (*foedera* as *genus*) to its components (*species*), but mentions potential sub-categories, called *genera*, as a means to bring

---

[31] English translation by Evan T. Sage, The Loeb Classical Library (London and Cambridge, Mass., 1953).
[32] Pomp. Dig. 49, 15, 5, 2 (37 ad Q. Mucium).
[33] English translation by Alan Watson, *The Digest of Justinian* (Philadelphia, 1985).

about a certain state of the law (*aequum foedus*; *sociale foedus*; *conventio*)[34] or as the description of these states themselves (*pax*; *amicitia*).

According to Livy, this confusion of only potentially systematic terms is uttered not by the Roman side but by the Hellenistic adversary, whose propensity for systematisation could be insinuated. Antiochus' envoys want to set forth that among equals the terms of the treaty would not be dictated and that hence Rome could not demand consent to clauses (here about the status of certain towns in Asia Minor) within an *amicitia*. Rome, however, ignores this and sets the terms of the matter – with downright ironic reference to the alleged system: 'vobis distincte agere licet et genera iungendarum amicitiarum enumerare' (34, 58, 1). Playing with the awareness of its own power, Rome even follows the envoys' main idea. Their tripartite distinction differentiates according to the balance of power – and Rome now treats Antiochus pursuant to the rules which he himself proposes for the defeated.

Thus, the basic tendency of the source is clearly antisystematic. Rome did not even think about discussing a subsumable concept of the treaty. Rome focused on its interests; the *formula iuris antiqui* is but one means among others to settle these interests. It is only mentioned in passing, its function remaining unclear[35] (*rerum repetitio*[36] or *reciperatio*?[37]). The

---

[34] The relationship of *rerum repetitio* and the restoration of the *possessio turbata* is just as unclear as the relationship of *conventio* and the *formula iuris antiqui*. *Et, si...* rules out an identity of both points. Later on, we will again have to deal with curiosities from the law of possession; a 'Romanist' analysis of the (alleged) application of possessory concepts in ancient international law does not exist.

[35] The questions start with the fact that in international law there were hardly any traditional bilateral structures. Some things seem to indicate that in its foreign relations Rome deliberately conserved archaic formulas which were put in structurally unilateral terms, thus aiming rather at ritualised law enforcement than at open conflict resolution. What exactly was meant by Livy we can perhaps better know for certain by examining more closely the phrase *formula iuris antiqui* in contemporary civil procedure.

[36] If Livy 34, 57, 8 is supposed to hint at the *rerum repetitio*, the formalised unilateral claim for damages (the wording of this passage suggests this indeed) we should at least have to bear in mind that this formal act used to precede a war, not to follow upon a war, just because the power which was politically agreed upon was in this way supposed to be legitimated at last. Cf. Jean-Louis Ferrary, '*Ius fetiale* et diplomatie' in E. Frézouls and A. Jacquemin (eds.), *Les Relations internationales. Actes du Colloque de Strasbourg 15–17 juin 1993* (Paris, 1995), pp. 411–32, at pp. 420–31; Baldus, *Regelhafte Vertragsauslegung*, pp. 364–5 (containing a misleading reference in note 190), 425, 429, 439–44 etc.; most recently Adalberto Giovannini, 'Le droit fétial et la déclaration de guerre de Rome à Carthage en 218 avant J.-C.', *Athenaeum* 88 (2000), 69–116 at pp. 86–94.

[37] Linguistically this is also conceivable and practically it is more obvious than a connection with the *rerum repetitio*. The term *reciperatio* designates the enforcement (supposedly of international origin) of claims for damages from consequences of war (in more detail

means to settle Rome's interests only have legal names. The use of legal concepts is therefore misleading. The terminological coherence of the formulations did not matter because the terms of the treaties were negotiated politically. In order to achieve the juridification of the different situations, it would according to Livy have been necessary to have a consensus of both parties.

The passage by Pomponius (the content and authenticity of which are hopelessly disputed) points to the same outcome. It revolves around questions of the *postliminium*, i.e. the restoration to his legal position by a captivated and afterwards returning Roman,[38] Dig. 49, 15, 5, 2, here in the difficult variation of the *postliminium in pace*. It is quite problematic whether there was a right to return outside the war, too. We cannot deal with this and related questions here.

The preliminary question is to find out on what terms Rome was to the community the Roman returned from. Was it a *hostis*? Could there be a *postliminium* even below this threshold to an armed conflict?[39] Was

see Baldus, *Regelhafte Vertragsauslegung*, pp. 325–35); thus, however, Livy would implicitly have said that such a *formula* was not necessarily equitable.

[38] The most recent monograph is Maria Floriana Cursi, *La struttura del 'postliminium' nella repubblica e nel principato* (Naples, 1996); previous references cf. with Baldus, *Regelhafte Vertragsauslegung*, pp. 257–65; on individual resultant problems of private law, Maria Virginia Sanna, *Ricerche in tema di redemptio ab hostibus* (Cagliari, 1998); Laura D'Amati, '"Pater ab hostibus captus" e status dei discendenti nei giuristi romani', *Index* 27 (1999), 55–85. The problem of *postliminium in pace* refers to that of 'natural hostility' (s.v. note 41): if strife is required for a *postliminium*, hence it can – in the absence of an agreement by treaty between Rome and the other community – be granted without any problem, just because in case of doubt hostility is the rule. But the premise that a *postliminium in pace* can only be constructed under such hostility is unproven: why should the favour under private law, i.e. the right to return home, have depended upon such a strict and politically highly sensitive theory of international law (which was not at all typical of Rome)? Semi-'official', semi-private capture and displacement were the order of the day. Reasoning in international law which has been trained by the nineteenth century is inappropriate here. By way of the *postliminium in pace*, the *de facto* power exercised by a third party could be recognised while avoiding that the home-comer's pecuniary interests suffer later on.

[39] Robbers (and pirates) were no *iusti hostes*. Ulpian points out in Dig. 49, 15, 24 (1 inst.) that those captured by *latrunculi vel praedones* remain free and therefore do not require the *postliminium*. Germans and Parthians serve as examples of *hostes* – without any reference to the respective legal status. The pirate, however, is certainly an 'enemy' to all communities, but his actions do not create captivity in a legal sense. In more detail, Karl-Heinz Ziegler, 'Pirata communis hostis omnium' in Manfred Harder and Georg Thielmann (eds.), *De iustitia et iure: Festgabe für Ulrich von Lübtow zum 80. Geburtstag* (Berlin, 1980), pp. 93–103 at p. 98. The question whether the categories *hostis* on the one hand and *latro* etc. on the other hand cover all conceivable cases does not need to be clarified here. The problem of pirates as a reflection of structural deficiencies in the Roman technique of governance or, in other words, the repeated systematic use of pirates for purposes of expansion and

it sufficient that none of the three treaties – *amicitia, hospitium, foedus* – had been concluded? Pomponius does not even try to find a generic term but simply juxtaposes the three terms. *Pax* remains separate from these – maybe as a mere factual situation. One of the treaty terms, by the way, the *hospitium (publicum)*, was supposedly no more than a historical reminiscence in the second century AD.[40] We cannot settle the problem on the basis of this source. Here the systematisation does not fail owing to the 'un-legal' usage of the terms but because of the limited meaning of the concepts. A positive definition of the treaties mentioned is not necessary for Pomponius' purposes.

These two sources – they are of a different type and more than a century apart from each other – have one thing in common. They are enumerations fulfilling a negative function. *Pars pro toto* concepts are enumerated in order to indicate the *totum* – not to structure it. For this there was no actual theoretical or political demand. The other sources in which we might find terms describing the international treaty do not show any systematising structure; such a structure can thus at best be extracted by an *ex post* survey of various texts.

Modern systematisations

We can now try to find out to what extent the numerous sources using different terms technically designated the peace treaty; thus a systematisation *ex post* would become possible. The terms which have to be considered have partly been mentioned (*foedus, conventio, pax, amicitia*); we must add *sponsio, hospitium, societas, pactum, deditio*.

It is evident that the peace treaty was of special importance at least as a means of control. This opinion is also held by researchers who are

---

creation of 'client kingdoms' has recently been examined by Raimund Schulz in several publications on the basis of his monograph *Herrschaft und Regierung. Roms Regiment in den Provinzen in der Zeit der Republik* (Paderborn etc., 1997; here pp. 246–85); it is in the centre of his 'Zwischen Kooperation und Konfrontation. Die römische Weltreichsbildung und die Piraterie, *Klio* 82 (2000), 426–40 and briefly in his 'Herrschaft und Dienst am Weltreich. Zum Regierungsstil des römischen Statthalters in der Zeit der Republik', *Gymnasium* 107 (2000), 481–96 at p. 495.

[40] A late and atypical case of the *hospitium publicum* is the person of L. Cornelius Balbus (F. III. 2 and Baldus, *Regelhafte Vertragsauslegung*, pp. 283–4). On his person (as an accomplice of Spanish pirates), most recently Raimund Schulz again in his 'Zwischen Kooperation und Konfrontation', *Klio* 82 (2000), 426–40 at p. 437. The private *hospitium* could also have diplomatic relevance. Cf. most recently Karl-Ernst Petzold, 'Die Freiheit der Griechen und die Politik der *nova sapientia*', *Historia* 48 (1999), 61–93 at pp. 61, 63 and 72.

sceptical about the phenomenon of 'ancient international law' as a whole. An extreme form of such scepticism is Mommsen's theory of 'natural hostility' between the ancient communities which – in a modified way – has been taken up by Laurens Winkel.[41] According to this theory, the peace treaty itself only creates the possibility of law, hence it is necessarily underlying every other agreement.

In modern secondary literature, different approaches can be found.[42] The above-mentioned two main currents of research also have different conclusions with respect to the *foedus*. The authors placing the emphasis on religious history assign a special role to it because of its sacral origins and its resulting compulsory forms (Catalano, in a certain manner also Watson and Giorgio Luraschi).

The authors having adopted the normative-political theory (Preiser, Ziegler, Nörr) rather tend to focus on the actual function of the individual treaty. If we follow the latter, we have fewer explanatory problems for the time after the High Republic. We do not have to explain why a formal sacral act is said to have been of central relevance, although the competent priests (the *fetiales*) were only of marginal importance in the sources (and hence, as we may conclude, in political reality),[43] and although the deity called upon was sometimes unknown to the parties to the treaty. Neither do we have to explain why by the imperial period more and more utterly unimportant treaties were called *foedera* and why the term *foederatus* increasingly declined to a mere honorary title void of any function – perhaps apart from indicating exemption from the provincial administration.[44] Furthermore, the researcher who is primarily orientated towards sacral aspects is confronted with the question whether the

---

[41] Laurens C. Winkel, 'Einige Bemerkungen über *ius naturale und ius gentium*' in Martin Josef Schermaier and Zoltán Végh (eds.), *Ars boni et aequi: Festschrift für Wolfgang Waldstein zum 65. Geburtstag* (Stuttgart, 1993), pp. 443–9; doubts in Baldus, *Regelhafte Vertragsauslegung*, pp. 193–5.

[42] An overview of the following can be found in Baldus, *Regelhafte Vertragsauslegung*, pp. 217–32.

[43] Cf. North, *Roman Religion*, esp. pp. 23–7: summarising at p. 27: 'The colleges reported back to the senate and seem to have had no power to reach an independent decision or act on their own initiative.' Mary Beard, 'Priesthood in the Roman Republic' in Mary Beard and John North (eds.), *Pagan Priests* (London, 1990), pp. 19–48, almost completely leaves out the *fetiales* (synoptical tables at p. 20). Previous literature is referred to in Baldus, *Regelhafte Vertragsauslegung*, pp. 412–17. The contemporary conditionality of Cicero's remarks on the *fetiales* is discussed by Ferrary, '*Ius fetiale* et diplomatie', p. 416.

[44] It is true, however, that other treaty-related terms could indicate internal autonomy, too; see with respect to the *societas sine foedere* at the time of the High Republic, Petzold, *Geschichtsdenken und Geschichtsschreibung*, p. 87.

solemnly concluded *foedus* was merely the form transporting a content to be laid down elsewhere (Luraschi).

All of this is much easier for the political approach: Rome may have named *deditio* what would have been called *foedus* earlier on, or formed compound terms just as it liked – if only the alliance made sense politically. It is undisputed, however, that the sacral element did have its significance as a means of sanction (and a means of psychology as regards domestic policy and military strategy). We can thus also follow this theory as for the content and the limits of the possibility to find terms from an *ex post* perspective.[45] Accordingly, the state of the law appears (of course in a simplified way) to be as follows.

The *hospitium publicum*, the 'guest treaty', is of limited importance in historic times.[46] *Amicitia* is a relation of friendship without any further concrete engagements, i.e. the mere exclusion of hostilities; according to the prevailing opinion it could be concluded by a treaty but also without.[47] *Societas*, to the extent that it is not a mere synonym or accompanying term of *amicitia*,[48] apart from being an obligation to peace and neutrality, also consists of a duty to grant military support. *Foedus* distinguishes itself because of its strict form: an oral oath by the *fetialis* to which the written documentation is only added. This form has often been described.[49]

---

[45] Karl-Heinz Ziegler, 'Das Völkerrecht der römischen Republik', in *Aufstieg und Niedergang der römischen Welt* (Berlin and New York, 1972), vol. I-2, pp. 68–114 at pp. 82–98. With respect to the early imperial period we can find similar basic structures – although with an increase in the significance of *deditio*. It might be sensible to scrutinise the treaty texts left to us from a terminological angle, for epochs and for authors (cf. for instance the compilations by Hermann Bengtson, *Die Staatsverträge des Altertums* (Munich and Berlin, 1962), vol. II, and by Barbara Scardigli, *I trattati romano-cartaginesi* (Pisa, 1991)). (In addition, cf. the helpful information on treaty negotiations with Greek legations in Reinhard Selinger's review of Filippo Canali de Rossi, *Le ambascerie dal mondo greco a Roma in età repubblicana, Anzeiger für die Altertumswissenschaft* 52 (1929), col. 53 *et seqq.*, at col. 55.)

[46] Cf. note 40.

[47] References in Baldus, *Regelhafte Vertragsauslegung*, pp. 218–20. Ivanna Savalli-Lestrade, *Les 'philoi' royaux dans l'Asie hellénique* (Geneva, 1998; review by M. M. Austin, *Classical Review* 50 (2000), 193) treats the followers of Hellenistic rulers, not the latter themselves, as Rome's friends.

[48] The proposition (most recently in Petzold, *Geschichtsdenken und Geschichtsschreibung*, p. 89) that the *amicitia et societas* was created 'by [Rome's] unilateral constitutive declaration ... and registration in the *formula sociorum*' cannot be taken as a statement of general theoretical significance. The fact, however, that from the Roman point of view the *formula* was central cannot be denied.

[49] For a comprehensive work in a comparative perspective and the English language, cf. Karl-Heinz Ziegler, 'Conclusion and Publication of International Treaties in Antiquity', *Israel Law Review* 29 (1995), 233–49.

According to Livy,[50] it is central to the binding effect that the *fetialis* pronounces a self-damnation at the expense of the Roman people in a sacrificial ritual. When it (i.e. the Roman people) 'on'[51] a public decision first defected in bad faith from the treaty', may Jupiter beat it just as the *fetialis* would now do to the sacrificial pig: 'Si prior defexit publico consilio dolo malo, tum illo die, Iuppiter, populum Romanum sic ferito ut ego hunc porcem hic hodie feriam.' The importance of the document increased over time;[52] that of the institution as such decreased. For one reason alone the sacral law stood in the way of itself. Since the *fetiales* were not allowed to leave Italic soil, no *foedera* observing the formal requirements could be concluded abroad. As has been hinted at, the main problem of the *foedus* is the relation between form and content. If we can trust the passage of Livy, it indicates a subjectivity of the binding form, thus a starting point for the introduction of arguments concerning the subject matter in the case of a conflict. However, there are doubts as to whether Livy here (and not only here) projects younger concepts into a more remote past – ultimately in order to legitimise Roman misbehaviour. Not even the private law of the time referred to knows the reservations being hinted at, let alone public law – as far as it can be separated from private law.

In archaic times the binding character of the form will have been at least as central as in private law. However, this does not imply a lack of detailed provisions articulating the content of a treaty. Even the first treaty between Rome and Carthage contains clauses about geographic and legal rules of maritime trade.[53]

We do not fully know the content of *foedera* passed on to us, but typically they contained a peace settlement: the renunciation of force; future friendship; collateral agreements concerning territorial or security issues such as hostage-taking; and the payment of reparations.

The self-damnation of the fetial priests in the case of a treaty violation, which the Roman community consciously (*sciens*) or *dolo malo* decided

---

[50] Livy 1, 24, 8.
[51] 'By a public decision' would be closer to modern legal thinking; however, what is meant here rather seems to be the concrete military action as a violation of treaty, and the competent authorities' decision is only the basis of this.
[52] On the practical importance of the (though theoretically not required) epigraphic inscription of *Greek* treaties, cf. Angelos Chaniotis, *Die Verträge zwischen kretischen Poleis in der hellenistischen Zeit* (Stuttgart, 1996), pp. 64 and 68.
[53] On this agreement (probably to be dated 509 BC) see most recently Lucia Ronconi, 'Sardegna e Corsica: colonizzazione negata', *Rivista storica dell'antichità* 29 (1999), 7–26 at p. 24.

upon, speaks against a complete separation of the *foedus* as a formal act on the one hand, and the determination of its content, for instance by means of *amicitia*, on the other hand. Only clauses the content of which has been defined can be violated. Furthermore, the reservations do not make any sense if they are related only to the binding form. There may have been supplements to the agreement, just as in private law the *pacta adiecta* gave additional shape to the *stipulatio*. But there are no compelling reasons for the *foedus* being only container, and not carrying content either.

It is alleged that a preceding *sponsio* may have to be distinguished from the *foedus*; we will have to come back to the dubious nature of the underlying sources later.

The treaties mentioned so far are usually supposed to guarantee peace. They may also contain specific post-war settlements. In addition, there are several types of agreements the peacemaking function of which is part and parcel of their nature: *pax, deditio, indutiae*.[54] It has been disputed in the modern literature whether *pax* was itself a treaty or whether this term could designate as well the peace situation created by other treaties. The first opinion mentioned presupposes the theory of 'natural hostility'. As a consequence, it has to be rejected too. Hence, *pax* can be both the state of peace and the means to achieve it by treaty. The *indutiae* (cease-fires) do not end the war as a whole, but interrupt the hostilities only temporarily.[55] In spite of its stipulation-like form, the nature of the surrender (*deditio*) as a treaty is disputed. By some it is regarded as a mere 'legal self-destruction' by the surrendering community. It seems convincing to follow Dieter Nörr[56] and focus on the inherent normative expectation that the victor would in any case spare the inhabitants' lives. Here, as often in the law of war, a minimum was touched which could well be in the personal interest of someone who – at a time of changing luck at war – wanted to be able

---

[54] In Ulp. Dig. 2, 14, 5 the *publica conventio* is furthermore mentioned in the context of *pax*, but supposedly not as a special form of a treaty. With respect to *pacta, pactiones* see above in the main text.

[55] Recently on a case of *indutiae* (between Rome and Macedonia 172/171 BC) see Petzold, *Geschichtsdenken und Geschichtsschreibung*, pp. 61–4.

[56] Cf. note 3. For the question whether the *deditio* had a self-destructive character, the *evocatio deorum*, the evocation ('calling out') by the Romans of the gods worshipped in the besieged town, is of importance (cf. for references Baldus, *Regelhafte Vertragsauslegung*, p. 234); recent research on this institution, the importance of which could be greater than has been assumed up to now, can be found in Alain Blomart, 'Die *evocatio* und der Transfer "fremder" Götter von der Peripherie nach Rom' in Cancik and Rüpke, *Römische Reichsreligion und Provinzialreligion*, pp. 99–111.

to win a town fast and without casualties.[57] In Livy's representation of the *deditio* in times of peace there are certain references to civil law which also support the point of view that, at the time of the turn of the calendar, Roman ideology regarded *deditio* as – or at least pretended it was – an immediately effective disposition by treaty.[58]

For the peace treaty this entails that even from an *ex post* perspective there is no contemporary typology. Many of the treaties mentioned in the sources are peace treaties in the sense of the modern concept; but as a matter of fact, such a classification was not made in Roman antiquity. Probably there was no political or theoretical demand for this,[59] however important the idea of *pax* may have been to Roman ideology.[60]

Thus, we have to form categories ourselves. Strictly speaking, we have to ask what corresponds to our category of the peace treaty when we want to know to what extent Rome offers historical illustrations of this category.

'Classical' Roman international law as a sociological system

How then can we surmount the interior barriers of access to 'classical' Roman international law? We cannot entirely take off our systematic spectacles, but we can look for criteria which abstract to the utmost from our contemporary understanding of the law. Here, legal sociology could provide an approach. This does not mean that legal sociology would be apt to serve as a 'meta-science' independent from any reference to time, nor does this mean that a certain sociological doctrine will receive theoretical credits. But if we regard the ongoing reception of Niklas Luhmann's 'system theory' (*Systemtheorie*) in legal history, we discover that not only

---

[57] Most recently see Karl-Heinz Ziegler, 'Vae victis – Sieger und Besiegte im Licht des Römischen Rechts' in Otto Kraus (ed.), *'Vae victis!' Über den Umgang mit Besiegten* (Göttingen, 1998).

[58] Cf. Baldus, *Regelhafte Vertragsauslegung*, pp. 240–9, as well on the anachronistic character of these intimations (see also the reference at note 18 above).

[59] Not least does the passage by Livy discussed above (34, 57, 7 *et seqq.*) support this view.

[60] Above all for Augustan ideology; critically of this most recently Michael Mause, 'Augustus: "Friedensfürst" in einer unruhigen Zeit', *Klio* 81 (1999), 142–55. Likewise against the common idea of peace as the main political objective during the Principate is Marcelo T. Schmitt, *Die römische Außenpolitik des 2. Jahrhunderts n. Chr.: Friedenssicherung oder Expansion?* (Stuttgart, 1997; reviews by Herbert Graßl, *Anzeiger für die Altertumswissenschaft* 52 (1999), col. 282 *et seq.*; critically Ulrich Lambrecht, *Gymnasium* 106 (1999), 471; Roland Schöffmann, *Zeitschrift der Savigny-Stiftung für Rechtsgeschichte, Romanistische Abteilung* 116 (1999), 615).

those legal historians pursuing a theoretical approach related to modern problems hope to gain scientific findings from this theory.[61]

'System theory' is also attractive for representatives of a modern 'historicism'[62] such as Mario Bretone.[63] It is not decisive for the utility of 'system theory' that Luhmann at times takes examples from Roman law,[64] even if this demonstrates that his argumentation is not limited to modern phenomena. Above all, Luhmann's theory is of interest to the legal historian because it deals with the autonomy of the law, i.e. with the identification and correct description of the object of our research. 'System theory' does not concentrate on (the formal quality of) the interaction of a 'whole' and its constituents. It rather asks how a system can be distinguished from its environment, how it reproduces itself and what functions it thus fulfils in society.

If we speak about the Roman legal 'system', this does not mean that we can infer its contents from a pre-existing objectivity – these contents are wittingly created by the system itself. We may take *exempli gratia* the creative usage of formulas from the early Republican period onward, which we also find – although with smaller variety than in private law – with the *foedus*. Religion had a strong political function in Early Rome, and at first it may have been used to a smaller extent for manipulative purposes than in the Classical period. The Roman citizens (a group which at the time was to a large extent still identical with the soldiers) and their Italic neighbouring peoples (the Italic-Etruscan *koine*) did not want to spoil things with the gods, especially Jupiter, and wanted to keep the *pax deorum*.[65]

Therefore, the formally duly concluded *foedus* actually represented a political factor: since the Roman community as a whole defined its relationship with the adversary in view of the *pax deorum*, the conclusion of a *foedus* had a preventive effect on future warfare, especially on the conduct of private wars by individual groups – just as the ceremonious opening of hostilities rather had the purpose to attribute responsibility

---

[61] Cf. (for a differentiation from anachronistic concepts of system) Baldus, 'Sistema giuridico europeo'.

[62] On the concept of 'historism' and recent trends in research cf. representative of all others the articles in Gunter Scholtz (ed.), *Historismus am Ende des 20. Jahrhunderts: eine internationale Diskussion* (Berlin, 1997), esp. the contributions by Georg Iggers, pp. 102–26, Volker Steenblock, pp. 174–91, and Gunter Scholtz, pp. 192–214; as well as Peter Burke, *New Perspectives on Historical Writing*, pp. 233–48.

[63] Mario Bretone, 'L'autonomia del diritto ed il diritto antico' in his *Diritto e tempo nella tradizione europea* (4th edn, Rome and Bari, 1999), pp. 111–22, at pp. 112–17.

[64] Niklas Luhmann, *Das Recht der Gesellschaft* (Frankfurt am Main, 1995), p. 122.

[65] Most recently on this, Rosenberger, *Gezähmte Götter*, pp. 17–21.

for the warfare on the home front than serve for the actual resolution of the conflict.[66]

Whatever we may think about 'natural hostility', the *foedus* at any rate put 'foreign' relations on a new foundation which was binding for the entire community. The same phenomenon will have applied to adversaries within the Italic *koine*.

With regard to this period we can thus summarise. There were treaties, the *foedera*, which channelled and impeded the use of force by means of their formalism. The law takes definite shape here: peace is kept owing to the inherent effect – although rooted in religion – of the formulas. Considering the recent availability of sources, we can only speculate about the effect of non-formal agreements at the time. But there is every reason to believe that at a time of heavily formalised legal reasoning they were of little effect. Hence the formalised treaty had a value of its own, corresponding to its function.

In the following, we will try to analyse the material from the sources with the help of a typical criterion of the legal system, i.e. reports on controversies over the interpretation and application of peace treaties. Typically, peace treaties intend to settle conflicts by withdrawing the controversial questions from the political discourse and by preparing them for legal examination. There are some suggestions in the sources on how this was done in Rome. Thus, we cannot identify a theoretical system, but we can see juridified patterns of behaviour and ways of formalising expectations, which we can sum up and examine *in toto*. After what has just been said, the structure of the following paragraphs can only be in accordance with substantial aspects, i.e. typical questions of controversy. Any 'types of treaties' or other formal aspects according to which we would have to organise our examination *ex ante* do not exist.

Peace treaties as a subject of legal discussion: examples

There are three areas in which, according to the sources, peace treaties were of importance to legal discussion:[67] first, Roman arbitration awards

---

[66] See with respect to the well-known problem of the *bellum iustum*, above all Alfons Bürge in a text not yet published; cf. Baldus, *Regelhafte Vertragsauslegung*, pp. 443–5.
[67] Merely rhetorical *exempla* will be excluded here even if later – preferably taken from international law (see Baldus, *Regelhafte Vertragsauslegung*, pp. 363–4; Gerhard H. Waldherr, 'Punica fides': Das Bild der Karthager in Rom', *Gymnasium* 107 (2000), 193–279 at p. 216) – they were passed on into modern times, sometimes in unchanged form;

between third parties,⁶⁸ second, debates about violations of treaties and, finally, disputes between Rome and its allies.⁶⁹

Roman arbitration awards between third parties

This field is dominated by the border dispute, which is the very reason for the infertility of the respective sources for our purposes: in modern times, the boundary *line* is a typical object of international conflicts.⁷⁰ Of course, there were disputes about borders in Antiquity too.⁷¹ There was, however, one significant difference: surveying – for instance in order to delimit private real estate or construct supply pipes and roads – was quite precise at the time; politically, however, the border was rather an area than a line. It was a zone of transition and of possible communication; often it was not even defended as a line either – this was all the more the case the weaker the Roman rule was or became.⁷²

cf. Klaus Luig, 'Paley's Rule und die Auslegung von Rechtsgeschäften' in Haimo Schack (ed.), *Gedächtnisschrift für Alexander Lüderitz* (Munich, 2000), pp. 471–86.

⁶⁸ There is no clear evidence of any submission of Rome to an international arbitral tribunal, in the form of a *recuperatio* (cf. note 37 above). As a party, Rome does not take part in the Greek tradition of arbitration (although she receives it into her own sphere of influence; cf. Ferrary, '*Ius fetiale* et diplomatie', p. 431). On this tradition see (apart from those referred to in Baldus, *Regelhafte Vertragsauslegung*, pp. 325–36 and 431) Jean Gaudemet, 'L'arbitrage dans les conflits territoriaux entre cités dans l'Antiquité gréco-romaine', *Recueils de la Société Jean Bodin pour l'Histoire Comparative des Institutions* 63 (1996), 1 (reviewed by Franz-Stefan Meissel, *Zeitschrift der Savigny-Stiftung für Rechtsgeschichte, Romanistische Abteilung* 116 (1999), 449–54); Sheila L. Ager, *Interstate Arbitration in the Greek World, 337–90 B.C.* (Berkeley, 1996; referred to by Kaja Harter-Uibopuu, *Zeitschrift der Savigny-Stiftung für Rechtsgeschichte, Romanistische Abteilung* 115 (1998), 660; reviewed by Everett L. Wheeler, *American Journal of Philology* 119 (1998), 642–6) – with the introductory indication (p. 3) that in Greece it was not the Great Powers which strived for arbitral conflict resolution. Mainly epigraphic: Kaja Harter-Uibopuu, *Das zwischenstaatliche Schiedsverfahren im achäischen Koinon* (Cologne and Graz, 1998); review by Karl-Heinz Ziegler, *Zeitschrift der Savigny-Stiftung für Rechtsgeschichte, Romanistische Abteilung* 117 (2000), 494–500); Petzold, *Geschichtsdenken und Geschichtsschreibung*, p. 90. Greek law of treaties is also discussed by Chaniotis, *Verträge zwischen kretischen Poleis* (review by Pierre Brulé, *Gnomon* 71 (1999), 674–9).

⁶⁹ We will leave aside the alleged interpretation of disputed treaties by the *fetiales*. If it can be proved at all, this does not concern peace treaties. Cf. in detail Baldus, *Regelhafte Vertragsauslegung*, pp. 412–60; and once again Ferrary, '*Ius fetiale* et diplomatie', p. 420.

⁷⁰ Cf. the recent monograph by Brigitte Daum, *Grenzverletzungen und Völkerrecht: eine Untersuchung der Rechtsfolgen von Grenzverletzungen in der Staatenpraxis . . .* (Frankfurt am Main etc., 1999).

⁷¹ Ager, *Interstate Arbitration*, p. 4.

⁷² On all of these aspects, cf. (apart from those quoted by Baldus, *Regelhafte Vertragsauslegung*, pp. 339–41) Aline Rousselle (ed.), *Frontières terrestres, frontières célestes dans l'antiquité*

Hence the typical dispute was not about the significance of such-and-such geographical detail in the wording of the treaty. As a recurrent pattern we can make out that the parties accused each other of violating the treaty in general – not a particular clause of the treaty. The function of the peace treaty is therefore not the precise geographical, and hence substantial and concrete, delimitation of interests. By reproaching each other for the violation of the treaty the parties referred to their underlying mutual relations in general.

At times the *status quo ante*,[73] i.e. the factual state, was discussed. But even this was not of real interest to Rome in the most famous of all border conflicts: the succession of conflicts between Carthage and Numidia – the latter supported by Rome – under Masinissa after 201 BC. Under the Roman–Carthaginian *foedus*, Carthage had to accept Numidian independence as well as a geographically determined prohibition to make war, and it had to make a treaty with Numidia. Functionally, this was a peace treaty with a trilateral effect – even if we do not know whether later on a Carthagian–Numidian *foedus* was concluded. In reaction to Numidian raids, Carthage disputed these border violations and with the *foedus*; Livy even mentions debates in which the terminology of claims for possession was used. Rome, however, manoeuvred to elude a legal decision, for taking the treaty seriously would have meant putting its *socius* Masinissa in his place.

(Perpignan, 1995): here above all the *présentation* and the article by Jean-Michel Carrié, '1993: ouverture des frontières romaines?', pp. 31–53, on the most recent history of research; Maïté Lafourcade (ed.), *La Frontière des origines à nos jours* (Bordeaux, 1998). For an archaeological perspective, cf. *Recherches sur les fortifications linéaires romaines* (Rome, 1997) by Joëlle Napoli and the reviews by Pol Trousset, *Latomus* 58 (1999), 699–702 at pp. 701–2; Günter Fischer, *Gnomon* 73 (2001), 91 at p. 92. Sceptical especially about the question of exact Roman maps is Kai Brodersen, *Terra cognita* (Hildesheim etc., 1995; critical review by Eckart Olshausen, *Klio* 81 (1999), 535). Modern international law has adopted the opposite position with respect to the linear character of the border: there is no point which is topographically situated 'on the border'. Because of its extension 'up and down', the border is, however, an area in the vertical sense (Kimminich and Hobe, *Einführung in das Völkerrecht*, pp. 82 and 100; for the historic roots of the civil law adage *cuius est solum, eius est usque ad caelum, usque ad inferos*, cf. the thesis by Ulf Goeke, *Luftraum und Erdreich als Inhalt des Bodeneigentums* . . . (Cologne etc., 1998)).

[73] It is disputed in this respect whether Rome, in determining the *status quo ante*, deliberately postponed the decisive moment. Cf. Baldus, *Regelhafte Vertragsauslegung*, pp. 344–6. On *uti possidetis* in modern international law see now Christiane Simmler, *Das uti possidetis-Prinzip: zur Grenzziehung zwischen neu entstandenen Staaten* (Berlin, 1999); indications of Roman law at p. 34, further references as well in the preface, p. 9. I have not seen Michael Weber, '*Uti possidetis iuris*' *als allgemeines Rechtsprinzip im Völkerrecht* . . . (Göttingen, 1999).

The treaty did not gain political substance, because its guardian power did not want this. This does not mean that *e contrario* Roman respect for a *foedus* necessarily had to be based on respect for law. It could well be politically advisable not to pressurise the other party excessively. In such cases the adherence to Roman virtues such as *fides* comes the way of the other party.[74]

Debates about violations of treaties

Structure of the argumentation

The sources are abundant in statements of the kind that certain polities were *foedifragi*, violators of treaties. Even linguistically, the *foedus* stands for all treaties, *pars pro toto*. Above all, such statements are made when war guilt is discussed, for a *bellum iustum* may be waged against the party violating the treaty. At this point, we must not expect any elaborate theory of justification as was known in contemporary private law; for the above-mentioned reasons, there was no political interest in such an autonomous theory. Unlike formalism in private law, the archaic formalism of the declaration of war by the fetial priests — without any discussion it simply says *foedus a vobis ruptum* — is not developed any further towards a differentiation of its contents.[75]

---

[74] Cf. in detail Petzold, *Geschichtsdenken und Geschichtsschreibung*, pp. 69, 75, 87–91 and *passim* for Roman politics as regards Greece in the early second century BC. For a long time, the Senate majority tolerated that Greek allies opposed certain Roman demands by invoking concluded *foedera* – this also reflects the fact that the Greeks attached another kind of importance to their *libertas* than did the Romans. In so far as the Senate as an arbitral tribunal delayed decisions between Greek communities, this did not necessarily have a unilaterally beneficial effect – contrary to the case of Masinissa. Of course this attitude came to an end when in Rome more direct interventions and negotiating techniques which were traditionally regarded as insidious (*nova sapientia*) asserted themselves as being desirable. Petzold can also be followed in his theory that for the appreciation of *libertas* and *auctoritas* the existence of a *foedus* was not important in the end (at p. 91 with correct reference to Proc. Dig. 49, 15, 7, 1). The propagandistic exploitation of the motive of *libertas* also varied according to the audience: late annalists writing for Roman recipients did not need the freedom of the Greeks for their theories of *bellum iustum* (cf. Ferrary, '*Ius fetiale* et diplomatie', pp. 429–30). This is one of the points in which an analysis of Polybius' patterns of assessment promises to be of particular use (cf. once again Eckstein, *Moral Vision in the Histories of Polybius*).

[75] The same is applicable to the preceding *rerum repetitio*. The peculiar parallel of *formula iuris antiqui* and the *commodum* of the parties in Livy 34, 57, 8 (see note 36 above) indicates that here a terminological relic was dragged along. Cf. once again the fundamental discussion of '*Ius fetiale* et diplomatie' by Ferrary.

Especially *topoi* like *fides* and *perfidia*, loyalty and disloyalty, are not specified as to their contents but are complemented by ethnic stereotypes. Their correspondence to reality and political function is intensively and sometimes controversially debated in recent research.[76] At any rate, the sources tend towards a surprisingly simple and plain argumentation. Thus, we have to wonder how narrow the theoretical basis of the peace treaty was in its political perception.

This is all the more astonishing since such politically active historiography – as we have to characterise the ancient historiography – had arguments to offer which could be taken seriously by an educated audience. Instead the authors, in particular of the Augustan era, present apodictic allegations and amazing legal constructions which hardly anyone can seriously have subscribed to in the past – at a time when Greek rhetoric and some basic knowledge of law were part of general education. Furthermore, Livy in particular shows a tendency to avoid questions of interpretation.[77]

Here we find unanswered questions concerning the communication between chroniclers and recipients, and underlying there are the questions – unanswered as well – of what was really being discussed in the historical cases of conflict and with what kind of expectation. We will come back to this point later.

The Punic Wars

Nevertheless, some debates abound in material, above all those concerning the relations with Carthage.[78] Several treaties gave rise to disputes;

---

[76] To the references in Baldus, *Regelhafte Vertragsauslegung*, pp. 366–9 add Martina Jantz, *Das Fremdenbild in der Literatur der römischen Republik und der augusteischen Zeit: Vorstellungen und Sichtweisen am Beispiel von Hispanien und Gallien* (Frankfurt am Main etc., 1995), esp. pp. 166–235 on characteristics such as *fides* and *perfidia*, reviewed by Gérard Freyburger, *Latomus* 58 (1999), 226 and (critically) José Carlos Fernández Corte, *Gnomon* 72 (2000), 715; Beatrix Günnewig, *Das Bild der Germanen und Britannier: Untersuchungen zur Sichtweise von fremden Völkern in antiker Literatur und moderner wissenschaftlicher Forschung* (Frankfurt am Main etc., 1998); reviews by Gerhard Dobesch, *Anzeiger für die Altertumswissenschaft* 52 (1999), cols. 246–58 and Waldherr, 'Punica fides'. Further details are given by Gerhard Dobesch, *Gnomon* 71 (1999), 529–34 and *Anzeiger für die Altertumswissenschaft* 51 (1998), cols. 100–5 on the work by Bernhard Kremer, *Das Bild der Kelten bis in augusteische Zeit* (Stuttgart, 1995). *Cantus firmus* of Dobesch's reviews is his plea for an approach to look for reflections of factually observed characteristics of the foreign peoples within the *topos*.

[77] Cf. for instance Baldus, *Regelhafte Vertragsauslegung*, pp. 374–5 and 389–94 (about the Third Punic War).

[78] The substantial debate in secondary literature concentrates on questions of war guilt. Robert Palmer, *Rome and Carthage at Peace* (Stuttgart, 1997; on the treaties, cf. primarily the historical overview pp. 15–30) recently endeavoured to elucidate the state of peace, of

however, the question whether after the so-called Treaty of Philinus of 306 Sicily belonged to the Roman or to the Carthaginian sphere, i.e. the question of guilt over the First Punic War, is – even by the ancient authors – primarily discussed from the point of view of whether this treaty had existed at all. Moreover the wording of this treaty is uncertain.[79]

With respect to the Second Punic War, the question of war guilt is classic. Did Carthage by attacking Saguntum violate the Treaty of Lutatius (concluded in 241 BC after the First Punic War) or the so-called Ebro Treaty (concluded in 226–225 BC by Hasdrubal)?[80] The Treaty of Lutatius guaranteed, among other things, 'the safety of the allies of both sides' (at the same time it did not allow any new alliances with third parties). The Ebro Treaty delimited Carthaginian (or rather the commander Hasdrubal's) interests in Spain from Roman interests by the course of a river named

course without meeting particular approval by the critics (see the reviews by Klaus Geus, *Gnomon* 72 (2000), 134–7 and Walter Ameling, *Klio* 81 (1999), 526). On the image of Carthage in Rome cf. most recently Waldherr, 'Punica fides', *passim*: according to him, wholesale defamation of Carthaginians, unknown to the older Roman historiography (though not the Greek), had its initial stages with Cato and Polybius and culminated in Livy's *ab urbe condita*.

[79] Briefly about this problem: Baldus, *Regelhafte Vertragsauslegung*, p. 380; the First Punic War has recently been dealt with by Bruce Dexter Hoyos in the first part of his *Unplanned Wars: The Origins of the First and Second Punic Wars* (Berlin and New York, 1997 [1998]; review by John F. Lazenby, *Classical Review* 49 (1999), 175); John Lazenby, *The First Punic War* (Palo Alto, 1996; review M. James Moscovich, *Phoenix* 51 (1997), 233), here pp. 31–42 for the legal situation.

[80] The references up to 1990 are given by Barbara Scardigli, *I trattati romano-cartaginesi*; especially references after 1990 can be found in Baldus, *Regelhafte Vertragsauslegung*, pp. 379–88. Further see Petzold, *Geschichtsdenken und Geschichtsschreibung*, pp. 538–63; Ursula Händl-Sagawe, *Der Beginn des 2. Punischen Krieges: ein historisch-kritischer Kommentar zu Livius Buch 21* (Munich, 1995; critical review by John Briscoe, *Gnomon* 71 (1999), 211–14); John Rich, 'The Origins of the Second Punic War' in Tim Cornell, Boris Rankov and Philip Sabin (eds.), *The Second Punic War: A Reappraisal* (London, 1996), pp. 1–37. (The fall of Saguntum would have induced Rome to declare war, not a violation of the Ebro Treaty; approving review by M. James Moscovich, *Phoenix* 51 (1997), 233, 235); Hoyos, *Unplanned Wars*, pp. 174–95; Martine Chassignet, 'La deuxième guerre punique dans l'historiographie romaine: fixation et évaluation d'une tradition' in David, *Valeurs et mémoire à Rome*, pp. 55–72. Cf. as well the commentary works by Christoph Leidl, *Appians Darstellung des 2. punischen Krieges in Spanien (Iberike c. 1–38, § 1–158a)* (Munich, 1996; review by Walter Ameling, *Klio* 81 (1999), 538) and P. Goukowsky, *Appien ... L'Ibérique* (Paris, 1997), both reviewed by J. S. Richardson, *Classical Review* 49 (1999), 30. For more detail about 'Le droit fétial et la déclaration de guerre de Rome à Carthage en 218 avant J.-C.' see Adalberto Giovannini, pp. 102–5, especially about the disputed clauses. The central theme of the discussion is brought out by Guido Rings, 'Der zweite punische Krieg zwischen Fiktion und Realität', *Storia della Storiografia* 34 (1998), 111–17. I have not seen Alberto Díaz Tejera, *El tratado del Ebro y el origen de la segunda Guerra Púnica* (Madrid, 1996; review Eric Foulon, *Latomus* 59 (2000), 447).

Iber. The content and the very existence of the latter treaty is dubious. Did it refer to the river Ebro or to the Segura (as it is called today)? According to Rome, Saguntum was – though only after 241 BC – its ally. It was successfully sieged by Carthage and not defended in good time by Rome. Rome went to war with Carthage *pro fide* in order to reconquer the town which is situated north of the Segura but south of the Ebro. We can only briefly treat one problem from this complex discussion:[81] According to Polybius (c. 200–120 BC),[82] after the occupation of the town Carthage intended to conclude *e contrario* from the wording of the Treaty of Lutatius that the safety clause would not apply to Iberian allies (and therefore not to Saguntum either). In Rome, however, the contrary was – only internally though – being considered: According to this view it could be inferred (also *e contrario*) from the treaty that, in the absence of an explicit prohibition to enter into new alliances and given the clauses about third-party contacts, it would have been allowed to ally with Saguntum.

We can ask now which of these two standpoints has to be understood *ex nunc* and which *ex tunc*, but that means overestimating the importance of legal logics. Rome did not even express the aforementioned considerations to Carthage: the attack was a manifest violation of the treaty. Here the weakness of the treaty becomes an argument. Either the alleged Roman reasoning is based on manipulations by historians. This would mean that Rome could not put forward any convincing arguments and the legal considerations were but invented for the purpose of legitimisation later on. Then again, it is possible that these considerations are historic but were not introduced into the political debate with the adversary at the time.

Things here are no different from the formalism of the *foedus* and the declaration of war. Roman international law did have its place in foreign affairs, but it mostly derived its significance and political reality from domestic affairs. There was no 'international community' which Rome would have had to convince of the lawfulness of its intentions (at the most,

---

[81] Principal outlines of the further argumentation in Baldus, *Regelhafte Vertragsauslegung*, pp. 380–7.

[82] Especially Polybius 3, 21, 4–7; 3, 39, 1–10. Livy only touches upon these problems (cf. the passages referred to by Baldus, *Regelhafte Vertragsauslegung*, pp. 383–5, and Händl-Sagawe, *Der Beginn des 2. punischen Krieges*, esp. p. 77). Among the secondary literature, cf. most recently Hoyos, *Unplanned Wars*, pp. 223 and 252. Of course it remains somewhat unclear to what extent Hoyos understands and accepts Roman as well as Carthaginian behaviour as a reference to the respective legal standpoint. This seems to be based on his assumption that 'arguments on treaties and legalities were for the outside world' (p. 253) – however, this implies fading out the question of credibility; see above in the main text.

there were allies who may have wondered whether in case of conflict they would be as well off as Saguntum).

However, there was a political *forum internum*, in which arguments of international law played their part, too. To an extent even greater than in modern international law, loyalty to the treaty in foreign relations was also the result of considerations of domestic utility. Utility has to be understood comprehensively here, including respect for tradition, religion and sense of justice. The peace treaty was another element to include – no more no less. Moreover, we can only see the Roman *forum internum* from the post-victory perspective; hence we do not have any reliable knowledge about the real value (positive or negative) ascribed to loyalty to the law when being in distress.

Finally, Rome destroyed Carthage after the Third Punic War. The legitimacy of the war was based (once again by avoiding any serious interpretation of the treaty) on the allegation that Carthage itself had employed military force (i.e. in defence against Masinissa). Rome was criticised within the Greek world for the devastation of the city in spite of the surrender which had taken place.[83] The discussion of this criticism by Polybius, however, does not yield any precise knowledge of the structure and legal effects of the *deditio*.[84]

Binding force of the commander's agreement

A special question of the problem of the violation of a treaty is whether Rome was bound by an agreement concluded by a field commander without approval of the Senate – typically an armistice concluded in distress and on unfavourable terms. Generally accepted principles of international law did not exist for this kind of situation. Rome is said to have adopted a practice which seems to take up domestic Roman civil law, but it placed the opponent at such a disadvantage that, even according to Roman sources, other peoples did not accept it.[85]

The Senate denied responsibility for the treaty because the action had allegedly been taken without the Roman people's order (*iniussu populi*). The army was saved (although disarmed and humiliated); Rome refused, however, to render the negotiated return and only offered the extradition of the commander. This construction does not appear as absurd to the

---

[83] In the analysis of such criticism and of the attempts to refute it we always have to raise the question of how far the audience, the ideas of which the historiographer had in mind, can be identified. On this problem, cf. for instance Ferrary, '*Ius fetiale* et diplomatie', p. 429.

[84] Baldus, *Regelhafte Vertragsauslegung*, pp. 376–8.

[85] Baldus, *Regelhafte Vertragsauslegung*, pp. 394–404.

modern civil lawyer as it may to the legal historian. The unauthorised agent is personally liable for the contract concluded by him but unapproved by the principal.[86] Thus, a certain deterrent effect against unauthorised actions would be conceivable.

From the perspective of international law, however, the *falsus procurator*'s personal liability does not make any sense for military reasons: it must be possible to act in a legally binding way through the person of the local commander. This is of even greater importance when – as in Antiquity – there is a lack of good means of communication between the units in the field and higher decision-making authorities. Uncertainty about the power of representation cannot – at least *vis-à-vis* third parties – be accepted. Therefore today the local commander has the relevant power under customary international law.[87]

For our purposes it is the pseudo-civil law character of the commander's surrender which is of interest. Rome did not actually have any elaborate law of agency, even at the time of the Republic.[88] To be precise, in classical times there was the *actio quod iussu* by means of which the master of a slave or the father of a son subject to parental authority (*filius familias*) could be made liable when the slave or the son-in-power had acted on his order. If such an order did not exist objectively, the business partner even in good faith was not protected. This civil law reasoning was not applicable to the circumstances of international law, provided that a rational conduct of war should remain possible.

Rome, however, combined the contractual argument that the *iussum populi* was missing with the extradition, a consequence taken from the law of torts – just as the owner of a slave could hand him over to the injured person instead of making reparation for the damage caused by the slave (*noxae deditio*). The application of this mechanism to a treaty under international law did not make any sense. The fear of being handed over might have prevented a slave from mistreating someone else's property, and in the end this may have resulted in sufficient protection for the potential victim. But in order to escape the consequence of extradition the commander

---

[86] For the Federal Republic of Germany, cf. Par. 179, *Bürgerliches Gesetzbuch*.
[87] More recent international law of peace has eliminated this problem by a formalisation of the powers of representation (cf. Arts. 7–8 of the Vienna Convention on the Law of Treaties). Pursuant to its Art. 73, the Vienna Convention is not applied to the international law of war. On customary law, cf. Alfred Verdross and Bruno Simma, *Universelles Völkerrecht* (3rd edn, Berlin, 1994), p. 443.
[88] Further Andreas Wacke, 'Die adjektizischen Klagen im Überblick. Erster Teil: Von der Reeder- und der Betriebsleiterklage zur direkten Stellvertretung', *Zeitschrift der Savigny-Stiftung für Rechtsgeschichte, Romanistische Abteilung* 111 (1994), 280–362.

would have had to bring about the destruction of the entire army or defect to the enemy.[89] Moreover, the logic of the commander's surrender had to turn out to be to Rome's disadvantage in the case of negotiations with enemy officers.[90]

After all, the classic case of a commander's *deditio*, the *pax Caudina* (allegedly 321 BC), has probably been invented for purposes of legitimisation. It was intended to legitimise an attempt to surrender which took place much later (and was unsuccessful, i.e. the extradition of Hostilius Mancinus to the Numantines in 136 BC). It follows that the legal distinction between a (binding) *foedus* and a mere *sponsio* to conclude a *foedus*, which Livy reports on while depicting the *pax Caudina*, might have been an invention, too. Thus an important source for our research on the types of treaties does not deserve much credit.

In conclusion we have to state on the one hand that what was wanted domestically exceeded the limit of what could be conveyed to third parties. The cases supported by historical evidence are from the second century BC, i.e. a time when to Rome it was of no importance any more to convince potential enemies.

On the other hand, we have to ask to what extent our sources have been written in order to convince a future Roman domestic audience or whether – in view of the amazing legal construction – we have to conclude that this purpose cannot seriously have been aspired to. Again, we will have to come back to this question.

Disputes between Rome and its allies

Obligation to lend military assistance

From time to time, Rome argued with its Italic allies about their obligation to lend military assistance,[91] the refusal of which was qualified as

---

[89] The latter was risky, of course, because in peace treaties the extradition of defectors (*transfugae*) was typically assured to Rome. To put it differently, an officer who deserted could at best have had an interest in a Roman defeat.

[90] On all of these questions, cf. Christian Baldus, review of Manfred Jäger, *Die Unverletzlichkeit der Gesandten zur Zeit der römischen Republik* (Münster and Hamburg, 1994) in *Seminarios Complutenses de Derecho Romano – Suplemento* 1994–95 (1996), pp. 93–114, at pp. 101–11; pp. 105–8 on Livy 9, 8,1 and 4–5; 9, 11 *passim*.

[91] The legal basis of the implementation of the prohibition of the Bacchic cult (186 BC) by non-subjugated communities in Italy is a related question. Cf. now an article dealing with the question of interference in 'internal affairs' of the *foideratei*: Olivier de Cazanove, 'I destinatari dell'iscrizione de Tiriolo e la questione del campo d'applicazione del Senatoconsulto *de Bacchanalibus*', *Athenaeum* 88 (2000), 59–68 (and an unnumbered page of maps), esp. at p. 67. According to this, the documented measures of prosecution possibly

defectio, defection from the treaty. In other words, here the function of the peace treaty to alter the legal state of affairs was debated. If we can trust the sources, it was certainly with the allies as it was with the colonies with which Rome had no treaty relations.[92] They had to obey, and their objections were mostly grounded on the impossibility of performance. Therefore, the legal basis of their obligation was not of primary importance.

Naturalisation

There was more discussion about the grant of citizenship to persons from allied communities which was sometimes subject to explicit restrictions by treaty. The original purpose of these clauses was to prevent uncontrolled Romanisation of foreign elites. But that was precisely the field wherein Rome wanted liberty; and the more the net of Roman alliances condensed to an empire, the more it was in the interest of the (formally still) foreign communities themselves that their elites were Romans and gained influence in Rome.[93]

Such an exponent was L. Cornelius Balbus from Gades (Cádiz); his Roman citizenship was questioned on a motive of domestic policy. Cicero (106–43 BC) defended him in his speech *Pro Balbo*, and felt compelled to argue down the accusation that Balbus had illegally become a Roman.[94] The core of the speech refers to the fact that certain other treaties contained saving clauses in favour of the party other than Rome:[95]

> Etenim quaedam foedera exstant, ut Cenomanorum ..., quorum in foederibus exceptum est, ne quis eorum a nobis civis recipiatur. Quod si exceptio facit ne liceat, ubi non sit exceptum, ibi necesse est licere. Ubi est igitur in foedere Gaditano exceptum, ne quem populus Romanus Gaditanum recipiat civitate? Nusquam.

only concerned places already directly controlled by Rome or (in the case of Latin colonies) culturally particularly close to Rome.

[92] On these, cf. most recently Randall S. Howarth, 'Rome, the Italians, and the Land', *Historia* 48 (1999), 282–300 (pp. 285–7 on the disputes about official duties); Aldo Petrucci, 'Colonie romane e latine nel V e IV sec. a.C.: i problemi' and 'Aspetti economici e problemi costituzionali nella deduzione di colonie dal 509 al 338 a.C.', both in F. Serrao (ed.), *Legge e società nella repubblica romana* (Naples, 2000), vol. II, pp. 1 and 95.

[93] Cf. on the continual effects of this tendency even after the provincialisation of an area, Schulz, *Herrschaft und Regierung*, p. 493: thus, the scope for action of the competent pro-magistrates was *de facto* limited.

[94] Cicero emphasises that not treaty law, but the law of citizenship was concerned (*pro Balbo* 29–30) and that Rome had an interest in everyone's possibility to become a Roman citizen (31). The *foedus*, however, could not completely be evaded.

[95] *Pro Balbo* 32.

> But there are in existence certain treaties, such as those concluded with the
> Cenomani . . . and in these treaties there is a saving clause that none of
> their people may be admitted by us to citizenship. But if a saving clause
> makes admission to citizenship unlawful, then, where there is no saving
> clause, admission must be lawful. Where, then, is there any saving clause
> in the treaty with Gades, under which the Roman People may not admit to
> citizenship any citizen of Gades? Nowhere.[96]

The rhetoric device is simple: The *argumentum e contrario* logically requires the existence of a rule and an exception; there could be no question of this in the law of citizenship, neither was there a general admissibility of naturalisation. The thesis, which Cicero sets up beforehand, that it always had to be possible to grant Roman citizenship to foreigners corresponded to political reality, but not even in principle to a fair treatment of other subjects under international law.[97] The function of the treaty here is purely a domestic one: the treaty constitutes the framework for admission to naturalisation. There was no conflict of interest between the two communities involved at the time of the proceedings. Similar to what we already have seen with Polybius, Cicero puts the *argumentum e contrario* – typically an ambivalent instrument of legal reasoning – into the service of a politically desired outcome. In substance, the argumentation is not marked by international law.

New findings for research in legal history

The texts discussed have often been interpreted as an expression of reckless power politics and hostility towards international law. Other authors regarded the mere observance of traditional formalities as such as a sign of respect for the law.[98] From the first mentioned perspective of *Realpolitik*,

---

[96] English translation on the basis of R. Gardner, The Loeb Classical Library (London and Cambridge, Mass., 1958).

[97] Cf. on the Romanisation, taking the elites in society as a starting point, Schulz, *Herrschaft und Regierung* and his 'Herrschaft und Dienst am Weltreich', both *passim*; furthermore, those quoted by Baldus, *Regelhafte Vertragsauslegung*, p. 282, and his 'Das *ius gentium*: Modernisierung des römischen Rechts als Globalisierungsphänomen?' in Martin Immenhauser and Jürg Wichtermann (eds.), *Jahrbuch Junger Zivilrechtswissenschaftler 1998* (Stuttgart etc., 1999), pp. 19–44 at pp. 23–4. The aspects which are of interest here are, however, not clear from the overview given by Peter Riesenberg, *Citizenship in the Western Tradition: Plato to Rousseau* (Chapel Hill etc., 1992), which is mainly based upon Cicero's philosophical writings and the speech *pro Archia* (see esp. pp. 75–8).

[98] In recent times, apparently only Michaela Kostial has tried to 'discuss away' Roman imperialism systematically, not least by having recourse to the *ius fetiale*: *Kriegerisches Rom?*

the peace treaty would at best have served to deceive other communities; from the second perspective we would be in the presence of a rather folkloric law not interfering with politics.

If we regard Roman conduct from a primarily domestic angle and ask about the significance of the legitimacy of international actions, this dilemma is diminished. The religious and traditional momentum remained a motivation for or a hindrance to, for example, the fighting spirit. Perhaps this was due to the fact that Roman religion was not concerned with personal revelation and could therefore coexist with more recent religious practices. To some extent there was consideration for third-party reactions. Throughout the Republican period we find traces of the endeavour to integrate on the inside, especially with respect to unauthorised actions of individuals who might cultivate separate relations to the outside world.

In archaic times the polity did not unhesitatingly want to be liable for the actions of the *gentes*, and the examination procedures entrusted to the fetial priests may have provided the framework for this purpose.[99] Later on, the Senate alone had to control the conduct of individual (pro-) magistrates with regard to foreign affairs. During the Principate this was no longer a problem. The maintenance of the *pax* was aspired to by means which structurally belonged to domestic policy. Among the latter there may have been – as paradoxical as it may sound – the *foedus*, degenerated to a mere testimonial of honour.

That the instruments of international law had not completely disappeared from Roman consciousness is, finally, shown by the late Principate and above all by the Dominate, when treaties were used in great numbers in order to integrate new centrifugal forces – sometimes successfully. International law with its traditional and power-related elements could after all form part of the political discourse – and this is quite something. The swift emancipation of private law from its archaic formalism is connected with the fact that independent instances – first the *pontifices*, then the 'secular' *iuris prudentes* – could have an integrating effect, by

Zur Frage von Unvermeidbarkeit und Normalität militärischer Konflikte in der römischen Politik (Stuttgart, 1995). In addition to the reservations hinted at by Baldus, *Regelhafte Vertragsauslegung*, pp. 414–15, 440, 467, cf. now the clear remarks in the review by William V. Harris, *Gnomon* 72 (2000), 561.

[99] On the institutionalisation of the priests' and magistrates' power *in sacris*, cf. (with respect to the interpretation of divine signs) Rosenberger, *Gezähmte Götter*, pp. 46–50, 65–6, 70–1 etc. The observation (p. 65) that it was just the imprecision of the priests' answers which gave the necessary scope of action to 'secular' decision-making authorities is presumably *ceteris paribus* applicable to issues of international law.

development and *interpretatio* of forms of contracts and of actions. At the international level, only an instance higher than Rome might have brought about a comparable achievement. This did not exist, and the centrifugal forces in the Mediterranean area were overcome not by an organised consensus but by the military rise of Rome. At the time, however, it was not the most natural thing in the world that this rise assumed legal forms and that he who negotiated with Rome obtained to a large extent certainty about the principal features of his future relationship with Rome.

Here the law has its own sphere, and it requires its specific argumentation. Not every politically desired behaviour is enforceable. This is nowhere as clear as just in those sources which have probably been disfigured or invented: even one to two centuries before the classics of private law, Livy perceived certain political realities to be unacceptable and impossible to be communicated to his audience.[100] If Roman international law had only been an apologetic instrument (or, in order to take up Koskenniemi's aporia,[101] a utopia without the capacity to shape reality), ancient writers would not have had to make such an effort.

From the perspective of the present this means that the tension between short-term utility and investment in long-term confidence-building structures, which is so typical of international law, did already exist in Rome – the mere particularity consists in the fact that the domestic forum, where this tension was being discussed, was of far greater importance than the external perspective. From a distance, this situation is similar to a regional sub-system today where a hegemonic power has a free hand because international bodies or superpowers do not want to intervene.

It could thus be interesting to find out about the domestic application of the law. But to this end we would have to know more about what is fact or fiction in our sources. And with respect to Rome, we would have to accept the fact that there is no strict borderline between international law and private law. On the contrary, the legally relevant ideas permeate both spheres.[102] Not only are the archaic formalities

---

[100] The same considerations could apply to Livy's own sources, which were historically closer to the actual events.

[101] Martti Koskenniemi, *From Apology to Utopia: The Structure of International Legal Argument* (Helsinki, 1989).

[102] The *punica fides* (i.e. *perfidia*), the 'idiomatic' Carthaginian lack of loyalty, forms a vivid and graphic example central to the political discourse of the time: at first related to fraudulent businessmen, i.e. the private sphere, it later became the standard reproach of hostility to international law identified with the Punic community. Cf. Waldherr, 'Punica fides', pp. 206–7 and 211–12.

similar,[103] but also the long-lasting concepts. Roman legal thinking leaves less freedom of development to international law than to private law, but unlike the extremely state-centred theory of the nineteenth century, it does not know any radical separation of the two spheres.[104]

Summarising our findings, we still find many unknown spots on our map of the legal landscape. We know only partially to what extent the peace treaty really was a legal act and subject to legal assessment – and to what extent only questions of power mattered. But it is precisely the task of our discipline, the history of international law, to determine more closely the relation of power and norm – and the peace treaty constitutes the classic object of this task.

Desiderata

The open questions touch on a problem which legal history and the Classics can only solve together. What urged an author to rig out the period described by him with – among other things – legal institutions and debates about which a modern legal historian can immediately say: it was not like this, and in fact nobody at the time of origin of the work can have believed that it was like this? If incorrect things have been voiced and believed, why? Which political function did the reference to law and to lawfulness have?

As has been explained at the beginning, we cannot primarily hope for new sources, but we can observe a process which at the moment is flowering in academic history, and we can ask whether it brings to light anything relevant from a legal perspective: the analysis of the sources as a process of communication at the time. Authors and recipients of works of history but also of court speeches mainly belonged to an educated upper class; some had themselves been making decisions with respect to legal matters or foreign affairs, some were at least close to such decision-makers. Information on contemporary history thus could be obtained from several independent sources. 'Public' law was passed on not least by means of historical cases;[105] knowledge of private law more likely belonged to a general

---

[103] Traditionally, this is discussed in the literature with respect to the *fetiales* – of course without any clear traces of private law reasoning being recognisable in the practice of international law.

[104] At least this is a stimulus for further reflection in the present. There are at any rate but few arguments in favour of the rejection – traditional since the nineteenth century – of private law analogies in international law. Cf. the pioneering study by Hersch Lauterpacht of *Private Law Sources and Analogies in International Law* (London etc., 1927) and Baldus, *Regelhafte Vertragsauslegung*, pp. 90–107 and 738–46.

[105] References in Baldus, *Regelhafte Vertragsauslegung*, pp. 404–5.

education than it does today. From private law some recipients were well acquainted with debates on legal issues which – as to subject matter as well as language – were highly demanding. Hence, the social subsystem in which our sources are to be placed was – having regard to the possibilities of the time – rather well informed. The question arises of what can be gained from the sources if we examine the statements from the history of international law for their credibility and if we extend our philological criticism to considerations of subject matter and communication.

In studies of ancient history, experiments are being carried out with structuralism and semantics, with hypertext and context – far beyond the questions of structures and events in history. Time will tell how much of this is merely fashionable and how much is really useful.[106] At any rate, we can discern a trend towards linguistics and the theory of communication. It is, however, striking about this contextualisation that the law is of hardly any relevance within the ongoing debate. Thus, we do not get any further than by means of purely philological criticism of the sources.

Let us first take the example of an individual institution. As has been shown, the commander's surrender was based on rules of the law of agency, a law which, at the time, did not exist – neither in private law nor in international law. The example of the *punica fides* is well suited to demonstrate the problems regarding the basic attitude of respect for the law.[107] Rome considered itself to be a people of (especially international) *fides*, but the reference to this value sometimes served domestic purposes rather than those related to foreign policy. This was increasingly so the more the real conflict with Carthage became history. Hence, all of this was more about the 'good Roman' than the 'bad Carthaginian'.

However, this self-portrayal of the political public in the early imperial period increasingly tended to hold the overlong period of peace responsible for the loss of traditional virtues. Ultimately, the renunciation of force,

---

[106] The aforementioned reviews are revealing in this respect, too: a reserved, cautiously open attitude towards the various institutions of the theory of communication dominates. As far as legal science is concerned, there is a tendency to distrust theories (like structuralism) which do not have an objective meaning of linguistic signs. It must be practically possible to lay down socially binding rules and enforce them, otherwise law loses its function. The same scepticism exists about the tendency of structuralism to concentrate on the procedures by means of which 'meaning' is determined. A lawyer (typically a judge) has to present within a reasonable time a result to society which can be expected to reach a broad consensus: thus, reflection about the procedures leading to such a result is functionally limited by this duty.

[107] Waldherr, 'Punica fides', pp. 214–15, 218, 221–2.

arranged by a treaty, was disapproved of.[108] Hence, the political discourse on the value of respect for the law is characterised by two opposite tendencies, and both wanted to exploit the perception of foreign affairs for their purposes.

If we desire to know about the function of the peace treaty in Rome, we will have to ask about the setting. We will have to know more about the presence of law in the (intellectual) day-to-day life of the educated; we will have to know to what extent they perceived law as a historical phenomenon and to what extent they thought of contemporary distinctions between legal history and the present, between private and public law, etc., when they listened to works of history which were read out to them.[109] Thus, we are dealing with communication about plausibilities, and this, to be more precise, within a quadrangle composed of specialist legal literature, historical writings, political expectations and the education of the recipients. Neither from a historical nor from a legal perspective has this field been explored satisfactorily.[110] Historical (re-)search for the collective memory of course requires contextualisation.[111] This means – with respect to reports on legal issues – that we have to make a comparison of the popular legal ideas at the time of the narration and the law of that time.

The perspective of the contemporary audience[112] in general is discussed just by those researchers who emphasise the creative element in ancient

---

[108] At least this is supported by Schmitt, *Die römische Außenpolitik des 2. Jahrhunderts n. Chr.*, conclusion p. 200; Ulrich Huttner, 'Zur Zivilisationskritik in der frühen Kaiserzeit: die Diskriminierung der *pax Romana*', *Historia* 49 (2000), 447–66 (on Seneca, from p. 463 on his further influence).

[109] A quick glance at Dig. 1, 2 reveals that these distinctions were treated by academic literature. Cf. representatively on this Dieter Nörr, 'Pomponius oder "Zum Geschichtsverständnis der römischen Juristen"' in Hildegard Temporini and Wolfgang Haase (eds.), *Aufstieg und Niedergang* (Berlin and New York, 1976), vol. II-15, pp. 497–604.

[110] With respect to the Greek court speech (not historiography) see, however, most recently Thomas A. Schmitz, 'Plausibility in the Greek Orators', *American Journal of Philology* 121 (2000), 47–77. The structuralistically influenced Schmitz regards the speech in court at least as close to fictional texts. He questions in general a concept of truth asking for agreement between text and reality (pp. 55–6). In legal history, however, there seems to be doubt about the question of the extent to which the description of contemporary events for a contemporary public can be regarded as being not (really) a reference.

[111] Uwe Walter, *Gymnasium*, 107 (2000), 339.

[112] Whether this was a public of readers or an auditorium cannot unhesitatingly be decided in favour of the second alternative – reading out of texts as a rule – any longer: Emmanuelle Valette-Cagnac, *La Lecture à Rome* (Paris, 1997; reviews by Catherine Salles, *Latomus* 59 (2000), 936; critically William V. Harris, *Klio* 82 (2000), 526). What is essential for our question: the listening, especially collective, draws less attention to dubious details in the text; consensus about the contents is reached far more spontaneously and less rationally.

writers.¹¹³ However, these considerations are seldom transferred to legal history. Any rigorous reading of the ancient writers from a legal perspective raises questions which, of course, cannot be answered by philologists or historians but which cannot be answered without them either. The answers which might be given to these questions could then give hints about what the events reported by the sources may have looked like.

Here it does not suffice to point out that ancient aspiration to truthfulness did in fact not correspond to our modern sense of objectivity.¹¹⁴ This can be well demonstrated by a passage from *De oratore* 2, 62 *et seq.*, which is usually cited in this context.¹¹⁵ Here Cicero makes Antonius first say:

> Nam quis nescit, primam esse historiae legem, ne quid falsi dicere audeat? Deinde ne quid veri non audeat? Ne qua suspicio gratiae sit in scribendo? Ne qua simultatis? Haec scilicet fundamenta nota sunt omnibus; ipsa autem exaedificatio posita est in rebus et verbis. Rerum ratio ordinem temporum desiderat, regionum descriptionem . . .

---

¹¹³ For instance, the thought that 'each reader's act of reading makes the story complete' is so central to Jaeger, *Livy's Written Rome*, that it appears in her conclusion (p. 178) just as the idea of contextualisation (p. 179): 'The *Ab urbe condita* thus schools its audience in the best way to meet a crisis: exemplary Romans view such situations with detachment, place events in context, and summon outside help even if they have to invent it. Adopting or creating detached and external points of view helps Romans recapture space and expand their territory.' If, of course, we relate this thought to a contextualisation of the considerations of international law referred to by Livy, at least some questions arise. The idea of a new arrangement of historical space by Livy which is central to Jaeger could also be considered with respect to international law. For an overview of demands and methods of the authors that are of interest here, cf. Flach, *Einführung in die römische Geschichtsschreibung*, pp. 5–18; in the chapter on Livy see esp. p. 152 – contemporary criticism.

¹¹⁴ Whatever objectivity may be in modern historical research (not to mention epistemologically). A classic of the *Annales*: Marc Bloch, *Apologie pour l'histoire ou Métier d'historien* (Paris, 1997; German edn. Munich, 1985), *passim*; from more recent theory representative of all others: Jörn Rüsen (ed.), *Historische Objektivität* (Göttingen, 1975); Charles-Olivier Carbonell, *L'Historiographie* (Paris, 1981); Christian Meier and Jörg Rüsen (eds.), *Historische Methode* (Munich, 1988; here primarily the chapter by Rüsen, pp. 62–80); Friedrich Jaeger and Jörn Rüsen (eds.), *Geschichte des Historismus* (Munich, 1992); on historicism cf. furthermore the collection cited above, Scholtz (ed.), *Historismus am Ende des 20. Jahrhunderts*; Reinhart Koselleck, Wolfgang J. Mommsen and Jörn Rüsen (eds.), *Objektivität und Parteilichkeit in der Geschichtswissenschaft* (Munich, 1977); Jörn Rüsen, *Grundlagen und Methoden der Historiographiegeschichte* (Frankfurt am Main, 1995). Examples from ancient history or from the theory of history are apparently of no importance to this debate.

¹¹⁵ Gordon Shrimpton, *History and Memory in Ancient Greece* (Montreal, 1997), p. 25 (with respect to Cicero, not the Greek authors). Cf. on his work and his central theory that the historian – at least the Greek one – saw himself primarily as a literary voice of collective memory, the review by Stewart Flory, *Phoenix* 53 (1999), 157–60.

For who does not know history's first law to be that an author must not dare to tell anything but the truth? And its second that he must make bold to tell the whole truth? That there must be no suggestion of partiality anywhere in his writings? Nor of malice? This groundwork of course is familiar to every one; the completed structure however rests upon the story and the diction. The nature of the subject needs chronological arrangement and geographical representation...'[116]

This description of the *res* to be depicted is followed by Cicero's remarks on the arrangement and the content of the text in which he encourages the *orator* to provide details: *non solum quid actum aut dictum sit, sed etiam quomodo*, and to give the *causae* of the events as well as the protagonists' *vita atque natura* (2, 63). In the *genus orationis fusum atque tractum*, however, the *orator* is urged not to treat anything as in court: *sine hac iudiciali asperitate, et sine sententiarum forensium aculeis*, i.e. without this judicial severity and without the acuity of speeches in court.

Hence, details embellish the story and improve the flow of speech; they are not pointed comments as needed in judicial argumentations. The criterion for the selection of what is to be told is not the success in judicial proceedings but the general persuasiveness. Through such a selection not only sharp remarks but also legally relevant points will get lost. For Antonius (whom of course we must not unreservedly regard as Cicero's mouthpiece),[117] there is no contradiction in this: only the well-told history is correctly told. The acuities of speeches in court are to be avoided in a historical text (merely) for stylistic reasons.[118]

Thus, for Cicero the historical text is subject to other rhetorical rules than the description of the legal and political present; neither may he simply collect facts in the style of Roman Republican annalists, nor may

[116] *De oratore* 2, 62–3. (This cannot directly be recognised from the secondary quotation in Shrimpton, *History and Memory in Ancient Greece*, pp. 24–5). Hence, the particularities of Greek historiography are not of importance to these considerations. For a parallel quotation of Cicero, cf. A. J. Woodman, *Rhetoric in Classical Historiography* (London, 1998), pp. 85–6. English translation by E. W. Sutton, in the Loeb Classical Library (London and Cambridge, Mass., 1959).

[117] Cf. in greater detail on this the analysis by Ferdinando Bona, 'L'ideale retorico ciceroniano ed il "ius civile in artem redigere"', *Studia et Documenta Historiae et Iuris* 46 (1980), 282–382; also a monograph, Bona, *Cicerone tra diritto e oratoria* (Como, 1984, pp. 62–162): the *perfectus orator* is embodied not by Antonius but by Crassus (let both of them be idealised); jurisprudence is represented by Q. Mucius Scaevola *augur* (pp. 296–331 and 348–49).

[118] Cf. in detail as well on the following Karl-Ernst Petzold, 'Cicero und Historie', *Chiron* 2 (1972), 253–76; quoted here as Petzold, *Geschichtsdenken und Geschichtsschreibung*, pp. 86–109.

he aim at impressing the reader by an excessive amount of (only probable) details. The detail, for instance from legal history, is permitted where it explains the course of events, and thus serves to shape the material; otherwise it must stand back because it spoils the arrangement of the narration. It should be examined whether in particular Livy follows similar maxims when he makes his protagonists argue about international law. Cicero, at any rate, who was more inclined to political and juridical rhetoric than to historiography, offers us – for instance in his *pro Balbo* speech – quite a lot of material; but precisely for this genre he exempts himself from the strict rules from *De oratore* 2, 62. Methodological postulate and practical implementation can thus not easily be paralleled.

A science such as Roman legal history, which is used to judging each linguistic sign in a normative way, faces a problem here: if we delete everything which could be purely ornamental, not enough will be left to gain an overall impression. A legal historian is also well acquainted with the fact that at times the ancient law employed legal fictions *bona fide*.[119] We therefore have to work with the rhetorical details, though not uncritically as regards ideology. To this end we need assistance from other disciplines.

An author deduced the following from the passage by Cicero: 'The *narratio* of the historian "convinces" by its correspondence, not to the events, as in modern theory, but to the people, times and places.'[120] Thus, to put it in modern terms, it is all about the (re-)presentation of structures. What can be the historical narration of law from such a perspective? It can, for example, depict certain legal proceedings such as the chronicler himself imagines them to be. Thus, we have come to the question of the history of events or of structure.

Legal history asks for what has been valid and why; it asks for theory, validity, demand for and effects of regulation. It asks for the substance of law. The substance of law is not an 'event' in the sense of an opposition to people, times and places as larger, structurally considered objects of

---

[119] Recent monographs: António dos Santos Justo, *A 'fictio iuris' no direito romano*... (Coimbra, 1988); Francesca Lamberti, *Studi sui 'postumi'*... (Naples, 1996), pp. 24–34; Ernesto Bianchi, *Fictio iuris* (Padua, 1997); for a classification within a greater methodological context, cf. further Karl Hackl, 'Vom "quasi" im römischen zum "als ob" im modernen Recht' in Reinhard Zimmermann *et al.* (eds.), *Rechtsgeschichte und Rechtsdogmatik: Festschrift für Hans Hermann Seiler* (Heidelberg, 1999), pp. 117–27: according to him, Roman 'fiction' with its element of comparability of the various constituents corresponds to what is known as 'analogy' today.

[120] Shrimpton, *History and Memory in Ancient Greece*, p. 25.

historical research. An individual conclusion of a treaty is an event – but it is of interest to the legal historian because of the possibility to draw conclusions about the underlying structure. The substance of law, however, refers to structure: norms in their continual application. Law is a structural feature of any given society, it would thus fall into the aforementioned categories of 'people' and 'time'. Individual legal cases can colour the description of a society; law as a structure, however, regulates and 'steers' society.[121] We can make use of the rhetorical detail not as a fact, but as an indicator of political and legal reasoning. The sources provide us with – compared to private law – fewer objective details and more theory instead. The invention of an anachronistic speech, the content of which concerns the law of agency or the law of possession, is a greater challenge to the ancient historiographer than the creative shaping of an event – which, according to contemporary categories, was permissible. In such an invention (or disfigurement) we find at the same time the construction of a fictitious context, and the reasons for such a construction are of interest to the researcher. The question of whether a source is 'lying' is less important than the question of why the improbable has been believed: why was it possible and did it make sense to build constructions which today appear dubious to us? Thus, the examination of the theoretical detail refers to the basic values of the examined society: to one of its structures.

The legal historian's task should not consist in being a dilettante in social history or linguistics. He may, however, carve out the conditions of a plausible argument with bits and pieces of law, especially private law. Philologists and historians can thereupon put these conditions into the communicative context of ancient society. If we succeed in this, the question about the historicity of individual events is of minor importance. If we know, for example, why it was possible for Livy to invent a certain commander's *deditio*, then we have found out what we are interested in: the norms that the writer (or Augustus) wanted to see laid down in history.

Thus, *vestigia pacis* are only at first sight traces of events in international law. Our doubts about the sources direct our eyes to the underlying theoretical structures. Whatever the *pax* 'primarily' may have been from a philological point of view – a treaty or a state of being – for the legal historian it is an organised situation, a regulatory mechanism. Legal

---

[121] But not taking a however modified *Volksgeistlehre* as a starting point.

history looks for this state of being – which is to be caught in theoretical categories and also in the light of modern international law. For the time being, however, we can but present a building site to today's positive law, in the hope that it will not be deemed pointless to look for its foundations – or, according to the respective standpoint, to lay these foundations.

6

The influence of medieval Roman law on peace treaties

KARL-HEINZ ZIEGLER

From *foedera pacis* to *foedera, paces*

Peace treaties (*foedera pacis*) are mentioned by St Isidore of Seville (*c.* 560–636), the last of the Latin Fathers of the Church, in his famous enumerative definition of the law observed by all peoples (*ius gentium*).[1] This text, written in the early seventh century, not only is a valuable example of the Roman law tradition within the Church,[2] but later also became a legal norm (*canon*) of the medieval law code of the Latin Church, the *Corpus iuris canonici*, owing to the fact that in the twelfth century the learned monk Gratian (*c.* 1100–60) in Bologna quoted it in his handbook of canon law, the *Decretum Gratiani*.[3] It is significant that the original Isidorian expression 'foedera pacis' in the official edition of the *Decretum Gratiani* in the sixteenth century, the so-called *editio Romana*, had been changed to 'foedera, paces'.[4] Obviously, *pax* had now acquired an autonomous meaning, which, as a legal term, it had never possessed in Roman times.[5] We will encounter that wide legal concept of *pax* when we touch on the activities of the public notaries after the twelfth century.

---

[1] Isidorus, *Etymologiae* 5, 6: 'Ius gentium est sedium occupatio, aedificatio, munitio, bella, captivitates, servitutes, postliminia, foedera pacis, induciae, legatorum non violandorum religio, conubia inter alienigenas prohibita. Et inde ius gentium, quia eo iure omnes fere gentes utuntur.'
[2] Karl-Heinz Ziegler, 'Die römische Grundlagen des europäischen Völkerrechts', *Ius Commune* 4 (1972), 1–27 at pp. 5–7; Ziegler, '*Ius gentium* als Völkerrecht in der Spätantike' in Robert Feenstra, A. S. Hartkamp, J. E. Spruit, P. J. Sijpesteijn and L. C. Winkel (eds.), *Collatio iuris Romani: études dédiées à Hans Ankum* (Amsterdam, 1995), vol. II, pp. 665–75 at p. 666.
[3] Ziegler, 'Römische Grundlagen', pp. 5–6.
[4] Aemilius Friedberg (ed.), *Corpus iuris canonici* (Leipzig, 1879, reprinted Graz, 1959), vol. I, cols. 3–4 at D. 1 c. 9.
[5] Karl-Heinz Ziegler, 'Das Völkerrecht der römischen Republik' in Hildegard Temporini (ed.), *Aufstieg und Niedergang der römischen Welt* (Berlin and New York, 1972), vol. I-2, pp. 68–114 at p. 97; Ziegler,'Friedensverträge im römischen Altertum', *Archiv des Völkerrechts* 27 (1989), 45–62 at p. 46.

The conclusion of treaties

International treaties – the solemn agreements between states or their rulers throughout the Middle Ages and into the sixteenth century – were concluded in the same way as in Antiquity,[6] namely through declarations of the treaty-making parties, solemnly confirmed by mutual oaths.[7] This means that the written declarations or formal documents so frequently used did not constitute the peace to be concluded by their own quality, but served as a mutual security in order to avoid misunderstandings or future problems of interpretation. An oath properly demanded and properly taken was binding, in whatever form the sworn agreement had been prepared and published. The Middle Ages had inherited this pattern of treaty-making from Rome, which itself had preserved a legal tradition leading back to the third millennium BC.[8] Of course, the formulas of the oaths used to corroborate international agreements had changed considerably since pagan times. But we can still observe the custom of the swearing party cursing itself for the case of perjury, i.e. violating the treaty. Such solemn self-cursing was obviously not regarded as being contrary to Christian faith. Documentary evidence is given by the Roman–Persian peace treaty of AD 562, concluded by Emperor Justinian I (527–65), Article 12 of which contained 'prayers to God and imprecations to the effect that may God be gracious and ever an ally to him who abides by the peace, but if anyone with deceit wishes to alter any of the agreements, may God be his adversary and enemy'. This Greek text was probably unknown to the medieval Latin world, while in Byzantine literature it had been kept alive.[9] But Justinian's Novel 8 (AD 535), the Latin version of which was a part of the medieval editions of the *Corpus iuris civilis*, contained also the formula of an oath to be taken by the imperial officers, beginning with the invocation of God Almighty, our Lord Jesus Christ, the Holy Spirit, the Virgin Mary, and the four Gospels held in hand,[10] ending with the curse

---

[6] Karl-Heinz Ziegler, 'Conclusion and Publication of International Treaties in Antiquity', *Israel Law Review* 29 (1995), 233–49.

[7] Althur Nussbaum, 'Forms and Observance of Treaties in the Middle Ages and the Early Sixteenth Century' in George A. Lipsky (ed.), *Law and Politics in the World Community: Essays on Hans Kelsen's Pure Theory and Related Problems in International Law* (Berkeley and Los Angeles, 1953), pp. 191–8 at pp. 191–6.

[8] Ziegler, 'Conclusion and Publication', and now also Karl-Heinz Ziegler, 'Biblische Grundlagen des europäischen Völkerrechts', *Zeitschrift der Savigny-Stiftung für Rechtsgeschichte, Kanonistische Abteilung* 117 (2000), 1–32 at pp. 8–10, 15–17, 21, 30–1.

[9] C. de Boor (ed.), *Excerpta historica iussu Imp. Constantini Porphyrogeniti confecta*, vol. I: *Excerpta de legationibus*, pars I (Berlin, 1903), pp. 170–88.

[10] Nov. 8: 'Iusiurandum quod praestetur ab his, qui administrationes accipiunt: Iuro ego per deum omnipotentem et filium eius unigenitum dominum nostrum Iesum Christum

that, in the case of perjury, the swearing party was to be held in common with Judas, suffering from the leprosy of Gehazi[11] and the trembling of Cain.[12] The Treaty (*pactio*) concluded in AD 587 between the Frankish kings Gunthramn of Burgundy (560–93) and Childebert II of Austrasia (575–95) was sworn by the partners in the name of God Almighty, the inseparable Trinity, everything which is holy and the terror of the Last Judgement.[13]

The more complicated procedure of treaty-making in the high and late Middle Ages, when duly empowered representatives conducted the negotiations and came to an agreement which was then ratified by the contracting monarch or state,[14] did not change the archaic basic structure. Very often the negotiators themselves took the oath that their ruler would ratify the treaty. The ratification itself often meant that the monarch himself also took an oath. A very instructive example is furnished by the Peace of Brétigny, which was concluded in 1360 between King Edward III of England (1327–77) and King John II of France (1350–64, who since 1356 had been in English captivity). The treaty, which also regulated the release of the French king, was agreed upon and sworn by Edward Prince of Wales (1330–76) and by the dauphin and French regent, Charles (later King Charles V, 1364–80). Article 38 provided that the Treaty should be approved, sworn and confirmed by the kings personally, who one month later were also to exchange letters of confirmation.[15]

The oath taken in person with the hand touching the Gospels was called 'iuramentum corporaliter praestitum', an expression taken from

---

et spiritum sanctum et sanctam gloriosam dei genitricem et semper virginem Mariam et quattuor evangelia, quae in manibus meis teneo.'

[11] 2 Kings 5, 20–7 at 27.

[12] Nov. 8 *Iusiurandum* f.i.: 'Si vero non haec omnia ita servavero, recipiam hic et in futuro saeculo in terribili iudicio magni dei domini et salvatoris nostri Iesu Christi et habeam partem cum Iuda et lepram Giezi et tremorem Cain.'

[13] The *exemplar pactionis* is quoted in *Gregorii Turonensis Historiarum* 9, 20: 'Iurant partes per Dei omnipotentis nomen et inseparabilem Trinitatem vel divina omnia ac tremendum diem iudicii, se omnia quae superius scripta sunt absque ullo dolo malo vel fraudis ingenio inviolabiliter servaturos.'

[14] The authors referred to in Karl-Heinz Ziegler, *Völkerrechtsgeschichte: ein Studienbuch* (Munich, 1994), pp. 98–9.

[15] 'Item quod praesens Tractatus approbabitur, iurabitur, et confirmabitur per duos Reges Calesii, cum ibidem fuerint in propriis Personis.

  Et, postquam Rex Franciae recesserit de Calesio, et fuerit in sua potestate, infra unum mensem, proximo sequentem dictum recessum, dictus Rex Franciae faciet inde literas confirmatorias, et alias necessarias Patentes, et illas mittat et liberabit, Calesii, dicto Regi Angliae, vel Deputatis suis in loco praedicto.

  Et similiter, dictus Rex Angliae, receptis dictis literis confirmatoriis, tradet literas confirmatorias consimiles illis Regis Franciae.'

Roman law, exactly from Justinian's *Codex*, where we find the expressions 'iusiurandum corporaliter praestitum'[16] and 'sacramentum corporaliter praestitum'.[17] In a Treaty of permanent peace (*pax perpetua*) concluded in 1435 between King Ladislas III of Poland (1434–44) and the Teutonic Order of Prussia the exchange of oaths was mentioned expressly ('iuramentis corporaliter praestitis').[18] In the Peace Treaty of Barcelona of 19 November 1493 between King Ferdinand (1474–1516) and Queen Isabella of Spain (1474–1504) and King Charles VIII of France (1483–98) the Spanish monarchs declared: 'We swear upon the four sacred Gospels of God which we really touched with our hands.'[19]

Ecclesiastical jurisdiction

Since legal disputes about an oath in the Middle Ages were considered a matter for the Church and were therefore subject to ecclesiastical jurisdiction, we can observe a widespread activity of popes and bishops in international affairs.[20] We will not delve into the numerous rules which were developed in canon law for the validity and the nullity of sworn promises, including such figures as the *reservatio mentali* and the *clausula rebus sic stantibus*.[21] But it was Pope Innocent III (1198–1216) who, in a famous decretal (*Novit ille*, X.2, 1, 13) addressed to the prelates of France, stated that it was the office of the Church to control whether sworn agreements in a peace treaty were violated.[22] The legal bond between the kings of France and England referred to in the decretal is quoted as 'peace treaties confirmed by both parties with an oath taken personally'.[23]

In some cases, the contracting Christian monarchs even consented to a clause stating that the party violating the treaty should be

---

[16] Cod. 2, 27, 1 (Alex.; interpolated?).
[17] Cod. 2, 42, 3, 4 (Diocl. et Max. a. 293; interpolated?).
[18] Also published in Erich Weise (ed.), *Die Staatsverträge des deutschen Ordens in Preußen im 15. Jahrhundert*, vol. I (Königsberg, 1939), pp. 197–212 (no. 181). For the problem of the date, Klaus Neitmann, *Die Staatsverträge des deutschen Ordens in Preußen 1230–1449* (Cologne and Vienna, 1986), pp. 208–19.
[19] Art. 19: 'pollicemur, promittimus, concordamus, firmamus et juramus super sancta Dei quatuor Evangelia, corporaliter et manualiter per nos tacta'.
[20] Nussbaum, 'Forms and Observance', pp. 192–3.
[21] Nussbaum, 'Forms and Observance', pp. 194–5.
[22] X. 2, 1, 13: 'Postremo quum inter reges ipsos reformata fuerint pacis foedera, et utrinque praestito proprio iuramento firmata, quae tamen usque ad tempus praetaxatum servata non fuerint, numquid non poterimus de iuramenti religione cognoscere, quod ad iudicium ecclesiae non est dubium pertinere, ut rupta pacis foedera reformentur?'
[23] X. 2, 1, 13.

excommunicated by the pope. As late as 1492, King Henry VII of England (1485–1509) and King Charles VIII of France had a clause inserted in the Peace Treaty of Etaples of 3 November 1492 ('tractatus pacis et amicitiae') that they should demand a sentence of excommunication against the one who would not observe the treaty, and in addition a sentence of interdict against his kingdom and his other territories.[24]

The parties to the treaties

Peace treaties were common practice in medieval societies. They belong to the sphere of international law as far as the persons or communities involved participated as autonomous powers in international life.[25] Sovereignty was not limited to the pope and the emperor or to the rulers of the major kingdoms as the kings of England, of France or of Spain. Powers of lesser rank were also participants in international relations as subjects of international law, as far as they were able to wage war and to conclude treaties with each other, with their own overlord or with foreign rulers. So, in the Middle Ages 'the line between national and international law was fluid'.[26]

It was not seldom that a medieval ruler, who, according to the doctrine of *bellum iustum*, could wage a 'just war' even against his own subjects rebelling against him,[27] concluded a peace treaty with the former rebels. Of course, the stylistics of such a treaty were often somewhat different from

---

[24] Art. 28: 'Et insuper uterque Principum praedictorum infra terminum instanter et cum effectu requiret sacrosanctam sedem Apostolicam et summum Pontificem, quod ferat sententiam excommunicationis nunc pro tunc, et tunc pro nunc in eum, ex praedictis Principibus, qui omnia et singula Capitula in praesenti Tractatu contenta, quatenus ipsum concernunt, non observaverit; praeter et ultra sententiam interdicti, in eius Regna, patrias, terras et dominia.'

[25] Wolfgang Preiser, 'History of the Law of Nations: Ancient Times to 1648' in Rudolf Bernhardt (ed.), *Encyclopedia of Public International Law* (Amsterdam, 1995), vol. II, pp. 722–49 at pp. 733–6; Ziegler, *Völkerrechtsgeschichte*, pp. 95–7.

[26] Preiser, 'History', pp. 734–5.

[27] Cf. the seven types of war (*bellum*) distinguished in the middle of the thirteenth century by Cardinal Hostiensis, now also quoted in Wilhelm G. Grewe (ed.), *Fontes historiae iuris gentium*, vol. I: *1380 BC–1493* (Berlin and New York, 1995), p. 572. A just war was also the *bellum iudiciale*. The distinction of Hostiensis was still quoted in the fourteenth and fifteenth centuries, by Johannes de Lignano in his *Tractatus de bello* of 1360 in chapter 76, and by Martinus Garatus Laudensis in his *Tractatus de bello* written before 1450 in Qu. 31 (see for both authors Karl-Heinz Ziegler, 'Kriegsrechtliche Literatur im Spätmittelalter' in Horst Brunner (ed.), *Der Krieg im Mittelalter und in der frühen Neuzeit: Gründe, Begründungen, Bilder, Bräuche, Recht* (Wiesbaden, 1999), pp. 57–71 at pp. 64 n. 67 and 68 n. 99 for the Latin texts.

a treaty concluded between monarchs of equal rank. However it is not the outer appearance that is decisive, but the real substance. A famous example is the Peace Treaty of Constance of 1183 between Emperor Frederick I (1152–90) and the Lombardic League, which is stylised as an imperial concession ('pacem nostram quam eis clementer indultam concessimus'). The political substance is visible in the armistice ('treuga') which the emperor had promised and sworn for six years with the Lombardic League in 1177,[28] as agreed upon in a clause of the Peace Treaty ('pax') of Venice between the emperor and Pope Alexander III (1159–81), also signed in 1177.[29] Another example shows the possible self-confidence of a vassal prince: in 1199 Count Balduin of Flanders (1171–1205) published the peace treaty he had made with King Philip II August of France (1180–1223): 'These are the terms of the peace between my Liege Lord Philip King of France and me' ('haec est forma pacis inter Dominum meum Philippum Regem Franciae et me').

Treaty-making forms

Making peace by an agreement sworn by the parties was also common in the non-statal wars or feuds so frequent in the feudal society. The Latin expression for promising peace after an armed conflict (German *urvede*, *urfehde*, Anglo-Saxon *unfáehda*) was 'iuramentum pacis'.[30] For such peace agreements, which are testified already for Frankish times,[31] we know formulas from different parts of Europe, even from the law book of medieval Iceland (the *Grágás*).[32]

Since also the Italian municipal communities were often troubled by violent armed conflicts between individuals, their families or even political parties, the learned notaries also used forms for peace agreements

---

[28] Text with German translation also in Lorenz Weinrich (ed.), *Quellen zur deutschen Verfassungs-, Wirtschafts- und Sozialgeschichte bis 1250* (Darmstadt, 1977), pp. 286–91. The truce is concluded with the words: 'Inter dominum imperatorem et suam partem ... et Societatem Lombardorum ... treuga constituta est ...'.

[29] The major part of the text with German and English translations in Grewe, *Fontes*, vol. I, pp. 387–90. In Art. 27, it is said: 'Imperator ... et treuquam Lombardorum a proximis scilicet Augusti usque ad VI annos firmabit iuramento suo et principum et faciet Lombardos qui ex parte sua sunt, sicut in communi scripto treuque dispositum et scriptum est, eamdem treuquam firmari.'

[30] S. C. Saar, 'Urfehde' in *Handwörterbuch zur deutschen Rechtsgeschichte* (Berlin, 1993), vol. V, cols. 562–70 at col. 562.

[31] Cf. the feud of Sichar reported in *Gregorii Turonensis Historia* 7, 47.

[32] Cf. the German translation in Andreas Heusler (trans.), *Isländisches Recht: die Graugans* (Weimar, 1937), pp. 191–2 (*Friedenssprüche*).

THE INFLUENCE OF MEDIEVAL ROMAN LAW 153

laid down in a notarial document ('publicum instrumentum'). So, the manual *Ars notariae* of Rainerius Perusinus, written around 1230,[33] gives a short 'Document of peace, amity or truce' ('Carta pacis, concordie sive treugue'),[34] which was definitively to put an end to all kind of quarrelling, fighting, or litigation arising from an injury. More elaborated is the form which repeats the most famous author on Roman canonistic procedure, Gulielmus Durantis (c. 1237–96), in his widely disseminated handbook *Speculum iudiciale* (c. 1290),[35] of a 'Public instrument for peace and amity' ('publicum instrumentum super pace et concordia').[36] The solemn promises of a 'stable and permanent peace, the end and remission and amity' ('fecerunt firmam et perpetuam pacem, finem, remissionem atque concordiam') are made also for the eventual heirs, and they are accompanied by the exchange of the kiss of peace ('pacis osculo vicissim et mutuo interveniente').[37] It is significant that Durantis reports this form of peace and amity under the heading 'De treuga et pace', which is the official title of rubric 34 in the first book of the compilation of decretals authorised by Pope Gregory IX (1227–41), the *Liber extra* of 1234. The two decretals constituting this rubric had both been pronounced by Pope Alexander III (whom we have mentioned above as the opponent and partner of the Emperor Frederick I) in the year 1179, regulating the times of truce ('treuga') prescribed by the Church, the punishments for those disturbing the peace,[38] and the persons who are to be safe in times of feud or war ('tempore guerrae').[39]

There can be no doubt that from the beginning of the new (i.e. medieval) legal science in Bologna learned jurists and public notaries were concerned with international affairs.[40] It is a well-known fact that in the conflicts and disputes between the kings of France and the Roman-German emperors the latter lost many a case because the French kings had the better chancery and more and better jurists trained in international

---

[33] Modern edition: Ludwig Wahrmund (ed.), *Die ars notariae des Rainerius Perusinus, Quellen zur Geschichte des römisch-kanonischen Prozesses im Mittelalter* (Innsbruck, 1917; reprinted 1962), vol. III-2.
[34] Wahrmund, *Die ars notariae*, pp. 54–5 (no. 51): 'Promittentes inter se et ad invicem stipulantes, dictam concordiam et omnia et singula, que in ea contenentur, rata et firma perpetuo habere atque tenere.'
[35] Edition used: Gulielmi Durandi Episcopi Mimatensis, *Speculum iuris* (Basel, 1574; reprinted 1975).
[36] Durandi, *Speculum*, pars 4 particula 1: *De treuga et pace*, p. 107.
[37] Cf. also the promise made by the parties: 'et dictam pacem, sive remissionem atque concordiam et omnia et singula supra scripta perpetuo grata, rata, et firma habebunt, et tenebunt, nec contraveniunt per se, vel alios aliqua ratione, vel causa de iure, vel facto.'
[38] X. 1, 34, 1.   [39] X. 1, 34, 2.   [40] Ziegler, 'Römische Grundlagen', p. 17.

negotiations.⁴¹ This does not mean that the practice of peace treaties was shaped or modelled in a decisive manner by Roman law. But legal arguments and juristic professional terms were now used, giving more precision and the possibility of rational control to the clauses agreed upon in the peace negotiations.

Roman law sources

Before we look for details of Roman law influence in medieval peace treaties, we shall have a glimpse of the first beginnings of a learned theory of international treaties in general, and peace treaties in particular. We must also keep in mind that the *Corpus iuris civilis* does not give much information about the law of nations recognised by the ancient Romans,⁴² and the rich tradition in Cicero, Livy and other ancient authors had mainly been exploited only after the age of humanism.⁴³ But in Justinian's *Digest* the jurists found hints about international relations founded upon amity (*amicitia*), hospitality (*hospitium*) and treaty (*foedus*),⁴⁴ the distinction between an equal treaty (*foedus aequum*) and a treaty between partners of different ranking,⁴⁵ and they found a classical definition of the armistice or truce (*indutiae*), which stops or interrupts fighting, but does not end war.⁴⁶ The medieval jurists could see that the Romans sometimes concluded peace treaties in which the release of the prisoners of war was expressly regulated.⁴⁷ Of systematic interest was a text where an agreement between the military leaders who want to promote peace is defined as 'public convention' (*publica conventio*).⁴⁸

---

⁴¹ Cf. only Fritz Kern, *Die Anfänge der französischen Ausdehnungspolitik bis zum Jahre 1308* (Tübingen, 1910), pp. 36–50 and *passim*.

⁴² Ziegler, 'Römische Grundlagen', p. 8.   ⁴³ Ziegler, 'Römische Grundlagen', pp. 21–4.

⁴⁴ Dig. 49, 15, 5, 2 (Pomp. 31 Muc.): 'In pace quoque postliminium datum est: nam si cum gente aliqua neque amicitiam neque hospitium neque foedus amicitiae causa factum habemus, hi hostes quidem non sunt.'

⁴⁵ Dig. 49, 15, 7, 1 (Proc. 8 epist.): 'Liber autem populus est is, qui nullius alterius populi potestati est subiectus: sive is foederatus est item, sive aequo foedere in amicitiam venit sive foedere comprehensum est, ut is populus alterius populi maiestatem comiter conservaret. Hoc enim adicitur, ut intellegatur alterum populum superiorem esse, non ut intellegatur alterum non esse liberum.'

⁴⁶ Dig. 49, 15, 19, 1 (Paul. 16 Sab.): 'Indutiae sunt, cum in breve et in praesens tempus convenit, ne invicem se lacessant.'

⁴⁷ Dig. 49, 15, 20 pr. (Pomp. 36 Sab.): 'Si captivus, de quo in pace cautum fuerat, ut rediret, sua voluntate apud hostes mansit, non est ei postea postliminium.' But cf. also Dig. 49, 15, 12 pr. (Tryph. 4 disp.): 'In bello postliminium est, in pace autem his, qui bello capti erant, de quibus nihil in pactis erat comprehensum.'

⁴⁸ Cf. Dig. 2, 14, 5 i.f. (Ulp. 4 ed.): 'publica conventio est, quae fit per pacem, quotiens inter se duces belli quaedam paciscuntur.'

In commenting on this last passage, Accursius (c. 1263) in his *Glossa ordinaria* gives a short summary of such conventions which belligerents might conclude: truces for a long time (*treugae*) or for a short time (*induciae*), treaties of friendship between equals or unequals (*foedera amicitiae aequalia, vel inaequalia*), mentioning also the possibility of tacit conventions.[49] Interesting is that Accursius in other glosses ranks the *treuga* amongst *foedera*:[50] he sees a difference between *treuga* and *indutiae*, limiting the latter to the Roman understanding of armistice or truce which does not create peace, while *treuga*, as a kind of *foedus*, acquires the character of a peace treaty limited in time. This obviously corresponds to the medieval practice and the use of *treuga* in the sphere of the Church.

Peace treaties and the learned *ius commune*

The first short monograph which we have on international treaties (including peace treaties) was written before the middle of the fifteenth century by a learned Italian jurist, Martinus Garatus, also called Laudensis (according to his birthplace Lodi), who had been professor of Roman law in Pavia, Siena, Bologna and Ferrara (c. 1453).[51] His 'Treatise on alliance, peace, and conventions of princes' (*Tractatus de confederatione, pace et conventionibus principum*)[52] was obviously satisfying practical interests, and far from academic curiosity. Twenty-four of the sixty-three questions (*quaestiones*) into which the treatise is divided are dedicated to peace (*pax*) and peace treaties, and five questions to the long-term truce (*treuga*).

The law sources referred to by Garatus belong to Roman as well as to canon law. The authors referred to are legists or canonists. But part of the 'Law of the Empire' referred to by Garatus consists of so-called extravagant constitutions of Emperor Frederick I, which had been incorporated into the medieval editions of the *Corpus iuris civilis*, namely the statute 'On peace to be kept between subjects and to be confirmed by oath' (*De pace tenenda inter subditos et iuramento firmanda*), inserted into the Books of

---

[49] Cf. Gl. *Paciscuntur* ad Dig. 2, 14, 5: 'ut treugas, quae sunt in longum tempus. Item inducias, quae sunt in breve' (Dig. 49, 15, 19, 1). 'Item foedera amicitiae aequalia, vel inaequalia' (Dig. 49, 15, 7). 'Et hoc in expressis. Tacite etiam pacisci videntur, eo quod legati hostium securi sunt, tacite eis securitate data per leges' (Dig. 50, 7, 18).

[50] Gl. *Lacessant* ad Dig. 49, 15, 19, 1: 'id est ad bellum provocent. Sed treugae in longum, et dicuntur foedera' (Dig. 49, 15, 7 and Dig. 49, 15, 24). Cf. also the Gl. *Foederati* ad Dig. 49, 15, 7: 'Foederati id est cum quibus fecimus treugas' (Dig. 49, 15, 19, 1).

[51] Ingrid Baumgärtner, *Martinus Garatus Laudensis: ein italienischer Rechtsgelehrter des 15. Jahrhunderts* (Cologne and Vienna, 1986).

[52] Text in *Tractatus universi iuris*, vol. XVI (Venice, 1584), fols. 302r–303r. See chapter 8 by Alain Wijffels, and the Appendix giving his edition of it.

Feudal law (*Libri feudorum*),[53] and the Peace of Constance concluded by the emperor in 1183 with the Lombardic City League mentioned above, which had become a separate *Liber de pace Constantiae*.[54] Amongst the papal constitutions, the decrete *Novit ille* of Innocent III (1204) mentioned above was of fundamental importance. Garatus concluded from it that the pope can force the princes to keep the peace which they have concluded, and the principle that peace is to be maintained even by enemies.[55] Therefore the crime of broken peace is to be persecuted by the Church.[56]

The much discussed *treuga* is constructed by Garatus (following Baldus) as a convention including the tacit agreement that, after its termination, the parties are again in a state of war (*guerra*).[57] So, the *treuga* has the character not of a definitive peace treaty, but more of a truce or armistice in the sense of the Roman *indutiae*. From canon law the principle is derived that a violation of the truce (*treuga*) by one party does not release the other party from its obligation until the *treuga* is terminated.[58] With Dig. 49, 15, 7 Garatus argues that an 'ally is called the people which has a *treuga* with another people or prince'.[59] He obviously follows the opinion of Accursius, who in the *Glossa ordinaria* had regarded the *treuga* as a kind of *foedus*. The remark that in the time of *treuga* merchants and peasants must be safe[60] again shows the close relation to the Roman *indutiae*, for the rule was developed by the Church for the time of feud or war.[61]

That a prince has to enforce peace between cities or subject states is derived by Garatus from a text in Justinian's *Digest*, which concerns the tasks of a provincial governor.[62] That Christian princes must strive for peace is proved by the peace treaties of the Emperor Justinian with the

---

[53] Cf. L.F. 2, 53.
[54] It had been commented with glosses by Odofredus (*c.* 1265) and Baldus de Ubaldis (1327–1400).
[55] Qu. 19 (Papa potest compellere Principes ad servandam pacem inter eos contractam ... et hostibus est pax servanda).
[56] Qu. 22 (Crimen fractae pacis inter Principes pertinet ad iudicium Ecclesiasticum).
[57] Qu. 9 (Principes invicem facientes treugam, vel confederationem tacite videntur inter eos agere, quod post treugam et confederationem finitam sint in guerra).
[58] Qu. 16 (In treugis est speciale, quod licet tu frangis fidem mihi, tamen non debeo tibi frangere, donec durat tempus treugae).
[59] Qu. 24 (Foederatus populus dicitur qui habet treugam cum alio populo vel Principe).
[60] Qu. 30 (Tempore treugae mercatores, et rustici debent esse securi).   [61] X. 1, 34, 2.
[62] Qu. 12 (Si dissensio sit inter duas civitates, Princeps debet eas compellere ad pacem). The *lex* referred to, Dig. 1, 18, 13, begins as follows: 'Congruit bono et gravi praesidi curare, ut pacata et quieta provincia sit quam regit.'

Persians and of Emperor Frederick I with the Lombardic cities.[63] From the latter treaty, it can also be argued that a peace treaty need not necessarily regulate the restitution of the party whose rights were violated.[64] The formal aspects of a peace treaty concern the rule confirmed with the statement of Justinian's *Codex* that an instrument has to close with the exact date of its perfection.[65] We can generally observe that the Roman law sources referred to very often have no direct connection with international questions. If two princes only agreed upon concluding a peace treaty, there is no perfect reconciliation, and as an argument Garatus refers to a Roman text concerning a case from the Roman law of divorce and dowry.[66] If the peace treaty states that there can be no peace without the adherents, they are included in the peace provisions, and this is substantiated by a text from Justinian's *Digest*, where building material belonging to a tomb shares its sanctity.[67]

Garatus mentions a legal rule of great practical importance with reference to the *Speculator* of Gulielmus Durantis. For peace negotiations a special mandate is required for the negotiators who act as procurators for their prince.[68] If we consider the *Speculum iudiciale* of Durantis, we read that such a mandate must also be expressly mentioned in the peace instrument.[69] And this rule was still observed in European peace treaties in the seventeenth century.[70]

---

[63] Qu. 37 (Principes debent diligere pacem: nam Imperator Iustinianus habuit pacem cum Persis ... et Federicus cum Lombardis pacem).

[64] Qu. 38 (Quando pax fit inter Principes, non habet locum regula, quod spoliatus ante omnia sit restituendus, si spolians habet bona iura in proprietate).

[65] Qu. 50 (Inspicitur finalis punctus pacis in ponendis hora et die in instrumento). The *lex* referred to is Cod. 4, 21, 17.

[66] Qu. 29 (Reconciliatio inter duos Principes habentes guerram non dicitur perfecte facta, licet invicem paciscantur de faciendo pacem). The text referred to is Dig. 24, 3, 38.

[67] Qu. 35 (Si paciscentur non potest esse pax sine adhaerentibus, verba pacis extenduntur ad adhaerentes). The *lex* referred to is Dig. 6, 1, 43, beginning as follows: 'Quae religiosis adhaerent, religiosa sunt et idcirco nec lapides inaedificati postquam remoti sunt vindicari possunt.'

[68] Qu. 59 (In pace fienda requiritur speciale mandatum. Spe. in tit. de treuga et pace. '1. ver.hoc.quoque. not. quod princeps mittit procuratorem pro capitula pacis).

[69] *Speculum* Lib. 4 particula I *De treuga et pace Rubrica*, at no. 4: 'Hoc quoque nota quod si haec fiant per procuratores, debent ad hoc speciale mandatum habere: de quo etiam in pacis instrumento fiat mentio specialis.'

[70] The best example is given by the Peace Treaties of Münster and Osnabrück of 24 October 1648. In the preambles it is expressly mentioned: 'mutuasque plenipotentiarum tabulas (quarum apographa sub finem huius instrumenti de verbo ad verbum inserta sunt) rite commutatas'.

The influence of classical Roman law on medieval peace treaties

When we study the medieval peace treaties in detail, we hardly discover any notable influence of Roman international law. If we ascertain traces of Roman law, they mostly concern Roman private law or procedure, seldom public law. This transfer from Roman private law to treaty law was recently studied in a comprehensive way by Christian Baldus.[71]

The influence of medieval Roman law can be observed in the construction that an ambassador acting politically for his prince or state is regarded as *procurator*,[72] who must present duly formulated letters demonstrating his authority – the *mandatum speciale*, as Durantis calls it, which must also be mentioned in the peace instrument. So, in the Peace Treaty concluded in 1325 between King Charles IV of France (1322–28) and King Edward II of England (1307–27), the authorisations by the two monarchs are quoted literally, showing that the 'true and legitimate procurators and special envoys' ('veri et legitimi procuratores ac nuntii speciales') had 'general, full and free power and a special mandate' ('generalis, plena et libera potestas ac speciale mandatum') for their negotiations and for reaching an agreement.[73] In a long list, all the necessary and possible activities are enumerated which can lead to the desired 'complete peace and amity' ('ad plenam pacem et concordiam').[74] The sealed instruments also included the promises of the kings to ratify the treaty concluded by their procurators.[75]

Another visible trace of Roman law is the frequent appeal to 'good faith' (*bona fides*) in peace treaties. Already the Peace of Constance of

---

[71] Christian Baldus, *Regelhafte Vertragsauslegung nach Parteirollen im klassischen römischen Recht und in der modernen Völkerrechtswissenschaft* (Frankfurt a. M., Berlin and Berne, etc., 1998).

[72] Donald E. Queller, *The Office of Ambassador in the Middle Ages* (Princeton, NJ, 1967), pp. 26–59.

[73] Arts. 11–12.

[74] Art. 11: 'Ac tractatum huiusmodi quacumque firmitate vallandi, petendi, stipulandi, recipiendi, retinendi, paciscendi, componendi, transigendi, concordandi et conveniendi ac in certos diem et locum, quibus nos et praefatus Rex Angliae personaliter conveniamus, si expedire viderint, consentiendi, ac eosdem diem et locum nostro nomine acceptandi, et treugas seu sufferentiam vallandi, firmandi, ac etiam roborandi; diem et treugas seu sufferentiam huiusmodi, semel et pluries, quoties expedire videbitur, prorogandi; ac omnia et singula faciendi, quae sunt pacis et concordiae, et ad plenam pacem et concordiam valent pertinere.' Art. 12 with the *mandatum* of the king of England differs only slightly.

[75] Art. 11: 'Ac promittentes pro nobis successoribusque nostris ratum et firmum habere et habituros, quicquid per dictos Consiliarios et Procuratores nostros ... gestum, actum et factum seu etiam procuratum fuit in praemissis et quolibet praemissorum.' Art. 12 differs slightly.

1183, concluded between Emperor Frederick I and the Lombardic City League mentioned above, was understood by both parties to be made in 'good faith' (*bona fide*).[76] And the Peace which Count Balduin of Flanders in 1199 made with his liege King Philip II of France was promised 'in good faith and without bad intention' ('bona fide et sine malo ingenio').[77] In the French–English Peace Treaty of 1325 mentioned above, the negotiators declared for themselves and for their sovereigns that all obligations would be fulfilled 'in good faith' ('en bonne foy').[78] In a peace treaty of 1374, between Wenceslas of Bohemia (Roman-German king 1378–1419) as duke of Brabant and Albert, duke of Bavaria, as count of Holland, the promises are given 'in good faith' ('en bonne foy'), too.[79] In his Peace Treaty with the Teutonic Order of 1435, King Ladislas III of Poland gives his promise 'in good faith, carefully and faithfully upon Our Royal word, without treachery or fraud' ('promittimus bona fide, attente et fideliter in verbo nostro Regio absque dolo et fraude'). And still in 1493, in the Spanish–French Peace Treaty of Barcelona the Spanish monarchs promised to carry out the clauses 'in good faith and with Royal word' ('bona fide et in verbo Regio'). That in the fifteenth century it became less frequent to invoke 'good faith' in peace treaties may be due to the fact that in the doctrine every promise a prince gives in a treaty is regarded as being ruled by the principle of *bona fides*: Garatus,[80] following Baldus, writes 'that all contracts, which are made with a prince, are made under the rule of good faith' ('omnis contractus, qui fit cum Principe, habet naturam contractus bonae fidei').

Looking into the various clauses to be found in medieval peace treaties, we find many details which are stylised in a very professional manner, according to patterns of Roman common law,[81] as it was studied in the

---

[76] 'Hanc igitur pacem . . . bona fide intelleximus . . . Lombardi eam bona fide intellexerunt.'
[77] 'Hanc pacem concessi tenendam bona fide et sine malo ingenio, et partem meorum hominum feci iurare, et partem iurare faciam, pacem tenendam Domino Regi, bona fide et sine malo ingenio.'
[78] Art. 10: 'nous devant dits Conseillers, Messagers et Procureurs des devant dits Roys de France et d'Angleterre avons promis en bonne foy, au nom de nos dits Seigneurs et pour eux, à tenir, garder et accomplir de poinct en poinct en bonne foy'.
[79] 'Lesquels points, conditions et accord, nous Duc et Duchesse susdits avons promis et promettons en bonne foy de tenir l'un l'autre pour ferme et inviolable.'
[80] The following quotation in Qu. 36.
[81] An early example of the use of Roman technical legal terms is furnished by the Peace Treaty (*pax et concordia*) which Count Balduin of Flanders concluded with Count Theobald of Bar and Luxemburg in 1199, where the instruments signed and sealed are described in the following way: 'scripto chyrographizato eas (scil. *conventiones*) commendari fecimus et sigillarum nostrorum appensionibus et testium subscriptionibus corroborari'. The

law schools of Italy and Western Europe. Such technical references are easily explainable in affairs such as payment of money (for whatever reason), transferring or ceding territory, restitution of property, release of prisoners, etc.

A last example of the practice of medieval notaries introducing a clause from Roman private law into international law will illustrate our observations. In the French–English Peace Treaty of 1325, both kings declared in their *mandatum* for their negotiators (inserted into the text of the treaty, as mentioned above) that for their promise to ratify the treaty for themselves and their heirs they forfeited or pledged all their possessions ('bona nostra omnia obligamus').[82] We can still observe pledge as a security for duties regulated in a peace treaty in the seventeenth century.[83]

Conclusion

The influence of medieval Roman law on peace treaties was rather limited if we consider most of the material provisions. On the other hand, this influence should not be underestimated. In the centuries before the new legal science evolved in the law school of Bologna (beginning about 1100), a considerable Roman law tradition had been preserved by the Latin Church. But since the age of the glossators of Roman law, the whole legal sphere of Latin Europe had been penetrated by Roman law, not in the sense of ancient law replacing or suppressing national or regional law, but as a process of a general rising of the scholarly standard, using a common law formed by Roman and Canon law (the *ius utrumque*).[84] In that sense, we share the critical remark which Hugo Grotius (1583–1645) made in the seventeenth century, namely that the medieval jurists 'wanted to decide all

---

terms *chirographum* and *chirographarius* were well known to learned jurists (cf. only the *chirographaria instrumenta* in Justinian's Constitution Cod. 4, 2, 17).

[82] Art. 11: 'Supra quibus approbandis, tenendis, servandis, faciendis et complendis, nos et successores nostros, bonaque nostra omnia obligamus.' In Art. 12 the same formula is used; only the English king speaks of 'nos et haeredes nostros'.

[83] In the 1648 Peace Treaty of Osnabrück, the German princes and states that were to pay a compensation to Sweden forfeited all their possessions as security; cf. IPO art. XVI para. 12: 'singuli septem dictorum circulorum electores, principes et status vigore huius conventionis se ad suam quisque quotam condicto tempore locoque bona fide solvendum sponte idque sub hypotheca omnium suorum bonorum obligant'.

[84] For the history of private law, this is a common opinion. For public law, cf. M. P. Gilmore, *Argument from Roman Law in Political Thought 1200–1600* (Cambridge, Mass., 1941); for international law, see Ziegler, 'Römische Grundlagen'.

disputes between kings and peoples with Roman law, adding sometimes rules of canon law'.[85]

The influence of Roman international law became stronger and more apparent sensible after the age of humanism. So, also for our theme we can end with Arthur Nussbaum's formulation written half a century ago: 'Roman law ... was an indispensable tool in the early development of a doctrine of international law.'[86]

---

[85] Hugo Grotius, *De iure belli ac Pacis libri tres* (Paris, 1625), Prol. 54: 'omnes regum populorumque controversias definire voluit ex legibus Romanis, assumtis interdum canonibus'.
[86] Arthur Nussbaum, 'The Significance of Roman Law in the History of International Law', *University of Pennsylvania Law Review* 100 (1952), 678–887 at p. 687.

7

The kiss of peace

HANNA VOLLRATH

> We advance our understanding of differences by seeking what is universal; and the attempt to find generalising language in terms of which to compare things as to their resemblances as well as their differences leads us back again to a recognition of universals or part-universals.[1]

Introduction

When today's media report the conclusion of a peace treaty, they invariably have their story accompanied by a ritualised scene: two or more dignitaries – usually middle-aged men – brandish their fountainpens (never ballpoints) and put what our legal experience tells us are their names to parallel arranged papers, after which younger men emerge from behind to assiduously blot the wet ink; then the older men get up and shake hands. The news factor cannot be high, as it is a standardised scene, at least in the Western world. The relevant information, the conditions that have been agreed upon for the peace to begin and to last, lies buried in a document with a multitude of paragraphs, of which the general public will only want to know those points which have been most controversial. Basically, the standardised scene conveys the very essence of what the elaborate document contains: that peace will begin, that the period of conflict has ended. The transition from one status to another is encapsulated in the scene, enacted for the public to look at and to be witness to.

Modern experience shows that the document and the staging of a scenic demonstration complement each other.[2] Because, in the earlier Middle Ages, most peace treaties were concluded without a written document,

---

[1] Robert Redfield, *The Primitive World and Its Transformation* (Ithaca, NY, 1963), p. 96.
[2] For the importance and the frequency of gestures in the modern world notwithstanding the prevalence of written communication, see Jean-Claude Schmitt, 'The Rationale of Gestures in the West: Third to Thirteenth Centuries' in Jan Bremmer and Herman Roodenburg (eds.), *A Cultural History of Gesture* (Cambridge, 1991), pp. 59–70; Jean-Claude Schmitt, *La raison des gestes dans l'Occident médiéval* (Paris, 1990).

there was no text to put names to.³ Other gestures were employed instead to validate the pact: oaths were sworn, hostages exchanged or sureties given,⁴ and very often the whole procedure was rounded up by a kiss of peace – *osculum pacis* – which could be supplemented or replaced by other gestures.

From the twelfth century onwards, university-trained legal experts began to reshape traditional legal practices into professional legal systems; part of this process was the splitting up of the entirety of earlier modes of action into definable elements and the establishment of their respective functions within the whole. It eventually became accepted that it was the signatures of the heads of state involved or proxies that validate a peace treaty; the act of signing may or may not be accompanied by gestures that signify peaceful relations such as the shaking of hands, but it is the signatures that are legally decisive and thus leave to the gestures the role of a merely ceremonial accompaniment.⁵ Is this changing today? When the American President George W. Bush made it known recently that he felt a handshake of himself and the Russian President Putin would suffice to seal a nuclear disarmament agreement, there was irritated rumour in the American Senate and Senator Robert Byrd declared himself shocked by the thought of an agreement without a written text. The German daily

---

³ For the emergence of written instruments of peace and their relation to corporeal gestures see Claudia Garnier, 'Zeichen und Schrift. Symbolische Handlungen und literale Fixierung am Beispiel von Friedensschlüssen des 13. Jahrhunderts', *Frühmittelalterliche Studien* 32 (1998), 263–87.

⁴ Wendy Davies, 'People and Places in Dispute in Ninth-Century Brittany' in Wendy Davies and Paul Fouracre (eds.), *The Settlement of Disputes in Early Medieval Europe* (Cambridge, 1986), pp. 65–84; Nicolas Offenstadt, 'Interaction et régulation des conflits. Les gestes de l'arbitrage et de la conciliation au moyen âge (XIIe–XVe siècles)' in Claude Gauvard and Robert Jacob (eds.), *Les Rites de la justice: gestes et rituels judiciaires au moyen âge occidental* (Paris, 2000), pp. 201–28.

⁵ 'Peace treaties' in modern state-structured societies will be international treaties regulated by international law. It is in the treaties between states that validation usually rests in the signatures of the heads of states or their especially authorised representatives, although more elaborate modes can be chosen, particularly when there are more than two parties involved; see Knut Ipsen, *Völkerrecht* (4th edn, Munich, 1999), pp. 103–14 on the Vienna Convention on the Law of Treaties of 23 May 1969, where this is laid down as a rule; for the still existing possibility of oral validation of international treaties, see Nguyen Quoc Dinh, Patrick Dailliers and Alain Pellet, *Droit international public* (6th edn, Paris, 1999), p. 120. By referring to the Vienna Convention the authors make it quite clear that, as a rule, an international treaty will be 'un accord conclut par écrit'. But while praising this convention for having combined customary definitions with formal elements, they do not completely delegitimise oral treaties: 'La convention définit le traité comme un accord conclu par écrit. Sans doute, son article 3 implique qu'elle n'ignore pas les accords qui n'ont pas été conclus par écrit – les accords verbaux – et qu'elle ne leur denie pas toute valeur juridique.'

newspaper *Frankfurter Allgemeine Zeitung* made it clear: 'Ein Handschlag genügt nicht.'[6] In the Middle Ages more often than not it was not a handshake, but a kiss – a kiss of peace.

Body language

What role did the kiss of peace play before signed written treaties came to dominate political peacemaking? It stands to reason that kisses or the swearing of oaths and the giving or exchanging of hostages or sureties are fundamentally different means employed to make a treaty stand. Hostages or sureties are given to inflict tangible material losses on the side that breaks a treaty, whereas oaths make God a party to it: they are sworn by touching sacred objects such as the Bible or a case of relics and by delivering oneself to God's damnation should one fail to fulfil what has been agreed upon.[7] What meaning did the kiss of peace convey? Was it just as binding as an oath? Could it be replaced by other gestures? Apparently the kiss of peace stood for the promise to keep the peace. Did people expect or demand sanctions if somebody did not act peacefully after having given the kiss of peace?

Our medieval historiographic sources tend to take notice of those treaties that were remarkable events belonging to the sphere of big politics, and many modern historians seem to follow suit. Ceremonies on such occasions are treated under the heading of 'ritual' or 'symbolic communication'.[8] It has its risks, however, when historians look exclusively at great men making history without taking into account that political rituals[9] are

---

[6] 17 November 2001. In private agreements regulated by civil law, a handshake or, in fact, a kiss would do if the parties concerned agreed to have it that way, as many other gestures or modes of ratification would do. For the stipulation in German civil law according to the *Bürgerliches Gezetsbuch*, see Dieter Medicus, *Allgemeiner Teil des BGB* (7th edn, Heidelberg, 1997), pp. 119–29.

[7] Paolo Prodi, *Das Sakrament der Herrschaft: der politische Eid in der Verfassungsgeschichte des Okzidents* (Berlin, 1997); Paolo Prodi (ed.), *Glaube und Eid: Treueformeln, Glaubensbekenntnisse und Sozialdisziplinierung zwischen Mittelalter und Neuzeit* (Munich, 1993).

[8] Gerd Althoff, *Spielregeln der Politik im Mittelalter* (Darmstadt, 1997); Althoff, 'Zur Bedeutung symbolischer Kommunikation für das Verständnis des Mittelalters', *Frühmittelalterliche Studien* 31 (1997), 370–89; Althoff, 'Das Privileg der "Deditio". Formen gütlicher Konfliktbeendigung in der mittelalterlichen Adelsgesellschaft' in Otto Gerhard Oexle and Werner Paravicini (eds.), *Nobilitas: Funktion und Repräsentation des Adels in Alteuropa* (Göttingen, 1997), pp. 27–52; Gerd Althoff (ed.), *Formen und Funktionen öffentlicher Kommunikation im Mittelalter* (Vorträge und Forschungen 51, Stuttgart, 2001).

[9] For the very problematic term of 'political rituals' see Philippe Buc, 'Political Rituals and Political Imagination in the Medieval West from the Fourth Century to the Eleventh' in Peter Linehan and Janet Nelson (eds.), *The Medieval World* (London and New York, 2000), pp. 189–213.

embedded in and form part of a cultural code shared by the whole society or by a community within a society. As patterned behaviour,[10] they are made up of components, of words and gestures[11] that belong to ordinary language[12] which members of a particular community use in all kinds of situations.[13]

Up to the present day, spoken language is accompanied by body language. It can be assumed that medieval people were more at the mercy of their bodies, that they were more aware of their bodies and therefore more used to express themselves with their bodies than we are today. If we see symbols as means to give a concrete form to an abstract reality,[14] we may assume that this mode of communication particularly fitted people in the earlier Middle Ages who found orientation in their world without taking recourse to abstract definitions. They rarely employed concepts to give order to their experiences but rather looked for 'meaning' behind the obvious. Body language is symbolic in itself: as soon as the

---

[10] Geoffrey Koziol, *Begging Pardon and Favor: Ritual and Political Order in Early Medieval France* (Ithaca, NY and London, 1992), p. 294.

[11] Jean-Marie Moeglin defines ritual as 'une séquence ordonnée de gestes et de rites' in 'Pénitence publique et amende honorable au moyen âge', *Revue Historique* 298 (1977), 225–69 at p. 226; Keith Thomas discusses gesture as part of culturally determined bodily comportment in his Introduction to Jan Bremmer and Herman Roodenburg (eds.), *A Cultural History of Gestures* (Oxford, 1993), pp. 1–14; Gerd Althoff speaks of rituals, 'wenn Handlungen komplexerer Natur, besser Ketten von Handlungen, von Akteuren in bestimmten Situationen in immer der gleichen oder zumindest sehr ähnlicher Weise wiederholt werden' in 'Die Veränderbarkeit von Ritualen im Mittelalter' in Althoff, *Formen und Funktionen*, pp. 157–76 at p. 157.

[12] Timothy Reuter defines rituals as a meta-language: 'Die Metasprache bestand aus Elementen natürlicher Sprache (geschrieben und gesprochen) aus bildlichen Darstellungen, aus Inszenierungen in der Form von "Drehbüchern" für Szenen und Handlungssequenzen und von "Requisiten": symbolisch beladenen Objekten und Orten', in ' "Velle sibi fieri in forma hac". Symbolisches Handeln im Becketstreit' in Althoff, *Formen und Funktionen*, pp. 201–25 at p. 203. I think it is misleading to distinguish 'natural' language from rituals as 'unnatural' language, i.e. deliberately invented means of communication. It is indicative of this 'Althoffian' approach that Reuter limits 'language' to 'written and spoken' communication without mentioning body language such as gestures.

[13] Here I differ from Gerd Althoff, presently the leading German expert on rituals, who maintains that rituals were a privilege of the nobility; cf. his *Spielregeln* and the criticism of Jean-Marie Moeglin, 'Rituels et Verfassungsgeschichte. A propos du livre de Gerd Althoff "Spielregeln der Politik im Mittelalter" ', *Francia* 10 (1998), 245–50; see also Theodor Bühler, 'Wenn das Recht ohne Schrift auskommen muß' in Louis Carlen (ed.), *Forschungen zur Rechtsarchäologie und zur rechtlichen Volkskunde* (Zurich, 1982), vol. IV, pp. 79–97, who maintains at p. 97: 'Ein großer Teil der Rituale ist nichts anderes als die formalisierte Reaktion auf eine jeweils gegebene Situation. Es ist in dieser Hinsicht unrichtig, sie als "Erfindung" einer Elite zu qualifizieren.'

[14] Jacques Le Goff, 'Le rituel symbolique de la vassalité', reprinted in Jacques Le Goff, *Pour un autre moyen âge* (Paris, 1977), pp. 249–420 at p. 352.

movements of the body are used as modes of communication, they are perceived as 'meaning' something, and what we call symbol as in symbolic communication is mostly rendered by the word *signum* = sign, because it signifies something beyond the perception of the gesture. To speak of body language means to ascribe the same faculties to bodily gestures as to spoken language, namely the faculty to convey or exchange messages, to be used as arguments, but also to misguide, to lie and to cover up intentions. In the twelfth century, intellectuals theorised about the fact that visible and audible expressions could differ considerably from what they were supposed to demonstrate. Eloise's self-accusation of being torn by sexual desire for her husband Peter Abelard (1079–1142), while appearing to be a pious abbess sunk in prayer before the high altar, will forever stand as the most moving tribute paid to this understanding.[15]

Abelard built his tract on ethics upon the difference between the inner disposition and the visible act and concluded that sin cannot be detected by looking at a person's outward appearance.[16] Medieval people knew very well that a *gestus corporis* was not necessarily a *signum mentis* even before theorists like Abelard conceptualised it. All plays or stage productions, be they ever so ecclesiastical, presuppose the difference between being and seeming, as do carnival masquerades.[17]

---

[15] 'The Personal Letters between Abelard and Heloise' (ed. T. S. Muckle), *Medieval Studies* 15 (1953), 47–94, especially Letter no. 3 at pp. 77–82.

[16] Petrus Abaelardus, *Ethica* (ed. David E. Luscombe, Oxford, 1971). Here Abelard expressed what was commonly accepted in the schools of the twelfth century; cf. Kurt Flasch, *Das philosophische Denken im Mittelalter* (Stuttgart, 1986), pp. 211–25.

[17] Klaus Schreiner tries to explain the importance of rituals and gestures in the Middle Ages by referring to medieval anthropology: 'Im Mittelalter besaßen Rituale, Gesten und Gebärden nur deshalb [*sic*] den Charakter von über sich hinausweisenden Handlungen, weil – im Lichte mittelalterlicher Anthropologie betrachtet – zwischen "actus animi" und "actus corporis", zwischen "homo interior" und "homo exterior" ein wechselseitiger Zusammenhang bestand. Aus der Einheit von Leib und Seele bedingte sich nach Auffassung mittelalterlicher Theologen, Philosophen und Moralisten die Möglichkeit . . . in der Haltung des Körpers ("gestus corporis") ein Zeichen innerer Gesinnung ("signum mentis") zu erblicken'; in '"Gerechtigkeit und Frieden haben sich geküßt" (Ps. 81, 11). Friedensstiftung durch symbolisches Handeln' in Johannes Fried (ed.), *Träger und Instrumentarien des Friedens im hohen und späten Mittelalter* (Sigmaringen, 1996), pp. 37–86 at p. 39. I find this explanation unacceptable. The importance of a feature as universal as gestures cannot be explained by intellectual constructs. Medieval people were much too shrewd to develop social practices out of intellectual assumptions, even though modern intellectuals like to think so. I do not mean to argue that there were no mutual influences of religion-based theorising and social practices; I think there were, as will become apparent a little later. I argue against the assumption that the meaningfulness of gestures was developed out of theological theorising.

I want to suggest that kisses should be understood as part of a highly developed body language. It was probably related to the as yet restricted use of literacy. It is only when spoken texts are transformed into written texts that the meaning, the message is exclusively conveyed by words and sentences. It is only the written text that completely dissociates what is being expressed by words from its physical presentation. A person who speaks will always support the meaning of his/her sentences by gestures, facial expressions, voice modulations and variations of speed. But modern people are so used to perceiving by reading and writing that the significance of body language has been greatly reduced. I want to suggest that the kisses of the Middle Ages were part of that very strong body language which our written sources but rarely carry. Both language consisting of words and body language can develop more or less fixed formulas and *topoi*.

Roman traditions and medieval practices

Roman grammarians distinguished three types of kisses: *oscula*, *basia* and *savia*; *osculum* was the term most frequently used. Although *basium* and *savium* can be further distinguished and *osculum* was in practice used for all kinds of kisses, *osculum* was certainly used with preference for kisses given and received in public as a strictly regulated social practice, whereas *basium* and *savium* referred to affectionate and erotic kissing.[18] *Osculum*-type kisses were subject to legal regulation: the *ius osculi* stipulated that blood relations up to the sixth degree and closely allied friends of a Roman lady could and even had to kiss her on the mouth every time they met her.[19] In the Roman world kisses had juridical implications in other situations too. In 336 the Roman emperor Constantine had it laid down as a law, that a bride whose fiancé had died before their marriage was only entitled to half her marriage portion if she had been kissed by her husband-to-be, a legal custom that remained valid right into modern times.[20] By the

---

[18] Philippe Moreau, 'Osculum, basium, savium', *Revue de Philologie* 3rd series 52 (1978), 87–97; Peter Flury, 'Osculum und osculari, Beobachtungen zum Vokabular des Kusses im Lateinischen' in Sigrid Krämer and Michael Bernhard (eds.), *Scire Literas: Forschungen zum mittelalterlichen Geistesleben* (Munich, 1988), pp. 149–57.

[19] Moreau, 'Osculum', p. 94.

[20] Hans-Wolfgang Strätz, *Der Verlobungskuß und seine Folgen rechtsgeschichtlich besehen* (Constance, 1979), p. 10; Hans-Wolfgang Strätz, 'Der Kuß im Recht' in Gisela Völger and Karin von Welck (eds.), *Die Braut. Geliebt, verkauft, getauscht, geraubt: Zur Rolle der Frau im Kulturvergleich* (Ausstellungskatalog, Cologne, 1985), vol. I, pp. 286–93 at p. 292; Hans Wieling, 'Kuß, Verlobung und Geschenk' in Hans-Georg Knothe and Jürgen Kohler (eds.), *Status familiae: Festschrift für Andreas Wacke zum 65. Geburtstag* (Munich, 2001), pp. 541–57.

kiss the bride had been received into the family and had become a part of it.

A fourth-century episode should be understood against this background. When Gregory of Nazianzus set out to demonstrate how saintly was the behaviour of his newly converted mother Nonna, he said that she refused to greet heathens with a kiss even if they were relatives.[21] Nonna's kissing habits sound very Christian, indeed. However, she was merely adapting pre-Christian Roman customs to her particular Christian needs. Nonna was demonstrating that the community into which she had been received by her conversion precluded the community with heathens and was more important to her than her belonging to her family.

In Roman society, kisses were not reserved for relatives. People were received with a kiss when entering a *collegium*, a college or fraternity. The kiss was a sign that one belonged, that one had become a member-brother.[22] Upon manumission, former slaves were kissed by all those present. Again, it was a kiss of reception, of receiving the former slave into the community of free Romans. It is against this background that the baptismal kiss is to be understood. Through baptism a human being was freed from Adam's chains and was made a member of the community of the brethren in Christ.

All family groups, fraternities and communities shared the notion that to be a member meant to live in peace with each other and to live in union with one's fellow-members. The kiss was the symbol thereof. This is what the Apostle Paul expressed when he demanded of his fellow Christians in Rome: 'Thou shalt greet each other with a holy kiss.'[23] It was a 'holy kiss', because Christians believed their community to be founded by Jesus Christ himself; their community was a spiritual, holy union, and therefore the kiss was spiritual and holy too.

To belong to a community included the obligation to live in peace with one's fellow members. The kiss was, therefore, quite naturally seen as a sign of peace. For Christians the teaching of Jesus Christ and biblical tradition had endowed the word peace with a spiritual meaning, signifying much

---

[21] Franz Josef Dölger, 'Nonna. Ein Kapitel über christliche Volksfrömmigkeit des vierten Jahrhunderts, 3: Verweigerung von Kuß, Händedruck und Salzgemeinschaft aus Gewissensbedenken' in Franz Josef Dölger, *Antike und Christentum* (Münster, 1936), vol. V, pp. 51–9.

[22] Franz Josef Dölger, 'Der Kuß im Tauf- und Firmungsritual nach Cyprian von Karthago und Hippolyt von Rom' in Franz Josef Dölger, *Antike und Christentum* (Münster, 1929), vol. I, pp. 186–96 at pp. 193–6.

[23] Romans 16, 16.

more than the absence of strife. Peace was a spiritual gift by Christ to those who belonged to Him for them to share. The *osculum pacis* charged pre-Christian social practices with Christian symbolism.

Kisses also demonstrated rank. A kiss on the mouth denoted equality; to kiss the lowest part, the feet, signalled submission.[24] Kisses on parts of the body between the mouth and the feet such as elbows, hands and knees constituted a hierarchy of kissing.

People, so it seems, kissed on a great many different occasions in the 'kissing-eager Middle Ages'.[25] It depended on the context, which aspects of the kissing tradition came to the fore. In more theoretical tracts of Christian instruction, Christian symbolism was paramount, of course. The beginning of St Bernard's (c. 1090–1153) first sermon on the Song of Songs is a good example. Solomon's Song of Songs begins with the well-known phrase: 'He shall kiss me with the kiss of his mouth' ('osculetur me osculo oris sui'). In his sermon Bernard states that this sentence, lacking an introduction, can only be understood in connection with the title – *Cantica canticorum Salomonis*. 'As Solomon is the name of "The peaceful", the beginning of the book appropriately starts with the sign of peace, a kiss.'[26] Bernard's English contemporary and fellow Cistercian Aelred of Rievaulx is more detailed in his explanation. He distinguishes between corporeal, spiritual and intellectual kisses. This is what he has to say about corporeal kisses:

> The corporeal kiss is given by the impression of the lips. It should only be offered and received for good and honest reasons. It is a sign of reconciliation when people become friends who have been enemies, it is a sign of peace: just as holy communion in church signifies inner peace, so the kiss

---

[24] A. Alföldi, Art. 'Fußkuß' in *Lexikon des Mittelalters* (Munich, 1989), vol. IV, cols. 1063–1165.

[25] Willem Frijhoff, 'The Kiss Sacred and Profane. Reflections on a Cross-Cultural Confrontation' in Bremmer and Roodenburg, *Cultural History of Gesture*, pp. 210–36 at p. 213; for a comprehensive treatment of medieval kissing practices, cf. Yannick Carré, *Le baiser sur la bouche au moyen âge: rites, symboles, mentalités à travers les textes et les images, XIe–XVe siècle* (Paris, 1992); this book supersedes the older work by N. J. Perella, *The Kiss Sacred and Profane* (Berkeley and Los Angeles, 1969).

[26] 'Titulum talis est: Incipiunt Cantica Canticorum Salomonis. Observa in primis Pacifici nomen, quod est Salomon, convenire principio libri qui incipit a signo pacis, id est ab osculo' in Bernhard von Clairvaux, *Sämtliche Werke* (ed. B. Winkler, Inssbruck, 1992), vol. V, p. 58; see also Klaus Schreiner, '"Er küsse mich mit dem Kuß seines Mundes" (osculetur me osculo oris sui, Cant. 1,1). Metaphorik, kommunikative und herrschaftliche Funktionen einer symbolischen Handlung' in Hella Ragotzky and Horst Wenzel (eds.), *Höfische Repräsentation: das Zeremoniell und die Zeichen* (Tübingen, 1990), pp. 89–132.

stands for outer peace; as a sign of love it is permitted between husband and wife just as it is offered to and received from friends after prolonged absences; it is a sign of catholic unity, when it is offered upon the arrival of a guest.

All these significations, he continues, belong to the kiss according to natural law. But just as other naturally good things can be perverted, so can the kiss. 'When it is joined to licentiousness to kiss is nothing else than adultery.'[27]

What the learned abbot explains theoretically is spelt out in practice on many occasions. Contracts seem to have been confirmed by kisses as a matter of course. When in 1108 a lay lord made a donation to the bishop of Grenoble, he promised to respect his gift 'by an oath delivered into the hands of the bishop and by a kiss with the promise of good faith'.[28] In this particular case there were only two men kissing each other. Often, however, a donation entailed a great number of kisses. When the abbot of Solignac and his monks gave their possessory rights of a church to a prior, the abbot was the first one to kiss the prior and then all the monks present kissed him one after the other.[29] The kiss confirming a gift was exchanged not only by monks or ecclesiastics but also by laymen. There were kisses of confirmation between a count and several knights,[30] but as ecclesiastics were more used to putting transactions into writing, we hear of kisses being exchanged between them far more often than of those kisses between laymen.

Donations as well as renunciations of possessory rights seem to have been sealed by kisses as a matter of course, and Klaus Schreiner maintains: 'Beim Abschluß privater und öffentlicher Verträge erfüllte der Kuß die Funktion eines rechtskonstitutiven Sinnzeichens, das die Geltungskraft und Einklagbarkeit vertraglicher Abmachungen verbürgen sollte.'[31] But kisses were exchanged on many other occasions as well. People greeted each other or welcomed somebody with a kiss. When William the

---

[27] Aelredi Rievallensis, 'De spirituali amicitia' in A. Hoste and C. H. Talbot (eds.), *Aelredi Rievallensis Opera omnia* (Corpus Christianorum Continuatio Medievalis, Turnhout, 1971), p. 307.

[28] Emile Chénon, 'Le rôle juridique de l'osculum dans l'ancien droit français', *Mémoire de la Société Nationale des Antiquaires de France* 82 sér. 6, 76 (1924), 124–55 at p. 126.

[29] Chénon, 'Le rôle', p. 128.   [30] Chénon, 'Le rôle', p. 130.

[31] Schreiner, 'Er küsse mich', p. 90. 'At the conclusion of private on public contracts, the kiss as a symbol held a constitutional value and provided the contractual stipulations with binding force and enforceability' (author's translation).

Conqueror (1066–87) came to London in 1068, 'he invited everybody to his kiss and showed them great affability'.[32]

It is well known that kisses were an essential part of establishing feudal ties. In twelfth-century France a formula developed, 'homme de bouche et de main', meaning a man who had performed the rite of vassalage and had exchanged a kiss with his lord.[33] To become a lord's man of mouth meant, of course, that lord and vassal had exchanged a kiss on the mouth, whereas the second component, man of hand, denoted that the man had put his folded hands into the lord's hand on bended knees, thereby performing the rite of homage.[34] The combination of these two elements made visible the concept of equality in submission; the kiss on the mouth stood for equality and was mostly the sign accompanying the mutual promise of fidelity (*fides*).[35] By the sixteenth century, mutual kisses on the mouth by strangers were considered indecent, and *homme de bouche* began to be understood as a man who had *spoken* the relevant formulas by word of mouth.[36] Sometimes the feudal kiss was specified as a 'kiss of good faith' or 'kiss of faith and peace'. The kiss was so much an element of the feudal rite that a German medieval law book stipulated that *ein ungekussed Lehen* was legally not valid.[37]

To kiss was the normal way of greeting people. It seems to have been such a regular part of the greeting ceremony that its mention could be packed off into subordinate clauses. When the archbishop-elect of York, Thurstan, was called by Pope Callistus II (1119–24) to meet him in Reims, Thurstan came with several other clerics: 'After having received them all with a kiss, the pope said . . .'.[38] In many texts it is said that people greeted each other with the kiss of peace (*osculum pacis*) or took leave with it. There is an interesting example for this in a twelfth-century letter: an unidentified clerk of the church of Freising tried to defend himself against accusations of having spread vicious slander about his bishop. He begins his letter to the bishop with the following sentences: 'O how gold is obscured and the best of colours changed. Having been dismissed with the kiss of peace I left you convinced that I enjoyed the full security

---

[32] Carré, *Le baiser*, p. 105.   [33] Carré, *Le baiser*, p. 26.
[34] Le Goff, 'Le rite symbolique', pp. 356–8.   [35] Le Goff, 'Le rite symbolique', p. 370.
[36] J. Russel Major, 'Bastard Feudalism and the Kiss: Changing Social Mores in Late Medieval and Early Modern France', *Journal of Interdisciplinary History* 17 (1987), 509–35.
[37] Strätz, 'Der Kuß im Recht', p. 289.
[38] 'Quibus in osculo susceptis hiisdem verbis inquit...' in C. Johnson (ed.), *Hugh the Chanter: The History of the Church of York 1066–1127* (London, 1961), p. 72.

of your highness's grace'[39] – when suddenly the rumour just mentioned undermined his position with his lord.

The kiss as a sign of communion could be used to express this without further explanation. After 1159 Latin Christendom was torn by a schism. The German king and emperor Frederick Barbarossa (1152–90) supported a man who was unable to win the support of most churches and countries and was considered an anti-pope by those who opposed him. When Bishop Ulrich of Treviso was called by the king to attend his court, he was horrified, 'because I knew the anti-pope to be there and I feared as everybody else did that I would be forced to adore and to kiss him' (i.e. the anti-pope).[40] To kiss the anti-pope would have meant to acknowledge him, of course, as a kiss was a sign of Christian unity, as Aelred of Rievaulx had put it. Unity in the faith meant peace and concord just as justice and right law did. The kiss could evoke and stand for these closely related notions of peace, justice and law in a circle of mutual references.[41]

Being aware of all this as every bishop would be, it is understandable that Bishop Ulrich was alarmed when Frederick Barbarossa called him to join his court. Not to follow the invitation would have meant a breach of his duties as a vassal. To go to court included the risk of meeting the anti-pope, with other risks in its wake. If he chose not to greet him appropriately in order to avoid an acknowledgement, he would have had to fear Barbarossa's wrath, who could rightly claim that his own honour had been hurt by the disrespect shown to his guest, the pope.[42]

Kisses, then, where ever-present in medieval communication. The 'normal' kiss was a kiss exchanged by men, and if the men were of equal rank it was given on the mouth. Were women greeted by a kiss on the mouth by men not related to them? It is hard to tell, but some episodes suggest that they were, as this one, for instance: Edward the Confessor's

---

[39] Günter Hödl and Peter Classen (eds.), *Die Admonter Briefsammlung* (MGH Epistolae: Briefe der deutschen Kaiserzeit, Hanover, 1983), vol. VI, Letter 15, p. 52.

[40] 'Ex vocatione siquidem domini mei imperatoris ad curiam veniens et ibidem eodem in tempore occursum suum venturum audiens, ne, sicut ab universis opinabatur, ipsum adorare et osculari cogerer, nimirum expavi...' in 'Die Salzburger Briefsammlung', Letter 27 in *Die Admonter Briefsammlung*, pp. 185–7 at p. 186.

[41] The Bologna Master Rufinus argues that kisses were given and exchanged in Holy Mass because the kiss of the mouth was the strongest expression of peace; an extensive quotation and interpretation is in Schreiner, 'Gerechtigkeit und Frieden', p. 42.

[42] For the importance of honour in twelfth-century relations and for the context of the letter, see Knut Görich, *Die Ehre Friedrich Barbarossas: Kommunikation, Konflikt und politisches Handeln im 12. Jahrhundert* (Darmstadt, 2001), esp. pp. 70–3 and 141–4.

(1043–65) wife Edith paid a visit to the monastery of St Riquier and as a matter of course offered a kiss to the abbot, who refused, however. The queen took this as an insult and became furious, but relented, of course, when she was told that the abbot was terribly pious and felt obliged by his vows as a monk not to kiss a woman. There are other examples of how all kinds of strategies were invented to spare monks the kiss of women, so we may assume that normally, i.e. when no monks were involved, women participated in the kissing rite just as men did.[43]

Kissing as politics

The kiss could denote peace and understanding, but could also be used to demonstrate rank. As such it made its way into 'political' communication. I will give some examples of this and I will then ask whether everyday 'non-political' kissing can help us to understand their meaning.

In 816 Pope Stephen IV (816–17) came to visit Charlemagne's son and heir Louis the Pious (814–40). There is a description by a poet, Ermold 'the Black', of how the two men met and greeted each other. The setting, he said, had been carefully arranged: both the pope and Louis arrived at the same time at the place set out for their meeting and embraced each other. Before that, Ermold explains, 'the wise king adores his guest three or four times with bended knee in honour of God and Saint Peter'. And then come the kisses. 'The king and the pious pontiff kiss each other's eyes, mouths, heads, breasts and throats. Then they take each other by the hand and walk towards the city of Reims.'[44]

The meeting between Pope Stephen and Louis the Pious has received a great deal of attention from modern historians, but all they can say about the reception is that it was done with great ceremony – the kisses are rarely mentioned.[45]

If modern historians do not seem to be interested in kisses, the Carolingian poet certainly is. Whenever he tells of Charlemagne or Louis the Pious taking counsel with his magnates, he has the magnates regularly kiss the

---

[43] Carré, *Le baiser*, pp. 203–4; Chénon, 'Le rôle', p. 135; Major, 'Bastard Feudalism', p. 521.

[44] Ermold Le Noir, ed. and trans. Edmond Faral, *Poème sur Louis le Pieux et Epîtres au Roi Pépin* (Paris, 1964), pp. 68–71.

[45] But Philippe Buc, 'Ritual and Interpretation: The Early Medieval Case', *Early Medieval Europe* 9 (2000), 183–210, for the meeting of Reims p. 189. Buc refers to the comparison of all the extant sources made by Mariëlle Hagemann at the NIAS Conference, Wassenaer, October 1997. I have not been able to get hold of this paper; also Achim Thomas Hack, *Das Empfangszeremoniell bei mittelalterlichen Papst–Kaiser–Treffen* (Cologne, Weimar and Vienna, 1999), pp. 458–64.

emperor's feet before they give counsel. Duke William of Toulouse 'kissed Charlemagne's feet with bended knee' before vehemently recommending an assault on Barcelona – a recommendation Charlemagne had wished to hear, by the way. At the end of his speech, the king embraced him and kissed his head. After that, 'all the magnates spoke to the same effect and they all kissed the feet of their benign lord'.[46]

The same is said of Einhard (c. 770–840), who was the first of the counsellors to speak when asked about Charlemagne's succession. Before he spoke, 'he fell to Charles' feet and kissed them'.[47]

When Louis the Pious made plans to invade Brittany, he made Count Lambert of Nantes come to inform him about the situation there. 'Lampert came and kissed the king's knees before he spoke.'[48] After that an abbot was sent to the Breton king Murman, to demand submission to the Franks. Murman returned the abbot's greetings with the kiss, 'as was the custom'.[49]

A little further on the poet describes a scene between Murman and his wife. Murman had almost made up his mind to submit to the Franks when his wife entered the scene and tried to keep him from doing so. Before talking to him she embraced him, 'and first kissed his knees, then his throat, and his beard and his hands'. Although these kisses from a wife might seem somewhat extravagant for our taste, the many kisses exchanged between men seem even more so; especially, I think, the kissing of a king's feet. When we think of Western European medieval noble retainers, we do not imagine them kissing their king's feet. This particular rite seems more at home in ancient oriental despotism than in the West.[50] It is known that it was part of the elaborate court ceremonial practised at the emperor's court in Byzantium; the Byzantine emperor was entitled to have his feet kissed, but it is also reported from late Antiquity that the Byzantine emperors are known to have kissed the pope's feet, a ceremony first recorded for Justinian (527–65) in 525.[51]

There is a well-known episode which suggests that in the Frankish kingdom noble vassals indeed kissed their royal lord's feet. When the

---

[46] Ermold Le Noir, *Poème sur Louis le Pieux*, p. 16.
[47] Ermold Le Noir, *Poème sur Louis le Pieux*, p. 52.
[48] Ermold Le Noir, *Poème sur Louis le Pieux*, pp. 100–1.
[49] Ermold Le Noir, *Poème sur Louis le Pieux*, p. 106.
[50] It was customary in ancient Persia, but it is not clear whether some phrases in the Old Testament also refer to the kissing of feet as a custom in ancient Israel, cf. August Wünsche, *Der Kuss in Bibel, Talmud und Midrasch* (Breslau, 1911), p. 14.
[51] Alföldi, 'Fußkuß', cols. 1063–65.

Viking Rollo was made count of Rouen to legitimise his conquests, he was asked to kiss King Charles' feet. Apparently he found this rather disgusting, so he made one of his retainers lift the king's foot to his mouth for the application of the kiss, which made the Frankish king fall on his back. This episode only makes sense if the Frankish king was indeed entitled to the kissing of his feet.[52]

The rite of kissing someone's feet seems to have continued in Western Europe. It is suggested by Gregory VII's (1073–85) *Dictatus Papae* of 1075, in which he outlines the hierarchical position he feels the pope should have in Latin Christendom. The ninth of the twenty-seven sentences reads: 'That the pope is the only one to have his feet kissed by all the princes.'[53] He might have copied this from a Byzantine ceremonial, but it seems more likely that Western practice supplied him with the example.[54]

Still, the question is whether Ermold with his many kisses is describing what actually happened or whether he gives us visual imagery. Considering the many 'business kisses' mentioned above, it is possible that the scenes happened as described, although the sheer quantity of the kisses could also suggest that they were part of Ermold's personal pictorial language. Anyway, what Ermold wanted to convey is quite clear when we compare the kisses of the pope and the emperor, on the one hand, and those of Charlemagne and Louis and their retainers on the other. The pope and the emperor kissed 'each other on the eyes, mouths, heads, breasts, and throats'. The kisses demonstrate equality, while the noble retainers acknowledge the hierarchical order with their kisses. Kisses demonstrated hierarchy.

When we take into consideration that body language was a language which was charged with meaning through everyday experiences, it is to be asked whether the people described actually used that language, and

---

[52] Dudo of Saint-Quentin, *De moribus et actis primorum Normanniae ducum* (ed. Jules Lair, Caen, 1865), p. 169; cf. Hermann Kamp, 'Die Macht der Zeichen und Gesten. Öffentliches Verhalten bei Dudo von Saint-Quentin' in Althoff, *Formen und Funktionen*, pp. 125–55.

[53] 'Quod solius papae pedes omnes principes deosculentur' in Erich Caspar (ed.), *Das Register Gregors VII.* (MGH Epistolae, Sel. 2, Berlin, 1920–23), vol. II, pp. 201–4 at p. 204.

[54] By the twelfth century, the kissing of the pope's feet had become a regular feature of the papal ceremonial. The well-known reconciliation of Pope Alexander III and the emperor Frederick Barbarossa in Venice where the emperor undoubtedly kissed the pope's feet must be seen against this background. For a synopsis and interpretation of the four independent eye-witness accounts, see Hack, *Empfangszeremoniell*, pp. 648–69 and Sebastian Scholz, 'Symbolik und Zeremoniell bei den Päpsten in der zweiten Hälfte des 12. Jahrhunderts' in Stefan Weinfurter (ed.), *Stauferreich im Wandel: Ordnungsvorstellungen und Politik vor und nach 1177* (Stuttgart, 2002), pp. 131–48 at pp. 132 and 142–5.

the contemporary writer was merely describing what had happened, or whether it was the writer who made use of body language to convey meaning.[55] In many cases it will be next to impossible to tell for sure even if there is parallel documentation; kisses and many other gestures were so much part of everyday communication that a contemporary writer might have chosen to omit the details he was familiar with, while another might have felt inclined to mention them for reasons that escape us today. In Ermold's text – which is poetical, after all – it seems to me that the poet uses the kisses as a literary tool to convey meaning, but we will never know for sure.

Just as body language could convey meaning, it could be used to fake meaning, as it does in the following episode, related by Ralph de Diceto.[56] Rainald of Dassel, the archbishop-elect of Cologne, came to England in 1164 to negotiate two engagements: Henry II's (1154–89) first-born daughter Mathilda was to become the bride of Henry the Lion, duke of Saxony and Bavaria (1139/54–80), while a younger daughter was chosen for Frederick Barbarossa's own son. 'When the English magnates came to meet him in a solemn ceremony, the king's justiciar Robert of Leicester refused to receive his kiss saying he was an arch-schismatic. Afterwards the altars were destroyed upon which the schismatics had celebrated Mass.' Apparently it was normal for the magnates to receive a stranger with a kiss. It is only because the justiciar refused to do so that the historiographer came to mention the kiss of welcome at all. Robert of Leicester was right in calling Rainald an 'arch-schismatic'. The papal schism mentioned above was still going on, and Rainald of Dassel was not only one of the staunchest supporters of Emperor Frederick Barbarossa but was also regarded as the driving force behind the enthronement of a new anti-pope after the death of the first one. One would expect that the refusal of the normal way of greeting would mean the refusal of friendly cooperation. But far from it: Rainald continued his journey to see the queen and her daughters with travel expenses paid by the English exchequer, then went home in the company of two English envoys who were to swear to the treaty for which the marriage alliance was a confirmation.[57] Does a kiss – or rather the

---

[55] Buc, 'Ritual and Interpretation', p. 184.
[56] 'Imagines historiarum (1148–1202)' in William Stubbs (ed.), *Symeonis Monachi Opera omnia* (London, 1876), vol. I, p. 318.
[57] For the alliance of 1164, see Timothy Reuter, 'The Papal Schism: The Empire and the West 1159–1169' (DPhil. thesis, University of Oxford, 1975); Joseph P. Huffman, *The Social Politics of Medieval Diplomacy: Anglo-German Relations (1066–1307)* (Ann Arbor, 2000), pp. 72–91 and my own assessment of the treaty: 'Lüge oder Fälschung? Die Überlieferung

refusal of a kiss – have a meaning at all if there are no actions linked to it? Among the German lay princes Henry the Lion was the staunchest supporter of Frederick's anti-pope. So, evidently, Mathilda's husband-to-be was a schismatic too. He would certainly receive his bride with a kiss, because, other than marital kisses, a kiss of betrothal was of juridical importance. Undoubtedly kisses would be exchanged between a German schismatic and the English king's daughter. What difference did it make that the king's justiciar refused the kiss of welcome to the envoy who had come to negotiate the treaty and the marriage?

Here body language was dissociated from the meaning it was standing for. The people concerned contented themselves with the empty performance of a rite without committing themselves to the consequences inherent in it.[58] It was a 'mere' ritual, a demonstration of political correctness. It seems that the people concerned felt free enough towards rituals to make them subservient to their own political ends, even if the ritual contradicted their actions.

The importance of kissing in the peacemaking process: Henry II and Thomas Becket

There is another example, in the Becket material, which shows what a ritual like the exchange of the kiss of peace could and could not do. Thomas Becket (1120–70) was having a conflict with King Henry II over a number of problems epitomised in the Constitutions of Clarendon of 1164. Becket fled into exile at the end of that year, and lived in various places in France. The exile dragged on for several years, and by 1169 many of those involved hoped and worked for peace: Pope Alexander III (1159–81) supported Becket on many essential points, and had made this public when first meeting Becket in Sens by kissing him 'on the lips as well as on the eyes and the face';[59] but eventually the pope had also come to doubt the archbishop's good judgement in dealing with the problems; besides, several of his cardinals were siding with the English king, and

---

von Barbarossas Hoftag zu Würzburg im Jahr 1165 und der Becket-Streit' in Weinfurter (ed.), *Stauferreich im Wandel*, pp. 149–71.

[58] For a discussion of the question of practical consequences of ritual performances, cf. Jean-Marie Moeglin, 'Harmischar, hachée. Le dossier des rituels d'humiliation et de soumission au moyen âge', *Archivum Latinitatis Medii Aevi: Bulletin Du Cange* 54 (1996), 11–65.

[59] Benet of St Albans, Life of Thomas Becket, in F. Michel (ed.), *Chronique des ducs de Normandie* (Paris, 1844), vol. III, p. 619b.

there was also Frederick Barbarossa's anti-pope to reckon with, although dangers from that side had substantially subsided by 1169. The French king Louis VII (1137–80) wanted peace, too – he had Becket living on his territory and paid for his household. So did several other exiles who wanted to go home to England, and members of the English episcopate, who saw the disastrous consequences the long exile of the primate had for the English Church. Peace talks had been going on since January 1169 and many obstacles had to be overcome. There was so much bitterness on both sides that tensions rather increased than subsided and confidence-building measures seem to have been just as important as the issues. Then, finally in November 1169, an agreement was reached. Shortly before, Becket had asked the pope's advice on what kind of guarantee to ask from King Henry, and the pope had mentioned several possibilities: a solemn oath, for instance; but then he advised him to be content with a kiss of peace.[60] To Becket's surprise Henry refused to give this kiss. He claimed to have made a vow – in a rage, so he is reported to have said – 'never to kiss that man again'. The pope did the obvious thing; he absolved him from the vow. But Henry still would not kiss. In a letter to the archbishop of Sens, Becket quotes the French king as having said that for all his weight in gold he would not advise Thomas to enter Henry's territories without having first received the kiss of peace. Others present at this meeting were of a different opinion. They recalled the case of one Robert de Sillé, one of Henry's rebellious vassals, who had been kissed in public when peace had been made and still had been thrown into prison shortly afterwards, where he had died.[61] They said, of course, that a kiss did not guarantee peace and security. Not even did the oath which Henry had sworn personally

---

[60] Herbert of Bosham, 'Vita S. Thomae' in James C. Robertson (ed.), *Materials for the History of Thomas Becket, Archbishop of Canterbury* (London, 1875–85), vol. III, pp. 155–534 at pp. 449–51.

[61] Anne Duggan (ed.), *The Correspondence of Thomas Becket, Archbishop of Canterbury 1162–1170* (Oxford, 2000), vol. II, no. 243, pp. 1044–55 at p. 1048; Becket describes his meeting with Henry II in great detail with a verbatim-style rendering of the conversation. He claims to have proposed an amicable settlement under certain conditions, namely that Henry 'would offer him his grace and peace and security by the kiss of peace'. But Henry would not receive him to the kiss of peace. 'The most Christian prince [Louis VII of France] immediately concluded that not for all his weight in gold would he advise us to enter his [Henry's] territory, without first receiving the kiss of peace in public. And count Theobald added that it would be a very foolish presumption, while many of those standing around recalled and reminded one another of what had happened to Robert de Sillé, for whom even the kiss had not seemed a sufficient guarantee of the maintenance of peace and safety.' In Duggan, *Correspondence*, p. 1051.

to his liege lord, the king of France.[62] Becket might as well return to England without the kiss. Robert de Sillé had died just recently in prison; the memory of his fate was still fresh. But Becket insisted on the kiss. The more he insisted, the more Henry resisted. To kiss or not to kiss became the question.

The unsolved matter of the kiss held up the conclusion of the peace treaty for over half a year. Finally, peace was made at Fréteval in July 1170. The king had prevailed – no kiss. William fitz Stephen, one of the Becket hagiographers, who was probably an eye-witness, has an interesting detail. He quotes Henry as having said: 'In my country I'll kiss his mouth, his hands and his feet a hundred times . . . To give the kiss in my own country will mean grace and benevolence towards him, whereas here it would simply be compulsion.'[63] Shortly afterwards, Thomas Becket went back to England and was murdered. Why was a kiss so important? Would the king have curbed his fury about Becket's actions in England if he had given him the kiss of peace?[64]

Although Becket himself felt that there could not be true peace without the kiss and that a kiss given by the king's son in the king's place would not do,[65] he did return without the kiss. None of the Becket biographers links the murder to the missing kiss. What kind of security could a solemn rite (*forma solemnis*) bring? Henry had refused the kiss, but offered another solemn rite instead. He had held the archbishop's stirrup to help him mount his horse and then had led the horse smilingly a short distance, a clear sign of his grace and benevolence. The meaning of this corresponded exactly to that of the kiss. As the second one is clearly 'an ordered sequence of gestures' and as it was just as clearly negotiated before its public staging,[66] it was what many modern scholars would call a 'ritual', whereas

---

[62] 'Robertus de Silliaco . . . quem nec pacis osculum publice datum, nec fides corporaliter regi Francorum prestita, fecit esse securum', from the letter of Thomas Becket to his clerks Alexander and John, in Duggan, *Correspondence*, no. 244, pp. 1054–67 at p. 1064.

[63] 'Vita S. Thomae auctore Willelmo Filio Stephani' in Robertson, *Materials*, vol. III, p. 111.

[64] The episode has received a lot of attention, most recently from Schreiner, 'Gerechtigkeit und Frieden', p. 82 and Reuter, 'Velle sibi fieri', p. 216. Neither of them takes the letter to the archbishop of Sens into consideration, i.e. the case of Robert de Sillé.

[65] Letter of March 1170 to Bishop Bernard of Nevers, who was acting as papal intermediary. As his second condition for an agreement Becket demanded 'that he receive the archbishop with the kiss of peace, which is a solemn rite (forma solemnis) among all peoples and in every religion, without which the peace of those formerly in dispute can never be confirmed', in Duggan, *Correspondence*, no. 274, pp. 1164–77.

[66] Gerd Althoff sees rituals ordered by rules, 'die vertrauliche Klärungen zwingend vorschrieben, ehe es zu öffentlichen Auftritten kam', in 'Zur Einführung' in Althoff (ed.), *Formen und Funktionen*, p. 9.

a kiss of peace as a single gesture might not have been seen as one. It does not seem wise, however, to put the two under different headings as they were meant to signify the same thing, namely to make visible the very essence of what had been achieved: the return of peace and amicable understanding. Why did Henry refuse to give the kiss of peace? What was so special about it?

There was probably nothing special about the kiss as such. Henry refused it, so it seems, because Becket demanded it. Henry's refusal was not a silly whim on his part, but based on a serious problem. He had accepted virtually all demands Becket had made with the aid of the pope. Henry had been forced to give in. The pope had threatened to put England under an interdict, as he had already done for Henry's continental dominions. Since the eleventh century, the Roman Church had been able continually to strengthen its hold on its 'subjects'; its sanctions could endanger the position of any lord as they could disrupt the bonds of allegiance medieval society was built upon. If people were made to choose between St Peter and their king, there was no way of knowing whom they would side with. The better part of the English bishops would almost certainly prefer to stay with Mother Church. The king had been made to surrender virtually without condition, and that, too, might prove dangerous for him. A king's honour demanded that he dealt with his people from an elevated position. This enabled him to show 'grace and benevolence', which would look ridiculous in a man who had proved to be a weakling. Henry seems to have felt that he had given in to such a degree that he could not afford to submit his oath to the pope's discretion. He therefore refused Becket's demand of the kiss.

Although this particular kiss was never given, the non-kissing episode is quite revealing as to the practical importance of the kiss of peace and, in fact, of rituals in the Middle Ages. The witnesses of the scene were not able to arrive at an agreement of what Becket should do. The fraction that recalled Robert de Sillé's fate advised him not to insist on the kiss of peace as it would not help him anyway; the others advised him not to return to England without having been kissed by the king. Were they saying that the kiss of peace would guarantee security because it was a 'rechtskonstitutives Sinnzeichen, das die Geltungskraft und Einklagbarkeit vertraglicher Abmachungen verbürgen sollte'?[67] I do not think so. Although the two groups arrived at opposite pieces of advice, they do not seem to ascribe to the kiss a particular power. It was rather King Henry's character that

---

[67] Schreiner, 'Er küsse mich', p. 90.

was under discussion. Robert de Sillé's fate proved to the first group that Henry would not let himself be stopped by no matter what solemn rite. He was a man who got away with a breach of the promise of peace the kiss stood for. The others who advised Becket not to be content without the kiss likewise seem to have had Henry in mind and not the rite as such. If Henry refused the kiss of peace, the normal way to seal a peace treaty, one should beware of the king's notorious slyness and be suspicious of his peaceful intentions.[68] Would people react all that differently today if one of the parties refused to sign an international peace treaty that had been negotiated?

Conclusion

In recent scholarship, rituals have been regarded as possessing law-enforcing powers. Klaus Schreiner is quite typical when he says that the kiss of peace was given to ensure legal consequences ('sollte Einklagbarkeit verbürgen'). I doubt it. How could a kiss of peace or any other ritual do that? Schreiner seems to regard the kiss of peace as a self-operating mechanism. But the performance of rituals should not be separated from the fundamental driving forces of human action such as love turned into hatred and hatred into love, brutal force and unexpected good fortune, considerations of interest, power and influence. I want to argue that legal consequences depend not on rituals, but on law-enforcing agencies. These agencies are not necessarily institutions like state-organised law courts; the members of a community can act as a law-enforcing agency as well. In Henry II's case this would have meant that his noble retainers, and especially Robert de Sillé's peers, would have had to see to it that Henry lived up to the promises signified by the kiss of peace. Apparently they had failed to do so, and Henry had got away with it. The reasons for this are not known, but it is probably not wrong to assume that they were in line with the established ways of medieval *politics* set out so brilliantly by the late Karl Leyser in regard to Ottonian kingship: the power of a king, so he said, rested in his capacity to inspire awe and fear. He had to make sure of being considered just, generous and terrifying to his enemies so that potential opponents would think twice before they would challenge

---

[68] In his letter to the bishop of Nevers quoted above, Thomas Becket is quite outspoken about his king: 'Because it is not easy to detect the manifold deceits of this monster, whatever he says and whatever appearance he puts on you should be suspicious both of him and of all that belongs to him and you should believe him to be a liar, unless he has proven himself trustworthy by manifest deeds', in Duggan, *Correspondence*, pp. 1164–65.

him.[69] The first years of a king's reign were usually the most difficult ones, as a new king had to establish his image as a powerful ruler. Henry II had been king for sixteen years in 1169. He had well established himself as a powerful monarch and thought he could afford to act contrary to the promise expressed by the kiss of peace, and even contrary to the oath sworn to the king of France. Apparently, his judgement had been correct.

If the kiss of peace as such could not ensure anything, what could? Why was so much importance attached to it? Again the Becket material suggests an answer. Instead of kissing Thomas Becket, which he had sworn never to do again, Henry had offered his first-born son Henry as a proxy. The future 'Young King' should act in his father's stead and give Becket the kiss of peace. Thomas Becket refused, because 'it will not appear that the archbishop has received peace from the king through a proxy kiss from the king's son, but rather that he has returned to the son's favour'.[70] The kiss of peace, like other corporeal communications, made visible what had been agreed upon, and made the public a witness to the agreement. The transition from a status of enmity to that of peace and concord was encapsulated in the scene, enacted for the public to look at and to be witness to. It was what people *saw* that counted, and in this case the appearance would be misleading, no matter what had been agreed upon by word of mouth. If, Becket goes on, something should happen to the archbishop, 'the king would not be considered infamous' on the pretext that he had refused the kiss.[71] Infamy was a legal term inherited from Roman jurisprudence with a distinct legal meaning in twelfth-century canon law. It made people dishonourable and deprived them of their place in Christian society.[72] The kiss Becket demanded was in his eyes 'a solemn religious pledge given in public'.[73] The terms Becket used show his intention. He wanted to ground Henry's kiss of peace in canon law. Whereas there had not been a court and a judge for Robert de Sillé, there would have been one for Thomas Becket. Thomas Becket had experienced before that papal jurisdiction had forced Henry into submission, and he seems to have counted on it to do so again.

---

[69] Karl Leyser, *Rule and Conflict in Early Medieval Society: Ottonian Saxony* (London, 1979), p. 35.
[70] Letter to the bishop of Nevers, in Duggan, *Correspondence*, p. 1166.
[71] 'Et si archiepiscopo, quod absit, secus accideret, rex sub pretextu negati osculi crederetur exemptus infamie', in Duggan, *Correspondence*, pp. 1166–68.
[72] F. Merzbacher, 'Infamie' in *Handwörterbuch der deutschen Rechtsgeschichte* (Berlin, 1978), vol. II, pp. 358–60.
[73] 'archiepiscopus publice religionis sollempnem exigat cautionem', from the letter to the bishop of Nevers in Duggan, *Correspondence*, p. 1168.

Was the kiss of peace all that different from the signatures under today's international treaties? Of course there are fundamental differences. As everybody seems to take them for granted, I want to point out remarkable parallels between modern peacemaking and the medieval evidence. Neither kiss nor signature guarantee peace nor, in fact, any treaty by itself. As long as there is no regular law enforcement, they remain subject to considerations of political interest. Depending on the particular circumstances, a breach of the peace that people have made would or would not have practical consequences. In the twelfth century, canon law began to be established as international law in certain legal fields, with ecclesiastical jurisdiction and ecclesiastical sanctions as a regular law-enforcing agency. Today we seem to witness a similar development, the transition from political law enforcement to juridical law enforcement on a global scale. According to our modern predilections, the focus has changed from marriage law to trade law and from blasphemy to human rights, and the respective courts operate not in Rome, but in Strasbourg, Geneva and The Hague. What the Roman Church started in Western European Christendom in the twelfth century is coming to be a global affair today.

8

Martinus Garatus Laudensis on treaties

ALAIN WIJFFELS

Introduction

Martinus Garatus Laudensis' *De confœderatione, pace et conventionibus principum* is widely acknowledged as one of the first monographic works on the law of treaties. Whatever the merits of such a characterisation, there is a risk that it may obfuscate some of that work's essential features in its proper legal-historical context. Before considering the substance of the work, it is therefore necessary to consider some of its formal features, if only as a general methodological caveat.[1]

Martinus Garatus on the prince and the law

Before the second half of the seventeenth century, legal monographs on treaties are scarce.[2] That, of course, does not mean that the rich civil and canon law literature of the later medieval centuries does not yield much

---

[1] An edition of Garatus' treatise is presented in the Appendix. The most important works on Garatus which will be referred to throughout this contribution are Ingrid Baumgärtner, *Martinus Garatus Laudensis: ein italienischer Rechtsgelehrter des 15. Jahrhunderts* (Cologne and Vienna, 1986); G. Rondinini-Soldi, 'Il diritto di guerra in Italia nel secolo XV', *Nuova Rivista Storica* 48 (1964), 275–306; Rondinini-Soldi, 'Ambasciatori e ambascerie al tempo di Filippo Maria Visconti (1412–1426)', *Nuova Rivista Storica*, 49 (1965), 313–44; Rondinini-Soldi, *Il tractatus De principibus di Martino Garati da Lodi: con l'edizione critica della rubrica De principibus* (Milan and Varese, 1968); Rondinini-Soldi, *Per la storia del cardinalato nel secolo XV (con l'edizione del trattato De cardinalibus di Martino Garati da Lodi)* (Milan, 1973). Both authors also refer to older works. References in the text and in the footnotes of this chapter to a *Quaestio* (Qu. followed by a number), without any further specification, are references to *De confœderatione*.

[2] Baumgärtner's assertion that, in the context of the continuous wars in fifteenth-century Italy and hence because of the importance of alliances, treaties and peaces, 'mehrere Autoren verfaßten deshalb zu dieser Thematik eigenständige Traktate' is hardly supported by the footnote attached to that proposition: only the treatises by Garatus and by Johannes Lupus de Segovia (both included in the 1584 Venice collection of treatises) are mentioned (Baumgärtner, *Martinus Garatus Laudensis*, p. 202 and n. 277).

material on questions related to the law of treaties. As for most questions on aspects of *ius gentium* (whether understood as 'law of nations' or in a less anachronistic sense) and, indeed, for what modern lawyers would be prepared to recognise as questions of international law, much of the material is scattered over a wide range of commentaries *in utroque iure*, *repetitiones, summae, consilia* and so on, even though in any of those works there may be privileged *loci* on particular questions. Medieval *tractatus*, many of which were included in the multi-volume collections printed in Lyons in 1535, 1544 and 1549, and in Venice in 1584, remained on the whole a marginal genre of legal literature, and, as those very collections testify, that was also by and large the case for *ius gentium* topics. Systematic, reliable indexes to the relevant scattered passages in that variegated 'ocean' of medieval legal works do not exist. Little wonder, then, that in a recent positivistic past, international lawyers were inclined to believe that international law, not only as a science, only started around Grotius' time: apart from the idea that a 'modern state' was a prerequisite for international law (obviously a self-restricting definition), a search for readily identifiable legal works specifically on international law topics would not yield many results. Thus, apart from a few notable exceptions (most of which in due time found their way into the libraries of the 'classics' on international law), the vast body of late medieval legal scholarship on the law governing the relations between more or less autonomous political actors ('international relations' will be used here as a convenient, albeit anachronistic shorthand) has long been overlooked by scholars writing on the history of international law. As a result, most of the medieval legal doctrines, which often appear to have been worked out and formulated in close connection with political events and developments (particularly in Italy), fell into oblivion, although they often lived on indirectly through early modern legal literature.[3]

These general remarks apply to Garatus' work. His work, as regards its variety on a par with the *opera* of some prominent authors of the *mos italicus*, consists of commentaries, *consilia* and treatises.[4] The latter, however, show a comparatively distinctive bent for topics of what a modern lawyer would regard as 'public law': the status of sovereigns and other political rulers, the organisation and status of major political bodies, the

---

[3] Alain Wijffels, 'Early-Modern Literature on International Law and the Usus Modernus', *Grotiana*, NS 16/17 (1995–96), 35–54.

[4] See the general survey in Appendix I of Baumgärtner, *Martinus Garatus Laudensis*, pp. 321–50.

status of the servants of those rulers and bodies, tax law – and so on. The 'international law' related topics (on war, embassies,[5] treaties) should be viewed in the line of these works on 'public law'. None of those topics, it should be remembered, was outside the traditional area of the civil and canon law traditions. What marks Garatus is his insistence on gathering so much of that *ius commune* material together in the less fashionable format of the *tractatus*. On the other hand, it will also be obvious that the material thus brought together in these *tractatus* was highly relevant to those civil and canon lawyers who were seeking a career in public office.

Whether *De confœderatione* should be seen as a distinct treatise is a moot question. The sixteenth-century Lyons and Venice collections of treatises certainly contributed to the establishment of the assumption that it is a treatise in its own right. Some manuscripts nevertheless suggest that it should be seen as a distinctive part of a wider work consisting of what the printed collections presented as separate *tractatus*. Thus, *De confœderatione* appears in the survey of some manuscripts as a title (*rubrica*) in a series of titles on the theme *De principibus*,[6] although even there the ambiguity is reinforced by the fact that the (first and) main title within that wider work is itself entitled *De principibus*.[7] Short of a satisfactory description of the various known manuscripts, the provisional evidence

---

[5] For Garatus' treatise on ambassadors, see the edition in V. Hrabar, *De legatis et de legationibus tractatus varii* (Dorpat, 1905). In spite of an important body of medieval legal doctrine *De legatis*, distinctive legal(-political) monographs on embassies only started flourishing during the latter part of the sixteenth century. Alain Wijffels, 'Le Statut juridique des ambassadeurs d'après la doctrine du XVIe siècle', *Publication du Centre Européen d'Etudes Bourguignonnes (XIVe–XVIe s.)*, 32 (1992), 127–42.

[6] E.g. PBN MS Lat. 4684, fol. 1r: Principium tractatuum domini Martini Laudensis pene viginti f. 1v: Sequntur omnes rubrice huius tractatus De confederationibus et conventionibus principum (wrongly headed, however, on fol. 28v, as De vasallis principum Rubrica); see also *in fine*, fol. 43ra: Conclusio huius libri De principibus. Also MBS MS clm 403, fol. 2v, which lists the Rubrice huius operis, as a whole, including *De principibus* and *De confœderatione*; TUB MS MC 299, fol. 1ra–rb: Incipit tractatus quidam pulcer et utilis per famosum utriusque iuris doctor. do. Martinum de Laude, intitulatus de principibus . . . Hec sunt Rubrice presentis tractatus videlicet De principibus . . . De confœderationibus et conventionibus principum . . . It is also the case in the Lyons 1530 edition of Garatus' *tractatus*: *Solemnes et quotidiani ac practicabiles Tractatus domini Martini de Cazariis Lauden. iurisconsulti* ([Lyons], 1530); although on the title-page, a list of the 'treatises' is given, the heading on fol. 32ra is *De confederatione: pace et conventionibus principum. Rubrica*.

[7] In order to avoid confusion, I shall therefore always refer to the *Rubrica De principibus* for that part of the treatise which gave its name to the whole, as a *pars pro toto*. Quotations and references to that *rubrica* will be based on Rondinini-Soldi's modern edition, *Il tractatus De Principibus di Martino Garato da Lodi: con l'edizione critica della rubrica De principibus*.

seems to confirm the close link between the various 'treatises' linked to *De principibus*, and therefore the need to consider *De confœderatione* in relation to those other parts, and to avoid presenting it too much as a separate work in its own right.

Garatus' successful academic career brought him into direct contact with several of northern Italy's principalities or 'states': Milan, Siena, Bologna, Ferrara. His calling as an author of legal opinions (*consilia*) confirms his acquaintance with litigation throughout northern Italy.[8] The *tractatus*, too, show that many of the questions Garatus considered were embedded in the shifting Italian politics of his time.

The major theme of *De principibus* (both as a separate rubric and as the common title for the various *tractatus* appearing in the same collections) is that of the *princeps* as a sovereign or quasi-sovereign authority in his relation to the pope, the emperor, other *principes*, other (non-sovereign) political actors and, partly through the intermediary of his agents, his subjects.[9] The constant and abundant references to the civil and canon law authorities emphasise that the author is considering the political issues in question neither by the standards of theologians or artists, nor as a contribution to the burgeoning genre of political monographs. Moreover, because the bulk of the material is not original, but recapitulates existing statements from the legal authorities, the issues are inevitably expressed in a way which fits in with the terminological and conceptual framework of legal studies.

The treatise entitled *De confœderatione*, like most of Garatus' other treatises, is not a treatise in the modern sense of a fairly comprehensive and, above all, systematic treatment of a particular topic. Indeed, the main, if not the only, element that gives the work its distinct character is that the issues it considers are (mostly) related to the theme announced

---

[8] Baumgärtner's work *Martinus Garatus Laudensis* is a major contribution to our understanding of the geographical area in which Garatus was active as the author of *consilia*: cf. the map on p. 254, and its discussion, pp. 240–1.

[9] A large number of the *quaestiones* in the *Rubrica De principibus* deal with either the prerogatives of the prince (e.g. Qu. 16, 35, 58, 65, 74, 83, 97, 103, 116, 141, 181, 349, 376, 384, 440, add. 14) or the restrictions on these prerogatives (e.g. Qu. 21, 27, 36, 58, 253, 257, 388). Some of these questions include characteristic features of the medieval attributes of sovereignty, such as the power to adjudicate as the final judge, against whose decisions there is no appeal; the authorities and principles quoted by Garatus often significantly express his views on the international community, e.g. Qu. 257, which states that only judgements by the pope and the emperor cannot be challenged, although Qu. 384 acknowledges that there is no appeal against the judgement of a king in his own realm (the 'supplication' referred to in the following part of the question should not necessarily be seen as a remedy before a superior judge).

in the title. Otherwise, the internal arrangement shows even less concern for systematisation than the *ordo legalis* (or *canonum*) within many of the titles of the *corpora iuris*. As a 'monograph', it simply consists of a series of mostly brief *quaestiones* (in total sixty-three); the sequence of these questions does not appear to follow any obvious coherent system, although now and again a cluster of questions on related issues appears; nor does the work seem to aim at a comprehensive treatment of the subject matter or of the legal authorities on the subject. Some questions could well have been treated in another treatise and, conversely, some of the questions treated in those other treatises are more relevant to the law of treaties.[10]

Not only are the *quaestiones* mostly very brief, but concision is sometimes sought to such a point that the answer is reduced to a simple reference to a doctrinal authority, without even being spelled out.[11]

As regards these legal authorities, they are on the whole fairly conventional.[12] The (glossed) *corpora iuris* are, of course, prominent. Not surprisingly, considering the theme and the author's approach, the *Libri feudorum* provide a substantial part of these references to the fundamental authorities. Among the civil law commentators, Bartolus (1314–57), Baldus (1327–1400) and Angelus (d. *c.* 1400) are the most frequently quoted authors; among the canon lawyers, there are Hostiensis (d. 1271), Pope Innocent IV (1243–54) and Johannes Andreae (*c.* 1270–1348); Barbatia, Zabarella (1360–1417) and Johannes de Lignano (d. 1383) appear less frequently. Among the *consilia*, those by Angelus de Ubaldis were obviously a major source to Garatus; Ludovicus Romanus (d. 1439) is also quoted. From the treatises, Garatus quotes Bartolus on tyrants and, as could be expected, the major single authority in his days on the law of treaties: Baldus' commentary *De pace Constantiae* (and Odofredus' notes). As in his other work, Garatus also refers, sometimes teasingly, to his own scholarly production, sometimes even to his 'work in progress'.

The methods applied by Garatus follow the general pattern of his time. On the one hand, the characteristic features of the *mos italicus* prevail: legal reasoning follows an 'open system' of argumentation, i.e. authorities

---

[10] E.g. *Rubrica De principibus*, Qu. 123, on the binding force of contracts concluded by the pope, the emperor and princes towards their successors; *De legatis maxime principum* (in Hrabar, *De legatis*, pp. 45–52); Qu. 18 (pacta vel legatorum capitula sunt conventio publica).

[11] E.g. Qu. 2.

[12] Cf. the authorities quoted in the *Rubrica De principibus*; Rondinini-Soldi, *Tractatus*, p. 48.

which have no substantive link *per se* with the issue under discussion may nevertheless be relevant, either because of an underlying general principle, because of an analogy, etc. On the other hand, because of the very fact that as a treatise the work focuses on questions around the same theme, there is also a greater (though not exclusive) focus on authorities which have a close link *ratione materiae* with the subject matter, e.g. the title (in the *Liber extra*) *De treuga et pace*; *consilia* dealing with treaties; and, as already mentioned, Baldus and Odofredus on *De pace Constantiae*.

Personae, modus, effectus

At the risk of imposing too much of a system upon *De confœderatione*, three main topics which appear throughout the sequence of questions will be dealt with here. First, who are the 'actors' involved in the 'agreements' under discussion and how are these actors related to each other? Second, which principles governing negotiations and the conclusion of treaties does the treatise discuss? And third, what is the scope of the agreements?

The range of actors who are in a position to conclude treaties

The community of actors which emerges from Garatus' work in general reflects the conventional historiographic concept of the *respublica christiana*. Actors from outside of Latin Christendom seldom, if ever, appear.[13] Within that Latin Christendom, the northern Italian peninsula seems to be the privileged reference for Garatus. Obviously, this is partly due to his personal experience and perspective, but it is also a consequence of the legal authorities which provided him with much of his primary material, viz. the works of Italian jurists who, particularly for questions on the relations between political actors, were themselves directly inspired by their own political context. However, occasional references to other princes of

---

[13] In spite of the medieval (canon) law's relevance to international law questions (e.g. on the law of war) with non-Christians: James Muldoon, 'Medieval Canon Law and the Formation of International Law', *Zeitschrift der Savigny-Stiftung für Rechtsgeschichte, Kanonistische Abteilung* 81 (1995), 64–82. In the *Rubrica De principibus*, the 'Greek' emperor appears in Qu. 84; occasional references to the Saracens, the Jews or infidels occur in Qu. 8, 48, 71, 345. In the *rubrica* of ambassadors (published in Hrabar, *De legatis*, pp. 45–52), the emphasis is also, as the title (*De legatis maxime principum*) implies, on the *princeps*, with occasional references to embassies from cities (*civitates*: Qu. 1, 17, 22), communities (*communitates*: Qu. 6; and Qu. 10 on embassies sent to such bodies), a *populus liber* (Qu. 29: qui habet auctoritatem principis). A hierarchy (at least, of honour) among princes is acknowledged in Qu. 27 and 35.

Western Christianity occur here, too.[14] Nevertheless, even the references to situations or events in Italy remain comparatively restrained: throughout the treatise the purported validity of both principles and examples remains applicable to Western Christian political actors in general.

Among those actors, the princes as autonomous political rulers (*principes*) are cast in the main (although not supreme) role.[15] Admittedly, their position is subordinated to the pope and to the emperor. But partly because the main focus of the work is on *principes*, partly because their autonomy is fully or largely identified as at least some form of sovereignty, it is their actions, such as their agreements and treaties, which take centre stage in the treatise. In Garatus' work, the term and concept of a ruler or political authority *non recognoscens superiorem* appears at different levels, and usually is to be understood (except for the pope) in a relative sense.[16] The prince's relations with other political actors, which can be established through treaties, are manifold and reflect different political and legal networks within his realm. In *De confœderatione* the emphasis is mainly on three categories of actors with whom the prince may have agreements: his *adhaerentes* or *sequaces*, cities (*civitates*, possibly also to be understood at times as city-states) and representatives of the feudal system, here mostly vassals of the prince as overlord. It is more difficult to assess the status of the *populus* when it is referred to as some political entity. The legal pluralism of this community of actors is emphasised by the fact that, against the position of the prince, all the other actors' standing

---

[14] This is also the case throughout the other titles of the treatise *De principibus*. In some cases, the *quaestio* refers to more or less recognisable events (e.g. the conflict between the duke of Burgundy and the king of France in *De bello*, quoted in n. 21); in other cases, the reference is more general and abstract (e.g. also in *De bello*, the Qu. inc., 'Si baro regis Francie vel alterius principis moverit guerram ipsi regi suo').

[15] There is, of course, the dedication of the work as such to the duke of Milan, and, as is made clear in the preface to the general work *De principibus* and throughout several *rubricae*, an emphasis on the prerogatives and duties of the *princeps christianus*. The term 'dux' may of course refer to very different positions: e.g. Qu. 6 (on a par with other princes), 18, 31, 56, 60 (the duke of Milan); cf. for example *De bello*: 'Dux belli potest facere treugam', which seems to refer to a military commander.

[16] The same remark applies in other contexts, e.g. reprisals (Rondinini-Soldi, *Tractatus*, p. 13), treason (p. 57), taxation (p. 59), etc. See also the *Rubrica De principibus*, Qu. 122 (regal and tax prerogatives of a city *non recognoscens superiorem*), 165 (prerogatives of a *populus non recognoscens superiorem*), 181 (reserved regal rights exercised by a *princeps non recognoscens superiorem*), 376 (mint, exercised by a city *non recognoscens superiorem*), 444 (limitations to the statute-making power of a city which is, on the contrary, *recognoscens superiorem*); and the question included 'Inferentes iniustam guerram' in *De bello* (TUB MS MC 299, fol. 21ra): a prince of a city in Italy 'que non recognosc[i]t superiorem' may prepare for war against an enemy.

appears to be hierarchically inferior, although this does not necessarily affect their capacity to negotiate and conclude treaties with the prince – a reminder that our modern distinctions between public international law and municipal public law cannot apply without seriously distorting the understanding of the political constellation Garatus was considering. To blur modern concepts even more, one should also consider that a political actor's position in the hierarchy was not only determined by his political authority or power. This becomes clear from remarks on the position of a *tyrannus*; the latter's authority while in power may come close to that of the prince, but the legitimacy of his rule is much more doubtful as soon as he is out of office.[17]

Whereas the emperor's role in *De confœderatione* is almost reduced to its vanishing point,[18] the pope as the supreme authority of the community of actors is strongly asserted.[19] His superiority *in iure* over the princes is unequivocally established, though the role ascribed to him often seems to take into account that his superiority is rather a matter of law, moral authority and religious duty than political (or military) clout.[20] In some

---

[17] Qu. 41.
[18] In the *Rubrica De principibus*, the pre-eminent position of the emperor (in law) is more marked: cf. Qu. 9, 16, 58, 168.
[19] The same strong emphasis is made in the *Rubrica De principibus*: see for example Qu. 485 (according to the common opinion 'imperium dependat a papatu'). See also the *Rubrica De principibus*, e.g. Qu. 6 (the pope's right to remove rulers from office), 9 (the pope's right to amalgamate two kingdoms under one ruler), 17 (general supremacy of the pope), 27 (the pope's jurisdiction over sovereigns), 46 (again, the pope as supreme judge), 74 (the anointment of kings), 90 (the pope's prerogative to allow derogations from the ordinary rules of proceedings), 459 (the pope's power to revoke a council's decree).
[20] Rondinini-Soldi, *Tractatus*, p. 36 ('nell'incertezza politica dello stato presente, rivivifichi il ricorrente motivo di una supremazia assoluta del pontefice sul mondo, quale limite naturale all'avidità ed all'instabilità dei sovrani della terra') and *De principibus*, Qu. 46: 'quotiescumque est necesse, recurrendum est ad papam, sive sit necessitas iuris, quia iudex dubius est de iure, sive facti, quia alius non sit iudex superior, vel propter negligentiam, vel vacantibus regnis et principatibus' (further qualified in the text). A very good example of Garatus' concern for both law and politics is a *quaestio* which occurs in the title *De bello* (quoted here from TUB MS MC 299, fol. 21ra–rb, with corrections or additions from MBS MS clm 403), although the appeal by the king of France to the emperor or the pope may seem to be a purely theoretical option: 'Dux Borgondie violenter et clam castra et urbes regis Francie occupavit deinde [post] multos annos rex Francie potuit de iure [MSB: iuste] movere bellum contra ducem Borgondie causa recuperandi castra sua. Et dico aut rex Francie potest habere recursum ad papam vel imperatorem et sic ad superiorem et tunc non debet indicere bellum propria auctoritate, secus si non potuit habere recursum vel non timeretur papa vel imperator a duce Borgondie, tunc rex possit indicere bellum et ratio [est] quia licet ex intervallo non liceat vim vi repellere in l. iii. § cum igitur ff. de vi. et vi ar. et glo. in l. i. C. unde vi, ymmo debet ire ad superiorem qui faciat restitui ablata c. novit de iudi. l. si pacto ff. de pac. tamen ubi papa vel imperator

of the treatise's questions, the pope's position appears more on a par with that of other territorial princes.

The most striking feature of the community of actors as it appears through the somewhat haphazard sequence of questions in Garatus' treatise is therefore that of the great versatility of 'treaties' for establishing agreements or relationships between actors of hierarchically widely differing positions. Even sovereignty in the relative sense of *superiorem non recognoscens* does not seem to be a requirement in a political world where most autonomous actors, including the princes, are deemed to fit within a superior *respublica*. This matches the political order which appears in the *Rubrica de principibus*, and which is not fundamentally different from that considered in *De confœderatione*: a clear indication that within the academic Roman-canonistic legal theory the principles governing both the individual, more or less autonomous territories and their rulers, and the superior *respublica* represented by the emperor and the pope, were largely shared. Garatus' legal authorities still reflect a concept of a Western Christian political system where there is comparatively little dualism opposing the constitutional foundation of the individual actors to that of the international community.[21]

Negotiations and the conclusion of treaties

The non-systematic, patchy approach of this format of treatise addressing more or less specific questions appears most clearly if one tries to work out the general principles governing the negotiations and the conclusion of a treaty. Only a few questions address specific aspects of the matter, and no general theory emerges.

The most general principle is no doubt the duty of Christian rulers to seek peace (within Christendom): whatever the ideology and mentalities

---

non timetur bellum est licitum licet ex intervallo postquam mediante iudice non potest ablata recuperare c. olim de resti. spol. per Inno. et no. Bal. in repe. l. i. C unde vi. in 3° fol. facit quod no. Bar. in l. si alius § bellissime ff. quod vi aut clam quod est notabile pro principibus quando occupantur sua castra et civitates a tiranno patenti quod ex intervallo potest indici bellum quando aliter superioris copia et defensio effectualis haberi non potest.'

[21] In that sense, Randall Lesaffer's accurate characterisation of the early sixteenth-century literature on international law and politics would also apply to Garatus' work: 'To the authors both in favour of and opposed to the sovereignty of the state and the decline of the universal monarchy, the international community was still a legal community with its own finality and its own normative system', Randall Lesaffer, *Europa: een zoektocht naar vrede 1453–1763 en 1945–1997* (Leuven, 1999), p. 116.

of an aristocratic ruling class defined as the fighting class within society,[22] the Christian political order puts the *bonum pacis* forward as its fundamental priority.

Incidentally, the questions confirm either that negotiations and the conclusion of treaties can be delegated or that the prince can take such tasks upon himself personally (in which case formal constraints will be relaxed). Otherwise, the questions remind the reader that the preparation and approval of such agreements will require discretion, trust and some clear, and therefore inevitably to some degree formal,[23] exchanges. A mere reconciliation does not amount to a peace.

Political expediency and legal principles may also clash in the case of several successive alliances.

The scope of the agreements established in treaties

The effects of treaties receive greater attention. From the outset a distinction is made between public and private interests. The crucial test for that distinction appears to be the sovereign's power. *Quaestio* 1 considers the scope of the usual clause in a peace treaty whereby damage and loss suffered by either party will not be actionable. Such a clause should not restrict the rights of private individuals, but here the more general principle that the prince can affect an individual subject's rights in the public interest is applied and takes precedence. Moreover, the law of war may have affected proprietary rights.[24] Similarly, provisions in a peace treaty regarding the status of a city will not *per se* affect its rights as a corporation: a clause placing the city under the protection of a prince, for instance, does not as such abolish or suspend the jurisdictional privilege of that city.[25]

The binding force of treaties is asserted in several questions. Predictably, the legal foundation for a prince being bound by contracts he has entered

---

[22] But the ideology was also shared within society at large: Rondinini-Soldi, *Tractatus*, pp. 31 and 37 (in the latter passage, on the pope's duty to intervene on behalf of peace).

[23] In spite of the decline of formalities in the general law of (private) contracts: J. Bärmann, 'Considérations sur l'histoire du contrat consensuel', *Revue Internationale de Droit Comparé* 13 (1961), 19–53 at p. 42.

[24] Qu. 38. The status of hostages (e.g. kept as sureties) contains some specific rules regarding their property and their right to dispose by will: Qu. 40, 54.

[25] *De confœderatione* Qu. 56. See also Qu. 54 (hostage's right to dispose by will once the peace is made); Qu. 30 (protection of landworkers and other categories).

into is not altogether free from ambiguities: some clusters of authorities emphasise that a contract made by a prince acquires *vis legis*,[26] while others point out that, while a prince may be 'above' the law(s), he is bound by contracts and by laws which are akin to contracts.[27] In spite of the obvious tension between the two theses, the terse formulation of the questions (which, remarkably, here only refer to civil law authorities[28]) does not provide sufficient grounds for a debate of doctrines. What is nevertheless clear is the intention to assert strongly the binding force of a treaty upon a prince. The use of the l. *Digna vox* (Cod. 1, 14, 4) in both clusters,[29] together with the authorities which underline the willingness of the prince to conform to his own laws[30] and the desirability that a prince should anyhow conform to *bona fide* contracts,[31] further adds to the onus on a prince to abide by his contracts and treaties.[32]

The obligations of a party to the treaty are, however, qualified by various means. In contrast to what was the case during later centuries, coercion seems to vitiate, if not the treaty itself, then at least the clauses unduly extracted from the other party. The 'good faith' which buttresses the binding force of the treaty also pervades its effects: perpetual treaties are

---

[26] Qu. 46, 47; see also Kenneth Pennington, *The Prince and the Law 1200–1600: Sovereignty and Rights in the Western Legal Tradition* (Berkeley, 1993), p. 206 on the binding force of treaties, and *passim* on the binding force of contracts in general.

[27] Under divine law: Qu. 5.

[28] On the canonistic foundations of the principle: Randall Lesaffer, 'The Medieval Canon Law of Contract and Early Modern Treaty Law', *Journal of the History of International Law*, 2 (2000), 178–98, also referring to earlier literature.

[29] In a different context, the l. *Digna vox* is also prominent in the *Rubrica De principibus*: e.g. Qu. 103 (*princeps solutus legibus*, followed by qualifications of the principle), 163 (the right of a prince to recede from a contract if it causes a major prejudice to his realm), 327 (again, qualifications of the principle *legibus solutus*), 434 (the prince is bound by his obligations towards his own subjects). On rulers' statutory powers, or prerogatives to act against statutory terms, see also Qu. 47, 53, 90, 275. On the binding forces of contracts made by a prince: Qu. 123.

[30] Cf. Cynus ad Cod. 5, 16, 26, quoted in Qu. 47.   [31] Qu. 36, 46.

[32] Both Allen Z. Hertz, 'Medieval Treaty Obligation', *Connecticut Journal of International Law* 6 (1991), 425–43 and Lesaffer, 'Medieval Canon Law of Contract' strongly emphasise the importance and influence of medieval canon law on the development of the law of treaties. This is, of course, justified when one considers textual and doctrinal authorities as sources of both the doctrine and, to some degree, the formal practice related to treaties, but, at the same time, it also reflects a certain ambivalence as regards the 'binding character' attributed to the canon law by secular rulers, even in their relations between each other. Garatus' *De confœderatione* illustrates both the importance of canon law as a legal authority and its somewhat idealistic normative force.

deemed to remain in force 'quamdiu fides servetur';³³ a treaty of alliance is incompatible with an alliance undertaken with an enemy of the party one is already allied to.³⁴ Obligations to an enemy (in the formal sense: *hostis*) are binding, though a distinction is made between the binding *publica fides* and private obligations.³⁵ Other qualifications appear to be more technical: for instance, the principle that an ally will only have to provide assistance when asked,³⁶ a qualification which, however, may not be applicable if the obligation is one not of an ally, but of a prince who has promised protection to a city.³⁷ An ally's obligation to intervene (e.g. in the context of an agreement of collective defence) in any case remains restricted by a common standard of care and capacity.³⁸

Some rules are specifically applicable to truces: e.g. the obligation to continue to observe the truce, even though the other party may have committed a breach;³⁹ the provision for a penalty;⁴⁰ and the protection of certain categories of persons.⁴¹

The questions relating to *adhaerentes et sequaces* refer both to prevailing practices and to non-legal obligations of the rulers to these categories. These non-legal obligations appear to be partly founded in morality, practical considerations and even a certain degree of *Realpolitik*.⁴² The definition of these categories remains sufficiently broad to allow some degree of interpretation and conflict, particularly if conventions do not refer to them *nominatim*. One of the crucial legal questions seems to be whether these categories (when not referred to individually and specifically) are included implicitly in treaty provisions. Since the question is raised,⁴³ one may be tempted to infer that their inclusion could not safely be assumed. Nevertheless, there is some emphasis that the pope's policy (according to Johannes Andreae⁴⁴) tended to include the followers (who, presumably, did or could normally not act as autonomous actors in their own right) explicitly, a practice which seems to be approved.⁴⁵ The practice of secular rulers, who also appear to refer to their followers, is referred to in vaguer

---

[33] Qu. 9, reference to Baldus on *De pace Constantiae*. This is a different problem from that which would become known as the validity of treaties *rebus sic stantibus*: Alain Wijffels, 'La validité *rebus sic stantibus* des conventions: quelques étapes du développement historique (moyen âge – temps modernes)', in F. Ost et M. Van Hoecke (eds.), *Temps et droit: le droit a-t-il pour vocation de durer?* (Brussels, 1998), pp. 247–70.
[34] Qu. 26.   [35] Qu. 49.   [36] Qu. 28.   [37] Qu. 43.
[38] Qu. 4.   [39] Qu. 16.   [40] Qu. 32   [41] Qu. 30.
[42] See for example Qu. 43 and 56 on cities that have been declared to be under the protection of an overlord, and Qu. 52, which expresses the prince's duty.
[43] Qu. 3 and 27.   [44] Ad Sextum, 2, 14, 2.
[45] Andreas Barbatia ad Clementinam 1, 3, 2, 2 (quoted in Qu. 3), and Qu. 21.

terms.[46] Whether because of a prevailing (or at least endorsed) practice, or because of its moral or political effects, some authorities (e.g. Angelus de Ubaldis[47]) suggest that there is at least an implicit argument for including the *adhaerentes* in those treaty provisions, which otherwise might prove ineffective. A prince's duty as regards these categories was probably in theory restricted to public matters.[48] Conversely, hostile relations could, of course, also affect both the prince and his following.[49]

Conclusion

Garatus' *Rubrica* of treaties is not a comprehensive treatise on the late medieval Roman-canonistic literature and doctrine on the law of treaties. It consists primarily in a series of specific questions, mostly derived from that literature, which deal with a variety of aspects of the law of treaties. Its main advantage point is that of the sequence of *rubricae* which, altogether, form the treatise *De principibus*, and which deal with the rights, prerogatives and duties of a prince, here considered mainly as a ruler within the northern Italian peninsula around the mid-fifteenth century. Since the other *rubricae* of the treatise follow the same unsystematic arrangement as in *De confœderatione, et pace conventionibus principum*, the treatise does not offer a comprehensive or systematically presented survey of the subject matter either.

What Garatus' *De confœderatione* does offer, however, is a variegated sample of late-medieval civil law and canon law authorities on a limited range of related issues. These are just loose fragments of a wider picture which was never assembled by late-medieval lawyers, nor by early modern legal authors; indeed, even modern historiography does not provide a full study of the medieval Roman canonistic doctrine on the law of treaties – a study which, of course, no modern historian would undertake without also undertaking the formidable task of studying the context of late-medieval treaty-making practice, in particular in the Italian political context of most late-medieval commentators and authors of *consilia*. Garatus' work may provide a first stepping-stone to such a study, though Baldus' commentary *De pace Constantiae* should take precedence as the fundamental single authority on the subject in *mos italicus* literature.

---

[46] At least in Qu. 27. Qu. 17, 39 and 57 may be seen as more specific cases.
[47] Ad D. 6, 1, 43, quoted in Qu. 35. [48] Qu. 63. [49] Qu. 51.

A provisional edition

The full edition of the *Rubrica* in the Appendix at the end of the book may facilitate such further studies. It is not a critical edition, as the Italian manuscripts of *De confœderatione* could not be taken into account. It is based on the most widely available edition, which figures in the collection of treatises published in Venice in 1584; a critical apparatus is based on a collation with the edition in the 1544 Lyons collection of treatises, with the 1530 Lyons edition of Garatus' *tractatus* and with the three known 'transalpine' manuscripts. The main added value of the present edition, however, will hopefully be the addition of quotations in full from the main doctrinal authorities referred to by Garatus.[50] It is hoped that, in the future, it will be possible to publish a full critical edition including the Italian manuscripts and other printed versions of *De confœderatione*.

[50] Several references remain doubtful or unidentified. This is partly due to the limited range of old editions I had at my disposal while preparing the Appendix, although I was occasionally able to consult a manuscript (e.g. Johannes de Lignano ad X) and some rare editions. Garatus' use of manuscript sources has also been the reason why, in some cases, the original reference may be erroneous. Finally, the limited collation of Garatus' text shows many disparities, particularly in the references to some authors. References to the manuscripts are abbreviated as follows: MBS (Munich, Bayerische Staatsbibliothek); PBN (Paris, Bibliothèque Nationale); TUB (Tübingen, Universitätsbibliothek).

9

The importance of medieval canon law and the scholastic tradition for the emergence of the early modern international legal order

DOMINIQUE BAUER

Introduction

It is becoming increasingly clear that the rise of the consensus-based early modern treaty and the law of nations was highly determined by the medieval tradition of canon and Roman law, and of scholastic philosophy and theology.[1] The role played by the principle of *pacta sunt servanda*, a basic principle of natural law,[2] as the cornerstone of early modern treaty law is one of the most striking examples of the way in which canon law influenced the early modern doctrine of treaty law. However, how must this medieval influence be understood? What did it mean? How can it be described?

These questions cannot easily be resolved because of the complex character of the various evolutions that took place. In this chapter, two central elements that emerged throughout the medieval period will be dealt with: natural law and voluntarism. More specifically, these two topics will be

---

[1] Robert Feenstra, 'Quelques remarques sur les sources utilisées par Grotius dans ses travaux de droit naturel' in *International Law and the Grotian Heritage: A Commemorative Colloquium Held at the Hague on 8 April 1983 on the Occasion of the Fourth Centenary of the Birth of Hugo Grotius* (The Hague, 1985), pp. 65–81; James Muldoon, 'The contribution of Medieval Canon Lawyers to the Formation of International Law', *Traditio* 28 (1972), 483–97, gives an account of the state of affairs. Muldoon, 'Medieval Canon Law and the Formation of International Law', *Zeitschrift der Savigny-Stiftung für Rechtsgeschichte, Kanonistische Abteilung* 81 (1995), 64–82, especially deals with the influence of the medieval legal and ecclesiological worldview; Randall Lesaffer, 'The Medieval Canon Law of Contract and Early Modern Treaty Law', *Journal of the History of International Law* 2 (2000), 178–98 focuses on the principle of *pacta sunt servanda*.

[2] Lesaffer, 'Medieval Canon Law', p. 180; E. Jiménez de Aréchaga, 'The Grotian Heritage and the Concept of Just World Order' in *International Law and the Grotian Heritage*, pp. 7–18 at p. 7.

treated from their close intertwinement with the legal order that came into being as an original product of the Middle Ages. This legal structure was based upon the antagonism between, on the one hand, the legal subject and, on the other hand, the public, objective legal order. This background is important in order to understand and to grasp the (historical) significance of the doctrinal legitimation of a consensus-based law of nations, of *pacta sunt servanda* as its formal principle, and to understand adequately the early steps of the law of nations in their uniqueness as well as in their being tributary to the Middle Ages. The analysis of these elements will be the subject of this chapter. Of course, a topic as broad as this one cannot be developed exhaustively and therefore its treatment remains inevitably incomplete. Moreover, some of the arguments need further research, as the study of the influence of the Middle Ages on the law of nations still has a long way to go.

The breakdown of the old medieval order as it had taken shape in the papacy and the Holy Roman Empire did not just necessitate new institutional forms and new legitimations that had to replace the diminishing powers of popes and emperors. The need for a new basis of legitimate power introduced into the law of nations and into treaty law the legal subject, with its medieval voluntaristic and consensualistic features. In its turn, early modern treaty law functioned as a catalyst of fundamental legal changes. With the gradual disappearance of the old framework, a few medieval attainments concerning the legal subject and its voluntaristic foundations were introduced into the international legal field. The shift from rights as things external to the legal subject and to the concept of subjective right as a *facultas*, referring to a capacity of the legal subject, was closely related to the legitimation of a voluntaristic law of nations. Moreover, with Hugo Grotius' (1583–1645) concept of *appetitus societatis* a new legitimation was created to found a new formal principle (*pacta sunt servanda*) on this subjective basis in order to intercept the breakdown of the traditional order.

Ever since the Middle Ages, an antagonism existed between the objective, public legal order above, which was external to the legal subjects, and the legal subject itself that had internal, legally sanctioned features and characteristics of its own. One of the most important of these legally sanctioned characteristics was personal will, which gave rise to the emergence of voluntarism and intentionalism. Within the scope of this chapter, it is impossible to go into detail here, but it must be stated that voluntarism and intentionalism were a part of the emergence of an independent human positive law that sprang from the acknowledgement of the personal, unique characteristics of every individual, from the human essence that was universally present in every human being before the Fall and from original human nature that had been blurred by original sin. This essence was a theological, an ecclesiological concept.

There are two aspects to medieval tradition that have to be taken into account. First, there is the Roman canonical tradition of the Middle Ages as it was formed from the twelfth century onwards. What matters here for our argument has already been mentioned: the formation of the antagonism between the public legal order and the legal subject himself, the formation of a voluntaristic subject and of a subjective concept of *ius* with its consequences for the relation between divine law, natural law and positive law. The relation between these three types of law reveals a complex eclectic synthesis of Roman law concepts of natural law, Christian moral precepts and ecclesiological concepts that led to as many interesting original combinations of thought as to, in our modern eyes, contradictory statements. This medieval synthesis was of great importance for the interpretation of seventeenth-century natural law thinking, which can be illustrated by Grotius' work and, especially as to the status of *pacta sunt servanda*, by Samuel Pufendorf's (1632–94) *De officio hominis et civis libri duo*.[3] The same goes for the works of the other members of the seventeenth- and eighteenth-century pantheon of the early law of nations, such as Christian Wolff (1679–1754).

Second, there was the further development, from the thirteenth century onwards, of the debate on the relations between reason and will. The tradition of the voluntaristic school of natural law originated in the Middle Ages and is rooted in medieval scholastic philosophy. Prior to the 'official' start of voluntaristic scholastic philosophy with Johannes Duns Scotus (1266–1308) and William of Ockham (1300–49), voluntarism had already formed an integral part of medieval thinking ever since its emergence in twelfth-century canon law. It had already reached a unique highlight well before the publication of the *Decretum Gratiani* (1140), which initiated classical canon law. Ivo of Chartres (*c*. 1040–1115) and Peter Abelard (1079–1142) can be considered to be the champions of this earliest voluntarism in the first half of the twelfth century. Well before the *doctor subtilis* Thomas Aquinas (1225–74) developed voluntarism throughout his endless and beautiful *distinctiones* at the end of the thirteenth century, the voluntaristic interpretation of *ius* and even of *dominium* had already taken shape within the work of John Peter Olivi (*c*. 1248–98), who seems

[3] 1682 (Classics of International Law 10, Oxford, 1927).

to deal with those concepts as if they evidently have to be regarded not as *res*, but as capacities, as subjective rights.⁴ In his *Quaestiones in secundum librum sententiarum*, he dealt with the question *Quid ponat ius vel dominium*⁵ in the framework of his elaboration on the *distinctio formalis*. In this *quaestio*, he treated the question whether rights and property (he also mentions *iurisdictio*, *auctoritas* and *potestas*) add something to the person who holds these rights or property. What is important from a legal point of view is the fact that *ius* and *dominium* were treated not as things, but as a (spiritual) capacity. This interpretation was an essential step in the development of natural rights. This is clearly illustrated by Grotius' *De iure belli ac pacis*. In the first book, that deals among other things with the definition of *ius*, this concept in its subjective meaning is described as a moral capacity, a *facultas* that, even if it refers to real rights, applies to the person that holds these rights.⁶

Voluntaristic natural law thinking developed in a constant struggle with the 'rationalistic' natural law thinking of Thomistic philosophy. The implications of Duns Scotus' voluntaristic philosophy for the formation of natural law were passed from thinkers such as Gabriel Biel (*c.* 1420–95) and Ferdinand Vasquez (1512–69) on to Martin Luther (1483–1546) and the secular natural thinkers such as Grotius, Hobbes (1588–1679) and Pufendorf. Starting from the medieval tradition and Johannes Duns Scotus and William of Ockham, one can follow the voluntaristic tradition from scholasticism to John Locke (1632–1704), John Austin (1790–1859)

---

⁴ Brian Tierney, *The Idea of Natural Right: Studies on Natural Rights, Natural Law and Church Law 1150–1625* (Atlanta, 1997), p. 42, deals with the works of John Peter Olivi in elaborating on the fact that *ius* was interpreted as a subjective right long before the rise of nominalism.
⁵ Brother Petrus Iohannis Olivi, OFM, *Quaestiones in secundum librum sententiarum* (ed. B. Jansen, Quarracchi, 1922); S. Belmond, 'Deux penseurs franciscains: Pierre-Jean Olivi et Guillaume Occam', *Etudes Franciscaines* 35 (1923), 188–97; W. Hoeres, 'Der Begriff der Intentionalität bei Olivi', *Scholastik* 36 (1961), 23–48; Hoeres, 'Der Unterschied von Wesenheit und Individuation bei Olivi', *Scholastik* 38 (1963), 54–61; B. Jansen, 'Beiträge zur geschichtlichen Entwicklung der Distinctio formalis', *Zeitschrift für katholische Theologie* 53 (1929), 317–544 at pp. 517–28; Jansen, 'Die Definition des Konzils von Vienne: Substantia animae rationalis seu intellective vere ac per se humani corporis forma', *Zeitschrift für katholische Theologie* 32 (1908), 289–306 and 471–87; C. Partee, 'Peter John Olivi: Historical and Doctrinal Study', *Franciscan Studies* 20 (1960), 215–60.
⁶ Hugo Grotius, *De iure belli ac pacis libri tres* 1, 1, 4 (Paris, 1625): 'Ab hac iuris significatione diversa est altera, sed ab hac ipsa veniens, quae ad personam refertur; quo sensu ius est qualitas moralis personae competens ad aliquid iuste habendum vel agendum. Personae competit hoc ius, etiam si rem interdum sequatur, ut servitutes praediorum quae iura realia dicuntur comparatione facta ad alia mere personalia: non quia non ipsa quoque personae competant, sed quia non alii competunt quam rem certam habeat.'

and Samuel Pufendorf.[7] An analysis of the antithesis of Thomas Aquinas' natural law thinking and the voluntaristic construction of Johannes Duns Scotus[8] from this perspective can be surprisingly illustrative.

The often problematical distinction between reason and will, set and integrated in the field of law and translated into legal concepts and terminology, seems to be an important criterion for separating and describing natural law and positive law and their mutual relations. The often confusing and vague distinctions between divine law and natural law, between natural law and natural positive law, between natural law and positive law, between natural and voluntary law, etc., can become very useful from the perspective of the relation between legal subject and objective, for public legal order from a legal perspective in law and for the relation between rationalism and voluntarism from a philosophical perspective.

Voluntarism and positive human law were in many respects the result of the secularisation of this theological framework. This unique kind of medieval secularisation is expressed by the historical cohesion of an essentialist view of what man is and the relevance of secular society for human essence. The original theological context had introduced into Western thinking a unique kind of political rationality that combined on the one hand moral and pastoral control of the individuals and, on the other, the legal construction of the state.[9] All of these features of man and society served in their increasingly secular forms as the basis of the nation-states and as the basis for the formulation of a common good, a common goal within society corresponding with the nature of man.

The latter evolution constitutes the historical background for seventeenth- and eighteenth-century natural law thinking. From this point of view, the formal principle of *pacta sunt servanda* was at the same time a remnant of the moral and religious connotations that had always, going back as far as classical Roman law, surrounded doctrinal reflections on natural law and the law of nations, as it was the translation into international law of the new subjectivism of natural philosophy that would shape the Enlightenment. The legal outside world, the public legal order, was legitimised and formally shaped after voluntarism itself. In this context, two things can be studied in more detail, especially with regard

---

[7] H. Schiedermaier, 'Hugo Grotius und die Naturrechtsschule' in B. Börner and H. Jahrreiss (eds.), *Einigkeit und Recht und Freiheit: Festschrift für Karl Carstens zum 70. Geburtstag* (Bonn and Munich, 1985); G. Stratenwerth, *Die Naturrechtslehre des Johannes Duns Scotus* (Göttingen, 1951), pp. 115–16.

[8] Stratenwerth, *Naturrechtslehre des Johannes Duns Scotus*, pp. 115–16.

[9] Michel Foucault, 'Omnes et singulatim. Vers une critique de la raison politique' in D. Defert and F. Ewald (eds.), *Dits et écrits (1954–1988)*, (Paris, 1994), vol. IV, pp. 134–61.

to Grotius' *De iure belli ac pacis*. First, the already mentioned medieval sense of *ius* as a subjective right should be dealt with and, second, Grotius' concept of *appetitus societatis* acquires prominence. The hypothesis can be formulated that the term *appetitus societatis*, as Grotius put it, served as a tool for expressing a view of man that could serve as the foundation for the law of nations. To that end, Grotius used the old scholastic term *appetitus*, which had an essential, constructive, positive and preserving role regarding human nature. Perhaps this can be illustrated further on the basis of the use of the term *appetitus* in the work of Grotius' countryman Baruch Spinoza (1632–77). Further investigation of the continuity and discontinuity of the concept of *appetitus* could be very illuminating regarding the fundamental changes in the interpretation of human essence during the seventeenth century, and its implications for legal doctrine.

The subjectivism of the seventeenth century within this legal context stands side by side with similar evolutions within political theory and philosophy. After Descartes' (1596–1650) *Meditationes de prima philosophia* (1641), the world is shaped on the bases of the features of the new human essence, the *cogito*. Political theorists such as Locke, Hobbes and Rousseau (1712–78) legitimise their states or social systems upon the universal features, upon the essence of man, upon man as he really is, in the state of nature, before he enters the state. Hobbes' *The Elements of Law Natural and Politic* (1640), consisting of *Human Nature* and *De corpore politico*, for example represents a very pure and radical case of the corresponding dualism of legal subject/human nature on the one hand and objective or public legal and political order on the other. The line of argument is the same here as later in his *Leviathan* (1651). Human nature only allows for the adoption of rational precepts without which there would be a constant state of war. The analysis of human nature precedes that of the state, because the construction of the state and the need for a state is preconditioned by the implications, necessities and possibilities given by human nature.

Rather than starting this analysis from an overview of the material definitions and descriptions of natural law, it is much more appropriate and effective, in order to grasp the relevant elements of the evolution and emergence of natural law for our central theme, to begin with a more formal treatment of natural law. Within a formal treatment of natural law, one has to search for the constitutive elements and relations that are at stake in any material definition of natural law. These components have to be, if not exclusively determinative, of essential importance to the formation of natural law and its legal and cultural features.

From the perspective of cultural history, natural law thinking is in keeping with natural philosophy, which was the cornerstone of political and philosophical thinking during the Enlightenment, as well as of enlightened legal doctrine, jurisdiction and jurisprudence. In this regard, natural law thinking appears as one of the constitutive elements, together with Cartesian philosophy, that shaped the intellectual context and challenges that the Enlightenment tried to deal with.

This approach has two significant advantages. On the one hand, it reveals the fact that the internal legal evolution cannot be separated and is profoundly influenced by this broader intellectual context. On the other hand, however, it will also appear that the emergence and evolution of the main legal 'protagonists', *pacta sunt servanda*, the legal public order and the legal subject in turn profoundly influence and are highly illustrative of the status of the human person, of human society and the legitimate exercise of power within society, and of morality.

Grotius' *De iure belli ac pacis* is generally considered an attempt to fill the legal gap that was caused by the breakdown of medieval legal *christianitas*. It is important to elaborate here in a few lines on what was at stake with the replacement of one criterion by another. What was at stake here was the need of a new foundation of legitimate power at the level of the nation-states. The exercise of legitimate power, however, is founded upon what is regarded, often implicitly, as the public order, as the overarching order that binds and defines the legal subjects, and upon society, which implies a specific view of what human persons are. From this perspective, the definition of legitimate power and, consequently, of the public legal order is closely related to the definition of the legal person and the human person. In other words, replacing the criterion of legitimate power is reshaping the status of society and of the individual. So one should always take into account that Grotius' masterpiece reveals in many respects a new world, carefully hidden behind its eclectic lines and definitions. The scope and content of the series of implications that flow from Grotius' work, however, is largely determined by the conditions given by the development of law set by the Middle Ages.

Natural law and the objective, public order

The inheritance of classical Roman and Justinian law

As is the case for the seventeenth and eighteenth centuries, there was no clear-cut definition of natural law available in medieval canon and in

Roman law. In classical and post-classical Roman law, with the medieval canonists as with the medieval legists, various, often even contradictory, definitions of natural law stood side by side. The same goes for the denomination of *ius gentium*. In describing the medieval inheritance of natural law thinking and its treatment of the *ius gentium* one should take into account a few decisive facts and evolutions: the discussion of natural law and the *ius gentium* with Gaius and Paulus; the influence and interpretation of the definition of Ulpian by the glossators; and finally, the definitions of Gratian and his influence on both decretists and glossators.[10] Although Ulpian's definition of natural law was of much more influence on the medieval tradition than those of Gaius and Paulus, it is very useful to mention them, because they point to a problem that was reinforced during the Middle Ages. With Gaius and especially with Paulus, natural law and the *ius gentium*, which are practically one and the same, are based upon or refer to non-legal concepts, such as the *naturalis ratio* (Gaius) or *aequitas* (Paulus) that stem from the Stoic and Aristotelian traditions respectively.

The interpretation of natural law as the expression of rationality present in things and living beings, or being founded in human nature, is integrated into the *Corpus iuris civilis*. In Justinian Roman law, however, this interpretation is accompanied by another, Christian interpretation of natural law. Natural law also appears to be based upon God as the highest legislator. The impact of this combination of two kinds of natural law can hardly be overestimated.

First, the idea of God as the foundation of natural law does not only give natural law and the law of nations – which in the *Corpus iuris civilis* is identical to natural law – a metaphysical dimension unknown to classical Roman law. It also gives natural law a moral connotation and connects it with lawgiving. Because of the former, moral precepts and rationality obtain a shared universality and therefore, in its moral capacity, natural law serves the project of the salvation of universal mankind. Because of the latter, will and reason are integrated as two cooperating powers in the construction of law.

Moreover, the image of God as a lawgiver was to become a model of lawgiving and constituted the basis of what Walter Ullmann called 'the descending theory of power'. Roman ideas of government, the imperial

---

[10] For an overview of natural law thinking with decretists and glossators, see R. Weigand, *Die Naturrechtslehre der Legisten und Dekretisten von Irnerius bis Accursius und von Gratian bis Johannes Teutonicus* (Munich, 1967). See also on *ius gentium*, chapter 10.

ideology and the biblical themes of power given from above, of *potestas* being awarded or transmitted by divinity, constituted the foundations of the descending, theocratical theme of government. This cluster of Roman and biblical elements served as a basis for the concept of sovereignty of the ruler as well as creating the relationship of complete submission of the subjects to their ruler.[11]

The more the lawgiving institutions regard themselves as the embodiment of the natural or the divine order, the more their efficient government and control of the *forum internum*, the level of conscience, is legitimised. In other words, the combination of these two kinds of natural law serves as the basis of Foucault's combination of the pastoral and legal field in Western political rationality.[12] The idea that the Church was founded by a divine act and that ecclesiastical power was given by God to the pope not only implied that the pope stood above the Church; it also meant that there could be no legitimate, independently existing corporations within Christianity, because the Church as a corporate body, as the *universitas fidelium*, could not generate any legitimate power, any rights within itself – nor could the individual members of the Church claim any such power or rights.[13] The Church as a corporation by definition was one and universal. The deduction from the corporational Church of the concept of the state as a fictitious legal person, being treated and acting as an individual entity, makes up the indispensable theoretical, legal and ideological background for the sovereignty of the nation-states.[14] The importance of the *universitas* and the entities that were modelled on it,[15] as the building stones of the modern legal construction of society, can hardly be overestimated. Regarding natural law thinking, this corporational development

---

[11] Walter Ullmann, 'Der Souveränitätsgedanke in den mittelalterliche Krönungsordines' in Peter Classen and P. Scheibert (eds.), *Festschrift für Percy Ernst Schramm* (Wiesbaden, 1964), pp. 72–89 at pp. 74–7; Ullmann, 'The Bible and the Principles of Government in the Middle Ages' in *Settimane di studio del Centro italiano di studi sull'alto medioevo* (Spoleto, 1963), pp. 181–227; Ullmann, *Law and Politics in the Middle Ages: An Introduction to the Sources of Medieval Political Ideas* (Cambridge, 1988), pp. 25–50.

[12] Foucault, 'Omnes et singulatim'.

[13] Walter Ullmann, 'Legal Obstacles to the Emergence of the Concept of the State in the Middle Ages', *Annali di Storia del Diritto* 13 (1969), 44–61; Ullmann, *The Individual and Society in the Middle Ages* (Baltimore, 1966); Ullmann, 'Papst und König', *Salzburger Universitätsschriften* 3 (1966), 21–3.

[14] Ernst Kantorowicz, *The King's Two Bodies: A Study in Medieval Political Theology* (Princeton, NJ, 1957).

[15] Dirk van den Auweele, 'De Renaissance van de twaalfde eeuw: een nieuwe orde als fundament der Westerse samenleving' in Raoul Bauer *et al.* (eds.), *De twaalfde eeuw: een breuklijn in onze beschaving* (Antwerp and Amsterdam, 1982), pp. 73–101.

and the creation of the state as a legal person reflects the institutional and political dimension of the definition of the legal subject and of the individual within law and society. The view of society and the view of man were not only very closely intertwined; through the evolution of legal doctrine, political theory and practice, human society became the 'natural', integrated framework of man as an essentially social and legal being. The essence of society and the essence of man were reciprocally denominated. During the Renaissance of the twelfth century this development led to a constructive and positive attitude towards political power, positive law and the organisation of society, which countered Augustian pessimism long before Aristotelian political thinking influenced medieval minds.[16]

As one of the most powerful mechanisms of secularisation, it created an unbreakable link between an efficiently politically and legally structured society and an essentialist view of man. To grasp this relation fully, we need to turn to yet another implication that directly relates to the emergence of natural law thinking and natural philosophy during the seventeenth and eighteenth centuries: the essentialist view of man. In Justinian law, and especially later in canon law, natural law referred to the essence of man within a moral and at the same time rational and legal project. The fact that morality as a social and legal project directly related to human essence, to what was good for man, led to the integration of social organisation into the scope of natural law and of legal thinking, and the other way around.

This situation not only contained the seeds of secularisation from the twelfth century onwards, but was in its turn reinforced secularisation throughout its different stages. Starting from these medieval preconditions, secularisation within Western culture regarded the shift from something external to human nature that determines human nature to human nature itself. This development led to a combined secularised morality and rationality based upon human nature. Seventeenth- and eighteenth-century natural law thinking and natural philosophy were the result of the latter. The attention for human nature and mankind in its original, natural setting, before entering the state and society, served as a new criterion for the constitution of the appropriate state and the just society.

The natural law thinkers and natural philosophers of the seventeenth and eighteenth centuries tried to elaborate the link that was created

---

[16] Dirk van den Auweele, 'De Renaissance van de XIIe eeuw en de Verlichting: ideologie, canonistiek en strafrechtsbedeling', *Panopticon. Tijdschrift voor strafrecht, criminologie en forensisch welzijnswerk* 4 (1993), 467–84.

between a secularised social institutionalism and an essentialist view of man that reflect each other reciprocally. This is not only a theoretical or doctrinal matter, but also a practical one. The existing political and institutional environment had a deep impact on the different natural law theories. This is why Locke's natural law thinking is undeniably related to his conception of the individual in his natural setting, completely equipped with the fundamental rights and liberties of the parliamentary state. It explains why Rousseau's abstract individual within an ahistorical natural state contained the preconditions for the aberration of the French Revolution during the *Terreur*. It clarifies the fact that with Montesquieu's carefully built-up and balanced political system corresponds a human being determined by history and by organically grown institutions.

The difficulties that are caused by this double definition of natural law for the glossators to offer a clear definition of natural law are aggravated by the existence of a third definition of natural law within classical Roman law, that of Ulpian. The definition of Ulpian was widely spread during the Middle Ages, among glossators as well as among canonists.[17] Ulpian divided law into three categories. First, there is natural law, common to both men and animals; second, he mentions the *ius gentium*, which only applies to human beings and which is based upon reason; and finally, there is civil law, by which the various states are governed internally. In Ulpian's triple division, the tension between a rational and even 'instinctive' interpretation of natural law and the later moral Christian interpretation is driven to a climax. The example of marriage, procreation and the education of children – which on the one hand is interpreted by Ulpian as a part of his conception of natural law and which on the other hand is based upon a highly moral natural law and on human, positive law in the later canon law – illustrates this.

This tension is illustrated as well by the status that is attributed to the law of nations, in between natural law and civil law.[18] Moreover, the law

---

[17] Dig. 1, 1, 1, 2–4: 'Privatum ius triplex est: collectum etenim est ex naturalibus praeceptis aut gentium aut civilibus. Ius naturale est, quod natura omnia animalia docuit: nam ius istud non humani generis proprium, sed omnium animalium, quae in terra, quae in mari nascuntur, avium quoque commune est. hinc descendit maris atque feminae coniunctio quam nos matrimonium appelamus, hinc liberorum procreatio, hinc educatio: videmus etenim cetera quoque animalia, feras etiam istius iuris peritia censeri. Ius gentium est, quo gentes humanae utuntur. Quod a naturali recedere facile inteligere licet, quia illud omnibus animalibus, hoc solis hominibus inter se commune sit.'

[18] This ambiguity will also be widely spread within medieval legal doctrine. The glossator Martinus for example describes the *ius gentium* as natural law, but at the same time places it between natural law and civil law. With Martinus, one can find an example of how the

of nations not only stands on the borderline between an amoral and even instinctive interpretation of natural law and a moral conception thereof, but also has to be situated between immutable law, transcending society, and a mutable, positive law that is the result of the particularities of space and time of the specific society in which this kind of law is created.

Apart from the tension between an amoral and a moral conception of natural law, between immutable and mutable law, the *ius gentium* has to be situated between yet two other elements, namely between a rationalistic conception of law and a voluntaristic conception of law. This distinction takes us to the heart of the antagonism between the legal subject and the public, objective legal order. Set in a medieval context, this matter is closely related to the tension between subject-based legal concepts on the one hand and the legal impact of the external legal order and society that binds the legal subjects and individuals on the other. This tension expresses the relation between voluntarism and rationalism in a legal context. It is very important to take this relation into account when dealing with the influence of Thomistic scholastic theology on canon law, with the legitimation of the law of nations through voluntarism,[19] with Vitoria (*c.* 1480–1546), Suarez (1548–1617), Vasquez and, finally, Grotius and his reference to positive law as *ius voluntarium*.[20]

Canon law and the glossators

The moral and ecclesiological concept of natural law mainly originated from canon law and largely influenced the glossators in their attempts to deal especially with Ulpian's definition and the dualism of Justinian law in a consistent way. The canon law doctrine of natural law was based upon the *Decretum Gratiani*, which initiated the classical period of medieval canon law. Throughout the *Tractatus de legibus* – containing the first twenty

---

law of nations was being divided into law that came into existence with mankind and law that was created afterwards by human reason; Weigand, *Naturrechtslehre*, p. 62. In the sixteenth and seventeenth centuries, thinkers such as Vitoria and Suarez and their successors created similar distinctions when dealing with the *ius gentium naturale* and the *ius gentium humanum* that is based upon consensus.

[19] Randall Lesaffer, *Europa: een zoektocht naar vrede?* (Leuven, 1999), pp. 83–8.
[20] Grotius, *De iure belli ac pacis* 1, 1, 9, 2: 'Iuris ita accepti optima partito est quae apud Aristotelem extat, ut sit aliud ius naturale, aliud voluntarium'; and 1, 1, 10, 4: 'Sciendum praeterea ius naturale non de iis tantum agere quae citra voluntatem humanam existunt, sed de multis etiam quae voluntatis humanae actum consequuntur. Sic dominium, quale nunc in usus est, voluntas humana introduxit: at eo introducto nefas mihi esse id arripere te invito quod tui est dominii ipsum indicat ius naturale.'

distinctiones of the *Decretum* – one finds the hierarchy of authorities, all the ingredients of the moral interpretation of canon law and its close relation to the construction of an institutionalised public legal order.

Within the framework of this chapter, it is most interesting to focus on the first nine *causae* of the first distinction. The first two distinctions are taken from Isidore of Seville's (560–636) *Liber ethymologiarum*. The confrontation of two elements of this eclectic background illustrate the shift to a moral concept of natural law: the definition of Ulpian[21] on the one hand, and the distinction between *ius* and *fas* on the other.[22] In Ulpian's triple division, natural law is a part of the law. Regarding the distinction between *fas* and *ius*, however, nature belongs to the level of divine lawfulness, while *ius* expresses human law. Through *fas*, a kind of natural law is introduced that is identical with divine law and a kind of nature comes into the picture that expresses divine lawfulness. So within law, a non-legal source of law is introduced, and next to legal validity comes lawfulness.

These conclusions lead us to the relation between natural law and divine law in the *Decretum Gratiani*. Although it has often been stated that Gratian confused divine law and natural law or that they are one and the same,[23] there is a substantial difference between them that is very relevant within the scope of this chapter. The complex relation between natural law and divine law can be clarified from the moral and religious integration of natural law as it appears from the tension between *ius* and *fas*.

Natural law came into existence together with mankind.[24] Because of its dignity and age, natural law differs from human law. Again, this illustrates the religious and moral meaning of natural law in the *Decretum Gratiani* and refers to the original state of mankind. This reference in the *Decretum Gratiani* has to be understood in two ways. First, it relates to an age prior to

---

[21] D. 1 c. 6: 'Ius aut naturale est, aut civile, aut gentium.'

[22] D. 1 c. 1: 'Fas lex divina est: ius est lex humana. Transire per agrum alienum, fas est, ius non est.'

[23] R. W. and R. J. Carlyle, *A History of Medieval Political Theory in the West* (Edinburgh, 1903), vol. II, p. 105; A. Wegner, 'Über positives göttliches Recht und natürliches', *Studia Gratiana* 1 (1953), 483–502. On the other hand S. Chororow, *Christian Political Theory in the West and Church Politic* (Berkeley and Los Angeles, 1972) analyses the difference between natural law and divine law in the *Decretum Gratiani*, and Weigand, *Naturrechtslehre*, p. 134, states that with Gratian natural law and divine law are materially one and the same, but formally different.

[24] D. 5 d. ante c. 1: 'Naturale ius inter omnia primatum obtinet et tempore et dignitate. Cepit enim ab exordio rationalis creaturae, nec variatur tempore, sed immutabile permanere.'

the foundation of society[25] and, second, it relates to the human condition before original sin. Within the Augustinian tradition, law and customs were the necessary means of organising a society poisoned by original sin. The long development of Augustine's (354–430) political thought had reached its final stages in the *De civitate Dei*, one of the most influential works of the Middle Ages. In this work, Augustine makes a clear distinction between society and the state. Whereas society is rooted in nature, the state is the result of original sin; it is the result of man's sinful condition. Society is interpreted as a harmonious whole of equals, whereas the state consists of unequals. Every institutional kind of submission to authority is unnatural. Political organisation is rooted in the chaos of the *saeculum* and cannot create order in which man can find rest. The state cannot achieve the right order in this world; it can only minimise disorder, and prevent tension and strife from becoming even worse.[26] In this way, the Augustinian legacy permeated the Middle Ages with a negative definition of political authority and political social organisation.

It is clear that Gratian and the decretists interpreted dignity and age of natural law within this framework. From the perspective of the Augustinian view of society and its negative legitimation of laws and customs, they did not discriminate between the state of men before society and the state of men before original sin. This is why in the *Decretum Gratiani* natural law and divine law are placed upon the same level, both in opposition to laws and customs.[27]

The theologically motivated difference between natural law and positive law and the interpretation of natural law as being valid before original sin determines the difference between natural law and divine law. This is very clearly elaborated by the early decretist Rufinus, who claimed that before original sin, mankind was governed by natural law, but that after original sin, men thought that everything was allowed. By the rules laid

---

[25] D. 6 dict. post c. 3: 'Naturale ergo ius ab exordio rationalis creature incipiens ... manet immobile. Ius vero consuetudinis post naturalem legem exordium habuit ex quo homines convenientes in unum ceperunt simul habitare; quod ex eo tempore factum creditur, ex quo cain edificasse legitur.'

[26] R. A. Markus, *Saeculum: History and Society in the Theology of St Augustin* (Cambridge, 1970), pp. 83–4 and 203–6; P. R. L. Brown, 'Saint Augustine and Political Society' in D. F. Donnelly (ed.), *The City of God: A Collection of Critical Essays* (New York, 1995), pp. 17–35 at pp. 27–8.

[27] D. 8 c. 3: 'Veritati et rationi consuetudo est posponenda'; D. 8 c. 3: 'Si consuetudinem fortassis opponas advertum est, quod Dominus dicit: "Ego sum veritas". Non dixit: ego sum consuetudo, sed veritas'; D. 8 c. 6: 'Itaque veritate manifestata cedat consuetudo. Revelatione ergo facta veritatis cedat consuetudoi.'

down in the New Covenant, however, natural law is repaired and even perfectioned.[28] Within this framework, natural law is interpreted in a moral and religious way. It is no surprise that the decretists saw natural law as the moral goal of any kind of law.[29]

The canon law conception of natural law highly influenced the legists and was combined with Ulpian's definition. In his *apparatus* to the *Digestum novum*, Accursius (d. 1263) for example often refers to the divine law that can be found in the Bible and that is identical to natural law. Decretists as well as legists saw God as the founder of natural law because he created nature: 'Natura, id est Deus.'[30] Within the late school of Bologna, Laurentius and Johannes Teutonicus situate natural law in God and see it taking part in God's being.[31]

Notwithstanding the equation between the *ius gentium* and natural law, no overall conclusive definition of the *ius gentium* exists. The *ius gentium* is generally floating between civil law and natural law. On the one hand, it shares with natural law its rational character and therefore takes part in its universality and unchangeability. On the other hand, materially it can hardly be separated from civil law and cannot be said to have been in existence before society emerged. The *ius gentium* as well as natural law itself keep holding this unsteady position. Vitoria, for example, who was a Thomist, disagreed with Thomas Aquinas about the status of the *ius gentium*. To Thomas, from his interpretation of Ulpian's definition, the *ius gentium* was clearly a part of natural law. To Vitoria, however, who agrees on this matter with Isidore of Seville, the *ius gentium* is a part of positive law.[32] This ambiguous position of the *ius gentium* will serve as the framework for the emergence of a consensus-based law of nations, next to the *ius gentium naturale*.

So, in canon and in Roman law, natural law and divine law were closely intertwined. Moreover, in canon law, natural law, divine law and positive canon law, being founded upon the authority of the pope, functioned as a whole of interchangeable types of law. In Gratian's *Tractatus de legibus*[33] and the canonical collections of the papal party during the

---

[28] Magister Rufinus, *Summa Decretorum* (ed. H. Singer, Paderborn, 1902), p. 6: 'Est itaque naturale ius vis quedam humane creaturae a natura insita ad faciendum bonum cavendumque contrarium . . . Hoc igitur ius naturale peccante primo homine eo usque confusum est, ut deinceps homines nichil putarent fore illicitum . . . Et propterea generalitatem reparatur et reparando perficitur.'

[29] Ullmann, *Medieval Papalism*, p. 38.   [30] Weigand, *Naturrechtslehre*, pp. 58–60.

[31] Weigand, *Naturrechtslehre*, p. 368.

[32] G. Otte, *Das Privatrecht bei Francisco Vitoria* (Cologne, 1964), pp. 26–7.

[33] With regard to the equality of natural law, divine law and ecclesiastical (papal) law, three important aspects can be mentioned. First, natural law, divine law and ecclesiastical (papal)

Gregorian Reform (from 1049 onwards), such as Anselmus of Lucca's *Collectio canonum*,[34] one can find the first traces and the theoretical legitimation of this equal treatment.

Two related questions need to be answered: first, why is the material equality of natural law and divine law and their formal distinction so important to the subject that is dealt with here, and second, what is the meaning of the strongly institutionalised public legal order?

In order to answer these questions, we need to recapitulate some elements. In the first place, the moralisation of natural law emerged side by side with the moralisation of human nature. Secondly, the public legal order in its moral and religious character and goal had taken an institutional form. The transcendent order was being personified by the institutional Church through its legal language. This identification was the result of institutionalist tendencies within the Gregorian Reform, which had become predominant by the middle of the twelfth century. With Pope Innocent III (1198–1216) and the statements of the fourth Lateran Council (1215), and with Innocent IV (1243–54), Christian society had become a legal entity, a legally structured right order based upon the absolutistic papal claims of universal jurisdiction and jurisprudence. As James Muldoon put it, the worldview and the theoretical preconditions on which authors like Juan de Solorzano Pereira built their theories about the legitimacy of the conquest of the Americas was in fact a statement about

---

law are defined in a positive way, in contrast to secular law. Secular law is defined in a negative way, as a kind of law that applies when it does not contradict natural law, divine law or ecclesiastical (papal) law. This can be illustrated by D. 9 dict. post c. 11: 'Constitutiones ergo vel ecclesiasticae vel seculares, si naturali iuri contrarie probantur, penitus sunt excludande', or D. 10 dict. post c. 6: 'Ubi autem evangelicis atque canonicis decretis non obviarint, omni reverentia digne habeantur.' Second, the superiority of ecclesiastical laws to secular law is based upon the *voluntas Dei*, which takes the first place in the hierarchy of authorities. This can be illustrated by D. 10, where the subordinance of secular rules to ecclesiastical rules is placed on the same level as the subordination of secular laws to evangelical rules. Moreover, in D. 10 dict. post 6, Gratian speaks of ecclesiastical laws in the sense of evangelical decrees: 'Ubi autem evangelicis atque canonicis decretis non obviarint, omni reverentia dignae habeantur'. This brings us to a third aspect of the equation of natural, divine and ecclesiastical law: the interchangeability of *leges ecclesiasticae* and *scripturae canonicae*. The latter seem to belong to the highest level of the hierarchy of authorities, but this category seems to apply to ecclesiastical laws as well.

[34] When one compares, for example, the canons that are used in the *Collectio canonum* with those in the *Collectio Lanfranci* (CC Book I [28], [29]; [32], [33], [34]; [14], [23], [39], [57], [62], [68] *Anselm II. Bischof von Lucca, Collectio canonum una cum collectione minore*, ed. F. Thaner, Innsbruck, 1906) it appears that in the former the canons are used to legitimise papal primacy, whereas in the latter they are used in a variety of contexts. Other interesting aspects that illustrate these Gregorian tendencies are analysed by K. C. Cushing, *Papacy and Law in the Gregorian Revolution: The Canonistic Work of Anselm of Lucca* (Oxford, 1998).

the medieval Christian theory of world order: 'This theory of world order was the product of the principles of the rightly ordered society that the canonists had developed in the course of the medieval church–state conflict when combined with Innocent IV's discussion of the nature of the relationship between Christian and non-Christian societies.'[35]

Both of these developments implied a kind of secularisation that integrated and transformed some theological preconditions. Social, secular organisation became an indispensable part of the ecclesiastical institutional programme. In this framework, positive law obtained a very ambiguous position. On the one hand, contrary to the Augustinian pessimism concerning political secular organisation and well before the influence of Aristotle's political works, secular organisation and positive law as the means to accomplish this were given a positive value in their own right, but, on the other hand, for a reason that could never be founded upon secular social organisation as such. This implied a constant tension between the status of human society and positive law on the one hand and the public legal order with its theological roots on the other.

What should be said for the status of positive law also goes for the status of the individual person, which determined the outlook of the legal subject as well. The broader development of secularisation from the twelfth century onwards was characterised by the strong dualism between the exterior and the interior,[36] as between a personal monastic vocation and the exemplary life on which it had to be modelled, between a person's intentions and his actions as such, between the corporate body and its members, between head and members, between the unique and the general. In its dealing with the relationship between the unique and the general, the parts and the whole, twelfth-century thinking was equally characterised by the attempt in metaphysical terms to describe independent, subsistent entities and clearly separate them from them by the definition of non-subsistent qualities.[37] In canon law, this dualism led to the creation of the

---

[35] Muldoon, 'Medieval Canon Law and the Formation of International Law'.
[36] C. W. Bynum, 'Did the Twelfth Century Discover the Individual?', *Journal of Ecclesiastical History* 31 (1980), 1–15.
[37] The philosophy of Gilbertus Porretanus offers a clear example of this evolution. His distinction between *id quod est* or *subsistens* and the *id quo est* or *subsistentia*, and his attempt to describe realities in their uniqueness through his concept of *totum quo*, clearly reflect the aspirations of the twelfth-century intelligentsia. A detailed analysis of his work is offered by H. C. Van Elsewijk, *Gilbert Porreta: sa vie, son œuvre, sa pensée* (Leuven, 1966). Similar attempts can be found with Anselm of Canterbury; see K. Jacobi, 'Einzelnes–Individuum–Person' in J. A. Aertsen and A. Speer (eds.), *Individuum und Individualität* (Berlin and New York, 1996).

legal personality and the distinction between natural persons and legal persons when discussing the juridical nature of corporate bodies and their relationship to their individual members.[38] The interior and the exterior, the subject and the object, the unique and the general, the secular and the transcendent were the new correlated abstractions the twelfth-century Renaissance brought into existence.

It is important to stress that twelfth-century individualism evolved alongside these metaphysical ambitions. The description of *dominium* as a *facultas*, pertaining to a (juridical) subject, from the thirteenth century onwards, would have been unthinkable without this step in the evolution of Western thought.

Legally, this dualism was expressed in three ways. In the first place, there is the tension between the valorisation and relevance of objective and subjective elements in legal figures and the interpretation of situations and acts. The relation between these subjective and objective elements was strongly elaborated and systematised, as can be illustrated by the case of liability for failure that regards the non-observance or the insufficient observance of an obligation in classical and medieval Roman law. The interpretation of liability underwent a fundamental development, starting from a purely objective conception of liability, through the introduction of a subjective notion of failure to the increasing importance of the question whether in a given case a moral error is involved. During the Middle Ages, the duty of *custodia*, which originally was a purely objective criterion of liability, connected with a limited number of specific cases, is interpreted in a subjective way. The criterion of liability shifts from objective cases and the external outlook of actions to personal error or the absence of error in various degrees.

Secondly, it is characterised by the tension between intentions and actions. This tension was further elaborated during the Middle Ages, often in a legal context or dealing with legal examples. This can be illustrated by Johannes Duns Scotus' *Quaestio XVIII*, which deals with the question *Utrum actus exterior addat aliquid bonitatis vel malitiae ad actum interiorem.*[39]

---

[38] From the latter half of the twelfth century on, the concept of 'legal person' was applied to groups such as monastic communities, and by 1200 a difference was made between natural and legal persons (*persona quoad iuris intellectum*); James Brundage, *Medieval Canon Law* (New York, 1995), p. 100.

[39] Joannis Duns Scoti doctoris subtilis, ordinis minorum, *Opera omnia editio nova*, XXVI, *Quaestiones quod libertales XIV–XXI – Conciliationes – Opusculum de contradictionibus. De perfectione statuum* (Paris, 1845), p. 228: 'Deinde quaeritur de comparatione actus

Thirdly, there is the antagonism between the legal subject and the objective, public legal order. Historically, this antagonism takes shape within the tension between voluntarism and consensualism on the one hand and institutionalisation on the other. The evolution of the legal interpretation of the foundation of marriage in the works of Gratian and the decretists illustrates this. Growing institutionalism and the diminishing relevance of voluntarism is expressed in the shift from a mere consensus between the parties to an (institutional) ratification of marriage.[40]

The legal subject

Twelfth-century dualism between the exterior and the interior, the division of realities into subsistent and non-subsistent and the reciprocal determination, within the field of society and law, of the strong dualism between the legal subject and the objective public legal order, provided the following centuries with a challenging intellectual framework. In dealing with the way in which they determined future thinking one also has to bear in mind the context of secularisation in which these dualisms emerged.

intrinseci voluntatis ad actus extrinsecum: Utrum actus exterior addat aliquid bonitatis, vel malitiae ad actum interiorem.'

[40] The treatment of marriage in the *Decretum Gratiani* offers a good example of this antagonism. In his *Tractatus matrimonii*, Gratian elaborates on some distinctions concerning *matrimonium* in order to resolve the problem of what constitutes a valid marriage. He discerns *matrimonium initiatum, ratum, consummatum* and *perfectum* (C. 27 q. 2: 'Sed sciendum est, quod coniugium desponsatione initiatur, conmixtione perficitur. Unde inter sponsum et sponsam coniugium est, sed initiatum; inter copulatos est coniugium ratum.') The *matrimonium initiatum* is constituted by the *desponsatio*, whereas the *matrimonium ratum* is established by sexual intercourse that perfects the *desponsatio*. A marriage that is *ratum* is called *perfectum* and fully accomplishes the sacrament of Christ and his Church. It is interesting that *ratum* is used in a double sense. It can refer to the consummation of marriage as well as to the unbreakability of marriage (Jean Gaudemet, *Le Marriage en occident* (Paris, 1987), pp. 175–6). In earlier, more purely voluntaristic interpretations of marriage (as one may find in the canonical collections of Ivo of Chartres, 1040–1115) there is legally speaking no difference between marriage and *desponsatio*. Both are based upon the consensus of the parties and are therefore unbreakable. Gratian's distinctions, however, constitute a fundamental difference between marriage and *desponsatio*, because the latter loses its legal relevance. The traditional consensualist foundation of marriage is being shifted to the legally irrelevant *desponsatio*. Ratification becomes the foundation of a valid, hence unbreakable marriage (which is, for example, illustrated by C. 28 q. 1 dict. post c. 18: 'Hoc inter infideles ratum non est, quia non est firmum et inviolabile ... Inter fideles vero ratum coniugium est, quia coniugia, semel inita intereos, ulterius solvi non possunt'). With the decretists, for example with Rufinus (Gaudemet, *Le Marriage en occident*, pp. 176–7), the link between *desponsatio* and *matrimonium ratum* becomes very thin and the institutional ratification of marriage becomes more and more important.

Especially with regard to the relation between the legal subject and the public order this background is very important. The legal relevance of subjective data such as intentions that founded a systemically articulated voluntarism was a part of the same historical framework that made possible the valorisation and definition of positive law as such. Moreover, the metaphysical attempt of describing subsisting individual entities and the moral and religious definition of human nature on the basis of Christian ecclesiology led to a many-sided essentialism. First, it implied the possibility and the necessity of an abstract and universal definition of what man is. Second, this definition had a profound social meaning. By virtue of the medieval ecclesiological view of man, human essence was defined in terms of penitence acting morally just in order to obtain salvation. With the Gregorian Reform, human society and earthly, temporal reality became very important in reaching this goal. As a result of this, this many-sided essentialism forced thinkers not only to define realities within the framework of this 'metaphysical individualism', but also, with regard to the individual human person, to define the latter in his relation to society and social organisation.

These various elements of twelfth-century dualism and the mechanism of secularisation can function as a framework for explaining and understanding the emergence of natural rights from the twelfth century onwards, the debate on what kind of 'things' rights are and the outcome of this debate. Finally, the analysis of this medieval legacy determines the way in which the definition of right as a *facultas* will find its counterpart in the foundation of natural law on the *appetitus societatis*.[41]

Ius *as a* facultas *and Grotius'* appetitus societatis

In the first book of his *De iure belli ac pacis*, Grotius defined and clarified the various meanings of *ius*. *Ius* can refer to a general notion of what is right, and more precisely to what is not unjust, what is not contrary to the nature of a community of reasonable beings.[42]

This general meaning of *ius* that applies to justice is followed by an analysis of the subjective meaning of *ius*. In its most perfect form, it is

---

[41] The traditional link between the emergence of natural rights and nominalism as opposed to realism fails to do this. First, as Tierney has pointed out, natural rights and the conception of a right as a *facultas* were already an evident part of medieval canon law culture long before Ockham; Tierney, *Idea of Natural Rights*, p. 42.

[42] Grotius, *De iure belli ac pacis* 1, 1, 3, 1: 'Nam ius hic nihil aliud quam quod iustum est significat: idque negante magis sensu quam aiente, ut ius sit quod iniustum non est.'

called *facultas*, in its less perfect form *aptitudo*. *Facultas* consists first of *potestas*, which is called freedom when it refers to oneself (*tuum in te*) and paternal power or the power of a master. It contains, second, the right to property (*dominium*) and, third, the right to demand something (*creditum*) and the obligation to respond to this demand (*debitum*).[43]

These two definitions of *ius* represent the two poles of the legal spectrum: the objective legal order based upon a supra-legal notion of justice, which in turn is based upon the nature of the community on the one hand, and *ius* based upon the legal subject on the other. The third definition Grotius deals with fits in with the first definition of *ius*: *ius* as justice. *Ius* in this definition functions as *lex*, which is a criterion for determining the moral character of actions as well as a law that obliges to what is just.[44] *Ius* in the first and third definitions refers to an extra-juridical as well as to a juridical order. It is important to bear in mind that *ius* in this sense is based upon the nature of the community. To Grotius, man is by nature a social being; he is characterised by an *appetitus societatis*. Natural or social law is based upon human essence itself, but inscribed into man by God.[45] On the basis of this human essence, people, a part of a people or different communities are by nature driven towards constituting a society.[46] By attributing to the scholastic notion of *appetitus* or desire a constructive, constitutive role towards human nature, Grotius seems to broaden the concept of human nature itself, which becomes more than reason alone.[47] By attributing a constructive meaning to *appetitus* with regard to human nature, Grotius creates the foundation of *pacta sunt servanda* as

---

[43] Grotius, *De iure belli ac pacis* 1, 1, 4: 'Ab hac iuris significatione diversa est altera, sed ab hac ipsa veniens, quae ad personam refertur; quo sensu ius est Qualitas moralis personae competens ad aliquid habendum vel agendum ... Qualitas autem moralis perfecta, Facultas nobis dicitur; minus perfecta, Aptitudo ... sub quo continentur Potestas, tum in se, quae libertas dicitur, tum in alios, ut patria, dominica: Dominium ... et creditum cui ex adverso respondet debitum.'

[44] Grotius, *De iure belli ac pacis*, 1, 1, 9, 1: 'Est et tertia iuris significatio quae idem valet quod Lex, quoties vox legis largissime sumitur, ut sit Regula actuum moralium obligans ad id quod rectum est ... Diximus autem, ad rectum obligans, non simpliciter ad iustum, quia ius hac notione non ad solius iustitiae, qualem exposuimus, sed et aliarum virtutum materiam pertinet.'

[45] Grotius, *De iure belli ac pacis, Prol.* 12: 'Sed et illud ipsum noster nobis irrefragabiliter dictat. Sed et illud ipsum de quo egimus naturale ius, sive illud sociale ... quamquam ex principiis homini internis profluit, Deo tamen asscribi merito potest.'

[46] Grotius, *De iure belli ac pacis* 2, 5, 17: 'Consociationes praeter hanc maxime naturalem sunt et aliae tam privatae tam publicae: et hae quidem aut in populum aut ex populis ... Omnino enim ea credenda est fuisse voluntas in societatem coeuntium.'

[47] H. Rapp, 'Grotius and Hume', *Archiv für Rechts- und Sozialphilosophie* 68 (1982), 372–87 at p. 375: 'Human nature, for Grotius, is not merely reason, or merely the passions, but both.'

the legal, voluntaristic cornerstone of the positive law of nations, which in this way gets an independent foundation, something that is foreign to, for example, Suarez or Vasquez,[48] which is constituted by the formal extrapolation of what is proper to man, namely the *appetitus societatis*. From this perspective – and the importance that can be attributed to the *appetitus societatis* – it could be very clarifying to compare the way in which the old scholastic term *appetitus* is used traditionally and the way in which it is used not only by Grotius but also by Baruch de Spinoza. The latter uses this term too when he describes the constitution of and the mechanisms within man's essence, in which the appetites play an important role in man's self-preservation and in that capacity are closely related to the human will.[49]

This corresponds with Grotius' interpretation of natural law, which, together with *ius voluntarium*, constitutes this third kind of law. As Suarez did, Grotius did not take an exclusively rationalistic or voluntaristic position towards natural law, but instead developed a flexible view on natural law that was closely related to human will.[50] In this sense, there is no clearcut distinction between the *ius naturale* and the *ius voluntarium*, because natural law applies not only to actions that do not follow on human will, but also to actions that do follow on human will. Property, for example, was introduced by human will, but if one takes away someone's property, this is a crime against natural law.[51] With Grotius, voluntarism seems to serve as a dominant criterion of his distinction between the various types of law, preceding the distinction between reason and will. He does not clarify, however, the relation between reason and will, or resolve the question of the origin of the *appetitus societatis*, which is at the same time inherently human and God given.[52]

The status of the signa voluntaria *and* ius *as a* facultas*: John Peter Olivi, Jean Gerson Francisco de Vitoria and Francisco Suarez*

Grotius' description of the subjective meaning of *ius*, of *ius* as a *facultas*, as well as his enumeration of its different fields of application, especially

---

[48] Lesaffer, *Europa: een zoektocht naar vrede?*, p. 88.
[49] Herman De Dijn, *Spinoza: The Way to Wisdom* (Princeton, NJ, 1985), pp. 241–2: 'According to Spinoza there is no fundamental distinction among will, appetite, and desire: will is the fundamental striving of the mind; appetite is this same striving as related to Mind and Body together'; and desire is 'appetite together with consciousness thereof'.
[50] Jiménez de Aréchaga, 'Grotian Heritage and the Concept of Just World Order', p. 18.
[51] Cf. n. 19.
[52] Grotius, *De iure belli ac pacis, Prol.* 10 and 12: 'quamquam ex principiis homini internis profluit, Deo tamen asscribi merito potest'.

potestas, paternal and *tuum in te*, and *dominium*, fits well into the scholastic tradition. Within the scholastic tradition, *dominium* could refer to property, as well as to dominion, to mastery. *Dominium* in the latter sense is often used as a synonym of *potestas* or *facultas*, and *facultas* is often used interchangeably with *libertas*. The works of Suarez brim over with examples of the varied use of these terms.[53]

Already in the thirteenth century, the designation of *ius* and *dominium* and related terms such as *facultas* was firmly rooted in canon law tradition and in scholastic philosophy. As has been mentioned above, Brian Tierney pointed out that Olivi treated *ius* and *dominium* very obviously in the sense of a subjective right, as many glossators, canonists and theologians did before the breakthrough of nominalism.[54] Concerning *ius*, *dominium* and *iurisdictio*, orally given and written orders, laws, contracts and wills, Olivi asks himself whether they add something to a person.[55] They are subject to the application of the *distinctio formalis*, a distinction that is not real, but not purely conceptual either. If between a person and the right he holds a formal distinction exists, this means that *aliquid reale* is added to that person but no new essence. It is very interesting to see that 'things' like *ius*, *dominium* and *iurisdictio* are designated as *signa voluntaria*, as signs that result from will. This problem of the link between internal intention and exterior act is very clearly defined in the work of Johannes Duns Scotus, who adopts Olivi's *distinctio formalis*. Duns Scotus' already mentioned *Quaestio XVIII*, which deals with the question *Utrum actus exterior addat aliquid bonitatis vel malitiae ad actum interiorem*, is a fine example of this.[56]

In the fifteenth century, it can be found in ecclesiological and political works, such as in *De potestate ecclesiastica* of Jean Gerson (1369–1429):

---

[53] Franciscus Suarez, *Opera omnia*, 3, 279, 6–7: 'Primo, igitur dicimus, capacitatem dominii convenire homini naturaliter ex eo quod ad imaginem Dei factus est'; in 3, 415, 10 property is indicated as *dominium proprietatis*; 15, 574: 'Potest dari res quae non sit sub dominio alicujus; in discussing 'Qualis esse debeat facultas eligendi confessorem ab homine concessa' (22, 568) *facultas* is used in the sense of *potestas*; 22, 568, 3: 'Secundo, certum est, facultatem hanc non posse excedere potestatem concedentis'; 22, 557: 'Quis possit facultatem eligendi confessorem concedere, et quomodo intelligenda sit.'

[54] Tierney, *The Idea of Natural Rights*, p. 42.

[55] Jansen, 'Beiträge zur geschichtlichen Entwicklung der Distinctio formalis', p. 518: 'Et consimiliter habet locum in tota materia iuris, an scilicet iurisdictio regalis vel sacerdotalis vel iurisdictio cuiuscumque dominii vel proprietatis addat aliquid ad personas, in quibus est huiusmodi iurisdictio, vel ad res, super quas habetur.'

[56] Joannis Duns Scoti doctoris subtilis, ordinis minorum, *Opera omnia editio nova*, *XXVI*, *Quaestiones quod libertales XIV–XXI – Conciliationes – Opusculum de contradictionibus. De perfectione statuum*, p. 228.

'Est autem potestas facultas propinqua ad exeundum in actum.'[57] When Fransisco de Vitoria deals with property, he describes *dominium* as *facultas quadam ad utendum re aliqua secundum iura*.[58]

So, Grotius' eclectic definition of his concept of *ius* as a subjective right in fact collects the different terminological elements of the old scholastic tradition. They are combined with the foundation of the international legal order and of the law of nations on the *appetitus societatis* that derives a moral, supra-legal and society orientated connotation from the medieval concepts of natural law and of the essence of man.

---

[57] Jean Gerson, *Œuvres complètes* (ed. P. Glorieux, Tournai, 1965), p. 211.
[58] Otte, *Das Privatrecht bei Fransisco de Vitoria*, p. 41.

10

The Peace Treaties of Westphalia as an instance of the reception of Roman law

LAURENS WINKEL

Introduction[1]

The role of Roman law in the development of international law has been appreciated in quite different ways. In some manuals, such as those by Nussbaum, Grewe and Truyol y Serra, this role has certainly been underestimated.[2] Another position is defended by Ziegler: from his earlier publications[3] until his recent general survey on the history of international law,[4] he has shown a wide variety of influences of Roman law on the development of international law. Of course, this difference in appreciation of the role of Roman law is closely linked with what I would like to call the 'minimalist' and 'maximalist' approaches to the history of international law. A 'minimalist' concept defines international law as law between sovereign states. Sovereignty in the modern sense does not appear before the sixteenth century, so, therefore, the 'real' history of international law does not start until the early modern period. In the minimalist opinion, there has hardly ever been any interest in the question whether the concepts of international law have been influenced by Roman law.

On the other hand, the 'maximalist' approach applies a wider concept of 'international', so that the earliest forms of peace treaties mark the beginning of the history of international law. The great problem for

---

[1] This chapter is dedicated to the memory of my mother, Dr Helena Winkel-Rauws, who was a specialist in seventeenth-century Dutch history and died in June 2001.
[2] Arthur Nussbaum, *A Concise History of the Law of Nations* (New York, 1954; repr. 1962); Wilhelm G. Grewe, *Epochen der Völkerrechtsgeschichte*, 2nd edn (Baden-Baden, 1988); English edition (Berlin, 2000); Antonio Truyol y Serra, *Histoire du droit international public* (Paris, 1995).
[3] The starting point was Karl-Heinz Ziegler, 'Die römischen Grundlagen des europäischen Völkerrechts', *Ius Commune* 4 (1972), 1–27.
[4] Karl-Heinz Ziegler, *Völkerrechtsgeschichte* (Munich, 1994).

the 'maximalist' approach concerns the Middle Ages, when the emperor of the medieval Holy Roman Empire of the Germanic Nation and the pope both claimed universal recognition, which seems to exclude the existence of international law. The champion of this maximalist approach was undoubtedly Ziegler's teacher, Wolfgang Preiser.[5] I cannot further explain this within the framework of this chapter, but I am quite convinced that the 'minimalistic' approach to the history of international law is in one way or another linked with legal positivism, whereas the 'maximalists' are more inclined towards natural law philosophy. The reason for this seems obvious: when some continuity in the development of international law is assumed, it certainly is embedded in the framework of theoretical concepts which were coined in the Middle Ages by natural law philosophy.

It is not surprising that the role of Roman law can be much more elaborated in the 'maximalist' view, although the latest survey of international law in Antiquity by David Bederman is disappointing in this respect.[6] Unfortunately, the controversy between 'minimalists' and 'maximalists' is not the only one there is. There has also been much dispute about 'international law' in the Roman history of Antiquity. Its very existence within the framework of the Roman Empire has been denied as well. Those authors based their opinion on a supposed 'Negation der Existenzberechtigung' of the non-Roman nations.[7] That there was international law in the Roman world was recently once again – and very convincingly – shown by Dieter Nörr.[8] In the following, I would like to go into the role of Roman law in the development of international law. Special emphasis will be put on the continuity of appearances of international law on the conceptual level between Antiquity and early modern times. To this extent, I fully adhere to the views of Ziegler: the main 'connecting link' between ancient and more modern international law lies in the Roman ambivalent conception of *ius gentium*: on the one hand a philosophical concept, on the other hand private law concerning *peregrini* and Roman

---

[5] Wolfgang Preiser, *Die Völkerrechtsgeschichte, ihre Aufgaben und ihre Methode* (Frankfurt am Main, 1963); see also his collected studies, *Macht und Norm in der Völkerrechtsgeschichte* (Baden Baden, 1978).
[6] David J. Bederman, *International Law in Antiquity* (Cambridge, 2001).
[7] See, e.g., S. Brassloff, *Der römische Staat und seine internationalen Beziehungen* (Vienna and Leipzig, 1928), following an earlier opinion of Theodor Mommsen; see also Hans Magnus Enzensberger, *Die grosse Wanderung: Dreiunddreissig Markierungen, mit einer Fussnote 'Über einige Besonderheiten bei der Menschenjagd'* (Frankfurt am Main, 1994).
[8] Dieter Nörr, *Aspekte des römischen Völkerrechts: die Bronzetafel von Alcántara* (Munich, 1989); Nörr, *Die Fides im römischen Völkerrecht* (Heidelberg, 1991).

citizens, developed after the creation of the *praetor peregrinus* in 242 BC.[9] *Ius gentium* occasionally also refers to 'international law' in the classical Roman legal sources, e.g. D. 50, 7, 18(17), but has mostly one (or even both) of the mentioned first meanings. The continuity of references to *ius gentium*, however, also has implications that are not fully explained by Ziegler, or by other scholars. I refer here to the analogies between international law and private law, which were analysed by Hersch Lauterpacht in his doctoral thesis of 1927.[10] Nevertheless, he – in his turn – does not give the historical reasons for this analogy. The analogy can be found not only between 'contract' and 'treaty' (hence the application of the maxims *pacta servanda sunt*,[11] the disputed *clausula rebus sic stantibus* and the *exceptio non adimpleti contractus*), but also in the field of 'tort' and 'law of succession' analogous with the doctrine of 'state succession'. The number of examples could even be extended.[12]

I will follow Ziegler's train of thought; I shall even quote some of the same texts as he did, but I would like to draw attention to some hitherto more or less neglected aspects of these texts, which could explain the rise of international law as a secular branch of science, even before the famous *Etiamsi daremus* by Grotius.[13] In doing so, I also want to shed some light on some more or less implicit references to Roman legal principles which can be found in the Peace Treaties of Westphalia. These references may show that Roman private law was also important in international law outside the concept of *ius gentium* in its original sense. The explanation for this phenomenon will be the conclusion of this short chapter.

---

[9] Max Kaser, *Ius gentium* (Cologne, Weimar and Vienna, 1993).
[10] Hersch Lauterpacht, *Private Law Sources and Analogies of International Law* (London, 1927, reprinted Hamden Conn., 1970); H. C. Gutteridge, 'Comparative Law and the Law of Nations' in William E. Butler (ed.), *International Law in Comparative Perspective* (Alphen and Rijn, 1980), pp. 13–24.
[11] J. Bärmann, 'Pacta servanda sunt', *Revue Internationale de Droit Comparé* 13 (1961), 18–53; see also J. H. W. Verzijl, *International Law in Historical Perspective* (Leiden, 1968), vol. I, pp. 244–55 and Grotius, *De iure belli ac pacis*, Prol. §8 and §15 and 3, 19, 2, 2.
[12] See, e.g., Axel Hägerström, *Recht, Pflicht und bindende Kraft des Vertrages nach römischer und naturrechtlicher Anschauung* (ed. Karl Olivecrona, Stockholm and Wiesbaden, 1965); Heinrich Triepel, *Delegation und Mandat im öffentlichen Recht* (Stuttgart, 1942); Laurens Winkel, 'Mandatum im römischen öffentlichen Recht?' in Dieter Nörr and S. Nishimura (eds.), *Mandatum und Verwandtes: Vorträge gehalten in Fukuoka/Japan, September 1991* (Berlin, Heidelberg and Tokyo, 1993), pp. 53–66; Christian Baldus, *Regelhafte Vertragsauslegung nach Parteirollen* (2 vols., Berne, 1998).
[13] *De iure belli ac pacis*, Prol. 11; see L. F. M. Besselink, 'The Impious Hypothesis Revisited', *Grotiana* NS 9 (1988), 3–63.

The conceptual development of *ius gentium*

In the history of ideas, there has been a gradual change of *ius gentium* as a philosophical concept. When *ius gentium* no longer refers to natural law innate in every human being, the way is paved for a more pragmatic and positivist approach to law between *gentes*. In this regard it is necessary to unfold the historical sequence of common definitions of *ius gentium*. Gaius (around 160 AD) still starts from a very cosmopolitic idea of *ius gentium*, certainly under the influence of Stoic philosophy.[14]

> G. 1, 1
>
> Omnes populi qui legibus et moribus reguntur, partim suo proprio, partim communi omnium hominum iure utuntur; nam quod quisque populus ipse sibi ius constituit, id ipsius proprium est vocaturque ius civile, quasi ius proprium civitatis; quod vero naturalis ratio inter **omnes** homines constituit, id apud omnes populos peraeque custoditur vocaturque ius gentium, quasi quo iure omnes gentes utuntur. Populus itaque Romanus partim suo proprio, partim communi **omnium** hominum iure utitur.
>
> Every people that is governed by statutes and customs observes partly its own peculiar law and partly the common law of all mankind. That law which a people establishes for itself is peculiar to it and is called *ius civile* (civil law) as being the special law of that *civitas* (state), while the law that natural reason establishes among all mankind is followed by **all** peoples alike, and is called *ius gentium* (law of nations, or law of the world) as being the law observed by **all** mankind. Thus the Roman people observes partly its own peculiar law and partly the common law of all mankind. This distinction we shall apply in detail at the proper places.[15]

Gaius defends a common position in popular philosophy of Antiquity with an accent on the rational character of human nature and behaviour. This way of thinking was especially developed in Stoic philosophy: the *logos* is the basic principle of cosmic order.[16] Hermogenianus, a Roman jurist of the second half of the third century AD, already has a more down-to-earth approach:

---

[14] H. Wagner, *Studien zur allgemeinen Rechtslehre des Gaius: ius gentium und ius naturale in ihrem Verhältnis zum ius civile* (Zutphen, 1978), pp. 51–73 at p. 57.
[15] My translation.
[16] E. J. H. Schrage, *Libertas est facultas naturalis* (Leiden, 1975), pp. 32–6.

Dig. 1, 1, 5 *Hermogenianus libro primo iuris epitomarum*.

> Ex hoc iure gentium introducta bella, discretae gentes, regna condita, dominia distincta, agris termini positi, aedificia collocata, commercium, emptiones venditiones, locationes conductiones, obligationes institutae; exceptis quibusdam quae iure civili introductae sunt.
>
> As a consequence of this *ius gentium*, wars were introduced, nations differentiated, kingdoms founded, properties individuated, estate boundaries settled, buildings put up, and commerce established, including contracts of buying and selling and letting and hiring (except for certain contractual elements established through *ius civile*).[17]

Kaser did not show much appreciation for this text. According to him, '[Hermogenian] weiß mit dem Begriff nichts mehr anzufangen.'[18] This text, however, contains a definition in the form of a *partitio*: the parts of which the object consists are enunciated by way of definition.[19] Moreover, there is a rather clear separation in this text between the first part, which undoubtedly refers to 'public international law', and the second part, starting with the ambiguous expression *termini positi*, which contains private law institutions. *Termini positi* itself refers to boundaries of different realms, but also to boundaries between private properties. References to the origins of *ius gentium* are made with the words *commercium* and the contracts of sale and hire, both of which emerged as consensual contracts after the creation of the *praetor peregrinus* in 242 BC.

It is interesting to see that this rational character of every human being is no longer defended by Isidore of Seville (*c.* 560–636):

> Isidore of Sevilla, *Etymologiae* 5, 6
>
> Ius gentium est sedium occupatio, aedificatio, munitio, bella, captivitates, servitutes, postliminia, foedera, paces, induciae, legatorum violandorum religio, connubia inter alienigenas prohibita; et inde ius gentium, quod eo iure omnes **fere** gentes utuntur.
>
> *Ius gentium* is occupation, construction, fortification, wars, captivity, the right of regaining citizenship after captivity, slavery, treaties, peace, armistice, the inviolability of ambassadors, the prohibition of mixed marriage; and it is [called] *ius gentium* because **nearly** every nation uses it.[20]

---

[17] Translation Alan Watson *et al.*, *The Digest of Justinian* (Philadelphia, 1985).
[18] Kaser, *Ius gentium*, p. 49: 'does not know what to do, with this concept any longer'.
[19] D. Nörr, *Divisio und Partitio: Bemerkungen zur römischen Rechtsquellenlehre und zur antiken Wissenschaftstheorie* (Munich, 1972), pp. 20–7.
[20] My translation.

This text has been analysed by De Churruca, word for word.[21] The word *fere* is explained by him – and had earlier already been by Alvaro D'Ors – as if it here refers to the barbarians, in contrast to Gaius, who, in their opinion, had referred only to the other Mediterranean people that were in regular contact with Rome. Not a word, however, is devoted to the fact that, in a philosophical sense, the *ratio* was supposed to be shared with every human being, independently from legal relations with Rome. Gaius' adherence to this Stoic concept is not discussed by these Spanish scholars, but cannot simply be denied.[22]

The definition of Isidore was also incorporated in the *Decretum Gratiani* of 1140 (D 1, c. 9), and therefore formed a part of the medieval Catholic doctrine, in which radical opinions were held about the status of non-Christians, for example those of Cardinal Hostiensis (c. 1280), who wrote that there was always a just war when Christians fought non-Christians.

Much later, Francisco de Vitoria (c. 1480–1546) is apparently under the spell of the discovery of the Americas when he delivers his famous lectures on the discovery of the Indies. In these lectures the main issue is whether a just war has been waged. At first Vitoria pays lip-service to the old definition of *ius gentium* of the *Digest*,[23] but later he denies practical application of the old cosmopolitic conception of *ius gentium* in clear terms:[24]

> Francisco de Vitoria, *Relectio de Indis* 3, 2
>
> Probatur primo ex iure gentium, quod vel est ius naturale vel derivatur ex iure naturali (Inst., De iure naturali et gentium): 'quod naturalis ratio

---

[21] J. de Churruca, 'Presupuestos para el estudio de las fuentes jurídicas de Isidoro de Sevilla', *Anuario de Historia del Derecho Español* 43 (1973), 429–43; J. de Churruca, *Las instituciones de Gayo en San Isidoro de Sevilla* (Bilbao, 1975), p. 28; de Churruca, 'La definición Isidoriana de ius gentium', *Estudios de Deusto* 30 (1982), 71–95, esp. p. 94, following A. D'Ors, 'En torno a la definición Isidoriana del "ius gentium" in *Derecho de gentes y organizacion internaciona*, vol. I (Santiago de Compostela, 1956), pp. 11–40, esp. pp. 33–7; see also J. de Churruca, 'Patrística y derecho romano', *Estudios de Deusto* 32 (1984), 429–44. I thank my friend and distinguished colleague Juan de Churruca for providing me with copies of these publications.

[22] See Wagner, *Studien zur allgemeinen Rechtslehre des Gaius*, p. 236.

[23] See P. Clementinus a Vlissingen, *De evolutione definitionis iuris gentium, Studium historico-iuridicum de doctrina iuris gentium apud Auctores Classicos Saec. XVI–XVIII* (Rome, 1940), p. 52. The opinion ascribed there to Vitoria is certainly incorrect and very incomplete; see also the important contribution by Ernest Nys, 'Les jurisconsultes espagnols et la science du droit des gens', *Revue de Droit International et de Législation Comparée*, 2nd series, 14 (1912), 360–87, 494–524, 614–42; he deals with Vitoria on pp. 518–24 and 614–16.

[24] A. E. Perez Luño, *La polémica sobre el Nuevo Mundo* (Madrid, 1992), p. 121; Nys, 'Les jurisconsultes espagnoles', pp. 619–25.

inter omnes gentes constituit, vocatur ius gentium. Sic enim apud omnes nationes habetur inhumanum sine aliqua speciali causa hospites et peregrinos male accipere.'

Proof of this may in the first place be derived from the law of nations (*ius gentium*) which either is natural law or derived from natural law (Inst. 1, 2, 1): 'What natural reason has established among all nations is called *ius gentium*. For, congruently herewith, it is reckoned among all nations inhumane to treat visitors and foreigners badly without some special cause.'[25]

F. de Vitoria, *Relectio de Indis* 3, 4

Et quidem multa hic videntur procedere ex iure gentium, quod, quia derivatur sufficienter ex iure naturali, manifestam vim habet ad dandum ius et obligandum. Et, dato quod non semper derivetur ex iure naturali, satis videtur esse **consensus maioris partis totius orbis**, maxime pro bono communi omnium. Si enim, post prima tempora creati orbis aut reparati post diluvium, maior pars hominum constituerit, ut legati ubique essent inviolabiles, ut mare esset commune, ut bello capti essent servi, et hoc ita e*xpediret, ut hospites non exigerentur, certe hoc haberet vim, etiam aliis repugnantibus.*

And, indeed, there are many things in this connection which issue from the law of nations, which, because it has a sufficient derivation from natural law, is clearly capable of conferring rights and creating obligations. And even if we grant that it is not always derived from natural law, yet there exists clearly enough **a consensus of the greater part of the world**, especially in behalf of the common good of all. For if after the early days of the creation of the world or its recovery from the flood the majority of mankind decided that ambassadors should everywhere be reckoned inviolable and that the sea should be common and that prisoners of war should be made slaves, and, if this, namely, that strangers should not be driven out, were deemed to be a desirable principle, it would certainly have the force of law, even though the rest of mankind objected thereto.

A majority of peoples are able to determine the content of *ius gentium*. The conclusion of the sequence of these texts can only be that from now on there is a positivist tendency in the conceptualisation of *ius gentium*. We clearly are at the roots not only of *ius gentium voluntarium*, which we find in the legal theory of a century later, but even also of the unwritten source alluded to in Article 38 of the Statute of the International Court of Justice, where we read that there are general principles 'recognised

[25] Translation John Pawley Bate (*Classics of International Law* 7, Washington, DC, 1917).

by civilised nations' as a subsidiary and ultimate source of international law.

Before we can go to the specific topic of the influence of Roman law on international law we can now explain why even in the Grotian system of *ius gentium* there is a distinction between *ius gentium necessarium* and *ius gentium voluntarium*.[26] This distinction must be a compromise between the idealistic concept of international law, based on ancient ideas of cosmopolitanism, and the practical realities of international law of Grotius' days, but is at the same time adapted to legal practice.[27] We have dealt briefly with the renewed interest in Stoic philosophy in an earlier publication, and refer to existing literature for the importance of the aforementioned distinction.[28]

Uti possidetis in the Westphalia Peace Treaties

In the Peace Treaties of Westphalia, which were recently analysed by Lesaffer and Ziegler,[29] we see at least two implicit references to institutions of Roman private law.[30] The first can be found in paragraph 3 of the Münster Treaty of 30 January 1648 between Spain and the Dutch Republic: the principle of *uti possidetis*,[31] which has since then known

---

[26] *De iure belli ac pacis* 1, 2, 4, 2.

[27] Christopher A. Ford, 'Preaching Propriety to Princes: Grotius, Lipsius and Neo-Stoic International Law', *Case Western Reserve Journal of International Law* 28 (1996), 313–67, esp. at pp. 343–8.

[28] Laurens Winkel, 'Parerga et paralipomena ad errorem iuris' in *Iurisprudentia universalis: Festschrift für Theo Mayer-Maly* (Cologne, Weimar and Vienna, 2002), pp. 901–10, esp. at p. 908; see also A. Finkielkraut, *L'humanité perdue* (Paris, 1985), pp. 21–8, who agrees with me on this, Karl-Heinz Ziegler, 'Völkerrechtliche Aspekte der Eroberung Lateinamerikas', *Zeitschrift für Neuere Rechtsgeschichte* 23 (2001), 1–30, does not deal with the controversy in Valladolid; nor does he allude to the revival of Stoic philosophy in the sixteenth century.

[29] Randall Lesaffer, 'The Westphalian Peace Treaties and the Development of the Tradition of Great European Peace Settlements prior to 1648', *Grotiana* NS 18 (1997), 71–96; Karl-Heinz Ziegler, 'Der westfälische Frieden von 1648 in der Geschichte des Völkerrechts' in Meinhard Schröder (ed.), *350 Jahre westfälischer Friede* (Berlin, 1999), pp. 99–117; Ziegler, 'Die Bedeutung des westfälischen Friedens von 1648 für das europäisches Völkerrecht', *Archiv des Völkerrechts* 37 (1999), 129–51.

[30] Ziegler, 'Bedeuting des westfälischen Friedens', p. 147.

[31] For a general survey, see F. Woolbridge, 'Uti possidetis doctrine', in Rudolf Bernhardt (ed.), *Encyclopaedia of Public Internatonal Law* (1st edn., Berlin, 1987), vol. X, pp. 519–21; see also Alessandra Bignardi, *'Controversiae agrorum'e arbitrati internazionali, alle origine dell'interdetto 'uti possidetis'* (Milan, 1984); Giuseppe Falcone, *Ricerche sull'origine dell'interdetto 'uti possidetis'* (Palermo, 1996); S. R. Ratner, 'Drawing a Better Line: *uti possidetis* and the Border of New States', *American Journal of International Law* 90 (1996), 590–624.

a remarkable application in the process of decolonisation, first in South America, later in other border disputes. It still plays an important role in Africa, now known under the ugly and grammatically incorrect Latin name *uti possidetis iuris*, implying that in cases of border disputes the old colonial boundaries have to be respected before peaceful settlement of the dispute can take place. The principle of *uti possidetis* as such implies that, before peaceful settlement of a border dispute by way of arbitration, the military situation is completely frozen on both sides. The original *interdictum uti possidetis* was from the beginning an *interdictum duplex*, addressing not only the claimant, but also the defendant in the future dispute on property rights. It was necessary in Roman private law to invoke this praetorian remedy because the *rei vindicatio* can only be instituted against a possessor.

In the case of the Münster Treaty, the dispute resolution was to be brought before the Chambre Mi-Partie, a mixed tribunal which indeed was active in the decade after the Peace Treaty.[32] In modern contexts, the principle is explicitly mentioned in the 1986 verdict of the International Court of Justice on the frontier dispute between Burkina Faso and Mali.[33] The comparison between the original function of the praetorian remedy preceding the *rei vindicatio* in Roman law and the modern use of this doctrine in international law can shed an interesting light on the evolution of this doctrine. The passage runs as follows:

> Uti possidetis
>
> Unusquisque habeat ac realiter fruatur ditionibus, urbibus, locis, terris, ac dominiis, quae impraesentarum tenet ac possidet, ita ut in eo non turbetur aut impediatur directe nec indirecte, quocunque id fuerit modo; sub quibus intelliguntur etiam vici, pagi, vicinitates & terrae planae ab iis dependentes: consequenter totus Majoratus Sylvaeducensis, ut & omnia Dominia, urbes, castella, vici, pagi, vicinitates & terrae planae dependentes ab eadem urbe & Majoratu Sylvaeducensis, urbe & Marchionatu Bergozomensi, urbe & Baronatu Bredano, urbe Trajectina ad Mosam ejusque jurisdictione, ut & comitatu Vronhovio, urbe Gravia & ditione Cuykia,

---

[32] C. Streefkerk, 'Cedant arma togae. De sententiën van de Chambre mi-partie, 1654–1657', *Verslagen en Mededelingen van de Stichting tot Uitgaaf der Bronnen van het Oud-vaderlandse Recht* 5 (1987), 103–16. He also mentions all the earlier literature on this tribunal.

[33] Judgement of the International Court of Justice, in *Reports of Judgments, Advisory Opinions and Orders, Case concerning the Frontier Dispute Burkina Faso/Mali*, 10 January 1986/22 December 1986, 563–70; see also the judgement in the border dispute between Cameroon and Nigeria rendered by the International Court of Justice, 10 October 2002, see *Nederlands Juristenblad* (2002), 2061–3.

Hulsta & Baillivatu Hulstae, & Ambachta Hulstensi, ut & Ambachta Axelia fita ad austrum & septentrionem ejus, cum fortalitiis, quae praefati Domini Ordines nunc tenent in ditione Waasia, & omnes alias urbes & locos quos vel quas dicti Domini Ordines possident in Brabantia, Flandria, & alibi, mancant penes praedictos Dominos Ordines in omnibus & iisdem juribus & partibus supremi Imperii & superioritatis, nihil excepto, & aeque ac possident provincias unitarium provincarium. Ita tamen ut omne reliquum ditionis Waesiae, exceptis dictis fortaliciis, maneat penes Regem Hispaniae. Quod attinet tres tracus Transmasanos nempe Falkenburgum, Daelhemum, & Rotulamducis, maneant in statu in quo nunc sunt: & in casu controversiae super iisdem remittantur ad decisionem camerae; dipartitae; de qua posthac dicetur.[34]

Uti possidetis

Each shall remain effectively in the possession and enjoyment of the countries, towns, forts, lands and dominions which he holds and possesses at present, without being troubled or molested therein, directly or indirectly, in any manner whatsoever; wherein villages, burghs, hamlets and flat country thereupon depending are understood to be comprehended. And next the mayoralty of Boisleduc, as also the lordships, cities, castles, towns, villages, hamlets and flat country depending upon the said city and mayoralty of Boisleduc, the city and marquisate of Bergen-op-Zoom, the city and barony of Breda, the city and jurisdiction of Maastricht, as also the country of Vroomhoff, the town of Grave, the county of Kuyk, Hulst and the bailage of Hulst, and Hulster Ambacht, situated upon the south and north of Guelder; and likewise the forts which the said Lords and States possess at present in the county of Waes, and all the other towns and places which the said Lords and States hold in Brabant, Flanders, and elsewhere, shall remain to the said Lords and States, in all the same rights, and parts of sovereignty and superiority, just in the same manner that they hold the provinces of the United Low Countries. But then it must be observed, that all the rest of the said country of Waes, excepting the said forts shall belong to the said Lord the king of Spain. As to the three quarters of the Over-Maze, viz. Fauquermont, Dalem and Roleduc, they shall remain in the state they are in at the present: and in case of dispute or controversy, the matter shall be referred to the Chambre My-Partie, or the indifferent and desinterested court, whereof mention shall be made afterwards.[35]

The comparison also shows an interesting form of continuity. The *interdictum uti possidetis* was originally a legal remedy between Roman citizens only and therefore it was part of the *ius civile*, and from another perspective

[34] Treaty of Münster of 30 January 1648, Para. 3.   [35] Translation from FHIG II, p. 418.

it belonged to the *ius honorarium*, the law established by the Roman magistrates. It never formed a part of *ius gentium*. Now it has been applied in a context of *ius gentium*, albeit in the new, nearly exclusive sense of international law. In this way, the Peace Treaties of Westphalia are a bridge between Roman law as it was received in the seventeenth century and the modern doctrine of international law. Military occupation (factual domination of a territory) can be compared with possession according to private law, another form of 'private law analogy'.

An indication of the reception of Roman law in this respect in 1648 can be found in a comparison with the earlier Peace Treaty of Crépy of 18 September 1544 between Spain and France. In this Treaty there is a clause of arbitration, though no reference to freezing the military situation in the meantime:[36]

> Et pour autant qu'il y a plusieurs différends concernant les limites d'entre de Roiaume de France, et lesdits Pais d'embas, et Comté de Bourgogne, et les sujets d'un côté et d'autre, sur aucuns desquels ont déjà été tenües Communications; et que le tems ne permet de presentement les apointer et vuider, a été accordé et traité, que l'on disputera aucuns bons Personnages d'un côté et d'autre, lesquels se trouveront au lieu de Cambrai, le jour et fête de Saint Martin prochain, pour iceux apointer amiablement, et autres touchant les dits Roiaume et Pais, et les Sujets d'un côté et d'autre, grevez à cette cause et occasion, dont ils auront entiere charge et commission de la part desdits Seigneurs Empereur et Roi: et s'il y reste quelque difficulté, en avertiront chacun endroit soi, pour en procurer la finale pacification, par le moien des Ambassadeurs de leursdites Majestez.[37]

---

[36] On medieval arbitration in general, see Karl S. Bader, 'Arbiter arbitrator seu amicalis compositor. Zur Verbreitung einer kanonistischen Formel nördlich der Alpen', *Zeitschrift der Savigny-Stiftung für Rechtsgeschichte, Kanonistische Abteilung* 77 (1960), 239–76; Karl-Heinz Ziegler, 'Arbiter, arbitrator und amicalis compositor', *Zeitschrift der Savigny-Stiftung für Rechtsgeschichte, Romanistische Abteilung* 84 (1967), 376–81; Ziegler, *Völkerrechtsgeschichte*, p. 157.

[37] FHIG II, p. 15. 'And in so far as there are various disputes concerning the boundaries between the Kingdom of France, and the said *Pais d'embas*, and the County of Burgundy, as well as between the subjects of both sides, about some of which there have already been talks; and in so far as time does not permit to treat and solve them at this time, it has been agreed and concluded, that some good persons from both sides will be appointed who will be in the town of Cambrai coming St Martin's Day, to treat in a peaceful way about these points and others which concern the said Kingdom and Lands, and the subjects of both sides, as well as about complaints at this event and occasion, for which they will have full charge and commission from the said Lords Emperor and King: and if a certain difficulty will subsist, each will warn his legal side, in order to obtain the final pacification, through the Ambassadors of the said Majesties.'

From this text it is not possible to deduce a direct proof of the reception of the Roman legal principle of *uti possidetis*, although arbitration is explicitly regulated. Maybe we should look at the legal literature of the later sixteenth century to investigate whether there were any contemporary publications on this legal remedy. In the well-known collection of the *Oceanus iuris* published in Venice in 1583, we find at least one elaborate treatise on the interdict of *uti possidetis*.[38] Notwithstanding the popularity and wide divulgation of the *Oceanus iuris*, clear evidence cannot be deduced from this publication only. But there is other evidence of interest in the practical application of this interdict, as appears from an unfortunately rather superficial survey by Ernst Holthöfer: at first sight, a great number of other specialised treatises on this topic must have been published at the end of the sixteenth century with a broad geographical spectrum of towns of edition,[39] but at least one of them, the *Tractatus de pacificis possessoribus* written by a well-known French jurist, Petrus Rebuffus (1487–1557),[40] has a completely different content. Nevertheless, some of the publications quoted by Holthöfer may have contributed to the practical application of the principle of *uti possidetis* in the Peace Treaty of Westphalia. The educational level of the ambassadors involved in the negotiations before the Peace Treaties is also important, and there is no reason to differ from the general patterns of the growing bureaucracies starting at the end of the Middle Ages: jurists became increasingly important and through them the process of the reception of Roman law has taken place.[41] However, Adriaan Pauw, one of the most important Dutch negotiators in Münster, was, for example, not a jurist.[42] In his apologetic pamphlet

[38] Verginius de Bocatiis de Cingulo, 'De interdicto uti possidetis sive de manutentione in possessione' in *Tractatus universi iuris = Oceanus iuris*, vol. III, Part II (Venice, 1583), *De iudiciis*, pp. 300–25.

[39] E. Holthöfer, 'Die Literatur zum gemeinen und partikularen Recht in Italien, Frankreich, Spanien und Portugal' in Helmut Coing (ed.), *Handbuch der Quellen und Literatur der neueren europäischen Privatrechtsgeschichte*, vol. II-1 (Munich, 1977), pp. 350–1: *Remedia possessoria*.

[40] Petrus Rebuffus, 'Tractatus de pacificis interdictis possessoribus', *Tractatus universi iuris = Oceanus iuris* xv, 2 (Venice, 1584), pp. 540–58; this volume, xv, 2, only contains treatises on *beneficia*; see for a biographical note E. Holthöfer, 'Rebuffi (Rebuffus) Pierre (1487–1557)' in Michael Stolleis (ed.), *Juristen: ein biographisches Lexikon* (Munich, 1995), pp. 513–14.

[41] See, e.g., Paul Koschaker, *Europa und das römische Recht* (Munich, 1966), pp. 178–80 and passim.

[42] A. J. van der Aa, *Biographisch woordenboek der Nederlanden*, vol. XV (Haarlem, 1872), pp. 134–7; W. van Ravesteyn, 'Adriaan Pauw' in *Nieuw Nederlandsch biographisch woordenboek*, vol. X (Leiden, 1937), pp. 714–17: Adriaan Pauw was curator of Leiden University from 1619.

concerning his activities as a negotiator in Münster there is no reference to the principle of *uti possidetis*.[43] We tried to investigate whether one of the Dutch or Spanish ambassadors in Münster was a graduate in law. This investigation was unfortunately unsuccessful: Bartold van Gendt, Johan van Matenesse, Johan de Knuyt, François van Donia, Willem Ripperda, Adriaan Clant and Godard van Reede van Nederhorst, the other Dutch ambassadors at Münster, are nowhere described as professional jurists.[44] On the Spanish side we only found that Don Gaspar de Bracamonte y Guzmán, earl of Peñaranda, had a degree in canon law from the university of Salamanca, whereas no detailed information could be traced about the background of the other Spanish ambassador Antoine Brun, or about the secretary of the embassy, Pedro Fernández del Campo.[45]

Further indirect proof of the reception of the principle of *uti possidetis* in international law can be found in the Peace Treaty of Breda of 31 July 1667, between England and the Netherlands, Article 3:

> Conventum praeterea est, ut utraque jam disignatarum partium cum plenario Jure summi Imperii, proprietatis et possesionis, omnes ejusmodi terras, insulas urbes, munimenta, loca et colonias, teneat et possideat in posterum, quotquot durante hoc bello aut ante hoc bellum ullis retro temporibus vi et armis aut quoquo modo abaltera parte occupavit aut retinuit, eum prorsus in modum quo ea 10/20 die Maii proxime occupaverat et possedit (nullis eorum locorum exceptis).
>
> It is further agreed that both of the aforesaid parties, or either of them, shall keep and possess hereafter, with plenary rights of sovereignty, property and possession, all such lands, islands, cities, forts, places, and colonies (how many soever) as during this war, or in any other war, by force of arms, or in any other way they have seized or retained from the other party, and this

---

[43] Adriaan Pauw, *Verscheyde stucken raeckende de vrede-handelinghe* (Amsterdam, 1647). See W. P. C. Knuttel, *Catalogus van de Pamfletten-Verzameling berustende in de Koninklijke Bibliotheek*, vol. I-2 (The Hague, 1889), p. 421, no. 5478.

[44] 'Bartold van Gendt' in *Nieuw Nederlands biographisch woordenboek* (Leiden, 1924), vol. VI, pp. 558–9; 'Willem Ripperda' in *Nieuw Nederlands biographisch woordenboek* (Leiden, 1914), vol. III, pp. 1192–3; 'Adriaan Clant' in *Nieuw Nederlands biographisch woordenboek*, vol. III, pp. 218–19; 'Godard van Reede van Nederhorst' in *Nieuw Nederlands biographisch woordenboek*, vol. III, pp. 1025–6 (all biographies written by W. M. C. Regt). The others could not be traced.

[45] José A. Carbezas, *Negociation of the peace of Westphalia. Action of the plenipotentiary D. Gaspar de Bracamonte, Earl of Peñaranda and participation of the secretary D. Pedro Fernández del Campo*, found on 5 December 2002 on www.fundaciongsr.es/pdfs/westphaliapdf. The English text is apparently a translation of two Spanish articles, published with the title *España en Westfalia I* and *II* in *Historia* 22, no. 18 (1998), 16–17 and 28–41 (not seen).

precisely in the manner in which they were seized of and possessed them on the tenth day of May last past, none of the said places being excepted.[46]

A particularity of this Treaty is the fact that the invocation of the principle of *uti possidetis* does not go together with a reference to arbitration. For this reason this Treaty is not mentioned by Lingens in his survey of the practice of arbitration after 1648.[47] Michael Weber[48] mentions another treaty in which the principle *uti possidetis* can be found, in this case together with arbitration.[49] It is the Peace Treaty of Pessarowicz, between Austria and the Ottoman Empire, of 21 July 1718, Article 1:

> Provinciae Moldaviae et Valachiae, partim Poloniae et partim Transylvaniae limitibus conterminae, interjacentibus, ut ab antiquo, montibus distinguantur et separentur, ita, ut ab omni parte antiquorum confiniorum termini observentur, nullaque in his nec ultra fiat mutatio, et cum partes Valachiae cis Alutam fluvium sitae cum locis et Munimento Temewarini in potestate et possessione Sacro Romano-Caesareae Regiaeque Majestatis sint, juxta acceptatum Fundamentum Pacis: uti possidetis, in ejusdem Potestate et Dominio permaneant, ita, ut a praedicti fluvii ripa Occidentalis ad Romanorum, ripa vero Orientalis ad Otomannorum Imperatorem pertineat.

> Let the provinces of Moldavia and Walachia, as in earlier times, be distinguished and divided by the frontier mountains in part from adjoining Poland and in part from adjoining Transylvania, so that the frontiers of earlier times will be kept in all places, and there may be no change either on one side or the other. And since the districts of Wallachia located on this side of the Aluta river with the places and fortifications of Temesvar are in the power and possession of His Majesty, the Holy Roman [i.e. Austrian] Emperor. In accordance with the accepted founded principle of the peace: As you now possess (*Uti possidetis*), let it remain in his power and sovereignty. Thus let the western bank of the aforementioned river belong to the Roman, and let the eastern bank belong to the Ottoman Emperor.[50]

From these examples, a clear conclusion can safely be drawn: the principle of *uti possidetis* belongs to the practice of international treaty law, at least

---
[46] Translation from FHIG II, p. 317.
[47] Karl-Heinz Lingens, *Internationale Schiedsgerichtsbarkeit und Jus Publicum Europaeum 1648–1794* (Berlin, 1988).
[48] Michael Weber, '*Uti possidetis iuris*' als allgemeiner Rechtsbegriff im Völkerrecht – Überlegungen zum Verhältnis von '*uti possidetis*', Selbstbestimmungsrecht der Völker und Effektivitätsprinzip (Göttingen, 1999), p. 4.
[49] Lingens, *Internationale Schiedsgerichtsbarkeit*, p. 42.
[50] Translation from FHIG II, p. 356, slightly altered here.

since 1648, often but not always in the framework of a clause concerning arbitration.

The restitution clause in the Westphalia Peace Treaties

The second instance of the reception of Roman law in the Treaties of Westphalia is a reference to the principle of *restitutio*, to be found in the Peace Treaty of Osnabrück between the Emperor and Sweden of 14 October 1648:

> Iuxta hoc universalis et illimitatae amnestiae fundamentum universi et singuli Romani imperii electores, principes, status (comprehensa immediata imperii nobilitate) eorumque vasalli, subditi, cives et incolae, quibus occasione Bohemiae Germaniaeve motuum vel foederum hinc inde contractorum ab una vel altera parte aliquid praeiudicii aut damni quocunque modo vel praetextu illatum est, tam quoad ditiones et bona feudalia, subfeudalia et allodialia, quam quoad dignitates, immunitates, iura et privilegia restituti sunto plenarie in eum utrinque statum in sacris et profanis, quo ante destitutionem gavisi sunt aut iure gaudere potuerunt, non obstantibus sed annullatis quibuscunque interim in contrarium factis mutationibus.

> General Restitution Clause; restoration of the estates of the Empire

> According to this foundation of a general and unlimited amnesty, all and every of the electors of the Sacred Roman Empire, the princes and states therein included, the nobility that hold immediately of the empire, their vassals, subjects, citizens and inhabitants, who upon occasion of the troubles of Bohemia and Germany, or upon the account of alliances contracted on the side and another, may have suffer'd any prejudice or damage from either party, in any manner, or under any pretext whatsoever, either in their domains, goods, fees, sub-fees, allodials, or in their dignities, immunities, rights and privileges, shall be fully re-establish'd on both sides, in the same state, both as to spirituals and temporals, which they enjoy'd, or could of right enjoy before those troubles, notwithstanding all the changes made to the contrary, which shall be annul'd and remain void.[51]

Although the restitution clause is rooted in the Roman remedy of *restitutio in integrum* of the praetorian Edict,[52] there is no direct line of influence here. This is due to the doctrine of the Spanish late Scholastic School, where the principle of restitution was developed under the influence not

---

[51] FHIG II, p. 191.
[52] Max Kaser, *Das römische Privatrecht* (2nd edn, Munich, 1971), vol. I, p. 252; Helmut Coing, *Europäisches Privatrecht* (Munich, 1985), vol. I, pp. 177–8.

just of this Roman legal remedy, but also of moral philosophy, linked back to Aristotle and Thomas Aquinas.[53] Here too we see a strong – most probably indirect – influence of private law doctrine on the development of the doctrine of international law. For an indirect influence we could invoke a commonly defended argument according to which there is no direct influence of Grotius' *De iure belli ac pacis* on the Peace Treaties of Westphalia.[54]

Conclusion

The slow shift of the meaning of *ius gentium* explains why at the beginning of the emerging positivism in 'classical' international law the full reception of Roman private law concepts in treaty law and elsewhere has taken place. In this respect, the Westphalia Peace Treaties, together with Grotius' *De iure belli ac pacis*, were absolutely crucial. In *De iure belli ac pacis* we find applications of the restitution clause, but we do not yet find applications of the principle of *uti possidetis*. We have not been able to trace back the origins of the rather sudden appearance of this principle in peace treaties of the seventeenth century, but in general terms the appearance of institutions of Roman law can be explained in the same way as the general reception of Roman law in Western Europe in the early modern period. As we have seen in the comparison between the Treaty of Crépy and the Treaty of Münster, the difference in wording certainly goes beyond what Daube once labelled as 'the self-understood in legal history',[55] and leads us to trace back the practical application of the *uti possidetis* principle to 1648.

In this respect at least, the Peace Treaties of Westphalia are also a noticeable but until now underestimated instance in the reception of Roman law.[56]

---

[53] Coing, *Europäisches Privatrecht*, vol. I, pp. 190–1.
[54] Heinhard Steiger, 'Konkreter Frieden und allgemeine Ordnung – Zur rechtlichen Bedeutung der Verträge vom 14. Oktober 1648' in Klaus Bussmann (ed.), *1648, Krieg und Frieden in Europa, I: Politik, Religion, Recht und Gesellschaft* (s.l., 1998), pp. 437–46 at p. 442. See also C. G. Roelofsen, 'Völkerrechtliche Aspekte des westfälischen Friedens in niederländischer Sicht', *Rechtstheorie* 29 (1998), 175–88 at p. 183.
[55] D. Daube, 'The Self-Understood in Legal History', *The Judicial Review* 85 (1973), 126–34 = *Collected Studies*, vol. II (Frankfurt am Main, 1991), pp. 1277–85.
[56] I wish to thank my friends Tammo Wallinga and Peter Haalebos for their kind help.

PART III

Thinking peace: towards a better future

11

Peace treaties, *bonne foi* and European civility in the Enlightenment

MARC BÉLISSA

Introduction

In the eighteenth century, diplomacy underwent a double transformation: it became permanent and it widened the scope of its interventions.[1] Publicists and philosophers did not fail to notice this increasing importance of interstate relations.[2] How did the men of the Enlightenment analyse this phenomenon?[3] Diplomacy had always been the private domain of kings and princes. Did philosophers consider it a peacemaking institution or one of the many elements of a European 'political system' serving the reigning families? Were the reinforcement of the links between the states and the increase in the number of treaties forming the *Droit public de l'Europe* since the Westphalian Treaties regarded as the progress of civilising between the peoples or as a start for new claims and new conflicts? Throughout the eighteenth century, this debate poses the central question of the moral legitimacy of diplomacy and its relations with the law of

---

[1] C. S. Blaga, *L'Evolution de la diplomatie: idéologie, mœurs et techniques* (Paris, 1938), vol. I; Lucien Bély, *Les Relations internationales en Europe XVIe–XVIIIe siècle* (Paris, 1992); Lucien Bély (ed.), *L'Invention de la diplomatie, moyen-âge – temps modernes* (Paris, 1998).
[2] The word 'philosopher' must here be understood in a wider sense as all the writers, journalists and intellectuals who participated in this debate.
[3] M. Bottaro-Palumbo, 'De justice paix, de paix abondance. Les projets de l'abbé de Saint-Pierre', *Studies on Voltaire and the Eighteenth Century* 346 (1997), 25–64; R. Derathé, *J. J. Rousseau et la science politique de son temps* (Paris, 1950); J. L. Lecercle, 'L'abbé de Saint-Pierre, Rousseau et l'Europe', *Dix-Huitième Siècle* 25 (1993), 23–39; G. Lepan, 'Guerre et paix dans l'œuvre de Rousseau', *Dix-Huitième Siècle* 30 (1998), 435–56; M. L. Perkins, 'Voltaire's Concept of International Law', *Studies on Voltaire and the Eighteenth Century* 26 (1963); Perkins, 'Montesquieu on National Power and International Rivalry', *Studies on Voltaire and the Eighteenth century*, 238 (1985), 1–94; F. S. Ruddy, *International Law in the Enlightment: The Background of Vattel's* Le droit des gens (Dobbs Ferry, 1975); E. V. Souleyman, *The Vision of World Peace in the XVIIth and XVIIIth Century in France* (New York, 1941).

peace.[4] Although philosophers are critical of the European order and of the Machiavellian politics of princes, they still notice that peace treaties – as remote from the 'true principles of morals' as they are – remain of a distinctly ambivalent nature. Gabriel Bonnot de Mably (1709–85) particularly dwells on the necessary transparency of peace negotiations. According to him, diplomats should do away with the practice of vulgar politics, which consists of making treaty articles obscure; they should turn *bonne foi* into the cornerstone of their peaceful intentions.

Treaties, public law and the process of civilising

For most philosophers, interstate negotiations stem from the objective interaction of powers, that is to say, from the action of their passions and not from reason. Politics concerns the private thing of the kings, but paradoxically it creates public law, for the sovereigns unwittingly reproduce in the articles of their treaties the very principles that aim to establish relations between peoples. Under the *ancien régime*, the fact that every new treaty confirmed the old ones contributed to the perpetuation of their basic principles. It was customary in European diplomacy when signing a fundamental treaty to renew the articles that had established the state borders, the claims of the monarchs and the mutual rights of their subjects. The Treaties of Westphalia, which had established the principle of religious plurality in Europe and the primacy of the secular law of nations, had been repeated in the Treaty of Utrecht. Similarly, the Treaty of Utrecht was reconfirmed in all the major treaties of the eighteenth century. This juridical corpus forms a precedent that was admitted by all the sovereigns and that could, according to Mably, be bettered in order to create a real European code of the law of nations as long as it was founded on the 'true principles of morality'. The principles of the law of nations – at least those that did not contradict natural law – tended to become a kind of European constitution, though an imperfect one, but on which one had to rely to civilise the political system of Europe.

The entry 'traité' of the *Encyclopédie*, written by Louis de Jaucourt (1704–79), equally stated the ambivalent nature of diplomatic conventions:

> Il est vrai que ce ne sont pas les traités, mais la nécessité qui lie les rois. L'Histoire nous apprend que tous les autres droits, ceux de la naissance, de la religion, de la reconnaissance, de l'honneur même, sont de faibles barrières,

---

[4] Marc Bélissa, *Fraternité universelle et intérêt national (1713–1795): les cosmopolitiques du droit des gens* (Paris, 1998).

que l'ambition, la vaine gloire, la jalousie, et tant d'autres passions brisent toujours. Cependant puisque les traités publics sont une partie considérable du droit des gens, nous en considérerons les principes et les règles, comme si c'étaient des choses permanentes.[5]

Sovereigns had to respect their promises, for 'nothing is more shameful for sovereigns who punish with such rigour their vow-breaking subjects than to neglect their own treaties and to consider them as a way to cheat on the others'.[6] Treaties were of the same nature as contracts between individuals. Reason of state, as distinguishing between moral obligations of the sovereign and those of individuals, was rejected. The natural obligation to keep one's word applied to sovereigns as justice was considered the basis of the society between men.[7] That was why honouring treaties, as Emer de Vattel (1714–67) wrote, was a question that went beyond the parties and involved the 'universal society of mankind'.[8] Although often disregarded in practice, this motto did not cease to be true, and nothing was worse for a sovereign than being called 'perfidious'.[9] The same idea is to be found in Mably, who wrote that 'to fulfil one's promises is the cement of the general society, it is the base of all the happiness of every particular society'.[10]

The *Encyclopédie* quoted Grotius and distinguished between two types of treaties: the first are those by which a sovereign was committed to matters that were already compulsory according to natural law. The other type consists of those in which one promised something more.[11] The more important for human society were those of the first category, that is to say, those 'by which people commit themselves purely and simply not to

---

[5] *Encyclopédie ou dictionnaire raisonné des sciences, des arts et des métiers* (Paris, 1751–80; reprinted Stuttgart, 1967), vol. XVI, pp. 533–5. 'It is true that kings are bound not by treaties but by necessity. History teaches us that all other rights, granted by birth, religion, gratitude or even honour are but weak dams that ambition, vain glory, envy and other passions always end up flooding. Still, inasmuch as public treaties are a significant part of the right of the people, we shall consider their principles and their rules as if they were permanent things' (author's translation). Jaucourt followed the same plan as Vattel in his conclusions.

[6] My translation, as with further English quotations.

[7] Jean Bodin, *Les Six Livres de la République* 5, 5–6 (1576, ed. Paris, 1993). Bodin thought that faith was the only cement of justice, which was itself the only link between the peoples. Wise princes would always refuse to promise something that contradicted natural law, for the good prince must always keep his faith, even towards his enemies.

[8] Emer de Vattel, *Le Droit des gens ou principes de la loi naturelle, appliqués à la conduite et aux affaires des nations et des souverains* 2, 15, 218 (Leiden, 1758).

[9] Vattel, *Le Droit des gens* 2, 12, 163.

[10] Gabriel Bonnot de Mably, *Le Droit public de l'Europe* (in *Œuvres complètes*, Paris, 1795), vol. V, p. 333.

[11] See also Vattel, *Droit des gens* 2, 12, 158.

harm each other and, on the contrary, to respect the duties of humanity'. This kind of treaty was an invention of modern Europe, for the ancients did not know such agreements: 'Common opinion was that one did not have to abide by the laws of humanity except for one's fellow citizens and that foreigners could be held as foes unless some contrary agreement had been reached with them.' In the second category, Jaucourt distinguished between equal and unequal treaties as well as between personal and real treaties. The practice of unequal treaties – that is to say, a treaty in which one of the two parties committed itself unilaterally without compensation – was condemned, for reciprocity of commitments must reflect the juridical equality of the sovereigns. Personal treaties were those in which a sovereign was committed and not his heirs, while real treaties remained valid after the death of the monarch who had signed them.[12] Real treaties contributed to the building of a more solid basis of public law and helped perpetuate the sovereigns' commitments to respecting the law of nations. Therefore, when there is doubt, the *Encyclopédie* advised to regard all treaties as real. The *Encyclopédie méthodique* also stressed the importance of the treaties for all the societies, whatever this sovereigns' will might be: 'L'intérêt des sociétés policées a toujours été de former entre elles, suivant leur situation, des alliances réciproquement utiles, tant pour assurer leur repos, favoriser leur prospérité au dedans, que pour étendre leurs relations au-dehors, et pour acquérir de la considération.'[13] The philosophers therefore imposed a moral obligation of civility upon diplomatic conventions. Peace treaties were 'intruments publics de bonne foi'.[14] When they reached a fair agreement, states formed between them a juridical link that created a public space of reciprocity beneficial to society.

Bonne foi and criticism of Machiavellian diplomacy

Actual interstate relations were far from this ideal representation. The passions of sovereign princes encouraged Machiavellian behaviour during

---

[12] See also Vattel, *Droit des gens* 2, 12, 183 and 185.
[13] *Encyclopédie méthodique: économie politique et diplomatique* (Paris, 1784–86); see the Introduction on 'diplomatique'. 'The interest of civilised societies has always been to enter into alliances among themselves, according to their situation; alliances that were mutually beneficial, so as to assure their domestic peace and enhance their domestic prosperity, as well as extend their relations and gain consideration abroad' (author's translation).
[14] Those are Mably's words; see below.

the drafting of the treaties. Treaties were all too often conceived in a quibbling spirit so as to allow the breaking of the treaty according to *convenance*. Mental and written reservations, additional articles that contradicted the core of the treaty, linguistic tricks and smokescreens, all such practices were opposed to the spirit that should govern sociability between peoples. Through the disastrous moral example they gave to the nations, these Machiavellian practices caused the dissolution of society.

As early as the end of the seventeenth century, François de Salignac de la Mothe Fénelon (1651–1715) had already dwelt on the *bonne foi* necessary for the negotiation of treaties:

> Votre ennemi est votre frère; vous ne pouvez l'oublier sans oublier l'humanité . . . Dans les traités, il ne s'agit plus d'armes et de guerre; il ne s'agit que de paix, de justice, d'humanité et de bonne foi. Il est encore plus infâme et plus criminel de tromper dans un traité de paix avec un peuple voisin, que de tromper dans un contrat avec un particulier. Mettre dans un traité des termes ambigus et captieux, c'est préparer des semences de guerre pour l'avenir; c'est mettre des caques de poudre sous les maisons où l'on habite.[15]

It did not suffice, however, to respect one's commitments to the enemy sovereign; one also had to respect them as regards the peoples.[16] The interpretation of treaties must be sincere and founded on the juridical practice that had followed the signature and, above all, 'il faut soumettre les coutumes et jurisprudences des pays particuliers au droit des gens, qui leur est infiniment supérieur, et à la foi inviolable des traités de paix, qui sont l'unique fondement de la sûreté humaine'.[17]

In his *Considérations sur les causes de la grandeur des Romains et de leur décadence* (1734), Charles de Secondat de Montesquieu (1689–1755) criticised the Machiavellianism that governed the negotiations of modern Europe, giving the Romans as an example: 'On pensait alors dans les Républiques d'Italie que les traités qu'elles avaient faits avec un roi ne

---

[15] François de Fénelon, 'Examen de conscience sur les devoirs de la royauté' (1699), in Fénelon, *Ecrits et lettres politiques* (Paris, 1981), vol. XXVI, pp. 56–7. 'Your enemy is also your brother – forget that and you forget humanity . . . Treaties are no longer about arms and wars, but peace, justice, humanity and sincerity. To use deception is more infamous and criminal in a peace treaty with a neighbour country than in a contract with a single person. To put ambiguous and specious terms in a treaty is sowing seeds for future wars; it is like storing powder kegs in the house where you live' (author's translation).

[16] Fénelon, 'Examen', p. 62. [17] Fénelon, 'Examen', p. 64.

les obligeaient point envers son successeur; c'était pour elles une espèce de droit des gens. Ainsi, tout ce qui avait été soumis par un roi de Rome se prétendait libre sous un autre et les guerres naissaient toujours des guerres.'[18] The Roman Senate always talked with the voice of the master through its envoys, which never failed to bring about hostile reactions, thus giving an easy excuse for making war.[19] The summit of hypocrisy was reached by the Romans, who thought themselves to be the very embodiment of *fides*, as they never failed to impose unacceptable conditions on their defeated enemies:

> Comme ils ne faisaient jamais la paix de bonne foi et que, dans le dessein d'envahir tout, leurs traités n'étaient proprement que des suspensions de guerre, ils y mettaient des conditions qui commençaient toujours la ruine de l'Etat qui les acceptait. Ils abusaient également de subtilités de langage indignes d'un grand peuple, ainsi ils détruisirent Carthage, disant qu'ils avaient promis de conserver la Cité, et non pas la ville.[20]

Vattel too denounced the 'Prétendus grands politiques qui mettent toute leur subtilité à circonvenir ceux avec qui ils traitent, à ménager de telle sorte les conditions du traité, que tout l'avantage revient à leur maître.' It gave a poor image of 'la foi des traités que de chercher à les dresser en termes vagues ou équivoques, à y glisser des expressions louches, à se réserver des sujets de chicane, à surprendre celui avec qui l'on traite, et faire assaut de finesse et de mauvaise foi'.[21] Nevertheless, he added

---

[18] Charles de Secondat de Montesquieu, *Considérations sur les causes de la grandeur des Romains et de leur décadence* (1734, ed. Paris, 1968), p. 26. 'It was then thought, in the Republics of Italy, that a treaty which had been signed with one king did not bind his successor. It was for them a kind of people's right. Thus, everything that had been submitted by one king of Rome claimed to be free under another, so that wars kept breeding wars' (author's translation).

[19] Montesquieu, *Considérations*, p. 61.

[20] Montesquieu, *Considérations*, pp. 61–2. 'Since they never made peace sincerely and that, with the design to invade everything, their treaties were properly nothing but suspensions of war, they added provisions that entailed the ruin of the state that accepted them. They also resorted to deceptive language subtleties, which was unworthy of a great people; so they destroyed Carthage, claiming that they had promised to preserve the City, but not the town' (author's translation).

[21] Vattel, *Droit des gens* 2, 15, 231. 'So-called great politicians who use all their subtlety to circumvent those with whom they deal, so that the provisions of the treaty are put in such a way as to profit their master.' '... the sincerity of the treaties, this way of writing them in vague or equivocal terms, of slipping weird expressions into them, of keeping in store reasons to quibble, of catching unaware the one with whom you make the treaty, of competing in deceit and insincerity' (author's translation).

that a mere *lésion* is not a sufficient cause to break a convention, but an obviously unfair or pernicious treaty should be considered void.[22]

To the Enlightenment debate on diplomacy and treaties, Mably's contribution was of major importance.[23] The success of his *Droit public de l'Europe* and of its preface shows that it fulfilled an intellectual demand of rationalisation.[24] *Le droit public de l'Europe* and *Les Principes des négociations* contributed to the establishment of a reference or a norm of the same importance – in a more restricted field – as Montesquieu's *L'esprit des lois* for the whole political thinking in the Enlightenment. Mably's *Le droit public de l'Europe* was the fruit of an evolution in Mably's thought between 1746 – the year of its first publication – and 1764.[25] Mably quoted and summarised thousands of modern European treaty articles, which formed the 'archives of the nations'. This first layer of the text represented roughly two-thirds of the whole book, being the part least modified between 1746 and 1764. The second layer consisted of commentaries on those quotations. Mably clarified obscure parts and described the practices of diplomacy. In the third layer he gave a more general overview and developed a historical discourse on the role of public law. Eventually, the fourth level laid the link between practical questions and general principles of moral philosophy. This structure revealed Mably's approach: he drew his philosophical conceptions and his principles on treaty practices from the existing practices of public law. In 1754, he decided to write a long preface on the relations between moral and public law, which became his *Principes des négociations*.

---

[22] Vattel, *Droit des gens* 2, 12, 158, 161 and 168.
[23] Gabriel Bonnot de Mably (1709–85) was born in Grenoble on 14 March 1709 in a family of the 'noblesse de robe'. He studied at the Jesuit college in Lyons, then at the seminary of Saint-Sulpice, but, like his brother Condillac, he never became a priest. Protected by Madame de Tencin, he was received in her famous Paris salon, where he met Montesquieu, Bolingbroke, Fontenelle and the abbé de Saint-Pierre as well as many other figures of the first generation of the Enlightenment. In 1742, he became secretary to Cardinal de Tencin, the new minister of foreign affairs in the Fleury government. Here Mably acquired diplomatic experience that heavily influenced the evolution of his thought. This experience was fundamental to the first version of *Le droit public de l'Europe*, published in The Hague in 1746. In 1747, he quit a promising diplomatic career and devoted himself to writing and to the study of politics. When he died in 1785, he had published fifteen books.
[24] See my introduction to the issue of Gabriel Bonnot de Mably, *Principes des négociations* (Paris, 2001).
[25] See Clay Ramsay, 'L'Europe, atelier de Mably: deux états du droit public de l'Europe, 1746–1764' in *La Politique comme science morale* (Bari, 1995), vol. I, pp. 101–14.

According to Mably, true diplomacy consisted of the application of rules that were aimed at common happiness. They had nothing to do with the intrigues and quibbles in which most diplomats excelled:

> Si on regarde l'art de négocier comme un moyen de faire réussir telle ou telle affaire en particulier, la politique n'a aucune règle à prescrire aux négociateurs. Mais quand on considère les négociations comme un moyen général qu'un Etat emploie ou pour agrandir sa fortune, ou pour la conserver, si on examine comment la politique doit s'en servir pour diriger la masse entière des affaires, et traiter les étrangers de façon qu'il en résulte un avantage général, durable et permanent, on commence à découvrir des principes qui sont autant de guides sûrs dans tous les temps et toutes les circonstances. On verra que toutes les négociations doivent être entreprises et conduites relativement à son intérêt fondamental. Chaque Etat tient de ses lois, de ses mœurs et de sa position géographique, une manière d'être qui lui est propre et qui décide seule de ses vrais intérêts. Si l'objet qu'il se propose dans ses négociations est contraire à cet intérêt fondamental, il demeure, malgré tous ses efforts et quelques succès passagers, dans l'impuissance de franchir l'intervalle qui le sépare de la fin qu'il veut atteindre.'[26]

Negotiation was useful for a nation if the nation's nature was respected. But for Mably, only what was just was useful, and reason and *bonne foi* formed the bases of such a negotiation. That is why he vigourously condemned the systematic use of secrecy and the Machiavellianism of the *ancien régime*'s diplomacy:

> Rien n'est plus digne d'un prince qui connaît le prix du sang humain que de publier dans un manifeste, les motifs qui le déterminent à prendre les armes. Il faudrait en même temps faire connaître ses prétentions, ou la réparation qu'on exige. La plupart des ministres ont regardé, au contraire, comme un trait d'habileté, de ne point déclarer nettement ce qu'ils demandent par la

[26] Mably, *Droit public*, vol. V, pp. 18–19. 'If the art of negotiation is seen as a means to succeed in some endeavour in particular, then politics has no rule to prescribe to the negotiators ... But when we consider negotiations as a general mean employed by a state to improve or maintain its wealth, and if we consider the way politics should use it to manage the whole bulk of the affairs and treat the foreigners in such a way that a general, long-lasting and permanent advantage should result, we then start to discover principles that are as many guidelines to be used at every time and in any circumstances. We then shall see that every negotiation should be started and led according to the state's fundamental interest. Every state derives from its laws, its character and its geographical situation a way of being that is proper to it, and which should be the sole determining factor of its true interests ... If the goal that is aimed at in the negotiations is adverse to this fundamental interest, it will remain, in spite of all its efforts and of a few short-lived successes, impotent in making the last step to meet the end it has pursued' (author's translation).

guerre; ils ont craint de se compromettre, si elle était malheureuse, et voulu se laisser la liberté d'étendre leurs prétentions, si les succès répondaient à leurs espérances.[27]

Secret diplomacy was opposed to the necessary transparency of the public space in the relations between peoples. This transparency must be evident through a clear manifesto stating the goals of war and through open negotiations in general congresses where the interests of all the parties were discussed. Those talks must lead to texts which contributed to the establishment of 'permanent principles between nations' and to the 'improvement of our law of nations where there still remain traces of our ancient barbarous customs'. Secret treaties contributed to 'the introduction of fraud and insincerity in negotiation and commitments'.[28] This habit was 'contrary to the rules of diplomacy whose goal is the happiness of the peoples'; it was also contrary to the true principles of the law of nations even if custom tolerated it, for 'the law of nations is not what is done but what should be done'.[29] Mably went even further where he expressed a desire for a radical change of diplomatic practices:

> Il serait bien digne de la sagesse des peuples dont le gouvernement n'admet aucun engagement secret, d'en proscrire l'usage de l'Europe entière. Sans doute, que la politique, débarrassée des soupçons, des défiances et des incertitudes qui l'environnent, se conduirait avec plus de bonne foi, et se hasarderait moins souvent à commettre des fraudes, parce qu'elle en craindrait moins de la part de ses alliés.[30]

Every treaty article should clarify and not make obscure the rights and the claims; the commitments must be clearly stated. That is why Mably rejected the practice of implied clauses:

---

[27] Mably, *Droit public*, vol. V, p. 167. 'Nothing is more worthy, for a prince who knows the price of human blood, than to publish in a manifesto the motives that drive him to take up arms... It should also be necessary for him to make public his claims, or the compensation he demands. Most ministers have considered, on the contrary, as a sign of cleverness, not to state clearly what is their goal in the war. For they did not want to get compromised if they lost, and wanted to be free to extend their claim, should they be as successful as they had wished' (author's translation).

[28] Mably, *Droit public*, vol. VII, p. 89. [29] Mably, *Droit public*, vol. VII p. 90.

[30] Mably, *Droit public*, vol. VII, p. 91. 'All the wise people whose government brooks no secret committment, would be well advised to forbid the use of secrecy in all of Europe. There is no doubt that, if politicians got rid of all the suspicion, distrust and uncertainty that hover around them, they would behave with more sincerity; they would resort less often to forgery, since they would expect less treachery from their allies' (author's translation).

> Ce n'est pas que je prétende qu'il ne puisse y avoir dans les traités, comme dans toutes les autres espèces de contrats, des conditions sous-entendues et qui sont présumées; mais il me semble que les politiques ont eu raison d'établir entre eux pour principe, de n'y avoir point égard. Plus la foi des traités est sacrée, plus il faut écarter avec soin tout ce qui peut y donner quelque atteinte. Faut-il exposer les traités à devenir le jouet des subtilités, des sophismes, et des chicanes de l'ambition et de l'intérêt? Il n'y a plus rien de stable entre les nations, si l'on admet dans leurs conventions, des conditions tacites; car, il n'est que trop prouvé, pour le malheur des hommes, que leurs passions les aveuglent même sur leurs engagements les plus clairs et les plus évidents.[31]

The practice of including articles that led to the violation of the treaty was a manifest contradiction to the spirit of peace negotiations:

> Il n'est pas rare de trouver dans des traités, des clauses dont les parties contractantes prévoient certainement l'inexécution. Elles rédigent même quelquefois des articles, de manière qu'elles ne sont pas obligées de les remplir. C'est apprendre aux hommes à se jouer des instruments de la foi publique. On ne concevrait pas les motifs d'une pareille conduite, si on ne savait qu'en de certaines mains, la politique ne devient qu'une petite finesse propre à déshonorer un gouvernement.[32]

Implicit language must be banished from the treaties, for 'what is not clearly written in a treaty is not there at all', 'nothing is expressed with too much precision in a treaty of alliance not only when they deal with the nature of help that is required but on the very way it must be commanded'.[33] When linguistic obscurities were allowed on purpose, that was

---

[31] Mably, *Droit public*, vol. V, pp. 329–30. 'It does not mean that there could not be in treaties, as in all kind of contracts, conditions that go without saying, that are assumed. Still, it appears to me that politicians were right in establishing as a principle between them that they should have no regard for such conditions. The more sacred is the trust in a treaty, the more careful one should be in discarding anything that could mar this sacred trust. Should treaties be exposed to the subtleties, the sophistry and the quibbles of ambition and interest? There will not remain a stable position between nations if we admit tacit conditions in their covenants; for it has all too often been proved, for man's misery, that his passion can blind him, even in his clearest and most obvious commitments' (author's translation).

[32] Mably, *Droit public*, vol. V, p. 465. 'It is not rare to find in treaties some clauses which both contracting parties certainly consider as ineffectual. Sometimes the parties even write provisions in such a way that they will never have to fulfil them. They thus show to mankind how to tamper with the very instruments of public trust. Such a conduct would be meaningless if it were not known that in some hands politics is but a way to finagle, which is also a way to dishonour a government' (author's translation).

[33] Mably, *Droit public*, vol. V, p. 153.

not, according to Mably, a simple manoeuvre, but the very expression of Machiavellian methods with which a strong nation should do away. Confusion in a treaty 'annonce infailliblement des ministres qui ont négocié au hasard, et sans avoir des idées nettes de l'affaire dont ils étaient chargés. Les uns veulent imprimer à leur traité le caractère des finesses et des subtilités qu'ils ont employé dans le cours de leurs négociations; ils évitent le terme propre quand ils n'ont même aucun intérêt d'être obscurs.'[34]

A contrario, Mably saw in the actions of the negotiators of the Treaties of Westphalia a model of clarity and peacefulness:

> Quel ordre, quelle précision, quelle profondeur ne remarque-t-on pas dans le plan de leur négociation, et dans la matière dont ils l'exécutent? Tandis que les uns ne cherchent qu'à faire naître des difficultés, et embrouiller les affaires pour en retarder la décision, les autres se gardent bien de vouloir lever en détail tous les obstacles qu'on leur oppose. C'est en ne s'attachant qu'aux points importants et décisifs de leur négociation, qu'ils cheminent et forcent leurs adversaires à les suivre. On embrasse à la fois toutes les faces d'une affaire; on examine ses rapports voisins et éloignés; on écarte les objets étrangers; on se hâte de finir, mais sans impatience; on veut rétablir la tranquillité de l'Europe, mais on ne veut point d'une paix qui rallume la guerre. De là cette sagesse admirable des articles de Westphalie, qui sont devenus autant de lois pour l'Europe, de là cet ordre lumineux qui règne dans les matières; de là ces expressions simples, claires et précises, qui ne laissent que très rarement quelque ressource aux subtilités de la chicane.[35]

To clarify the obscure part of the treaty, Mably relied on natural law. It must be a constant reference in the negotiator's mind so as to avoid confusion brought on by the proliferation of positive law between states. Contrary to

[34] Mably, *Droit public*, vol. V, p. 330. 'Is infallibly the sign that ministers have negotiated in confusion, with no clear idea of the case they were in charge of. Some want to leave into their treaty a trace of all the tricks and subtleties they employed in the course of the negotiations. They avoid using the proper term even when they have no interest in being obscure' (author's translation).

[35] Mably, *Droit public*, vol. V, pp. 329–30. 'What an order, what precision, what depth is shown in the plan of their negotiations, and in the way they carry it out! While some only try to create new difficulties and muddle up all the affairs so as to delay the final decision, others refuse to examine in detail every obstruction. By sticking to the important and decisive points of the negotiation, they are moving forward, forcing their adversaries to follow their progress. Every aspect of a case is so embraced; every close or remote relation is examined; alien subjects are left out; they make haste, but with no impatience. No one wants a peace that would breed a new war. Hence the admirable wisdom of the articles of the Peace of Westphalia, which have become so many laws for all Europe; hence this luminous order that reigns in the matters; hence these simple, clear and precise expressions, which leave so little room for the subtleties of quibbles' (author's translation).

the positive law, which was but the expression of the balance of power and of the passions of the sovereigns, natural law was the product of natural reason. This is the reason why Mably advised to start by thinking within the framework of natural law to elucidate or invalidate an obscure point of positive law, whereas Vattel used natural law only *a posteriori*.

The programme set forth by Mably was an ideal that one should try to achieve so as to leave the vicious circle of the treaties, which imposed no law and bred future wars. The treaties, which should be charts of the law of the nations, were unfortunately only short-lived truces in a system of latent hostilities.

Although the practice of treaties improved during the eighteenth century, philosophers kept on insisting on the contradictions between the principles of juridical equality of the nations and the unequal or exclusive articles of the treaties. To sum up, they reproached the sovereigns for not going far enough in the achievement of a spirit of necessary reciprocity in the relations between peoples. The example of the *droit d'aubaine* can illustrate this. Indeed, throughout the eighteenth century, the kings of France signed conventions of abolition of the *droit d'aubaine* with many European states, but they never had the intention of completely suppressing such a 'gothic right'. The persistence of this right in an enlightened century was for the *Encyclopédie* an enigma and a source of shame.[36] For Mably, 'le droit d'aubaine est un reste de l'ancienne barbarie du gouvernement féodal. On a prouvé que ce droit est contraire aux lois de l'humanité, au progrès du commerce, et aux intérêts bien entendus de chaque prince; il subsiste cependant toujours.'[37]

Conclusion

Peace treaties were regarded by the Enlightenment philosophers as the deformed expression of a European civility which naturally tended towards peace. These 'archives of the nations' were the product of the sovereign passions, but they were also a juridical corpus creating law where beforehand only a state of war reigned. For philosophers, it was a kind of 'nature's trick', an instance of what Immanuel Kant (1724–1804) called the 'unsociable sociability of man'. Peace treaties formed the juridical basis for a proclamation of a code of law of nations founded on the 'true principles of moral'. To pacify relations between the peoples, this dialectical contradiction had to be solved through the rejection of secrecy and quibbles of

[36] *Encyclopédie*, article 'aubaine'. [37] Mably, *Droit public*, vol. VII, p. 7.

vulgar Machiavellianism. In spite of the passions and vices of the men who preside over their drafting, treaties were 'public instruments of *bonne foi*', hence the necessity to rely on these 'acquis de civilisation' to improve even more the relations within European society. Nevertheless, this approach to diplomacy was not hegemonic among philosophers (some like Simon Nicolas Henri Linguet (1736–94) or Jean-Jacques Rousseau (1712–78) for different reasons denied their 'progressist' nature) but it is widely admitted, for example by Montesquieu or Vattel. Late eighteenth-century revolutionaries would revive this debate. For example, American revolutionaries elaborated a new conception of active diplomacy founded on the progress of the law of nations, whereas their French counterparts aimed at a radical transformation of the European diplomatic order.[38]

[38] See Bélissa, *Fraternité universelle*.

12

Peace, security and international organisations: the German international lawyers and the Hague Conferences

INGO HUECK

Introduction[1]

The centenary celebration of the birthday of Walther Schücking (1875–1935) led Ulrich Scheuner, the distinguished German international lawyer and historian, to declare tersely in 1975: 'The relationship which Germany has to the establishment of a generally unified state has never had the depth and the character of an idealistic, moralistic movement as it had in other countries, especially in England.'[2] He primarily based this finding, almost certainly correctly, on Germany's external relationships, including the two World Wars, which resulted in the brief though not particularly favourable era of the League of Nations and the division of Germany after 1945.[3] Within these time frames, with their important international law turning points and events, the international law theory supported neither official German politics nor the idea of achieving peace and security in the international community. It was for this reason that the international lawyer, politician and pacifist Walther Schücking played a particularly important role, not only during his lifetime, but also into the years of

[1] This chapter draws on research carried out for a book project on the development of international law in Germany during the nineteenth century (see: http://www.ingohueck.com). In this context, I would like to thank the participants in the international legal history project at the Frankfurt Max Planck Institute for European Legal History (1998–2001). I owe a special debt to Professor Martti Koskenniemi (Helsinki University and New York University) for our discussions at Harvard in the spring of 2000, which deeply influenced my further research.

[2] Ulrich Scheuner, 'Die internationale Organisation der Staaten und die Friedenssicherung. Zum Werk Walther Schückings (1875–1935)', *Die Friedens-Warte* 58 (1975), 7–22 at p. 8 (my translation).

[3] Scheuner, 'Internationale Organisation der Staaten', pp. 8–9.

the construction of the Federal Republic – the role more or less of an outsider.[4]

Where are the inner motivations for these developments? Why indeed did the strongest maritime and colonial power, Britain, develop a stronger notion of securing peace and building international relationships in the age of imperialism, while the young German Empire was devoting itself to glorifying war? The early and publicly effective German peace movement only had a minimal influence on German international law thought. Whilst German international law teaching in the eighteenth and nineteenth centuries was marked by a 'European' line of thought, after the establishment of the Empire the cries changed to that of state power and nationalism. This tendency, which remained a powerful and special influence in German international law, can nevertheless only be explained convincingly by the construction of a German nationalist state with world domination as its goal.

The separation of international law from the philosophy of international law, completed well before the establishment of the *Kaiserreich* in the nineteenth century, was decisive in the inclusion of international law as a permanent component of jurisprudence. Not only did a new type of international law practitioner and a juristic-pragmatic approach to questions of international law emerge from this development. With the increasing importance of the practice of international law and international relations, a closer relationship between international law and political decisions also developed. In Germany, from an academic and institutional perspective, this tendency resulted in a special marriage between public law and international law, which continues up to the present.[5]

The protection of international peace in the context of the Hague Conferences of 1899 and 1907

The contemporary system of peace with which we are familiar was not developed in the nineteenth century, and, even until well after the Hague Peace Conferences of 1899 and 1907, was not practically applied. The reforms these Conferences brought regarded less the *ius contra bellum*

---

[4] Detlev Acker, *Walther Schücking* (Münster, 1970).
[5] Ingo Hueck, 'Die Gründung völkerrechtlicher Zeitschriften im internationalen Vergleich' in Michael Stolleis (ed.), *Juristische Zeitschriften: die neuen Medien des 18.–20. Jahrhunderts* (Frankfurt am Main, 1999), pp. 379–420 at pp. 380–4 and 398–9.

than the *ius in bello* and the problem of the peaceful settlement of disputes. The Hague Conferences were not yet about trying to avoid war through the creation of international organisations, as was first approached gradually after the First World War with the establishment of the League of Nations and the 1928 Briand–Kellogg Pact.[6] Prior to this, it was not only the relevant moral, social and political framework which was lacking, but also a theory of international law with corresponding concepts and vision. Despite some nation-specific interest in the development of the theoretical discipline of modern international law, securing international peace was not of primary importance in the minds of the European international legal community. This idea of securing international peace was formulated and propagated in this period by the international peace movement, minorities and independence movements, revolutionary committees and 'peace clubs', as well as by naïve world-changers or fanatical utopians. The majority of international lawyers tended to work pragmatically and directed their scholarly work primarily towards national interests and foreign policy. Many worked not as scholars, but as diplomats or legal advisers for government officials and conference delegations. They travelled not as friends of peace, but rather as government representatives to the Hague Peace Conferences of 1899 and 1907. The Hague Conferences developed remarkably quickly into an international platform for fundamental debates regarding the international law of peace, and were significantly influenced by the conference experience itself, not to mention the active peace movement and public interest. Accordingly, the Hague Conferences were of great importance, not least because of their results in the sphere of international law. They constitute a particularly momentous event from a historical, academic perspective in that they established the study of international law as a specific academic area in and of itself. The Hague Conferences not only reinforced the aim of securing international peace, but also promoted a new direction for international law which articulated the concept of the establishment of international peace: so-called academic pacifism.[7]

---

[6] Clive Parry, 'League of Nations' in Rudolf Bernhardt (ed.), *Encyclopaedia of Public International Law* (2nd edn, Amsterdam, 1997), vol. III, pp. 177–86; Cynthia D. Wallace, 'Kellogg–Briand Pact (1928)' in Bernhardt (ed.), *Encyclopaedia of Public International Law*, vol. III, pp. 76–9; see also Wilhelm G. Grewe, *The Epochs of International Law* (Berlin, 2000), pp. 575–9 and 585–8.

[7] From a German perspective, see Hans Wehberg, *Die Führer der deutschen Friedensbewegung (1890 bis 1923)* (Leipzig, 1923) and Hans Wehberg, 'Die deutsche Friedensbewegung 1870–1933', *Die Friedens-Warte* 48 (1948), 247–51.

International politics in the Age of Imperialism

The long nineteenth century, until the First World War (1815–1914), is generally referred to as the Age of Imperialism. The great European powers expanded their power and influence worldwide, as the USA and Japan did in their own parts of the globe. International politics served the primary purpose of territorial and economic expansion. The states with strong economic and military support were looking for international markets and sources of raw materials. These policies implied a significant potential for crisis and conflict. Crises and conflicts up until the First World War, however, did not lead to widespread war, but remained regional or concerned only two countries. In particular, between the Crimean War, 1853–56, and the First World War there were very few wars involving a great number of superpowers simultaneously. In contrast, a certain tendency to show restraint when it came to conflict between states was typical for this so-called Age of High Imperialism. The German historian Jost Dülffer developed a convincing basic model justifying this situation, which points to the impressive industrial economic growth and technological progress, and the resulting social and political implications.[8] Despite the increasingly vehement tensions in the world, in particular in relation to the race to conquer Africa, and the increasing frequency of serious crises and serious threats of war, it was only in 1914 that the First World War commenced. In Europe, as well as overseas, the political desire to avoid war, or at least to limit it to regional disputes, was predominant.

This period of relative stability was also one during which international law – following the Congress of Vienna of 1815 – was strengthened. Parallel to the economic and territorial expansion of states, the importance of international law continued to grow. Numerous international law contracts and agreements were created, both bilaterally and multilaterally. Arthur Nussbaum reports on estimates that in the period between the Congress of Vienna and the First World War between 10,000 and 16,000 contracts alone were made.[9] Technical and economic progress demanded international agreements on standardisation and norms. International trade resulted in the foundation of the first international organisations, the so-called administrative unions, such as the International Telegraph Union (1865), the General Postal Union (1874, after 1878 called

---

[8] Jost Dülffer, *Regeln gegen den Krieg? Die Haager Friedenskonferenzen von 1899 und 1907 in der internationalen Politik* (Berlin, 1981).
[9] Arthur Nussbaum, *A Concise History of the Law of Nations* (New York, 1947), pp. 191–2.

the Universal Postal Union), the Convention on Transport of Goods by Rail (1890) and Radiotelegraphy (World Transmission Contract 1906), as well as the Convention on Automobile Traffic (1909).

As serious conflicts could be avoided, old mechanisms for the peaceful settlement of disputes were rediscovered and introduced. It was in this context that the Jay Treaty of 1784 between the United States and Great Britain was considered to be the hour of the birth of modern arbitration. This agreement was intended to establish numerous mixed commissions, some of which were also to assume the role of judicial arbitrators.[10] It was on this basis that a whole series of judicial treaties emerged in the nineteenth century – treaties which gave the mixed commissions, neutral governments or individual people the authority to make binding decisions in cases of conflict. These jurisdictional arbitrators were not equally established across the superpowers in the nineteenth century. The numerous and, most importantly, successful arbitration mechanisms between the United States and Great Britain were, however, an important prerequisite for the 1899 Hague Arbitration Convention and the 1907 Hague Conventions.

International law in superpower Europe

How did the increasingly important role of international legal practice in the individual European states affect their practices in diplomacy and international law? To what extent did it affect the development of international law as an academic subject and did it change the role of its representatives?

Above all, there was one particular trend: the professionalisation of the study of international law. After the initial critical approaches of the natural law theory in the eighteenth century, the study and literature of international law now became a far more systematic-analytical and practical discipline within the context of state practice. In addition, the methods used in the sciences increasingly pervaded the juristic and political culture of knowledge and communication.

These influences encouraged the radical search for new theoretical arguments which was undertaken in the context of international law in the late eighteenth century by John Austin (1798–1859), the leading scholar in British legal positivism and founder of the English analytical school

---

[10] For further details, see Grewe, *Epochs of International Law*, pp. 517–24.

of jurisprudence.[11] Generally, presentations of natural justice and views regarding legitimate war slowly began to take the back seat in academic discussions. The so-called 'art of diplomacy', that is, the art and technique of diplomatic transactions, can still be found in the textbooks of the nineteenth century, but is nevertheless strictly separated with regard to subject matter.[12] Only the legal status of diplomatic staff was still considered to continue to be a part of and was dealt with in the context of international law. The conviction that private law concepts did not provide optimal solutions to public international law situations and problems ultimately prevailed. These opinions resulted in an early separation from international private law and the establishment of a completely separate discipline differentiated linguistically; they manifested themselves in the names 'private international law' and 'public international law'. In conjunction, these legal, practical and intellectual changes during the nineteenth century led to a clear creation of public international law as a branch of the legal disciplines and to its final emancipation and separation from philosophy, theology and politics.

With this development of the subject, the function and purposes of public international law, as well as the way in which the public international law theorists perceived themselves, also changed. A perfect example is Johann Ludwig Klüber (1762–1837). Both a diplomat and a legal adviser, as well as Professor of Constitutional Law at Heidelberg University, he became well known upon the publication of the files of the Vienna Conventions.[13] He gained access to the materials thanks to his personal connections with the Prussian State Chancellor Hardenberg. In this connection, Klüber was described as the master of the treatment of

---

[11] John Austin, *Lectures on Jurisprudence or the Philosophy of Positive Law* (1830–31; ed. Robert Campbell, London, 1861).

[12] For example, see one of the most influential textbooks in Europe in the nineteenth century, written by August Wilhelm Heffter, *Das europäische Völkerrecht der Gegenwart* (Berlin, 1844). Heffter's textbook went through eight German editions, two of them posthumous (1881 and 1888); in addition, four French editions appeared and the book was translated into Greek, Hungarian, Polish, Russian, Spanish and Japanese. It has frequently been cited also by English and American academics. For further details of Heffter's theoretical background and influence, see my forthcoming article in a new German book series on the history of international law (*Studien zur Geschichte des Völkerrechts*, ed. by the Frankfurt Max Planck Institute for Legal History); see also my 'Pragmatism, Positivism and Hegelianism in the Nineteenth Century: August Wilhelm Heffter's Notion of Public International Law' in Michael Stolleis and Masaharu Yanagihara (eds.), *East Asian and European Perspectives on International Law* (Baden Baden, 2004), 41–55.

[13] Johann Ludwig Klüber (ed.), *Akten des Wiener Congresses in den Jahren 1814 und 1815* (Erlangen, 1815–35).

current public law, a person who could deal excellently with the enormous amounts of sources and who was an 'author without the frills'.[14] This is also an apt description for one of Klüber's successful works, *Droit des gens modernes de l'Europe* (1819), the first German edition of which was published in 1821.[15] Its impact was not a result of the book's original thought. In his groundwork, Klüber, like the German diplomat and scholar Georg Friedrich von Martens (1756–1821) before, founded his international law theories on natural law theory. He also presented international law as a part of diplomacy. The work was particularly successful thanks to well-founded documentation of pacts and conventions from the time subsequent to 1815. It was also for this reason that it received international recognition, to the extent that a Russian edition was published in 1828. This text remained the only systematic treatise of international law in the Russian language until 1880. It was then that the Russian edition of Heffter's work appeared on the scene.

Klüber and Heffter were German scholars who, like Moser and Martens in the eighteenth century, turned to constitutional law and the politics of public international law.[16] Their textbooks appeared in numerous editions and countless languages and dominated German writings on international law well into the nineteenth century. These authors not only represent a humanistic, natural law and later positivistic tradition in public international law; they also represent a tradition that places European public international law and the European superpowers in the spotlight of their public international law observations. In connection with the securing of international peace, this tradition continued to be uncontroversial up until the mid-nineteenth century. An observer of the overall European situation could only have been satisfied: the Vienna Congress was the beginning of one of the longest periods of peace in European history. This peace was protected, more or less, by the five European superpowers (Great Britain, France, Austria, Prussia and Russia) and created the conditions for a rapid industrial improvement and technological progress. This industrial and economic progress, however, demanded social and political changes. Free trade and economic strength benefited only a limited

---

[14] See Michael Stolleis, *Geschichte des öffentlichen Rechts in Deutschland* (Munich, 1992), vol. II, p. 83.
[15] Johann Ludwig Klüber, *Droit des gens modernes de l'Europe; avec un supplément contenant une bibliothèque choisie du droit des gens* (Stuttgart, 1819); Johann Ludwig Klüber, *Europäisches Völkerrecht* (Stuttgart, 1821, 2nd edn Morstadt and Heidelberg, 1847).
[16] For further information on Moser and Martens, see e.g. Nussbaum, *Concise History of the Law of Nations*, pp. 163–70 and 170–7.

part of Europe, particularly the West European countries. The securing of peace was clearly in the hands of the five superpowers, of which three, namely Austria, Prussia and Russia, were governed by absolute monarchies. It was the Crimean War (1853–56) which was to demonstrate just how fragile this international system really was.

The influence of the international peace movement

Critical assessments of the state practice of public international law in Europe were in fact only made by the freedom movements. They were in part radically religious (such as William Penn's movement in the United States), in part radically democratic.[17] They stood up for political freedom and liberal ideas. Initially, they were badly organised, but from the middle of the nineteenth century on, regional conferences and world congresses were organised (around 1850 in Frankfurt) at which resolutions of peace and non-violence were discussed and agreed upon, and which, of course, were seldom heard of in diplomatic circles.

On the other hand, a group of critical public international scholars had been forming since the 1860s. Most of the initiators came from countries with a more liberal tradition, among which were the founders and founding members of the *Institut de Droit international* established in Ghent, Belgium, in 1873.[18] This international group met annually to delve into and resolve current international law problems, and was, even up until the League of Nations era, a very important and influential society of internationally recognised international law experts. As an independent, international committee, these lawyers provided expert opinions on and suggestions for individual states or groups of states, and developed drafts of codifications, in particular for the Law of War for both land and sea (1880 and 1913). According to its statutes, the *Institut* was intended to serve the general interest and encourage academic work in the area of public international law. Johann Caspar Bluntschli (1808–81), the German founding member – originating from Switzerland – had hoped that the

[17] For example, William Penn, *Essay towards the Present and Future Peace of Europe* (American Peace Society, ed., Washington, DC, 1912); Irwin Abrams, 'A History of European Peace Societies 1867–1899' (PhD, Harvard University, 1938); Abrams, 'The Emergence of International Law Societies', *Review of Politics* 19 (1957), 361–80; see also Richard Barkeley, *Die deutsche Friedensbewegung 1870–1933* (Hamburg, 1948).

[18] For further details of the initial ideas, concepts, and vision, see Martti Koskenniemi, *The Gentle Civilizer of Nations: The Rise and Fall of International Law, 1870–1960* (Cambridge, 2002), pp. 39–51; with a special focus on the German influence and contributions, see Fritz Münch, 'Das Institut de Droit international', *Archiv des Völkerrechts* 28 (1990), 76–105.

independent body could present itself as a permanent committee, established for the resolution of international conflicts.[19]

The initiators, the Dutchman Tobias M. C. Asser (1838–1913), the Belgian Gustave Rolin-Jacquemyns (1835–1902) and the Englishman John Westlake (1828–1913), had a very specific goal: the liberalisation and the reform of existing public international law on the basis of humanitarian and democratic concepts. Most importantly, they feared that the existing European system of safeguarding the peace was being jeopardised by extreme economic, social and political changes which had been characterising the last third of the nineteenth century. In contrast to the majority of public international lawyers, who predominantly worked from a national perspective, these three young international lawyers criticised the increase in international crises and conflicts from an overall European perspective, especially in the context of the arms race of the superpowers and the unequal distribution of economic and technical achievements. These three jurists, who first met at the meeting establishing the 'British Association for the Promotion of Social Science' in Brussels in 1857, in subsequent years developed the idea of founding the first public international law journal. The *Revue de Droit International et de Législation Comparée* was first published in 1869.[20] The journal was intended to deal particularly with current problems of law resulting from national legislation and international economic transactions. The community of states and national jurists were to be encouraged, particularly in the area of economics, to try to create congruent legal standards in order to diminish or avoid political or social conflicts. In addition, Westlake established that the journal was to encourage international thought, especially in view of the nationalistic state tendencies in Italy, Germany and Central Europe: nations and minorities were to define public international law principles and values, and cease to file away public international law to be used only for the purposes of national interests.

Asser, Rolin and Westlake did not take part in the established study of public international law prior to the foundation of the *Institut de Droit international*, or after the publication of the journal. They were practising and politically thinking lawyers. Rolin and Westlake worked as lawyers; Asser became Professor of Comparative Law in Amsterdam. The foreword to the first issue clarified that the new journal was to be a forum for

---

[19] Koskenniemi, *Gentle Civilizer*, pp. 42–7.
[20] See Hueck, 'Gründung völkerrechtlicher Zeitschriften', pp. 385–6; Koskenniemi, *Gentle Civilizer*, pp. 12–19.

liberal legal reforms, primarily in the area of private international law, for which a comprehensive agenda was immediately suggested.[21] Within public international law, a more international humanitarian law in the context of war was suggested, which was to go somewhat further than the relatively recent 1864 Geneva Convention for the Amelioration of the Condition of the Wounded and Sick of Armies in the Field.[22] They highly criticised diplomacy as an instrument for resolving conflicts and avoiding war. The concept of the Holy Alliance was viewed with great ambivalence and judged as dangerous, as it was particularly interest-based and exclusive. It was with these goals that the *Revue*, and later also the *Institut de Droit international*, primarily targeted reform-orientated and internationally equipped jurists.

Asser, Rolin and Westlake sought comrades who were equally critical and forward-looking, and less bound by tradition. It therefore comes as no surprise that in the programme for the opening speech of the first *Revue* there are no references to traditional European writings, but merely short references to Rousseau and Kant in connection with humanitarian and federalist thought. The German public international law literature was completely ignored. In the opinion of Asser, Rolin and Westlake, the German writings were antiquated, based on established European state systems, and therefore offered no suggestions of reform. This did not mean, however, that there was no German participation whatsoever. Bluntschli, both in a political and in a public international law sense a particularly liberal and open-minded contemporary, was President of the *Institut de Droit international*. In addition, August von Bulmerincq (1822–90) and Franz von Holtzendorff (1829–89) were amongst the first members, who were particularly noticeable through their desire to reform and commented critically on the state of contemporary public international law within German academia.[23]

Alongside these academic movements for reform, the peace movement in particular began to organise itself towards the end of the nineteenth century. This movement resulted in the creation of its own organisations,

---

[21] Hans Wehberg, 'Völkerrechtszeitschriften und Annuaires' in Karl Strupp (ed.), *Wörterbuch des Völkerrechts und der Diplomatie* (Berlin, 1924–29), vol. III, pp. 302–4; Paul Fauchille, *Traité de droit international public* (Paris, 1922), vol. I, pp. 141–3.

[22] See Grewe, *Epochs of International law*, p. 513.

[23] For example, August von Bulmerincq, 'Die Lehre und das Studium des Völkerrechts an den Hochschulen Deutschlands', *Schmollers Jahrbuch für Gesetzgebung, Verwaltung und Volkswirtschaft* NS 1 (1877), 457–64; for further details of these aspects, see Hueck, 'Gründung völkerrechtlicher Zeitschriften', pp. 386–7.

which initially hardly ever sought contact with the public international law movements of reform, such as the *Institut de Droit international* or the American International Law Association, also founded in 1873. In 1892, the author and pacifist Bertha von Suttner (1843–1914) published the first monthly magazine of the European peace movement under the name of her successful novel, *Die Waffen Nieder!* (*Lay Down Your Arms!*, 1889).[24] It was in the very same year that the *Bureau international de la Paix* was established in Berne; in 1903 the *Institut international de la Paix* was created in Monaco. Along with Suttner, the German peace movement was represented primarily by Alfred Hermann Fried (1864–1921), Ludwig Quidde (1853–1941) and Otto Lehmann-Rüssbüldt (1873–1964).[25]

Despite these strong movements for reform in public international law, the subsequent improvements of the study of public international law seemed to have no substantial impact. This was the case not only in Germany, but also in Great Britain and France. Germany, however, was relatively lucky, particularly Prussia and Bavaria as a result of their long traditions of international law, their numerous universities and their federal structure after the establishment of the Empire. Public international law was, at least in written form – as already discussed – dealt with as a part of national law and diplomacy. In France, public international law was taught as a part of natural law, strictly separated from the art of diplomacy and predominantly taught at faculties of philosophy.[26] The worst off was Great Britain, the European superpower of the nineteenth century. Neither Oxford nor Cambridge offered public international law lectures. There was practically no university education for public international law until the middle of the nineteenth century. One used the English translations of Grotius, Bynkershoek and Vattel. This, however, was to change rapidly.

After a comprehensive curriculum reform, in 1859 Oxford (the Chichele Chair with Montague Bernard) and in 1866 Cambridge (the Whewell Chair with William Harcourt) each created for the first time a special teaching position in public international law. In Edinburgh, it

---

[24] Bertha von Suttner, *Die Waffen nieder! Eine Lebensgeschichte* (Dresden and Leipzig, 1889).
[25] Hueck, 'Gründung völkerrechtlicher Zeitschriften', pp. 395–8.
[26] See Koskenniemi, *Gentle Civilizer*, pp. 28–35 ('An amateur science'), which gives an excellent overview of the situation of the discipline of international law in Europe, especially in German, French and British academia; for the British situation, see also Eric W. Beckett, 'International Law in England', *The Law Quarterly Review* 55 (1939), 257–72; Sir Arnold McNair, 'The Wider Teaching of International Law', *Journal of the Society of Public Teachers of Law* 2 (1952), 10–14.

was Sir James Lorimer (1818–90) who obtained a teaching position in the Law of Nature and the Law of Nations in 1862. Special professorships were established through private sponsorship at other universities. In contrast to the German tradition of the university-educated diplomat or legal adviser who also worked as a representative of the state, the British public law professor tended to work only within the context of the university. They were all educated within the Vattel tradition, and until the late 1880s had arguments – completely in contrast to the majority of their continental European colleagues – based on the foundations of the law of nature and God's will.[27] Accordingly, the interest of practice-orientated jurists wanting to participate in government and diplomacy was minimal. This attitude, particularly from a leading superpower such as Great Britain, had little to do with a simple lack of interest. The leading economic, military and hegemonic powers could not simultaneously be advocates of a better form of international law; primarily, it was about maintaining power and expansion. On the other hand, Great Britain was no longer an absolute monarchy. The British government thus sought, in the power politics context, from time to time legitimisation in public international law. From the English perspective, public international law was therefore an instrument of power and *Realpolitik*.

The Hague Conferences of 1899 and 1907

At the Hague Peace Conferences of 1899 and 1907, the United Kingdom and Russia were the positive players, the German Empire the spoilsport. It was in fact Russia that initiated the process that led to the 1899 Conference. In the summer of 1898, the Russian czar's comments regarding peace shook the diplomatic world. Russia of all countries, one of the most extensively armed superpowers of the time, sent out invitations to a disarmament conference. Great Britain, which like other superpowers had conquered a great empire and held formidable naval forces, was not particularly interested in disarmament. It was Britain, however, that was the proponent of the introduction of an international court of arbitration. Particularly sensitised to the crisis management involved in avoiding war, Britain together with the United States encouraged such a system politically and morally. It was primarily the British effort that led to the

---

[27] For the contrasts in many respects, see Nussbaum's excellent descriptions in his *Concise History of the Law of Nations* on Bynkershoek (pp. 142–8), Wolff (pp. 148–55) and Vattel (pp. 155–63).

establishment of the Hague Permanent Court of Arbitration. The superpowers were even interested in the possibility of giving the court obligatory jurisdiction in areas clearly defined, in order to protect the interests of individual states through the inclusion of relevant exceptions. Of the important European superpowers, only the German Empire opposed this fundamental consensus – the introduction of the obligatory international arbitration court failed in 1899 as a result of the lack of the German vote. The German government continued to harp on the principle of absolute sovereignty of the superpowers, and, as a result, at both Hague Conferences was responsible for bringing negotiations to a standstill, including negotiations which would have resulted in steady progress towards avoiding war and managing conflicts. Behind this were, of course, Germany's interest in uninhibited expansion and the domestic concern that concessions in the arbitral or armament issues would strengthen the social democratic party, as well as the pacifist movement within the German Empire.[28]

It was perhaps in spite of, or even because of, such domestic political developments that the government was unable to maintain its extreme stance. Already during the first Hague Conference of 1899, there were open controversies in matters of international dispute resolution between two academic representatives within the German delegation, both of them conservative German professors: Karl von Stengel from Munich University and Philipp Zorn from Bonn University. Stengel supported the German government and rejected obligatory international arbitration on the basis of the teachings of sovereignty ('He who has the power, has the right').[29] Zorn, who served the young crown prince Wilhelm as well as the sons of Emperor Wilhelm II as a teacher and who was known for his state-centric views, was, in the words of one of his students, Hans Wehberg, 'sucked into the whirlpool of enthusiasm for the arbitral jurisdiction'.[30]

Zorn opposed the rejection of the permanent arbitration court according to the instructions of the German foreign minister, and so mitigated

---

[28] The history of the Hague Conferences, including the political and legal discussion and policy, is excellently described and analysed in Jost Dülffer's book on the *Haager Friedenskonferenzen*. In addition, cf. Philip Zorn, *Weltunion, Haager Friedenskonferenzen und Völkerbund* (Berlin, 1925), p. 29 ('unverkennbares Misstrauen des offiziellen kaiserlichen Deutschlands... auch einflussreiche militärische Kreise'); Hans Wehberg, 'Zur Erinnerung an die erste Haager Friedenskonferenz (1899)', *Die Friedens-Warte* 49 (1949), 212–14; see also a longer version of this chapter in *Neue Züricher Zeitung*, 19 June 1949, no. 1256.

[29] Karl von Stengel, 'Die Haager Friedenskonferenz und das Völkerrecht', *Archiv für Öffentliches Recht* 15 (1899), 139–201 at p. 197 (my translation).

[30] Wehberg, 'Zur Erinnerung', p. 213 (my translation).

GERMAN INTERNATIONAL LAWYERS AND HAGUE CONFERENCES 267

the strong German stance otherwise taken.[31] Along with other German liberal or open-minded public international law scholars, such as Josef Kohler, Franz von Liszt and, primarily, Walther Schücking and Hans Wehberg, Zorn was involved with the ideas of peace movements and the Hague Conferences. Other liberal and critical German international lawyers were August von Bulmerincq and Franz von Holtzendorff mentioned above.[32] Already early on, they complained of the lack of support of public international law in research and teaching, especially in the light of its increasing practical and international importance. Especially since the time of the establishment of the Empire, politically and morally the atmosphere differed from that of other states such as the United Kingdom and small states such as Belgium and the Netherlands, where the liberal movement and liberal traditions were probably far more conspicuous.[33]

It was Philipp Zorn who warned, with Walther Schücking and Hans Wehberg, his particularly active students, that, with all too openly liberal tendencies, one could not have a career in the study of law in Germany.[34] Those who set the course took quite a different view until the First World War, a view which the Hague Conferences of 1899 and 1907 documented with particular clarity: the German historian and winner of the Nobel Prize in Literature 1902, Theodor Mommsen (1817–1903), decried the first Hague Conference as an error in world history,[35] and a particularly renowned Heidelberg law professor, Ernst Immanuel Bekker (1827–1916), warned against attending public international law lectures. They were both useless and dangerous, he is said to have told his students regularly, sending them on their way. Even if described with slight exaggeration, it was impossible for the study of public international law to bloom under such conditions during the era of the German Empire.[36] The traditionally active study of public international law was therefore tainted with

[31] For further information about Zorn's life, and his political and professional career, see the published thesis by Julia Schmidt, Konservative Staatsrechtslehre und Friedenspolitik: Leben und Werk Philipp Zorns (Ebelsbach, 2001).
[32] For German academia on public international law during this period, see Hueck, 'Gründung völkerrechtlicher Zeitschriften', pp. 395–8 and 407–10, and Koskenniemi, Gentle Civilizer, pp. 213–22.
[33] See Koskenniemi, Gentle Civilizer, pp. 88–97.
[34] See Hans Wehberg, '50 Jahre Friedens-Warte', Die Friedens-Warte 50 (1950/51), 1–7 at p. 4.
[35] Jürgen Kuczynski, Theodor Mommsen: Porträt eines Gesellschaftswissenschaftlers (Berlin, 1978).
[36] E.g., see the study of the discipline of public international law in Germany by Moritz Liepmann, a distinguished law professor from Kiel University, Die Pflege des Völkerrechts an den deutschen Universitäten (Berlin, 1919).

a hint of antagonism. There were numerous standard publications, in particular textbooks on international law, such as those of August Wilhelm Heffter (eight German editions between 1844 and 1888) as well as those of Franz von Liszt (twelve German editions between 1898 and 1925), which through translation into countless languages enjoyed a very good reputation.[37] In the theory of public international law, Carl Magnus Bergbohm (1849–1927), Georg Jellinek (1851–1911) and Heinrich Triepel (1868–1949) enjoyed particular notoriety and, along with others, presented the theoretical basis for the positivistic establishment of public international law.[38] On the other hand, it was a new Hegelian position, particularly popular after the establishment of the Empire in Germany, which supported the official German stance taken at the Hague Conferences, in that people such as Adolf Lasson (1837–1917) and Erich Kaufmann (1880–1972) placed the state's individual sovereignty central and propagated war ('Only he who can, may!').[39] Furthermore, they remained supportive of an older German tradition, and, as already mentioned in connection with the *Institut de Droit international*, defined their public international law position from a particularly narrow connection between constitutional foundations (sovereignty, equality, equality between states).

Conclusion

Along with Ulrich Scheuner's description of 'external relationships' – such as the European nation-state movement, the establishment of the German

---

[37] For further details on Heffter's textbook, see Hueck, 'Pragmatism'; about the backgrounds of Liszt's successful textbook, see Florian Herrmann, *Das Standardwerk: Franz von Liszt und das Völkerrecht* (Baden Baden, 2001).

[38] See the main writings of Carl Magnus Bergbohm, *Staatsverträge und Gesetz als Quelle des Völkerrechts* (Dorpat, 1876); Georg Jellinek, *Die rechtliche Natur der Staatsverträge* (Vienna, 1880); and *Die Lehre von den Staatenverbindungen* (Vienna, 1882); Heinrich Triepel, *Völkerrecht und Landesrecht* (Leipzig, 1899). For further details of the works of Jellinek, see Jochen von Bernstorff, 'Georg Jellinek – Völkerrecht als modernes öffentliches Recht im fin de siècle' in Stanley L. Paulson and Martin Schulte (eds.), *Georg Jellinek: Beiträge zu Leben und Werk* (Tübingen, 2000), pp. 183–206; for further information on the foundation of *Gesetzpositivismus*, see Koskenniemi, *Gentle Civilizer*, pp. 186–8.

[39] Adolf Lasson, *Prinzip und Zukunft des Völkerrechts* (Berlin, 1871); about Lasson's works, see Klaus Lüderssen, 'Anerkennungsprobleme im Völkerrecht' in *Genesis und Geltung in der Jurisprudenz* (Frankfurt, 1996), pp. 223–47, and Heinhard Steiger, 'Völkerrecht und Naturrecht zwischen Christian Wolff und Adolf Lasson' in Diethelm Klippel (ed.), *Naturrecht im 19. Jahrhundert* (Goldbach, 1997), pp. 45–74 at pp. 64–74. Erich Kaufmann, *Das Wesen des Völkerrechts und die Clausula rebus sic stantibus* (Tübingen, 1911); about Kaufmann's early main work, see Koskenniemi, *Gentle Civilizer*, pp. 249–61.

Empire, and the two World Wars – there were also structural and socio-cultural reasons which were responsible for Germany, in comparison with the United Kingdom, asserting the idea of securing international peace through establishments within the theory of public international law much, much later. From an academic perspective, the close link between public international law and constitutional law also resulted in the fact that visionary thoughts were hardly provoked and rather that within this framework the attempt was made simply to reconstruct the relationship perceived. Despite socio-cultural conditions being similar to those in the United Kingdom, in particular with the presence of the German peace movement, prior to the First World War and the era of the League of Nations these circumstances had no effect either in the political or in the academic arena in Germany. Primarily, extreme concepts of sovereignty, the glorification of violence and the minimisation of the harm of war characterised German public international law both in theory and in practice, even until as late as 1945.[40]

[40] See Jochen A. Frowein, 'Bilanz des Jahrhunderts. Verfassungsrecht und Völkerrecht' in Hartmut Lehmann (ed.), *Rückblicke auf das 20. Jahrhundert* (Göttingen, 2000), pp. 35–53; Ingo Hueck, 'Die deutsche Völkerrechtswissenschaft im Nationalsozialismus' in Doris Kaufmann (ed.), *Geschichte der Kaiser-Wilhelm-Gesellschaft im Nationalsozialismus* (Göttingen, 2000), vol. II, pp. 490–527; Hueck, '"Spheres of Influence" and "Völkisch" Legal Thought: Reinhard Höhn's Notion of Europe' in Christian Joerges and Navraj Singh Ghaleigh (eds.), *The Darker Legacy of Law in Europe: The Shadow of National Socialism and Fascism over Europe and Its Legal Tradition* (Oxford, 2003), 71–85.

13

Consent and caution: Lassa Oppenheim and his reaction to World War I

MATHIAS SCHMOECKEL

Introduction

World War I left the world in shock.[1] Major violations of international law such as the German occupation of neutral Belgium and the atrocities of warfare left the impression that the consensus of the civilised world had been destroyed. Evidently, more had been dishonoured than just the law. For the European victors it was evident who the main culprit was. Before any historical research was done, Germany had to admit its responsibility for the war and thus for any losses and damages resulting from it in Article 231 of the Versailles Treaty.[2] Thus, the Peace Treaty of Versailles between the Allied Powers and Germany decided on a question of guilt. In Article 227, the former Kaiser Wilhelm II (1888–1920, died 1941), was accused of a supreme offence against international morality and the sanctity of treaties. Hereby, the Treaty of Versailles itself also treated questions of morality. As it was felt that the German state had failed to observe the standards of European civilisation, it was consistent to argue that institutions other than those of this German state should deal with the German individuals thought to be responsible for war crimes.

---

[1] Geoffrey Best, *War and Law since 1945* (Oxford, 1994), p. 53. This may have been a diplomatic way to bar excessive damages claims; see William R. Keylor, 'Versailles and International Diplomacy' in Manfred Boemeke, Gerald Feldman and El Glaser (eds.), *The Treaty of Versailles: A Reassessment after 75 Years* (Cambridge, 1998), pp. 469–505 at p. 500. But the denial of any attribution of war guilt (see p. 501, and then at p. 504: 'There was no war-guilt clause in the treaty of Versailles') is difficult to understand.

[2] Cf. 'Commission on Responsibility of Authors of the War', *American Journal of International Law* 14 (1920), 95–154 at pp. 98–104. For an evaluation of the war guilt clauses see Francis H. Hinsley, *Power and the Pursuit of Peace* (Cambridge, 1963), pp. 293–303. On the peace treaty, see Elinor von Puttkammer, 'Versailles Peace Treaty' in Rudolf Bernhardt (ed.), *Encyclopaedia of Public International Law* (Amsterdam, 2000), vol. IV, pp. 1277–83.

Consequently, in Articles 228–30 Germany was required to hand over nationals accused of war crimes to the victorious nations.

Already during the war, in order to ensure peace, democracy and justice, plans had been drafted for an international organisation through which conflicts could be solved before a war arose.[3] So, before dealing with Germany in any way, the Peace Treaty of Versailles established the League of Nations as a means to advance international cooperation and to ensure peace (Part I of the Treaty), but also as a way to entertain international relations based on justice and honour.[4] The Articles on the League of Nations were called the rules of future international politics and as such would have to be closely observed.[5] Thus, the Treaties of Paris in 1919/20 undertook to re-establish that which once had existed, before something had gone wrong with civilisation.[6]

But in doing so, they changed the very structure of international law. An American internationalist stated that, from the standpoint of international law, it might be claimed that no modern treaty of peace had ever violated this system.[7] Indeed, according to Wilhelm Grewe, the 1919/20 Treaties mark the transition from classical to post-classical international law.[8] 'Classical' international law of the nineteenth century was characterised by the prevalence of the doctrines of capitalism, economic liberalism, the principle of the sanctity of private property and the limitation of international personality to sovereign states.[9] In contrast, 'modern'

---

[3] For the plans and the drafting of the League see Alfred Zimmern, *The League of Nations and the Rule of Law 1918–1935* (London, 1936), pp. 215–63; Matthew S. Anderson, *The Rise of Modern Diplomacy* (London and New York, 1993), pp. 281–90.
[4] Cf. Wilhelm Grewe, *Epochen der Völkerrechtsgeschichte* (Baden-Baden, 1984), pp. 691–4. Antoine Fleury, 'The League of Nations: Towards a New Appreciation of Its History' in Boemeke, Feldman and Glaser, *Treaty of Versailles*, pp. 507–22. For the text of the Versailles Treaty the *Traité de paix entre les puissances alliés et associées et l'Allemagne* (Paris, 1919) and *Reichsgesetzblatt 2* (1919), 687 were also used.
[5] Above Art. 1.   [6] Best, *War and Law since 1945*, p. 56.
[7] Professor Sterling E. Edmunds of the St. Louis University Law School, quoted by Warren F. Kuehl, *Seeking World Order* (Nashville, Tenn., 1969), p. 341; F. N. Keen, *Revision of the League of Nations Covenant* (London, 1919), pp. 6–7, cited by Anderson, *Rise of Modern Diplomacy*, p. 289.
[8] Grewe, *Epochen*, p. 683.
[9] Josef L. Kunz, *The Changing Law of Nations: Essays on International Law* (Columbus, Ohio, 1968), pp. 6–7; see also Karl-Heinz Ziegler, *Völkerrechtsgeschichte* (Munich, 1994), pp. 240–4; David Kennedy, 'International Law and the Nineteenth Century: History of an Illusion', *Nordic Journal of International Law* 65 (1996), 385–420 at pp. 386–90, explains the differences between classical and modern international law. For the variety of new approaches, see Martti Koskenniemi, *From Apology to Utopia: The Structure of International Legal Argument* (Helsinki, 1989), pp. 154–6.

public international law is marked by, among other things, the loss of certain common cultural and moral standards.[10] Moreover, the creation of international organisations and courts changed the structure of the international community. As the Peace Treaties, as well as the League and the movement for the codification of international law, tried to secure the law against potential violations, there was also a tendency to restrict the freedom of sovereign states.

How could the study of international law at the end of the World War I cope with these major changes in the structure of international law? Were internationalists able to insert these new issues into the old system of international law or were they forced to admit a major rupture in the development of law? In this chapter, the focus will be on Lassa Oppenheim as a famous representative of the traditional view on international law.

Lassa Oppenheim was born near Frankfurt am Main in 1858 and died in Cambridge shortly after World War I, in October 1919.[11] After his doctoral thesis in Göttingen in 1881, supervised by Heinrich Thöl, he became closely attached to the famous criminal lawyer Karl Binding in Leipzig and specialised in criminal law. After his *Habilitation*, Oppenheim was appointed *Extraordinarius* Professor of Criminal Law in Freiburg in 1889 and in Basel in 1892, where he was made full professor one year later. Thanks to British relatives, liberal inclinations, financial independence and perhaps a propensity for the British way of life, he resigned his position in Basel and moved to London in 1895. There he started a completely new career as an international lawyer. He quickly gained expertise and built up a vast library, from which at some point even the Foreign Office started to borrow books. Oppenheim was naturalised quite quickly, becoming a British citizen on 31 December 1900. In the beginning, he taught evening classes, and he later taught at the London School of Economics. With the publication of his *International Law* in 1905/6, he gained a fine reputation in England and abroad. Thanks to John Westlake's recommendation, he was appointed Professor of International Law at Cambridge University in 1908. He held this chair until his death in October 1919.

[10] Kunz, *Changing Law of Nations*, p. 6.
[11] See Monika Kingreen, *Jüdisches Landleben in Windecken, Ostheim und Heldenbergen* (Hanau, 1994), pp. 112–14; Andreas Zimmermann, 'Oppenheim, Lassa Francis Lawrence', in *Neue deutsche Biographie* (Berlin, 1999), vol. XIX, pp. 566–7; Mathias Schmoeckel, 'The Story of a Success: Lassa Oppenheim and his "International Law"', *European Journal of International Law* 11 (2000), 699–712; Schmoeckel, 'The Story of a Success. Lassa Oppenheim and his "International Law"', in Michael Stolleis and Masaharu Yanagihara (eds.), *East Asian and European Perspectives on International Law* (Baden-Baden, 2004), pp. 57–138.

His later fame was mostly based on his treatise on international law. His book was unusually successful, as it presented a good overview of the vast field and gave the impression of comprehensive and unbiased information. Oppenheim always looked for the basic rules of international law, which he illustrated or proved with cases and their exceptions. He rarely failed to indicate divergent opinions. The reason for Oppenheim's success may be the lucidity of his conceptions, which, although never presented directly in the book, always led to a simplicity and precision of statement. A second edition, which was published in 1912, was sold out quickly, just like the first one. Oppenheim died while preparing the third edition – which was finished by his former student Ronald Roxburgh, who stuck closely to the ideas of his teacher.

Against all critics of the existence of any international law, Oppenheim affirms that the international practice of states shows that they acknowledge some rules. The absence of a legislative authority is not essential; a rule of law can also be asserted when there is common consent that such rules will be enforced.[12] Yet the international community is a rather primitive community, as there are no institutions that will guarantee the law. Only the states themselves enforce the rules, because in international politics they pursue shared interests. Owing to the common European tradition, they have similar notions of justice, and hereby form a 'Family of Nations', based on the same notion of civilisation.[13]

Thus, law only exists on the basis of the common will of states, namely of civilised states, which stick to the tradition. Furthermore, international law is based exclusively on the free will of states. They must be sovereign in order to be equipped with equal rights, regardless of their actual political power, and be responsible for their actions.[14] Vice versa, if universal international law has to be ratified by every civilised state, it does not solely assure the sovereignty of states;[15] it also guarantees that the law is based on a common conception of morals and prevents law from becoming isolated from the ethical level.[16] As Oppenheim traced law back to the common consent of states, the principle of sovereignty held a paramount

---

[12] Lassa Oppenheim, *International Law* (1st edn, London, 1905), I Par. 4, p. 7.
[13] Oppenheim, *International Law* (1st edn), I Par.Par. 7–9, p. 12.
[14] Oppenheim, *International Law* (1st edn), I Par. 116, p. 163.
[15] Lassa Oppenheim, 'Lectures on the International Law of the Present War' (unpublished, Trinity College, Cambridge, Wren Library, Add. MS 338, 2/1–2/21), 2/3, p. 4; Oppenheim, 'The Science of International Law: Its Task and Method', *American Journal of International Law* 2 (1908), 313–56 at p. 331.
[16] For a critique, see Hans Kelsen, *Théorie du droit international coutumier* (Geneva, 1939), pp. 19–21.

position in his theory. The logic of his assumption gave Oppenheim no alternative explanation for the existence of law.

As Oppenheim only acknowledges as law what has previously been accepted as such by the states, the exclusive subjects of international law, his position has been called extremely 'statist'.[17] Oppenheim's view is marked by a nineteenth-century perception of the world.[18] In the legal doctrine of the nineteenth century, the original attributes of utmost political power were transformed into the abstract quality any independent state assumed as a member of the Family of Nations. Hereby the notion of sovereignty became an abstract quality, which could be universally found and applied.[19] The more this quality became uniform and a 'social function',[20] the more every participant in world politics was compelled to adopt it as a criterion of his own international legal personality.

Looking at Oppenheim's reaction to the peace treaties of 1919, the question is to what extent he could incorporate the new subjects into his system of international law. The League of Nations seems to impose one of the major changes. Oppenheim responded directly to this new issue several times. As it restricts the freedom of the states, the main question here is how he could combine this organisation with his theory of sovereignty. Furthermore, the Peace Treaties raised the problem of morality and personal liability for their breach. Here again the notion of sovereignty was challenged as the state's exclusive jurisdiction over its subjects was challenged. Moreover, the accusation of the Kaiser raised the question of the legal status (*Deliktsfähigkeit*) of individuals; evidently, individuals, not only states, were now capable of liability under international law.

Inserting the League of Nations in the legal framework

At first sight, it may be astonishing to see Oppenheim among the supporters of the League. He had indeed been very much in favour of such a

---

[17] Anthony Carty, 'Why Theory? The Implications for International Law Teaching', in his *Theory and International Law: An Introduction* (London, 1991), pp. 75–99 at p. 77.

[18] Morton A. Kaplan and Nicholas Katzenbach, *The Political Foundations of International Law* (New York, 1961), pp. 85–94; for the philosophical background, especially in Germany, see Léon Duguit, 'The Law and the State', *Harvard Law Review* 31 (1917), 77–129. Jens Bartelson, *A Genealogy of Sovereignty* (Cambridge, 1995), pp. 188 and 237–40, places this concept in an epistemological context.

[19] Kennedy, 'International Law', p. 406.   [20] Kennedy, 'International Law', p. 404.

development for a long time.²¹ Already in 1911, he had advocated the creation of international courts and organisations.²² As Oppenheim regarded the sovereignty of states as the major guarantee of order and legality in world order, he opposed the idea of a world state.²³ The association which he envisaged would not form a world-wide covering state.

Instead, he proposed an organisation uniting all sovereign states. This would be the final step towards the creation of a universal legal order,²⁴ the principal rules of the organisation forming the constitution of the new society.²⁵ He regarded the establishment of the Permanent Court of Arbitration as the beginning of a development²⁶ which would lead from a rather anarchic community²⁷ to an organised international society.²⁸

Furthermore, the founding of such organisations would increase the chances of a peaceful resolution of conflicts.²⁹ Actually, the Covenant of the League stated that all disputes between members should be brought before the League, which had to take effective actions to prevent war.³⁰ Oppenheim, likewise, regarded the establishment of the Permanent Court of International Justice as a means to a peaceful settlement of hostilities and to preventing wars.³¹ So, in 1919 Oppenheim could see his visions come to life.

For this reason, he was ready to admit that the League launched a new age of international law.³² In the Council he saw a novel kind of executive

---

[21] For the diplomatic background to Wilson's proposal, see Thomas J. Knock, 'Wilsonian Concepts and International Realities at the End of the War', in Boemeke, Feldman and Glaser, *Treaty of Versailles*, pp. 111–29; Kuehl, *Seeking World Order*, pp. 232–5.
[22] Lassa Oppenheim, *Die Zukunft des Völkerrechts: Festschrift für Karl Binding* (Leipzig, 1911), pp. 141–201 and 157–62.
[23] For this idea, see Johann Baptist Müller, 'Weltstaat contra Nationalstaat – die geistesgeschichtlichen Wurzeln der Vereinten Nationen', *Politische Studien* 47 (1996), 9–18; for Oppenheim and Carl Schmitt, see Mathias Schmoeckel, *Lassa Oppenheim: The Story of a Success. Lassa Oppenheim and His 'International Law'* (Baden-Baden, 2004), pp. 75, 85.
[24] For a detailed catalogue of proposals, see Oppenheim, *Zukunft*, p. 159.
[25] Oppenheim, *Zukunft*, p. 160.
[26] Oppenheim, *Zukunft*, p. 157; Oppenheim, *International Law* (1st edn), I Par. 51, p. 75.
[27] Oppenheim, *Zukunft*, pp. 150–1.
[28] Oppenheim, *Zukunft*, p. 152.   [29] Oppenheim, 'Science', p. 322.
[30] Lassa Oppenheim, *International Law* (3rd edn, London, 1921), II Par. 25 c, p. 35.
[31] Oppenheim, *International Law* (3rd edn), I Par. 51 as n. 6, 101 s (= 4th edn, London, 1928, I Par. 51, p. 102); contrary to what Michael W. Reisman holds in his 'Lassa Oppenheim's Nine Lives', *Yale Journal of International Law* 19 (1994), 255–80 at p. 269, this is not a later addition by Hersch Lauterpacht.
[32] Oppenheim, *International Law* (3rd edn), I Par. 167 t, p. 300. These passages are written by Oppenheim himself, see Roxburgh in Oppenheim, *International Law* (3rd edn), p. x.

for the Family of Nations.[33] Such new bodies were to bring about great changes in international law.[34] But most importantly, he felt that the structure of the international community itself had been changed:[35]

> the conclusion is obvious that the League of Nations is intended to take the place of what hitherto used to be called the Family of Nations, namely, the community of civilised States, for the international conduct of which International Law has grown up. The Covenant of the League is an attempt to organise the hitherto unorganised community of States by a written constitution ... this constitution will gradually become more complete and perfect, and the time may not be very distant when all civilised States, without exception, will be members.

According to Oppenheim, the establishment of the League meant that the international community had ceased to be a primitive society and had acquired a more definite structure. This is something a natural lawyer would have called the transition from the state of nature to society. In the Covenant of the League, Oppenheim saw a written constitution for the whole world. He called the disadvantage of many unsolved problems an 'absence of rigidity', which gave room for future development of the Covenant.[36] All states, as soon as they acquired enough culture and stability of order to be called civilised,[37] would eventually participate. The League could not merely be called the club of the victorious states, as already thirteen neutral nations had entered the League. Oppenheim remained rather optimistic that even Germany would eventually become a member.[38]

Especially this last point indicates an idealised, or at least rather personal, view of Oppenheim, as indeed it was one of the major shortcomings of the League that it never included all major states.[39] On the other hand,

---

[33] Oppenheim, *International Law* (3rd edn), I Par. 167 t, p. 300.
[34] Oppenheim, *International Law* (3rd edn), I Par. 167 i, p. 280.
[35] Oppenheim, *International Law* (3rd edn), I Par. 167 c, p. 269.
[36] Oppenheim, *International Law* (3rd edn), I Par. 167 t, p. 301. Contrarily Hinsley, *Power and the Pursuit of Peace*, p. 319, points to the attempts after 1919 to scale down the obligations implied by the Covenant.
[37] So, on the whole, the notion of the 'civilised state' may lose its importance (see Grewe, *Epochen*, pp. 687–690), yet Oppenheim still retains it.
[38] Lassa Oppenheim, 'Le caractère essentiel de la Société des Nations', *Revue Générale de Droit International Public* 26 (1919), 234–44 at p. 241; Oppenheim, *International Law* (3rd edn), I Par. 167 r, p. 292.
[39] For a list of the member states, see Francis P. Walters, *A History of the League of Nations* (Oxford, 1960), pp. 64–5; on the question of universality, see Paul Barandon, 'Völkerbund', in Karl Strupp and Hans-Jochen Schlochauer (eds.), *Wörterbuch des Völkerrechts* (Berlin, 1962), vol. III, pp. 597–611 at p. 601.

Oppenheim criticised the League several times. He did so at length even in his treatise, although such harsh disapproval was rare in his *International Law*. The fact that not all states were members of the League conflicted with Oppenheim's view of a world united in a legally organised society. Therefore, this constituted a major shortcoming of the League for him. The possibility of even excluding members again collided with Oppenheim's vision,[40] but this he thought would remain mere theory.[41] Likewise he rejected the criticism that the League formed a society of governments and not of the people, as he correctly argued that members of the government also represent the people.[42]

In several respects the Covenant, according to Oppenheim, did not provide enough means to ensure peace. The jurisdiction of the Permanent Court of International Justice was not compulsory,[43] so in spite of the existence of this means to prevent war, states had the possibility of waging war immediately.[44] Oppenheim was disappointed that the Covenant did not give the Council the right to intervene if a belligerent violated fundamental rules of warfare, or the right to undertake the punishment of war crimes.[45] Finally, the structure of the League was defective in some respects. Oppenheim regretted that there was no separate Council of Conciliation.[46] In the existing Council of the League Oppenheim feared the influence of the Great Powers and thought that the Council might be prejudiced; this is exactly the view later taken by historians.[47] Especially because of the importance of the Council,[48] the League could only become a society of Great Powers and not a society of all states.[49] But Oppenheim hoped that the Great Powers would not abuse their possibilities, and

---

[40] Oppenheim, 'Caractère essentiel', 243–4.
[41] Cf. Hinsley, *Power and the Pursuit of Peace*, p. 316. According to Hinsley, the exclusion meant an intensification of the struggles and the extension of wars.
[42] Oppenheim, 'Caractère essentiel', 243. Yet this sums up the critique reiterated by Hinsley, *Power and the Pursuit of Peace*, p. 311.
[43] Oppenheim, *International Law* (3rd edn), I Par. 167 s, p. 298.
[44] Oppenheim also thought the Assembly unfit to pronounce on the validity of law; this should be left to the Court of Justice instead, cf. Oppenheim, *International Law* (3rd edn), I Par. 167 s, p. 299.
[45] Oppenheim, *International Law* (3rd edn), I Par. 167 s, p. 295.
[46] Best, *War and Law since 1945*, p. 56, points to the example that the great powers fuelled the civil war in Russia.
[47] Anderson, *Rise of Modern Diplomacy*, p. 288, states that the League was dominated by a handful of great powers in a way which most internationalists had tried to avoid. Hinsley, *Power and the Pursuit of Peace*, p. 318, calls it an enforcement machine of the politics of the Great Powers.
[48] Oppenheim, *International Law* (3rd edn), I Par. 167 f, p. 277.
[49] Oppenheim, 'Caractère essentiel', p. 242.

pointed to the fact that, as a rule, in Council meetings all members had to agree.[50] By such assertions he tried to increase the chances of the League's acceptation.

So Oppenheim remained remarkably sceptical of the League even after it had come into existence.[51] Although he hoped that the League would develop into a more complete system, he expected the process to be a very slow one. For this reason, he gave his book on this subject the motto *festina lente*.[52] He even considered the possibility that the League of Nations would be dissolved,[53] although it ought to be indissoluble.[54] He reminded the victorious states of the fact that the League would only work once all states had become members.[55] Nevertheless, he did not expect the states to cease their secret negotiations after the establishment of the League of Nations.[56]

It becomes obvious that, in order to identify the League with his ideal, Oppenheim interpreted the Covenant in a special way. The League had to be more than an alliance as it was open to all civilised states and was intended to be universal.[57] On the other hand, the League could not be a state, a federal state (*Bundesstaat*) or a confederation of states (*Staatenbund*).[58] A confederation would be constituted by a certain number of states which form a union in order to look after common interests. But Oppenheim denied the notion that the League had received any power over its member states; in this respect the League could not be a state. He clearly opposed the idea of considering the League a world-wide

---

[50] Oppenheim, *International Law* (3rd edn), I Par. 167 r, p. 294.
[51] Oppenheim, 'Caractère essentiel', p. 236.
[52] Lassa Oppenheim, *The League of Nations and Its Problems: Three Lectures* (London, 1919).
[53] Roxburgh, 'Introduction', in Oppenheim, *International Law* (3rd edn), I, p. xii.
[54] Oppenheim, *International Law* (3rd edn), I Par. 167 c, p. 279.
[55] Oppenheim, 'Caractère essentiel', p. 240.
[56] Oppenheim, Lecture on Diplomacy (unpublished, Trinity College, Cambridge, Wren Library, Add. MS 338, 1/1–1–21), 1/1, p. 18: 'the League of Nations and an International Council of Conciliation would grant the chance of settling the difference and restrict the opportunity for secret negotiations, but "secret negotiations would always play a certain part in diplomacy"'. This was a common assumption; cf. Zimmern, *League of Nations*, pp. 480–1.
[57] Oppenheim, 'Caractère essentiel', p. 238.
[58] Oppenheim, *International Law* (3rd edn), I Par. 167 c, p. 269; Oppenheim, 'Caractère essentiel', p. 237. The literature in English did not pronounce on this special German distinction. James L. Brierly, *The Law of Nations* (5th edn, Oxford, 1955), p. 103, attributed hardly any corporate capacity to the League. This was contested by Zimmern, *League of Nations*, p. 285 n. 2, but on pp. 277–85 he closely follows Oppenheim and qualifies the League as the society of states.

superstate, because it lacked the structures and the competence of states.[59] In 1911, Oppenheim had even been afraid of such a universal state, as it would bring death instead of life in mixing people and abolishing those structures which up to then had guaranteed a minimum of order.[60] After the League had been created, Oppenheim admitted that it had a certain competence and even the right of intervention. Thus, it could exercise rights which otherwise only sovereign states possessed.[61] But it could assume sovereign power only where there was no sovereign power, such as in the Saar Basin.[62]

The reason why the League could not assume the rank of a state is that this would endanger Oppenheim's theory of sovereignty. Only states can be considered full members of the international community, whereas the League is only a legal framework. So, while Oppenheim could not deny that the League was a new subject of international law,[63] he could only concede a form of legal personality *sui generis*.[64]

In international law all decisions had to be reached by a unanimous vote; majority votes could only bind the members of the majority.[65] In order to apply a rule of international law to a state, it first had to be ascertained whether this state had openly or tacitly consented to accept the norm as binding. Oppenheim's conception could not permit a majority decision to be binding on dissenting states.[66] International law as developed over time could not be changed by the will of new sovereign states.[67]

---

[59] Oppenheim, *Zukunft*, p. 153; later, 'Caractère essentiel', p. 237; *International Law* (3rd edn), I Par. 167 r, p. 294.
[60] Oppenheim, *Zukunft*, p. 153.
[61] Oppenheim, *International Law* (3rd edn), I Par. 167 c, p. 270.
[62] Oppenheim, 'Caractère essentiel', p. 239. In 1911 Oppenheim (*Zukunft*, p. 161) was not willing to grant any executive power to the League.
[63] Oppenheim, *International Law* (3rd edn), I Par. 167 c, p. 268.
[64] As in Oppenheim, 'Caractère essentiel', p. 238; Oppenheim, *International Law* (3rd edn), I Par. 167 c, p. 269. Without hesitation Karl Strupp, in *Grundzüge des positiven Völkerrechts* (2nd edn, Bonn, 1922), p. 163, called the League a 'Staatenbund sui generis'.
[65] Oppenheim, *Zukunft*, p. 159.
[66] This has been ridiculed by Leonard Nelson, *Die Rechtswissenschaft ohne Recht* (Leipzig, 1917), pp. 116–18.
[67] Oppenheim, *International Law* (1st edn), I Par. 13, p. 18. For a similar notion of Jellinek, see Jochen Graf Bernstorff, 'Georg Jellinek – Völkerrecht als modernes öffentliches Recht im fin de siècle?' in S. Paulson and M. Schulte (eds.), *Georg Jellinek: Beiträge zu Leben und Werk* (Beiträge zur Rechtsgeschichte des 20. Jahrhunderts 27, Tübingen, 2000), pp. 183–206 at p. 194; for Triepel's more moderate approach, see Ulrich Gassner, *Heinrich Triepel: Leben und Werk* (Tübinger Schriften zum Staats- und Verwaltungsrecht 51, Berlin, 1999), p. 452.

He could not deny that the League might impose obligations on the member states,[68] such as a reduction in arms.[69] This touches a sensitive part of the politics of any sovereign state and follows from the obligation of the League to protect its members.[70] But it is crucial that the member states decide for themselves. By entering the League, states consented to any legal decisions by the League that followed,[71] as far as these were covered by the original consent.[72] So, future changes to the Constitution of the League would bind only those members who consented to the new rules.[73] Furthermore, Oppenheim stated that unanimous votes were the rule in the Council and the Assembly if not otherwise stated, whereas the majority could only decide on procedural matters.[74] Other authors, meanwhile, stressed the importance of these majority decisions.[75]

Oppenheim may have been right not to overestimate the power of the League. Indeed, some believe that the League could be a loose association and would not have worked if it had had more power.[76] But Oppenheim's view was not based on a clever political assessment. Rather, he tried to incorporate the League into his system and his views on the composition of the international community and the function of international law. Obviously, he could not ignore those circumstances that stood in opposition to his ideas. But as an academic, he was free to interpret the new law. However, this is no scholastic controversy, which would have hardly any significance.[77]

Oppenheim succeeded in presenting the League in such a way that no major changes to the framework of his textbook, such as the theory of sovereignty, were necessary. Although he admitted that the League constituted a major transformation of the law, he could insert the new provisions into the already existing structures of his textbook. To this end, he interpreted the Covenant in a special way and clearly stated what he approved of and what might have negative impacts. Contrary to the usual, neutral presentation of subjects in his book, Oppenheim was very

---

[68] See Oppenheim, *International Law* (3rd edn), I Par. 167 i, p. 281.
[69] Oppenheim, *International Law* (3rd edn), I Par. 167 l, pp. 284–5.
[70] Oppenheim, *International Law* (3rd edn), I Par. 167 l, p. 285.
[71] Oppenheim, *Zukunft*, p. 152. [72] Oppenheim, *Zukunft*, p. 159.
[73] Oppenheim, *International Law* (3rd edn), I, Par. 167 d, p. 271.
[74] Oppenheim, *International Law* (3rd edn), I, Par. 167 f, p. 275.
[75] Barandon, 'Völkerbund', p. 602, points to several instances in which the majority could decide; furthermore, it proved to be difficult to decide whether it was a question of substance or only of procedure.
[76] Hinsley, *Power and the Pursuit of Peace*, pp. 312 and 315.
[77] Oppenheim, *International Law* (3rd edn), I Par. 70, p. 133.

outspoken in support of his position on this issue. None the less, his reader is well informed on the new law, and is able to grasp the significance of the new provisions and to get an understanding of the prospects of this new institution.

Divisibility of sovereignty

Oppenheim did not always succeed in shaping the new law in accordance with his system and his views. The provisions on the mandates posed more difficulties for him. According to Oppenheim, history teaches that states less than fully sovereign are not durable. Yet, the facts forced him to acknowledge that sovereignty is divisible.[78] For this reason, he had to discuss the mandates, protectorates and other forms of non-sovereign states such as the peculiar case of Andorra.[79] But he did so separately from the assertion of the principal rules. These examples might contradict his convictions, but it becomes clear that they remain an anomaly.[80] Most of all, it did not result in a change in the framework of Oppenheim's book. Oppenheim thought that strange phenomena might arise, but might again lose their relevance in the greater historical perspective. Here again history proved Oppenheim to be right. The models of protectorate and mandate turned out to be rather unsuccessful in the course of the twentieth century. For this reason the structure as asserted by academics may in the long run be more important than new law and cases.

Opposition to prosecution for war crimes

The prosecution of war crimes created even more problems for Oppenheim. The subject evokes several difficult questions of international law, which have increased in importance ever since, while staying controversial. The definition of war crimes was as difficult, as the question of jurisdiction was contested.[81] It was principally a right of a state to judge its nationals for actions committed during the war. Since the 1870s war between

---

[78] Oppenheim, *International Law* (3rd edn), I Par. 70, p. 133.
[79] Oppenheim, *International Law* (3rd edn), I Par. 92, p. 166, where he states that the notion of 'protectorate' lacks exact juristic precision.
[80] Oppenheim, *International Law* (3rd edn), I Par. 65, p. 128; unchanged from 1st edn, I Par. 65, p. 102.
[81] Hermann von Mangoldt, 'Das Kriegsverbrechen und seine Verfolgung in Vergangenheit und Gegenwart', *Jahrbuch für Internationales und Ausländisches Öffentliches Recht* 2/3 (1948), 283–334 at pp. 288–95, describes the slow development of the discussion after World War I, especially on basic notions.

France and Germany, an increasing number of states had assumed the right to sentence captured foreign soldiers.[82] Oppenheim supported this position,[83] which he thought to be a necessity of war.[84] He argued for a general prosecution of war crimes, and similar positions were expressed in Germany.[85]

But if the accused were judged according to the criminal law of the land, how could one hold to the fact that, as long as they had acted in accordance with the laws of war, they had acted lawfully and had committed no crimes?[86] If they had acted on orders from their superiors, could they be convicted? Oppenheim, siding with American authors and disagreeing with his British colleagues,[87] was opposed to their punishment.[88] As international criminal law was *in statu nascendi*,[89] so was the differentiation between an act of a corporate body and the actions of an individual of his own free will (*delicta iuris gentium*).[90]

Any criminal liability of individuals in international law raised the question whether individuals could be subjects of international law. The Hague Peace Conferences of 1899 and 1907 neither clarified nor limited the basic principle that criminal responsibility attaches to war crimes.[91]

---

[82] See James Garner, 'Punishment of Offenders against the Laws and Customs of War', *American Journal of International Law* 14 (1920), 70–94 at pp. 73–7. For an early plan for criminal prosecution of war crimes, see Nicasio de Landa, 'Droit pénal de la guerre. Projet de classification des crimes et délits contre les lois de la guerre, selon la déclaration de Bruxelles', *Revue du Droit International et de Législation Comparée* 10 (1878), 182–9.

[83] Oppenheim, *International Law* (3rd edn), II Par. 251, p. 342.

[84] See Oppenheim, *International Law* (3rd edn), I Par. 445, p. 609 n.1, against Strupp; II Par. 251, p. 342; Lassa Oppenheim, 'On War Treason', *Law Quarterly Review* 33 (1917), 266–86 at p. 284 for war treason.

[85] Alfred Verdross, *Die völkerrechtswidrige Kriegshandlung und der Strafanspruch der Staaten* (Berlin, 1920), pp. 30–1 and 92.

[86] Garner, 'Punishment of Offenders', p. 73.   [87] Garner, 'Punishment of Offenders', p. 86.

[88] Oppenheim, *International Law* (3rd edn), II Par. 253, p. 342; of the same opinion Verdross, *Völkerrechtswidrige Kriegshandlung*, p. 58.

[89] Admitted by A. de Lapradelle and F. Larnaude, 'Examen de la responsabilité pénale de l'empereur Guillaume II d'Allemagne', *Journal du Droit International* 46 (1919), 151–9 at p. 156.

[90] There is very little information in Ingo von Münch, *Das völkerrechtliche Delikt in der modernen Entwicklung der Völkerrechtsgemeinschaft* (Frankfurt am Main, 1963), pp. 4–5; Heiko Ahlbrecht, *Geschichte der völkerrechtlichen Strafgerichtsbarkeit im 20. Jahrhundert* (Juristische Zeitgeschichte 2, Baden Baden, 2000), pp. 18–19.

[91] Hans-Heinrich Jescheck, 'War Crimes', in Bernhardt, *Encyclopaedia of Public International Law*, vol. IV, pp. 1349–54 at p. 1350; for the 1899 conference, see the contributions in Arthur Eyffinger, *The 1899 Hague Peace Conference* (The Hague, 1999); Jörg Manfred Mössner, 'Hague Peace Conferences of 1899 and 1907', in Bernhardt, *Encyclopaedia of International Public Law*, vol. II, pp. 671–7.

Therefore, an individual's responsibility in international law was considered to be utterly new.[92] The American delegates in the Commission on Responsibility of Authors of the War were opposed to an indictment of the Kaiser, one argument being that, traditionally, heads of state were considered to be immune in international law and exempt from international prosecution; they were held responsible only according to the national law.[93] But the majority of the Commission was not influenced by the legal arguments put forward by the American delegates.[94]

Such uncertainties opened the possibility for different interpretations of Article 227. The French internationalist De Lapradelle argued that the basic question was already decided: Article 227 of the Versailles Treaty stated that the Kaiser would be prosecuted for crimes against international law.[95] The American delegate of the Commission stressed the fact that this Article adopted a political, not a judicial sanction;[96] consequently, he did not regard the tribunal established by Article 227 as a court of legal justice.[97] Following this argument, the Netherlands later refused to extradite the Kaiser.[98]

But it was not merely the number of difficult questions that made it hard for Oppenheim to express his views on this development. Already during the war, he had been severely attacked by a British colleague for presenting the subject in a German and utterly un-British way.[99] So, any statement on this matter was difficult for him, and Oppenheim hesitated to perform this duty during his lifetime. After his death, Roxburgh stepped in, but he did so in a way which would have been typical for Oppenheim. In the first volume he simply gave an account of the contents of the Versailles

---

[92] Garner, 'Punishment of Offenders', p. 71, with further references. For the German literature, see Strupp, *Grundzüge*, pp. 128 and 210. Strupp maintained that it was impossible to punish individuals and that the state was responsible for the wrongs of individuals.

[93] Garner, 'Punishment of Offenders', p. 92; Robert Lansing, 'Some Legal Questions of the Peace Conference', *American Journal of International Law* 13 (1919), 631–50 at pp. 644–45; Verdross, *Völkerrechtswidrige Kriegshandlung*, p. 66.

[94] See 'Commission on Responsibility', Annex II: Memorandum of reservations presented by the representatives of the United States, p. 148.

[95] De Lapradelle and Larnaude, 'Examen de la responsabilité pénale', p. 152.

[96] Lansing, 'Some Legal Questions', p. 648; of the same opinion was Garner, 'Punishment of Offenders', pp. 90–1.

[97] Lansing, 'Some Legal Questions', pp. 647–8.

[98] See Ahlbrecht, *Geschichte der völkerrechtlichen Strafgerichtsbarkeit*, p. 38.

[99] For the attack of J. H. Morgan, see Oppenheim, 'On War Treason', pp. 266–7. The propaganda against Germany and the Kaiser is shown by Erik Goldstein, 'Great Britain: The Home Front', in Boemeke, Feldman and Glaser, *Treaty of Versailles*, pp. 147–66 at pp. 151–2.

Peace Treaty,[100] in the second volume he left the chapter on war crimes nearly unchanged.[101] Just a footnote informs the reader of Article 227, but, as Queen Wilhelmina (1898–1948) refused to extradite the Kaiser in 1920, this section is seen to be no longer of any practical importance.[102] This appears to be no comment at all. As we nowadays regard Article 227 as the forerunner of the Nuremberg trials, it becomes evident that Roxburgh/Oppenheim tried to minimise its importance.

Roxburgh gives a clue for understanding this position. Oppenheim wanted to rely on the work of his friend James Garner, whose views he shared to a great extent.[103] Sharing Garner's point of view, it would have been easy for Oppenheim to show that Article 227 was opposed to the traditional assumptions of international law. For Oppenheim, the international personality of individuals was still inconceivable; rights given to monarchs were conveyed not to them as persons, but to their states.[104] Therefore, individuals could have neither rights nor duties.[105] But it was far easier to state that Article 227 was one of the many oddities to be found in the history and practice of international law which lost its importance if understood properly. The same could have been said about Articles 228–30. Here again, after a list of 896 officers and politicians was handed over to the German representative, uproar in Germany convinced the Allies not to pursue their extradition claim; the trials were left to the German *Reichsgericht*.[106] And so, even in the third edition, Oppenheim could maintain the principle that international law remains a law only between states.[107]

---

[100] Oppenheim, *International Law* (3rd edn), I Par. 568e, p. 722, reference is given to II Par.Par. 251–7. This passage was written by Roxburgh; see his 'Introduction' to Oppenheim, *International Law* (3rd edn), I, p. x.

[101] Cf. Oppenheim, *International Law* (1st edn), II Par.Par. 251–7, pp. 263–4; Oppenheim, *International Law* (3rd edn), II Par. 251, pp. 341–8.

[102] Oppenheim, *International Law* (3rd edn), II Par. 253, p. 343 n.1.

[103] James Garner, *International Law and the World War* (2 vols., London, 1920). Oppenheim had seen the manuscript (see Roxburgh, 'Introduction' in Oppenheim, *International Law* (3rd edn), II, p. v), and had perhaps given Roxburgh some help.

[104] Oppenheim, *International Law* (1st edn), I Par. 14, p. 19; I Par. 288, p. 341; (3rd edn), I Par. 14, p. 19; I Par. 288, p. 457.

[105] Oppenheim, *International Law* (3rd edn), I Par. 289, p. 460.

[106] Cf. Dirk von Selle, 'Prolog zu Nürnberg – Die Leipziger Kriegsverbrecherprozesse vor dem Reichsgericht', *Zeitschrift der neueren Rechtsgeschichte* 19 (1997), 193–209 at pp. 195–6; Kai Müller, 'Oktroyierte Verliererjustiz nach dem ersten Weltkrieg', *Archiv des Völkerrechts* 39 (2001), 202–2, according to whom this national court did not pronounce effective sentences for the crimes.

[107] Oppenheim, *International Law* (3rd edn), II Par. 254, p. 345.

Indirectly, Oppenheim reacted to the far greater assault on international law implied by Article 227. What could a lawyer make of the 'sanctity of treaties', if it was not the violation of Belgium's neutrality[108] or the Hague Treaties that were meant? What on earth was a 'supreme offence against international morality'?

The so-called Martens clause in the preamble to the 1899 Hague Treaty mentioned 'the laws of humanity and the dictates of the public conscience'. This vague provision was adopted, following difficult negotiations, as the only means of securing agreement to the Treaty.[109] The notion had become increasingly attractive;[110] consequently, the 'Commission on Responsibility of Authors of the War' also mentioned the violation of the 'Laws of Humanity'.[111] But still the American delegates maintained that the 'laws of humanity' did not constitute a definite code and that there was no fixed and universal standard of humanity.[112]

Whereas the notion of 'humanity' gradually became a term of international law,[113] still no clues were developed to identify the crimes named in Article 227. The American delegation again was quite explicit. The members expressed their understanding that some tended to mix law and politics,[114] but upheld the supremacy of the law over the natural impulse.[115]

Oppenheim was ready to condemn appalling violations of international law committed by the German forces and did so even more explicitly in his lectures.[116] But fervently he tried to uphold the distinction between law and morality. To talk of 'morality' would negate the binding force of law, which Oppenheim also claimed to be the basis of international law.[117] For him even World War I had proven the validity of the laws of war: even when

---

[108] The 'Commission on Responsibility', p. 120, was convinced that the Kaiser could not be accused of the breach of Belgium's neutrality.
[109] See V. V. Pustagarov, 'The Martens Clause in International Law', *Journal of the History of International Law* 1 (1999), 125–6.
[110] See, e.g., the assertion of Freiherr Marschall von Bieberstein, a German delegate speaking at the Hague Conference of 1907, that the German navy would fulfil the principles of humanity as the surest guides for the conduct of sailors; cf. 'Commission on Responsibility', p. 118.
[111] 'Commission on Responsibility', pp. 121–4, Annex II, pp. 150–1.
[112] Lansing, 'Some Legal Questions', p. 647.
[113] Oppenheim, *International Law* (3rd edn), I Par. 137, p. 229, on the intervention in the interests of humanity.
[114] Lansing, 'Some Legal Questions', p. 643; Garner, 'Punishment of Offenders', pp. 93–4.
[115] Lansing, 'Some Legal Questions', p. 644.
[116] Oppenheim, *International Law* (3rd edn), II Par. 250, p. 341.
[117] Oppenheim, 'The Science of International Law', p. 332.

Germany violated a rule of law, it agreed on its existence, but interpreted it in favour of its own position.[118] Yet, as according to Oppenheim the foundation of a rule of law was common international consent, there was no unilateral conception of law. Only what is commonly considered to be binding can be regarded as law. Interventions to stop cruelties in other countries occurred in the nineteenth century, but instead of assuming a right of intervention in the interest of humanity Oppenheim just did not exclude the possibility that in the future the states would commonly agree on such a rule.[119] Law can punish only what is usually considered to be punishable.[120] So, the lawyer must draw a sharp line between questions of morality and law. Some state practices may be considered to be immoral, but, as long as there is no common consent as to illegality, they may yet be called law.[121]

Conclusion: with consent and caution

Summing up, we see an independent approach to interpretation, in which Oppenheim reshaped the Versailles Treaty to a considerable extent. In some instances, he reshaped the provisions by means of interpretation; in others he presented facts as divergences from principles or as insignificant. We also notice that peace treaties are only as good as their interpreters. Sometimes they may even be improved in so far as they are put into accordance with the legal framework of international law. Though this may seem a commonplace, it encompasses a question of method. It is also the result of Oppenheim's understanding of the task of any international lawyer who has to expound the existing rules and to criticise them in order to help the progress of international law. He himself had to distil the main principles so that codification would eventually become possible. All this would clarify the law so that differences could be avoided or at least be settled more easily through arbitration and international judicature. As law became easier to understand, it would become better known by the world at large.[122]

This is what Oppenheim did with the Peace Treaty of Versailles. He regarded it as his duty to evaluate the results of the conferences and to insert the new rules into a system of international law.[123] This was to help

---

[118] Oppenheim, *International Law* (3rd edn), II Par. 10 n.1, pp. 13–14.
[119] Oppenheim, *International Law* (3rd edn), I Par. 137, p. 229.
[120] Oppenheim, 'On War Treason', p. 286. [121] Oppenheim, 'On War Treason', p. 286.
[122] Oppenheim, 'The Science of International Law', p. 314.
[123] Oppenheim, *Zukunft*, p. 149.

a better understanding of the multitude of cases and rules to be found in this subject. The internationalist had to show what was congruent and what conflicted with the older notions of law. In all cases, the scholar acted as a sort of filter. Sometimes he gave his consent to the new rules or shaped them by means of interpretation so that they fitted into a coherent concept of international law. This Oppenheim did with the Covenant of the League of Nations, to the effect that even such a major transformation could be explained and integrated into a rational and consistent view. In so far as he did not agree with the innovations, he presented them as an anomaly, independent of the principles. He would hope that the anomaly would soon become irrelevant, but he could not ignore it, given his duty to inform the reader of the current state of the law. It was also open to the international law to point out the practical irrelevance of certain cases where the new 'rules' did not conform to the principles.

Nevertheless, his evaluation was wrong sometimes. In the case of Article 227 of the Versailles Treaty, Oppenheim and Roxburgh proved to be wide of the mark, as this provision turned out to be very important as the legal basis for the Nuremberg trials. And yet, Oppenheim's contribution, as that of any textbook,[124] to the understanding of the new law was important. His contemporaries consulted Oppenheim's *International Law* in order to understand the law and its developments before, perhaps, studying the treaty itself. And explaining and ascertaining the law may have helped to absorb the shock left by World War I better than statements on morality and guilt. I do not have the means of assessing the success of the so-called 'peace through law' movement.[125] But for more than 3,000 years, people have resorted to law when questions of morality arise. They expect that a body of more or less coherent rules, which are less convincing when

---

[124] On the textbook tradition, see Anthony Carty, 'A Colloquium on International Law Textbooks in England, France and Germany: Introduction', *European Journal of International Law* 11 (2000), 615–19.

[125] Jost Delbrück, *Die Konstitution des Friedens als Rechtsordnung* (Schriften zum Völkerrecht 121, Berlin, 1996), pp. 275–92; Walter Poeggel, *Der Völkerbund als zwischenstaatliche Organisation für den Weltfrieden und die Haltung Deutschlands* (Texte zur politischen Bildung 20, Schkeuditz, 1995), p. 15; Volker Rittberger, 'Frieden durch Weltorganisation?', *Die Friedenswarte* 74 (1999), 371–8; Patricia Schneider, *Frieden durch Recht: ein historischsystematischer Abriss* (Hamburger Beiträge zur Friedensforschung und Sicherheitspolitik 117, Hamburg, 1999); Schneider, 'Frieden durch Recht. Von der Einhegung des Krieges zur gewaltfreien Konfliktbeilegung', *Sicherheit und Frieden* 18 (2000), 54–66; Hidemi Suganami, 'The "Peace through Law" Approach: A Critical Examination of Its Ideas' in T. Taylor (ed.), *Approaches and Theory in International Relations* (London, 1978), pp. 100–20.

drafted on the spot, will be more convincing and will persuade more people not to take up arms.

And all the time specialists are needed to make the law comprehensible and to decide on its application. According to Oppenheim, the internationalist has to proceed with great caution in view of the importance of his task.[126] His statements will be an interpretation. But the clearer and less biased it is, the more it may convince the reader and thus be influential. This may just be the point to understand, as Philip Allott once put it, the 'enigma Oppenheim', to understand how his concise writing was considered to be reliable and comprehensive at the same time. The more complex a society is, the more it needs specialists who inform the greater public or provide the means to gather the necessary information. Oppenheim had to discuss the principles so that the new law became intelligible.[127]

As Heraclitus declared war to be the father of all things,[128] the Peace Treaty of Versailles introduced considerable changes to international law. But treaties on their own do not constitute the law. It is the task of academics to discuss and to ascertain the law and, among other things, a good historical overview is needed to do this job. In doing so, academic learning helps to interpret what has been introduced through practice, and here will lie its importance as long as it exists.

---

[126] Reisman, 'Lassa Oppenheim's Nine Lives', p. 272.
[127] It is of little importance whether science is regarded as an independent source of law or – as Oppenheim, *International Law* (3rd edn), I Par. 19, p. 23, did – as a means to perceive the law so that it gradually becomes accepted through consent or custom.
[128] Heraclitus, 29 fr. 53.

14

Talking peace: social science, peace negotiations and the structure of politics

ANDREAS OSIANDER

Introduction

In this chapter, an attempt is made to place the general subject matter of this volume, peace negotiations and treaties, within a theoretical framework. Such a framework should clarify basic issues such as why we should look at peacemaking processes in the first place, and, if so, what we should look for, and why.

The chapter is divided into five parts. The first section discusses and challenges the traditional separation of the treatment of social phenomena into historiography on the one hand and social studies on the other. I contend that this dichotomy causes historiography to shun systematic, theory-guided analysis, while it prevents social studies from being able to deal with long-term change and to place the phenomena it observes in a larger historical context. The second section discusses the role of fundamental assumptions in any endeavour to understand social phenomena past or present. I suggest that a common problem in dealing with past social phenomena (history) is a lack of reflection on the assumptions underlying their narration by both historians and social studies authors. The third section proposes that the best way of avoiding the distortion caused by applying anachronistic and arbitrary assumptions and concepts to past phenomena is to bear in mind that, just as much as present social reality, any past social reality was a collective construct based on assumptions shared by people at the time. It further proposes that a Constructivist approach that pays attention to the key role of such assumptions is capable of integrating historiography and social studies to their mutual benefit. The fourth section discusses, from a Constructivist point of view, the problem of social change, of understanding why structural and procedural patterns of social interaction never remain constant for long but evolve continuously. Finally, the fifth section sketches the way in which the methodology suggested here may be applied to gain an understanding of social and political change in Europe over the past ten or fifteen centuries, and how the examination of peacemaking processes fits into such an endeavour. Throughout the chapter, special attention is paid to theorising within the discipline of International Relations, as it is that part of social studies that is most relevant to any discussion of peacemaking.

Historiography versus social studies: a questionable dichotomy

In Western civilisation, historiography and social studies have always been set apart, which appears normal because we are used to it. Indeed, the divide between the two goes back to the very beginnings of both types of enquiry in pre-Christian Greece – Herodotos and Thucydides on the one hand, Plato and Aristotle on the other. Yet this separation is actually somewhat odd if we consider that historiography and social studies both deal with the same general subject matter, social phenomena: political, economic, cultural. One of the rare bridges between the two appears to be legal history, marrying as it does jurisprudence on the one hand and historiography on the other.[1]

Jurisprudence is concerned with a particular kind of norm – law – governing social relations. In this sense and although this is an unusual way of classifying it, it can be placed under the general heading of social studies. It is true that other disciplines falling under that heading, like sociology, political science and economics, are cast in a less normative and more empirical mould than jurisprudence, but that difference is one of degree. I do not know whether there is such a thing as normative sociology, but political science includes political philosophy, an eminently normative endeavour, and the main ambition of economists is to give policy recommendations to enable governments to control the economy. Conversely, jurisprudence has an empirical aspect since it is concerned not only with norms that ought to be followed but (in particular in the case of 'positivistic' international law) with finding out what the norms are that are actually followed ('state practice'). And all four disciplines share the aspiration for systematic thinking, the ordering of their subject matter into internally coherent intellectual edifices that abstract from particular phenomena and put the emphasis on general patterns.

---

[1] I employ the word 'historiography' to distinguish the purposive recording of events, as well as organised academic enquiry into the past, from their subject matter. The word 'history' should properly be limited to designating the latter.

Regarding historiography, on the other hand, the difference between it and social studies is one of timeframe and approach. Social studies is usually concerned with the present only, where present is in practice defined as extending to a scholar's own life and possibly that of his immediate teachers or predecessors. It is, I suppose, this difference of timeframe, potentially long in the case of historiography, and, by comparison, negligible in the case of social studies, that usually causes historiography to privilege chronology over analysis and conversely causes social studies to privilege analysis over chronology. That in turn goes hand in hand with the tendency of historiography to privilege the particular over the general and of social studies to do the reverse.

Historians tell stories: not for nothing do the word history and the word story share the same root. Social studies authors, on the other hand, think systematically. Unquestionably, good historiography must be analytical too. But it has to grapple with the temporal dimension in a way that social studies does not. Historiography has to grapple with how we got from point A in time to point B – hence the tendency for its analysis to serve primarily to document that rather than to elucidate some abstract theoretical proposition. Immanuel Wallerstein (in line with other social studies authors) has called the method usually followed by historians idiographic, while he refers to that found in social studies as nomothetic.[2] Placing the period of origin of this divergence much later than I have done above, in the era of their institutionalisation as autonomous academic disciplines and epistemic communities that essentially took place in the industrial period, Wallerstein explains that

> [i]n the nineteenth-century world-view history was the reconstruction of the particular by its isolation from more general trends, and the social sciences attempted to discover universal laws . . . The name of the first game was to identify uniqueness; the name of the second was to establish abstract propositions.[3]

He argues that both the separation of social studies into distinct disciplines and the separation of social studies from historiography are arbitrary and unjustified.

---

[2] Immanuel Wallerstein, 'Some Reflections on History, the Social Sciences, and Politics' in *The Capitalist World Economy: Essays by Immanuel Wallerstein* (Cambridge, 1979), pp. vii–xii at p. viii. The two categories were originally introduced by the philosopher Wilhelm Windelband (1848–1915) to describe the respective methods of the natural sciences on the one hand and the arts and humanities (*Geisteswissenschaften*) on the other. See his inaugural address as rector of Strasbourg University, *Geschichte und Naturwissenschaft* (Strasbourg, 1894).

[3] Wallerstein, 'Some Reflections', p. xi.

> I believe ... that history and social science are one subject matter, which I shall call ... historical social science ... One cannot talk about (analyse) any particular set of occurrences without using concepts that imply theorems or generalisations about recurrent phenomena. Thus all 'history' is based on 'social science'. However, conversely, not only is all 'social science' a set of inductions from 'history', but there are *no* generalisations which are a-historical, that is, universal. Concepts and theorems are historically rooted and valid only within certain parameters of time and space, however broad ... I do not deny that in a piece of research one might not be more immediately concerned with explaining why a certain sequence of events occurred and that, in another piece of work, one might be more immediately concerned with identifying the patterns that are similar in several sets of events. But to reify the motives of scholars in doing particular research into two disciplines – the first history, the second social science – is to give misleading substance to the accidental and passing, and to miss the intellectual unity of the two enterprises.[4]

A good example of a generalisation, indeed a very sweeping generalisation of a social studies type in historiography is the idea of 'feudalism'. Conversely, a good example of a social studies generalisation that is in fact rooted in specific historic experience is the Realist paradigm in the discipline of International Relations. Both, but in particular the latter, will be discussed at greater length further on.

While he asserts the underlying unity of historiography and social studies, Wallerstein does not spell out the consequences of their separation. But the effect of this compartmentalisation is not only that neither field exploits its full potential, but also that both are prone to produce and perpetuate erroneous information.

Social studies literature tends to be stuck in the present and, hence, to be unable to gauge change, more especially long-term change (what it can accommodate is small-scale change within a general context assumed to be stable over time). While it normally operates within an explicit theoretical framework, most social studies literature does not employ that theoretical framework to study past phenomena. By the same token, it does not *test* its theoretical framework against past phenomena, nor can it, with any methodological rigour, situate the results of its analyses within a larger temporal context. This explains the tendency of social studies literature to do one of two things uncritically and without much

---

[4] Wallerstein, 'Some Reflections', pp. ix–x.

attempt at verification: ascribing trans-historical validity, timelessness to certain phenomena, and novelty to others.

It must be admitted that neither is, in general, of any particular importance to social studies. An apparent exception will be found in that part of social studies that is to political science what international law is to jurisprudence, the discipline of International Relations (IR). IR has long been dominated by the so-called Realist paradigm, which posits that, regardless of place and period, certain invariable structural and behavioural patterns will be found wherever and whenever autonomous political units interact in the absence of a common government. According to IR Realism, actors in such an anarchical environment (the expression 'anarchical' is used in IR in the strictly technical sense of 'without government') cannot trust each other, and must constantly be on their guard against attack and therefore ready to defend themselves. Even if their intentions are not aggressive, their necessary military preparedness means that they cannot help but threaten each other. And because of the general lack of security and the absence of any mechanism to enforce peaceful compromise they are prone to recurrent warfare. Apart from the constant readiness for defence, the chief means of ensuring their own survival is to balance, singly or in alliance with others, against preponderant power, in other words to try to preserve an equilibrium (the famous 'balance of power').[5]

---

[5] The best-known statement of what is today, in IR, called 'classical Realism' is Hans J. Morgenthau, *Politics among Nations: The Struggle for Power and Peace* (6th edn, ed. Kenneth W. Thompson, Chicago, 1985; 1st edn 1948); another is Raymond Aron, *Paix et guerre entre les nations* (8th edn with new preface by the author, Paris, 1982; 1st edn 1962). The more recent reworking of the paradigm, known as neo-Realism, started with the, in IR, enormously influential book by Kenneth N. Waltz, *Theory of International Politics* (New York, 1979). For discussions of IR Realism see, e.g., Jack Donnelly, *Realism and International Relations* (Cambridge, 2000); Stefano Guzzini, *Realism in IR and IPE: The Continuing Story of a Death Foretold* (London, 1998); Alexander Siedschlag, *Neorealismus, Neoliberalismus und postinternationale Politik* (Opladen, 1996); Michael Smith, *Realist Thought from Weber to Kissinger* (Baton Rouge and London, 1986); Roger D. Spegele, *Political Realism in International Theory* (Cambridge, 1996). For brief introductions see, e.g., Scott Burchill, 'Realism and Neo-Realism' in Scott Burchill and Andrew Linklater (with Richard Devetak, Matthew Paterson and Jacqui True), *Theories of International Relations* (New York, 1996), pp. 67–92; Ole R. Holsti, 'Theories of International Relations and Foreign Policy: Realism and Its Challengers' in Charles W. Kegley (ed.), *Controversies in International Relations Theory: Realism and the Neoliberal Challenge* (New York, 1995), pp. 35–66; Jack Donnelly, 'Twentieth-Century Realism' in Terry Nardin and David R. Mapel (eds.), *Traditions of International Ethics* (Cambridge, 1992), pp. 85–111; Andrew Linklater, 'Neo-Realism in Theory and Practice' in Ken Booth and Steve Smith (eds.), *International Relations Theory Today* (University Park, Pa., 1995), pp. 241–62.

This Realist paradigm extends its purview to the past by claiming, routinely and explicitly, that its tenets are applicable to all ages.[6] Yet what I said about social studies being stuck in the present applies to it. Realist IR theory subsumes history into an everlasting present: history is the minutiae, literally the 'small change' that cannot affect the big picture provided by insight into the timeless and inescapable principles of international politics. So certain is Realist IR literature of the truth of its tenets that while their applicability to any period is posited emphatically it has never, to my knowledge, been rigorously examined within IR.[7]

[6] E.g. Morgenthau, *Politics*, pp. 4, 38, 52; Waltz, *Theory*, pp. 66, 110, 127.
[7] In a recent volume on the current situation of the discipline, Fred Halliday urged IR to engage more with history 'as a corrective both to presentism (everything is new) and to transhistorical complacency (nothing is new)'. F. Halliday, 'The Future of International Relations: Fears and Hopes' in Steve Smith, Ken Booth and Marysia Zalewski (eds.), *International Theory: Positivism and Beyond* (Cambridge, 1996), pp. 318–28 at p. 324. In the same volume, Barry Buzan, himself what might be described as a moderate or eclectic Realist, also raised the issue, as he had done on previous occasions. B. Buzan, 'The Timeless Wisdom of Realism?' in Smith, Booth and Zalewski (eds.), *International Theory*, pp. 47–65. He and Richard Little, in their recent book *International Systems in World History: Remaking the Study of International Relations* (Oxford, 2000), apply their modified Realism to the entire history of mankind, in the process rejecting some tenets of mainstream Realism. But they retain others (in particular the notion that bounded, centralised entities recognisably similar to the modern 'state' have existed and interacted since the beginning of civilisation) that – as I intend to show in more detail in a future work – rest on conceptually biased projection rather than on unprejudiced examination of the evidence. A similar problem undermines the article by Markus Fischer, 'Feudal Europe, 800–1300: Communal Discourse and Conflictual Practices', *International Organization* 46 (1992), 427–66, in which he seeks to show that (neo-)Realist theory is applicable to the relations among autonomous medieval lords. Again, this article is not an unprejudiced examination of the evidence (as in the book by Buzan and Little, there is no engagement with primary sources) but an attempt to find corroboration for a preconceived theory in the writings of well-respected historians. See the rejoinder by Rodney Bruce Hall and Friedrich V. Kratochwil (with a reply by Fischer), 'Medieval Tales: Neorealist "Science" and the Abuse of History', *International Organization* 47 (1993), 479–500, and my own remarks on Fischer in A. Osiander, 'Before Sovereignty: Society and Politics in Ancien Régime Europe', *Review of International Studies* 27 (2001), 119–45 at pp. 120–1, 124 and 143. To my knowledge, the only other systematic examination of the applicability of (neo-)Realism to the historical record comes from a historian, Paul W. Schroeder, whose 'Historical Reality vs. Neo-Realist Theory', *International Security* 19 (1994), 108–44, is a searing critique of the theory covering the period 1648–1945; but see the rejoinder by Colin Elman and Miriam Fendius Elman (with a reply by Schroeder), 'History vs. Neo-Realism: A Second Look', *International Security* 20 (1995), 182–95. The recent symposium 'History and Theory', *International Security* 20 (1997), 5–85 (with contributions by Colin Elman and Miriam Fendius Elman; Jack S. Levy; Stephen H. Haber and David M. Kennedy; Stephen D. Krasner; Alexander L. George; Edward Ingram; Paul W. Schroeder; John Lewis Gaddis) I find disappointingly arid and without much bearing on what I discuss in this chapter. I have suggested elsewhere that the reluctance of IR Realism to test its hypotheses against history in any very serious fashion stems from a latent

From a methodological viewpoint, despite its apparent interest in even rather remote history (Thucydides and the Greek politics of his day are routinely invoked), IR Realism is thus really the antithesis of historiography. It is an admirably pure embodiment of the combination, characteristic of social studies, of ahistoricism and systematic abstraction.

Social studies authors dread being thought of as too descriptive. Perhaps for this reason they generally avoid giving their work much of a temporary dimension at all, lest it become too narrative. Even Realist IR authors do not normally discuss the past in any depth, but merely allude to it in a mostly rather haphazard manner. Conversely, it is as if among historians it were somehow in bad taste to preface publications with a truly theoretical discussion of what they are trying to achieve. Historiography is mostly in a narrative mode, with little effort made at linking its focus on change and on past phenomena to any sort of explicit theoretical framework, and with little attention (certainly no systematic attention) paid to what might be called the social studies aspect of the subject matter. This double extremism on the part of both social studies authors and historians has unhappy consequences.

Historiography, social studies and the problem of fundamental theoretical assumptions

Concerning the general subject matter of this volume, 'diplomatic' history, and more particularly the history of negotiations between at least partly autonomous actors (if they did not have a degree of autonomy, negotiations would serve no purpose), it is precisely that in which IR authors are also interested. Yet historians writing on such topics who could name (let alone who have read) those IR authors most commonly cited in IR journals must be extremely few. Certainly it is extremely rare to come across references to IR authors in this branch of historiography (let alone any other branch).[8] A consequence of this weakness in terms of theory is that when historians – in this as in other fields – select, process and comment

---

ideological stance, a conservative desire to defend the classical sovereign state against the challenge of industrialisation and growing interdependence. Andreas Osiander, 'History and International Relations Theory' in Beatrice Heuser and Anja V. Hartmann (eds.), *War, Peace and World Orders in European History* (London, 2001), pp. 14–24.

[8] Barry Buzan and Richard Little, too, note that 'big names' in IR theory such as Hedley Bull, Hans Morgenthau, Robert Gilpin, Stephen Krasner, Robert Keohane, James Rosenau and Kenneth Waltz are virtually unknown outside the discipline. B. Buzan and R. Little, 'Why International Relations Has Failed as an Intellectual Project and What to Do about It', *Millennium* 30 (2001), 19–39 at p. 21.

on their raw data, the theoretical criteria applied usually remain unstated. They are not worked out in any explicit fashion and often reflect some kind of *Zeitgeist.*

The unspoken assumptions underlying such work may thus really be just as arbitrary and anachronistic, indeed not infrequently the same, as those current among IR authors. Realist IR theory itself adopted its tenets not after weighing and rejecting other possible ones, but because those particular assumptions were in line with the most generally accepted 'reading' of international politics, so much taken for granted as to be considered timeless – though this reading, far from being found in any period, has been dominant in Western civilisation only since the latter part of the nineteenth century.[9]

Realist IR authors, when they think they have evaluated 'history', really have been looking at standard nineteenth- and twentieth-century historiography. Much of that literature is based on a view of international politics dominant especially in the late nineteenth and the early twentieth century (though still widely accepted today): on this view international politics takes place between sovereign, tightly bounded, territorial and, preferably, 'nation' 'states', enjoins on those 'states' to seek their own preservation in the face of permanent foreign threats, of necessity entails rivalry between them, and revolves around the problem of war. There is no question that, for much of the period since the mid-nineteenth century, this view was not just that of observers of politics but corresponded to the thinking of many important actual decision makers themselves (and it is no doubt still held by some today).

What *should* be in question is whether the same view can simply be assumed to be applicable to any historical period, as many historians have done and still do. Although, put on the spot, they might well deny this charge and insist each on the peculiarities and uniqueness of the period in which they specialise, they are still likely to be guided by assumptions in line with the view outlined above but at once so fundamental and so taken for granted as to escape their notice.

The 'timeless' principles of IR Realism are, then, distilled not from history, but from the perception and discourse prevailing among writers of history that are contemporaries or near-contemporaries of the IR authors themselves. When it takes itself to be looking at history IR Realism is in fact looking at a mirror reflecting dominant assumptions of its own

---

[9] Cf. Osiander, 'History', and Andreas Osiander, 'Rereading Early Twentieth-Century IR Theory. Idealism Revisited', *International Studies Quarterly* 42 (1998), 409–32.

period. Conversely, much historiography concerning the relations among (part-)autonomous actors in any period tends to be suffused with what are, in fact, Realist assumptions. Even in recent historiography we often find it taken for granted that actors *always* compete for power, balance against and seek to outwit each other, etc., with much less attention being paid to issues like how they happened to be actors in the first place, what their means of action, their degree of control over, and their importance to, society at large were, or whether the image of power-maximising, exclusively self-regarding actors that Realist assumptions lead us to expect is not modified, if we care to look, by instances of voluntary cooperation, indeed subordination, or instances of avoidance of conflict or of limiting its conduct to mutually acceptable and recognised means and objectives.

Similarly, historiography tends to have a 'statist' and a national bias, causing it to consider, for example, efforts to create an effective central government to be 'good' (especially if the dominion in question can be considered the forerunner of some present-day 'nation') while secessionism or revolt against the central authority (like that of the 'king' or 'crown', expressions that are almost always used with positive connotations) is 'bad' (unless it happened to be at the origin of some modern 'nation'). The same bias is found in IR Realism, which is explicitly statist and less explicitly, indeed in this particular case latently, national in orientation.[10] The historical sociologist Michael Mann makes a similar point:

> Sociological theory cannot develop without knowledge of history. Most of the key questions of sociology concern processes occurring through time; social structure is inherited from particular pasts; and a large proportion of our 'sample' of complex societies is only available in history. But the study of

[10] A good example of this bias is provided by so perceptive a historian as Georges Duby in his famous work *La Société aux XIe et XIIe siècles dans la région mâconnaise* (Paris, 1982; 1st edn 1971). While attuned to every nuance and semantic peculiarity of the archival record of the period under scrutiny, in his larger, political judgements Duby reflects assumptions and attitudes that are very much those of his own period; the main thesis being that the phenomena observed, in particular the political phenomenon of the decentralisation and 'privatisation' of power, are the result of the 'failure' of the Frankish 'state'. Cf., e.g., the following excerpt from his *Conclusion générale*: 'Cet aménagement de la société est la conséquence directe d'un fait politique, la décomposition de l'Etat carolingien. La faillite de l'institution royale entraîna d'abord l'affaiblissement du pouvoir comtal, le fractionnement du *pagus*, le partage des droits régaliens qui, lorsque la présence du souverain ne fut plus sensible, devinrent aux mains des châtelains des droits privés . . .' (p. 480). Describing the Carolingian realm as a 'state' with a 'sovereign' is applying to it modern concepts assumed to be transhistorically valid, while terms like 'décomposition' or 'faillite' imply value judgements and political preferences which are, again, those of the contemporary period.

history is also impoverished without sociology. If historians eschew theory of how societies operate, they imprison themselves in the commonsense notions of their own society. In this volume, I repeatedly question the application of essentially modern notions – such as nation, state, class, private property, and the centralized state – to earlier historical periods.[11]

Indeed, the view that politics is always focused on something called the 'state' is a prime case of interpretation being influenced by the *Zeitgeist* or what Mann terms 'common sense notions' of the modern period. To judge by the larger part by far of nineteenth- and twentieth-century historiography, the 'state' must indeed represent something that is timeless in its essence, since most historians, just like IR authors, do not for a moment doubt that this concept is applicable to any but the most distant pre-civilisational past, and indeed central to any understanding of the past ever since civilisation began. So much so, that the concept usually goes undefined, introducing into any discussion of, say, the relations among pre-Christian Greek *poleis*, routinely described as 'city *states*', a great deal of unacknowledged intellectual baggage: about what 'states' are and do, and about what their 'interests' or 'motives' are, and so on. That seemingly anodyne, taken-for-granted concept thus purveys a false sense of familiarity and may seriously distort our perception of past social and political structures and processes.

Conversely, IR authors, even if they are interested in the more remote past and refer to it in corroboration of some point or other, do not in general adduce specialist and/or recent historiographical literature. Mostly they content themselves with conventional textbook wisdom. This may be buttressed by references to some well-known (and therefore usually not recent, or indeed deceased) historians, but such references are usually ornamental and may well be missing altogether.[12]

---

[11] Michael Mann, *The Sources of Social Power*, vol. I, *A History of Power from the Beginning to A.D. 1760* (Cambridge, 1986), p. vii.

[12] It is no doubt unfair to single out any authors, and doing so cannot replace systematic statistical analysis. But even if this evidence is anecdotal, Robert Gilpin with his, in IR, well-known book *War and Change in World Politics* (Cambridge, 1981) may serve as an illustration – which, subjective as this may be, I do consider representative. At the outset, Gilpin, a Realist, states unambiguously that 'the fundamental nature of international relations has not changed over the millennia . . . The classic history of Thucydides is as meaningful a guide to the behaviour of states today as when it was written in the fifth century B.C.' (p. 7). At the same time, the main purpose of the book, filled with references to the last 2000 or 3000 years of (mostly western) history, is to show this, and for Gilpin it does. Certainly, towards the end of the book the premise just quoted reappears as a conclusion ('Ultimately, international politics can still be characterized as it was by Thucydides', p. 228). The bibliography at the end of the book contains 276 titles. Out of those, some 200 belong under the heading social studies (with some of course being

Some social science authors have made efforts to marry social studies and historiography. Immanuel Wallerstein applied his ideas on 'historical social science' in developing his well-known world-system theory that posits the emergence of a 'capitalist world economy' in the West from the late Middle Ages onwards, and seeks to account for social and political developments as a function of the evolution of this underlying economic structure. Michael Mann provided a *History of Power* from the dawn of civilisation to the present day that is hardly less monumental or ambitious than the work of Wallerstein.

Barry Buzan and Richard Little, despite the provocative title of their recent article on the 'failure' of IR, have similarly ambitious designs for this discipline. According to them, the offer of macro-theory that makes sense of the 'big picture' is the reason why Wallerstein has been widely noted and discussed across disciplinary boundaries, while IR, unable to come up with any comparable 'grand theory', has been ignored by other branches of social studies and historiography alike, taking on a 'ghetto like character'.[13] However, in their estimation, thanks to the debate on 'globalisation' in the 1990s IR has increasingly overcome its narrow fixation on inter-'state' relations and has made 'steady progress towards taking as its subject the question of how humankind is organised politically, economically, socially, and ecologically and how the different aspects of its organisation play into each other'. They assert their belief that IR

> has the potential, and arguably the obligation, to become a kind of meta-discipline, systematically linking together the macro-sides of the social sciences and history . . . Its comparative advantage lies in its potential as a holistic theoretical framework, which should be able to speak equally well to political scientists, economists, lawyers, sociologists, anthropologists, and historians.[14]

---

borderline cases, so that others might count slightly differently). Many of these titles are on economics, a field Gilpin is particularly interested in. Some thirty titles are the kind of historiography, often with a wide chronological and/or interpretative focus, that must be largely based on secondary literature (e.g. Perry Anderson, *Lineages of the Absolutist State* (London, 1972), or William H. McNeill, *The Rise of the West* (Chicago, 1963)). Only some twenty titles are what I would call historical monographs that are or at least should be based to a significant extent on primary sources from the period under consideration. Note that despite the repeated references to Thucydides, no specialist literature on him is cited, and only three monographs on pre-Christian Greece are (two of them on economic aspects). Much of the remainder consists of period sources (e.g. Thucydides, Montesquieu, Mill, Marx, Lenin).

[13] Buzan and Little, 'Why International Relations Has Failed', p. 19, n. 1.
[14] Buzan and Little, 'Why International Relations Has Failed', p. 22.

They are in agreement with Wallerstein and Mann that no grand theory is possible in social studies without taking account of as much of history as possible.[15] Their recent book, encompassing no less than the past 60,000 years of human history, is an illustration of what they have in mind.[16]

All these authors, however, look at society (past and present) from the outside, as it were. They regard it as an object of inquiry that exists, and may be observed, quite independently of their mind or that of their readers, and to the analysis of which, as interpretive tools, it is both possible and necessary to bring concepts of their own making.

Constructivism as a means of merging historiography and social studies

This seems to me to be a serious weakness. Everybody who writes on history inevitably and necessarily does so with certain assumptions in mind. Failure to reflect on those assumptions may mean that we fail to employ the best possible assumptions. Authors like Mann do reflect on the concepts that they use to shed light on past social phenomena, and yet in choosing concepts alien (at least in part) to the cultures observed they still introduce an unnecessary element of arbitrariness into their analysis.

If it is granted that to interpret the past with explicit assumptions is better than to do it with latent, indeed unreflected assumptions, then how can we possibly determine which assumptions are best? Can the element of arbitrariness be avoided at all? It seems to me that there is a way at least to minimise it. Non-Realist IR theory offers a promising approach to this problem. However, in typical social studies fashion it has not so far applied the relevant ideas to past phenomena; indeed as far as I can see it has not even grasped the potential of this approach for historiography.

It will be agreed that the best assumptions to use in dealing with social phenomena are those that provide maximum understanding of those phenomena. I contend that the best assumptions in this respect are those of the people who produced the social phenomena that we happen to be dealing with, and not others. Scholars studying the past should seek to identify the key assumptions – and concepts (which generally imply, and are shorthand for, key assumptions) – of the people who made the history they are looking at in preference to their own assumptions and

---

[15] 'In our opinion, conceptual frameworks in mainstream IR are hamstrung by their failure to build on a long view of history'; Buzan and Little, 'Why International Relations Has Failed', p. 26.

[16] Buzan and Little, *International Systems*.

concepts, and wherever possible should use those assumptions and concepts, not their own, to interpret the behaviour of past social or political actors. So, to the extent that the approach that I am here suggesting is predicated on assumptions made a priori, they are on a meta-theoretical level. It is this recognition of the importance of meta-theoretical assumptions that is perhaps the greatest achievement of recent theoretical debate in IR.[17]

The Realist school of IR, still enormously influential, but also some of its challengers (like neo-liberalism) use what in current theoretical debate in the discipline is called a 'positivistic' approach. By contrast, the new mode of theorising is known in IR as 'post-positivistic'. Until recently, IR theory took for granted (as, I suspect, virtually all historians still do) that the assumptions it makes about the world reflect the world as it is: for it, its subject matter, the world of international politics, was really 'out there', like some kind of natural phenomenon quite independent of the mind of those trying to interpret it. Conversely, the starting point of an important branch of post-positivistic IR theory is that social structures and social actors are *not* 'out there' but exist only in our minds. Dependent as they are on shared assumptions, social structures and actors have no reality other than as collective mental constructs; hence the name Constructivism for this school of thought.

In an early formulation of this approach, Robert Cox put it thus:

> Historical structures, the cumulative result of innumerable often-repeated actions, are discoverable through the common understandings and common expectations of behavior that provide the common framework for actions. Another way of saying this is that historical structures are revealed as intersubjectivity. Language; patterns of response to stimuli considered as normal behavior; institutions like the family and the state; as well as less formally defined but nevertheless recurrent practices of personal morality and international behavior – all are constituted by intersubjectivity. Intersubjectivity does not mean approval or consensus, just common recognition of the existence of these things. Intersubjectivity makes them objective independently of individual wills.[18]

---

[17] Fred Halliday has criticised the recent preoccupation of the discipline with meta-theoretical debate as 'epistemological hypochondria' (Halliday, 'Future', p. 320; the expression is credited to Ernest Gellner). Yet I am inclined to see precisely this sensitivity to questions of method as a major achievement in itself, even if no consensus has as yet emerged on which approach to follow.

[18] Robert W. Cox, 'Production, the State, and Change in World Order' in Ernst-Otto Czempiel and James N. Rosenau (eds.), *Global Changes and Theoretical Challenge: Approaches to World Politics for the 1990s* (Lexington, Mass. and Toronto, 1989), pp. 37–50 at p. 38.

In making assumptions about the natural world, people merely interpret it. But in making assumptions about the social world, they create (or, in historiography, re-create) it. While the natural world may be studied with a positivistic approach, the social world cannot.

Take, once more, that key notion of political science, but also of much historiography, the notion of state. What we know as a state does not exist the way a tree or a table does. It cannot be touched; all it is is what people think it is. People make assumptions about it; when enough people make the same assumptions about something they are agreed to call a state, then and only then that something will have being. When those shared assumptions change, so will the state, or whatever other social structures we are dealing with. On a different plane, what we often call the international system, the larger system encompassing a plurality of self-confined political units, or a plurality of autonomous actors, is likewise based on assumptions; and in the same way, far from having some immutable, timeless essence, when assumptions about it change, so does the system.

It might be objected that it can also change through coercion being applied, indeed that that is an important, perhaps the most important, cause of change. Yet just as a government cannot function in the long run if it is based exclusively on coercion, so it is difficult to defend areas conquered unless there is a minimum degree of consensus on the legitimacy or at least utility (which in itself is something subjective, dependent for its meaning in given historical circumstances on both individual perception and prevailing values) of empire among those concerned (who may be the subjects, but also those in control). History abounds in object lessons to this effect. The Athenian Empire in the fifth century BC (and again the Spartan Empire that succeeded it in the early fourth century BC) was fragile, short-lived and small because of its tendency, inherent in the way it was constructed, to ignore the wishes and notions of legitimacy of those whose liberty was taken away or curtailed. Conversely, the Roman Empire grew and endured because, again owing to the specific circumstances and character of its construction, it left its subjects largely alone, brought them benefits that were perceived by important elements of the population as outweighing the negative aspects of Roman rule and, specifically, allowed the local elites to run most of their own affairs as they saw fit. Existing elites were not demoted but co-opted, especially through the offer to selected non-Roman subjects of Roman citizenship and its attendant privileges; this key plank of Roman imperial policy would have been unthinkable in classical Greece, where citizenship was much more exclusive.¹⁹ In a related fashion, the Soviet Empire after 1945 endured (despite hostility among the 'subjects') as long as, at least, the elites (both within the Soviet Union itself and in the satellite countries) maintained their belief in the system; it disintegrated when they lost that belief, rather than because of any external coercion.

A social system not predicated on the existence of a central, authoritative government, the kind of system that IR theory calls anarchical, may change in less coordinated – or perhaps it would be better to say in more complex – fashion than does a system that is under some form of central control. Yet the reasons for its transformation are not fundamentally different. We may think that a state undergoes a given change because the government wills that change, but that cannot be an exhaustive explanation. To account fully for change within a state we need to know on the basis of what principles of legitimacy the government is accepted by a majority of the population (or at least its more important elements), what possibilities and constraints those particular principles of legitimacy bestow on the government, how it happened to have the ideas of desirable change that it does, and so on. Any analysis of social phenomena boils down to assumptions made by those that are significantly involved in those phenomena.

Likewise with an anarchical system, such as, say, the European system of the eighteenth century or the global system of the twentieth. It takes the form we observe because of the shared assumptions of the people who think, live, express, and thereby create and perpetuate this system, and the eighteenth-century European system looks different from the

---

¹⁹ This type of argument is not new but was current in the pre-Christian Graeco-Roman world. It is made for example by the Greek orator Aelius Aristides in his *Roman Oration* (*Eis Rhomen*) of 143 AD. For the suggestion that Athenian military weakness, harsh treatment of non-Athenian subjects and the smallness of the fifth-century BC Athenian empire were interrelated, see especially ch. 57 of that text; for the success of Rome being based on the inclusive character of Roman rule and the nature – restricted yet accessible – of Roman citizenship, especially chs. 59 and 64–5. For similar, somewhat earlier ideas on the character of the Athenian (and then Spartan) system of rule on the one hand and the Roman Empire on the other, see Tacitus, *Annals* 11.23–4, and compare Tacitus, *Histories* 4.74. The view that both Sparta and Athens lost their hegemonial position in the fourth century BC (Sparta through its defeat at Leuktra in 371 at the hands of its erstwhile client Thebes, Athens through its defeat in the 'Social War' of 357–355 against a coalition of its own allies) at least partly because of disregard for the interests and dignity of those they dominated was already expressed by contemporary observers. See, e.g., the powerful indictment of Athenian (and Spartan) policy by Isocrates (b. 436) in his *Oration on the Peace*, the peace in question being that of 355 which ended the so-called Social War.

present-day global one because there are, to some extent, different underlying assumptions.

If, in making certain fundamental, widely shared assumptions, people create and perpetuate the social structures within which they live, then to understand those structures, both their being at a given moment and their evolution over time, we need to know what those fundamental assumptions were. If we neglect those assumptions and substitute our own, then what we get is not an understanding of history but something called myth. Instead of entering the past that people inhabited at the time we create a past that is artificial, mythical, precisely to the extent to which it mirrors present assumptions rather than those prevailing at the time. Yet precisely because this kind of historiography echoes familiar assumptions, it may appear the more plausible. Reading nineteenth-century historiography, we are often aware of a 'dated', 'old-fashioned' quality about it that results at least partly from the fact that, to the extent that the assumptions underlying it strike us as peculiar, we *notice* them. But much of twentieth-century historiography is likely to suffer a similar fate a hundred years hence.

Historians reflecting on this might be inclined to accept it as inevitable, arguing that every age has to rewrite, indeed 'reconstruct' its own history. For example, Luise Schorn-Schütte writes in the introduction of her recent biography of the emperor Charles V:

> Historians remain contemporaries, and present historical research, too, follows guiding concepts specific to our period. This insight does not by any means render historical research superfluous. The inference is merely that it is the attempt, to which every new generation is entitled, to reconstruct its past afresh.[20]

I think Schorn-Schütte is right to stress the character of historiography as a social construct. We can make sense of past social phenomena only by reconstructing past social structures, which we do in exactly the same way that we construct our present social reality, i.e. by making assumptions about it. But whereas assumptions we make about present-day structures are the result of our constant exposure to, and participation in, a huge volume of social communication, of discourse purveying those assumptions,

---

[20] 'Historiker bleiben Zeitgenossen, und auch die gegenwärtige historische Forschung folgt zeitgebundenen Leitbildern. Diese Einsicht macht historische Forschung keineswegs überflüssig. Es wird lediglich deutlich, daß sie der – jeder Generation zustehende – Versuch ist, ihre eigene Vergangenheit neu zu konstruieren.' L. Schorn-Schütte, *Karl V. Kaiser zwischen Mittelalter und Neuzeit* (Munich, 2000), pp. 8–9.

readers of historiographical literature are not in touch with, not communicating with past social actors. To the extent that they consist of text, historical sources are relics, and more or less representative samples, of the social and political discourse of their period. But almost all historiographical literature interposes itself between that discourse and its readers. It filters the original discourse as though through a prism, introducing its own social and political assumptions for interpretive purposes. In doing so, it replaces to a greater or lesser extent those assumptions and concepts that are conveyed in the original discourse. As a consequence, whereas our perception of present-day social reality is checked against the social communication to which we are continuously exposed, what historians tell us about the past is not similarly checked against past social discourse. The natural tendency is for historians to reconstruct the past in accordance with their own assumptions, and for readers to find that reconstruction plausible because of the familiarity of the assumptions implied.

Although this will often be the case, assumptions are not necessarily familiar because they are contemporary. There are familiar assumptions that have become customarily associated with given past phenomena but which reflect neither the social reality of today nor that of the period being discussed. A good example is the idea of 'feudalism'. As is well known, that term did not exist in the Middle Ages, the period with reference to which it was coined; it is the invention (in its French form *féodalité*) of seventeenth-century scholars. Some of the numerous assumptions and concepts associated with it are earlier but still anachronistic, i.e. post-Reformation, while other terminology is indeed found in pre-Reformation sources, though not necessarily with the meaning assigned to it in post-Reformation (or, for that matter, even pre-Reformation) scholarly systematisation. Among specialists this entire tangle of technical language and concepts has in recent years been the object of some debate, but both the bulk of even recent historiographical literature and the general public take its validity for granted. This is unjustified, as Susan Reynolds has argued in her work on relations between lords in Latin Christianity:

> Fiefs and vassalage, as they are generally defined by medieval historians today, are post-medieval constructs, though rather earlier than the construct of feudalism. Historians often refer to both fiefs and vassals when neither word is in their sources . . . Even when the historians follow the terminology of their documents and take pains to establish the phenomena recorded, they tend to fit their findings into a framework of interpretation that was devised in the sixteenth century and elaborated in the seventeenth

and eighteenth ... We cannot understand medieval society and its property relations if we see it through seventeenth- and eighteenth-century spectacles. Yet every time we think of fiefs and vassals we do just that.[21]

But once a simplistic paradigm like the idea of feudalism (or, in IR and diplomatic history, Realism) has become entrenched, no amount of evidence will of itself dislodge it:

> Just as the image of feudal society was composed syncretically to fit a thousand years of the history of all Europe, so the vast increase of knowledge about the middle ages has since then gone on being accommodated syncretically to fit an image which changed by accretion but not by radical revision. The middle ages have been taken as the age of feudalism, and so whatever does not form part of the image of feudalism is filtered out of the view or adapted to fit into the background.[22]

Reynolds argues that 'feudalism' is not even useful as a Weberian 'ideal type' — according to her it is too complex for that — or as what Abraham Kaplan has called a 'descriptive generalisation' designed to 'inform us of what manner of creature we may expect on our travels':

> What the concept of feudalism seems to have done since the sixteenth century is not to help us recognize the creatures we meet but to tell us that all medieval creatures are the same so that we need not bother to look at them. Put another way, feudalism has provided a kind of protective lens through which it has seemed prudent to view the otherwise dazzling oddities and varieties of medieval creatures.[23]

This quality of providing a 'protective lens' that insulates from the actual historical evidence is very much applicable to the Realist paradigm in IR as well.

My contention here is that, although it will never be possible for those writing about past social phenomena to escape completely the preoccupations of their own time, the attempt should at least be made to minimise the contamination. To do this, and thus to understand (rather than recreate) any social system past or present, including any political system, we need to look *consistently* at the assumptions on which that system was (is) based, where those assumptions came from, how they were (are) communicated, how on occasion they clash(ed) and compete(d). To the extent that it is not concerned exclusively with material or technical aspects of

---

[21] Susan Reynolds, *Fiefs and Vassals: The Medieval Evidence Reinterpreted* (Oxford, 1994), pp. 2–3.
[22] Reynolds, *Fiefs*, p. 9.   [23] Reynolds, *Fiefs*, p. 11; Kaplan quoted there.

past phenomena, this should be a chief focus of any historiographical inquiry. In particular, any reconstruction and evaluation of political processes must not be undertaken without constant attention to the basic concepts, values (notions of right and wrong), objectives and interests of the relevant actors as perceived by themselves. It must never ignore their terminology. At the very least, if anachronistic concepts are introduced, they should be labelled as such: 'When the subject under investigation involves notions or attitudes held by people in the society concerned it is vital to distinguish whether a concept is ours or theirs.'[24]

While every effort should be made to do so, it will not always be possible to demonstrate those concepts, values, objectives and interests in a satisfactory manner. But any attempt to substitute conjecture for secure evidence from period discourse should be explicit and reasoned rather than tacit as is so often the case in conventional historiography. Historiography that seeks to throw light on past political processes should, to the extent to which this is possible, be based on the explicit analysis of extant discourse from the period in question.

Constructivism and social and political change

The social reality of any period is the result of the constant interaction of forces of inertia and forces of change, the two aspects of social reality that, precisely, gave rise to the dichotomy between historiography and social studies with which our discussion began. But why should assumptions, and with them the social and political structures that they create, change once they are in place? Why do they, in fact, change all the time? To this question, Alexander Wendt gave the following answer:

> Culture is constantly in motion ... Despite having a conservative bias ... culture is always characterized by more or less contestation among its carriers, which is a constant resource for cultural change. This contestation has at least five overlapping sources. One is internal contradictions between different logics within a culture. Cultures consist of many different norms, rules, and institutions, and the practices they induce will often be contradictory. A second is the fact that agents are never perfectly socialized, such that they only have shared beliefs. Every one of us has private beliefs that motivate us to pursue personal projects that can change our environments. The unintended consequences of shared beliefs are a third source of conflict. A tragedy of the commons can be rooted in a shared understanding of

[24] Reynolds, *Fiefs*, p. 13.

something as a commons, but produce an outcome that eventually causes a change of that belief. Exogenous shocks are a fourth factor. A revolution, cultural imperialism, or an invasion by conquistadores can all transform cultural order. And finally there is creativity, the invention of new ideas from within a culture.[25]

I can think of two further rubrics that should perhaps be added. One, which might also be thought of as an elaboration of the first and last source of change given by Wendt (contradictory competing logics within a culture, and the emergence of new ideas), and which, again, may interlock with others, is the possibility that the evolution of the assumptions underlying social and political structures is governed by an intrinsic dynamic of its own that is partly, or perhaps even largely, independent both of material factors – other than those with a bearing on the transmission of information – and of conscious human agency. We may think of such assumptions as similar to genes in biology. Assumptions condition a social system in much the same way as different genes produce different phenotypes in biology.

It has been proposed recently that, indeed, there are important parallels between genes and copiable artefacts called 'memes' – a category that includes abstract notions like ideas, assumptions, concepts, norms and the like – that form the myriad and disparate elements of human culture. On this view, the human species is unique in its capacity to learn by imitation, which is the foundation of culture. Even the most creative human individuals copy, rather than invent, all but a vanishingly small portion of their language, behaviour, attitudes and convictions. Socialisation, from this perspective, is simply the process of acquiring such memes through observation (sometimes reinforced by purposive teaching) and imitation.

Memes compete – although, like genes, memes also co-act for the very purpose of competition. Even simple life forms are created by amalgams, as it were cooperatives, of myriad genes that evolutionary biology refers to as geneplexes (short for co-adapted gene complexes); similarly, memes combine into memeplexes governing complex, composite cultural phenomena, e.g. religions or technologies. A concomitant of this competition is that almost always we choose from among several available memes or memeplexes that are more or less different from each other. We may all dress in a similar fashion, but our dress is rarely identical (certainly strict

[25] Alexander Wendt, *Social Theory of International Politics* (Cambridge, 1999), p. 188. This book, by the way, is an interesting attempt by an IR writer to reconcile Realism and Constructivism.

vestiary uniformity, as in an army or Mao's China, has to be imposed through disciplinary pressure); similarly, a (variable) degree of heterogeneity is present in virtually every part of culture, owing to the availability of rival memes or memeplexes. Memes replicate, survive, through being copied, but since the copying often involves a greater or lesser extent of variation, mutations constantly occur entering the competition among memes. This in turn creates an intrinsic evolutionary logic and dynamic similar (though not identical) to that causing biological evolution, since memes share with genes their fundamental quality of being self-replicating yet mutable.[26]

This logic may account, most obviously, for cultural change that has little evident necessity or utility. There is really no very compelling reason why people should dress so differently today from a hundred or two hundred or five hundred years ago – even if, on reflection, the semiotics of dress may, to some extent, mirror general social change and the assumptions underlying it. The same holds for speech, music and many other things subject to 'fashion' or 'style' – in quite the same way, perhaps, as biological species succeed each other without one being more evidently 'needed', or even only better adapted, than the other (e.g. dinosaurs may dominate in one evolutionary epoch, mammals in the next).

However, self-propelled, quasi-automatic memetic evolution rather than self-conscious, controlled human agency may also explain the spread of 'serious' ideas, including those with a bearing on politics. As an example, I have attempted elsewhere to account in memetic terms for the takeover, until recently almost inexplicably successful, of Western civilisation by Christianity, drawing on the perception of religions as contagious and, especially in the case of Christianity and later Islam, highly aggressive and resilient 'mind viruses' (the expression is from Richard Dawkins, who also coined the term 'memes' in 1976).[27]

The other possible source of change is the evolution of the framework of material constraints and opportunities within which any society operates. Needless to say, the assumptions underlying the social order do not exist in a material vacuum. Karl Marx rightly emphasised the influence of the way in which society reproduces itself materially on the way in

---

[26] This approach, known as memetics, has been gathering momentum since the late 1970s but has as yet made almost no impact on either social studies or historiography. The brief outline given here cannot do justice to the complexities of the theory. For a brilliant exposition see Susan Blackmore, *The Meme Machine* (Oxford, 1999).

[27] Andreas Osiander, 'Religion and Politics in Western Civilisation: The Ancient World as Matrix and Mirror of the Modern', *Millennium* 29 (2000), 761–90.

which it reproduces itself ideationally. The means available for producing goods, for waging violent conflict, and, certainly not least, the methods available for sharing information, do have a potent impact on what kind of assumptions underlie social and political structures.

Yet Alexander Wendt (following Douglas Porpora and David Rubinstein) has pointed out that Marxian 'historical materialism' is not in fact as purely materialistic as that label might suggest:

> Marxism defines the material base as the mode of production, and locates ideology, culture, and other ideational factors in a non-material superstructure. 'Materialism' thereby becomes identified with explanations by reference to economic factors... The problem is that Marxism defines the mode of production not only in terms of forces but also in terms of *relations* of production. Forces of production ('tools') are plausible candidates for being brute material forces. But relations of production are thoroughly ideational phenomena, namely institutions or rules – which are ultimately shared ideas – that constitute property and exchange relationships, who works for whom, class powers and interests, and so on. The fact that relations of production are ideational means that capitalism is mostly a *cultural* form, not material, and as such Marxism's 'material base' actually is shot through and through with ideas.[28]

This may serve as a reminder that it is probably in most instances impossible to separate material factors neatly from ideational ones. They interrelate, with material factors becoming as it were enmeshed or encrusted with ideational ones, in a way that appears variable and unpredictable. A given technological breakthrough will not, on its own, cause social change. Thus, to cite a commonly given example, the invention of movable type in eleventh-century China (and then of metal type in thirteenth-century Korea) apparently had little impact on society there, whereas, for reasons not readily apparent, the same invention revolutionised Western civilisation.[29] And though it could easily have been copied from there, printing was slow to have much cultural impact outside Christendom.[30]

---

[28] Wendt, *Social Theory*, p. 94–9; original emphasis.

[29] For a penetrating analysis see Elizabeth L. Eisenstein, *The Printing Revolution in Early Modern Europe* (abridged edn, Cambridge, 1983). Not the least merit of this book is to make clear how differently, including in the purely intellectual field, a scribal culture will function from one heavily reliant on printing as Western civilisation has been from the fifteenth century onward. We are so accustomed to the availability of print that we hardly ever stop to reflect on how a material constraint like the absence of printing will cause a society not only to operate differently, but to *think* differently from our own.

[30] For example, the first printing press in the Ottoman Empire was set up, possibly as early as 1493, by Jewish immigrants at Thessalonike, following the settlement there by sultan

It is somewhat similar to the other obvious example, gunpowder. Introduced to Europe some time after 1300, metal ordnance over time contributed to revolutionising both warfare and the political structures of Christendom.[31] It failed, however, to have a comparable impact elsewhere. Both military-grade gunpowder and metal ordnance were used in thirteenth-century China, some decades before they appeared in Christendom, and the technology was also copied, from either culture, in the Muslim world and in Japan. But again major political change was only triggered within Christendom. Despite their competent mastery of it, both China and Japan had largely abandoned the technology by 1600, while the Muslim world (e.g. the Ottoman Empire or Mughal India) failed to attain durably the expertise in producing and deploying ordnance possessed by Christian Europe. Geoffrey Parker analysed the reasons for this differential impact, suggesting administrative factors, political developments and local traditions of warfare, part of which at least must rank as non-material.[32]

It has often, and of course rightly, been emphasised that the evolution of the early modern European state was potently conditioned by such inventions as gunpowder and printing. But even though some have tried, to my mind it is not possible to account for the development either of the modern European state or of the larger political system within which it evolved without recognising the prime importance of shared assumptions. There are those who have written on the evolution of the modern state purely in terms of its capability to wield coercive power, extract revenue from its subjects and wage war. Others have focused on the institutional developments leading from the 'feudal' system to the modern state. But this kind of argument, highly significant though it may be, does not exhaust the topic nor does it even go to the heart of the matter.[33]

Bayezid II of many of the Jews expelled from Spain in 1492. But Ottoman literary culture continued to be scribal until well into the eighteenth century. The geographical treatise *Cihân-numâ* by Mustafa b. Abdullah (1609–57) was one of the first Ottoman works to appear in print, in 1732. Suraiya Faroqhi, *Geschichte des osmanischen Reiches* (Munich, 2000), pp. 33 and 72.

[31] Geoffrey Parker, *The Military Revolution: Military Innovation and the Rise of the West, 1500–1800* (2nd edn, Cambridge, 1996). For an overview of the controversy generated by this book, see Clifford Rogers (ed.), *The Military Revolution Debate: Readings on the Military Transformation of Early Modern Europe* (Boulder, Colo., 1995).

[32] Parker, *Military Revolution*, pp. 115–45.

[33] A good example of the former approach is Charles Tilly, *Coercion, Capital and European States AD 990–1990* (Oxford, 1990), and of the latter, Gianfranco Poggi, *The Development of the Modern State: A Sociological Introduction* (Stanford, Calif., 1978). I am not suggesting that either writer regards his approach as exhaustive or incompatible with other accounts.

It is a bit like studying medicine before the invention of the microscope. It is possible to have theories, and they may even be true, but much better theories become possible once it is understood that underlying larger phenomena there are such crucial basic units as cells or indeed genes. However, in social studies, or historiography, no special tools are necessary: since social phenomena are constructed in the mind, the mind is also able to deconstruct and thereby understand them.

Change in the European system

Concerning the subject matter of the present volume, what were the assumptions of the evolving European system? Where did those assumptions come from, how were they communicated, and how and why did they change? Evidently, and not least because I do not wish to encroach on the areas of expertise of other contributors to this volume, only the briefest sketch can be given here, for illustrative purposes.

For much of the earliest history of the European system after the end of Roman rule in the Latin West, those assumptions were communicated, and in part also supplied, by the Church. The Church was extremely potent in an era when it had a near-total if gradually weakening monopoly on written culture and higher learning (in other words, on account of its disposal of superior means for storing, processing and spreading information, it had what could be called a position of great *memetic* power). At the same time, and most importantly, the Church was one. Although there were always plural political units and (part-)autonomous actors in pre-Reformation Christian Europe, they were within the Church. This means that those units and actors shared a common source of basic assumptions, which in turn goes a long way to explain why they developed in parallel fashion and were always more alike than different – even after both the intellectual monopoly and the unity of the Church at last came to an end.

The Church did not itself create all of the assumptions that it promoted, but adopted many from elsewhere. For example, ideas of monarchy were influenced on the one hand by the model of kingship offered by the Old Testament, but also merged with Germanic traditions of kingship and, last but not least, Roman traditions. Roman law itself, after the rediscovery of the Digest in the eleventh century, and Aristotelian political philosophy, after the translation of the relevant writings of Aristotle in the thirteenth century, were spread via people who, for a long time, were mostly clerics, servants of the one church.

It is certainly true that both the reintroduction and the study of the Digest (and the rest of the Justinian Code) and the Aristotelianism of the scholastics helped promote a process of intellectual emancipation from the Church, but because the Church had been universal even the new intellectual paradigms that came to some extent to compete with its teachings remained universal; universal in the sense that they were shared throughout European society regardless of political boundaries, which socially were not very important in any case before the nineteenth century.

What we have established, in the course of the past millennium, is a system, the European social and political system, in which individual political units gradually become more important than the whole that they make up, more important first politically and then also socially. At the same time, however, they do so under the influence of the same shared ideas and with results that, for all the variations from one individual case to the next, retain many fundamental similarities in the assumptions on which they are based and in the institutional arrangements resulting from those assumptions.

This means that although these political units – which eventually begin to take the shape of what we call states – grow more distinct and separate from each other, they continue to speak the same language in terms of basic concepts. Historians and also IR scholars are apt to pay too much attention to conflict, because it is so dramatic and visible, while at the same time they overlook the importance of fundamental structures that both enable and accommodate as well as outlast those conflicts. We have to bear in mind that the basic structures of pre- and post-Reformation Europe were not created by war so much as it was those structures that conditioned the kind of violent conflict observable in a given place or period – for example, the very different modes of warfare between thirteenth-century knights, eighteenth-century mercenary armies and twentieth-century conscript armies. Those striking differences cannot be explained without reference to the basic assumptions underlying thirteenth-, eighteenth- or twentieth-century society.

Where do we find those assumptions? As pointed out, such assumptions only create durable social and political structures if they are widely shared, which means that they must be communicated. We therefore find them in discourse that people of a given period and community address to each other. Among the sources for such discourse, as far as the overarching, 'international' system is concerned, peace talks are among the most fruitful because the record of the negotiations will reflect the views of those actually in a position to take important decisions. Thus I think we can learn much more about the assumptions underlying European politics in the mid-seventeenth century by studying the wealth of documentation left by the Peace Congress of Münster and Osnabrück than we can by studying, say, the (near-)contemporary writings of Hugo Grotius (1583–1645). The problem with the thinking of intellectuals like Grotius is that, while they were clearly widely read, and their ideas must have been influential, it is hard to determine just how great their impact was on given policy-makers at given key junctures in history. To put it in pointed fashion, political thinkers are good, but actual political discourse, where we have enough of it to form a reliable database, is better.

When we are concerned with understanding the European system as a whole, and the politics of its component autonomous actors, peace conferences are evidently among the best sources of the relevant kind of political discourse, especially peace conferences where the fate of the system as a whole was at stake, or at least the fate of important parts of the system. What people tell each other during negotiations of that kind will tell us exactly what common conceptual language, which common assumptions, they thought the system was, could or should be based on. And it is those assumptions that tell us most about why the system took the shape that it did and why that shape evolved.

In this context a point concerning the way the records of such negotiations are used bears emphasising. In the past, historians have almost always used those documents to distil some kind of inherent 'truth' more or less distinct from the actual semantics of the text being studied. For example, in a diplomatic note they would try to look 'beyond' the niceties of protocol, or the attempt to disguise something potentially embarrassing through conciliatory verbiage, and to get to the core, the 'real' intentions encrypted in the documents. They shunned the rhetorical wrapping, as it were; they were wary of being misled by mere justificatory phraseology; they may well have been bored by the way certain phrases and concepts recurred in ritualised, incantatory and therefore monotonous fashion.

All that is treated as superficial, even as hypocritical, deception surely being an important ingredient of diplomacy. But, from the perspective of the approach suggested here, the rhetorical wrapping, the self-justification of the negotiators through the invocation of certain principles that everybody acknowledges, even their adversaries, are no less important than the specific messages that documents contain. I have shown in my work on European peace conferences how the way negotiators justify themselves is different from one period to the next. The principles invoked in justification are different. This mirrors, indeed at least in part accounts for, the way the system itself evolves.[34]

---

[34] Andreas Osiander, *The States System of Europe 1640–1990: Peacemaking and the Conditions of International Stability* (Oxford, 1994).

Whatever the intentions and private interests of the parties, to reach a compromise that is acceptable to all involved and that can be 'sold' to the wider public that is not directly involved but may be important nevertheless, requires finding an outcome that is in line with general principles, basic assumptions about the common political ('international') system shared by all. To give just one example, the negotiations leading to the Peace Treaties of Utrecht of 1712–15 were caused by the semi-defection of the British Crown from the anti-Bourbon alliance and its readiness to make considerable concessions to Louis XIV (1643–1715) to bring about an end to the war, urgently desired by the new Tory government that had replaced the pro-war Whigs in power. Yet in the course of the negotiations the British foreign minister, Bolingbroke, warned that the French ought not to overplay their hand and rely too much on British readiness to indulge them, writing to one of the British plenipotentiaries at Utrecht that 'France must come to form such a project as the queen [Anne of Britain] will accept, *and can justify herself to her allies, to God, and to all the world.*'[35]

As those principles or assumptions change, so does the system, and to trace that it is necessary to look at the general terms of reference that, for example, diplomatic correspondence exhibits, and not just at specific content. It is in this sense and in this context, then, that the study of concepts and norms in peacemaking processes can elucidate the evolution of the European system. On their own they will not account fully for that evolution, since the discourse of 'official' politics is more shaped by the general discourse underlying society and its component units (autonomous or not) than the other way around. It is probably true that, except in special, revolutionary circumstances, politics is shaped by the social context in which it takes place more than that context is shaped by politics. But that is no reason for not studying politics in its own right, and, while the impact of political interaction and processes on social structures should not be overestimated, neither is it unimportant.

---

[35] Quoted in Osiander, *States System*, p. 153; emphasis added. I have sought to document in the book (*States System*, ch. 3) how this meant that any decision in the peace treaties had to be in line with, or at least not contradict too visibly, the notions prevailing in early eighteenth-century Europe of what ought or ought not to be done in dealings among autonomous actors.

PART IV

Making peace: aspects of treaty practice

15

The *ius foederis* re-examined: the Peace of Westphalia and the constitution of the Holy Roman Empire

RONALD G. ASCH

Introduction

The Peace of Westphalia occupies a special place among the early modern peace treaties. The agreements signed in Osnabrück and Münster on 24 October 1648 were both international contracts and fundamental laws of the Holy Roman Empire. In fact, it would be difficult to find another legal document in the early modern period in which these two aspects, domestic constitutional settlement and international agreement, are so closely combined. Of course, it is not easy to take a fresh look at this important treaty three years after the prolonged and sometimes perhaps even slightly excessive festivities which marked the 350th anniversary of the Westphalian Peace.[1] One might very well feel that everything that could be said on this subject has indeed been said. I shall therefore try to concentrate on one aspect of the Peace Treaties, which – although frequently discussed – has remained particularly controversial: the *ius foederis*, the *Bündnisrecht der Reichsstände*. First, however, we will have to examine the character of the war which preceded the conference in Münster and Osnabrück, as the settlement achieved in 1648 can only be understood in the context of the conflict it sought to end.

---

[1] See, in particular, Klaus Bußmann and Heinz Schilling (eds.), *1648: Krieg und Frieden in Europa* (3 vols., Münster, 1998); Heinz Duchhardt (ed.), *Der westfälische Frieden: Diplomatie, politische Zäsur, kulturelles Umfeld, Rezeptionsgeschichte* (Munich, 1998) and Klaus Garber and Jutta Held (eds.), *Der Frieden: Rekonstruktion einer europäischen Vision* (2 vols., Paderborn, 2001), in particular vol. II, dealing with the political and legal aspects; Ronald G. Asch, Wulf Eckhart Voss and Martin Wrede (eds.), *Frieden und Krieg in der frühen Neuzeit: die Staatenordnung Europas und die außereuropäische Welt* (Paderborn, 2001).

The Thirty Years War

The Thirty Years War was ended by a peace conference in which most of the major European powers took part. However, the Thirty Years War had begun – at least to some extent – as an internal conflict in the Holy Roman Empire. Admittedly, Spain had been involved right from the beginning as the emperor's ally and because it took a keen interest in the supply routes for its armies in the southern Netherlands.[2] Nevertheless, in its earlier phases the Thirty Years War can be described as a civil war, not entirely unlike other civil wars which had gone on in Europe earlier such as the French Wars of Religion, or were to break out some years later such as the English Civil War or the *Fronde*. Historians have repeatedly tried to find a common denominator for the various domestic conflicts of this period. One of the solutions they offered is the famous crisis of the seventeenth century.[3] Allegedly, structural tensions, which had their origins not least in social and economic change, undermined the stability of the great European monarchies in the early seventeenth century, causing a series of domestic conflicts and revolts. It has always been difficult to fit the Thirty Years War into this model; to depict the war as a social conflict is hardly possible and, moreover, all the other major civil wars and rebellions took place in the 1640s while the war in Germany began twenty years earlier. In fact, to some extent the *Fronde* in France or the provincial rebellions in the Spanish Empire[4] were a result of the Thirty Years War, of the fiscal burdens it had forced governments to impose and the political change that it had created, rather than the expression of a major social and political crisis that preceded the war.

---

[2] For the history of the war, see Geoffrey Parker *et al.*, *The Thirty Years' War* (2nd edn, London, 1997); Johannes Burkhardt, *Der Dreißigjährige Krieg* (Frankfurt am Main, 1992); Georg Schmidt, *Der Dreißigjährige Krieg* (Munich, 1995); Ronald G. Asch, *The Thirty Years War: The Holy Roman Empire and Europe, 1618–1648* (Basingstoke, 1997); and most recently, Gerhard Schormann, 'Dreißigjähriger Krieg 1618–1648' in Wolfgang Reinhard (ed.), *Gebhardt Handbuch der deutschen Geschichte* (Stuttgart, 2001), vol. X, pp. 207–79.

[3] Most recently, Sheila C. Ogilvie, 'Germany and the Seventeenth-Century Crisis', *Historical Journal* 35 (1992), 417–41, with references to older publications.

[4] For Spain, see John H. Elliott, *The Revolt of the Catalans* (Cambridge, 1963); Jean-Frédéric Schaub, 'La crise hispanique de 1640. Le modèle des "révolutions périphériques" en question', *Annales Economiques Sociologiques Culturelles* 49 (1994), 219–39; John H. Elliott *et al.* (eds.), *La monarquía hispánica en crisis* (Barcelona, 1992); M. Angels Pérez Samper, *Catalunya i Portugal en 1640: dos pobles en una cruilla* (Barcelona, 1992) and I. A. A. Thompson and Bartholomé Yun Casalilla (eds.), *The Castilian Crisis of the Seventeenth Century: New Perspectives on the Economic and Social History of Seventeenth-Century Spain* (Cambridge, 1994).

Nevertheless, the early seventeenth century was clearly a time of great political instability, and the Thirty Years War can to some extent be considered part of a series of internal conflicts in many parts of Europe. Although the model of the composite monarchy or the great dynastic union of states comprising a number of distinct principalities and dominions is certainly not tailor made for the Holy Roman Empire – it fits the Spanish Empire or the realm of the German Habsburgs or even the Stuart monarchy much better – the tensions which gave rise to violent conflict in Germany before 1618 are not altogether dissimilar from the structural problems of the great dynastic state, and the Bohemian rebellion of 1618 is, of course, a classical example of a provincial rebellion defending regional autonomy and privileges.[5]

But even in the Empire we find, on the one hand, a central monarchical power asserting its authority and, on the other hand, local or regional centres of power trying to defend their own position. Recent interpretations have stressed that the Thirty Years War has to be seen as a *Staatsbildungskrieg*, a war that was brought about by and was part of a process of state building.[6] Although the author of this thesis, Johannes Burkhardt, possibly overestimated the extent to which the idea of a universal monarchy, an Empire claiming a supreme authority over the entire Christian world, was still a viable model in the early seventeenth century, he was probably right in assuming that in many ways it was the deficiencies of the existing state structure that had caused and prolonged the Thirty Years War, and not so much the conflicting interests within a fully established system of sovereign states. However, as opposed to Burkhardt, I would emphasise more strongly the fact that the war effort itself led to an escalation of the conflict. Limited conflicts in central Europe and elsewhere became part of an all-embracing war which could no longer be controlled or contained, because the political and fiscal efforts which were necessary to fight even the initially more limited campaigns undermined the stability of the existing political structure and gained a momentum of their own.

---

[5] For the composite monarchies of the early modern period, see Helmut G. Koenigsberger, 'Dominium Regale or Dominium Politicum et Regale? Monarchies and Parliaments in Early Modern Europe' in Helmut G. Koenigsberger (ed.), *Politicians and Virtuosi* (London, 1986), pp. 1–26; John H. Elliott, 'A Europe of Composite Monarchies', *Past and Present* 137 (1992), 48–71.

[6] Burkhardt, *Dreißigjährige Krieg*, pp. 63–89; Johannes Burkhardt, 'Der Dreißigjährige Krieg als frühmoderner Staatsbildungskrieg', *Geschichte in Wissenschaft und Unterricht* 45 (1994), 487–99; and Johannes Burkhardt, 'Die Friedlosigkeit der Frühen Neuzeit. Grundlegung einer Theorie der Bellizität Europas', *Zeitschrift für Historische Forschung* 24 (1997), 509–74 at pp. 513–35 and 570–74.

This is most clearly visible in the case of the Spanish monarchy, which concentrated a very considerable percentage of its immense force on the attempt to prevent a rebellious province, the Northern Netherlands, from achieving full sovereignty or in fact any sort of sovereignty under conditions which were unacceptable to Madrid. The ensuing Eighty Years War forced Spain to coordinate its military effort from Portugal over Naples to the Franche Comté much more consistently than in the past and to reassert its hegemony in northern Italy, thereby giving more coherence to the Empire but also causing fresh conflicts with smaller dynasties and neighbouring powers, as in the case of Mantua in 1627/28 or with regional interests as in Catalonia and Portugal in 1640.[7]

Although France was much more of a unitary state than the Spanish Empire, the series of revolts, which culminated in the *Fronde* in 1648, were also to a large extent reactions to the enormous pressure the war effort exerted on the social and political fabric.[8] In Germany, the war had its origins in confessional and political tensions, which had gradually escalated since the 1580s. The reason, however, that it proved impossible to end the war once it had begun lay to a considerable extent in the fact that the war effort tended to create new problems. The need to finance vast armies and to reward their leaders – be they princes of the Empire like Maximilian of Bavaria (1598–1651) or military entrepreneurs like Wallenstein (1583–1634) – both politically and financially, undermined the traditional constitution of the Empire. This is particularly visible in the 1620s, when the war effort got totally out of hand and swept away all constitutional constraints – although the dismissal of Wallenstein in 1630 was certainly a belated attempt to impose some political control on

---

[7] For warfare, in general see Ronald G. Asch, 'Warfare in the Age of the Thirty Years War 1598–1648' in Jeremy Black (ed.), *European Warfare, 1435–1815* (Basingstoke, 1999), pp. 45–68 and 250–6; for its effect on the Spanish monarchy, see most recently I. A. A. Thompson, 'The Impact of War and Peace on Government and Society in Seventeenth Century Spain' in Asch *et al.* (eds.), *Frieden und Krieg*, pp. 161–79, as well as I. A. A. Thompson, 'Aspectos de la organization naval y militar durante el Ministerio de Olivares' in John H. Elliott and Angel Garcia Sanz (eds.), *La España de Conde Duque de Olivares* (Valladolid, 1990), pp. 249–74 and Juan Gelabert, 'El impacto de la guerra y del fiscalismo en Castilla' in Elliott and Garcia Sanz, *La España*, pp. 555–74. See also John H. Elliott, *The Count-Duke of Olivares: The Statesman in an Age of Decline* (New Haven, Conn., 1986), in particular pp. 244–77, 337–45 and 553–71. For the impact of the war outside Spain, see Antonio Calabria, *The Cost of Empire: The Finances of the Kingdom of Naples in the Time of Spanish Rule* (Cambridge, 1991).

[8] For the *Fronde*, see most recently: A. Lloyd Moote, *The Revolt of the Judges: The Parlement of Paris and the Fronde (1643–52)* (Princeton, 1971); M. Pernot, *La Fronde* (Paris, 1994); Orest A. Ranum, *The Fronde: A French Revolution 1648–1652* (New York, 1993).

warfare once more.⁹ Not until the Peace of Prague in 1635 did the emperor and most of the German princes reach some sort of consensus on the way in which to organise the war in such a way that effective warfare and the raising of contributions remained compatible with the legal structure of the Empire. It may seem a paradox, but clearly the war could not be ended before an acceptable solution had been reached on how to fight it and before a consensus had been achieved about the specific roles the emperor, the imperial circles and the princes were to play in organising the war effort. Although recent research has shown that the system of financing the war effort established in 1635 was at least to some extent a success, matters had already gone too far and the Peace of Prague proved abortive.¹⁰

Thus, one of the essential problems which the Treaty of Prague had tried to address remained on the agenda in Osnabrück and Münster: the problem of the *ius armorum* and the *ius foederis* for the Estates of the Empire. What type of *Kriegsverfassung* (military constitution) was the Empire to adopt: the type of centralised organisation which the Peace of Prague had tried to establish or a much more decentralised structure which left each Estate of the Empire at liberty to make its own political and military arrangements?

The Peace of Westphalia and the constitution of the Empire

This decision on the future *Kriegsverfassung* of the Empire had serious implications for the constitution of the Empire, for its ability to survive

---

⁹ For this phase of the war, see Asch, *Thirty Years War*, pp. 98–100 and 158–60. For the entrepreneurial system of warfare and its impact, see F. Redlich, *The German Military Enterpriser and His Workforce: A Study in European Economic and Social History* (2 vols., Wiesbaden, 1964–65). Still useful is Moriz Ritter, 'Das Kontributionssystem Wallenstein', *Historische Zeitschrift* 90 (1903), 193–249. For the resistance against Wallenstein's methods to finance his army, see Dieter Albrecht, *Maximilan I von Bayern 1573–1651* (Munich, 1998), pp. 673–9.

¹⁰ For the Peace of Prague and its impact, see Heiner Haan, 'Kaiser Ferdinand II. und das Problem des Reichsabsolutismus. Die Prager Heeresreform von 1635', *Historische Zeitschrift* 207 (1968), 297–345; Albrecht, *Maximilian*, pp. 907–48, and, most recently, Kathrin Bierther, 'Einleitung' in Kathrin Bierther (ed.), *Briefe und Akten zur Geschichte des Dreißigjährigen Krieges, Neue Folge: die Politik Maximilians I. und seiner Verbündeten 1618–1651*, Section II, vol. X: *Der Prager Frieden 1635* (4 parts, Munich and Vienna, 1997), part I, pp. 11–241 (hereinafter referred to as II BA NF). For the effect of the military reforms undertaken in Prague, see Hubert Salm, *Armeefinanzierung im Dreißigjährigen Krieg: der niederrheinisch-westfälische Reichskreis 1635–1650* (Münster, 1990) and Cordula Kapser, *Die bayerische Kriegsorganisation in der zweiten Hälfte des Dreißigjährigen Krieges 1635–1648/49* (Münster, 1997).

as an autonomous political system, possibly even perhaps as a type of federal state within the European system of states. A traditional interpretation widely current before World War II but still influential after 1945 argued that the Westphalian Peace was the first step in a long-term process transforming the Empire, which could have developed into a state instead into a mere confederation of almost independent separate principalities.[11] Recently, however, the opposite interpretation has been much more influential; an interpretation which considers the Empire as a true though highly decentralised state, in many ways comparable to other early modern states. This is definitely a new perspective, which has managed to provoke not only a great deal of new research but also a heated intellectual debate.[12]

Undoubtedly, there is a certain tendency among younger German historians these days to celebrate the Holy Roman Empire as a wonderful work of art in which the privileges of the individual princes and Estates, the authority of the Imperial Diet and the power of the emperor created a most miraculous balance and equilibrium.[13] Thus, the Empire is no longer seen as a somewhat chaotic and difficult to define political system

---

[11] Even Fritz Dickmann, who did a great deal to revise the traditional image of the Westphalian Peace, still subscribed to this view; Fritz Dickmann, *Der Westfälische Frieden* (6th edn, Münster, 1972), p. 494: 'Der Frieden bedeutete für unser Volk ein nationales Unglück und für das Heilige Römische Reich, in dem es bisher seine staatliche Form gefunden hatte, den Anfang der tödlichen Krankheit, der es schließlich erlag.' ('For our nation the peace was a disaster and for the Holy Roman Empire, in which our nation had in the past found its political organisation, the beginning of a deadly disease, to which it was to succumb eventually.')

[12] Georg Schmidt, 'Der Westfälische Friede – eine neue Ordnung für das Alte Reich?' in Ernst-Wolfgang Böckenförde and Reinhard Mussgnung (eds.), *Wendemarken in der deutschen Verfassungsgeschichte* (= *Der Staat*, Beiheft 10, Berlin, 1993), pp. 45–72; Georg Schmidt, *Geschichte des alten Reiches: Staat und Nation in der frühen Neuzeit 1495–1806* (Munich, 1999), pp. 177–93; Schmidt, 'Deutschland am Beginn der Neuzeit: Reichsstaat und Kulturnation?' in Christine Roll, Bettina Braun and Horst Rabe (eds.), *Recht und Reich im Zeitalter der Reformation: Festschrift für Horst Rabe* (Frankfurt am Main, 1996), pp. 1–30; for a position directly opposed to Schmidt's interpretation, see Heinz Schilling, 'Reichs-Staat und frühneuzeitliche Nation der Deutschen oder teilmodernisiertes Reichssystem. Überlegungen zu Charakter und Aktualität des alten Reiches', *Historische Zeitschrift* 272 (2001), 377–95; but see also Schmidt's reply, *Historische Zeitschrift* 272 (2001), 377–95.

[13] See, for example, Wolfgang Burgdorf, 'Nationales Erwachen der Deutschen nach 1756. Reichisches gegen territoriales Nationalbewußtsein. Imitation eines Schweizer Vorbildes oder Inszenierung des kaiserlichen Hofes?' in Marco Bellabarba and Reinhard Stauber (eds.), *Territoriale Identität und politische Kultur in der frühen Neuzeit* (Bologna and Berlin, 1999), pp. 109–32 and Wolfgang Burgdorf, ' "Reichsnationalismus" gegen "Territorialnationalismus". Phasen der Intensivierung des nationalen Bewußtseins in Deutschland seit dem Siebenjährigen Krieg' in Dieter Langewiesche and Georg Schmidt (eds.), *Föderative Nation: Deutschlandkonzepte von der Reformation bis zum ersten Weltkrieg* (Munich, 1999), pp. 157–89.

which managed to preserve some degree of stability and peace in Central Europe but which fell far short of the criteria a proper state would have to meet; instead, it is depicted by Georg Schmidt and others as a *Reichs-Staat*, or rather as a *komplementäre Reichs-Staat* – a political structure which was at once an Empire (that is, at the same time more and less than a mere state) and a 'normal' state, and in which the imperial institutions and those of the individual principalities and territories complemented each other, each fulfilling certain distinct functions.

In this development of the Empire towards statehood, the Westphalian Peace is seen no longer as a set-back but rather as a step forward, as a legal settlement which gave the Empire a constitution at last and which at the same time managed to integrate northern and eastern Germany, which had allegedly played no real part in the late medieval and in the sixteenth-century Empire.[14]

It is beyond the scope of this chapter to discuss these matters very deeply, but in the present context it is mainly the impact of the Westphalian Peace which is of interest. Quite clearly the *ius foederis* and its treatment in the *instrumenta pacis* have always held a particularly prominent place in the debate about the constitutional impact of the Peace of Westphalia. As is well known, the treaty conceded the full *ius foederis*: the right to conclude alliances with other Estates or indeed European princes as long as these alliances were not directed against *Kaiser und Reich*, the emperor and the Empire as a body politic.[15] If one looks at the older interpretation in,

---

[14] Georg Schmidt, 'Der westfälische Friede als Grundgesetz des komplementären Reichs-Staats' in Bußmann and Schilling (eds.), *1648: Krieg und Frieden*, vol. I, pp. 447–54, in particular p. 453: 'Ob das strukturbedingt nicht angriffsfähige Reich ein Staat war, bleibt eine Definitionsfrage. Auch wenn der komplementäre Reichs-Staat die Kriterien eines National-, Macht- oder Steuerstaates nicht unbedingt erfüllte, war er doch ein politisch zielgerichtet handlungsfähiges System mit kaiserlicher Spitze – ein Staat.' ('Whether the Empire which was structurally incapable of attacking its neighbours was a state is a matter of definition. Even if the *komplementäre Reichs-Staat* did not meet the criteria of national or fiscal state or of a state acting as a great power on the international stage, it certainly was a political system which was fully capable of defending its interests under the emperor's leadership – in other words it was a state after all.') Interestingly enough, Schmidt had taken a different, more cautious line a few years before. See Schmidt, 'Eine neue Ordnung', p. 71: 'Er [Der westfälische Friede] machte das Reich keineswegs überflüssig, sondern garantierte dessen Fortbestand in seiner bewährten Form. Er blockierte allerdings dessen Staatswerdung [sic] oder die Umwandlung in ein monarchisches System.' ('The Westphalian Peace did not make the Empire obsolete; rather it secured its survival in its traditional well-established form. However it did prevent its transformation into a proper state [sic!] or into a purely monarchical system.')

[15] The words of the IPO, Art. 8 (2) were: 'Cumprimis vero ius faciendi inter se et cum exteris foedera pro sua cuiusque conservatione ac securitate singulis Statibus perpetuo liberum esto; ita tamen, ne eiusmodi foedera sint contra Imperatorem et Imperium pacemque

for example, Ernst Wolfgang Böckenförde's famous article in *Der Staat* of 1969, the *ius foederis* is seen as one of the hallmarks of sovereignty. Böckenförde recognised that this was not yet the case in the fifteenth and sixteenth centuries, when formal alliances were not all that different from feudal obligations or from the type of cooperation between princely dynasties which was based on kinship and personal friendship. In the course of the seventeenth century, however, the quality of diplomatic alliances changed. In Western Europe mere noblemen and princes now lost the ability to take part in international European politics; the sovereign states which enjoyed both full *ius foederis* and *ius belli et pacis* were the sole actors left on the European state. Not so, however, in Central Europe, where the Westphalian Peace gave the German territorial princes a status not altogether dissimilar from that of sovereign rulers, in spite of the fact that in theory at least they remained the Emperor's liegemen and subjects.[16]

---

eius publicam vel hanc imprimis Transactionem fiantque salvo per omnia Iuramento quo quisque Imperatori et Imperio obstrictus est.' ('Firstly the individual Estates of the Empire shall enjoy forever the right to conclude alliances among each other or with foreign powers for defensive purposes; in such a way, however, that such alliances should not be directed against the Emperor or the Empire as such and its peaceful order and in particular this treaty. Moreover they should not violate the oath by which each Estate has sworn allegiance and fealty to the Emperor and the Empire.') For the text, see also Heinz Duchhardt (ed.), *Der westfälische Frieden: das münstersche Exemplar des Vertrages zwischen Kaiser/Reich und Frankreich vom 24. Oktober 1648* (2 vols., Wiesbaden, 1996), vol. I.

[16] Ernst-Wolfgang Böckenförde, 'Der westfälische Frieden und das Bündnisrecht der Reichsstände', *Der Staat* 8 (1969), 449–78, in particular at pp. 458–63 and 477: 'Indem der westfälische Frieden das Bündnisrecht der Reichsstände anerkannte und des Kaisers ständischer Zustimmung unterwarf, hat er die Staatwerdung der Territorien sanktioniert, das föderative Element der Reichsverfassung wesentlich verstärkt und dem Reich Züge einer Staatenföderation angeheftet.' And – summing up – 'Lehensrechtliche, königsherrschaftliche, ständisch-territoriale und die nun verstärkten föderativen Strukturen zusammen bildeten und bestimmten den Verfassungsbau des Reiches. Der staatsrechtlich-völkerrechtliche Zwischenzustand war weiterhin das signum für den politischen Status des Reichs.' ('Because the Westfalian Peace acknowledged the right of the individual Estates to conclude alliances and restricted the Emperor's right to do so by forcing him to act with the consent of the Estates, it accepted the character of the various territories and principalities as states. Moreover it reinforced the federal element of the imperial constitution and transformed the Empire to some extent into a federation of individual states.' And, summing up: 'Structures which rested on feudal law, royal authority, the power of the territorial princes and the now increasingly federal character of the entire system made up – taken together – the constitutional fabric of the Empire. In terms of public and international law the ill-defined half-way position of the Empire [between state and confederation] remained unchanged and was indeed the characteristic mark of the Empire's constitution.')

Against Böckenförde, Georg Schmidt has argued in particular, but also other scholars have said that all alliances the princes of the Empire wanted to conclude remained subject to the principle of *Reichstreue* (loyalty to the Empire). This would not have been the case had they been truly sovereign. Moreover, Schmidt, but also Dickmann and Ruppert before him, have pointed out that the imperial delegation in Osnabrück and Münster accepted the French and Swedish proposals to concede the *ius foederis* to the Estates without much reluctance. In fact, some of the resistance against these proposals came not so much from the Emperor but from some of the princes, the Electors in particular.[17] Thus, the *ius foederis* in this perspective was not much more than a return to the *status quo ante* which had obtained before the Peace of Prague in 1635, when all alliances of princes within the Empire had been officially dissolved. Compared to the situation before 1618 nothing much had changed; on the contrary, the ancient constitution of the Empire had been re-established.[18]

To assess these arguments, first I want to examine the Peace of Prague and its origin, which had clearly prohibited alliances within the Empire and, secondly, I want to look at the discussions on the *ius foederis* in Osnabrück and Münster.

The *ius foederis* in the Peace of Prague

When Saxony entered into negotiations with the emperor in 1634, with the objective to end the war by finding a compromise for the controversial confessional and constitutional issues, the Saxon delegation already favoured a solution which would end the existence of all special confederations and alliances within the Empire.[19] Quite clearly, this proposal was directed primarily against the Catholic League led by Bavaria. On this point, the interests of Saxony and those of the emperor and the House of Austria were not all that different. Johann Caspar von Stadion, Grand Master of the Teutonic Order (1627–41), had already submitted a detailed memorandum to the emperor in December 1634, in which he argued that the imperial war effort was much hindered by the independent position which Bavaria

---

[17] Schmidt, 'Eine neue Ordnung', pp. 68–70; Karsten Ruppert, *Die kaiserliche Politik auf dem westfälischen Friedenskongreß* (Münster, 1979), p. 113.
[18] For the pre-1648 situation, see Dirk Götschmann, 'Das Ius Armorum. Ausformung und politische Bedeutung der reichsständischen Militärhoheit bis zu ihrer definitiven Anerkennung im westfälischen Frieden', *Blätter für Deutsche Landesgeschichte* 129 (1993), 257–76.
[19] Bierther, 'Einleitung', p. 239.

and its immediate allies still maintained. This excessive autonomy had been the reason why all attempts to put more pressure on the Republic of the Netherlands and defend the fortress of 's-Hertogenbosch (1629) had failed, for example. Only if all German armies were united under one imperial high command could the war be pursued successfully and the enemies of the Empire be forced to retreat and leave German soil.[20] Stadion's chancellor Eustachius Soll had pointed out, moreover, that the continued existence of the League posed a considerable danger should the emperor die before his successor had been elected. In this case, Saxony and Bavaria would act as regents or *Vicarii* in the Empire and could possibly prevent the election of another Habsburg prince.[21]

On the other hand, Soll was fully aware that the League was far less powerful in 1634 than it had been in the 1620s. Effectively, only the ecclesiastical principalities ruled by Wittelsbach bishops really cooperated with Bavaria, that is, primarily Cologne and Osnabrück (the latter ruled by Franz Wilhelm von Wartenberg, 1625–61, who was the offspring of a *mésalliance* between a Wittelsbach and a woman of lesser status). All the others had either been forced to flee into exile because their dominions were occupied by French or Swedish troops, or had been inclined to co-operate directly with the emperor, and not with Bavaria. However, according to Soll this very weakness of the League had to be exploited cautiously; a direct dissolution of the alliance would provoke a strong anti-Habsburg reaction.[22]

In this discussion, the legal question whether princes such as the Elector of Bavaria were entitled to conclude alliances with other Estates or not did not really play a very prominent role. Political and military considerations were much more important. Nevertheless, Stadion pointed out that the League had initially been approved by the emperor to maintain the political balance between the Protestants and Catholics, but that the continued existence of this alliance without imperial consent – and Stadion was clearly in favour of withholding this consent – would be illegal.

---

[20] Memorial by Deutschmeister, 16 Dec. 1634, II BA NF vol. IX: Juni 1634–Mai 1635 (Munich and Vienna, 1986), no. 176, pp. 392–8. The Grand Master had argued the league should be dissolved, 'weil sonsten in dem Römischen Reich niemand anders [als] dem Kaiser die waffen zu führen und einem ieden rechtens zu verhelfen, obligen und gebühren thuet' (p. 395) ('because otherwise in the Roman Empire only the Emperor is allowed to employ force of arms for purposes of law enforcement').

[21] Notes by Dr Johann Eustachius Soll for planned discussion with General Gallas, 20 Dec. 1634, II BA NF vol. IX, no. 178, p. 405.

[22] II BA NF vol. IX, no. 178, p. 406.

Only the emperor had the right to recruit armed forces in Germany and to maintain justice and peace.[23]

After the Habsburg victory over the Swedes in the battle of Nördlingen (1634), such a position was much more realistic than in the past. The Treaty of Pirna signed in November 1634 between Saxony and the emperor had indeed declared illegal all special alliances and confederations in the Empire. However, at Saxony's insistence a paragraph had been inserted into the treaty, which declared that the Protestant Estates should remain entitled to co-operate more closely among themselves to defend their interests. This Article 135 carefully avoided the word *Bündnis* or *foedus*; instead it spoke of 'einigkeit und aufrichtiges, freundliche[s] vertrawen', but what the difference between this mutual trust and a full-scale alliance was remained somewhat unclear.[24] Initially, Saxony had even demanded that all imperial mandates against such a closer cooperation among the Protestants should automatically be invalid, as long as this co-operation remained defensive in character. This proposal was not accepted; nevertheless, the Treaty of Pirna, which clearly abrogated the League, was favourable enough for the Protestants on this point.[25]

The final Peace Treaty signed in Prague in 1635 omitted the special pro-Protestant clause, which was plausibly enough seen by some of the imperial councillors as a belated justification for the military actions the Protestants had taken in the earlier stages of the war, in the 1620s and after the Swedish intervention in 1630 in particular.[26] Nevertheless, the League was dissolved and officially a unified imperial military command for all

---

[23] Memorandum by Deutschmeister, pp. 395–7.
[24] Treaty of Pirna, Art. 133: 'Es sollen auch inn und mit aufrichtung dieses friedensschlußes und deßen publication alle und iede uniones, ligae und foedera ... aufgehoben sein'; cf. Art. 135: 'Sondern es soll auch von den catholischen ständen nicht übel aufgenommen werden, daß die Augspurgische confessionsverwandte und protestierende eine gute einigkeit und aufrichtiges, freundliches vertrawen unter sich erhalten und keiner den anderen, das publicum betreffent verlaße.' ('By this peace treaty all alliances, confederations and leagues ... are void'; cf. Art. 135: 'However the Catholic Estates shall take no offence, that the Protestants who adhere to the Confessio Augustana maintain a good understanding, unity and friendly trust among themselves and that none of them deserts the other in public matters.')
[25] Saxon demands, II BA NF vol. X, part 3, no. 448, p. 1025 (June 1634) in particular Art. 26, p. 1027; if the Catholics were to conclude an alliance of their own – against the letter and spirit of the treaty – the Protestants were to have the same right. Imperial mandates against them were to be regarded as if they had never been issued, 'alß ob sie nie ergangen von maniglichen geachtet und gehalten werden'. This paragraph provoked a strong protest by the archbishop of Cologne. See part 4, no. 348, p. 788 (October 1634).
[26] Treaty of Prague, Art. 85. For the reservations the imperial councillors had about the earlier Treaty of Pirna, see the Memorandum by imperial envoys 20 Jan. 1635, II BA NF

armed forces in the Empire was created. In practice, Saxony and Bavaria continued to command large forces independently or almost independently. Officially, these forces were part of one and the same imperial army under the emperor's high command. In practice, however, the Bavarian troops in particular were not fully integrated into the imperial army. Maximilian of Bavaria was prepared to accept that he himself now had a position similar to that of an imperial general. In fact, such a position offered definite advantages, as it allowed him to collect taxes and raise contributions in the Empire's name, something the Elector very successfully did after 1635, as recent research has shown. But Maximilian insisted that all imperial orders should be addressed to him and not directly to his troops or commanders. As long as the emperor did not command the *Reichsarmee* in person – the future Ferdinand III (1637–57) did so for a short time in his capacity as king of Hungary before he succeeded his father – Maximilian retained his freedom of action.[27] Maximilian therefore in the end managed to benefit from the constitutional and military arrangements of the Treaty of Prague.[28] As the League had already largely fallen apart, its dissolution was no great sacrifice to him, and the new arrangement gave him the necessary legal authority to raise contributions outside his own dominions, in the Bavarian, Swabian and Franconian circle, to finance his troops.[29]

Historians would nowadays be very reluctant therefore to see the Peace of Prague as an attempt to establish a sort of *Reichsabsolutismus*, imperial absolutism in Germany,[30] not least because clearly the articles of the treaty were first and foremost an expression of the military and political situation in 1635 and of the desire on the part of the emperor and his councillors to mobilise all forces against the French, and – though less so – against the Swedes and the States General. Nevertheless, the Peace of Prague did

---

vol. X, part 2, no. 106, p. 157 and the instruction for the imperial envoys 12 March 1635, II BA NF vol. X, part 2, no. 128, p. 242, and in particular 285–6.

[27] Kapser, *Kriegsorganisation*, pp. 15–29, cf. Haan, 'Reichsabsolutismus', and Andreas Kraus, 'Zur Vorgeschichte des Prager Friedens von 1635. Die Entstehung der Kommandoregelung nach Artikel 24' in H. Dickerhof (ed.), *Festgabe H. Hürten zum 60. Geburtstag* (Frankfurt am Main, 1988), pp. 265–99.

[28] Albrecht, *Maximilian*, pp. 924–33, in particular p. 933: 'Im Grunde hat er [Maximilian] das reichsfürstliche *ius armorum*, das ihm 1619 zu Beginn des Krieges von Ferdinand II. bestätigt worden war, in seiner Praxis weiterhin behauptet.' ('Essentially he managed to maintain the princely *ius armorum* which had been confirmed in his favour at the beginning of the war in 1619 by Emperor Ferdinand II.')

[29] Kapser, *Kriegsorganisation*, pp. 123–65.

[30] These problems are discussed by Burkhardt, *Dreißgjährige Krieg*, pp. 92–9.

provide a new model for the Empire's constitution. On the one hand, Prague had created a stronger central authority, and on the other hand it confirmed the special position of a select circle of princes identical more or less with the secular Electors who shared in this authority and who could expect to reinforce their own position by claiming to act in the Emperor's name. Military and political events were to ensure that this model had no really lasting impact, and it may therefore seem that Pirna and Prague were only a short-lived episode and that Osnabrück and Münster really marked the return not only to the *status quo* but also to the normal way of managing matters in the Empire.

Nevertheless, one should bear in mind that federations of Estates such as the League and the Union which had played such an important part in the politics of the Empire before 1618, and, as far as the latter is concerned, in the 1620s as well, were much less prominent after 1648 with the exception of the short-lived *Rheinbund* in the late 1650s.[31] The prohibition of alliances in the Peace of Prague was, of course, aimed particularly at the League, not at the more temporary *ad hoc* alliances between individual princes.

The *ius foederis* and the Peace of Westphalia

When the foreign Crowns of France and Sweden in 1645 demanded that a clause be inserted into the peace treaty which would grant all estates of the Empire the right freely to conclude alliances – a right which the French delegates expressly described as *droit de souveraineté*[32] – the reaction of

---

[31] For the Rheinbund, see Anton Schindling, 'Der erste Rheinbund und das Reich' in Volker Press (ed.), *Alternativen zur Reichsverfassung in der frühen Neuzeit* (Munich, 1995), pp. 123–9.

[32] French Proposition, June 1645, Johann Gottfried von Meiern (ed.), *Acta Pacis Westphalicae Publica oder westphälische Friedens-Handlungen und Geschichte* (Hanover, 1734–36), vol. I, p. 8: 'Que tous le princes et Estats en general en en pariculier seront maintenus dans tous autres droits de Souveraineté, qui leur appartiennent et specialement dans celuy de faire de Conféderations tant entre eux qu'avec les Princes voysins, pour leur conversation et secureté.' ('That all princes and Estates in general and in particular should be defended in their possession of all other rights of sovereignty which they have, and in particular in their right to conclude alliances among themselves and with neighbouring princes for their security.') Quite similar is the Swedish proposition; Von Meiern, *Acta*, vol. I, p. 437: 'Sicut autem dictis statibus omnia ipsis de iure competentia regalia perpetuo illibata manebunt, ita et ius faciendi cum exteris foedera pro sua cujusque conservatione et securitate, singulis perpetuo liberum esto.' (In the same way in which the abovementioned Estates shall enjoy all their rightful prerogatives for ever in peace, they should also have the freedom to conclude alliances with foreign powers for their security.')

the German princes and Estates was remarkably unenthusiastic.[33] Some of this lack of enthusiasm can by explained by the fact that the imperial representatives made no great efforts to defend the provisions of the Peace of Prague regarding the *ius foederis*. On the contrary, they quickly conceded the French and Swedish demands as long as alliances remained defensive and compatible with the obligations the princes owed to the Empire and its ruler.[34]

The Electors clearly preferred an arrangement which allowed them to control the emperor's foreign policy as well as that of the other princes and Estates to a solution which gave each Estate almost unlimited freedom of action in foreign affairs.[35] For the Electors it was important to impose limitations on the emperor's right to take political decisions for the Empire, to declare peace or war or conclude alliances.[36] Such limitations, however, were worth little if the emperor could act freely in his capacity as archduke of Austria and king of Bohemia.[37] The fact that Ferdinand III was extremely reluctant to abandon the alliance with Spain which threatened to undermine the peace settlement, was understandably a cause for grave apprehensions on the part of the Electors. They therefore argued that alliances with powers outside the Empire were really unnecessary and perhaps even dangerous, even if they remained officially defensive in character.[38]

---

[33] Dickmann, *Frieden*, pp. 326, 329–30; cf. Von Meiern, *Acta*, vol. I, p. 813, votum by the Protestant Estates: 'Contra imperium et rem publicam gebühret niemandem, weder haupt noch gliedern, wer der auch seyn mege, einige Bundniß zu machen.' (Against the Empire and the commonwealth, nobody, neither the supreme head nor the members, should conclude an alliance.')

[34] Ruppert, *Kaiserliche Politik*, pp. 114–15; cf. Von Meiern, *Acta*, vol. II, pp. 919–20, votum by the representatives of the prince Electors.

[35] Dickmann, *Frieden*, p. 330.

[36] Von Meiern, *Acta*, vol. II, pp. 919–20, Electoral votum, April 1646. The envoys stressed that the Electors were entitled to control imperial policy but that the policy of the princes was subject to imperial control; cf. Brandenburg's opinion, Von Meiern, Acta, vol. II, p. 936, April 1646, and APW III, *Protokolle, Verhandlungsakten, Diarien, Varia*, Section A, *Protokolle*, vol. I, *Die Beratungen der kurfürstlichen Kurie*, part i, 1645–47 (ed. Winfried Becker, Münster, 1975), p. 471.

[37] Of course, France was greatly interested in ending the alliance between Spain and the emperor. The French envoys welcomed a solution which permitted defensive alliances but prohibited alliances undertaken by Estates of the Empire which were offensive in character – such as the alliance between Austria and Spain (according to the French interpretation). See APW III, section C, *Diarien*, vol. III, *Diarium Wartenberg*, part ii, 1647–48 (ed. Joachim F. Foerster, Münster, 1988), pp. 723 and 1129.

[38] Cf. Von Meiern, *Acta*, vol. II, pp. 919–20.

The only justification for such alliances would be a situation where the emperor himself exceeded his authority and acted as a tyrant so that the estates had to appeal to a right of resistance. The Electors of Mainz and Saxony both argued that even if the emperor were to break the law, the Electors would be powerful enough to defend the Empire's well-established constitutions; no alliance with external powers should be necessary for this purpose 'weil daß reich vor sich selbsten mächtig genug, der gleichen beginnen zu begegnen'.[39] Saxony argued that a formal right for the Estates to conclude alliances with foreign powers could easily provoke a rebellion against the emperor, and was therefore not advisable.[40] The Elector of Trier was somewhat more cautious; after all, he had been taken prisoner by imperial troops during the war. Although he admitted that it was preferable to settle all conflicts in Germany without an appeal to outside help, it might well happen that the just privileges of an Estate were attacked so fundamentally that foreign assistance became indispensable. It could happen that an Estate was forced to take appropriate action, if 'lex defecto omnis iustitiae also enormiter laedirt, daß er zu imploration außwertiger zuläßiger assistenz getrungen würde'.[41]

However, Trier as well as Bavaria agreed that the allegiance the Estates owed the Empire and its ruler always had priority and had to be respected in treaties of alliance.[42] Although some of the members of the *Fürstenrat*, the Council of Princes, such as Hesse were much keener than the Electors to reduce the emperor's authority, an unlimited right to conclude alliances found no great favour with them either. In the Council of Princes, delegates argued that to grant the princes and Estates officially the right to conclude alliances even against the emperor, as the Swedish delegation had demanded, would undermine the imperial constitution. Even to discuss the question of what measures were fit to be taken if an emperor were to act illegally would only create unnecessary controversies: 'Wann ein Röm. Kayser etwas exorbitiere ... würden sich eveniente casu schon solche Mittel

---

[39] 'Because the Empire in itself is capable and powerful enough to deal with such matters'; APW III A, vol. I, part i, pp. 482–3, February 1646.
[40] APW III A, vol. I, part i, p. 783, 6 May 1647.
[41] It could happen that an Estate 'would be forced to implore foreign help because the law had been broken so blatantly and justice neglected so clearly that there was no other way out'; APW III A, vol. I, part i, p. 783, 24 April 1647.
[42] APW III A, vol. I, part i, p. 476 Kurbayern and p. 474 Trier, February 1646. Here Trier argued that emperor and Estates should jointly decide whether alliance was compatible with this allegiance or not.

finden, daß man dergleichen bündnissen gar nicht bedürffen würde.' This was an opinion which most members of the *Fürstenrat* shared (at least they did not openly contradict it), and the Württemberg representative went on record saying 'falls aber exorbitantien fürgiengen, hätte es schon allenthalben sein geweiste wege'.[43] Given the enormous conflicts of the last twenty-five years, this statement was rather surprising, but it shows that there was a general desire to leave well alone and to accept that peace could only be re-established if some of the most fundamental constitutional questions remained once and for all happily unresolved and were not even mentioned in polite company.

What needs to be emphasised is that both the prince electors and the princes or their representatives discussed the *ius foederis* not so much in the context of sovereignty but in the much more traditional context of the *Widerstandsrecht*, the right of resistance. Before 1618 even scholars who saw the Empire as a genuinely monarchical state had accepted that the Estates and princes as *magistratus inferiores* were – under certain circumstances – entitled to defend themselves against a ruler who acted as a tyrant. In many ways, this position was quite traditional before 1618. The truly controversial point was whether, at a given moment in time, the conditions for claiming a right of resistance were really met.[44]

On the other hand, the world was no longer the same in 1648 as in 1618. At the beginning of the seventeenth century, armed protests against unpopular political decisions and open rebellions had, even in a country such as France, been almost a well-established part of the political game. The line dividing the loyal courtier from the rebellious nobleman and *frondeur* remained a very fine one, as the late 1640s and early 1650s were once more to show. However, at this stage the rules of the game had

---

[43] 'Should a Roman Emperor do something illegal . . . ways and means certainly would be found in such a case to deal with such an emergency without such alliances.' And 'if exorbitant acts were committed, there were well established procedures to deal with such a situation'; Von Meiern, *Acta*, vol. II, pp. 318–19, Jan. 1646; cf. APW III A, vol. III, part ii, *Protokolle des Fürstenrates zu Osnabrück, 1645–46* (ed. Maria-Elisabeth Brunert, Münster, 1998), pp. 91–3, Nov. 1645; but cf. p. 549, where Lampadius (the envoy for the dukes of Brunswick) took a much more critical line and argued that the old laws and constitutions of the Empire should not be identified with the illegal practice of the last thirty years. 'Peccata' should not be identified with 'iura'. If the emperor did not claim the rights Tiberius had enjoyed in Rome, he had certainly acted in the past like Diocletian, who had persecuted the Christians.

[44] For discussion on the right of resistance, see most recently Robert von Friedeburg, *Widerstandsrecht und Konfessionskonflikt: Notwehr und Gemeiner Mann im deutsch-britischen Vergleich 1530 bis 1669* (Berlin, 1999).

already begun to change, and after 1660 in France as well as in other monarchies open revolt implied that one had abandoned all hopes for political advancement within the existing political system.[45]

In the Empire, on the other hand, older forms of resistance against unjust rulers continued to have some legal backing, as the *ius foederis* had clearly been understood in 1648 as part of this right of resistance. This interpretation of the *ius foederis* survived well into the eighteenth century. In 1709 Heinrich Henniges (d. 1711), a legal scholar and lawyer who served – for part of his career – Brandenburg-Prussia, argued in his well-known *Meditations on the Instrumentum Pacis* that the Estates of the Empire had the right to create a confederation against the emperor if the emperor ignored or attacked their well-established privileges, for example by supporting rebellious noblemen against the princes. Henniges thought that the way the emperor abused his position as supreme judge – the judgements given by the *Reichshofrat* in Vienna in favour of the *Reichsritterschaft* and other noblemen were in his opinion unfair and unjust – could well provide estates of the Empire with sufficient reasons to exercise their right of resistance and conclude appropriate defensive alliances:

> Aliquando etiam iudex ipse suspectus est alterius parte favore, vel quadam status ratione corruptus ut ius aequum et rectum ab eo frustra expectetur. Quod cum sit, sine crimine et maleficio est statibus, suis amicorum viribus se contra id genus injuriae et subita crudaque mandata iudicis munire, quando manifestum est, non modo contra leges iudicari, verum etiam occulte agi, ut iuris dicendi . . . auctoritas et iura statuum paulatim frangantur.[46]

In the past, Protestant confederations against the Catholics such as the Schmalkaldic League or the *Leipziger Konvent* of 1630 had also been

---

[45] For this point, see Arlette Jouanna, *Le Devoir de révolte: la noblesse française et la gestation de l'état moderne, 1559–1661* (Paris, 1989).

[46] 'Sometimes the judge himself is suspected of favouring unduly one of the two parties or is corrupted by political considerations so that one cannot expect a just sentence from him. In such a case the Estates have a right to defend themselves by their own and their friends' power against such an injustice and such sudden and cruel sentences, without committing a crime, when it is obvious that these sentences are given not only against law but with the secret intention to infringe the right of judicature and the prerogatives of the Estates'; Heinrich Henniges, *Meditationum ad instrumentum pacis caesaro-suecicum specimen I–IX* (s.l., 1706–12), vol. II (1709), Specimen VII regarding the *ius foederis*, p. 900.

justified for similar reasons. On the other hand, Henniges was careful to stress that in the last resort all Estates had to remain loyal not so much to the emperor but to the Empire as an institutional framework of politics.

This was a question of considerable importance when Henniges wrote in 1709, as Bavaria and Cologne were allied with France against the Empire. Such alliances, according to Henniges, were clearly inadmissible even if the Empire could not be considered a real state, 'una respublica' but only as a system of several states, 'systema plurium civitatum', for even this system was founded on certain permanent legal principles and mutual obligations, 'certis et aeternis pactis compositum', which could not be ignored.[47] This last remark clearly shows that it would be wrong to jump to the conclusion that the Empire remained or indeed became a genuine state in 1648, because its members were not entirely free to conclude whatever alliances they wished but had to remain loyal to the Empire; such, according to Henniges, could well be the case in a mere *systema plurium civitatum* which was not *una res publica*.[48]

Of course in practice only a small minority of the *Reichsstände* was able to pursue its own independent foreign policy after 1648. Bavaria tried to do so, but its attempt ended more or less in disaster in the War of the Spanish Succession (1700–13). In the last resort, only those prince Electors who also held royal titles outside the Empire could really act independently like other European rulers. In the eighteenth century this held good for Brandenburg and Hanover, and to a lesser extent for Saxony. For the other principalities of the Empire the *ius foederis* was much more a theoretical privilege than a right which really created new political chances and options.[49]

---

[47] Henniges, *Meditationum*, vol. II (1709), Specimen VII pp. 905–6.
[48] For the idea of the Empire as a *systema civitatum*, see Severinus de Monzambano [Samuel Pufendorf], 'De statu imperii Germanici' in Notker Hammerstein (ed.), *Staatslehre der frühen Neuzeit* (Frankfurt am Main, 1995), pp. 568–931 at pp. 831ff. (caput vi, § 9): 'Imo si tollas mutuam illam inter Imperatorem et Ordines renitentiam, iam erit revera Germania corpus aliquod seu systema sociorum inequali foedere nexorum.... Ergo commodissime Statum Germaniae possimus designare, quod proxime accedat ad systema aliquod plurium civitatum.' ('Indeed if you overcome the antagonism between the Emperor and the Estates, Germany will in fact be a body politic or a system of allies which are bound by an inequal treaty ... Therefore, we can most conveniently describe the constitution of Germany in such a way that it comes nearest to some sort of political system which comprises several states.)'
[49] This has recently been strongly emphasised by Heinhard Steiger, 'Die Träger des *ius belli ac pacis* 1648–1806' in Werner Rösener (ed.), *Staat und Krieg: vom Mittelalter bis zur Moderne* (Göttingen, 2000), pp. 15–135.

Conclusion

The *ius foederis* had become an explosive issue in the course of the Thirty Years War, not least because of the important and controversial role which the confessional alliances played, but also because the war forced all states and political powers in Europe to reorganise their military infrastructure. At the end of the war, most princes and Estates were quite happy to let this question again recede into a murky twilight, where most clear legal distinctions were blurred. Hardly any prince of the Empire wanted to achieve a truly sovereign status. Even for the prince Electors the added legitimacy, which the Empire's constitution could bestow on their policy, was too valuable. The negotiations in Osnabrück and Münster did demonstrate, however, that the political language in which the *ius foederis* was discussed in Germany was not the language of international diplomacy; rather, it was the language of the right of resistance. One could argue that this specific pattern of discourse provides more than enough proof that the Empire was and remained indeed a genuine state after 1648. However, the opposite conclusion is equally possible and perhaps more appropriate, that lawyers and political theorists in the Holy Roman Empire continued to use ideas and categories of thought in the later seventeenth century which had largely become obsolete in Western Europe, where the idea of undivided sovereignty as articulated first by Bodin and later by Hobbes became much more influential. To the extent that political discussions in the Empire were rooted in older traditions of thought, it remained a political system *sui generis* that was separated from the modern states of Western Europe by a widening gulf.

16

The peace treaties of the Ottoman Empire with European Christian powers

KARL-HEINZ ZIEGLER

Introduction

The Ottoman Empire was the only non-Christian European power which, from the Middle Ages to the early twentieth century, has ever been a permanent factor in the political system of Europe. The early state which the Turkish sultans belonging to the house of Osman had formed in Asia minor was transformed into an Empire by fighting against and conquering Byzantium and other Christian states in the Balkans. From 1365 the Ottoman rulers had their residence in Adrianople/Edirne, and from 1453 continuously in Constantinople/Istanbul, in Europe. In the sixteenth century, when their rule was extended to Syria-Palestine, Mesopotamia, Arabia and Egypt, the Ottoman sultans also laid claim to the Caliphate. As caliphs they were regarded as nominal successors to the Prophet Muhammad and therefore as the religious leaders of the whole Muslim community. But throughout the centuries, there have always been important Muslim states which did not recognise the Ottoman sultan–caliph as their supreme authority (such as Persia, Morocco, or the Mogul Empire in India).

The fact that, after the conquest of Constantinople in 1453, Turkish imperial armies had even besieged the Habsburg capital of Vienna in 1529 and once more in 1683 had contributed to the sentiment of mortal menace by Islam, which was widely spread in the *respublica christiana*. Only in the eighteenth century could the idea of coexistence and good neighbourliness between Christian Europe and the Muslim Turkish Empire become more effective.

Peaceful relations with Christian princes and communities regulated by international treaties were practised from the first by the first Ottoman rulers.[1] They followed a long practical legal tradition supported by spiritual authorities of Islam, namely that Muslims could conclude binding treaties with non-Muslims under certain conditions, suspending for a limited time the usual state of war between the Muslim world and the world of the 'unbelievers'.[2] So the peace treaty between Muslims and Christians, who did not submit to the Muslim ruler, originally was only an armistice or truce, not a definite peace treaty in the sense of definitely ending the war. The latter developed, as we shall see, from long-term truces. The binding force of such treaties (which were for a long time, as in the Christian world, regularly confirmed by oaths) had found expression in the holy scripture of the Muslims, the Quran: treaties must be kept, even treaties with idolators,[3] and an oath invoking God (Allah) must never be violated.[4]

Treaties regulating peaceful relations with Muslim rulers or states had also met ideological reservations in the Christian tradition. It was the Latin Church which had coined the term 'impious treaty' (*impium foedus*).[5] But the Fathers of the Church had established a biblical foundation for the principle that binding treaties could be concluded with 'pagans' (swearing by their 'false gods'), a principle confirmed by medieval canon law.[6]

The numerous truces and peace treaties which, in the course of more than six centuries, Ottoman sultans had concluded with Christian states cannot be thoroughly discussed in the following pages. We must content ourselves with a brief survey of a number of important and instructive examples.

The late Middle Ages: conflicts and treaties (1300–1500)

The expansion of the first Ottoman sultans to the west was accompanied by a number of treaties which they had concluded with the emperors

---

[1] Cf. the 'répertoire chronologique' in RAI I: 1300–1789, pp. 3–20 (for the period from 1307 to 1481).
[2] For the Muslim conceptions of war and peace, see the authors referred to in Karl-Heinz Ziegler, *Völkerrechtsgeschichte* (Munich, 1994), pp. 76–81 and 116–19. Cf. also Guido Komatsu, 'Die Türkei und das europäische Staatensystem im 16. Jahrhundert. Untersuchungen zu Theorie und Praxis des frühneuzeitlichen Völkerrechts' in *Recht und Reich im Zeitalter der Reformation: Festschrift für Horst Rabe* (Frankfurt am Main and Berlin, 1996), pp. 121–44 at pp. 134–40.
[3] Cf. Quran s. 9, 4.   [4] Cf. Quran s. 16, 93.
[5] Cf. Giulio Vismara, *Impium foedus* (Milan, 1950), now also in Giulio Vismara, *Scritti di storia giuridica* (Milan, 1989), vol. VII, pp. 1–114.
[6] Cf. Karl-Heinz Ziegler, 'Biblische Grundlagen des europäischen Völkerrechts', *Zeitschrift der Savigny-Stiftung für Rechtsgeschichte, Kanonistische Abteilung* 117 (2000), 1–32 at pp. 9–10 and 16–17.

of Byzantium, a regional power which degenerated into a petty state. The prince of Constantinople, the 'New Rome', although still addressed as 'emperor of the Romans' (Greek: *basileus Rhomaion*) and 'unlimited ruler' (Greek: *autokrator*),[7] in fact had become a vassal of the Turkish sultan.[8]

The Ottomans did not hesitate to use the Greek language in their international affairs, too. A most instructive example is the Peace Treaty which Mehmet II (1444–45 and 1451–81, ruling for his father Sultan Murat II, reigned 1421–51) had concluded with Venice in 1446.[9] The Greek document which the sultan had handed over to the Venetian ambassador begins with the invocation of God: 'In the name of the Great God, Amen.' Then the form of the oath follows:

> I, the Great Ruler and Great Emir Sultan Mehmet-Bey, son of the Great Ruler and Great Emir Sultan Murat-Bey, swear in the name of the Creator of heaven and earth, of our great Prophet Muhammad, of the seven parts of the Quran which we Muslims have and believe in, of the 124,000 prophets of God, Adam being the first of them, Muhammad (who confirmed the faith of us Muslims) the last, of the faith which I confess, of the life and the head of my father, and my own life, my head and the sword at my side.

Between the sultan and Venice there will be a 'valid and sincere, just and good peace by land and sea'.[10] It is remarkable that the duke of Venice is courteously called 'Father of my Highness'. The Greek expression for 'Highness' in the sense of independent rulership or sovereignty (*authentia*) is used by the sultan to refer both to himself and to the Republic of Venice. In the separate sections of the treaty (which also allowed free trade to Venetian merchants), the rights and duties are formulated on the basis of equality. In the last paragraph, Sultan Mehmet II confirms the agreements, and he refers expressly to the oath in the Preamble.[11] In

---

[7] For the Byzantine ideology of universal monarchy, see Ziegler, *Völkerrechtsgeschichte*, pp. 111–12. In Roman and Byzantine times, the Greek *autokrator* was the equivalent of the Latin *imperator*.

[8] Georg Ostrogorsky, 'Byzance, état tributaire de l'empire turc', *Recueil des Travaux de l'Institut d'Etudes Byzantines* 5 (1958), 49–58, now also in Georg Ostrogorsky, *Zur byzantinischen Geschichte* (Darmstadt, 1973), pp. 235–44.

[9] The treaty, missing in the chronological survey of RAI I, was published and commented on by Franz Babinger and Franz Dölger, 'Mehmed's II. frühester Staatsvertrag (1446)', *Orientalia Christiana Periodica* 15 (1949), 225–58, now also in Franz Dölger, *Byzantinische Diplomatik* (Ettal, 1956), pp. 262–91. The text, with a German translation, can also be found in FHIG I, pp. 375–8.

[10] The Greek word used for peace and peace treaty is *agape*.

[11] The document was written in Adrianople, on 23 February 1446.

his last years, the conqueror of Constantinople had concluded one more peace treaty with Venice, confirming it by a document in Greek, dated 25 January1479. Again we find the oath of Mehmet II at the beginning – it is practically identical to the one taken in the treaty of 1446 and it is this oath that is referred to. In the Preamble, the sultan also mentions the former 'peace and friendship'[12] with Venice, expressing his sworn determination to conclude again a good and stable peace 'by land and sea'. The expression 'written old and new chapters'[13] already shows the conception of the later Ottoman 'capitulations' with European powers.

Sultan Bayezit II (1481–1512), who in 1481 succeeded his father Mehmet II, renewed the peace treaty with Venice at the beginning of his reign. The Greek document, which was signed in Adrianople on 12 January 1482, follows the Turco-Byzantine patterns which we have observed in the two peace treaties of Mehmet II. The Preamble begins with the sultan remembering the good and peaceful relations which his ancestors and his late father Sultan Mehmet (II) had maintained with Venice and his own determination to confirm peace and friendship anew.[14] The oath of the Sultan contains elements similar to the form used by Mehmet II: 'Bayezit II swears upon the sword at his side, upon the soul of his father and his own soul, upon the prophets of God until Muhammad, upon the seven pieces of the Quran, upon the faith which he confesses, and upon God, the Creator of heaven and earth.' He promises 'good and permanent peace and friendship'.[15] With the last paragraph, the 'Great Ruler and Great Emir Sultan Bayezit Khan' confirms the agreements put under oath. Sultan Bayezit II concluded another peace treaty with Venice in 1502. He used Greek imperial titles, calling himself 'Sultan Bayezit Khan, by the grace of God supreme Emperor and unlimited ruler of the two continents of Asia and Europe and other possessions'.[16] It is clear that the Ottoman sultan, who had already used these titles earlier in his diplomatic correspondence,[17] presented himself as the legitimate successor to the Byzantine emperors. He undertakes that he will keep 'peace' or 'friendship and peace',[18] swearing 'great oaths' to God creator of heaven and earth.[19]

---

[12] Greek: *agape kai philia*.   [13] Greek: *gegrammena kephalaia, palaia te kai nea*.
[14] Greek: *nea agape kai kale philia*.   [15] Greek: *kale kai sterea agape kai philia*.
[16] The Greek titles cannot be exactly translated: *basileus* in classical Greek means 'king', but in Byzantine Greek also 'emperor'; *autokrator* in Roman and Byzantine times is the equivalent of Latin *imperator*, i.e. it also has the significance of 'emperor'.
[17] Ziegler, *Völkerrechtsgeschichte*, p. 141.   [18] Greek: *agape; philia kai agape*.
[19] The words of these *megaloi horkoi* are not reported in the document.

Similar treaty relations existed with other Christian powers and communities.[20] Genuine peace treaties with Christian states which had been invaded by Turkish armies must have been rare. If the Christian enemy was not defeated or did not become an Ottoman vassal, he could only get an armistice or truce as permitted by the legal theories of Islam. In the case of Hungary, no real peace treaty with the Ottomans is reported for the Middle Ages.

Friendship with France and neighbourly relations with the Roman-German emperor (1500–1648)

The power of the Habsburg monarchs, reigning as kings in Spain, as emperors in the Holy Roman Empire but also as kings in Hungary, had led to very friendly relations between the Ottoman Empire and France. The first 'Capitulation' which in February 1535 was concluded for 'the most Christian King',[21] Francis I of France (1515–47), and Sultan Süleyman I (1520–66) 'Emperor of the Turks',[22] by the French ambassador in Constantinople and the Turkish commander-in-chief (*serasker*) was not formally ratified, but 'its contents were considered as binding between the parties'. According to Article 1, 'a valid and sure peace and sincere concord'[23] was made for the lives of the contracting monarchs, guaranteeing free navigation, travel and trade to their subjects. The provisions of Article 16 (inviting the pope and the kings of England and Scotland to adhere to the treaty) and of Article 17 (for ratification and publication of the peace treaty) remained dead letters. The acceptance of French consuls and their jurisdiction over French subjects in civil and criminal cases between them (Article 3) and other rights for Frenchmen in the Ottoman Empire could, on the other hand, be interpreted as a kind of privilege granted to French subjects by the sultan (who, as caliph was not interested in imposing Muslim law on 'unbelievers').

The importance of the Capitulation of 1535 is confirmed by the second Capitulation with France, which was agreed by Sultan Selim II (1566–74) with King Charles IX of France (1561–74) and was signed in Constantinople on 18 October 1569. The French translation of a Turkish

---

[20] Cf. the Greek correspondence of the Ottomans in ADGMA III, and the notices in RAI I, pp. 8–23.
[21] *Rex Christianissimus* was a special title of the French kings also in European diplomacy. In the capitulation of 1535, it is used in its French version: *roi de France très-chrétien*.
[22] In the Preamble in French: 'trés-puissant et invincible grand seigneur Sultan Suléiman empereur des Turcs'.
[23] French text: 'bonne et sûre paix et sincère concorde'.

document is in the form of a unilateral declaration of the sultan, who in the Preamble also mentions the 'highest capitulations and orders' which his father and predecessor Süleyman (II) had 'granted to the ambassadors of the Emperors of France, their consuls, interpreters, merchants and other persons'.[24] The sultan calls himself 'by the grace of God, Emperor and King, Sultan Selim',[25] but he also uses titles from other traditions, such as 'King of Kings' or 'donator of the crowns of the White and the Black Sea, of the countries in Greece, Asia, Arabia and other countries'.[26] It is remarkable that the title of 'emperor' is used by the sultan for the king of France, who is also described as 'the greatest amongst the greatest princes of the religion of Jesus'.[27] The equal ranking of the Ottoman Empire and France is also clearly expressed by the remark about 'the perfect friendship and mutual agreement between two so great emperors'.[28] This, at the same time, was a political affront to the only emperor of the Latin world, the *imperator Romanorum* Ferdinand I (1555–64), ruling the Holy Roman Empire: owing to the fact that he was also king of Hungary, which the Ottomans regarded as their vassal state, the Sublime Porte denied to him the title of emperor.[29]

The Capitulation which Sultan Ahmet I concluded with King Henry IV of France (1589–1610) in 1604 is styled as a 'peace treaty and capitulation'.[30] The Treaty begins with the invocation: 'In the name of God'.[31] The titles which the sultan uses correspond to the Ottoman tradition, but also reflect the newer position as caliph: 'Emperor of victorious Emperors, distributor of crowns to the greatest princes on earth, servant to the two most holy and most august cities Mecca and Medina, protector and governor of holy Jerusalem', etc.[32] Article 1 contains the sultan's formal

---

[24] French: 'les très-hautes capitulations et commandements . . . qui auparavant et du temps de feu mon père Suléiman . . . ont été concédés aux ambassadeurs des empereurs de France, à leurs consuls, interprètes, marchands et autres personnes'.
[25] French: 'par la grâce de Dieu, empereur et roi, Sultan Sélim'.
[26] 'Moi, qui suis roi des rois . . . donateur des couronnes de la Mer Blanche et Noire, des pays en Grèce, Asie, Arabie et autres pays, etc.'.
[27] 'Entre les grands princes de la religion de Jésus, le plus grand, et des plus grands princes chrétiens le majeur, l'empereur de France, etc.'.
[28] '. . . la parfaite amitié et mutuelle intelligence des deux si grands empereurs, etc.'.
[29] Karl-Heinz Ziegler, 'Völkerrechtliche Beziehungen zwischen der Habsburgermonarchie und der hohen Pforte', *Zeitschrift für Neuere Rechtsgeschichte* 18 (1996), 177–195 at p. 182, and Komatsu, 'Die Türkei', p. 126.
[30] Arts. 48 and 50: 'traité de paix et de capitulation'. Cf. also Art. 2.
[31] 'Au nom de Dieu.'
[32] 'Moi . . . empereur des victorieux empereurs, distributeur des couronnes aux plus grands princes de la terre, serviteur des deux très-sacrées et très-augustes villes Mecque et Médine, protecteur et gouverneur de la sainte Jérusalem, etc.'

greeting of the French king: 'To the most glorious, magnanimous and great ruler of the religion of Jesus, chosen amongst the princes of the nation of the Messiah, mediator of the differences which occur in the Christian people, ruler of grandeur, majesty and richness, glorious guide of the greatest grands, Henry IV, emperor of France. May the end of his days be fortunate!'[33] Article 2 reports the wish of the 'emperor of France', 'that the treaties of peace and capitulations which have existed long since between our empire and that of the said ruler, should be renewed and sworn by our highness'.[34] The details of the separate articles show the leading political role of France in the Ottoman world. Article 27 grants the French ambassador in Turkey pre-eminence over all other European diplomats. It is also remarkable that Article 20 allows France to wage war on a limited scale against the Ottoman vassal-states Algiers and Tunisia if their corsairs violate the capitulation: this would not touch 'the friendship which exists between our Imperial Majesties'.[35] Article 49 underlines not only that the present Capitulation is binding, but also that the capitulations of the sultan's predecessors will be 'observed and kept in good faith'.[36] The confirmation of the treaty by oath is expressed in Article 50: 'We promise and swear on the truth of God Almighty, creator of heaven and earth; and on the soul of the chief of his prophets; and on the head of our ancestors' to keep the treaty, as long as the 'emperor of France' cultivates the sultan's friendship.[37]

Ottoman capitulations were also concluded (and several times renewed) with England after 1580[38] and the Netherlands after 1612. Their structure corresponds to the capitulations with France: to the subjects of

---

[33] 'Au plus glorieux, magnamine et grand-seigneur de la croyance de Jésus, élu entre les princes de la nation du Messie, médiateur des différends qui surviennent entre le peuple chrétien, seigneur de grandeur, majesté et richesse, glorieux guide des plus grands, Henri IV, empereur de France. Que la fin de ses jours soit heureuse!'

[34] Art. 2: 'que les traités de paix et capitulations, qui sont de longue mémoire entre notre empire et celui de son dit seigneur, fussent renouvelés et jurés de notre hautesse, etc.'.

[35] Art. 20: 'l'amitié qui est entre nos majestés impériales, etc.'.

[36] Art. 49: 'observées et entretenues de bonne foi'.

[37] Art. 50: 'Nous promettons et jurons par la vérité du Dieu tout-Puissant, créateur du ciel et de la terre; Et par celle de l'âme du chef de ses prophètes; Et par la tête des nos aieux et bis-aieux, De ne contrarier ni contrevenir à ce qui est porté par ce traité de paix et capitulation, tant que l'empereur de France sera constant et ferme à la conservation de notre amitié.'

[38] The Capitulation concluded by Sultan Murat III with Queen Elizabeth I of England is discussed in the Preamble and confirmed in Arts. 1–20 of the Capitulation which Sultan Mehmet IV concluded with King Charles II of England in 1675.

the sultan the capitulations are presented as imperial commandments; to the European powers they were treaties of peace and friendship.[39]

A genuine peace treaty was concluded by Sultan Süleyman I after a war with Venice, on 20 October 1540. Venice had to cede territories in Dalmatia and Greece to the sultan and pay a tribute, but received 'capitulations' in favour of the Venetian merchants and travellers. Sultan Selim II renewed the capitulation with Venice on 24 June 1567.

No real peace treaty was concluded in the entire sixteenth century between the Ottoman Empire and the Habsburg monarchs.[40] In the person of Emperor Charles V (reigning 1519–55), the kingdoms of Spain and the Holy Roman Empire were united. In 1526, his brother Ferdinand had become king in Bohemia and in Hungary (which was also claimed by Sultan Süleyman I). The first siege of Vienna by the Turkish army in 1529 was the answer of the sultan, who was supported by a Hungarian king ruling as an Ottoman ally and vassal in the eastern parts of Hungary. Only in 1547 was a written treaty concluded between Sultan Süleyman I and Emperor Charles V (who was called 'king of Spain' by the Ottoman chancery) and his brother Ferdinand I of Hungary (who, since 1531, as 'king of the Romans' was also designated successor to the imperial throne of the Holy Roman Empire). The time limit of five years and the annual payment of 30,000 florins which was brought to Constantinople clearly show that the treaty was in reality an armistice or truce. If the court of Vienna interpreted the regular payments as 'gifts of honour', the Sublime Porte and European observers also saw them as tributes. The eight-year truce which the ambassador of Emperor Ferdinand I agreed upon in Constantinople with the grand vizier of Sultan Süleyman I in 1562 also regulated the annual payments to the sultan, and we find the same arrangements in the following eight-year truces which were concluded between the Habsburg emperors and the Ottoman sultans in 1568, 1573, 1576, 1584 and 1591.

The first real peace treaty was signed by representatives of Emperor Rudolph II and Sultan Ahmet I in Hungary on 11 November 1606, the Peace of Zsitvatorok. Official recognition of the Habsburg emperor's rank by the Sublime Porte was given in Article 2, which determined 'that both should address each other as emperor, not just as King'.[41] Article 4

---

[39] Cf. the Preamble of the Capitulation with England of 1675: Queen Elizabeth proposed to Sultan Murat III, 'une bonne et ferme paix et une amitié parfaite'.
[40] For the following see Ziegler, 'Völkerrechtliche Beziehungen', pp. 181–2, and, more detailed, Komatsu, 'Die Türkei', pp. 123–32.
[41] Art. 2: 'et unus alterum Caesarem appellat, non autem Regem'.

constituted 'peace between the two emperors in all regions ... by land and sea'.[42] Article 12 limited the Peace to twenty years,[43] but included also the heirs and successors of both parties. The requirement of payments by the Roman emperor was lifted, but according to Article 12 the emperor had to send to the sultan a single 'gift of honour' amounting to 200,000 florins.[44] The formal promise of the emperor's representatives to keep the peace in Article 17 is formulated under the condition that the Turks also keep the peace.[45] This corresponds to the Ottoman tradition which we observed in the Capitulation with France of the year 1604.[46] In his ratification, Emperor Rudolph II (1576–1612)[47] mentions Sultan Ahmet I (1603–17) as the 'emperor of the Turks and of Asia and Greece'.[48]

After some incidents, the Peace of 1606 was renewed by Emperor Matthias and Sultan Ahmet I with the treaties concluded in Vienna in 1615 and 1616. In his Latin confirmation of the Treaty of 1616, the emperor also calls the sultan 'neighbour and friend'.[49] Article 1 renews the 'holy peace' (*sancta pax*) of Zsitvatorok for another twenty years. Article 7 promises freedom of worship for Roman Catholics in the Ottoman Empire. Article 10 sets rules for free trade of merchants travelling under the flag and with papers of the Roman emperor. The Habsburg–Ottoman neighbourliness was a great advantage for the Roman emperors during the Thirty Years War. The Peace of Zsitvatorok was confirmed and prolonged by Treaties in 1618, 1625, 1627[50] and 1642.[51] It is significant that in the Treaty which representatives of Emperor Ferdinand III and of Sultan Ibrahim I concluded on 19 March 1642 in Hungary, Article 1 expressly mentions the Treaties of 1606, 1615, 1625 and 1627, prolonging the peace for another twenty years.

In the sixteenth and early seventeenth centuries, Poland was a neighbour of the Ottoman Empire, since the Ukraine still was not part of

---

[42] Art. 4: 'Ut inter istos duos Imperatores sit pax in omnibus locis ... tam in mari quam in terra, etc.'
[43] Art. 12: 'Ut pax duret per annos 20 etc.'
[44] Art. 11: 'Ut nunc legatus Suae Majestatis Caesareae adferat Constantinopolim munus valoris ducentorum millium florenorum juxta promissum, semel pro semper.'
[45] Art. 17: 'nos obligamus, certoque promittimus, praescriptos ... articulos ... donec ex parte Turcarum non infringentur, in omnibus punctis et clausulis observabimus, et per eorum quoque supremum Scerdar ... firmiter et inviolabiliter observabuntur'.
[46] See n. 37 above.   [47] Latin text of the *confirmatio caesarea* in RAI I, p. 107.
[48] 'Serenissimum ac Potentissimum Principem Dominum Sultanum Achimetem Imperatorem Turcarum ac Asiae et Graeciae.'
[49] 'Serenissimum Sultanum Achometem Turcarum Imperatorem, Vicinum et Amicum nostrum.'
[50] Ziegler, 'Völkerrechtliche Beziehungen', p. 183.
[51] Latin text in CUD VI-1, pp. 245–6; French translation in RAI I, pp. 120.

Russia. The political situation was far from stable. The Ottoman vassal state of the Crimean Tatars was partly independent. On the other side, the Cossacks did not altogether accept Polish authority (as they later defended their autonomy against the Russian czars[52]). With Stephen Bathory, Poland for more than a decade had a king (1575–86) who, as prince of Transylvania, was already an Ottoman vassal. In the Thirty Years War, Poland not only supported the Roman emperor, but also went to war against the Turkish power, which was ended by the final Peace Treaty signed on 9 October 1621 for Sultan Osman II (1618–22) and King Sigismund III (1587–1632) at Khotin/Dnestr, confirming the Ottoman positions.

Power politics and peace policy (1648–1815)

In the course of the late seventeenth and the eighteenth centuries, the position of the Ottoman Empire in Europe changed from that of a powerful 'enemy of Christianity' to a partner in the European system. In the Napoleonic period Turkey was led into short and limited wars with France and England (for the first and the last time before 1914). But generally, England, France and the Netherlands were European powers cultivating peaceful relations with the Ottoman Empire and therefore also acting several times as successful mediators for peace treaties between Turkey and the Habsburg monarchy (1699, 1718, 1739, 1791) or Turkey and Russia (1712, 1739).

The Ottoman capitulations with European states kept their traditional character until the later eighteenth century. Even if there had been no war, the agreement with the European partner was sometimes described as a treaty constituting or confirming peace as the fundamental foundation for trade and commerce by land and sea; or the agreement was expressed in the form of a sultan's order in favour of a friendly king. Instructive examples are three capitulations renewing old and friendly relations in the reign of Sultan Mehmet IV. The Capitulation with King Louis XIV of France (1643–1715), dated 5 June 1673, begins with a Preamble in the traditional imperial style: Sultan Mehmet, 'emperor of emperors',[53]

---

[52] Hedwig Fleischhacker, *Die staats- und völkerrechtlichen Grundlagen der moskauischen Außenpolitik (14.–17. Jahrhundert)* (Breslau, 1938; reprinted 1959), pp. 163–224: 'Die völkerrechtliche Stellung des Azaporoger Heeres'.

[53] 'Moi . . . Empereur des Empereurs, Distributeur des Couronnes, Serviteur des deux très augustes et sacrées villes de la Mecque et Médine, Protecteur et Gouverneur da la Sainte Jérusalem, etc.'

tells how the ambassador of 'Louis, emperor of France',[54] had requested that 'the capitulations which have been existing for a long time between our ancestors and the emperors of France should be renewed'[55] and that the sultan had 'the inclination to conserve this old friendship'.[56] The special relations are also indicated by the pre-eminence of the French ambassador in Istanbul over all other diplomats – confirmed with Article 19.[57] The new chapters added to the former, renewed chapters close with the sultan's solemn self-obligation: 'We promise on the truth of the mighty Creator of heaven and earth and on the souls of our ancestors' to keep the treaty as long as the 'emperor of France' cultivates the sultan's friendship.[58]

The detailed Capitulation which Sultan Mehmet IV granted to England in September 1675[59] refers to the former relations since the first 'peace and friendship' concluded with the Sublime Porte by Queen Elizabeth I (1558–1603). King Charles II (1661–85) too is called by honourable titles, without reaching the position of the French king.[60] In the separate chapters, several times the establishment or renewal of 'peace and friendship' is mentioned.[61] In the last chapter, the sultan commands that the capitulations shall be observed as long as the English king 'maintains that friendship and good understanding with our Sublime Porte which had

---

[54] 'La gloire des plus grands Monarques de la Terre de la croyance de Jésus, choisi entre les Princes glorieux de la religion du Messie ... Louis, Empereur de France.'

[55] '... que les Capitulations qui ont longtemps duré entre nos ayeuls et les Empereurs de France, fussent renouvellées'.

[56] '... et par l'inclination que nous avons à conserver cette ancienne amitié, Nous avons accordé ce qui s'ensuit'. Cf. also in Art. 2: 'l'ancienne amitié que les Empereurs de France ont eue avec nostre Porte'.

[57] Art. 19: 'que son Ambassadeur qui réside à nostre heureuse Porte, aie la Préséance sur tous les autres Ambassadeurs des autres Roys et Princes, soit à nostre Divan public, ou autres lieux où ils se pourront trouver'.

[58] New Art. 15: 'Nous promettons par la vérité du Puissant Créateur du Ciel et de la Terre et par les ames de nos Ayeuls et Bis-Ayeuls, de ne contrarier ny contrevenir à ce qui est porté par les Nobles Capitulations, tant que l'Emp. de France sera constant et ferme à la conservation de Nostre Amitié; Acceptons dès à présent la sienne, avec volonté de la tenir chère et en faire estime: Telle est nostre promesse Imperiale.' Cf. Art. 50 of the capitulation of 1604.

[59] See n. 38 above.

[60] Preamble: 'Au glorieux entre les grands Princes de Jésus, révéré par les hauts potentats des peuples du Messie, seul directeur des affaires importantes de la nation nazaréenne ... Charles II, Roi d'Angleterre et d'Ecosse, de France et d'Irlande etc.'

[61] Art. 20: 'la paix et amitié déjà contractée ... que ladite paix et amitié fussent renouvelés et fortifiés'; Art. 33 in fine: 'notre présente paix et amitié'; Art. 46: 'établissement de paix et d'amitié ... la paix et amitié contractées de longtemps'.

been maintained in the fortunate time of our glorious predecessor',[62] and the sultan promises and swears on God Almighty that he will not allow any violation of the capitulation.[63]

A renewed capitulation with the Netherlands was concluded by Sultan Mehmet IV (1648–87) on 15 September 1680. It follows the pattern of the other capitulations. The style of the sultan's chancery is almost more decorative: in the Preamble, Mehmet IV is also called 'Caesar of Caesars of Mankind', his role as caliph is stressed by a quotation from the Quran, and the title of 'Padishah' is used, too.[64] But the Republic of the Netherlands also receives titles appropriate to a monarch: 'glory of the great Princes of the religion of Jesus', 'arbitrators of state affairs of the Christian people, wearing the robe of magnificence and majesty'.[65] In the last Article, the Sultan again 'accepts' the friendship of the Netherlands as long as they remain in their 'loyal friendship', and he swears on God that the capitulation shall be kept.[66]

In the eighteenth century, we can observe the first commercial Ottoman treaties which were concluded separately from peace treaties. But the tradition of the capitulations still prevailed. So in 1740, Sultan Mahmut I (1730–1754) renewed the Turkish-French capitulations with King Louis XV (1715–1774).[67] The French king is called by the traditional Ottoman titles, including 'Emperor of France', but also as 'our most magnificent,

---

[62] Art. 75: 'Nous avons de nouveau accordé ces sacrées Capitulations, et nous ordonnons qu'elles soient observées aussi longtemps que le susdit Roi continuera de maintenir cette amitié et bonne intelligence avec notre Sublime Porte, qui était maintenue dans l'heureux temps de notre glorieux Predécesseur; laquelle amitié, nous, de notre part, acceptons.'

[63] '... nous promettons et jurons, par le seul Dieu Tout-Puissant, Créateur du Ciel et de la Terre et de toutes les Créatures, que nous ne permettrons pas que rien ne soit fait ni transgressé contrairement à la teneur des articles et stipulations ci-dessus faites et contre ces Capitulations impériales'.

[64] Preamble: 'Le César des Césars du genre humain ... l'habitant de l'éminent séjour de la Loi sainte, d'après le passage du Coran: "Je constituerai mon Vicaire sur la terre" ... le Padichah juste et le souverain victorieux de ... le Sultan Méhémed Khan'.

[65] Preamble: 'ceux qui sont la gloire des grands Princes de la Religion de Jésus ... les arbitres des affaires des Républiques du peuple nazaréen; revêtus de la robe de la magnificence et de la majesté ... les Etats généraux et Souverains des provinces de Gueldres, de Hollande, de Zélande, etc.'.

[66] Art. 59: 'Tant que ... les Etats Généraux seront fermes et constants dans leur loyale amitié, de mon côté aussi j'accepte cette amitié, et je jure par le Dieu ... que de Notre part aussi on ne se permettra rien qui fût contraire à ce pacte et à ces promesses'.

[67] Partly also in FHIG II, p. 361. The Treaty was signed in Constantinople on 28 May 1740.

most honourable, sincere and old friend Louis XV'.[68] The old and solid friendship between France and the Ottoman Empire is not only emphasised in the Preamble,[69] but also in separate chapters.[70] The special rank of the French ambassadors and consuls is confirmed by Article 44, which also mentions that their King is recognised as 'Emperor' by the Sublime Porte according to old custom.[71] It is also old Ottoman tradition that the capitulation of 1740 in the last chapter is characterised as the renewal of peace once concluded with France.[72] The Sultan also promises solemnly (by oath) to keep the capitulation for himself ('our sacred Imperial person') and also for his successors.[73]

In the same year, Sultan Mahmut I had also concluded a treaty of 'peace and friendship, of commerce and navigation' with King Charles IV of Naples-Sicily (a kingdom which was connected with Spain by the same dynasty, the Spanish Bourbons).[74] Article 1 states 'Between the Kingdoms of the ... King of both Sicilies and the Ottoman Empire by the will of God, beginning with the arrival of the ratifications, has been established peace following the form and model of other friendly powers, as France, England, Holland, and Sweden'.[75] In the 'conclusion' of the Treaty, ratification is mentioned and the exchange of signed and sealed instruments in the Italian and Turkish languages.

Significant is also the famous short Treaty of Friendship and Commerce which was concluded in 1761 between the Ottoman Empire

---

[68] Preamble: 'l'empereur de France ... notre très magnifique, très honoré, sincère et ancien ami Louis XV'.

[69] E.g., 'les fondements de l'amitié qui, depuis un temps immémorial, subsistent avec solidité entre la cour de France et notre Sublime Porte'.

[70] Cf. the beginnings of Art. 55: 'La cour de France étant, depuis un temps immémorial, en amitié et en bonne intelligence avec ma Sublime-Porte'; and of Art. 83: 'Comme lamitié de la cour de France avec ma Sublime Porte est plus ancienne que celle des autres cours'.

[71] Art. 44: 'très magnifique empereur de France, comme le titre d'empereur a été attribué, ab antiquo, par ma Sublime Porte à Sadite Majesté'.

[72] Art. 85: 'La ... Sublime Porte ayant à présent renouvelé la paix ci-devant conclue avec les Francais'.

[73] '... de la part de notre Majesté Impériale, je m'engage sous notre auguste serment le plus sacré et le plus inviolable, soit pour notre sacré personne impériale, soit pour nos augustes successeurs'.

[74] Treaty signed at Constantinople on 7 April 1740. In the Preamble, the contracting monarchs are called, 'Mahmoud Khan, Sultan et Empereur des Ottomans, de l'Asie, de Grèce, de l'Egypte etc.', and 'Charles, Roi des Deux-Siciles et îles adjacentes, Infant d'Espagne, Duc de Parme, etc.'. Between them 'on a traité et contracté une paix éternelle et amitié'.

[75] Art. 1: 'Entre les royaumes du ... roi des Deux-Siciles et l'Empire Ottoman, par la volonté de Dieu, à partir de l'arrivée des ratifications a été établie la paix dans la forme et le modèle des autres puissances amies, comme la France, l'Angleterre, la Hollande, et la Suède; etc.'

and the young European power Prussia.[76] This capitulation of Sultan Mustafa III (1757–1774) and King Frederick II of Prussia (1740–1786) is still stylised as a treaty constituting peace and friendship as the foundation for free commerce and navigation. Article 1 begins: 'There will be constant peace, friendship and mutual sincerity between the . . . King of Prussia and the . . . Ottoman Empire'.[77] It is remarkable that the official instruments were written in Turkish and in Italian (not in German nor in French).

In 1782 a Treaty of Peace and Commerce was concluded between Sultan Abdülhamit I (1774–1789) and King Charles III of Spain (1759–1788).[78] Article 1 begins: 'By the will of God and beginning with the day when the ratification of this treaty has arrived, peace will be established between the two powers, following the form and model of other friendly nations.'[79] In the chapters, the parties are called the 'Ottoman Empire' or 'Sublime Porte' and 'His Catholic Majesty'. In Article 21, the Spanish king also expresses his willingness for friendly démarches against the activity of privateers from Malta, Genoa and the Papal States.[80]

In the second half of the seventeenth century, the Ottoman Empire concluded a number of real peace treaties with Western powers. A brief war with the Holy Roman Empire and Hungary was ended in 1664 with the Peace of Vasvár,[81] which once more confirmed the Ottoman position in Transylvania. In the names of Sultan Mehmet IV and Emperor Leopold I (1658–1705), Article 10 promised 'peace and good friendship'[82] for twenty years. For the regular exchange of embassies, it was provided that they were to bring proper presents.[83] In Article 10 also, the Peace of Zsitvatorok (1606) and later agreements are recalled.

---

[76] The Treaty was signed in Constantinople, 23 March 1761.
[77] The French translation, 'une paix constante et une amitié réciproque et sincère', is not exact. The official Italian text mentions 'una forte pace, amicizia e reciproca sincerita'.
[78] The Treaty was signed in Constantinople, on 14 September 1782.
[79] Art. 1: 'Par la volonté de Dieu et à compter du jour de l'arrivée de la ratification de ce traité, la paix sera établie entre les deux Puissances, dans la forme et à l'instar des autres nations amies; etc.'
[80] Art. 21 in fine: 'Enfin S.M.C. ne se refusera pas à faire des démarches amicales pour éviter la course des Maltais, des Romains, des Génois dans l'Archipel et en fera connaître le résultat à la Sublime Porte.'
[81] The Treaty was signed at Vasvár on 10 August 1664 and ratified on 25 September 1664.
[82] Latin: 'pax et bona amicitia'.
[83] Art. 10 states that the ambassador of the 'Roman Emperor' will bring presents amounting to 200,000 piastres 'as spontaneous gift and sign of friendship' ('in signum amicitiae, spontaneum munus'); meanwhile the Turkish ambassador will bring presents appropriate to the dignity of the Ottoman Empire.

The long war with Venice, which the Ottoman Empire had to fight for its Greek possessions, ended with the Turkish conquest of Crete which was accepted by Venice in the Peace Treaty of Candia on 5 September 1669. Articles 1 and 3 to 7 of the Treaty between the 'Ottoman Porte' and the 'Republic of Venice' made provision for the surrender of the fortress of Candia. The exchange of hostages as guarantee for the correct fulfilment of the agreements (Article 8) is remarkable. Other chapters give rules for the exchange of prisoners (Article 13) and mutual amnesty (Article 14). Article 15 confirms all treaties which had been valid before the war.[84] According to Article 16, the treaty instruments were to be in the Turkish and the Italian languages.

A war with Poland arose from the situation in the Ukraine, where the Cossacks accepted Ottoman help to secure their independence from Poland and from Russia. In the Peace Treaties of Buczacz (1672),[85] Zoravno (1676)[86] and Constantinople (1679)[87] the government of Sultan Mehmet IV secured its conquests in and influence over the Ukraine.

The Turkish invasion of Hungary and Austria, with the second siege of Vienna in 1683, was followed by a close cooperation between the Holy Roman Empire, Poland and Venice, uniting in 1684 in the 'Holy League',[88] in which the members of the League also promised expressly not to conclude peace separately, but only by common consent.[89] Consequently, the Peace of Karlowitz[90] was achieved through three treaties, which the representatives of Sultan Mustafa II concluded, near the frontier of the Habsburg and the Ottoman empires, on 26 January 1699, with the diplomats of Emperor Leopold I and of King Augustus II of Poland (1697–1733, also Elector of Saxony, 1694–1733),[91] acting also for the Republic of Venice. The Peace had been successfully mediated by England (ruled

---

[84] Consequently, in 1670 the capitulations with Venice were confirmed and extended: cf. the notes of RAI I, p. 51.
[85] Peace Treaty with King Michael Wisniowiecki of 18 October 1672. According to Art. 2, Poland had to pay 22,000 ducats to the sultan annually.
[86] Peace Treaty with King John Sobieski of 16 October 1676. In Art. 1 no tribute is mentioned any more.
[87] Peace Treaty with King John Sobieski of 12 September 1679. At the end of the treaty text, the sultan also confirms the 'peace and union' ('pac et unio') by oath ('iuramentum') invoking God and the prophet Muhammad.
[88] This offensive and defensive alliance against the Ottomans, concluded on 5 March 1684 in Linz, included the pope as protector and guarantor.
[89] Cf. Art. 5: 'partes nullo modo ... acceptabunt pacem nisi simul et semel in eandem omnes tres consenserint eandemque acceptaverint'.
[90] Today Sremski Karlovci, on the Danube in Serbia.
[91] As Art. 11 shows, the treaty had no time limit.

by William III, 1689–1702) and the Netherlands.[92] The Treaty between Emperor Leopold I and Sultan Mustafa II follows the Habsburg–Ottoman tradition: for both rulers the imperial titles are used. In the Preamble, the sultan is called 'Sultan Mustafa Khan, Emperor of the Ottomans, and of Asia and Greece',[93] his diplomats, those of the 'Imperial Ottoman Majesty'.[94] Peace is stipulated for twenty-five years (Article 20). In the Latin version the treaty is called *armistitium* ('truce')[95] as well as *pax* ('peace'),[96] but it is also called *tractatus pacis* (in the Preamble). With Article 13, the sultan again confirms freedom of worship for Roman Catholics in the Ottoman Empire. And Article 14 grants mutual freedom of commerce, the sultan conceding to the Roman emperor's subjects the same rights as the subjects of other friendly nations enjoy in the Ottoman Empire. Article 16 states rules for the exchange of embassies that will bring 'as a sign of friendship a spontaneous gift . . . appropriate to the dignity of both emperors'.[97] In Article 19, the ratification by the contracting monarchs is promised.[98] As Article 20 shows, signed and sealed instruments in Turkish and in Latin were exchanged by the negotiators.[99]

Russia had not participated in the Peace of Karlowitz, but in 1700 Czar Peter I (1682–1725) concluded peace for thirty years with Sultan Mustafa II.[100] In Article 1 it is stated, that 'the two States will respect in a scrupulous manner the conditions of the peace',[101] but the 'prolongation of the truce'[102] is also mentioned. At the end of the text, the treaty is

---

[92] Both states are expressly mentioned in the Preambles of the three treaties.
[93] 'Sultanus Mustaffa Han Ottomanorum Imperator, ac Asiae et Graeciae.'
[94] '. . . legati . . . Nomine vero Imperialis Ottomanae Majestatis'. Cf. also 'Imperium Ottomanicum' in the Preamble and in Art. 2, 'Ottomanorum Imperator' in Arts. 4 and 10, etc.
[95] We find 'armistitium' also in Arts. 11 and 16.
[96] Cf. Art. 18: 'Pax ista'.
[97] Art. 16: 'in signum amicitiae spontaneum munus . . . utriusque Imperatorus consentaneum'. The expressions used are already found in Art. 10 of the Treaty of Vasvár of 1664.
[98] Art. 19: 'Has vero conditiones et articulos ad formam hic mutuo placitam a Majestatibus utriusque Imperatoris ratihabitum iri . . . legati plenipotentiarii utriusque Imperii sese infallibiliter praestituros obligant atque compromittent.'
[99] Art. 20: 'Plenipotentiarii Ottomannici . . . instrumentum turcico sermone exaratum et subscriptum legitimum et validum . . . nobis exhibuerunt, nos quoque . . . propriis manibus et propriis sigillis subscriptas hasce pactorum litteras in latino idiomate tanquam legitimum et validum vicissim instrumentum extradidimus.'
[100] The Treaty was concluded in Constantinople on 13 June 1700.
[101] Art. 1: 'les deux Etats respecteront scrupuleusement les conditions de la paix'. Cf. also Arts. 5, 8 and 9: 'la présente paix'; Art. 11: 'durant le terme de cette paix'; Art. 14: 'les articles de paix'.
[102] Art. 1: 'Si . . . les deux parties désiraient la prolongation de la trève'.

described as 'the peace and truce'.[103] In Article 2, the treaty partners are described as 'the Czar of Russia' and 'the Sublime Porte'. A passage in Article 8 is remarkable, showing that the sultan's chancery knew of the former vassalage of the Moscow rulers to the Tatars, whose khanate of Crimea since the days of Mehmet II had been an Ottoman vassal state.

> Since the Empire of Russia is an independent state, the Czar and his successors will have no obligation to pay (neither for the past, nor in present or in future) the tribute which was paid every year to the khan of Crimea and the Crimeans until now. But also for their part the khan of Crimea, the Crimeans and the other Tatar peoples will respect the present peace and not violate it by asking tribute or on other pretexts.[104]

Article 12 permitted Russian subjects the pilgrimage to Jerusalem. Article 14 provided for the exchange of the peace instruments and the exchange of the letters of ratification with the Russian ambassador in Constantinople. This Peace Treaty was renewed in Constantinople in 1710 with Sultan Ahmet III (1703–30),[105] but soon the war broke out again. A final peace treaty, mediated by Great Britain and the Netherlands, was concluded for twenty-five years by Czar Peter I with Sultan Ahmet III in 1712,[106] but was renewed by another treaty for twenty-five years already in 1713.[107] In this 'peace treaty',[108] Peter the Great is still called 'Czar of Muscovy', but also 'Czar's Majesty',[109] while for the sultan's part the old expression 'Sublime Porte'[110] is used. One year later, in 1714, Sultan Ahmet III renewed the Peace of Karlowitz with Poland.[111]

A new war of the Ottoman Empire with Venice and the Holy Roman Empire was ended by the Peace of Passarowitz in 1718, which had again

---

[103] After Art. 14: 'la paix et trève convenue et renouvelée d'après les articles qui précèdent'.
[104] Art. 8: 'L'Empire de Russie étant un état indépendant, le Tzar et ses successeurs n'auront pas l'obligation de payer ni pour le passé, ni pour le présent, ni pour l'avenir le tribut annuellement donné jusqu'ici au Khan de Crimée et aux Criméens. Mais de leur côté aussi, le Khan de Crimée, les Criméens et les autres peuples Tatars respecteront la présente paix et ne la violeront pas par les demandes de tribut ni sous d'autres prétextes.'
[105] Preamble and final part in French translation, the text being identical with that of the Treaty of 1700. Dated 1 April 1710 (?).
[106] The Treaty was signed in Constantinople on 16 April 1712. According to Art. 7, instruments in Turkish and in Russian (with Italian translation) were exchanged by the negotiators.
[107] The Treaty was signed in Adrianople on 5/16 June 1713 (5 July 1713?).
[108] Arts. 1, 3 and 8: 'Traité de paix'; Art. 11: 'la paix, le présent traité'.
[109] Preamble, Arts. 2, 3, 7, 8 and 11: 'Czar de Moscovie'; Preamble, Arts. 3, 4 and 8: 'Sa Majesté Czarienne'.
[110] Preamble, Arts. 3, 7, 8 and 11: 'Sublime Porte'.
[111] Cf. the note of RAI I, p. 61. Treaty missing in CTS. Date: Constantinople, 22 April 1714.

been mediated by Great Britain and the Netherlands and was composed of two treaties: one between Sultan Ahmet III and Emperor Charles VI (1711–40)[112] and the other between the sultan and the Republic of Venice.[113] The 'peace' and 'truce'[114] between the emperor and the sultan, who were called by their usual titles, was stipulated for twenty-four lunar years (Article 20). The plenipotentiaries exchanged instruments in Turkish and in Latin.[115] An interesting detail of the European legal tradition is shown by Article 1 quoting the principle *Uti possidetis*.[116] Regarding the freedom of commerce confirmed by Article 13 of the peace treaty, a few days later a separate commercial treaty ('tractatus commercii') was concluded for the two empires.[117] Here is a last detail of the Peace Treaty: Article 16 mentions the proposal of the Roman emperor's plenipotentiaries that Poland too should be included in the peace, to which the sultan's diplomats replied that this was unnecessary because of the constant and stable peace with the king and the republic of Poland.[118]

In 1720 Sultan Ahmet III again concluded a peace treaty with Czar Peter I of Russia.[119] It was a treaty without time limit, a 'perpetual peace', which was concluded for 'His Imperial Ottoman Majesty and his glorious successors and His Majesty the Czar of the whole of Russia and his glorious successors'.[120] The Preamble also reported the Peace Treaties of 1700, 1710, 1712 and 1713. As a consequence of the perpetual peace and friendship, Article 12 allowed a permanent Russian embassy in Istanbul, and the ambassador was to be treated like the ambassadors of 'other monarchs who were friends of the Porte'.[121]

---

[112] Signed Passarowitz, 21 July 1718.   [113] Signed Passarowitz, 21 July 1718.
[114] The treaty mentions 'pax' (e.g. Arts. 1, 3, 4, 7, 12 and 20) and 'armistitium' (e.g. Arts. 17 and 20).
[115] The end of Art. 20 is identical with the end of Art. 20 of the Peace of Karlowitz.
[116] Art. 1: 'iuxta acceptatum fundamentum pacis: Uti possidetis'. This principle is also alluded to in Arts. 3 and 4. Ziegler, 'Völkerrechtliche Beziehungen', p. 186 with n. 71.
[117] French translation in RAI I, pp. 220–7: 'Traité de commerce et de navigation avec l'Autriche'. Signed Passarowitz, 27 July 1718.
[118] Art. 16: 'responsum est: inter regem Poloniae eiusdemque dictam rempublicam pacem perpetuam et firmam et nullas cum Ottomanico Imperio controversias versari'. For the Peace Treaty with Poland concluded in 1714, see n. 111 above.
[119] The Treaty was signed in Constantinople on 5/16 November 1720.
[120] Art. 1: 'Les conditions de la paix perpétuellement présentement conclue entre S.M.I. Ottomane et ses glorieux successeurs et S.M. le Czar de toute la Russie et ses glorieux successeurs'.
[121] Art. 12: 'Ledit Ministre sera traité de la même manière qu'on traite les Ministres des autres Princes amis de la Porte.'

A war which the Roman emperor and the Russian czar as allies had led against the Ottoman Empire was ended in 1739 by the Peace of Belgrade, achieved by two peace treaties mediated and guaranteed by France: a treaty between Sultan Mahmut I and the Roman Emperor Charles VI,[122] and a treaty between the sultan and the Russian empress Anne (1730–40).[123] The treaty with Emperor Charles VI shows the titles for the contracting monarchs and the terminology which we have observed in the earlier Habsburg–Ottoman peace treaties: both monarchs are 'emperors'.[124] The 'peace' and 'truce'[125] is stipulated for twenty-seven years (Article 23). The special role of the French ambassador also becomes clear from the fact that the peace negotiations had been held in his tent in the Turkish camp near Belgrade,[126] and that there the negotiators had also exchanged the instruments in the Turkish and the Latin languages.[127] In his brief statement in French, signed and sealed, the French ambassador confirmed that the peace had been concluded with the mediation and the guarantee of the 'emperor of France'.[128] The treaty with the Russian empress Anne shows the use of the imperial title introduced by Peter the Great.[129] In Article 1, the contracting monarchs are described as 'Her Imperial Majesty' and 'His Sultan Majesty'.[130] The peace contracted between them not only ends all hostilities, but also has the consequence of 'perpetual oblivion' and amnesty.[131] The peace is not limited, but 'perpetual, constant and inviolable by land and sea'.[132] The French ambassador in the Ottoman

---

[122] Signed near Belgrade, 18 September 1739.   [123] Signed at Belgrade, 18 September 1739.
[124] Cf., e.g., in Art. 23: 'pacta inter Majestatem ... Romanorum Imperatoris et Majestatem ... Ottomannorum Imperatoris et haeredes eorundem, imperia quoque et regna ipsorum, etc.'.
[125] In Art. 23, both expressions, 'pax' and 'armistitium', are used.
[126] Cf. in the Preamble of the Treaty: 'ad castra Ottomannica ad Belgradum et in Gallici oratoris ibi degentis tentoria'. According to Art. 1, the Roman emperor had to renounce the fortress at Belgrade, which was to be restored to the Sultan.
[127] Cf. Art. 23 *in fine*.
[128] 'Nous ... déclarons que le traité de paix ci-dessus a été conclu entre l'Empereur des Romains et la Porte Ottomane, par la médiation et sous la garantie de l'Empereur de France.' Cf. also the French *Acte de garantie*, signed 18 September 1739, RAI I, p. 255.
[129] Preamble, French translation: 'Anne, Impératrice et Autocratice de toutes les Russies'.
[130] Art. 1: 'les deux hautes parties contractantes, Sa Majesté Impériale et Sa Majesté Sultane, leurs Héritiers et successeurs'. Art. 12 of the Treaty regulates expressly the use of the imperial title for the Russian empress.
[131] Art. 1: 'que toutes les hostilités et contrariétés, commises par l'une ou l'autre des parties ... soient mises dans un oubli perpétuel, et qu'on ne cherche en aucune manière à tirer vengeance etc.'. This oblivion clause is typical for the European tradition. Jörg Fisch, *Krieg und Frieden im Friedensvertrag* (Stuttgart, 1979) pp. 103–7.
[132] Art. 1: 'la paix soit maintenue perpétuelle, constante et inviolable sur terre et sur mer'.

camp near Belgrade, who had presided over the negotiations for the sultan's peace treaty with the Roman emperor, was also plenipotentiary of the Russian empress.[133] So the French ambassador, on behalf of the Russian empress, received from the Ottoman grand vizier the peace instrument in the Turkish language, and handed over to the grand vizier the peace instrument in the Italian language,[134] with a brief statement in French that, in case of Russian ratification, the 'emperor of France' would guarantee the peace.[135]

Meanwhile, the peace between the Ottoman Empire and the Habsburg Empire lasted longer than the time stipulated in Belgrade, namely for half a century; the perpetual peace with Russia ended in 1768. The Peace Treaty of Kücük Kainarci was concluded on 21 July 1774 for the new Sultan Abdülhamit I and the Russian Empress Catherine II (1762–96), in the Russian camp in Bulgaria in the presence of the Russian commander-in-chief, while the grand vizier was represented by two Turkish diplomats. The peace clauses in Article 1 correspond to the Ottoman–Russian Treaty of Belgrade: a 'perpetual, stable and unchangeable peace by land and sea'[136] is contracted between 'Her Imperial Majesty' and 'His Majesty the Sultan' and their successors.[137] According to Article 3, the khanate of Crimea was to be an independent state, although Russia retained some fortresses. As to religious ceremonies, Article 3 recognised the rights of the sultan as caliph in the sense of religious leader of the Muslim community. With Articles 7, 8 and 14, Russia became a kind of protector of the Orthodox Christians in the Ottoman Empire and, moreover, Article 16 gave to Russia the position of quasi-protector of the principalities of Moldavia and Valachia, which were restored to the Ottoman Empire. That the Russian court still wanted full recognition of its equal rank with the Sublime Porte is shown by the curious Article 13: 'The Sublime Porte promises to employ the sacred title of the Empress of all the Russias in all public acts and letters, as well as in all other cases, in the Turkish language, that is to say, "Temamen Roussielerin

---

[133] Cf. the Preamble of the Ottoman–Russian Treaty. [134] Art. 15 *in fine*.
[135] '... ayant recu l'instrument authentique écrit en langue turque, signé et scellé par le susdit Grand Vizir de l'Empire Ottoman. Nous lui avons remis le présent instrument écrit en italien et souscrit par Nous en francais et scellé ... Nous réservant néanmoins la ratification de Sa Majesté de toutes les Russies, et au cas qu'elle soit donnée, nous promettons de garantir ledit traité pour et au nom de l'Empereur de France, etc.' Cf. also the French *Acte de garantie*, signed Constantinople, 28 December 1739, RAI I, p. 266.
[136] Art. 1: 'une paix perpétuelle, stable et inalterable, tant par terre que par mer'.
[137] Art. 1: 'Sa très haute Majesté impériale et Sa Majesté le Sultan, leurs successeurs et descendents, et aussi entre les Empires, etc.'.

Padischag"'.[138] According to Article 28, the peace instruments signed and sealed by the Russian commander-in-chief (in Russian and Italian) and the grand vizer (in Turkish and Italian) were to be exchanged. In a separate Article 2, added to the Peace Treaty, the Ottoman Empire was obliged to pay in the following three years a war indemnity of 7.5 million piastres (corresponding to 4.5 million Russian rubles).

When in 1787 the Ottoman Empire declared war on Russia, the Roman emperor Joseph II (1765–90), because of his alliance with the Russian empress Catherine II, became involved in this war.[139] In 1791 the Roman emperor Leopold II (1790–92) concluded the Peace of Sistova[140] with the new Sultan Selim III (1789–1807), which was mediated by Great Britain, Prussia and the Netherlands.[141] It is significant that the court of Vienna did not use Latin for the treaty text, but French: according to Article 14, the instruments signed and exchanged were written in Turkish and in French. The Preamble of the Treaty begins with the words: 'The Imperial and Royal Court and the Ottoman Sublime Porte, inspired by the mutual desire to restore the fortunate bonds of peace, friendship and good neighbourhood which have existed between the two Empires during half a century . . .'[142] Article 1 constituted 'perpetual and universal peace', 'true and sincere friendship', a 'perfect and close union'[143] between the two Empires and their subjects. Throughout the Treaty, the principle of *status quo* (*ante bellum*) is quoted as its basis.[144] With the Peace of Jassy, signed 9 January 1792, the diplomats of Sultan Selim III and Empress Catherine II brought an end to the Russian–Turkish war. In the Preamble, the contracting monarchs are called the 'Ottoman emperor' and the 'empress of all the

---

[138] Art. 13: 'La Sublime Porte promet d'employer de titre sacré d'Impératrice de toutes les Russies dans tous les actes et dans toutes les lettres publiques, comme aussi en tout autre cas dans la langue turque, savoir: Temamen Roussielerin Padischag.'

[139] For the situation and the Prussian–Turkish alliance of 1790 against Austria and Russia, see Ziegler, 'Völkerrechtliche Beziehungen', p. 188.

[140] Signed Sistova, 4 August 1791.

[141] A short declaration of the mediators is added to the treaty text (*Déclaration des Ministres-Médiateurs*).

[142] Preamble: 'La Cour Impériale et Royale et la Sublime Porte Ottomane, animées d'un désir égal de rétablir les liaisons heureuses de paix, d'amitié et de bon voisinage, qui avaient subsisté pendant un demi siècle entre les deux Empires'.

[143] Art. 1: 'une paix perpétuelle et universelle . . . entre les deux Empires, leurs sujets et vassaux, une amitié vraie et sincère, une union parfaite et étroite'.

[144] Art. 2: 'Les deux Hautes Parties contractantes reconnaissent et admettent, pour base commun de la présente pacification, le status quo strict antérieur à la guerre.' Cf. the expression 'status quo strict' also in Arts. 4, 6, 7, 9 and 12.

Russias';[145] in Article 13, which regulates the ratification, 'Their Majesties the Great Sultan and the empress of Russia'.[146] Article 1 does not expressly mention perpetual peace, but it is used in Article 13.[147] Article 2 confirms the Russian–Turkish Peace Treaty of 1774 and some later treaties and agreements, thus ratifying also the incorporation of the Crimea into the Russian Empire.[148]

The expedition of Napoleon Bonaparte (1769–1821) to Egypt in 1798 resulted in the only war between France and the Ottoman Empire before 1914. With the Peace Treaty of Paris concluded on 25 June 1802, this war finally ended. As the Preamble shows, Bonaparte as the First Consul of the French Republic (1799–1804) and Sultan Selim III wanted to 're-establish the original relations of peace and friendship which have existed since time immemorial between France and the Sublime Porte'.[149] The Treaty itself is short and precise. Article 1 states: 'In future there will be peace and friendship between the French Republic and the Sublime Ottoman Porte. Hostilities between the two states end from now and forever.'[150] Article 2 regulates the renewal of all treaties or capitulations which had existed. The Ottoman subjects were granted equal rights in French territory.[151] With Article 5, territorial integrity was mutually guaranteed.[152] Article 9 contained a most-favoured-nation clause for both parties.[153]

A brief war between the Ottoman Empire and Great Britain was ended by the Peace Treaty which was signed at the Dardanelles on 5 January 1809, by a British diplomat and a high Turkish official on behalf respectively of Sultan Mahmut II (1808–39) 'Emperor of the Ottomans'[154] and King

[145] Preamble: 'Le très-puissant Empereur Otoman et la très-puissante Impératrice de toutes les Russies'.
[146] Art. 13: 'LL. MM. le Grand Sultan et l'Impératrice de Russie'.
[147] Art. 13: 'Le présent Traité ... qui asssure aux deux Empires une paix perpétuelle'.
[148] Art. 2: 'l'Acte conclu le ... 8 janvier 1784 ... relatif à l'incorporation à la Russie de la Crimée'.
[149] Preamble: 'Le Premier Consul de la République Française, au nom du Peuple francais, et le Sublime Empereur Ottoman, voulant rétablir les rapports primitifs de paix et d'amitié qui ont existé de tout temps entre la France et la Sublime Porte'.
[150] Art. 1: 'Il y aura à l'avenir paix et amitié entre la République Française et la Sublime Porte Ottomane. Les hostilités cesseront désormais et pour toujours entre les deux Etats'.
[151] Art. 2 *in fine*: 'Il est entendu que les avantages assurés aux Francais par le présent article dans l'Empire Ottoman sont également assurés auy sujets et au pavillon de la Sublime Porte dans les mers et sur le territoire de la République Francaise.'
[152] Art. 5: 'La République Francaise et la Sublime Porte se garantissent mutuellement l'intégrité de leurs possessions.'
[153] Art. 9: 'se placer dans les Etats l'une de l'autre sur le pied de la Puissance la plus favorisée'.
[154] Preamble: 'Sa Majesté, le ... Sultan Mahmoud Khan II, Empereur des Ottomans'.

George III of Great Britain (1760–1820). In the Preamble to the Treaty, which is less concise and more 'conservative', the 'sincere desire' of the Sublime Porte and the Royal Court of Great Britain is also expressed to 're-establish the ancient friendship which had existed between them'.[155] It is remarkable that in Article 4 especially the Ottoman–English Capitulation of 1675 is again confirmed and still valid.

The war between Russia and the Ottoman Empire (which had broken out in 1806) was ended by the Peace signed in Bucharest on 28 May 1812. The 'emperor of all the Russias', Alexander I, and the 'emperor of the Ottomans', Mahmut II, concluded 'peace, friendship and good understanding for perpetuity'.[156] Article 16 regulates the ratification of the 'treaty of perpetual peace'.[157]

The European Concert (1815–1914)

The nineteenth century was a period of further decay of Ottoman power, but also a time of inner reforms and of still closer connections with Europe, into the international system with the Ottoman Empire being invited at the Peace Congress of Paris in 1856, after it had won the Crimean war against Russia thanks to its military allies France and Great Britain. So, the few great peace treaties of the Ottoman sultans in that period were all concluded with Russia, the only European power which had not fully accepted the existence of the Turkish Empire as a necessary part of the balance of power in Europe.

The intervention of France, Great Britain and Russia in the Greek struggle for independence had not led to a general war with the Ottoman Empire. Only Russia waged war, conquered the ancient capital Adrianople/Edirne and threatened even Constantinople/Istanbul. The peace treaty which the diplomats of Sultan Mahmut II and the Russian emperor Nicholas I concluded in Adrianople on 14 September 1829 was moderate in its conditions: Russia had to take into account that France, Great Britain and Austria would not have accepted Russian rule on the Bosporus. The pattern of the peace treaty followed the Russian–Ottoman tradition. In Article 1 it is stipulated that 'there will be peace, friendship and good understanding for perpetuity, between His Majesty the

---

[155] '... ces deux Puissances, également animées du désir sincère de rétablir l'ancienne amitié qui subsistait entre Elles'.
[156] Art. 1: 'La paix, l'amitié et la bonne intelligence règneront désormais à perpétuité'.
[157] Art. 16: 'Le présent traité d'une paix perpétuelle sera confirmé et ratifié'.

Emperor and Padishah of all the Russias and His Highness the Emperor and Padishah of the Ottomans, their heirs and successors to the throne, as well as between their Empires'.[158] The title *Padishah* for the Russian emperor[159] was obviously used following Article 13 of the 1774 Peace Treaty of Küçük Kainarci. The confirmation of all former treaties between Russia and the Ottoman Empire, as far as they were not abrogated, was expressly stipulated in Article 15 of the 1829 Treaty of Adrianople.

The Peace Treaty of Paris, concluded on 30 March 1856 'In the Name of God Almighty',[160] has a non-typical character owing to the fact that it was also signed by the representatives of two European powers which had not been belligerents, namely Austria and Prussia. The Preamble explains the invitation of Austria to the congress with the desire of the former belligerents of 'securing through effectual and reciprocal guarantees the Independence and Integrity of the Ottoman Empire'.[161] The invitation of Prussia was explained by the reasoning that it had also signed the Straits Convention of 1841 (concerning shipping through the Dardanelles and the Bosporus). Article 1 constitutes perpetual 'peace and friendship'[162] between the emperor of France (Napoleon III, 1852–70), the queen of Great Britain (Victoria, 1837–1901), the king of Sardinia (Victor Emanuel II, 1849–78) and the sultan (Abdülmecit I), on the one part, and the emperor of Russia on the other part, and between their heirs and successors. Instead of single peace treaties with the former enemy states, Russia concluded one treaty with them together – a model for the future. The title used for Sultan Abdülmecit, 'His Imperial Majesty the Sultan',[163] corresponds to the firm European tradition of the Ottoman rulers. The famous Article 7 reached beyond a mere peace treaty, in which the monarchs of Austria, France, Great Britain, Prussia, Russia and Sardinia

> declare the Sublime Porte admitted to participate in the advantages of the Public Law and System of Europe. Their Majesties engage, each on his part,

---

[158] Art. 1: 'il y aura à perpétuité paix, amitié et bonne intelligence entre Sa Majesté l'Empereur et Padichah de toutes les Russies et Sa Hautesse l'Empereur et Padichah des Ottomans, leurs héritiers et successeurs au trône, ainsi qu'entre leurs Empires'.
[159] Used also in Art. 2.
[160] Heading: 'Au nom de Dieu Tout-Puissant'. This form was acceptable for both Christians and Muslims.
[161] Preamble: 'en assurant par des garanties efficaces et réciproques l'indépendance et l'intégrité de l'Empire Ottoman'.
[162] Art. 1: 'paix et amitié . . . à perpétuité'.
[163] Art. 1: 'S.M.I. le Sultan'. In the Preamble, the title of the sultan was 'Sa Majesté l'Empereur des Ottomans'.

to respect the Independence and the Territorial Integrity of the Ottoman Empire, guarantee in common the strict observance of that engagement, and will, in consequence, consider any act tending to its violation as a question of general interest.[164]

That this guarantee was no dead letter, but was meant seriously, is shown by the short treaty concluded between Austria, France and Great Britain in Paris on 15 April 1856, in which they confirm their guarantee of the independence and integrity of the Ottoman Empire already given in the Peace Treaty of 30 March 1856 and make clear that a violation of the Paris Peace Treaty on this matter would be a *casus belli*.[165]

The only major peace treaty which the Ottoman Empire had to conclude in the nineteenth century was again included in a convention of the leading European powers. The crisis in the Balkans, where the Christian vassal states and Christian populations in Ottoman provinces claimed independence even with local wars and insurrections, resulted in the Ottoman war against Russia (1877/78), with disastrous results for the Turkish Empire. The Russian army once more conquered Edirne, and reached the periphery of modern Istanbul, San Stefano,[166] where the diplomats of Sultan Abdülhamit II (1876–1909) had to accept conditions of peace, dictated by the diplomats of the Russian emperor Alexander II (1855–81), which Great Britain and Austria-Hungary were not willing to tolerate in this form. So the Peace Treaty of San Stefano of 3 March 1878 led to the conference of Berlin, where a treaty was concluded on 13 July 1878, 'In the name of God Almighty', between Germany, Austria, France, Great Britain, Italy, Russia and the Ottoman Empire, incorporating the Russian–Turkish peace into a wider European solution of the so-called 'Oriental question'. This is demonstrated also by the Preamble to the Berlin Treaty, according to which the contracting parties were 'desirous to regulate, with a view to European order, according to the stipulations of the Treaty of Paris of 30 March 1856, the questions raised in the East

---

[164] Art. 7: 'déclarent la Sublime Porte admise à participer aux avantages du droit public et du concert européens. Leurs Majestés s'engagent, chacun de son côté, à respecter l'indépendance et l'intégrité territoriale de l'Empire Ottoman, garantissent en commun la stricte observation de cet engagement, et considéreront, en conséquence, tout acte de nature à y porter atteinte comme une question d'interêt général.'

[165] Art. 2: 'Toute infraction aux stipulations dudit traité sera considérée par les Puissances signataires du présent traité comme un casus belli.' The Treaty was ratified on 29 April 1856.

[166] Today Yesilköy, beside the airport of Istanbul.

by the events of the past few years and by the war terminated by the preliminary Treaty of San Stefano'.[167] So the territorial losses, especially the independence of Montenegro, Serbia and Romania, lost some of their bitterness for the Ottoman Porte. Generally, the treaty partners of 'His Majesty the Emperor of the Ottomans'[168] tried to respect the sentiments of the sultan-caliph. Therefore, Bulgaria was 'constituted an autonomous and tributary principality under the suzerainty of His Imperial Majesty the Sultan'.[169]

The further decline of the Ottoman power before World War I was not accompanied by great wars. The few peace treaties which the last sultans who officially participated in the 'European Concert' had to sign followed traditional European patterns. So we need not discuss the Ottoman Peace Treaty with Greece concluded in Constantinople in 1897, the Peace Treaty with Italy concluded in Ouchy in 1912, the Peace Treaty with Bulgaria, Greece, Montenegro and Serbia concluded after the first 'Balkan War' in London in May 1913, and the new border agreed upon with Bulgaria after the second 'Balkan War' in the same year.

Conclusion

The role of the Ottoman Empire during World War I as ally of Germany, Austria-Hungary and Bulgaria also included participation in the Peace Treaties concluded in 1918 with Russia, with the Ukraine and with Romania, before the war was lost.[170] The Peace Treaty of Sèvres, which the government of the last 'Ottoman emperor', Sultan Mehmet VI (1918–22), had to sign on 10 August 1920, was drawn up in three languages (French, English and Italian)[171] and concluded between 'The British Empire, France, Italy and Japan ... Armenia, Belgium, Greece, the Hejaz, Poland, Portugal, Romania, the Serb-Croat-Slovene State and Czecho-Slovakia ... of the one part; and Turkey of the other part'.[172] The declared

---

[167] Preamble: 'désirant régler dans une pensée d'ordre européen, conformément aux stipulations du Traité de Paris du 30 Mars 1856, les questions soulevées en Orient par les événements des dernières années et par la guerre dont le Traité préliminaire de San Stefano a marqué le terme, etc.'.
[168] Preamble: 'S.M. l'Empereur des Ottomans'.
[169] Art. 1: 'La Bulgarie est constituée en principauté autonome et tributaire sous la suzeraineté de S.M. Impériale le Sultan.'
[170] Karl-Heinz Ziegler, 'Deutschland und das Osmanische Reich in ihren völkerrechtlichen Beziehungen', *Archiv des Völkerrechts* 35 (1997), 255–72 at p. 271.
[171] Cf. the final clause following Art. 433.   [172] Preamble.

intention of the 'Allied Powers' to grant a 'firm, just and durable Peace'[173] was hardly to be discovered in the conditions set by the Treaty of Sèvres. It reduced the former Empire to a Turkish state with Istanbul and the greater part of Anatolia without real sovereignty, divided by the victors into spheres of influence. France and Great Britain, for centuries the 'friends' of the Sublime Porte, were rather narrow-minded victors after World War I. So, neither the sultan's government nor the revolutionary national movement led by Mustafa Kemal Pasha (later Atatürk) ratified the Treaty of Sèvres. In 1922, when the Kemalist forces entered Istanbul, the last Ottoman sultan (Mehmet VI) left Turkey forever, on board a British warship. The Peace Treaty of Lausanne concluded on 24 July 1923 between 'The British Empire, France, Italy, Japan, Greece, Romania and the Serb-Croat-Slovene State, of the one part, and Turkey, of the other part' was a treaty in a better tradition. The Preamble expressly mentioned the consideration that normal international relations 'must be based on respect for the independence and sovereignty of States'. So, the Turkish Republic (*Türkiye Cumhuriyeti*), which was proclaimed on 29 October 1923,[174] from its beginning was an equal member in the international community and in Europe, without the shadow that the unsuccesful Treaty of Sèvres had thrown on the dying Ottoman Empire.

[173] Preamble.   [174] The Sultanate had been abolished already on 1 November 1922.

17

Peace and prosperity: commercial aspects of peacemaking

STEPHEN C. NEFF

Introduction

Peacemaking may be seen in either narrow or broad terms. In narrow terms, peacemaking consists of the settlement of the particular issue or issues over which the war in question has been fought. Peacemaking in the broader sense may be taken to refer to the full 'normalisation' of relations between the erstwhile enemy states. 'Normalisation' is not a legal term of art; it comprises a range of matters, from cultural ties and diplomatic links to tourism and trade. The present discussion will focus on commercial ties.[1]

The relationship between the political and economic aspects of peacemaking, i.e. between peacemaking in the narrow and in the broad senses, has a certain intrinsic interest. But it also has a deeper significance: as a means of tracking or mirroring the changes that have taken place in the legal nature of war itself. This discussion will identify several historical phases. First there were the medieval and early modern periods, in which the medieval philosophy of just and unjust wars lay at the basis of legal thought about war and peace. In the seventeenth and eighteenth centuries, war was thought of in different terms, as a form of civil litigation. A third phase is comprised by the nineteenth century (up to World War I), when war was seen as a tool for the pursuit of national interests, largely to be wielded at the will of the individual states. Finally, in the twentieth century, ideas reminiscent of the medieval just-war outlook returned to international relations with the UN Charter's prohibition against the use of force.

---

[1] This discussion will not be concerned with indemnity or reparations aspects of peacemaking, which, although economic in nature, clearly do not fall into the category of 'normal' economic relations.

The Middle Ages

Two features of the European Middle Ages are particularly relevant to the subject at hand. First was the inauguration of the practice of regulating economic relations between states by way of framework treaties between their rulers. This practice began with the trading activities of the Italian cities in the eleventh century, and became more general during the following centuries.[2] The typical arrangement was that each ruler would guarantee that traders from the other state would be entitled to a number of basic protections, so that trade could take place with a minimum of disruption. These arrangements, which gradually became more elaborate, came to be known generically as treaties of friendship, commerce and navigation, or simply as FCN treaties.

The second notable feature of medieval Europe was the just-war doctrine, which was inherited from classical thought and further elaborated under the auspices of the Catholic Church. The principal objective of the just-war theory was to delineate objective criteria for the justifiable resort to armed force. For present purposes, however, the important feature of the concept was that it did not envisage a complete rupture of *all* relations between the warring states. In the just-war outlook, war was seen as essentially a remedial or punitive measure taken (always with reluctance) against a legal wrongdoer, in response to some specific violation of law. The medieval just war, in short, was essentially a law enforcement operation.[3]

A consequence of this medieval conception of war as law enforcement was that the warring states, throughout their struggle, never ceased to be fellow members of the same legal and moral community. By analogy, criminals did not cease to be members of society by virtue of their crimes – they merely became subject to lawful sanctions. Once the legal wrong had been corrected, for example by the infliction of appropriate punishment on the wrongdoing state, full normal relations should automatically resume, in the manner in which ex-criminals automatically resume their status as full members of society after undergoing their prescribed penalties.

It may be noted that this law enforcement model of war effectively precluded any idea of a state of war or of total war, i.e. of complete hostility

---

[2] On the early history of FCN treaties, see François L. Ganshof, *The Middle Ages: A History of International Relations* (New York, 1970), pp. 141–4.
[3] For a general survey of medieval just-war thought, see Frederick H. Russell, *The Just War in the Middle Ages* (Cambridge, 1975).

between the warring sides in all walks of life. In particular circumstances, of course, economic relations might be broken or economic treaties denounced or suspended, as a means of warmaking, i.e. as a utilitarian stratagem for defeating the enemy. The important point, though, is that the medieval just-war outlook did not necessitate an *automatic* rupture of economic relations between the warring states. In sum, the general nature and structure of medieval thought about war prevented the restoration of economic relations at the conclusion of the conflict from being problematic in principle. On the contrary, full normalisation of relations (i.e. peacemaking in the broader sense) was an automatic consequence of the ending of wars.

The seventeenth and eighteenth centuries

By the seventeenth century, several important changes had taken place in the field of international relations amongst the major European states. Two of these changes call for particular attention. First is the fact that, in this period, the concluding of FCN treaties became, for the first time, a routine and well-nigh universal feature of relations amongst the major European maritime states – so much so that FCN treaties came to be in virtually standard form. The second important feature of this period was the frequency of warfare amongst the major Western European states, with rivalry between Britain and France being the single most persistent feature.

In terms of international legal theory, the most important development of the period, for present purposes, was a change of ideas about the nature of war itself. The medieval just-war outlook, with its law enforcement ethos, had faded and had been replaced by a view of war as a clash of rival national interests without general moral or legal significance for the international community as a whole. More specifically, the idea of a *state* of war made its appearance, most notably in the writings of Hugo Grotius (1583–1645) and Thomas Hobbes (1588–1679).[4] This meant, in essence, that war was now seen as a situation in which there is a global transformation of legal relations between the contending states, into one of across-the-board hostility.

This new way of thinking directly implied a total-war outlook, which (as noted above) had been distinctly foreign to the medieval just-war theory. Of course, the technology and administrative capacity for waging total war

---

[4] Hugo Grotius, *De jure belli ac pacis libri tres* 3, 20 (Paris, 1625) and Thomas Hobbes, *Leviathan* (Oxford, 1957), p. 82.

in the twentieth-century sense was lacking. Nevertheless, it is fair to say that there was a total-war ethos in this period, in the sense that wars were commonly seen as contests not simply between uniformed armed forces but rather between the economies of the states. The common methods of waging war included the disruption of the enemy state's maritime trade by the systematic capturing of enemy property at sea. This style of economic warfare reached its climax in the wars of the French Revolution period, when Napoleon's Continental System was matched against British blockade policies.[5]

In the light of this total-war mentality, it is not surprising that one feature of a state of war was held to be the automatic and total abrogation of *all* peaceful relations between the warring states. More specifically, it meant the automatic abrogation of all pre-war treaties, including, of course, FCN treaties. A determined state could even exploit this doctrine by instituting a war for the very purpose of terminating an inconvenient economic treaty. Britain did just this in 1780, when it declared war against the Netherlands on, effectively, spurious grounds. Britain put forward some grievances against the Dutch for the sake of appearances. But there is no serious doubt that the real purpose of its declaration of war was to put an end to an FCN treaty of 1674, which Britain found to be inconvenient because of its provision that 'free ships make free goods' (i.e. that Britain, when it was a belligerent, could not capture enemy goods that were being carried on Dutch ships when the Netherlands was neutral).[6]

In all events, this doctrine of automatic abrogation of treaties by a state of war made the full normalisation of relations at the conclusion of a war more difficult than before. Conscious steps had to be taken to restore full economic relations, separately from the termination of the war itself (i.e. separately from peacemaking in the narrow sense). These two conceptually distinct steps could, of course, be embodied in the same instrument. For example, the Peace Treaty of Madrid of 1630 between England and Spain provided for a full resumption of economic relations.[7] So did the Treaty of the Pyrenees of 1659 between France and Spain.

The more common practice by far, however, was for the peacemaking states to conclude a new FCN treaty separate from, but in tandem with,

---

[5] The best description of this contest from the economic and legal standpoints is still Eli F. Heckscher, *The Continental System: An Economic Interpretation* (Oxford, 1922).

[6] Treaty of Commerce and Navigation of 10 December 1674, Art. 8. On the legal problems involving FCN treaties during this period, see Stephen C. Neff, *The Rights and Duties of Neutrals: A General History* (Manchester, 2000), pp. 27–43.

[7] Art. 7.

the peace treaty itself. In other words, the distinction between peacemaking in the narrow and the broader senses commonly found institutional expression in the resort to a two-stage peacemaking process. One treaty – the peace treaty properly speaking – would terminate the armed conflict and thereby bring peace in the narrow sense. It might transfer territory from one state to the other or settle the succession to a crown. The second stage – the conclusion of a separate FCN treaty – would bring about peace in the broader sense by placing the economic relations between the countries on a stable footing.

Sometimes the two separate treaties were concluded on, literally, the same day. This was the case on several occasions in which France and the Netherlands brought wars to an end. In 1678, the Peace of Nijmegen comprised two simultaneous treaties, one of peace and the other of commerce.[8] The same was true of the Peace of Ryswick in 1697[9] and of the Peace of Utrecht in 1713.[10] The Peace of Utrecht also comprised simultaneous bilateral treaties of peace and commerce between France and Britain.[11]

On other occasions, some interval of time separated the two. The Second Anglo-Dutch War, for example, was terminated in July 1667 by the Treaty of Breda, with the corresponding FCN treaty concluded early the next year.[12] When the Third Anglo-Dutch War was ended in 1674, the peace treaty preceded the commercial treaty by some ten months.[13] In the case of the Utrecht Peace Treaties following the War of the Spanish Succession, a gap of some five months separated the peace treaty between Britain and Spain from the FCN treaty.[14] After France and Britain brought their conflict over American independence to an end in 1783, three years elapsed before the conclusion of a commercial treaty.[15] Similarly, in December 1814, Britain and the United States ended a war between them with the Treaty of Ghent, with a Convention of Commerce following seven months later.[16]

---

[8] Both 10 August 1678.   [9] Both 20 September 1697.
[10] Both 11 April 1713.   [11] Both 11 April 1713 as well.
[12] Treaty of Breda of 31 July 1667 and Treaty of Commerce of 17 February 1668.
[13] Treaty of Peace of 19 February 1674 and Treaty of Commerce and Navigation of 10 December 1674.
[14] Treaty of Peace and Friendship of 13 July 1713 and Treaty of Commerce and Navigation of 9 December 1713.
[15] Definitive Treaty of Peace of Paris of 3 September 1783 and Treaty of Commerce and Navigation of 26 September 1786.
[16] Treaty of Ghent of 24 December 1814 and Treaty of Commerce of 3 July 1815.

When new FCN treaties were concluded in conjunction with peace agreements, they sometimes simply replicated the ones that had been abrogated. The Treaty of Commerce and Navigation between Britain and Spain in 1713, for example, following the War of the Spanish Succession, reproduced an earlier FCN treaty of 1667 word for word.[17] Straightforward reinstatement was not, however, the universal practice. If bargaining power had shifted since the conclusion of the previous treaty, the new one might be more favourable to the one side, and less favourable to the other, than the previous arrangement had been.

As always, we should beware of overestimating the consistency of state practice – especially since we are concerned here more with usage than with actual law. Peace treaties were not always accompanied by commercial treaties. For example, the termination of the First Anglo-Dutch War of 1652–54 was not accompanied by an FCN treaty between the two states.[18] Nor did the British–French component of the Peace of Ryswick of 1697 include a commercial treaty.[19] Also, in 1784, when Britain and the Netherlands concluded their conflict – entailing, as noted above, the abrogation of their existing FCN Treaty of 1674 – they did not conclude a replacement commercial treaty.[20] Nevertheless, it is broadly true to say that, in the seventeenth and eighteenth centuries, peacemaking practice was a two-stage process, directly reflecting the distinction between peace in the narrow sense and peace in the broader sense.

The nineteenth century

The nineteenth century witnessed the culmination of the positivist tendency in international law – including its view of war as a clash of rival national interests, devoid of any wider moral or legal significance. War was seen, now more than ever, as an unavoidable fact of international life, in which legal and moral notions such as fault, or guilt and innocence, were not applicable. An important departure from the previous centuries, however, was the discarding of the total-war mentality of the preceding era. It was replaced by a belief that war is – or at least should be – a contest between the professional armed forces of the two societies, with minimal disruption of civilian life. The professionalisation of war had, of course,

---

[17] Treaty of Commerce and Navigation of 9 December 1713.
[18] For the peace treaty, see Treaty of Westminster of 5 April 1654.
[19] For the peace treaty, see Treaty of Peace of 20 September 1697.
[20] For the peace treaty, see Definitive Treaty of Peace and Friendship of 20 May 1784.

been long in the making. But only in the nineteenth century was it fully articulated as a principle of law, most outstandingly by the Declaration of St Petersburg of 1868, which expressly stated that 'the only legitimate object' of war is 'to weaken the military forces of the enemy'.[21]

Reinforcing this limited-war outlook was the general trend towards economic liberalism. The liberal political economists of Britain and France envisaged the integration of the world into a single economic unit, suffering as little disruption as possible from political rivalries. This trend was naturally favourable towards increased rights of neutrals at the expense of belligerents, and of tightly confining warfare to professional armed forces, with as little disruption of civilian economic life as possible. This is an interesting demonstration of the way in which material modes of thought had replaced the moral ones of the Middle Ages. In the Middle Ages, the world had been seen as a single moral community, bound together by the ties of natural law, which subsisted even during war. In the materialistic nineteenth century, it was increasingly held that the world was – or at least was becoming – a single *economic* community, and that intermittent wars were merely, so to speak, temporary disturbances on the surface which should not affect that underlying unity.

One consequence of these interlocking trends was to cast doubt on the continued validity of the traditional rule that war automatically abrogates treaties between the contending parties. On the doctrinal side, there was, broadly speaking, a split between Anglo-American and continental European writers. English-speaking writers tended to adhere to the older doctrine of automatic abrogation, even into the twentieth century.[22] Continental European scholars, however, generally held that the automatic-abrogation principle was now obsolete. On this view, treaties between warring states (including economic treaties) were merely suspended during the conflict, but not terminated. As a result, they automatically came back into full effect when the state of war was terminated, unless the peace treaty itself provided otherwise. This view was essentially endorsed by the Institute of International Law in 1912. It pronounced, broadly speaking, that only political treaties are terminated by war, not commercial ones.[23]

---

[21] A. Roberts and R. Guelff (eds.), *Documents on the Laws of War* (3rd edn, Oxford, 2000), p. 55.
[22] See, most notably, John Westlake, *International Law* (2nd edn, Cambridge, 1913), vol. II, pp. 32–5.
[23] Resolution of 31 August 1912, Art. 2, in Institut de Droit International, *Tableau général des résolutions (1873–1956)* (Basel, 1957), p. 174.

The doctrinal positions on this automatic-abrogation issue appear to have had relatively little impact on state practice. In the face of uncertainty as to the general rule, it became the common practice for warring states to make provisions regarding pre-war treaties on an ad hoc basis. The result was a welter of different approaches.

Sometimes, peace treaties expressly endorsed the older automatic-abrogation rule by expressly stating that the war had terminated all prior treaties between the parties. An example is the Treaty of Frankfurt of 1871, which concluded the Franco-Prussian War.[24] Another example is the Treaty of Shimonoseki of 1895, concluding the Sino-Japanese War.[25] The peace arrangement between Britain and Venezuela in 1903 took an interestingly cautious middle course on the automatic-abrogation question. Noting that 'it might possibly be contended' that the conflict between the two states had abrogated all treaties, it proceeded to reinstate two identified FCN agreements between the two states.[26]

More in tune with the newer spirit were provisions for the revival or continuation of earlier treaties. It was often difficult to be certain whether those prior treaties were being re-concluded (after having been terminated), or whether they were being re-activated after a period of suspension or dormancy. In all events, some peace treaties stated that *all* prior agreements between the parties were now revived (or re-concluded), with no special consideration given to economic agreements. For example, a peace treaty of 1883 between Chile and Spain restored 'the state of things' from before the war pending new treaties – not expressly referring to economic agreements as such but clearly encompassing them.[27] Other examples of revival (or re-conclusion) include the peace treaty between El Salvador and Nicaragua in 1886, as well as the Treaty of Lausanne of 1912 between Italy and Turkey.[28] Sometimes, this mass revival of pre-war treaties was done by way of a protocol accompanying the peace treaty, as in the case of the peace made in 1859 between France and Austria, in which

---

[24] Treaty of Frankfurt of 10 May 1871, Art. 11.
[25] Treaty of Shimonoseki of 17 April 1895, Art. 6.
[26] Exchange of Notes Reserving and Confirming Former Treaties of 13 February 1903 between Great Britain and Venezuela. See also the Treaty for the Settlement of British Claims of 13 February 1903, between Great Britain and Venezuela, Art. 7. The two earlier FCN treaties that were revived were the Treaty of Amity, Commerce and Navigation of 18 April 1825 between Colombia and Great Britain and the Convention of Amity, Commerce and Navigation of 29 October 1834 between Great Britain and Venezuela.
[27] Treaty of Peace and Amity of 12 June 1883, Art. 3.
[28] Treaty of Amapala of 13 January 1886 between El Salvador and Nicaragua, Art. 1; and Definitive Treaty of Peace of 18 October 1912 between Italy and Turkey, Art. 5.

the peace treaty was accompanied by a Protocol Reviving Conventions Existing before the War.[29]

Some peace treaties, instead of reviving pre-war treaties *en bloc*, provided for the revival (or continuation) of specified pre-war commercial agreements. An example is the Treaty of Adrianople of 1829 between Russia and Turkey.[30] A peace treaty of 1864 between Colombia and Ecuador provided that an identified pre-war FCN treaty 'remains in full rigour' (apparently suggesting that the war had not actually terminated it).[31] The peace agreement of 1903 between Italy and Venezuela expressly revived an 1861 FCN treaty between the two states.[32]

Another common practice could be described as a sort of 'half-way house' between the older rule of automatic abrogation and the (arguably) newer rule of automatic revival. This was the provisional revival of pre-war treaties, pending the conclusion of new agreements in the future. The peace between Spain and France in 1814, for example, provided that a treaty of commerce would be concluded as soon as possible – but that, in the meantime, economic relations between the countries would be conducted on the pre-war basis.[33] The treaty of peace of that same year between Spain and Denmark restored relations between the two countries in the area of commerce and navigation to the pre-war status and then went on to provide that any extension of those arrangements would be achieved by means of a separate treaty.[34] The peace treaty between Denmark and Prussia of that year provided for a general restoration of relations to the pre-war position, and then provided that, in order to expand commercial relations, the two states would conclude a separate treaty of commerce without delay.[35] A similar arrangement was concluded that same year between Chile and Peru, providing that commercial relations would revert to their pre-war footing, pending the conclusion of a 'special treaty' on the subject.[36] The Bulgaria–Turkey Peace Treaty of 1913 provisionally revived a pre-existing commercial treaty for one year – with the parties then to negotiate a new and permanent treaty as soon as possible.[37]

---

[29] Treaty of Peace of 10 November 1859 and Protocols of Conference of 10 November 1859.
[30] Treaty of Adrianople of 14 September 1829, Art. 7.
[31] Treaty of Peace of 1 January 1864, Art. 3.
[32] Treaty for the Settlement of Italian Claims of 13 February 1903, Art. 8.
[33] Treaty of Peace and Amity of 20 July 1814, 2 of Additional Articles.
[34] Treaty of Peace of 14 August 1814, Arts. 4–5.
[35] Treaty of Peace of 25 August 1814, Arts. 2–3.
[36] Treaty of Peace and Amity of 20 October 1883, Art. 11.
[37] Treaty of Peace of 29 September 1913, Art. 4.

Some peace treaties dealt with economic relations between the parties not by reviving earlier treaties but rather by including economic and commercial arrangements in the peace treaty itself. This occurred in several treaties concluded in 1815–16 between Algiers and various Western powers – with the United States, Sardinia and the Kingdom of the Two Sicilies.[38] Another instance of this practice is found in a peace treaty between Ecuador and Peru in 1860.[39] The Treaty of Frankfurt of 1871 between France and Germany at the end of the Franco-Prussian War, after confirming that pre-war treaties had been annulled, provided that the most-favoured nation principle would henceforth form the basis of the relations between the two states.[40] In the Treaty of Peace between Russia and the Khanate of Khiva in 1873, the majority of articles concerned economic matters.[41] The Peace Treaty between France and China of 1885 contained several provisions regarding trade between the two countries.[42] (The two states concluded a full commercial treaty the following year.[43])

A variant of this practice was for the peace treaty to contain a mutual grant at first instance (i.e. not reviving a pre-existing treaty) of most-favoured nation status, pending the conclusion of a separate, fully fledged FCN agreement in the future. Examples include peace treaties between France and Mexico in 1839, between Buenos Aires and France in 1840 and between Peru and Spain in 1879.[44] In much the same vein, a peace agreement between Buenos Aires and Spain in 1823 contained various commercial provisions, while envisaging a later 'special convention' on maritime commerce.[45]

Sometimes, peace treaties simply envisaged the conclusion, in the near future, of a treaty on economic relations, but without including any provisional arrangements in the peace treaty itself. Examples include a peace treaty of 1829 between Colombia and Peru, as well as peace treaties

---

[38] Treaty of Peace of 3 July 1815 between Algiers and the United States; Treaty of Peace and Amity of 3 April 1816 between Algiers and Sardinia; and Treaty of Peace of 3 April 1816 between Algiers and the Kingdom of the Two Sicilies.
[39] Treaty of Peace, Friendship and Alliance of Guayaguil, 25 January 1860, Arts. 13–15 and 24.
[40] Treaty of Frankfurt of 10 May 1871, Art. 11.
[41] Treaty of Peace of 24 August 1873, Arts. 5–13.
[42] Treaty of Peace, Friendship and Commerce of 9 June 1885, Arts. 6–7.
[43] Commercial Convention of 25 April 1886.
[44] Treaty of Peace and Friendship of 9 March 1839 between France and Mexico, Art. 3; Convention of 29 October 1840 between Buenos Aires and France, Art. 5; and Treaty of Peace of 14 August 1879 between Peru and Spain, Arts. 3–4.
[45] Preliminary Convention of 4 July 1823, Art. 5.

between Peru and Spain in 1865, between Italy and Ethiopia in 1896 and between Greece and Turkey in 1897.[46] Sometimes, specific time limits were fixed for the conclusion of economic agreements. A protocol to the Peace Treaty of 1897 between Greece and Turkey, for example, provided that an FCN treaty was to be concluded between the two states within two years.[47] (In the event, some five and half years elapsed before the treaty envisaged was actually signed.[48])

In sum, the nineteenth century presents a wide spectrum of devices for supplementing peace arrangements in the narrow sense with provisions for full normalisation of relations. A common element – and perhaps the only one – was a definite awareness on the part of statesmen that peace in the fullest sense entailed more than merely terminating the hostilities and resolving the immediate issue which had given rise to the war.

The twentieth century: the era of the world wars

The peacemaking at the conclusion of the First World War marked a sharp departure from the immediately preceding period. When the peace was negotiated in 1919, the conflict was not treated as a mere clash of national interests; instead, it was agreed (by the victorious Allied Powers, of course) that the conflict had been the exclusive responsibility of the German side. As a result, the Versailles Treaty assumed an overtly punitive character more in tune with the medieval just-war philosophy of war than with the positivist ethos of the preceding era. The most famous indication of this new (or old) outlook was the imposition on Germany of a duty to pay reparations.[49] This development understandably caused deep resentment in Germany.

More pertinently for present considerations, it may be noted that the Versailles Treaty contained a host of economic arrangements. There were detailed provisions barring discriminatory treatment of post-war German commerce with the Allied states. The treaty granted most-favoured nation status unconditionally to the Allied states and guaranteed fair treatment of Allied nationals doing business with Germany. Germany was required

---

[46] Treaty of Peace of 22 September 1829 between Colombia and Peru, Art. 15; Preliminary Treaty of Peace and Friendship of 17 January 1865 between Peru and Spain, Art. 4; Treaty of Peace of 26 October 1896 between Ethiopia and Italy, Art. 6; and Treaty of Peace of 4 December 1897 between Greece and Turkey, Art. 11.
[47] Treaty of Peace of 4 December 1897, Protocol B.
[48] Treaty of Commerce and Navigation of 12 April 1903.
[49] Treaty of Versailles of 26 June 1919, Arts. 231–2.

to protect goods from Allied countries from 'unfair competition in commercial transactions'. There was to be no state immunity for German governmental acts in the field of international trade. There were also detailed provisions on freedom of transit and aerial navigation.[50]

Another notable feature of the Versailles Treaty was the way that it dealt with pre-existing economic treaties – with different treatment for multilateral and bilateral treaties. Regarding multilateral treaties, some twenty-six such agreements were singled out as continuing in force for Germany. Moreover, Germany was obligated to become a party, over the five years following the treaty, to any general conventions concluded by the Allies with the approval of the League of Nations.[51] The Treaty of Lausanne with Turkey, in 1923, similarly included a list of multilateral treaties that were to continue in force, as well as a list of agreements that Turkey undertook to become a party to. In addition, Turkey undertook specifically to adhere to the Barcelona Convention on Freedom of Transit, to the Convention and Statute on International Waterways and to the recommendations of the Conference of Barcelona on International Railways.[52]

As for bilateral treaties, the Treaty of Versailles granted to the victorious powers the right to designate which pre-war treaties with Germany would be revived or retained. (German bilateral treaties with Russia and Romania were specifically stated to be abrogated.)[53] Similar provisions were included in the Treaties of St-Germain-en-Laye and Neuilly with Austria and Hungary respectively.[54]

After the Second World War, the so-called 'little peace treaties' of 1947, concluded with five axis Powers, contained provisions on future economic relations. They set out a number of provisional economic arrangements, which were stated to be of eighteen months' duration. These were most-favoured nation treatment regarding trade and tariffs, a ban on 'arbitrary discrimination' against goods from Allied states and a ban on discrimination or exclusivity regarding civil aviation rights. (All of these requirements were subject to conditions of reciprocity on the part of the Allied states.) Regarding pre-war bilateral treaties, the Versailles Treaty approach

---

[50] Part X.   [51] Arts. 282 and 379.
[52] Treaty of Lausanne of 24 July 1923, Arts. 99–101 and 104.
[53] Treaty of Versailles of 28 June 1919, Arts. 289 and 292.
[54] Treaty of Saint-Germain-en-Laye of 10 September 1919, Art. 241 and Treaty of Neuilly of 27 November 1919, Art. 168.

was adopted, of granting the victors the option of selecting which treaties would be revived (or continued).[55]

The Japanese peace treaty concluded with the Western powers in 1951 also set out a number of provisional economic arrangements, to last for four years. These included most-favoured nation treatment on customs matters and national treatment with regard to shipping, navigation, taxation, access to courts, contracts and property. As in the European treaties, these arrangements were subject to reciprocal treatment of Japan by the Allied Powers. Regarding the longer term, Japan was to enter into negotiations with the victorious states to put commercial relations on to 'a stable and friendly basis'. More specifically, it was promptly to enter into negotiations on a fishing agreement with the Allied Powers. [56]

The separate arrangement between Japan and the Soviet Union in 1956 was to much the same effect. Although there has not yet been a fully fledged peace treaty between Japan and Russia (because of a continuing dispute over the Kuril Islands), the state of war was terminated in 1956 by means of a joint declaration. This declaration included an agreement to enter into negotiations for putting trade, navigation and commercial relations on to 'a firm and friendly basis'.[57] An accompanying protocol, concluded the same day, contained a provisional arrangement for most-favoured nation treatment regarding customs duties and vessels in ports.[58] (A bilateral treaty of commerce was duly concluded the following year.[59]) In bilateral peace treaties with Burma and Poland, Japan entered into similar commitments.[60] (In the Polish case, as in the Soviet one, a commercial treaty was duly concluded the following year.[61]) The general peace agreement between El Salvador and Honduras of 1980 similarly contained a commitment to conclude a bilateral trade treaty later (with the negotiators

---

[55] See, for example, Treaty of Peace of Paris with Bulgaria of 10 February 1947, Arts. 8 and 29. See, to the same effect: Treaty of Peace of Paris with Hungary of 10 February 1947, Arts. 10 and 33; Treaty of Peace of Paris with Italy of 10 February 1947, Art. 44, Part VIII; Treaty of Peace of Paris with Romania of 10 February 1947, Arts. 10 and 31 and Treaty of Peace of Paris with Finland of 10 February 1947, Arts. 12 and 30.
[56] Treaty of Peace with Japan of 8 September 1951, Arts. 9 and 12–13.
[57] Joint Declaration of 19 October 1956, Arts. 1 and 7.
[58] Protocol concerning the Expansion of Trade of 19 October 1956, Art. 1.
[59] Treaty of Commerce of 6 December 1957.
[60] Treaty of Peace of 5 November 1954 between Burma and Japan, Arts. 3–4 and Treaty on the Re-establishment of Normal Relations of 8 February 1957 between Japan and Poland, Art. 5.
[61] Treaty of Commerce of 26 April 1958.

to be appointed within three months of the entry into force of the peace treaty).[62]

The twentieth century: the United Nations era

In the meantime, the United Nations Charter was concluded in 1945 containing an express prohibition against the use of force in international relations – with the two outstanding exceptions of self-defence and enforcement action by (or under the approval of) the UN itself. This prohibition went far towards eliminating, at least formally, the concept of a state of war between countries. Instead, war (or the use of force) was now to be seen as a delict, apart from the two exceptions just noted. The UN Charter therefore also, in effect, went far towards reinstating the medieval just-war outlook. Not only was there now a distinction between just and unjust – or, more strictly, lawful and unlawful – wars, but also the idea took hold that, as in the Middle Ages, the eruption of an armed conflict did not automatically entail a comprehensive break in relations between the states concerned. For example, diplomatic relations continued between Iraq and Iran for the major part of their epic conflict of the 1980s.

It is therefore now widely, if tacitly, agreed that an armed conflict does not automatically terminate pre-existing treaties. This conclusion is reinforced by an important change in the legal character of international economic relations. Instead of being organised on a bilateral basis, by means of FCN treaties, the legal framework of international economic relations, since 1945, has been multilateral in nature – first under the General Agreement on Tariffs and Trade (of 1947) and, since 1995, under the World Trade Organisation (WTO). If the parties to a conflict are both WTO members, there will be, in effect, an automatic resumption of economic ties when a conflict ends.

The effect of these developments has been that post-1945 peace agreements have often consisted of little more than arrangements to halt the hostilities. This was the case, most obviously, with the Israel–Arab armistice agreements of 1949, as well as with the Israel–Syria Disengagement Agreement of 1974.[63] The same was true of the armistice in Korea

---

[62] General Peace Treaty of 30 October 1980, Art. 41.
[63] General Armistice Agreement of 24 February 1949 between Egypt and Israel; General Armistice Agreement of 23 March 1949 between Israel and Lebanon; General Armistice Agreement of 3 April 1949 between Israel and Jordan; General Armistice Agreement of 20 July 1949 between Israel and Syria and Agreement on Disengagement of 30 May 1974 between Israel and Syria.

in 1953.[64] The Paris Peace Agreement of 1973, concluding the American phase of the Vietnam War, contained many details of a political and military character but none of a commercial nature.[65] Nor did the arrangements for the termination of the Gulf War in 1991, which were highly detailed, contain any commercial provisions (although there were provisions regarding compensation for damage committed and Iraq's honouring of pre-war debts).[66]

The Falklands conflict offers a particularly instructive illustration of this UN-era style of peacemaking. During the conflict, Britain broke diplomatic relations and also instituted a number of economic measures. But these economic measures are best seen (it is submitted) as an integral part of Britain's effort to win the conflict, rather than as an automatic consequence of a state of war. Indeed, Britain was always careful to characterise the conflict as an exercise in self-defence on its part rather than as a war in the traditional sense. The termination of the conflict took the form of a simple military surrender by the Argentine armed forces on the islands.[67] Argentina described the situation in modest terms as 'a *de facto* cessation of hostilities', insisting that a full peace could not be said to exist until Britain lifted its economic measures and its maritime exclusion zone. (In due course, Britain did lift these measures.)

The effect, therefore, has been that the distinction between a peace treaty and an armistice agreement, which had been very sharp in the nineteenth century, now became indistinct. This point is illustrated by the debate at the UN in the 1950s over whether a state of war persisted between Israel and its neighbouring Arab states notwithstanding the conclusion of four bilateral armistice agreements of 1949. The conclusion of the UN Security Council on the point, expressed in a resolution in 1951, was that the 'armistice régime' was of a 'permanent character', with the consequence that there should be no exercise of traditional belligerents' rights by any of the countries concerned.[68]

As always, one cannot be too categorical, since we are dealing more with (so to speak) styles of peacemaking than with actual legal rules. Some

---

[64] Agreement Concerning a Military Armistice of 27 July 1953.
[65] Agreement on Ending the War of 27 January 1973.
[66] SC Res. 687 of 3 April 1991, in Karel C. Wellens (ed.), *Resolutions and Statements of the United Nations Security Council (1946–1992): A Thematic Guide* (2nd edn, Dordrecht, 1993).
[67] Instrument of Surrender of 14 June 1982.
[68] SC Res. 95 of 1 September 1951 in Wellens, *Resolutions*, p. 648. The immediate issue at stake was Egypt's subjection of Suez Canal traffic to belligerent measures, which the resolution specifically disapproved.

post-1945 peace agreements have contained economic provisions, most notably in cases in which no prior commercial treaties existed between the parties. An example is the Tashkent Declaration of 1966, terminating boundary hostilities between India and Pakistan. It provided, though only in the most general terms, that the parties would 'consider measures toward the restoration of economic and trade relations'.[69] But no economic agreement actually emerged between the two.

The most outstanding examples of peace treaties that contained significant economic components are the two peace treaties that emerged from the Middle East conflicts. In both cases, there had not been merely a lack of prior official economic ties. There had been formal boycott campaigns in place, expressly intended to inflict economic injury even when military hostilities were not occurring. The 1979 Treaty between Egypt and Israel provided that the 'normal relationship' which was being inaugurated by the Treaty was to include 'full ... economic ... relations'. In particular, it specified that there should be no economic boycotts or 'discriminatory barriers to the free movement of people and goods'. There were also specific provisions regarding Israeli use of the Suez Canal, and freedom of navigation and overflight through the Strait of Tiran and the Gulf of Aqaba. The treaty contained annexes setting out detailed arrangements in these areas. Furthermore, the parties were to enter into negotiations, within six months, for a treaty on trade and commerce generally and a treaty on civil aviation in particular.[70]

The Peace Treaty of 1994 between Israel and Jordan was to much the same effect on economic issues. Economic boycotts and discriminatory barriers were to be removed. Specific provisions dealt with road and rail links, freedom of navigation and access to ports, civil aviation links, communications, tourism and energy. It was also provided that, within six months, the parties would conclude (not merely commence negotiations for) agreements on economic cooperation in such spheres as trade, investment, banking and labour matters. [71]

Regarding the UN period in general, it may be concluded that, with the founding of the United Nations, we have created (or we like to believe that we have created) a world in which peace is the norm and armed conflict is pathological. Similarly, in the WTO we have created a world in which a very full degree of economic contact is normal and in which,

---

[69] Tashkent Declaration of 10 January 1966, Art. 6.
[70] Treaty of Peace of 26 March 1979, Arts. 3 and 5, Annex III.
[71] Treaty of Peace of 26 October 1994, Arts. 7, 13–17 and 19.

correspondingly, the lack of full economic relations is seen as abnormal. Consequently, detailed attention to economic matters in peace treaties is now seen as necessary only in marginal or special cases, such as the Israel–Egypt and Israel–Jordan cases, in which those normal economic relations had never previously been present. The general practice would seem to be, however, that the simple halting of military hostilities should entail, more or less automatically, the resumption of normal economic relations.

Conclusion

It is apparent that there is not, and never has been, a body of rules instructing states as to how to proceed when dealing with commercial aspects of peacemaking. This is a matter of practice rather than of strict law. Nevertheless, it should be apparent that the practice of states in this area has not been random. On the contrary, the economic aspects of peacemaking have reflected broader ideas which have prevailed in international law from time to time regarding the nature of war itself, as well as ideas about what constitutes normal relations between states. The economic aspects of peacemaking are therefore not a subject of study in their own right, divorced from the other aspects of war termination. Instead, the economic component of peacemaking forms an integral part of the study of peacemaking – and also of warmaking – in general.

18

The 1871 Peace Treaty between France and Germany and the 1919 Peace Treaty of Versailles

CHRISTIAN TOMUSCHAT

The historical background of the Peace Treaties

The war of 1870–71 between France and Germany did not last long. Hostilities began after France had declared war on Prussia on 19 July 1870. Two months later, an all-German military force had already defeated the main French armies. A truce was agreed on 28 January 1871, six months after the outbreak of the armed conflict. On 26 February 1871, the two parties signed a preliminary peace treaty. Thereafter, negotiations for a definitive treaty of peace were opened in Brussels. These negotiations dragged on for a while without making any significant headway. As a consequence, Bismarck convened a new conference in Frankfurt, which started on 6 May 1871. Four days later, on 10 May 1871, the final peace treaty was signed, and the exchange of instruments of ratification took place on 20 May 1871. Thus, less than four months after the end of the armed hostilities normalcy in the French–German relationship had been formally restored.

It should be recalled that the French–German war of 1870–71 was a bilateral war in which no other European power intervened. This fact certainly facilitated the conclusion of a peace treaty. It also contributed to the relatively modest dimensions of the two instruments. The Preliminary Peace Treaty consisted of ten articles, while the Frankfurt Peace Treaty encompassed seventeen articles. The conditions imposed on France were simple and straightforward. France had to renounce certain territories in the east of the country (Alsace and Lorraine), and it had to make a payment of 5 billion French francs. Additional provisions dealt with issues of nationality. All the other clauses were of secondary importance. Essentially, the Frankfurt Peace Treaty rested on these three pillars.

The First World War started in July 1914 with Austria's declaration of war on Serbia. A few days later, all major European powers were at war with one another. Fighting went on for more than four years. Eventually, Germany requested a truce, which came about on 11 November 1918. The Allied Powers did not invite Germany to participate in the negotiations on the Peace Treaty, which they opened soon thereafter. The draft treaty was handed over to the German delegation on 7 May 1919. No room for any subsequent negotiations was allowed. Germany was given the opportunity to make representations in writing, of which it availed itself repeatedly, but the Allied Powers retained their unreserved right to accept or dismiss the German counter-proposals. In fact, very little of the original substance of a complex legal regime reflected in no fewer than 440 articles of the main body of the Treaty and numerous annexes was amended. The Allied Powers then summoned Germany by an ultimatum of 16 June 1919 to accept the Peace Treaty within five days. This deadline was extended by a few days. On 22 June 1919, the German *Reichstag* adopted the Peace Treaty with a broad majority of 237 against 138 votes. On 28 June 1919, two delegates of the *Reichstag* put their signature to the document. Again, formal normalcy had been restored.

Guiding principles for peace treaties

It is not our aim to evaluate the two Peace Treaties from a historian's viewpoint. Rather, the perspective is a juridical one. However, this implies considerable difficulties since few legal standards existed at the time to assess the legal qualities of a peace treaty.

First of all, a trivial observation should be made. The legal, political and mental environment of the conclusion of a peace treaty varies considerably according to whether the waging of war is considered to be just a fact of international life or whether it falls under a general ban, making it an unlawful occurrence.

In that regard, the legal position of belligerents did not give rise to any doubts in the second half of the nineteenth century. War was certainly not welcomed as a normal state of affairs between nations, but it did not carry any mark of legal or moral reprobation either. All the textbooks agreed that a nation, with a view to enforcing its rights or interests, was entitled to engage in warfare.[1] Famous is a passage from Erich Kaufmann's

---

[1] See, for instance, Johann Caspar Bluntschli, *Das moderne Völkerrecht der civilisirten Staten als Rechtsbuch dargestellt* (Nördlingen, 1868), p. 290, paras. 515–16; August Wilhelm Heffter and F. Heinrich Geffcken, *Das europäische Völkerrecht der Gegenwart* (8th edn, Berlin, 1888), pp. 244–5.

monograph on the *clausula rebus sic stantibus* in international law, written in 1911, in which war is praised as the ultimate challenge where a nation can validly demonstrate its inherent strengths and virtues.[2]

Notwithstanding Kaufmann's eulogy of war, the general climate of social psychology had considerably changed in Europe during the last years before the outbreak of the First World War, not least under the impact of the two Hague Peace Conferences of 1899 and 1907.[3] Intuitively, the European nations had become aware of the fact that the classical system of the balance of power did not suffice any more to maintain peace and stability. They realised that the spectre of war was constantly hovering over Europe and could have disastrous consequences. The outbreak of the war in 1914 confirmed all of these fears. Consequently, at Versailles the question of responsibility for all the material losses and human suffering which Europe had endured for many long years arose by necessity. This was all the more understandable since the First World War had gone beyond anything that Europe had witnessed during the last 200 years, reminding observers of the horrors of the Thirty Years War. But in fact, as all lawyers know, a definitive ban on war did not come into existence prior to 1928, when the Briand–Kellogg Pact was made. Thus, to speak of responsibility in 1919 was to some extent premature, although based on sound political reasons. It was in fact the First World War which pushed the international community into adopting a new attitude *vis-à-vis* the phenomenon of war, which until then had been a routine feature of European history, albeit, after the Thirty Years War, in a somewhat more civilised version. The conclusion of the Versailles Treaty marked a decisive turning point. But the political evaluation of war on the one hand, and its legal evaluation on the other, still differed. It stands to reason that this discrepancy, which is reflected in the Treaty, could not but lead to tremendous tensions.

It is, furthermore, significant that before the conclusion of the Briand–Kellogg Pact of 1928, international treaties were considered to be perfectly valid even though their conclusion had been brought about by the use or threat of use of military force. The rule today laid down in Article 52 of the Vienna Convention on the Law of Treaties, according to which a treaty concluded under such coercion is void, derives as a logical consequence

---

[2] Erich Kaufmann, *Das Wesen des Völkerrechts und die clausula rebus sic stantibus* (Tübingen, 1911), p. 146.
[3] See Arthur Eyffinger, *The Hague Peace Conference: 'The Parliament of Man, the Federation of the World'* (The Hague, 1999), pp. 2–14.

from the ban on the use of force as enshrined in the UN Charter. Thus, before 1928 or 1945, victors could compel a defeated enemy to accept the conditions of peace, which they had established unilaterally. Peace treaties brought into being under such circumstances of inequality could not be objected to on legal grounds. The only constraints on a victor's power were considerations of political wisdom and expediency. No great foresight is needed to predict that a peace treaty the clauses of which are too harsh may carry the seeds of new conflict. Today, under the regime of the new 'moralising' international law, it has proven increasingly difficult to conclude at all a formal peace treaty after a major armed conflict. Recognising the possible unfortunate consequences of Article 52 of the Vienna Convention on the Law of Treaties, the International Law Commission suggested an additional provision, now Article 75, which sets forth special rules permitting sanctions against an aggressor state. However, this normative complement to Article 52 is drafted in such an infelicitous manner, and is consequently so hard to understand, that it can hardly fulfil the function which it is expected to fulfil.[4] In any event, the circumstances surrounding the conclusion of a peace treaty did not matter in legal terms at the time, nor in 1871 or 1919.

Lastly, in attempting to evaluate the two peace treaties of 1871 and 1919 the student must take into account the weakness of the principle of self-determination at that time. Germany reached national unity by claiming the same rights as such traditional nation-states as France and Great Britain, but at a time of sovereignty of kings and other monarchs its claim was not based on the principle of self-determination of the German people. Again, in this respect, the general climate changed in the early twentieth century. In particular, US President Wilson publicly proclaimed that after the war the new European System was to be based on free decisions of peoples, who should not be shoved around 'as if they were mere chattels and pawns in a game'.[5] Consequently, the German government and people trusted that the later peace treaty would be founded on the concept of self-determination. But in 1919 that concept constituted no more than a political guideline, so that no objections could be raised on legal grounds against treaty clauses providing for the separation of parts of German territory together with their population from the

---

[4] See the commentary by the International Law Commission on former article 70, *Yearbook of the ILC* (1966), vol. II, p. 268.
[5] Speech of 11 February 1918, point 2, reprinted in Herbert Kraus and Gustav Rödiger (eds.), *Urkunden zum Friedensvertrage von Versailles vom 28. Juni 1919* (Berlin, 1920), vol. I, pp. 2–3 at p. 3.

German mainland, without any consultation of the population and even against its wishes.

Of course, even in the absence of legal principles to preside over the conclusion of peace treaties, many recipes of a political nature may be found.[6] Essentially, peace treaties are designed to pave the way for firm and lasting peace; they are not meant to become the starting point of a new round of war, in accordance with the adage: 'the time after the war is the time before the war'. No reasonable government can wish to live under a permanent state of war. However, there is a basic alternative regarding which a choice must be made by a victorious power.

On the one hand, a state that has defeated an adversary may seek to create conditions of stability by suggesting a peace treaty, which both sides consider just and equitable. In this perspective, even a defeated state should be treated as a partner who, after the peace regime has been put into place, will enjoy a status equal to that of the victors. As was pointed out by Immanuel Kant (1724–1804) in his treatise 'On Perpetual Peace', a certain measure of confidence in the enemy must exist for peace to be restored.[7] Admittedly, a great amount of self-denial is necessary for a victor or a victorious alliance to extend its hand to the defeated nation, inviting it to join in a common project of cooperation. After many hesitations, which marred the first years after 1945, France had the good idea of proposing to Germany participation on equal terms within the framework of the European Coal and Steel Community. Of course, in the sovereignty-orientated mind-frames of the second half of the nineteenth century such ideas were still out of place and could not appear to provide a reasonable choice. In 1919, on the other hand, the establishment of the League of Nations amounted to a first great experiment in international cooperation. Indeed, the Covenant of the League of Nations was adopted as part and parcel of the Versailles Treaty.

---

[6] See, for instance, Jost Dülffer, 'Versailles und die Friedensschlüsse des 19. und 20. Jahrhunderts' in Gerd Krumeich (ed.), *Versailles 1919: Ziele – Wirkung – Wahrnehmung* (Essen, 2001), pp. 17–34; Christian Tomuschat, 'Die Kunst, Frieden zu schließen und zu sichern', *Friedens-Warte* 74 (1999), 361–8.

[7] Immanuel Kant, *Zum ewigen Frieden* (1795, ed. Wilhelm Weischedel in Immanuel Kant, *Werke in sechs Bänden*, Darmstadt, 1964, vol. VI, pp. 193–251 at p. 200): 'Denn irgend ein Vertrauen auf die Denkungsart des Feindes muß mitten im Kriege noch übrig bleiben, weil sonst auch kein Frieden abgeschlossen werden könnte' ('At least same trust in the attitude of the enemy must remain during war; if not, making peace becomes impossible'), with comment by Jörg Fisch, 'When Will Kant's Perpetual Peace Be Definitive', *Journal of the History of International Law* 2 (2000), 125–47 at p. 132. For a modern version of this idea see the memorandum of the German Catholic bishops of 27 September 2000, *Gerechter Friede* (Bonn, 2000), paras. 108–113.

On the other hand, a different peace strategy may seek to weaken potential adversaries to the greatest extent possible ('*Ceterum censeo* . . .'). A victor may avail himself of the opportunities provided to him by his military success to destroy once and for all the military power of his succumbed enemy by subjecting him to a straitjacket of legal constraints set forth in the relevant peace treaty. Such a strategy is dangerous. In particular, it may easily backfire if the vanquished state is able to recover strength and to emancipate itself from the constraints which were designed to keep it down.

The two Peace Treaties compared

Procedures employed may testify to the fairness of the substantive solutions eventually agreed upon. It is undeniable that between a victorious power and a defeated nation invariably a factual difference in status exists. None the less, even a victor may be prepared to listen to arguments put forward by the weaker party. He may do so in his own interest if he is intent on finding a long-lasting solution that will not be challenged on political grounds immediately after the conclusion of the peace treaty concerned.

In this regard, the process as it evolved after the Truce of 28 January 1871 provides a picture which shows a reasonable measure of German generosity. Thiers, the French prime minister, met Bismarck at Versailles a few days before the conclusion of the Preliminary Peace Treaty,[8] and was able to discuss with him the main points of the peace regime envisaged by the German Empire. He was not able to convince Bismarck that Metz should not pass under German sovereignty, but he succeeded in persuading him that France should keep Belfort.[9] Germany was also prepared to commence the negotiations for the definitive peace treaty in Brussels, i.e. in a neutral country, not on German soil. No definitive answers were framed during that first stage, a fact explained not least by the Commune of Paris, which badly affected the authority of the French government and made Bismarck fear that he would not be able to find a reliable interlocutor. Although the last and decisive round of negotiations took place in Frankfurt, where Bismarck put time pressure to bear on the French delegation, the eventual outcome was indeed the fruit of some compromise. Whereas Germany had originally requested 6 billion francs, the

---

[8] The three acts bringing to an end the Franco-German war of 1871 constitute the most illustrative example of the practices of the nineteenth century; see Fisch, 'Kant's Perpetual Peace', p. 130. On peace preliminaries in general see Paulus Andreas Hausmann, 'Friedenspräliminarien in der Völkerrechtsgeschichte', *Zeitschrift für Ausländisches Öffentliches Recht und Völkerrecht* 25 (1965), 657–92.

[9] M. Thiers, *Notes et souvenirs 1870–1873* (Paris, 1904), pp. 111–26.

sum definitively agreed upon amounted to only 5 billion francs. Thus, on balance, Thiers characterised the Frankfurt Peace Treaty as 'un vrai soulagement pour nous'.[10] To be sure, his judgement should not be taken for the whole truth, since Thiers bore the responsibility for coming to terms with Germany and could not *ex post* discredit his own role.[11] None the less, this is a statement of considerable weight, which shows that moderation had prevailed.

As has already been hinted, the making of the Versailles Treaty followed a different course. Germany had no say whatsoever in the elaboration of the texts. Consequently, the moment of handing over the finished drafts to the German delegates on 7 May 1919 was a moment of great tension, and the German foreign minister Brockdorff-Rantzau, in his response to the short introductory speech by the French prime minister Clemenceau, spoke of 'Wucht des Hasses, die uns hier entgegentritt'[12] – an observation which certainly was not very wise within the given context.[13] But Germany could indeed feel treated unfairly. The fact that it was given two weeks to comment in writing – in French or English – on the draft which the victors had worked on for almost four months put it into a position of inequality. It was not respected as a sovereign nation on a par with the states belonging to the victorious Alliance.[14] Even moderate voices in Germany, including some from the peace movement,[15] initially rejected the draft peace treaty quite emotionally.[16]

---

[10] Thiers, *Notes et souvenirs*, p. 183.
[11] In fact, Jules Valfrey, *Histoire du Traité de Francfort et de la libération du territoire français* (Paris, 1874), vol. I, p. 122, writes: 'Il n'y en a pas de plus douloureux ni de plus écrasant dans notre histoire.'
[12] Reprinted in Friedrich Berber, *Das Diktat von Versailles: Entstehung – Inhalt – Zerfall* (Essen, 1939), p. 52. 'Forces of hatred that come forward now.'
[13] See today's evaluation by Michael Dreyer and Oliver Lembcke, *Die deutsche Diskussion um die Kriegsschuldfrage 1918/19* (Berlin, 1993), p. 137, and the vitriolic comment by Georges Clemenceau, 'Foreword', in André Tardieu, *La paix* (Paris, 1921), pp. IX–XXXII at p. XXII: 'Le début ne fut pas très heureux avec M. de Brockdorff-Rantzau, tout drapé de brutale impudence, qui vint nous accuser de "haïr" l'Allemagne pour n'avoir pas prêté la gorge à ses bourreaux.' ('The negotiations with M. de Brockdorff-Rantzan did not start in a very fortunate way. He was very impudent, accused us of "hating" Germany for not having offered its neck to the executioners'.)
[14] On the French war objectives see David Stevenson, 'French War Aims and Peace Planning' in Manfred Boemeke, Gerald Feldman and Elisabeth Glaser (eds.), *The Treaty of Versailles: A Reassessment after 75 Years* (Cambridge, 1998), pp. 86–109; Georges-Henri Soutou, 'The French Peacemakers and Their Home Front', in Boemeke *et al.*, *Treaty of Versailles*, pp. 167–88.
[15] Alfred H. Fried, editor of *Die Friedens-Warte*, in his article 'Aus meinem Kriegstagebuch', *Friedens-Warte* 21 (1919), 119–27 at pp. 119 and 121.
[16] Thus, Prime Minister Philipp Scheidemann exclaimed in a speech before the German National Assembly held in the meeting hall of the University of Berlin a few days after the

As far as substance is concerned, a great discrepancy exists between the two treaties, not only in terms of quantity but also in terms of quality. The overall framework of the Frankfurt Peace Treaty had been delineated by the Preliminary Peace Treaty of 26 February 1871, and no great changes were effected in the subsequent negotiations. As far as the peace settlement of 1919 is concerned, Germany had received certain assurances from US President Wilson before agreeing to the armistice on 11 November 1918. In the so-called Lansing note,[17] the US pledged that the peace would be concluded not only on the basis of Wilson's Fourteen Points, specified in a speech before the US Congress on 8 January 1918,[18] but also on 'the principles of settlement enunciated in his subsequent addresses'.[19] Immediately after the publication of the draft treaty, a controversy arose as to its conformity with this agreed framework. Germany's delegation at Versailles challenged it, whereas the Allied Powers rejected that charge.[20] Because of the generality of all of the twenty-seven points, many of which did not concern Germany, it is almost impossible to arrive at a clear-cut conclusion regarding this issue.

The centrepiece of the two peace agreements ending the Franco-German War was the cession by France of almost the entire territory of Alsace and large parts of Lorraine. Such cessions of territory constituted a routine element of all peace treaties of the eighteenth and nineteenth centuries. Obviously, although the German language was still widely spoken in the ceded region, and although all of its component parts had formerly belonged to the Holy Roman Empire of German Nations for many centuries, the decision of annexation was not terribly wise – in any event not without a free consultation of the population concerned. Regarding Metz, an integral part of 'Lorraine française', the decision was even less justifiable since neither linguistic nor historical reasons could be adduced. By virtue of the Westphalian Peace Treaties of 1648 Metz had been confirmed as a French city. But the German military felt that Metz was necessary on security grounds and the request was supported by German ultra-nationalists

---

publication of the draft treaty: 'Welche Hand müßte nicht verdorren, die sich uns diese Fessel anlegt?'; see Andreas Hillgruber, '"Revisionismus" – Kontinuität und Wandel in der Außenpolitik der Weimarer Republik', *Historische Zeitschrift* 237 (1983), 597–621 at p. 597.

[17] Reprinted in Kraus and Rödiger, *Urkunden*, p. 10; German translation: Ernst Rudolf Huber, *Dokumente zur deutschen Verfassungsgeschichte* (3rd edn, Stuttgart, 1990), vol. III, p. 289.

[18] Reprinted in Kraus and Rödiger, *Urkunden*, p. 1; FHIG III–1, p. 670; Marjorie M. Whiteman, *Digest of International Law* (Washington, DC, 1965), vol. V, p. 42.

[19] Speech before Congress on 11 February 1918, Mount Vernon speech of 4 July 1918, speech in New York of 27 September 1918, all reprinted in Kraus and Rödiger, *Urkunden*, pp. 2–3.

[20] Note of 16 June 1919, reprinted in Berber, *Diktat von Versailles*, p. 76.

like Heinrich von Treitschke.[21] In addition, according to views widely held at that time, cessions of territory were a necessary element of a peace settlement to demonstrate that the victory achieved was indeed a true victory.[22] With the acquisition of Alsace and Lorraine, Germany seemed definitively to have gained the upper hand over France, possessing now a surface of 540,858 square kilometres against France's 538,085 square kilometres.

Through the Treaty of Versailles, Germany suffered territorial losses of roughly 70,000 square kilometres (being reduced to 470,545 square kilometres). Some of these losses were a natural consequence of the former annexation policy. It was clear that the large majority of the inhabitants of Alsace and Lorraine wished to return to France.[23] In some smaller areas, referendums were held, i.e. in some southern parts of East Prussia, in Schleswig and in Upper Silesia. But many decisions were taken against the wishes of the populations concerned. Thus, the establishment of the Free City of Danzig (Art. 102–3) or of the autonomous territory of Memelland (Art. 99) did not correspond to the will of its inhabitants. No referenda were held in West Prussia or in Eupen and Malmedy.[24] Some of the territorial provisions were openly vexatious.[25] Fortunately for Germany, the United States successfully opposed plans by France to place all the territories on the left bank of the Rhine under a special regime, creating autonomous protectorates under Allied control. On the whole, in spite of the bitterness which they aroused, the losses can be deemed to be moderate, above all if compared to what would happen twenty-six years later, after the Second World War, although a foreign observer commented on the isolation of East Prussia from the main body of the Reich through the Polish 'corridor': 'Never before in the history of war or diplomacy was similar violence done to the integrity of a highly civilised State.'[26] In

---

[21] See, e.g., his article 'Was fordern wir von Frankreich', in his *Zehn Jahre deutscher Kämpfe: Schriften zur Tagespolitik* (3rd edn, Berlin, 1897), vol. I, pp. 321–69 at pp. 335–6.

[22] See Eberhard Kolb, 'Der schwierige Weg zum Frieden. Das Problem der Kriegsbeendigung 1870/71', *Historische Zeitschrift* 241 (1985), 51–79 at pp. 61–2.

[23] See F. Roth, 'Die Rückkehr Elsaß-Lothringens zu Frankreich', in Krimeich, *Versailles 1919*, pp. 126–44.

[24] It should not be overlooked, in this connection, that Imperial Germany had pursued truly megalomaniac annexationist war objectives especially to the detriment of Belgium; see Fritz Fischer, *Griff nach der Weltmacht: die Kriegszielpolitik des kaiserlichen Deutschland 1914/18* (special edition, Düsseldorf, 1967), pp. 87–8.

[25] Thus, by virtue of Article 97 East Prussia was granted access to the Weichsel (Vistula) of a width of – four metres!

[26] William Harbutt Dawson, *Germany under the Treaty* (London, 1933), p. 12.

THE 1871 PEACE TREATY AND THE 1919 VERSAILLES TREATY   391

retrospect, the territorial provisions of the Versailles Treaty appear as a strange conglomerate of determinations in perfect harmony with the latest political tendencies regarding self-determination and decisions solely motivated by the will of the victors to reduce the size of Germany in pursuance of an overall strategy intended to weaken the ex-enemy as far as possible.[27]

The 'war contribution' imposed by the two treaties of 1871 on France (5 billion francs) was rooted in a tradition of peace treaties which invariably put the financial burden of the past war on the losing party. No questions were raised regarding the responsibility for the outbreak of hostilities. The stronger state decided, and the succumbing party had to bow to its requests. Consequently, no controversy arose in February 1871 as to the origin of the contribution to be paid by France. The French representatives confined themselves to questioning the size of that contribution. Contrary to their complaints, 5 billion francs constituted a burden which France could easily shoulder. Immediately after the conclusion of the Frankfurt Peace Treaty, a loan was launched by the government, and within days 4.9 billion French francs were thus made available.[28] In other words, within an extremely short time span France had fully recovered economically.

Within the Treaty of Versailles, the issue of reparations played a pivotal role. In order to obtain a legal basis justifying claims for the full reparation of all injury suffered, the Allied Governments included the following provision in the Versailles Treaty (Art. 231):

> The Allied and Associated Governments affirm and Germany accepts the responsibility of Germany and her allies for causing all the loss and damage to which the Allied and Associated Governments and their nationals have been subjected as a consequence of the war imposed upon them by the aggression of Germany and her allies.

Notwithstanding its original connotation as a clause meant to make a determination solely on Germany's financial liability, Article 231 was read – and certainly could be read – as a clause establishing Germany's sole and exclusive guilt for the outbreak of the First World War. This

---

[27] See also Thomas Würtenberger and Gernot Sydow, 'Versailles und das Völkerrecht', in Krumeich, *Versailles 1919*, pp. 35–52 at pp. 45–6. According to William R. Keylor, 'Versailles and International Diplomacy' in Boemeke *et al.*, *Treaty of Versailles*, pp. 469–505 at p. 496: 'The principle of national self-determination was applied with great selectivity at the peace conference that was expected to enshrine it as the foundation of the "new" diplomacy.'
[28] See Thiers, *Notes et souvenirs*, p. 195.

was an absolute novelty in the European history of peace treaties. The trenchant proposition aroused bitter resentment in Germany, where a majority felt that the country had been dragged into the war by an unfortunate interconnection of circumstances. It is well known that controversy still rages among historians since Fritz Fischer attempted to prove in a well-documented monograph that Germany had indeed been intent on winning through war the stature of a true world power.[29] In any event, the so-called 'lie of war guilt' (*Kriegsschuldlüge*) discredited the Versailles Treaty, not only in the eyes of radical nationalists but also among broad groups of ordinary middle-class Germans.

Furthermore, it was a logical but misconceived idea to make Germany liable for all the losses which the Allied Powers had sustained. The financial burden resulting from that statement of principle was so huge that the young democratic regime of the Weimar Republic was driven into financial chaos.[30] Internal unrest was the unavoidable consequence. In that respect, the authors of the Treaty, in particular the French government, acted without paying any heed to the possible political consequences of their stubbornness. They wished retroactively to win the battles of the past instead of building the future.

The 1871 Peace Treaties said nothing about the size of the French Armed Forces. In 1871, Germany felt so powerful after its victory over France that it did not see any necessity to impose restrictions in that regard on France. Moreover, in all probability France would not have accepted any condition in that regard and, lastly, other European powers might have intervened to prevent such an emasculation of France's military power. By contrast, the Versailles Treaty set strict limits on Germany's military potential. It is common knowledge, in particular, that the maximum number of personnel in the German Armed Forces was fixed at 100,000 men (Art. 160). Germany was not allowed to possess any tanks (Art. 171 (3)) or submarines (Art. 191). Again, this regime of control of armaments was greatly resented in Germany. Instead, Germany could have understood this regime of demilitarisation as a chance to spend its public money on more sensible or profitable purposes. This chance was not perceived, however. Germany felt adversely affected above all because it viewed the military clauses of

---

[29] Fischer, *Griff nach der Weltmacht*.
[30] Gerald Feldman, 'A Comment' in Boemeke *et al.*, *Treaty of Versailles*, pp. 441–7 at p. 441, characterises the territorial as well as the economic and financial settlements as 'horrendous failures by any standard one wishes to employ'. But some other voices suggest that to pay the reparations imposed by the Treaty would have been a realistic option for Germany; see Keylor, 'Versailles and Diplomacy', pp. 502–3.

the Versailles Treaty as another sign of deliberate discrimination. In fact, the clauses served a policy of 'keeping Germany down', a policy which was understandable, but obviously short-sighted as everyone knows with hindsight.

More burdensome and discriminatory were the provisions concerning the occupation of the entire German territory situated to the west of the Rhine, together with several bridgeheads east of the Rhine, for a period of at least fifteen years (Art. 428), a proviso which was complemented by a reservation to the effect that the occupation could be renewed in the case that Germany did not fully comply with its obligation to make reparation (Art. 430). In fact, this clause was invoked in 1923, when French military forces took control of the Ruhr area. Additionally, the Saar basin was separated from Germany and placed under the authority of the League of Nations in order to permit France to exploit the local coalmines, which Germany had to cede to it. Vainly the French government had attempted to obtain full sovereignty over the Saar, the US government objecting to such a far-reaching measure which France in an official memorandum had claimed by contending that the Saar 'a été pendant de longs siècles unie à la France et n'a été séparée d'elle que par la force'[31] – a curious figment of the imagination which could not even persuade the other Allied participants in the peace conference.

Lastly, the clauses providing for the extradition of the German Kaiser (Art. 227) and for the prosecution of perpetrators of war crimes (Art. 228–9) are worthy of particular mention. In 1870, Napoleon III (1852–70) had been made prisoner of war after the defeat of his army at Sedan, with all the consequences of such a status, but no additional consequences. Nobody even aired the notion that Napoleon III might be put on trial. In fact, the Franco-German War was considered to be a war as occurred from time to time between European nations, a fact of life. In the early twentieth century, by contrast, waging war had certainly taken on features of immoral conduct and could therefore be viewed as a breach of common standards of European civilisation. It was in particular with the fact that Belgium's neutrality had not been respected, as had been guaranteed by a multilateral treaty regime, that Germany was charged. However, it was a hazardous adventure to affirm that the Kaiser was liable to criminal prosecution on account of 'a supreme offence against international morality and the sanctity of treaties'. Until that time, heads of state had always been granted immunity from any kind of criminal

---

[31] 'Mémoire présenté par la délégation française' in Tardieu, *La paix*, p. 279.

prosecution. Furthermore, it was totally unclear what kind of legal charges could be brought against the Kaiser. During the relevant period from 1914 to 1918, no international penal law had existed. To be sure, Germany had violated Belgium's neutrality, but its military operations on Belgian territory amounted to nothing more – but also nothing less – than a breach of international law for which Germany was responsible as a collective entity. Individual criminal responsibility is a different matter altogether. The flaws of Article 227 were sharply highlighted by the Netherlands when its government declined to comply with an extradition request by the Allied Governments.[32] All in all, Article 227 was largely seen by the German people as a deliberate manoeuvre to humiliate Germany in the person of its former head of state. And it is certainly hard to deny that some element of such an intent had crept into the drafting of Article 227.

It is much less understandable why the German public resented in a similar fashion the Articles providing for the prosecution of members of the Germany military who had committed war crimes. To be sure, Articles 228 and 229 symbolised a definite departure from a tradition of earlier peace treaties, which invariably contained sweeping amnesty clauses. What had happened during a war was to be forgotten and deleted from memory. However, the First World War had shown such a high degree of savagery and barbarian ruthlessness, in particular by German forces, that it was clear now that the existence *vel non* of the applicable regime of humanitarian law hinged on appropriate sanctions to be imposed on perpetrators.[33] Wishing to be recognised as a state abiding by the rule of law, Germany should not have opposed the notion of trials against war criminals. It is true that Articles 228 and 229 originally provided for prosecution by Allied tribunals. But even after subsequent negotiations had permitted the transfer of jurisdiction to the German *Reichsgericht*,[34] prosecution remained lenient and half-hearted. Only a handful of the officers referred to in the lists made available to the German prosecutorial authorities were convicted and sentenced. Out of a general sentiment of being treated unfairly, Germany missed the opportunity to show that, on its part at least, it was committed to a better future of international cooperation in accordance with principles of law and justice. It does not add to the reputation of a nation if it backs those who

---

[32] See note of 21 January 1921, reprinted in FHIG III-2, p. 730.
[33] See, for instance, Gerd Krumeich, 'Versailles 1919. Der Krieg in den Köpfen', in his *Versailles 1919*, pp. 53–64 at pp. 54–5.
[34] Letter by British Prime Minister Lloyd George to the German Chancellor, of 13 February 1920, reprinted in Kraus and Rödiger, *Urkunden*, vol. II (Berlin, 1921), p. 948.

engaged in war crimes; on the contrary, by taking appropriate sanctions it is able to restore its reputation, which may have been tainted by such offences.

Conclusion

The two Peace Treaties of 1871 and 1919 are embedded in widely divergent political and legal contexts. During the second half of the nineteenth century, war was still accepted as a natural component part of relations among states. Therefore, to conclude peace after war amounted to an undertaking of rational *Realpolitik*. No issues of international morality were raised. Thus, many risks could be avoided which later threatened peacemaking during the entire course of the twentieth century. In 1871, Germany was solely interested in establishing a new balance of power ensuring German superiority. At the same time, France was respected as a party with equal rights. After the conclusion of the Frankfurt Treaty, French sovereignty over the entire national territory was fully restored. Germany did not seek to keep any leverage over French domestic affairs. Thus, a new era of relationships on the basis of sovereign equality could begin – an era which remained overshadowed, however, by France's legitimate refusal to accept the loss of Alsace and Lorraine.

The Peace Treaty of Versailles came into being at the end of a war that had definitively rebutted the already shattered dogma of moral irrelevance of war. For the first time, actual inferences were drawn from the proposition that to launch war deserved reprobation in a community of civilised nations. However, the two articles establishing the sole and exclusive responsibility of Germany and its allies for all the loss and damage caused by the war, and charging the German Kaiser with 'a supreme offence' of a criminal nature, had weak factual and legal bases. Indeed, they lacked a firm foundation in general international law except for the Versailles Treaty itself. War became subject to a legal ban not earlier than 1928 and could hardly constitute a criminal offence before that date. Both of those key provisions remained therefore in the twilight, which subsequently could not but lead to requests for change. Today, under the Charter of the United Nations and after the lessons of Nuremberg, it seems almost natural that an aggressor is liable for the damage he has caused, and that persons committing crimes under international law should be liable to punishment irrespective of their rank within the organisation of the state concerned. In 1919, all of this looked like a deliberate policy of discrimination against Germany.

Notwithstanding its objectionable aspects, the Versailles Treaty could probably have paved the way for a new and peaceful climate in Europe if Germany had immediately been admitted as a member of the League of Nations, the new world organisation whose Covenant was enacted as part and parcel of the Treaty. Unfortunately, this was not the case. The Versailles Treaty was dominated by a backward-looking philosophy. France, in particular, still regarded Germany as a hereditary enemy which it wished to surround by a tight network of legal constraints,[35] and the League of Nations was entrusted with implementing a considerable number of those constraints by acting, for instance, as trustee for the Saar, the Memelland and the Free City of Danzig. Consequently, the League never became really popular in Germany even after membership was obtained in 1926.[36] No offer was made to Germany to become associated with a common European project. For a couple of years, it remained, so to speak, an outcast within Europe, having a status of less-than-equal rights. To relegate Germany to such a secondary position within Europe was probably the most serious defect of the Versailles Treaty.[37] Eventually, the Treaty contributed to weakening the political forces which had voted for its acceptance and thereby to undermining the fledgling democracy in post-war Germany, with all the disastrous consequences well known to us.

[35] See the criticism by Wolfgang J. Mommsen, 'Der Vertrag von Versailles. Eine Bilanz' in Krumeich, *Versailles 1919*, pp. 351–60 at p. 353. Similarly, David Stevenson, 'French War Aims', pp. 86–109 at p. 88 writes: 'French policy . . . was not merely security-conscious and defensive, but included elements of anti-German imperialism fired by a conviction of cultural superiority and memories of historical greatness.'

[36] See inaugural speech by German Foreign Minister Gustav Stresemann before the Assembly of the League of Nations on 10 September 1926, reprinted in Berber, *Diktat von Versailles*, pp. 146–50 at p. 149.

[37] See also the assessment by Würtenberger and Sydow, 'Versailles und das Völkerrecht', pp. 48–52.

PART V

Conclusion

19

Conclusion

RANDALL LESAFFER

The revolution of the twentieth century

Here are no lessons for the world, no disclosures to shock peoples. It is filled with trivial things, partly that no one mistake for history the bones from which some day a man may make history, and partly for the pleasure it gave me to recall the fellowship of the revolt. We were fond together, because of the sweep of the open places, the taste of wide winds, the sunlight, and the hopes in which we worked. The morning freshness of the world-to-be intoxicated us. We were wrought up with ideas inexpressible and vaporous, but to be fought for. We lived many lives in those whirling campaigns, never sparing ourselves: yet, when we achieved and the new world dawned, the old men came out again and took our victory to re-make it in the likeness of the former world they knew. Youth could win, but had not learned to keep: and was pitiably weak against age. We stammered that we had worked for a new heaven and a new earth, and they thanked us kindly and made their peace.[1]

As Lawrence of Arabia's experience of the Great War was far different from what most young British officers lived through in the trenches of Flanders and France, so his assessment of the peace must have seemed strange to many of his readers. Historians and international lawyers have considered and still consider the Peace Treaties of Paris of 1919/20 a watershed in the history of international law, their failure to achieve lasting peace notwithstanding. If anything, few would call them the 'remaking in the likeness of the former world they knew'. Though the American President Woodrow Wilson did not convince his European allies to turn their back on the old world and sacrifice their traditional interests on the altar of his new world order, the peacemakers of Versailles and the other Parisian suburbs did implement or at least paid lip service to some of his ideas and principles. The League of Nations was meant to provide an institutional

[1] T. E. Lawrence, *The Seven Pillars of Wisdom* (London, 1935), pp. 6–7.

framework for collective security and a limitation on the liberty of states to resort to war. The ascendancy of right over might, which was to be the cornerstone of the new international community, was declared *post factum* over Germany and its allies. They were said to be solely responsible for the war. From their side, the war had been an infringement of international law, an accusation which in its turn served as the juridical basis for making the losers of the war liable for all the damages it had caused. The Peace Treaty of Versailles made a sharp inroad on state sovereignty, the hallmark of the Westphalian order, as the German Kaiser and German leaders would not benefit from the individual immunity and impunity state authority granted to them under the old law, but became subject to criminal prosecution.

The emergence of international organisations, the limitation of the right to wage war and the rebirth of the individual as a subject of international law – first through his liability for international crimes, later in the international protection of human rights – are the three paramount features of the dramatic change international law is traditionally said to have undergone since 1919. And indeed, these three elements were for the first time present in an important international instrument that year.[2]

---

[2] Many international lawyers and legal historians considered or still consider the Peace Treaties of Versailles to be a fundamental watershed in the development of international law: George Abi-Saab, 'Whither the International Community?', *European Journal of International Law* 9 (1998), 248–65; Antonio Cassese, *International Law* (Oxford, 2001), pp. 30–1; Charles de Visscher, *Théories et réalités en droit international public* (Paris, 1953), pp. 69 and 74–80; Wolfgang Friedman, *The Changing Structure of International Law* (London, 1964); Hersch Lauterpacht, 'The Reality of the Law of Nations' in Elihu Lauterpacht (ed.), *International Law: Being the Collected Papers of Hersch Lauterpacht* (Cambridge, 1975), vol. II, pp. 22–9; Peter Malanczuk, *Akehurst's Modern Introduction to International Law* (7th edn, London and New York, 1997), pp. 23–32; Alistair McNair, *Oppenheim's International Law: A Treatise* (4th edn, London, 1928), vol. I, pp. 87–99; Alfred Verdross, *Völkerrecht* (Berlin, 1937), pp. 11–20; Wilhelm Wengler, *Völkerrecht* (Berlin, Göttingen and Heidelberg, 1964), p. 131. The view also took root among the main historians of international law: Fritz Dickmann, 'Krieg und Frieden im Völkerrecht der frühen Neuzeit' in his *Friedensrecht und Friedenssicherung: Studien zum Friedensproblem in der Geschichte* (Göttingen, 1971), pp. 116–39; Wilhelm G. Grewe, 'Was ist klassisches, was ist modernes Völkerrecht?' in Alexander Böhm, Klaus Lüdersen and Karl-Heinz Ziegler (eds.), *Idee und Realität des Rechts in der Entwicklung internationaler Beziehungen: Festgabe für Wolfgang Preiser* (Baden Baden, 1983), pp. 111–31, at p. 117; Arthur Nussbaum, *A Concise History of the Law of Nations* (New York, 1947), pp. 238–92; Wolfgang Preiser, *Die Völkerrechtsgeschichte: Ihren Aufgaben und Methoden* (Wiesbaden, 1964), p. 36; Carl Schmitt, *Der Nomos der Erde im Völkerrecht des Jus Publicum Europaeum* (4th edn, Berlin, 1997), pp. 200–57; Antonio Truyol y Serra, *Histoire du droit international public* (Paris, 1995), pp. 133–66; Karl-Heinz Ziegler, *Völkerrechtsgeschichte* (Munich, 1994), pp. 240–4.

This assessment of the Peace Treaties of Paris of 1919/20 had an enormous impact on the historiography of international law. It has caused international lawyers and legal historians to draw sharp distinctions between the periods before and after World War I. Owing to this, the significance of late nineteenth- and early twentieth-century tendencies and events that prepared the way for what happened in 1919/20 has been somewhat underrated, and have been called marginal and radical in the context of their times.[3] More importantly, the opposition of the 'old' pre-Versailles order to the 'new' twentieth-century order has tempted scholars to overemphasise the dominance of state sovereignty as the undisputed guiding principle of the Westphalian order and its law of nations. This discourse that followed tends to consider all historical ideas and practices that limit or contradict this sovereignty as marginal, exceptional and un-influential.[4] Of course, the legal positivists of the nineteenth century in their close alliance with the defenders of absolute state sovereignty offered ammunition to the student of nineteenth-century international law. However, this hardly accounts for the fact that most scholars quite unconsciously transferred these ideas from the heyday of the sovereign state and of the 'classical' law of nations to the previous century and a half (1648–1815).

No proponents of Versailles as a fundamental watershed have turned a blind eye to the failure of the peace settlement. Nevertheless, not a few historians and international lawyers have understated the deficiencies of the peace settlement and have too readily attributed its failure to external, political factors. For a peace to be successful and to guarantee stability, it needs to be based on a sincere consensus about the main political, moral and juridical principles it is founded on.[5] Such a consensus was clearly not present at Versailles. Not only did the German losers of the war not truly accept the *Diktat* of Versailles; many of the belligerents fighting on the side of the Allies, such as Lawrence's Arabs, also had cause to feel deep disappointment. But worse than that, even among the main victorious states involved – the US, Britain and France – there was no real consensus about the main principles and the main points of decision. As such, the Peace Treaty was not only a mixture of old and new

---

[3] For a survey of the doctrine of that period: Martii Koskenniemi, *The Gentle Civilizer of Nations: The Rise and Fall of International Law 1870–1960* (Cambridge, 2001).
[4] Randall Lesaffer, 'The Grotian Tradition Revisited: Change and Continuity in the History of International Law', *British Yearbook of International Law* 73 (2002).
[5] See Andreas Osiander's chapter 14 in this book as well as his *The States System of Europe 1640–1990: Peacemaking and the Conditions of International Stability* (Oxford, 1994).

ideas and principles, it was also inconsistent. The principle of the self-determination of the peoples was paid lip service to, but was often put aside, to the detriment not only of the losing powers, but also of some of the victorious ones.[6] Collective security was interpreted in a totally different way in Paris, London or Washington. For France it proved little more than the redressing of the balance of power through an Anglo-American safety guarantee – the balance of power the American President so much abhorred.

The failure of Versailles did not end the march of the Wilsonian ideas about the international community and its laws. After World War II and then again after the Cold War, many of its features were revived. The international protection of human rights and the emergence of a multitude of international organisations, some of them with clearly supra-national and law-making authority, have brought fundamental change. Nevertheless, international law remains that same mixture of old and new that characterised Versailles. Today, the principle of state sovereignty gives way to opposing ideas about *ius cogens*, individual rights protected by international law or individual criminal responsibility.

Many scholars of international law struggle with this inherent duality of the current international legal order. Many express a profound discontent with this state of affairs and do not seem to accept that this mixture is viable. There are the advocates of a new order that can only successfully end in a world state of world citizens. For those adherents of the Kantian tradition the remnants of the old sovereign state system are just that and will gradually (have to) disappear. Their Hobbesian opponents, who are on the moral low ground, tend to ridicule the importance and real impact of international organisations and international law. Of course there is a middle ground where the inherent duality of the system is accepted as viable and durable. The Grotian tradition accepts the coexistence of sovereign states with an international community based on the solidarity of the states.[7] While states remain the primary subjects, authors and enforcers of international law, it is recognised that the international community as such – mainly through international organisations – also has law-making and low-enforcing powers. And while individual persons cannot be said to be fully fledged subjects

---

[6] Sharon Korman, *The Right of Conquest: The Acquisition of Territory by Force in International Law and Practice* (Oxford, 1996), pp. 135–78.

[7] Martin Wight, *International Theory: The Three Traditions* (ed. Gabriele Wight and Brian Porter, Leicester, 1991).

of international law, they clearly have some rights and duties under that law.

As much debate about these three traditions as there has been – on a theoretical level mainly among International Relations theorists, and on a pragmatic level mainly among international lawyers – genuine empirical historical research into legal practice which tries to explain the inherent duality of current international law is still scarce. Recently, some scholars have brought to the fore the significance of the world beyond Europe for the development of international law from the sixteenth century onwards.[8] One of them, Edward Keene, elaborated on the thesis that the newer elements like the international protection of human rights originate in the 'colonial' law of the sixteenth to nineteenth centuries. In this view, twentieth-century international law results from the merging of the *ius publicum Europaeum* of the *ancien régime* and the laws and principles the European states laid down for their relations outside Europe, with one another and with the peoples they colonised and ruled.[9] In this perspective, the historic concept of the 'line' dividing the European from the world beyond Europe regains relevance.[10]

The Westphalian order and further back

This thesis certainly has merit. But at the same time it threatens to underpin the traditional view of the Westphalian order (1648–1815) as the absolute heyday of the free arbiter of states. For the history of peace treaties, this period has always been considered extremely important, and justly so. The later seventeenth and eighteenth centuries saw several important peace congresses and peace treaties that articulated the basic principles of the European states system and the *ius publicum Europeaeum*, the law of nations that paradoxically enough is referred to both as 'classic' and as 'modern'. The traditional starting points of most historical studies on that modern law of nations are the works of Hugo Grotius (1583–1645) and

---

[8] Antony Anghie, 'Francisco de Vitoria and the Colonial Origins of International Law', *Social and Legal Studies* 5 (1996), 321–36; Heinhard Steiger, 'From the International Law of Christianity to the International Law of the World Citizen', *Journal of the History of International Law* 3 (2001), 180–93; Richard Tuck, *The Rights of War and Peace: Political Thought and the International Order from Grotius to Kant* (Oxford, 1999).
[9] Edward Keene, *Beyond the Anarchical Society: Grotius, Colonialism and Order in World Politics* (Cambridge, 2002).
[10] Jörg Fisch, *Die europäische Expansion und das Völkerrecht* (Stuttgart, 1984), pp. 75–82 and 96–9.

the Peace Treaties of Westphalia (1648). Over the twentieth century, the vast majority of students of the history of international law have come to accept and defend that Grotius' thought was largely tributary to writers of the sixteenth century, the Spanish neo-scholastics first and foremost among them. This acceptance of continuity in doctrine has, however, hardly been followed up by research on the continuity in legal practices.

This study on modern European peace treaty practice has tried to do just that. By going further back in time, beyond Westphalia, the authors of the book have tried to establish the links between the pre- and post-Westphalian orders and have drawn their conclusions from this for the interpretation of the latter. It is time to summarise the main results.

First, the peace treaties after Westphalia in many respects draw on an older tradition of peacemaking that goes back to the Renaissance (c. 1450–1648) and even beyond, to the late Middle Ages (c. 1100–1450). The basic structure of treaties, which became truly standardised after Westphalia and remained so until the early twentieth century, was already largely present in the peace treaties of the late fifteenth and sixteenth centuries. Important concepts and clauses such as *amicitia*, amnesty, and oblivion and restitution were already fully developed in the treaties of the Renaissance period. Other modern practices such as written ratification and approval by estates and legislative bodies – though they were very different from late medieval customs – nevertheless had older roots. More generally, one could say that the origins of much of the juridical-technical aspect of peacemaking of the post-Westphalian *ancien régime* have to be sought in the pre-Westphalian period. When during the late Middle Ages the large dynastic power complexes from which the modern states were to emerge were formed, they started to develop a customary law of peacemaking from which elements lived on. Concepts and institutions were changed to fit a new political and intellectual context, but they do not belie their origins.

Second, as is the case for other aspects of international law, the modern doctrines on peace treaties and treaty law are traditionally traced back to the sixteenth century. Legal thought about peacemaking is hardly ever taken into account for the Middle Ages. Nevertheless, such thought existed and was elaborated upon. The learned *ius commune* of Roman and canon law – and even through the *Libri feodorum* some feudal law – of the late Middle Ages was concerned with all the main issues of relations between 'sovereign' rulers and political entities. Above the multitude of national, regional and local law systems – the so-called *iura propria* – the *ius commune* hovered as a kind of ideal system of law and functioned as a common point of reference in all intellectual debate about the law. This was as much the case for conflicts and matters between sovereign princes as it was among private persons. In the absence of a strict dividing line between private and public law, between municipal and 'international' law, the concepts, rules and principles of the *ius commune* which originally were mostly meant to apply to private matters were readily transferred to the field of relations between princes and rulers. Treaty law as an autonomous discipline would only emerge from the seventeenth century onwards. But the Roman and canon law of contracts provided more than enough substance to approach the relevant questions reality confronted the jurists with. While in most parts of the Latin West, Roman law was only a learned law studied and taught at the universities, canon law was also applicable law. As the jurisdiction of the Church *ratione peccati* spread over treaty law and the laws of war, this implied that canon law often was the peremptory law governing the relations between sovereign rules and political entities. As canon law was to a large extent influenced by and articulated in constant dialogue with Roman law, many precepts and institutions of the latter system found their way to 'international' legal practice as well. In short, a *ius gentium* did exist during the late Middle Ages. From the doctrinal side, it was inextricably bound to the *ius commune*. From the practical side, it was an amalgam of that *ius commune* and customary practices.

Third, the sixteenth and early seventeenth centuries form an important period of transition for the legal order of Europe. During the first half of the sixteenth century, the Reformation and the clash between the two leading powers of Europe, the Emperor Charles V (1519–58) and the French Kings Francis I (1515–47) and Henri II (1547–59), wrecked the old medieval order of the Latin West. By 1550, the major dynastic rulers of Europe had shed the last remnants of the universal authority of the emperor and the pope. Though the learned *ius commune* would remain an intellectual inspiration for generations of lawyers to come in addressing problems of international relations and law, it lost its peremptory authority and statute. The Reformation brought an end to the direct application of canon law as the hard core of the *ius gentium*, first among Protestant powers and between Catholic and Protestant powers, then also among Catholics. Through this, Roman law lost its main channel from doctrine to legal practice. All this implied that by 1550 the main basis that the order of the Latin West, the *respublica christiana*, was founded upon had crumbled. The challenge to the old system was even greater as the Age of Discoveries confronted the European lawyers and theologians with new problems that the old *ius gentium*, modelled on the Latin Christian world, did not provide answers for.

If in the history of modern Europe there has been one single period in which the sovereign rulers of Europe were truly 'sovereign' in the sense that there was neither an effectual authority nor a paramount legal system to curb their freedom, it was the century between 1550 and 1648. The medieval order of the *respublica christiana* was disrupted and the new order had not yet taken shape. This caused a deep crisis and even chaos in the international system of Europe. The century between 1550 and 1648 was marked by many religious wars. Most major territories of Europe were wrecked by endemic wars, civil strife and rebellions. This political instability prevented the creation of a new order. Nor was the crisis of the *respublica christiana* easily overcome in terms of the formulation of a new doctrine. The feeling of crisis, more than the promise of a new system, stimulated many theologians and lawyers to address problems of diplomacy and the law of nations during that century.

The peace treaty practice of the period clearly reflects that this was an era of crisis and transition. The continuous references to *amicitia* and the generalisation of the inclusion of third powers indicated that the mere existence of legal order was not felt to be natural or self-evident any longer. Though the political instability within the great European countries prevented the emergence of a new, stable international legal order, the treaty practice of the period shows some evolution towards what was to become the modern system of sovereign states and the *ius publicum Europaeum*. Since because of the collapse of the old system of the *respublica christiana*, external sovereignty had been achieved quite suddenly, this development almost exclusively concerned aspects of internal sovereignty and the monopolisation of international relations in the hands of central governments.

Fourth, the significance of the Peace Treaties of Westphalia of 1648 has to be reassessed. Traditionally, Westphalia has been considered the starting point of the modern European states system. In many works on international law, diplomatic history and International Relations theory it has been stated that the Peace Treaties of Münster and Osnabrück laid down the basic principles that the *ius publicum Europaeum* was to rest upon, such as sovereignty, equality and religious neutrality.[11] Some even

---

[11] E.g. 'The peace of Westphalia 1648, may be chosen as the epoch from which to deduce the history of the modern science of international law': Henry Wheaton, *History of the Law of Nations in Europe and America from the Earliest Times to the Treaty of Washington* (New York, 1845), p. 69. See also Abi-Saab, 'Whither the International Community',

went as far as calling it the 'constitution' of the European states system. Upon close analysis of the Peace Treaties, it becomes clear, however, that they do not contain these principles, at least not as principles of the law of nations. At the most, these concepts are present in the parts of the Treaties that deal with the constitution of the Holy Roman Empire and its religious pacification. In their international dimension, as peace treaties between the major European powers, the Westphalia instruments prove to be rather traditional and classic peace settlements which largely drew on sixteenth-century and even late medieval practices.[12] However,

pp. 250–1; Calvo, *Droit international*, vol. 1, pp. 35–7; Cassese, *International Law*, p. 21 (with more care for historical accuracy and counterargument than many other international lawyers); Richard A. Falk, 'The Interplay of Westphalia and Charter Conceptions of International Legal Order' in Richard A. Falk and Cyril E. Black (eds.), *The Future of the International Legal Order* (Princeton, 1969), vol. I, pp. 43–8; Paul Fauchille, *Traité de droit international public* (8th edn, Paris, 1921), vol. I-1, p. 75; Leo Gross, 'The Peace of Westphalia, 1648–1948', *American Journal of International Law* 42 (1948), 20–41; Otto Kimminich, 'Die Entstehung des neuzeitlichen Völkerrechts' in Iring Fetscher and Herfried Münkler (eds.), *Handbuch der politischen Ideen* (Munich, 1985), vol. III, pp. 73–100; Franz von Liszt and Max Fleischmann, *Das Völkerrecht systematisch dargestellt* (Berlin, 1925), pp. 21–2; Malanczuk, *Akehurst's Introduction*, pp. 9–11; Nussbaum, *Concise History of the Law of Nations*, p. 86; Andrea Rapisardi Mirabelli, 'Le congrès de Westphalie. Ses négociations et ses résultats au point de vue de l'histoire de gens', *Bibliotheca Visseriana Dissertationum Ius Internationale Illustrantium* 20 (1929), 7–18; Robert Redslob, *Histoire des grands principes du droit des gens* (Paris, 1923), p. 213; Ernst Reibstein, 'Das europäische öffentliche Recht, 1648–1815', *Archiv des Völkerrechts* 8 (1959/1960), 385–420; Nico Schrijver, 'The Changing Nature of State Sovereignty', *British Yearbook of International Law* 70 (1999), 65–98 at pp. 65–9; Truyol y Serra, *Histoire du droit international public*, p. 95; A. Wegner, *Geschichte des Völkerrechts* (Stuttgart, 1936), p. 173.

[12] Recently the 'Westphalian myth' has been examined and at least to some extent challenged by: Stéphane Beaulac, 'The Westphalian Legal Orthodoxy – Myth or Reality?', *Journal of the History of International Law* 2 (2000), 148–77; Derek Croxton, 'The Peace of Westphalia of 1648 and the Origins of Sovereignty', *International History Review* 21 (1999), 569–91; Arthur Eyffinger, 'Europe in the Balance: An Appraisal of the Westphalian System', *Netherlands International Law Review* 45 (1998), 161–87; Peter Haggenmacher, 'La paix dans la pensée de Grotius' in Lucien Bély (ed.), *L'Europe des traités de Westphalie: esprit de diplomatie et diplomatie de l'esprit* (Paris, 2000), pp. 67–79 at pp. 68–9; Randall Lesaffer, 'The Westphalian Peace Treaties and the Development of the Tradition of Great European Peace Settlements prior to 1648', *Grotiana* NS 18 (1997), 71–95; Andreas Osiander, 'Sovereignty, International Relations and the Westphalian Myth', *International Organization* 55 (2001), 251–87; Meinhard Schröder, 'Der westfälische Friede – eine Epochengrenze in der Völkerrechtsentwicklung?' in Schröde (ed.), *350 Jahre westfälischer Friede: Verfassungsgeschichte, Staatskirchenrecht, Völkerrechtsgeschichte* (Berlin, 1999), pp. 119–37; Heinhard Steiger, 'Der westfälischen Frieden – Grundgesetz für Europa?' in Heinz Duchhardt (ed.), *Der westfälische Friede: Diplomatie, politische Zäsur, kulturelles Umfeld, Rezeptionsgeschichte* (Munich, 1998), pp. 33–80; Karl-Heinz Ziegler, 'Die Bedeutung des westfälischen Friedens von 1648 für das europäische Völkerrecht', *Archiv des Völkerrechts* 37 (1999), 129–51; Ziegler, 'Der westfälischen Frieden von 1648 in der Geschichte des Völkerrechts' in Schröder, *350 Jahre westfälischer Friede*, pp. 99–117.

the demystification of Westphalia is only partial. Though its position as the 'constitution' of the modern European legal order must be challenged, Westphalia remains a caesura in the history of the law of nations. Although it may not be the real starting point of the modern system of sovereign states, one cannot overlook the fact that since at least the last decades of the seventeenth century it has been considered as such. In other words, once the European diplomats and lawyers started to think in terms of an emerging system based on treaties concluded at major peace conferences, Westphalia became the historical point of reference *par excellence*.

How then do the Peace Treaties of 1648 constitute a caesura in the development of the law of nations? The answer to that question can be found in their political significance and their timing. However divergent views can be on their juridical originality and importance, one can hardly deny that Westphalia marks the end of the long period of religious and civil wars that had wrecked Europe since about 1550 and succeeded in laying down a constitutional order for Central Europe that would for a century and a half provide at least some stability. This pacification of Central Europe proved the beginning of a larger European process. By the late 1660s, almost all the large-scale civil wars and rebellions that had plagued the major European powers like Spain, France and England were over, sometimes because of the victory of the central government as with the *Fronde* in France (1653) or the rebellion of the Catalans in Spain (1653), sometimes with the constitution of a new power as with the Republic (1648) and Portugal (1668). Until the French Revolution, the great powers of Europe would be spared large-scale rebellions and civil wars.

Seen from this perspective, it is more easily understandable why Westphalia so readily became the point of reference for the beginning of a new era. Even if Westphalia did not lay down the basic features of the modern law of nations, it did lay down the political conditions for the new system to be formed. In fact, it was the main peace conferences of Nijmegen, Ryswick, Utrecht and the like that for the first time articulated and/or implemented the basic principles of the modern law of nations. Westphalia was the starting point of the formative period of the modern states system and not the constitution of that system.

Fifth, this reassessment of Westphalia and the period directly preceding it allows for a more nuanced approach to the modern law of nations of the 'Westphalian era' (1648–1815) itself. As was stated above, nineteenth- and twentieth-century historiography has interpreted this period as the era of the sovereign state and of a law of nations that could hardly limit the free arbiter of states. Seen within the wider context of developments since the end of the Middle Ages, this interpretation seems too one-sided. Although it cannot be denied that sovereignty was the single most important feature of the Westphalian system, its articulation was at least to some extent understood by the lawyers and diplomats as an attempt to reorganise Europe and to limit the freedom of sovereigns in their dealings with one another. The balance of power theory and the continuous references to the security of peace and tranquillity in Europe aimed – as historians have stressed – at safeguarding the sovereignty of all European powers, but at the same time expressed the recognition of limits to that sovereignty. Sovereignty and voluntarism were of course served by the ascendancy of treaties as the main constitutive instruments of the law of nations, but at the same time they were curbed by the custom to attribute a kind of paramountcy to some fundamental peace treaties. This more balanced view on the era of the *ius publicum Europaeum* plays down somewhat its historical uniqueness and allows us better to indicate the continuities with the periods preceding and following it.

Sixth, according to traditional historiography, the law of nations of the Westphalian period and the nineteenth century was almost completely formed by treaty and customary law. Only through their consent could sovereign rulers be bound by law. Even before the seventeenth century, this confronted the proponents of sovereignty with problems regarding the binding character of the law of nations. For the writers of the sixteenth, seventeenth and eighteenth centuries, the answer to that question was to be found in natural law. Grotius was not the first nor the last to vest the binding character of agreements in the natural law precept of *pacta sunt servanda*. From treaty practice, it becomes clear that self-defence was another natural precept that was commonly accepted. Fundamental and necessary though the role of natural law may have been, it was only marginal in terms of the articulation of particular rules of the law of nations. Now that the authority of the *ius commune* had collapsed, the sovereign rulers of Europe had to build a new body of law through treaties and customary practices. This did not imply, however, that they could not or did not turn to the old concepts, ideas and principles from the old doctrine. Even the modern natural lawyers and the Enlightened *philosophes* did not shed all traditional concepts and principles. They might disrobe a concept like *bona fides* of almost all its historical features, but that still does not prevent us from considering the basic concept itself an inheritance from Roman and canon law. In treaty practice, many elements of Roman and canon law were adopted and adapted.

Peace treaties in the Era of World Order

The Peace of Versailles of 1919 was a punitive and discriminatory peace. The Allies that had won the war erected themselves as the judges over their equals and thus struck at the very heart of the modern states system. In restoring the discriminatory character of war and peace, they returned at least in this one respect to the medieval just-war doctrine. The articles of the Peace providing for the foundation of the League of Nations introduced a framework for the peaceful settlement of disputes and collective security and implied important limitations to the freedom of member states to resort to war. The Peace of Versailles was not the first attempt of the era to curb the right to wage war and would not be the last. The Peace Conferences of The Hague of 1899 and 1907 were the most significant previous attempts. The Briand–Kellogg Pact of 1928 and the UN Charter of 1945 would further outlaw war.

As a punitive and discriminatory peace treaty, Versailles remains until today the most striking example. Only World War II and the Second Gulf War of 1991 ended with peace agreements – in the latter case in the form of a UN Security Council Resolution (no. 687) which was accepted by the losing belligerent – that are comparable to the Versailles Peace Treaty. Most peace treaties and peace settlements were much more classical and were largely reminiscent of nineteenth-century practices and traditions. Nevertheless, the new doctrine of *ius ad bellum* and the new world order have had their impact on peacemaking.

Though the twentieth-century doctrine of *ius ad bellum* is far different from the medieval doctrine of *bellum iustum*, it too led to a similar juridification of warfare and of peace. War is no longer total war, in which the belligerents break all juridical relations with one another and return to a kind of Hobbesian natural order. War is a partial disruption, often an illegal one, of a world order that is quite clearly defined and expressed in international law. Under the doctrine of the just war, war moreover was a means to enforce the law. Under the UN Charter, war can sometimes be the same.

The boundaries between war and peace have become more fluid than before. The greater involvement of civil populations and the emergence of non-state actors are of course other, even more important factors that have caused this, other than the re-juridification of war. This juridification, together with the emergence of a world order vested in permanent organisations and permanent rules, has diminished the significance of peace treaties as constitutive acts of the international order and of international law. Indeed, in many cases, peace treaties in the true sense – or even comparable settlements through elaborate UN Security Council Resolutions – have not proven necessary or desirable. Nevertheless, even over recent decades, wars have been ended by peace treaties, some of which were remarkably 'classic' in their structure and contents.[13] Peace treaties have lost their monopoly on peacemaking and have become just one means to that end. Moreover, treaty partners have lost much of their autonomy in framing peace, as they have to do it in the context of an established legal world order. The most striking novelty as opposed to the centuries before is the re-emergence of the individual as a holder of rights and duties under international law. The international protection of human rights as it emerged after 1945 – for the first time since the monopolisation of warfare by the state during the seventeenth century – makes the private individual a player in international law, even during war. States can waive their claims for the benefit of one another, but international law makes it harder and harder to barter the rights of their subjects. To some it might be a shred of hope that a Kantian world order of world citizens can be more than a dream, but it is surely reminiscent of the medieval and early modern debates on the rights of princes to dispose of the rights of their subjects. In this, as in many other respects, history seems to have come full circle and the sovereign state loses somewhat more of its myth. The era of the sovereign state loses its uniqueness and shrinks further back to what, after all, it is: just another episode in history.

[13] Like the Peace of Arava of 26 October 1994 between Israel and Jordan. Professor W. E. Voss (University of Osnabrück) elaborated on this during the March 2001 conference in Tilburg.

Appendix

ED. ALAIN WIJFFELS

{302rb}[a] TRACTATUS de confederatione, pace, & conventionibus Principum, *Disertissimi in utroque iure Doctoris D. Martini Laudensis*

¶ De confederatione, pace, & conventionibus[b] Principum. Rub.[c]

Quaestio. I.[d]

¶ Quando fit pax & remissio damnorum inter Principes, non[e] intelligitur in praeiudicium iurium privatorum[f]. Io. And. in c. quanto, de iureiur.[1] Bald. in l. venia. C. de in ius vocan.[2] & faciunt no. in c. in nostra, de iniur.[3] quod sane limitarem verum, nisi magna publica utilitas expresse & clare suaderet etiam[g] remissionem damnorum privatorum, quia utilitas publica prefertur private.[h] l. utilitas.[i] C. de [primipilo][j] lib. 12.[4] Nam Princeps ex causa potest remittere ius subditi sui[k], ut no. in l. rescripta. C. de preci. Impe. offeren.[5] & in l. fi. C. si contra ius vel util. publ.[6] faciunt no. per Bal. in l. quicunque. C. de servis fugi.[7] & l. si domus. ff. de servi. urbanorum prediorum,[8] l & in l. conventionum. ff. de pact.[9]

Quaestio. II.

¶ Si quis faciat confederationem cum pluribus successive, quem potius debeat iuvare, vide sing. Ludo. consi. 47.[10]

---

[1] Joannes Andreae ad X. 2, 24, 18, f. 189vb, No. 3: «[Assensu populi] quasi dicat, ex quo fit praeiudicium populo, non debet fieri sine suo assensu, ar. de offi. Archid. ad hoc .§. fi. et est arg. secundum Host. quod principes per se non [possunt] componere de damnis populo datis ratione guerrae, de quo remittit ad sum. de poeni. § fi. sub §. fi. versi. Sed pone, quod guerra».

[2] Baldus ad Cod. 2, 2, 2, f. 110vb, No. 3: «[...] not. quod quando ecclesia componit de delictis, non intelligitur componere de poenis et iuribus singularium personarum, nec potest hoc licite fieri in praeiudicium singularis personae cui est ius quaesitum [...]».

[3] X. 5, 36, 8.   [4] Cod. 12, 62, 3. The title of Cod. 12, 62 reads *De primipilo.*
[5] Cod. 1, 19,7.   [6] Cod. 1, 22, 6.   [7] Cod. 6, 1, 4.   [8] Dig. 2, 8, 21.   [9] Dig. 2, 14, 5.
[10] Ludovicus Romanus, Consilium 47 (inc. In Christi nomine. Amen. Visis necessariis pro habenda veritate), ff. 34vb–35rb, *quasi per totum,* esp. No. 1, f. 34vb; Nos. 6–7, f. 35rb

Quaestio. III.

¶ Pax facta cum principali, an extendatur ad adherentes, vide no. in c. ad Apostolicae, in fi. de iud. 6.[11] Barbacia. in cle. ne Romani.§. sane, de ele.[12] Lud. consi. 47.[13] & qualiter intelligatur promissio pacis facta pro se & adherentibus suis, vide Bal. in l. fi. circa finem. C. de edili. actio.[14] m

Questio. IIII.

¶ Si plures Principes fecerunt invicem colligationem de defendendo unu[m] alterum sub certa pena, non incurrunt penam, si faciunt, quod possunt pro adiuvando offensum. Ange. iuncta gl. in l. si ideo. C. de his quib. ut indig.[15]

(«[...] Ex quibus omnibus quo ad hoc primum concludo ambas confederationes per prefatum comitem contractas validas censeri: sed in secunda tacite ius primae confederationis semper intelligi repetitum. Et ideo prima haec confederatio secunda validior est censenda, et hoc de isto articulo consultationis dixisse sufficiat»).

[11] Sextus 2, 14, 2.

[12] Andreas Barbatia ad Clementinam 1, 3, 2, 2, f. 62va, No. 31: «... sed potius confederate ut invicem se conservent, licet palium vel aliam rem transmittant in signum preeminentie casum dicit esse valde nota. in l. non dubito ff. de capti. vide Bart. & Bal. exclamantes de illo tex. in l. cunctos populos C. de summa trinita. & faciat sing. dictum, ut refert Joan. And. in c. ad apostolice de re iudi. in vi. ubi commendatur fidelitas ecclesie romane que in capitulis pacis semper permittit terras adhaerentes recomendatas & confederatas, quia aliter pax facta cum civitate maiori non videtur facta cum civitatibus recomendatis, sive adherentibus, quod bene notabis ad capitula pacis formanda».

[13] Ludovicus Romanus, Consilium 47 (*supra*), No. 8, f. 35rb: Quo ad secundum breviter est dicendum praedictum comitem utriusque regis respectu in pace inter eos inita fore comprehensum. Quilibet enim ex his regibus pro se et suis confoederatis pacem contraxit: sed iste utrique regi est confederatus, ut late ex supradictis manifestum est. ergo in pace utriusque respectu comprehenditur. Ex quo amborum verba de confederatis generaliter loquuntur. ff. de leg. praestan. l. i. §. generaliter. ff. de testa. mili. l. in fraudem .§. fi. ff. de leg. 3. l. non aliter, et l. ille aut ille .§. cum in verbis, cum simil.».

[14] Baldus ad Cod. 4, 58, 5, ff. 130va–131rb, No. 27, f. 131rb: «Facit ad quaestionem de eo, qui promisit pro suis adhaerentibus, quia intelligitur promisisse de non offendendo occasione guerre, nec de aliis inimicitiis singularib. hominis ad hominem. Tene menti. Id .n. quod non subiicitur materie belli, non venit in natura pacti, vel pacis».

[15] Cf. Angelus de Ubaldis ad Cod. 6, 35, 7, f. 171ra: «Non imputatur quicquam facienti illud quod potest, sic supra de inof. testa. l. contra maiores. Et allegatur quod syndicus non tenetur denunciare maleficia quorum authores reperiri non possunt, sic infra eo l. cum fratrem .ff. eo. l. propter veneni ff. quod vi aut clam l. semper § si in sepulcro. Attende tamen ad formam practicandi, quia syndicus debet congregare universitatem suam et facere explorationem quam potest ab eis et ipsam redigere in publicam scripturam, et deinde debet accedere ad iudicem maleficiorum et narrare delictum commissum et se explorasse de authoribus quicquid potuit et explorationis chartulam dimittere apud acta et quod plus invenire non potest, et hoc facto relevatus erit a pena: quia nulla potest sibi negligentia imputari patet ex legibus allegatis coniuncta l. divus ff. de custo. reo.»; glossa 'est desiderata' ad Cod. 6, 35, 7.

Quaestio. V.

¶ Contractum non potest Princeps infringere nisi ex causa, quia licet Deus subiecerit leges principibus, non tamen subiecit^n contractus c. i. & ibi Bal. de natura feud.^{o} [16] & not. per Docto. in l. digna vox. C. de legi.[17] propterea si lex transit in contractum vel quasi non potest infringere^p secundum [Bar.]^q in l. omnes populi. ff. de iusti. & iure,[18] & videatur Bal. in l. qui se patris. C. unde libe. ver. sed quid si pater decedit.[19] ubi pulchre.

Quaestio. VI.

¶ Rex, dux vel alius Princeps vasallus Imperatoris vel Pape, qui sine licentia Domini sui superioris, a quo habet feudum, infeudavit castrum^r vel unam civitatem de feudo suo consiliario suo^s vel alteri, non dicitur cecidisse a feudo, quia licet hodie vasallus non possit alienare, c. i. de prohi. feu. alie. per Fede.[20] tamen vasallus potest in feudum dare his concurrentibus que ponit gl. in §. praeterea. c. i. de capitulis Corradi. quam gl. communiter sequuntur feudiste,[21] & ita publice disputavi Papie.[22] Advertendum tamen est, quod licet Principes possint donationes & alienationes facere, tamen non possunt, quando dignitatem regiam, Ducalem, vel Marchionalem graviter ledunt. c. Abbate sane, de re iud. lib. 6.[23] c. intellecto, de iureiu.[24] & l. dona.^{t} C. de dona. inter vi. & uxo.[25] &

---

[16] L.F. 1, 7; Baldus *ibidem*, s.v. Natura feudi, No. 2, f. 20vb: «Querunt Doctores utrum Imperator obligetur praecise ex suo contractu, et hic sunt opin. C. de legib. l. digna vox, quae quaestio videtur determinari quod sic infra, de nova forma fidelita. Et no. hic quod princeps tenetur servare suas consuetudines et sic ius consuetudinarium concludit principi. hoc no. supra, qui feu. da. pos. c. i. §. fi».

[17] Doctores ad Cod. 1, 14, 4.

[18] Cf. Bartolus ad Dig. 1, 1, 9, ff. 3rb–15ra, in particular f. 11rb–vb, on the case where a statute «transit in contractum vel quasi».

[19] Baldus ad Cod. 6, 14, 3, ff. 40rb–42rb, Nos. 33–4, f. 41va: «Sed quid si pater decedit in monasterio [. . .] dominus etiam Imperator non potest auferre feudum sine causa, nisi sit feudum precario concessum, argument. ff. de dolo. l. Lucius, seu per privilegium, quia speciale ius est in Principe, ut possit revocare suum privilegium, ex quo est alteri quaesitum, etiam sine causa, ut infra de omni agro. deser. l. qui fundos, libro undecimo. Sed si non est privilegium, sed conventio, tunc non potest revocare, nisi secundum ipsius rei naturam, ut l. fundi infra de fund. patri. libro. ii. Hoc scias, quod si Princeps recipit pretium, significat venditionem, et si uteretur verbo, indulgemus, vel simili verbo, esset irrevocabilis contractus, et non privilegium argu. infra de praecuria. l. fi. lib. decimo [. . .] Item, in concessis absque praeiudicio superioris, ut in iurisdictionalibus, nam in eis semper authoritas superioris reservatur, et nisi eius authoritate non potest exerceri, cum in eo residat suprema potestas inseparabilis, unde potest iurisdictiones supprimere aliorum, non solum singularium personarum, sed etiam civitat[u]m, ut no. in l. omnes populi per Doct. de iust. et iur. In translatis vero quo ad directum dominium, vel utile, non habet locum penitentiam, cum de iuregentium teneatur ex suo consensu, ut no. per Cy. supra de legi. l. digna vox».

[20] L. F. 2, 54   [21] L. F. 2, 40; cf. glossa 'feudi factas' *ibidem*; feudistae *ibidem*.

[22] See the passage quoted *infra*, n. 31.   [23] Sextus 2, 14, 3.

[24] X. 2, 24, 33.   [25] Cod. 5, 16, 26.

l. bene a Zenone. C. de quadri. praescri.²⁶ quod no. contra Principes in diminutionem dignitatum suarum alienantes modo unam civitatem, modo aliam, & modo unum castrum, modo aliud intricando dignitatem, arg. l. summa^u cum ratione. ff. de pecu.²⁷ & quod no. Bal.^v & Ange. in l. 2. C. de repu. haeredi.²⁸ & no. in l. nomen. ff. de leg. 3.²⁹ no. in c. grandi. de supplen. negli. praela.³⁰ Et dixi plene in proemio feudorum, hoc anno in hac civitate Senensi. & paucissima dixi in hoc opusculo de materia feudali,³¹ quia tractabo in materia feudali iam incepta & nondum finita.^w

Quaestio. VII.

¶ Ratione confederationis attribuitur iurisdi[ctio] alias non habenti. l. non dubito. ff. de capti.^x & postlimi. reversis.³² Nam quando Principes vel civitates sunt confederat[i],^y primo est considerandus tenor conventionum, l. i. in

---

[26] Cod. 7, 37, 3.   [27] Dig. 15, 1, 21.
[28] Cf. Baldus ad Cod. 6, 31, 2 (f. 111rb–va), Cod. 3, 3, 2 (f. 182)? Cf. Angelus de Ubaldis ad Cod. 6, 31, 2, f. 168va: «Et colligitur mala fides ex infrascriptis quatuor aut quinque. Primo si omnia bona emit ff. qu. in frau. cred. l. omnes § lucius. Idem credo si emisset omnia meliora, quia par ratio fraudis est. tex. est sing. et non est alibi in l. summa cum ratione in prin. ff. de pecu. Secundo si emit per interpositam personam ut supra de natu. li. l. i. et l. iii. § et quod de subeundo eo. ti. Tertio si post abstentionem emit incontinenti nam vicinitas temporis operatur hanc presumptionem de privile. credito. l. si venter § in bonis ff. de divortiis l. iii. Quarto et ultimo si emit clandestine de adm. tu. l. non estimo et si bene muneras sunt quandoque in glo. fi. ibi l. sicut § illud dic ille § nihil facit sed glo. dicit veritatem, quia retro fingitur fuisse dominus: ergo non tenuit emptio et hoc tenent Cy. et Bar.»?
[29] Dig. 32, 1, 34.   [30] Sextus 1, 8, 2.
[31] Comp. with Martinus Garatus, Lectura in Opere Feudorum, L. I, T. 1, s.v. Quia de feudis, Nos. 30–31, p. 16, ad v. 'Dignitas': «.[...] An princeps possit alienare ea quae sunt principatus? Concludit Bal. secundum veteres, quod aut princeps alienat expropriando et penitus abdicando dominium, iurisdictionem, et dignitatem, et tunc non potest: quia esset deformare principatum: c. intellecto et ibi not. de iureiur. vii. q. i cap. in apibus. ubi gl. notanter dicit, quod Imperator graecus non est proprie Imperator, sed Imperator Romanus. Aut alienat princeps retinendo directum dominium, vel saltem superioritatem: et tunc valet alienatio, ut in hoc c. nemo. in principio, et c. i. § praeterea. in gl. de capitulis Corradi. et in c. i. qui dicitur dux, vel marchio. Limitate Bald. Nisi infeudatio vergeret in detrimentum vel in incommodum principatus vel regni. l. summa cum ratione. ff. de pecul. puta, si rex passi, daret in feudum, nunc unam civitatem, nunc aliam, annihillando regnum: secundum plene scripta in c. grandi. et ibi Ioan. And. de supple. negli. praela. li. vi. et d. c. intellecto»; on the same theme, see also Nos. 57–58, p. 22 (granting of lower fiefs). The prohibition of disposing of fiefs in general is a recurrent theme in the *lectura*, e.g. p. 118, Nos. 17–18; p. 120, No. 1; p. 149, No. 17; p. 155, Nos. 37–38; L. I, T. 13, p. 172 ss.; p. 187, No. 2; p. 206 Nos. 3 ss.; p. 218, No. 5; pp. 294–5, Nos. 18–20; p. 310, No. 9; p. 381, No. 11 («Consuetudo de alienando feudo, valet»); p. 484, No. 20; pp. 520 ss., Nos. 6 ss.; p. 586, No. 2; L. III, T. 30, p. 634 ss.; L. III, T. 33, p. 641 ss. On the division of fiefs: e.g. p. 207, No. 15 («... nisi sit feudum regale ducatus»); p. 655 ss.
[32] Dig. 49, 5, 7.

prin. ff. de pact.³³ Et ipsis deficientibus, natura federis haec est, quod unus^z adiuvat alium, si requiratur, secundum Bald. in l. executorem. C. de execu. rei iudi.³⁴ vide Bart. in d. l. non dubito.³⁵

Quaestio. VIII.

¶ Civitas vel populus non potest conventionem facere [de]^{aa} recognoscendo alium in Dominum, quasi^{bb} Principem suum in preiudicium Principis sui, sicut non potest fieri prorogatio simplicis iurisd[ictionis] in preiudicium {**302va**} Domini, ut no. in c. significasti. in fi. de fo. comp.³⁶ & in c. ceterum. de iudi.³⁷ in novella, & fuit no. Bal. in l. 2. C. de ope. liber.³⁸

Quaestio. IX.³⁹

¶ Principes invicem facientes treugam, vel^{cc} confederationem tacite videntur inter eos agere, quod post treugam & confederationem finitam sint in guerra.

---

³³ Dig. 2, 14, 1.
³⁴ Baldus ad Cod. 7, 53, 8, ff. 74va–77rb, No. 33, f. 76ra–rb: «Sed quaero, quid de civitatib. confoederatis, nam natura federis haec est, persequi hostes alterius, ut proprios, ut ff. de cap. l. non dubito, nam confaederatio non est aliud, quam facere quasi ex duob. corporib. unum corpus, ad invicem se protegendum contra hostes, et inimicos cuiuslibet excollegatis, nec est novum quod de duab. civitatib. et duab. provinciis fiat unum corpus: nam si unio perfecta fieri potest, in Auth. ut iud. sine quoquo suffra. §. illud tamen diximus. ergo multo fortius quaedam confaederatio sociabilis. sed tu dic, quod confaederatio non operat plus, vel minus, quam dictent pacta confaederatorum, quicquid dicat Bar. in .§. ratione non obstat l. non dubito. quia ibi loquitur de confederatione Romani populi, qui in plenam tutelam populi erant recepti, vel ibi loquitur interveniente requisitione confaederatorum, sed sine requisitione non tenetur, nec debet puniri, vel dic quod ibi dicit, fiunt apud nos rei, id est possumus procedere contra delinquentes in terra faederata...».
³⁵ Bartolus ad Dig. 49, 15, 7, f. 145ra, No. 3: «[...] dico quod ex speciali statuto civitatis hoc potest fieri ut delinquentes de federatis civitatibus possint apud nos puniri per hunc tex. ita de termino in l. cunctos populos. posset etiam iste tex. aliter intelligi. ut hic tex. velit dicere quod contra homines de civitatibus federatis non procedimus tanquam contra hostes. sed si delinquunt de iure ordinario proceditur contra eos reos sicut contra nostros reos et sic poterit puniri sicut quilibet forensis delinquens non hostis».
³⁶ X. 2, 2, 18.   ³⁷ X. 2, 1, 5.
³⁸ Baldus ad Cod. 6, 3, 2 f. 20ra–rb, No. 6, f. 20ra–rb: «Sed nunquid civitas, vel castrum possit recognoscere aliquem in superiorem, qui non est: & videtur quod sic. ff. de capti. l. non dubito. sicut libertus et vasallus meus potest recognoscere et confiteri se plurium esse libertum, vel vasallum. So. si de iure, vel de commodo principalis et veri domini aliquid minuatur: talis recognitio non valet: ut ff. de aqu. plu. ar. l. in concedendo et ff. si quid in fraudem patro. l. 1 §. si quis. cum etiam prorogatio simplicis iurisdictionis non teneat in praeiudicium superiorum, ut no. extra. de iud. c. ceterum in novel. si autem vasallus potest omnibus integraliter satisfacere, tunc valet quo ad obligationem personalem, non quo ad realem seu vasallaticam, quia quatenus est unius, alterius esse non potest, nec etiam ad possessionem, ut l. fi. de acq. pos. de hoc in Spe. de feud. §. quum versi. ii. quaeritur».
³⁹ See also *De bello*, Qu. inc. «Finito tempore treugue...».

Bal. in l. illud. in fi. ff. de acq. here.⁴⁰ & vide no. in c. i. de treuga & pace,⁴¹ & an sit necessaria differentia, vide Bal. in c. nos Romanorum ver. non admittendum. de pace Constan.⁴² ᵈᵈ

Quaestio. X.

¶ Filii regis vivo rege consentiente possunt inter seᵉᵉ dividere baronias pro litibus futuris tollendis ipso rege perseverante usque ad mortem in eadem voluntate. l. fi. C. de pac.⁴³ & Bal. in auth. hoc amplius. C. de fideicom.⁴⁴ vide Alb. in l. fi. C. de don. inter virum & uxo.⁴⁵

---

⁴⁰ Baldus ad Dig. 29, 2, 77, f. 117ra, No. 3: «Et inducitur ista l. in arg. quod si non habentes guerram faciunt treugam, quod tacite videtur agi, quod post tempus treuge sint in guerra, de hoc hic per Cy. et l. si unus § i. de pac. sup.».
⁴¹ X. 1, 34, 1.
⁴² Cf. Baldus, De Pace Constantiae, f. 97 ra, Nos. 7–8: «[Nos Romanorum] Hic dicit Imperator, quod vult istam pacem esse perpetuam, idest quamdiu fides servetur, ut ff. loca. l. quaero .§. inter locatorem. Instit. eo .§. adeo. [In perpetuum] Per praesentem mundi aetatem et futuram, idest sine praefinitione temporis, quia Imperator facit hanc pacem nomine sedis, non nomine proprio tantum, et Imperium non moritur ut ff. de leg. 2. l. quod Principi. et in Auth. quomodo opor. epis. in fi. et no. per Cy. C. qui test. facere pos. l. si quis imperatorem, et in cap. si gratiose, de rescrip. lib. 6 et hoc ex parte Imperii. Sed ex parte civitatum...».
⁴³ Cod. 2, 3, 30.
⁴⁴ Baldus ad auth. *amplius hoc* [Cod. 6, 42, 31], ff. 155rb–156rb, Nos. 9–10, f. 155vb: «Quaero, an filii Regis vivo Rege possint inter se dividere Baronias pro futuris dissensionibus declinandis, Respondeo sic, de consensu Regis: tamen in eo requiritur perseverentia Regis usque ad mortem, ut l. fi. sup. de pac. non tamen Rex potest promittere, sed permittere, quia permissio, in qua potest habere locum poenitentia, non aufert libertatem testandi .i. heredem instituendi, vel codicillandi forte illa l. fi. potest tolli per statutum Regium, c. i § preterea. qui mo. feu. amit. quia Rex est lex animata in regno suo, et potest plus quam ius communis, vel consuetudo, et ideo quando primogenitus esset insufficiens, posset secundo genito regnum dare, ut fecit Rex David, nam consuetudo regni de praeferendo primogenitum non debet interpretari contra utilitatem totius regni, ut sup. de legi. l. quod favore».
⁴⁵ Albericus ad Cod. 5, 16, 26, ff. 263va–264va, No. 4, f. 263vb: «Item iure naturali omnes filii pariter succedunt et etiam positivo: ut ff. unde libe. l. scripto, et infra de libe. praete. l. maximum vitium, et probant etiam per philosophum 8. Ethicorum adeo quod etiam patre vivente dicuntur quodammodo domini, ut ff. de libe. et posth. l. in suis. Sed quia commodius regitur per unum, quam per plures, ut 7. q. 2 c. in apibus ext. de off. ordi. c. in plerisque, et de orig. in l. 2 § deinde. Quia difficile, ubi de hoc tetigi deventum fuit ad res, et aliquibus vium est probabilibus rationibus, reges per electionem assumendos, tamen usitatum est, quod per successionem transeunt, et idem videtur fuisse in imperatore: ut dixi infra ad l. Fal. 4 de hoc in us. feu. qui. mo. feu. acquir. § genera feudorum et § Item potest dari in feudum Marchio. et plene dixi. infra. de quadri. praescri. l. bene a Zenone, et ne discordia oriretur inter filios, transeunt ad primogenitum, et ad hoc potuit esse duplex ratio [...]».

Quaestio. XI.

¶ Princeps donavit Titio civitatem mille millium marcharum, valet haec donatio, licet non sit insinuata iure singulari in Principe secundum Ba[r].^ff & Fran. Tig. qui ita consuluerunt,^46 ut refert [Bal.]^gg in l. sancimus. C. de dona.^47 facit auth. igitur. C. de dona.^48 ^hh & l. dona. C. de dona.^ii inter virum & uxo.^49 dixi in rub. de Dominis^jj & principibus, conclusione. 13.^50

Quaestio. XII.

¶ Si dissensio^kk sit inter duas civitates, Princeps debet eas compellere ad pacem. [Bar].^ll in l. congruit. ff. de offi. praesi.^51

Quaestio. XIII.

¶ Princeps superior debet deponere tyrannos. l. in nomine Domini. C. de off. praefe. praeto.^52 & ex exercitio cognoscitur tyrannus, puta quia servat

---

[46] Bartolus; Franciscus de Tigrinis: cf. the following reference to Baldus.
[47] Baldus ad Cod. 8, 53, 34, ff. 182rb–183ra, No. 5, f. 182va: «Quidam dominus donavit alicui quoddam castrum valens decem millia marcharum. Iste dominus habebat merum, et Mixtum imperium in donato castro, donatio non fuit insinuata, agebatur coram superiore, et petebatur, quod ista donatio declararetur nulla, eo quod non erat insinuata, dicebatur, quod erat insinuata apud magistratum municipalem illius castri. Nam ipse donans erat magistratus municipalis, et habebat merum et mixtum imperium, et cum isto esset actus voluntariae iurisd. poterat fieri insinuatio apud se ipsum, ut ff. de adop. l. si consul. Odofr. determinat non valere, quia si speciale est in Principe, quod ipse idem posset esse donator, et iudex insinuationum, ergo secus in isto casu in alio inferiore, qui habet supra se superiorem. Et si dicatur, quod actus voluntarie poterat fieri apud seipsum, ut ff. de adop. l. si consul, non est verum, ubi requiritur authoritas superioris, unde dicit Odofr. si speciale est in principe, secus est secundum ius commune in quolibet alio habente superiorem. Recordor quod Bar. et Fran. de Pisis in testamento, quod fecit quidam de Ursinis in quodam castro, in quo habebat merum imperium et omnimodam iurisdictionem, et consuluerunt, quod illud testamentum valeret».
[48] Cf. Auth. Item et a privatis, ad Cod. 8, 53, 34.
[49] Cod. 5, 16, 26.   [50] Martinus Garatus.
[51] Cf. Bartolus ad Dig. 1, 18, 13, ff. 39vb–40ra, No. 4, f. 40ra: «Et inducitur in argumentum ad questionem, quod potestates provinciarum sive terrarum possunt cogere cives, et provinciales suos ad faciendam pacem, quod no. in corpore de mand. prin. § deinde et no. infra de usufru. l. si ususfructus §. inter duos alias est l. aequissimum. Contra hoc facit in Auth. ut lit. iu. § fi. colla. 9 et ideo dic, quod interdum quaeritur de pace fienda inter unam civitatem et aliam, et hoc casu preses sive potestas debet se interponere ut fiat, ut est tex. in §. deinde, preall. Quinque queritur de pace fienda inter singulares personas, et tunc, aut quaestio vertitur criminalis, aut civilis. Primo casu debet interponere se, et eos cogere, ut infra de usuf. l. si ususfructus §. si inter quos. secundo casu debet movere partes ad concordiam, maxime ubi iura partium conservarentur illaesa, alias non, et ita intellige d. §. fi. in fi. ut liti. iurent».
[52] Cod. 1, 27, 2.

partialitates inter civitates,^(mm) & non vult sapientes penes se, ut plene per Bar. in tract. de tyranno.⁵³ & Bar.^(nn) in l. decernimus. C. de sac. san. Eccle.⁵⁴

Quaestio. XIIII.

¶ Rex Fran.^(oo) vel alius Princeps non potest vendere vel alienare unam ex civitatibus regni vel ducatus, ne^(pp) habeant graviorem Dominum. l. invitus. in^(qq) gl. ff. de fideicom. lib.⁵⁵ & vide Host. & Io. An. in c. dilecti. de ma. & obed.⁵⁶

Quaestio. XV.

¶ Papa non potest alienare, & donare pecuniam suis nepotibus. c. non licet. 12. q. 2 ubi Archi.⁵⁷ quod Papa aliter faciens quamvis peccet & puniatur a Deo, tamen non subiicitur penae alicuius legis positivae; quia Papa est supra ius in

---

⁵³ Bartolus, Tractatus de tyrrania, ff. 113va–115vb, esp. f. 114vb.
⁵⁴ Bartolus ad Cod. 1, 2, 16, f. 15rb: «[. . .] Not. quod omnia facta tempore tyrannidis superveniente iusto domino debent cassari et irritari, quod not. Item quando supervenit iustus dominus etc.». Cf. infra, Qu. 41.
⁵⁵ Dig. 40, 5, 34; glossa 'non est' ibidem.
⁵⁶ Cf. Henricus de Segusio ad X. 1, 33, 13, ff. 160rb–161ra [Paris, J. Petit], f. 160rb: «(Praeiudicium) quia nova servitus imponebatur, et est ar. quod si aliquis nobilis velit se et terram suam subiicere alieno dominio hominum suorum contradictio admittet. Quia et interest sua quod dominus eorum sit liber et tot dominos non habere, ar. ad idem infra e. c. fi. et ff. de appella. non tantum et quia quod omnes tangit etc. ut no. supra de tempo. ordi. si archiepiscopus § fi. Et est expressum quod dominus in alium feudum non transferat sine vasalli voluntate, ut in lib. feu. de feudo non alie. sine consensu. ma. do. imperialem § preterea ducatur; cf. Ioannes Andreae ad X. 1, 33, 13, f. 268ra, No. 4: «[Praeiudicium] no. per hoc. Host. quod si aliquis dominus velit subiicere terram suam alieno domino, admittetur contradictio hominorum suorum, quia et interest sua, quod dominus ipsorum sit liber, et tot dominos non habere. ad idem infra c. fi. ff. de app. non tantum. et quia quod omnes etc. ff. de reg. iu. quod omnes. et videtur expressum, quod dominus sine voluntate vasalli ius suum non transferat in alium, in libro feu. de feu. non alie. sine volun. ma. do. imperialem .§. praeterea ducatus».
⁵⁷ Decretum Gratiani, c. 12, q. 2, c. 43; cf. Guido de Baysio ibidem, f. 225ra–rb: «Non liceat pape i. non debeat credere sibi licere. Hu. alienare ad malos usus non dico in casu non concesso nam posset de non concesso facere concessum per constitutionem immo dico quod h. natura turpe est alienare res ecclesie in casu non concesso, et ideo non potest ei licere ff. de ver. sig. . . . aliqua necessitate hoc videtur falsum ut no. supra e.q. in sum. Sed dic secundum hu. quod hoc non removet quando papa possit statuere vel invenire novum casum alienandi, sed ostendit alienationem aliis prohibitam pape non licere, sicut enim est peccatum in aliis alienare res ecclesie sine utilitate et sine causa rationabili et honesta, ita immo multomagis et in papa qui mortaliter peccat si vult res ecclesiasticas consumere in turpes usus vel dare consanguineis ut eos dicites pro aliis faciat vel ut ipsi inde construant palatia et huiusmodi secundum h. nec in ver qua lege, ver. custodes .i. ecclesiarum prelati et qui ver. nisi restituatur arg. contra hoc xvii. q. iiii. c. i. So. ibi loquitur de pena dispositionis, hic autem de pena excommunicationis [. . .]».

c. proposuit. de conces. praeb.⁵⁸ & vide Io. de Lig. in c. i.ʳʳ de reb. Eccl. non alie.⁵⁹

Quaestio. XVI.

¶ In treugis est speciale, quod licet tu frangisˢˢ fidem mihi, tamen non debeo tibi frangere, donec duratᵗᵗ tempus treugae, secundum Anto. de But. in c. pervenit. de iureiur.⁶⁰

Quaestio. XVII.

¶ Est conventio, quod civitas Florentina non possit derogare iurisdictionemᵘᵘ potestatis Aretii, deinde civitas Florentina mittitᵛᵛ vicarium ad unum castrum subiectum dictae civitati Aretii. Quaeritur, an fiat contra conventionem? Vidi consilium eximii Doctoris, quod non fiat contra conventionem, per casum,ʷʷ & ibi Bart. in l. tam collatoresˣˣ. §. pe. C. de re mili. lib. 12.⁶¹ ʸʸ

Quaestio. XVIII.

¶ Si invadat Princeps castra aliena, & nolit restituere nisi aliquo [accepto]ᶻᶻ ex conventione, & quidemᵃᵃᵃ tenetur Princeps acceptum reddere, quia turpiter

---

⁵⁸ X. 3, 8, 4.
⁵⁹ Ioannes de Lignano ad X. 3, 13, 6 (!), MBS Ms. CLM 8687, f. 35ra: «Sed potestne papa alienare et intelligere de bonis que sunt de mensa ecclesie Romane vel de bonis patrimonialibus que sunt specialiter de patrimonio ecclesie? Et nunquam [?] potest dare pecunias nepotibus et filiis ut emant castrum, textus est quem no. in c. non licet ubi no. Archidy. xii. q. ii, papa tamen aliter faciens tamen quamvis adeo puniendus et peccet, non tamen subicitur pene alicuius legis positive quia est supra ius ut supra de concess. preben. proposuit. Si alienet sine causa, et iam non subest legi positive sed iudicem divin[e] sic quamvis possit facere legem permittente[m] alienationem in causa nov[a]». See also ad X. 3, 8, 4 (quoted in the previous passage and by Garatus), f. 24ra: «Sed nunquid potest dispensare in omnibus, dic quod non in naturalibus quia solius dei est illa immutare [...] naturalibus tamen actibus potest aliquando per legem immutare licet non tollere. Sed si loquimur quo ad actus divinos non, quia non potest dispensare ut mortaliter peccem stante peccato sed in lege positiva potest bene dispensare quia illam potest tollere ergo effectum ipsius».
⁶⁰ Antonius de Butrio ad X. 2, 24, 3, No. 6, f. 73va: «Oppo. quod non servanti fidem fidem servare tenear xxiii. q. i. noli estimare cum si. glo. dicit quod regulariter procedit tex. ad quod xxv. distin. esto. de regulis iuris lib. sexto. casualiter procedit contra vel particulariter ad ca. noli dic quod concordat, quia hosti fides est servanda, si hostis fidem servat ca. quod deo. dic quod vota coniugum diriguntur in deum, nec unum prestatur ad implementum alterius respective, ideo nec resolvuntur vel conditionantur ad implementum alterius, ut si aliqua conditio inserta in iuramento et acceptata per aliam partem non servatur c. de condi. insertis. l. i. xxxii. quaestio. ultima c. fi. vel si iuravi fidelitatem propter feudum et aufert mihi feudum, ad hoc de loca. potuit, de feudis c. i. [...]».
⁶¹ Bartolus ad Cod. 12, 35, 18, f. 50rb: «[...] No. ex isto tex. quod si alicui officiali committitur cognitio alicuius cause et potestas cognoscendi tollitur capitaneo Perusii per hoc. non dicitur derogari iursditioni capitanei. ratio est quia civis de causa cognoscens subditus est ipsi capitaneo».

accepit & ideo per pacis capitula non firmatur talis contractus impressivus &^bbb turpis. Bal. in l.i.^ccc C. de condi. ob. tur. cau.^62 quod tene menti contra invadentes civitates alienas. facit l. fi. ff.^ddd de condi. ob. turp. ca.^63 propterea alias vidi consilium Illu. Doct.^64 quod cum multi de facto rebelles ducis^eee & de iure subditi ipsius ducis fecerunt conventionem cum ipso duce & Principe suo de restituendis^fff civitatibus & castris^ggg cum pacto, quod dicti rebelles retineant aliqua castra ducis, & etiam habeant^hhh aliqua bona civium, consultum fuit, non valere dictam conventionem tanquam meticulosam, & posse revocari. l. metum .§ volenti. ff. quod me. cau.^65 & faciunt no. in l. interpositas. C. de transact.^66 iii

Quaestio. XIX.

¶ Papa potest compellere Principes ad servandam pacem inter eos contractam. c. novit. de iud.^67 & hostibus est pax servanda, secundum Ant. de But. in d. c. novit.^68

Quaestio. XX.

¶ Barones civitatis^jjj tres vel plures si faciant ligam sine Principis maioris auctoritate, non valent tales conventiones. Inn. in c. dilecta. extra de exces. prela.^69 quod limita. nisi non recognoscant superiorem, secundum Bar.^kkk in l. fi. ff. de

---

[62] Cf. Baldus ad Cod. 4, 7, 3, f. 17va–rb: «Officialis, qui praetextu officii aliquid per concussionem accepit, accepta restituit, et criminaliter punitur. h.d. Tyrocinii .i. novae militiae. Idem si aliquid dedit, ne mitteretur in exercitu. vel non crearetur syndicus per impressionem superioris, et contra iustitiam, nam hic sola turpitudo, et barattaria recipientis versatur instantia .i. solicitudine, ut ff. de usu. l. si bene ff. de pig. ac. l. fi. § fi.».
[63] Dig. 12, 5, 9.   [64] Illustris[ssimi] Doctor[is].
[65] Dig. 4, 2, 9, 4.   [66] Cod. 2, 4, 13.   [67] X. 2, 1, 13.
[68] Antonius de Butrio ad X. 2, 1, 13, Nos. 24–26, f. 18vb: «Nota quod est pax quia vinculum est caritatis. Caritas autem est dilectio dei et proximi sui secundum Pet. et cum caritas sit specialis virtus qua salvamur, et fides. Ideo circa pacem et iuramentum specialis cognoscit ecclesia, ad hoc de electio. venerabilem, de treu. et pa. c. secundo et est pax etiam hosti servanda xxiii q. i Joan. et c. se.».
[69] Innocentius ad X. 5, 31, 14, No. 3, f. 200vb: «[...] Sed contra .ff. de colle illi. collegia in prin. ubi dicitur quod collegia non debent fieri absque autoritate senatusconsul. vel principis. sol. omnia predicta collegia. que fiunt pro bono ad malum non procedunt: dicimus esse concessa autoritate senatusconsul. qui sola illicita prohibet. et ideo licita concedere videtur .ff. de colle. illi l. i. sicut per idem senatusconsultum concessa sunt collegia processionum et negociationum et burgorum et villarum. C. de iurisd. om. iu. l. fi. supra de procura. quia .ff. quod cuius. univer. l. i. ff. ad trebel. omnibus .ff. de lega. i. si heres .§. vitiis. C. de natu. libe. l. si quis sen. et in l. quoniam. autoritate autem principis possent et deberent fieri collegia si homines parum habent facere simul ut si barones vel civitates vel tres vel plures coeant collegium. nam huiusmodi collegium non valeret sine autoritate principis, quia nec multum simul facere habent nec hoc faciunt causa religionis [...]».

colle. illici.⁷⁰ & faciens ligam contra Imperatorem incidit in crimen lesae ma. l. i C. ut armorum usus. lib. 11.⁷¹ secus si contra alium, tex. in l. non dubito. ff. de cap.⁷² & Bald. no. in l. conventionum. in recolle.ˡˡˡ ff. de pact.⁷³ ᵐᵐᵐ

Quaestio. XXI.

❡ Papa non vult pacem sine adhaerentibus suis, & eorum tutissima securitate. vide Inn. & Bal. in c. ad Apostolicae. de re iudi.⁷⁴

Quaestio. XXII.

❡ Crimen fractae pacis inter Principes pertinetⁿⁿⁿ ad iudicium Ecclesiasticum. Inn. in c. novit. de iud.⁷⁵

---

⁷⁰ Bartolus ad Dig. 47, 22, 4, ff. 157va–159ra, esp. Nos. 10–11, f. 158ra: «[. . .] Item iste lige que fiunt inter civitates et inter principes et barones non valent. ita tenet Inno. in c. dilecta. extra de exces. prelato. nec ob. l. non dubito. infra. de cap. ubi dicitur quod civitates invicem federantur et colligantur quia istud est verum quando civitates alie non amice vel libere federantur populo romano habenti imperium. sed plures civitates vel plures barones qui essent sub uno rege domino vel principe non possunt invicem facere illam federationem. Ista enim sunt sodalicia et collegia prohibita. ut supra l. i. Ex istis colligitur quod civitates tuscie que non recognoscunt de facto in temporalibus superiorem possunt invicem simul federari tanquam libere, sed plura castra vel ville que essent sub una civitate vel uno domino hoc non possent. ut dictum est».

⁷¹ Cod. 11, 47, 1.   ⁷² Dig. 49, 15, 7.

⁷³ The *recollectio* could not be found. Comp. with the lecture of Baldus ad Dig. 2, 14, 5, ff. 124vb, 124vb–125ra, which, however, is not directly relevant for the principle here at issue: «In tex. publica. non capitaneum, seu ducem exercitus posse pacisci etiam cum hoste, h.d. unde dicit Bart hoc, quod capitaneus guerrae potest dare securitatem bannito. et quod talis habens securitatem non potest capi, licet sit bannitus, et histis, et dicit quod ista q. fuit de facto. In gl. ibi, faedere, haec tamen non debent fieri sine iussu populi, et populo inconsulto, et ponit Salust. in Iugurtino exemplum de Aulo Duce exercitus Romanorum cum Iugurta, quia faedus quod pepigit Aulus cum Iugurta fuit rescissum, quia factum fuit sine iussu populi Romani. Extra quaero quando fiunt paces utrum damna illa singularib. personis possint remitti per syndicos generales pacis? et responde, ut colligitur extra de iniur. c. in nostra. in tex. et per Inn. gl. quae est in l. ii C. quae sit lon. consue. facit quod non, tamen contrarium est verum propter publicam utilitatem, quae in pace consistit. Bald. [Additio Bal.] In tex. ibi Publica. postquam facta est pax quid iuris sit de damnis tempore guerrae illatis? Vide per Inn. extra de iniuriis, et dam. dato, ca. in nostra».

⁷⁴ Innocentius ad Sextum 2, 14, 2? Cf. f. 121vb–122rb, f. 122ra, No. 3: «(Adhaerentes) no. fidelitatem ecclesie romane, quia nunquam voluit habere pacem nec pacis tractatum, nisi prius exprimeret et premitteret de pace sibi adherentium et de perpetua securitate eorum»; cf. Baldus ad X. 2, 26, 30, f. 244rb–vb, No. 7?

⁷⁵ Innocentius ad X. 2, 1, 13, f. 75ra–va, f. 75rb–va, No. 7: «(Iuramenti) no. crimen pacis fracte et periurii directe pertinere ad iudicium ecclesie, ut hic, idem in crimine symonie. sacril. usurarum. hereseos. separationis matrimonii ad thorum propter adulterium xxii. q. i. c. pe. xii. q. i. nulli liceat».

Quaestio. XXIII.

¶. §. si quis°°° quinque solidos. in c. i. de pace tenen.ᵖᵖᵖ in usib. feudo-{**302vb**} rum⁷⁶ ᑫᑫᑫ non servatur de consuetudine, secundum Alb. in l. quicunque. C. de servis fugi.⁷⁷ & secundum Bal. in auth. sed novo iure. C. eo. tit.⁷⁸

Quaestio. XXXIIII.

¶ Federatus populus dicitur qui habet treugam cum alio populo vel Principe. l. non dubito. ff. de capti.⁷⁹ & federati, & milites pro libertate reipubl. debentʳʳʳ pugnare contra hostes, in auth. ut neque milites, neque federati, in princ.⁸⁰ ˢˢˢ

Quaestio. XXV.

¶ Pacta, quae facit Papa,ᵗᵗᵗ vel Imperator cum civitate sunt servanda, nisi adsit dolus. Bal.ᵘᵘᵘ in l. fi. C. de trans.⁸¹ & si fiat in c.ᵛᵛᵛ pacis: ut castrum destruatur, intelligitur in perpetuum. Ang. in l. si fideiussor. §. meminisse. ff. de leg. i.⁸²

---

⁷⁶ L. F. 2, 27, 18.
⁷⁷ Albericus ad auth. Sed novo iure [ante Cod. 6, 1, 4], No. 1, f. 3vb; «[. . .] Sed hodie iure novissimo videtur quod pro furto quinque solidorum quis suspendatur, ut in usib. feud. de pa. tenen. § si quis quinque solidos, et ibi in gl. et intellige solidum pro auro, ut not. infra. l. proxima, alias de quo solido debet intelligi, cum secundum diversas regiones diverse expendantur monetae. Sed iure canonico videtur quod furi eruantur oculi, et virilia abscindantur, ut extra de homi. c. tua nos § fi. Sed dic quod ibi fuit sic punitus de facto, vel forte ex forma statutorum communis Vincentiae, ubi furtum fuerat perpetratum. de hoc qualiter hodie puniantur furta, vide plene de pace iuramento firmanda. ver. iniuria seu furtum, ubi plene de hoc. et etiam tangitur in Spec. de accu. § i. ver sed. pone. Tit. accusatur de furto. communiter tamen circa furta provisum est ex forma statutorum [. . .]».
⁷⁸ Baldus ad auth. 'Sed novo iure' [C. 6, 1, 3], ff. 5rb–6ra, No. 5, f. 5va: «Sed videtur etiam, quod pro furto quinque solidorum debeat ad mortem puniri, ut in titu. de pace te. §. Si quis quinque solidos, col. 10. Sol. ille .§ non servatur de generali consuetudine, et ideo de illa .§ non est curandum, ar. ff. de dolo, l. id est usque et not. in tit. de pac. iur. fir. c. i. § iniuria. col. 10».
⁷⁹ Dig. 49, 15, 7.   ⁸⁰ Collatio 8, 9 (Nov. 116).
⁸¹ Baldus ad Cod. 2, 4, 43, f. 142vb, No. 6: «Ultimo quaeritur, apostolicus dicit, quod quaedam civitas est sua illa civitas hoc negat, et sic est quaestio de statu, nunquid de ista quaestione potest transigi? verbi gratia: quod civitas faciat quaedam servitia, et non alia, vel quod data certa annua quantitate non compellatur ulterius. Respond. quod valeat transactio, et regulam istius legis: et ideo capitula quae facit apostolicus et Imperator cum civitatibus, sunt servanda: hoc intellige, nisi intervenerit dolus, ut notat Cy. supra de legi. l. digna vox. supra, eo. l. sub pretextu, et quod ibi no. Bal.[!]».
⁸² Angelus de Ubaldis ad Dig. 30, 1, 49, 8, f. 9va: «Damnatus vendere, intelligitur damnatus iusto pretio vendere h.d. et immediate cum vendit satisfactum est voluntati defuncti et libertatis est venditor ab actione ex testamento, unde licet postea res evincatur ex testamento non potest agere, sed potius ex empto, unde dicit Bar. quod si arbiter condemnavit titium ad locandum mihi domum per quiquenium, et titius locavit, et deinde locationi non stat, non potest pena peti compromissi, sed tantummodo pena adiecti in contractu locationis de quo per eum hic et per eum et per me in l. in numerationibus in fin. de solu. ubi dixi de

Quaestio. XXVI.

¶ Si quis facit confederationem cum inimico, praesumitur inimicus, quia confederati sunt eiusdem intentionis,^{www} & voluntatis, Bal. in l. liberi.^{xxx} C. de inoff. testa.^{83}

Quaestio. XXVII.

¶ Quia sepe in ligis^{yyy} & confederationibus^{zzz} Principum fit mentio de adhaerentibus, & sequacibus, & participibus, ideo sciendum est, quod adhaerentes dicuntur, qui sunt sub eodem velle, cuius est principalis tex. in c. ad Apostolicae. de re iud. li. 6.^{84} & de sequacibus habetur in c. conquesti. de sen. excom.^{85} & de participibus in l. i. C. si rector provinc.^{86} & plenius haec omnia^{aaaa} ponit Ang. in auth. de haere. & fal. §. etiam Principum.$^{87\ bbbb}$

> pace facta inter ianuenses et venetos in qua continetur quod castrum Tenedos [?] deberet discarcari, nam illud capitulum importat ut etiam in perpetuum non possit refici, et ita in alia causa fuit determinatum ut refert Cy. in l. servus C. de penis et dicit verum, quia non posset ianuensibus aliter esse succursum nisi ageretur ex illo capitulo et ideo non obst. iste § quia hic potest agi act. ex empto, omissa ac ex testamento. Et pro opi. Bar. adde de contrahen. emp. l. si fundus § fin. vonjuncta gloss. et de pac. l. ab emp. in glo. mag. et c. si adver. vendi. aut. sacramenta in glo. fi. et quod no. Spec. in ti. de arbi. § sequitur, ver. sed pone arbiter. Veritas [. . .] enim est quod ubicumque ex laudo vel ex contractu quis est obligatus ad actum qu. de sui natura habet successionis effectus nunquam ille actus impletus momento l. iii.. dare supra de usufru. supra, si servi. ven. l. si a te supra de arbi. l. inter castellianum. Et ideo non sufficit facere nisi duret factum. Sed ubi actus expeditur momento quo ad totalem sui perfectionem et causam propter quam utitur, hoc casu sufficit actum fecisse, licet non duret factum, ut hic et d. l. in numerationibus in fi. cum aliis concor.».

^{83} Baldus ad Cod. 3, 28, 23, f. 220vb, No. 3: «Quarto not. quomodo probatur inimici[ti]a probatur enim ex offensione, vel nisi offensionis, puta ex insidiis. Item probatur inimicitia, si quis contrahit parentelam, vel facit confederationem cum inimico nam coniuncti et confederati praesumuntur eiusdem intentionis: quod est nota. et ideo ex hoc casu debent amittere feudum, quod est not. ut dicit glo. et probatur in usi. feu. in tit. quae sit pri. causa ami. feu. col. x. facit l. iiii. ff. de leg. i. cum simi.».

^{84} Sextus 2, 14, 2. ^{85} X. 5, 39, 22. ^{86} Cod. 5, 2, 1.

^{87} Angelus de Ubaldis ad Coll. 1.1 (Nov. 1): In prooemium, s.v. 'Occupantis nobis', No. 3, f. 2va–vb: «[. . .] Quaero de intellectu huius literae. gl. variavit, et hoc propter diversitatem, nam quidam libri habent, quam nunc, et tunc dicit gl. quod intellectus est literae, quia debet subaudiri per q.d. per hanc meam obligationem habeant libertatem, quod Deus hactenus nec ipsis concessit, nec etiam nobis, quia nunc primum facti sunt subiecti reipublicae. Et hunc intellectum dicit glo. esse necessarium, alias oporteret nos dicere, quod semper fuissent servi etiam antequam capti fuerunt a populo Romano, quod est falsum. Alio modo intelligitur iste tex. prout est in litera quam primum, et tunc dicit gl. quod intellectus huius literae est planus. q.d. ita recuperaverunt libertatem Archidonei, sicut nobis noviter adhaerentes retinent libertatem, quam habent, et hoc placet. Ex hoc nota significatum verbi, adhaerentes, nam dicuntur qui sunt sponte eiusdem velle, cuius est principalis, de hoc est tex. in c. ad apostolicae. de re iudi. lib. vi. et hoc no. pro capitulis pacis, quae inter communitates communiter fiunt quotidie, nam una alteri et altera alteri promittit non

Quaestio. XXVIII.

¶ Confederatus non tenetur Dominum^{cccc} iuvare, nisi sit requisitus. Bal. in c. i. de nova for. fide. no.[88] pro capitulis lige.

Quaestio. XXIX.

¶ Reconciliatio inter duos Principes habentes guerram non dicitur perfecte facta, licet invicem paciscantur de faciendo pacem. Ange. in l. Lucius ff. sol. mat.[89] ubi de Domino Bervaboe^{dddd} viceco[mite].^{eeee}

Quaestio. XXX.

¶ Tempore treugae mercatores, & rustici debent esse securi, & multa de treuga & pace per Archi. 24. q. fi. c. illi oratores.[90]

---

offendere civitatem, nec suos adherentes. intelliguntur enim adherentes omnes subditi civitati, et qui sponte sunt eiusdem velle, cuius ipsa civitas. Quid enim importetur per hoc verbum, sequaces? vide tex. in c. conquesti extra de sen. excom. Item qui dicantur participes et ad se attinentes? vide tex. in l. i. C. de recto. provin. caporales autem dicuntur illi, qui caput et principium alicuius rei factisve negocii tenent. pro hoc videtur tex. in l. i. § si quis non honores ff. vi bo. rap. Tertia lectura huis tex. est, quam nisi nunc [...]».

[88] Baldus ad L.F. 2, 7pr., s.v. Est et alia, No. 7, f. 39ra: «[Requisitus] No. quod maxime ad offerendum non tenetur quis iuvare alium ex promissione vel confederatione, nisi fuerit requisitus. tene menti ad ligas terrarum».

[89] Angelus de Ubaldis ad Dig. 24, 3, 38, f. 11ra: «Lucrum dotis pertinens ad maritum propter divortium factum mulieris culpa non perditur per sponsalia subsequentia facta per patrem filio ignorante, vel etiam sciente et tacente, vel etiam expresse, consentiente. h.h. tex. et gl. secundum verum intellectum. Ratio autem huius est: quia per sola sponsalia per verba de futuro contracta non potest dici ad plenum uxor reconciliata viro, et ideo non ponitur uxor in statu repetendi dotem, secus cum plene reconciliata est, ut l. si uxor § fi. infra de adul. que est contra. Et per hunc tex. dico sequendo hanc lec. que est ipsa veritas, quod si duo facientes ad invicem guerram pollicentur se facturos pacem adhuc non dicuntur ad invicem reconciliati plene. Et istud iam vidi de facto in curia que do. Barnabas pepigerat cum ecclesia se non contracturum ligam seu confederationem cum aliquo inimico ecclesie non plene reconciliato [...]».

[90] Guido de Baysio ad Decretum Gratiani, c. 24 q. 3 c. 25 (which deals extensively with questions *de treuga*), f. 315ra: «[...] Item no. quod tempore treuge mercatores gaudent securitate, ut extra eo. ti. c. ulti. Sed ibi querit Goffre. et ho. quid ad papam de illis cum sint layci, et de foro alieno. Resp. multum quo ad pacem, xc. dist. statuendum extra de iudi. novi. et de transactio. c. ulti. secundum ho. Item animalia quibus rustici arant eadem securitate gaudere debent, ut in pre. c. de treu. et pa. c. ulti. Sed pone quod aretur in bove et asino nunquid asinus habebit privilegium bovis. dicit vin. quod sic. quia locum illius tenet ff. de contra. emp. l. ul. ar. extra de sen. ex. in audientia et in eo quod leg. et no. xciii. di. c. ulti. et xciiii. di. c. i. Item si uxor rustici portat semen habet hoc privilegium sicut uxor militis. C. de uxo. mil. l. i secundum Vincen. alii ver. infregerit dicit Hug. in derivationibus suis quod infringere est intus frangere vel infringendo illudere [...]».

Quaestio. XXXI.

¶ Decedente rege vel duce, relicta uxore pregnante, homagia, & fidelitates debent fieri ventri;^{ffff} quia habetur pro nato, Bal. in l. pen. ff. de sta. ho.[91] in l. fi. ad fi. C. de test. mili.[92] ^{gggg}

Quaestio. XXXII.

¶ Transgressor treugae, punitur in^{hhhh} pena 10.^{iiii} librarum auri. c. i. § si quis vero temerario. de pa. iu. fir.[93] & vide Bal. in rub. extra de treuga, & pace.[94]

Quaestio. XXXIII.

¶ Pax potest fieri inter civitates & nobiles & castra: quia pax est iure naturali approbata^{jjjj}, tex. not.^{kkkk} in c. i. §. si quis vero. de pace iura fir.[95] & Bal. in rubrica de treuga & pace.[96]

Quaestio. XXXIIII.

¶ Ad Papam pertinet pacem facere^{llll} inter Principes Christianos gl. in cle. i. de iureiu.[97] & Papa est Christi Vicarius non Petri, nisi improprie. tex. & gl. in verbo, Christus, in d. cle. i. de iureiur.[98] ^{mmmm}

---

[91] Baldus ad Dig. 1, 5, 26, f. 33a, No. 1: «In fi. huius l. no. argu. quod mortuo Rege relicta uxore praegnante fidelitates et homagia debentur ventri, ut deberentur filio, si iam natus esset in Mundo [...] Quaero quidam Florentinus fecit testamentum, et dixit, si Rex Parthorum decesserit sine filiis ex se legitime natis, instituo haeredem sanctam Iustinam de Padua. modo Rex Partorum decessit relicta uxore praegnante, quae postea peperit, quid iuris? Respondeo, non habetur pro nato: quia non agitur de commodo uteri, quia sibi nihil est relictum, cum verba sint negativa, ut l. ex facto, infra de hae. insti. et no. in l. Lucius, eo. titu. et ideo cum non agatur de commodo partus, debet inspici veritas verborum, sed non est natus, ergo admittitur Sancta Iustina, et idem in si. ut no. supra eo. l. qui in utero. Nam exempla ponimus, non ut ita sint, sed ut sentiant qui addiscunt. Bal.».

[92] Cod. 6, 21, 18.   [93] L. F. 2, 53, 1.

[94] Baldus ad X. 1, 34, f. 120vb, Nos. 1 ss. (definitions of, a.o., 'treuga', 'pax', 'concordia', and on the difference between a *pax* and a *confoederatio*); f. 121r, No. 9: «Quaero qua [p]ena puniantur transgressores treuge? Resp. pena talionis ut quemadmodum ipsam non servant, ita nec eis servetur. Item puniantur pena centum libris auri, ut in aut. de pace iura fir.§. si quis vero temerario. et sic in quintuplo punitur plus civitas quam castrum, et damnum passis tenetur resarcire. tex. ibi est valde notabilis et per illum apparet quod pax et treuga potest fieri inter intrinsecos et extrinsecos civitatis quia pax et concordia iure naturali approbantur quamvis proprie isti non dicantur hostes sed inimici et partiales, ut ff. de capti. l. si quis ingenuam. in civilibus et l. hostes. et ibi no. [...]».

[95] L. F. 2, 53, 1.

[96] Baldus ad X. 1, 34: see the passage quoted *supra*, n. 93 *in fine*.

[97] Cf. notata ad § Dudum («No. quod ad papam spectat reformare pacem inter christianos, et sedare discordias et scandala...»), glossa 'pace' ad Clementinam 2, 9, 1.

[98] Clementina 2, 9, 1; glossae 'Christus', 'vicarium', *ibidem*.

Quaestio. XXXV.

¶ Si paciscenti[nnnn] non potest esse pax sine adherentibus, verba pacis[oooo] extenduntur ad adherentes. Ang. in l. quae religiosis. ff. de rei vendi.[99]

Quaestio. XXXVI.

¶ Omnis contractus, qui fit cum Principe, habet naturam contractus bonefidei. Bal. in extravag. de pace Constan. §. si qua vero.[100] [pppp]

Quaestio. XXXVII.

¶ Principes debent diligere[qqqq] pacem: nam Imperator Iustinianus habuit pacem cum Persis. l. in nomine Domini. C. de off. praefec. praeto.[101] Et Federicus cum Lombardis pacem[rrrr] in extravag. de pace Constan. in prin.[102] Nam Princeps omnia debet[ssss] recognoscere a Deo nostro Iesu Christo. l. i. in prin. C. de vete. iure enucle.[103]

Quaestio. XXXVIII.

¶ Quando fit pax inter Principes, non habet locum regula, quod spoliatus ante omnia sit restituendus, si spolians[tttt] habet bona iura in proprietate. tex.

---

[99] Angelus ad Dig. 6, 1, 43, f. 171ra: «Lapides sepulchrorum sunt religiosi, et ideo exempti non vendicantur sed act. in factum domino succurri: secus si non sint religiosi h.d. In tex. ibi adherent No. idem esse iudicium de adherentibus quod de principalibus, et sic est argumentum quod pax facta [...] cum principali intelligatur facta cum adherentibus et in ea intelligatur introclusi virtute adherentie, ut hac l. facit infra de cloacis l. i § tribus infra commun. divi. l. arbor. de vestibulo et hoc credo verum si verba pacis in rem concepta sunt ar. infra de adve. l. hec verba infra de vi et vi ar. l. i § deiecisse in glo. secus si in personam et maxime si est stipulatione vallata cum stipulationis natura extensionem non patiatur: ut in l. quicquid astringende infra de ve. ob. et ideo moris est semper stipulari pro adherentibus et fieri adherentium declarationem ad quorum tuitionem et conservationem multum intendit et studet ecclesia: ut no. Inn. et Jo. An. in c. ad apostolice. de re iudi. li. vi. ubi text. dicit quod papa non facit pacem cum inimicis nisi adherentes faciat primo securos quod no. bene et etiam si verba fuerint concepta in personam includuntur adherentes si paciscenti, non posset esse pax sine adherentibus ut supra. de arbi. l. adversus C. de usu. rei iudi. l. fi. in fi. et est casus infra de verb. oblig. l. si stipulatus fuero per te non fieri, facit infra de pac. l. et heredi in princip. et l. cum unus sicut res eo. tit. facit etiam l. refectionis § si per fundum in li. infra commu. predi.».

[100] Baldus, De Pace Constantiae, s.v. 'Si quis vero', f. 102va, No. 1: «Hic dicitur quod si aliqua civitas de dicta societate Lombardiae non servat statuta pacis, ceterae civitates de societate compellant illam ad observandam. [Bona fide] No. quod bona fides debet servari, cui interdum non congruit de iuris apicibus disputare, ut ff. mand. l. si fideiussor §. quaedam. et est arg. quod omnes contractus qui fiunt cum Principe, habeant naturam bone fidei contractum».

[101] Cod. 1, 27, 2.   [102] De Pace Constantiae, proh.   [103] Cod. 1, 17, 1.

& ibi Odof. in extravag. de pace Constan.¹⁰⁴ & vide Bal. ibi,¹⁰⁵ & Princeps potest habere regem, vel civitatem socium, vel amicum. l. postliminium .§. postliminio^uuuu ff. de capti. & postli. rever.¹⁰⁶

Quaestio.XXXIX.

¶ Terrae recommendatae Florentinis^vvvv non dicuntur de districtu Florentino, sed dicuntur confederate,^wwww l. non dubito. de capti.¹⁰⁷ & Franci. Zaba. in cle. ne Romani. de electio.¹⁰⁸

---

¹⁰⁴ Cf. De Pace Constantiae, s.v. 'sententiae quoque'; Odofredus *ibidem*, s.v. 'restituantur': «hoc nisi ablator iure se posset tueri in causa proprietatis: tunc enim restitutio impeditur, ut inf. eo .§ si qui. Et cave, quia hic dicit de anlatoribus, seu suasoribus qui non sunt de societate. Sed ego idem puto, & de eis, qui sunt de societate, cum in d. § si qui generaliter loquatur, & non specificet, an de societate sit, vel non, sic ergo generaliter, et indistincte debent intelligi, ut ff. de publi. l. de precio. et intelligendum est, Imperatorem in hoc casu idem statuisse in suis, quod in aliis, et idem in aliis, quod in suis, causa aequalitatis hinc inde servandae, ut arg. ff. de arbit. l. si cum dies § fi. C. de fruct. et lit. expen. l. fi. C. de prox. sacrosacri. l. in sacris li. 12, et ff. mand. l. 3 in fi. et C. commu. div. l. pen. § fi. et ar. ff. fam. ercisc. l. in hoc iudicio. Odof. [...]».

¹⁰⁵ Baldus, De Pace Constantiae, s.v. Omnes, f. 102rbva, No. 1: «[Restituatur] Hoc nisi causa in principali iure se tueri possit possessor, nam tunc impeditur restitutio, ut sequitur, quod quidem est contra alia iura, nam et si quod ius haberet per ingressum violentum amisisset, et tamen restituere tenetur ei, cui per vim abstulisset, vel occupasset, ut C. unde vi. l. prima, et si quis in tantam, et in Lombar. de invasionibus. l. finali [...]».

¹⁰⁶ Dig. 49, 15, 19, 3.   ¹⁰⁷ Dig. 49, 15, 7.

¹⁰⁸ Franciscus Zabarella ad Clementinam 1, 3, 2, No. 24 (§ Sane), f. 13vb: «Sexto quaero circa id quod dixi in proxi. q. statuto cavetur quod nullus de civitate vel comitatu certum quid faciat, nunquid comprehenduntur hi qui sunt de districtu et non sunt de civitate vel comitatu. Respondet Pau. quod non, dicens ita sepe obtentum Bononie, pro hoc quia statuta sunt stricti iuris, de iniur. in nostra, ergo non extendenda l. quicquid astringende ff. de ver. obl. ff. ad muni. l. constitutionibus, et haec determinatio placet, sed dicta in precedentibus q. non faciunt nisi per quamdam similitudinem, sed ad determinandum vere hanc questionem videri oportet quid sit comitatus et quid civitas, de secundo est tex. in l. ii. ff. de ver. sig. et in c. si civitas de sen. excom. lib. vi. de primo .s. comitatu est tex. in l. una C. quando imperator inter pupil. et vidu. et XXIII q. VIII. si vobis. In quibus capitur comitatus pro curia seu residentia principis, sed non sic sumitur in terminis statuti premissi, quid ergo impostat comitatus quando ponitur in statuto vel alia dispositione, dic quod importat territorium villarum vel castrorum quod est pertinens ad civitatem, ita quod gaudet eisdem privilegiis et constituit eandem republicam, et per hoc potest contingere quod aliquid est de civitate et non de districtu quia districtus concernit tantum id quod actualiter a civitate distringitur sed comitatus non sic stricte accipitur, unde aliqua castra sunt de comitatu Imole, que sunt de districtu Bononie, et hoc modo dicimus quod que est ex vico intelligitur de illa civitate cui vicus subest, ff. ad municip. l. qui ex vico. Et hec lex videtur destruere premissa per quam potest inferri qu. omnis qui est de districtu dicitur de comitatu et dicitur eiusdem reipublice, sed defendendo determinationem dic quod in statutis et in aliis dispositionibus cum apponuntur verba significationis ambigue recurrimus ad commune modum intelligendi de spon. ex litteris. l. cum de lanionis § asinam ff. de fun. instru. ac Bononie fit illa diversitas inter comitatum

Quaestio. XL.

¶ Obsides qui dantur^{xxxx} Principi pro aliquo pacto servando sunt liberi; quia capite non^{yyyy} minuuntur, & bonorum, quae relinquunt domi, retinent [d]ominium, quae autem acquisiverunt in obsidatu sunt fisci: nisi concesso eis usu togae ab Imperatore, & non possunt testari. l. divus. cum seq. & ibi gl. ff. de iure fisci.[109]

Quaestio. XLI.

¶ Veniente pace debent cassari^{zzzz} omnia facta praetextu tyrannidis. l. decernimus.^{aaaaa} C. de sacrosan. Eccle.[110]

Quaestio. XLII.

¶ Quando in concipiendis capitulis pacis est contentio inter Prin-{**303ra**}cipes quo ad formam ligandi dirimitur hec causa arbitrio iudicis,^{bbbbb} secundum Ang. in d. l. de die. in prin. ff. qui satis. cog.[111] & si creditor tradit, vel resignat instrumenta Principi, sub cuius protectione est debitor,^{ccccc} videtur remittere

---

et districtum: alibi autem ut hic Padue quicquid est de districtu dicitur de comitatu et in illis locis non procederet determinatio predicta, et pro predictis que dixi de comitatu est quod dixi de rescrip. Rodulfus. Et ex his que dixi quod aliqui sunt de districtu qui non sunt de civitate vel comitatu videret quod terre recommendate que in signum preeminentie aliquid offerunt alteri civitati ut sunt plures recommendate Florentinis essent censende de districtu. Contrarium tamen tenet Pe. de Anch. et bene, quia tales potius dicuntur confederate ff. de cap. l. non dubito, facit ad predicta quod no. Bar. ff. de verbo. signi. [...]».

[109] Dig. 49, 14, 31–32; glossae 'bona', 'captivorum' ibidem. [110] Cod. 1, 2, 16.
[111] Angelus de Ubaldis ad Dig. 2, 8, 8pr., ff. 37va–38ra: «[. . .] Et istud principium legitur duobus modis. uno quod loquitur de die in stipulatione interponenda quo casu si est diversitas inter partes totum dirimitur iudicantis arbitrio, altero de duobus modis vel quod solum iudex declarat, vel declarat primo stipulator, etsi non declarat eque reductio fit per iudicem et in idem recidit. et quilibet modus est bonus secundum Jac. Bu. et quodlibet istorum modorum figurari potest casus in hoc principio et ista lec. sine dubio est vera maxime per tex. hic dum dicet de die ponenda [. . .] Et reducans predicta ad practicam: Nam in multis civitatibus vigent statuta quod iudex faciat litem compromitti inter consortes: et ubi inter eos esset guerra compellat, eos ad certam treugam temporalem. Nam si in componendo capitula compromissi vel treuge inter partes discordia versatur dirimenda est iudicantis arbitrio, ut hac l. cessante consuetudine. Sed si de more esset certam formam observari non esset recedendum ab ea, ut infra de evic. l. si fundus venierit et de edil. edict. l. quod si nolit § qui assidua. Et loquor de more universali, quia mos singularium non esset attendendus, ut extra de rescrip. ex parte el. i. Idem intelligo quando locus non est rebellis imperio, quia omnes leges et consuetudines talis loci intelliguntur reprobate per principem, et ideo ad talem morem non est recurrendum, sed potius ad arbitrium boni viri secundum Bart. qui ita no. in l. quia latronibus infra. de testa. dicam in d. l. si fundus [. . .]».

debitum,^ddddd secundum Ang. in l. Labeo. ff. de pactis.¹¹² quod. not. quia extenditur. d. l. Labeo.¹¹³

Quaestio. XLIII.

¶ Princeps, qui accepit civitatem sub protectione^eeeee per pactum, debet^fffff etiam defendere cum armis, casus in l. i. & rub. C. de domesti. & protecto.¹¹⁴ &^ggggg Ray. in l. non omnes.^hhhhh §. qui. ff. de re mili.¹¹⁵ non ob. c. 2. de privileg.

---

[112] Angelus de Ubaldis ad Dig. 2, 14, 2, ff. 56vb–57ra: «Pactio potest fieri inter presentes et absentes tacite et expresse. et si debitori redditur cautio debiti tacite dicitur factum pactum de non petendo h.d. Idem si non restituatur debitori, sed illi sub cuius generali protectione debitor est, ut no. per Inn. in c. cum pridem extra de pac. et infra dicam. Vel sic per redditionem cautionis factam debitori a creditore dicitur factum pactum de non petendo, secus si solum pignus reddatur nisi aliud actum sic. h.d. cum le. se. Et per hunc tex. dicit Inn. in c. cum M. de consti. in gl. qu. incipit, aliud est canonica quod si aliquis est receptus in canonicum et in fratrem, et eidem assignatus est stallus in choro et locus in capitulo, qu. per hoc facit que pertinet ad chorum secundum ordinem, ut legre et canere et que pertinent ad capitulum ut interesse electionibus et alienationibus rerum ecclesie, quia per talia signa tacite factus est de conventum et congregatione collegii, allegat etiam ad hoc infra de contrahen. em. l. clavibus. Sequitur in littera, et ideo si debitori meo. No. quod si creditor reddit instrumentum debiti debitori per hoc videtur remittere debitum. [...] et idem si non restituat debitori, sed illi sub cuius generali protectione debitor est, exemplum si creditor reassignavit pape instrumentum debiti ad quod erat aliqua ecclesia sibi obligata secundum Inn. ita apostillantem haec l. extra e. ti. c. cum pridem. Sed pone quod in instrumento erant obligati duo et ex diversis causis et uni redditus instrumentum an uterque erit liberatus, de illo enim cui est redditum instrumentum constat quod sic, sed de alio potest esse dubium, dic ut ibi per Guli. Et eodem modo hic decidi secundum eum si creditor habet duo instrumenta et unum restituit debitori et aliud penes se retinuit, an habeat locum hec lex, et dicit, quod sic et bene. Et eodem modo decidi secundum eum si restituto instrumento debitori: debitor illud reddat creditori, an obligatio renascatur, quia non renascitur secundum quosdam, ipse autem tamen oppositum, et eius opi. est vera ubicunque debitum descendit ex causa que per pactum non tollitur actio ipso iure sed solum paratur pacti exceptio, qui tunc non renascitur actio, sed solum removetur exceptionis obstaculum quod fieri potest, ut infra eo. l. si unus § pactus sed ubi tolleretur ipso iure, tunc esset vera opi. illorum, quia actio semel extincta non potest resuscitari nedum per pactum tacitum, imo nec per expressum, ut infra e. l. si tibi.§ quidam infra de sol. l. qui res .§ aream».

[113] Dig. 2, 14, 2.   [114] Cod. 12.17; Cod. 12, 17, 1.

[115] Raynerius de Forlivio ad Dig. 49, 16, 6, 1, 8, f. 136va: «Glo. quaerit quid si intulit manus et non occidit. respon. pisis antequam recederem per octo dies fuit talis questio: dominus comes pisanus nomine raynerius dederat civitatem sub protectione domini pape et dederat sibi multam pecunie quantitatem, dominus lucinus de mediolano miserat circa pisanos tria milia militum, commune pisanum volebat quod dominus papa defenderet eos cum armis, papa dicebat quod non tenebatur, ego fui inter ancianos et allegavi istum §. quod papa tenebatur, et c. de dome. et prote. in rubrica, et l. i. li. xii. et ibi no. quod no. de imperatore in constitutionem .ff. in princi. Quidam galicius advocatus qui fuerat vicarius bavari et erat de aritia gibellinus arrabiatus quia ibi sunt gibellini imperiales et gibellini arrabiati et illi erant inquantum poterant contra comitem, inducebant contra me extra de privi. c. i lib. vi. et faciebat ad hoc ut induceret populum contra comitem. tunc ego sibi respondi quod ibi videbatur casus huius questionis quod ibi in privilegiis

lib. 6.[116] quia loquitur in privilegio, non[iiiii] in pacto, vide Anto. de But. in c. accepimus. de privile.[117]

Quaestio. XLIIII.

¶ Quod facit maior pars confederatorum Principum, vel communitatum[jjjjj] debet haberi ratum, licet minor[kkkkk] pars confederatorum contradicat: quia reguntur[lllll] ad instar unius corporis, & Princeps, vel communitas, qui est nobilior vel potentior[mmmmm] in liga, intelligitur superior[nnnnn] ad convocandos alios confederatos, secundum Bal. in extravag. de pace Constan. in verbo maior.[118] & capitula cum subditis non potest Princeps revocare nisi ex iusta & probata causa, secundum Bal. in l. pe. C. de dona. inter virum & uxo.[119]

> quorum interpretatio pertinet ad papam. in reg. iur. neratius, hic in pacto quod fecit papa, quod debet interpretari contra eum ut l. veteribus. supra de pac. et ita commune pisanum acquievit dicto meo».
[116] Sextus 5, 7, 2.
[117] Antonius de Butrio ad X. 5, 33, 8, No. 11, f. 89va: «Oppo. de C. uno de peregrina So. ibi loquitur quando specialiter sub protectione recipitur ratione absentie, hic de generali protectione, unde dicit glossa quod talis protectio parum valet, sicut et generalis confirmatio, nisi quia aliqua reverentia magis illis debetur quam alii arg. per tuas supra de confir. uti. vel inuti. et forte citius papa movetur pro eis ad literas concedendas cum iniuste gravantur et ad vibrandum gladium censure. Nec mirum cum etiam domini temporales nisi his quos sub sua protectione recipiunt satisfiunt, guerram faciunt. Si ergo ab ecclesia neminem securat aut securatum defendat ne laqueum iniiciat xxvii. q. i. de viduis, vel fraudem adhibeat, de dona. et hoc secundum Hostien. qui consuluit quod ecclesia neminem nisi ex magna causa sub protectione sua recipiat, et raro si tamen recipiat defendat receptos in ere et personis iuxta nota. in capitu. ad liberendam in parte decisa. versi. quorum persona. de iudeis».
[118] Baldus, De Pace Constantiae, s.v. Ego, f. 103rb–va, No. 1: «[Maior] Quod enim maior pars facit, tota universitas fecisse videtur, ut ff. ad mu. l. quod ma. Odof. No. ego, quod illud quod facit maior pars collegiatorum, seu confederatorum, minori parte contradicente, ratum quo ad omnes debet haberi, quia omnes collegiati rediguntur ad instar unius corporis, quod est no. ex his, s. quae pertinent ad totum corpus ligae, et ille qui est nobilior et potentior in liga, intelligitur superior ad convocandum alios, arg. ff. de fide insrum. l. fi. et c. i. de maio. et obed. per Innoc.».
[119] Baldus ad Cod. 5, 16, 26, f. 198ra: «Contractus, qui celebratur cum Imperatore, vel Augusta, habet vim legis. h.d. Et hunc tex. non habes alibi. Unde no. quod contractus transit interdum in legem, et econtra quandoque transit in contractum nominatum, ut not. in l. quod semel. de decr. ab ordi. fa. vel innominatum, ut si resultat facio ut des, vel alius contractus innominatus, unde illi commitatenses qui fuerunt recepti a civitate per legem aliquo dato, non possunt revocari in Comitatum: quia facta relatione donationis ad legem, res transivit in contractum innominatum. Unde facta est irrevocabilis: nam nec Imperator potest revocare contractum secum delebratum, nisi ex causa: quia sibi non impletur quod impleri debet, ut no. Cy. supra. de legi. l. digna vox. Interdum lex stat in finibus contractus, et isti contractus sunt clari. Et no. ista verba. Quid de contractu, qui fieret inter aliquos Barones, utrum habeat vim legis? Consuluit Bart. quod sic, per hanc l. Pet. et Cy. notant contrarium in l. ea lege supra de condict. ob cau. quia in contrahendo non versatur publica utilitas, nisi in Imperatore, vele Rege, vel alio qui non ligatur legibus in suo territorio, sicut sunt multis Duces, et Marchiones».

Quaestio. XLV.

¶ Si facta est liga inter Principes, non potest alter princeps facere legem, vel aliud, per quod conditio legatorum[ooooo] reddatur deterior. Bal. in l. i. ff. si ex noxa. causa agatur.[120]

Quaestio. XLVI.

¶ Pacta facta a principe, licet non sint vestita stip[ulatione] tamen sunt servanda. l. donationes. C. de don. inter vi. & uxo.[121] quia praesentia Principis supplet omnem solennitatem. l. omnium. C. de testa.[122] nam si pactum nudum habet effectum agendi, si fiat in iudicio. gl. in auth. generaliter. C. de epis. & cler.[123] quanto magis si fiat coram Principe.[ppppp]

Quaestio. XLVII.

¶ Pacta & capitula Principum habent vim legum. Bart. in l. Cesar. ff. de publica.[124] vide Cy. in l. pen. C. de don. inter virum & uxo.[125]

Quaestio. XLVIII.

¶ Propter bonum pacis multa conceduntur, que alias non concederentur. gl. in c. ubi non est. de despon. impu.[126]

---

[120] Baldus ad Dig. 2, 9, 1, f. 97ra–rb, No. 5, f. 97rb: «Extra collige argu. ex illo tex. ad duas q. primo quae est causa, quod hic dicatur, quod inspici debet conditio personarum tempore contractus, quod si facta est liga inter duas civitates, non potest altera civitas facere statutum, per quod conditio colligatorum reddatur deterior, quam esset tempore ligae, et hoc tenet Bar. in quadam extravaganti Henrici, quam voluit glossare».

[121] Cod. 5, 16, 26.   [122] Cod. 6, 23, 19.

[123] Glossae 'conscribat', 'officii' ad auth. 'Generaliter autem' [Cod. 1, 3, 25].

[124] Bartolus ad Dig. 39, 4, 15, No. 3, f. 59rb: «Item no. quod dicta que apponuntur in contractibus factis ab eo quibus potestatem condendi. l. habent vim legis ad ligandos alios ut hic patet in glo. que exponit legem id est pactum. et est text. C. de dona. inte vi. et ux. l. pe. et sic factum quod facit publicanus vel alius contrahens cum civitate habet vim statuti quo ad omnes».

[125] Cynus ad Cod. 5, 16, 26, f. 317ra: «Not. hic. quod contractus Imperatoris obtinet vicem l. Et sic colligitur hic argu. quod si Imperator facit pactum, debet servari: quia pactum habet vicem legis, et ipse profitetur, se velle legibus vivere, ut supra de legib. l. digna vox, de quo ibi dixi. Secundo colligitur hic aliud arg. Quidam sunt domini, qui de facto non recognoscunt superiorem. Pone modo, quod talis dominus dedit terram in dotem filiae suae, eo pacto, quod non alienet eam, deinde filia alienat, nunquid transfertur dominium? Ista lex facit quod non, quia ubi l. prohibet, non transfertur dominium: sed contractus habet vicem legis, ut hic. Et talis dominus, qui non recognoscit superiorem, est princeps in terra sua de facto, et eodem errore non transfertur dominium contra eius conventionem. De hoc dixi supra, de condictio. ob causam. l. ead. l. dic ut ibi».

[126] Glossa 'pacis' ad X. 4, 2, 2; cf. notata, *ibidem*, pr.: «Nota quod pro bono pacis reformando toleratur matrimonium quod alias fieri interdiceretur. Ber.».

Quaestio. XLIX.

¶qqqqq Hosti publica fides est servanda, licet privata fides non sit servanda. l. i. § non fuit. ff. de dolo.[127] & Bal. in l. pacisci. ff. de pactis.[128] rrrrr

Quaestio. L.

¶ Inspicitur finalis punctus pacis in ponendis hora[sssss] & die in instrumento. l. contractus. ubi. Bal. C. de fide instru.[129]

Quaestio. LI.

¶ Quando Princeps diffidatur, omnes eius complices intelliguntur diffidati. Bal. in repe. l. si aquam. C. de servi. & aqua.[130]

Quaestio. LII.

¶ Tanta debet esse dilectio Principis erga adherentes suos, quod sine ipsis[ttttt] non debet facere pacem, nisi primo eos reddat tutos, & securos. c. ad Apostolicae. de re iud. li. 6.[131] secundum[uuuuu] Ang. cons. 289 quod incipit inter capitula pac[is][132] & ibi etiam dicit Ang. quod adhaerentes, vel sequaces Principis

---

[127] Dig. 4, 3, 1, 3.
[128] Baldus ad Dig. 2, 14, 31, f. 144va, No. 1: «Secundo quia hic versatur ius publicum. nam bannitus tanquam publicus hostis offenditur, et hosti non est servanda fides privata, licet sit servanda fides publica, ut infra de dolo l. i § non fuit».
[129] Baldus ad Cod. 4, 21, 17, ff. 61ra–62rb, No. 14, f. 61va: «Quaero, quid de die. pone quod fit contractus quidam pacis, cuius dictatio durat per mensem, quaero quis dies apponitur in instrumento. Respondeo dies conclusionis pacis, ut hic, quia quicquid agitur, dependet ex momento, in quo concluditur. ad hoc facit quod no. Bart. ff. de testib. l. testium».
[130] Baldus, repetitio ad Cod. 3, 34, 2. Cf. the commentary, *ibidem*, No. 76, f. 253rb: «Et no. quod quando aliquis diffiditur, et inciditur contra eum bellum, videntur similiter diffidati omnes eius complices, et auxiliantes secus in sententia lata in iudicio, quae non afficit nisi illos contra quos est nominatim factus processus, c. olim causam. de resti. spo. per Innoc. [...]»; the commentary further considers the situation of the subjects, the requirement of a *diffidatio* and the 'three types of war' (*defensionis, recuperationis, invasionis*).
[131] Sextus 2, 14, 2.
[132] Cf. Angelus de Ubaldis, Consilia (1539), Cons. 257 (inc. (i) Inter capitula pacis; (ii) Quia consultatio multum generalis), ff. 105va–107ra, No. 5, f. 106va: «[. . .] quod illi dicuntur adherentes et sequaces alterius qui intention[e] et operibus illius adherent et eam sequuntur. Et quod tales dicuntur sequaces est tex. in epistola inter claras et C. de rap. vir. l. i. § si autem ingenuam. Et quod hi dicantur etiam adherentes probatur C. de discor. l. ne in casu lib. X. per Inno. de re iudi. ad apostolice. causatur ex eo quod debet esse delectio principis erga adherentes suos et quod sine illis non debet facere pacem nisi primo eos reddat tutos atque securos, casus est in d. c. ad apostolice hi etiam sequaces et adherentes complices nuncupantur de fo. compe. ex parte quando autem ponit dictus Paulus intentiones et opera domini comitis ferventius sequi et sue intentioni ardentius inherere quam suam primam oppugnare studendo per secretorum revelationem et consiliorum renunciationem per quam crimen proditionis incurritur ac

dicuntur,^{vvvv} qui intentione & operibus illi^{wwwww} adherent, & eum sequuntur, ut in epistola inter claras. & ideo ille dicitur adherens & de sequacibus Principis, qui intentiones, & opera^{xxxxx} Principis ferventer sequitur, puta per secretorum revelationem & consiliorum renunciationem, & ibi vide, qui dicantur proditores: & vide Ang. con. 293.[133] ubi ponit, qui dicantur^{yyyyy} rebelles & forestati, & quod pacta inter Principes & communitates valentes^{zzzzz} condere legem habent vim legis. l. Caesar. ff. de pub.[134] iudicatur tamen ut de contractu non ut de lege, quod patet, quia non potest ad libitum revocari. d. l. Cesar.[135]

> etiam falsitatis ff. de re mili. l. omne delictum explioratores ff. de penis l. si quis aliquid § i et § si quis instrumentum et facit C. de advo. diver. iudi. l. i et C. de commer. et mer. l. i et ff. de privari. l. iii. et in x. col. quib. mod. feu. amit. § si capitanei. Et quod tales proditores ex adversa parte consistant et per consequens ipso facto sint partes adverse adherentes atque sequaces probatur ut ff. de infa. l. athletas c. item, prevaricatur quia in hostium numero se contulit dictus Paulus opere et sermone, ut patet ex processu et sententia ff. de re mili. proditores et C. de delato. l. fina. lib. x. et ff. de capti. l. post biennium § transfuge. et in x. col. quib. mod. feu. amit. § item si fratres in glos. et in ea col. de eo qui interfecit fratrem domini sui c. i. ibi litera loquitur de traditore et facit ff. de questio. l. i. § cum quis de istis etiam proditoribus tangit Bart. de pe. l. respiciendum§ delinqunt de his etiam habetur in divina scriptura Judicum IIII. c. sic et Judas adherens erat et sequax inimicorum Christi, et tamen cum eo corpore consistebat, et ideo scriptum est quod nulla peior pestis ad nocendum quam familiaris inimicus». See also Angelus de Ubaldis, Cons. 391 (1539), (inc. Sub aliis quidem termini), ff. 168vb–170ra, No. 4, f. 169ra–rb (on the question, who have to be considered as *adhaerentes* and *sequaces*, and f. 169rb: «. . . complices et sequaces et adhaerentes dicti domini ducis tales enim presumuntur in guerra intervenisse quales fuerant interclusi in pace et treuga»), No. 5, f. 169rb: «[. . .] et ideo nullus princeps belli etiam si sit imperator vel papa debet facere pacem cum inimicis nisi primo adherentes et sequaces faciat optima securitate gaudere de re iudi. c. ad apostolice ubi habetur de adherentibus et complicibus de fo. compe. c. ex parte et de sequacibus in epistola inter claras C. de rap. vir. l. i. § sinautem de ipsis etiam adhaerentibus habetur C. de discussoribus l. iii. lib. x».
>
> [133] Cf. Angelus de Ubaldis, Consilia (1539), Cons. 257 (*supra*), No. 4, f. 106rb: «[. . .] Forestati enim illi sunt quos forestare ex aliqua causa oportet, arguendo ab ethymologia vocabuli quod argumentum est validum ubi de significato verbi aliud non imponitur aut diffinitio non contradicit ei ut l. ii. § appellata si cer. pe. et ibi no. [. . .]»; Cons. 261 (inc. (i) Punctus est in anno Domini MCCC. indictio. xii. vii. calendis augusti; (ii) Thema predictum est dubium), ff. 108va–109va: f. 108vb, No. 1 (rebelles et forestati); No. 5, f. 109rb–va: «Omnes enim loquuntur in dispositione legali que regulariter licet lata sit per verba presentia tamen extenditur ad futura eo quod semper loquitur lex C. de here. arriani licet interdum regula illa fallit ut no. per Cyn. in l. leges C. de legi. per Barto. plenius in repeti. l. omnes populi. Sed dicta pacta et stipulationes dictorum communium Ianue et Pisarum licet observentur pro lege sicut et observantur pacta privatorum inter se ut l. legem C. de pac. et l. i § si convenerit deposi. non sunt tamen ll. cum nullum commune in alterum habuerit vel habeat postestatem legem condendi et licet esset lex quod est falsum tamen ex quo lex transit in contractum iudicatus de ea ut de contractu et de lege ut patet quia non potest ad libitum revocari etiam si sit lex cesaris ut d. l. cesar [. . .]».
> [134] Dig. 39, 4, 15.   [135] Dig. 39, 4, 15.

secundum Ang. cons. 283.¹³⁶ ᵃᵃᵃᵃᵃᵃ & de ligisᵇᵇᵇᵇᵇᵇ & confederationibusᶜᶜᶜᶜᶜᶜ ponit etiam Ang. cons. 278.ᵈᵈᵈᵈᵈᵈ quod incipit. in nomineᵉᵉᵉᵉᵉᵉ Domini.¹³⁷ ubi concludit, quod si maior pars Principum ligae confederantisᶠᶠᶠᶠᶠ est praeposita & magistraᵍᵍᵍᵍᵍᵍ ligae per pactum, tunc facta a maiori parte ligae praeiudicant reliquis alligatis,ʰʰʰʰʰʰ etiam non vocatis. l. item magistri. ff. de pac.¹³⁸ ubi est casus: & an ista probent, vide l. sed cum patrono .§. fi. & ibi Bar. ff. de bo. pos.¹³⁹ servarem tamen in his consuetudinem, arg. c. cum dilectus. de fide instrumentorum.¹⁴⁰ ⁱⁱⁱⁱⁱ

Quaestio. LIII.

¶ Si Princeps capitula civitatis producta coram se approbat in parte, caetera capitula videtur improbare.ʲʲʲʲʲ l. tribunus.§. fi. ff. de testa. mili.¹⁴¹ & Bar. in l. legata inutiliter. ff. de lega. i.¹⁴²

Quaestio. LIIII.

¶ Facta pace a Principe obsides possunt testari. Ang. in l. obsides. ff. de testamen.¹⁴³ ᵏᵏᵏᵏᵏᵏ

---

¹³⁶ Cf. the passage quoted from Angelus de Ubaldis, Cons. 261, *supra* (n. 133).
¹³⁷ Angelus de Ubaldis, Consilia, Cons. 269 (inc. (i) Punctus est anno Domini Mccclxxxix commune Anchone; (ii) Non est quod civitas Anchonitana), ff. 111vb–112ra, No. 2, f. 112ra: «[. . .] Ratio me movens est unica quod ipsum corpus societatis et lige quo ad potentiam recipiendi dominos vel communitates in colligatos preposuit maiorem partem unde maior pars societatis velut preposita et magistra societatis totius potest reliquis colligatis preiudicare ff. de pac. l. item magistri. per hoc apparet esse responsum ad l. quod maior cum suis concordan. ad municipales, loquuntur enim in ipsis que fiunt per maiorem partem et hoc usu de plano fatendum est alios de societate et corpore requirendos. Sed cum maior pars non facit simpliciter ut maior pars sed ex eo quod est preposita et magistra ipsius societatis per pactum prout est in casu proposito tunc factum a maiori parte preiudicat reliquis etiam non vocatis ut d. l. item magistri. per quam deciditur ista quaestio potissime [. . .]».
¹³⁸ Dig. 2, 14, 14.   ¹³⁹ Dig. 37, 1, 6, 1; Bartolus *ibidem* (f. 185vb)?
¹⁴⁰ X. 2, 22, 9.   ¹⁴¹ Dig. 29, 1, 20, 1.
¹⁴² Bartolus ad Dig. 30, 1, 19, f. 10ra, No. 7: «Ultimo Dy. inducit hanc l. adunam. q. quidam comes reprobavit quaedam facta in castro. an videatur alia approbare. Et videtur quod non. quia facta ad diminutionem non inducunt augmentum. ut hic cum similibus. In contrarium quia cum prohibeat un uno in aliis dicitur permittere. ut l. cum pretor. supra. de iudi. et l. tribunus .§. i supra. de testa. mili. et supra de test. l. ex ea. Potest dici quod si plura capitula fuerunt coram eo exposita. tunc quedam reprobanda alia videtur approbasse. Ita dicit Dy. facit extra de presump. c. nonne. et supra. de mino. l. et si sine .§ sed quod pap.».
¹⁴³ Angelus de Ubaldis ad Dig. 28, 1, 11, f. 17rb: «In gl. ibi facta tenenda Bald. dubitat super hoc qu. erat pax facta ergo illi desierant hostes esse, nec obsides essentes apud eos sue potestatis sunt quod puto verum cum pax sit causa reconciliationis ad benivolentiam principis aut pape cum civitatibus sibi subditis ut videmus fieri quotidie. Sed si fierent causa sedationis cuiusdam guerre, puta cum turchis apud quos nullum est commercium vel hospitium, sunt casus in l. postliminii § i. infra de capti. et hoc modo procedat Jo. opi.».

Quaestio. LV.

¶ Qualitas tractandae pacis^(lllllll) inter Principes exigit, ut tractetur secrete^(mmmmmm) & familiariter. tex. in cle. i. de iureiur.¹⁴⁴ & ibi vide tex. quod ab Ecclesia translatum fuit Imperium a Graecis in Romanos.^(nnnnnn)

Quaestio. LVI.

¶ Si in capitulis pacis continetur, quod talis civitas^(oooooo) sit sub protectione regis, vel ducis, rex, vel dux non habet iurisdictionem in tali civitate. ca. ex parte tua. el i. de privilegiis.¹⁴⁵ sed habet potestatem defendendi vel de facto cum armis, vel etiam de iure in iudicio not. in cap. ad audientiam. de^(pppppp) praescript.¹⁴⁶ quid autem si ponantur illa verba, sit in^(qqqqqq) regimine. vide Bart. in l. i. C. de excu. mili. lib. 10.¹⁴⁷ ^(rrrrrr)

---

¹⁴⁴ Clementina 2, 9, 1.   ¹⁴⁵ X. 5, 33, 13.   ¹⁴⁶ X. 2, 26, 13.
¹⁴⁷ Bartolus ad Cod. 10, 48, 1: «... ex hoc dicebam in questione de facto. dicitur in capitulis pacis factis cum archiepiscopo mediolanensi. quod omnia castra occupata per Ubaldinos remaneant sub protectione et regimine ipsorum. dubitatur quid important ista verba protectio et regimen. dico quod per ista verba non debetur eis: nec habent aliquam iurisdictionem. [...] Sed ex eo quod dicitur sub regimine eius est magis dubium. nam rector loci idem est quod preses, ut no. glo. de offi. rec. provin. in rubro et nigro et ff. de offi. presi. l. illicitas §. que universitas. et sic nota quod ibi dicitur regunt et sic videtur qud ex natura dicti verbi possunt omnia facere que potest preses. et sic habent merum et mixtum imperium. In contrarium facit quia est verum quod dictum est quando regimen committitur provincie, sed quando committitur regimen civitatis non venit merum imperium vel mixtum. et idem si committitur regimen castrorum vel villarum, ut supra de defen. civi. per totum. et melius in corpore de defen. civi. § ius. et § audient. et supra de man. prin. per totum. et ibi per glo. et Azo in summa. et hoc videtur verius quod sit speciale in urbe Roma. ut si eius committatur regim videatur committi merum et mixtum imperium, ut ff. de offi. prefec. urbis. l. i. et maxime cum ista verba dubia debent interpretari contra eum qui profert. ut. ff. de pac. l. veteribus. Sed posito quod habeat merum et mixtum imperium pene et mulcte que imponuntur in dictis locis erunt eorum. et certe non quia non sunt presidis seu rectoris sed eius qui in illis locis habet ius fiscale ut l. mulctarum supra de mo. mulc. et in x. col. que sint rega. [...]». See also Baldus *ibidem*, f. 270va: «Etiam hi, qui gerunt negotia Principis, habent vacationem a muneribus, nisi sint ex illis officialibus, quibus specialiter est concessum. h.d. Quaero, quid sit dictum, protectoribus? Gl. dicit, dic de hoc ut infra de domest. et protect. super gl. Rub. ubi exponit protectores, illos ad custodiam Principis, ut sunt macerii, et alii similes. Et ex hoc dicebam, quod dicitur hodie in capitulis factis cum Archiepiscopo Mediolanensi, quod omnia castra occupata per Ubandinos, remaneant sub protectione, et regimine ipsorum: dubitatur, quid important ista verba, protectio et regimen? et ideo dico, quod per ista verba non debetur eis, nec habent per hoc aliquam iurisdictionem, casus est in c. ex parte tua, extra de pri. Sed habent potestatem se defendendi de facto cum armis et militibus, quod est offitium protectionis, ut no. super rub. infra de protec. et dome. lib. xii. et potest etiam defendere in forma iuris, et iudicii, ut no. in c. audientes, extra. de appell. Sed ex eo, quod dicit sub regimine, est maius dubium, nam rector loci, idem est, quam

{303rb} **Quaestio. LVII.**

¶ Terrae recommendate Principi, quae tenentur praestare auxilium, non prescribuntur etiam per mille annos, si Princ[eps]^sssss non requisivit^ttttt auxilium. c. i. de feu. sine culpa non amit. in fi.¹⁴⁸ & Bar. in l. cum scimus. C. de agri. & censi.¹⁴⁹

Quaestio. LVIII.

¶ Si duo Principes faciunt invicem pacem cum pacto, quod liceat vendicare impune rumpentem pacem, non valet pactum tale, nisi quatenus de iure permissum^uuuuuu sit vendicare. Bal. in auth. sacramenta puberum. C. si adver. vendi.¹⁵⁰

>Praeses, ut supra de offi. Rect. provin. in rubro, et nigro. et ff. de offi. praesi. l. illicitas § qui universas, et sic no. quod ibi dicit regunt, et sic videtur quod ex mente dictorum verborum possint omnia facere quae potest Praeses, et sic habent merum, et mixtum imperium. In contrarium facit, quia verum est, quod dictum est, quando committitur regimen provinciae, sed quando committitur regimen civitatis, non venit merum, vel mixtum imperium? et idem si committitur regimen castrorum, vel villarum, ut supra de defen. civi. per totum, et melius in corpore, in Auth. de defen. civi. §. iusiurandum et § audientiam et supra de magistr. mu. per totum, et ibi per glo. et Azo. in Summa. et hoc videtur verius, quia cum speciale sit in urbe Romana, et si eis commitatur regimen, videatur committi merum, et mixtum imperium, ut ff. de offic. praefec. urn. l. i. maxime cum ista verba dubia debeant interpretari contra eum, qui profert, ut ff. de pact. l. veterib. Sed posito, quod habeat merum, vel mixtum imperium poenae et mulctae, quae imponuntur in dictis locis, nunquid erunt eorum? Certe non, quia non sunt Praesidis, seu Rectoris, sed eius, qui in dictis locis habet ius fiscale, ut l. mulctarum supra de modo mul. et x. col. quae sint regalia. c. i. ubi expresse dicitur quod talia non veniunt, nisi expresse concedantur. Sed quero, utrum huiusmodi personae poterunt imponere collectam in dictis locis? Resp. non, quia praeses provinciae non potest imponere collectam, ut infra eod. l. placet et de supeindic. l. i. remanet ergo apud eos. ad quos primo pertinebat ius collectandi. Cetera dic ut in glo.».

¹⁴⁸ L. F. 1, 20.
¹⁴⁹ Bartolus ad Cod. 11, 48, 22, f. 37vb: «In tex. ibi illud quoque ex h. §. sumitur optimum arg. quod si terre recommendate tenentur dare civitati perusii subsidium in cavalcantibus et exercitibus extra civitatem euntibus et per centum annos steterunt quod non prestiterunt ex eo quod civitas Perusina non requisivit cum de suis gentibus esset copiosa nimis. ut non propter hoc terre prescripserint libertatem dicti servitii. nulla enim causa desidie potest communi Perusii imputari ex quo necessitatem dicti subsidii non habuit. de quo dixi in l. in filiis supra. de decurionibus ubi videtur casus».
¹⁵⁰ Baldus ad auth. 'Sacramenta puberum' [Cod. 2, 26, 1], No. 2, f. 169va: «[. . .] Et ideo si duae civitates habuerunt inter se guerram, et dum faciunt pacem apponunt pactum, quod liceat alteri se vindicare, vel rumpere federa pacis: istud pactum non valet. nisi in casu in quo esset permissum de iure, quia ius bene potest deduci in pactum, et etiam augeri per aditionem poene: ut ff. de pac. l. non impossibile».

Quaestio. LIX.

¶ In pace fienda^{vvvvvv} requiritur speciale mandatum. Spe. in tit. de treuga & pace .§. i. ver. hoc quoque.¹⁵¹ not. quod princeps mittit procuratorem pro capitulis pacis.^{wwwwww}

Quaestio. LX.

¶ Dux Mediolani primo fecit confederationem cum Ianuensibus,^{xxxxxx} secundo fecit aliam confederationem^{yyyyyy} cum rege Francorum. prima confederatio praefertur secundae, per regulam l. qui prior. ff. de reg. iur.¹⁵² nam ex hac confederatione causatur^{zzzzzz} obligatio^{aaaaaaa} personalis ad faciendum, puta ad prestandum auxilium in bello. ergo prior tempore potior iure l. in operis. ff. loca.¹⁵³ & determinat Io. An. in c. recolentes. de sta.^{bbbbbbb} mo. in novella.¹⁵⁴ ubi quando quis est colligatus duobus^{ccccccc} insolidum est ligatus secundo^{ddddddd} salvo iure primi, & colligatus^{eeeeeee} dicitur legalitatem servans in fidelitate ac^{fffffff} auxiliis praestan. nam confederatis & colligatis^{ggggggg} unius potest aliam confederationem facere salvo iure primi. c. i.§ . fi.^{hhhhhhh} de no. for. fide. quod not.¹⁵⁵ ^{iiiiiii}

Quaestio. LXI.

¶ Confederationes non dicuntur iustae, neque^{jjjjjjj} ad bonum finem regulariter, quando fiunt contra Papam, vel Imperatorem. Ang. in l. i. ff. quod cuiusque^{kkkkkkk} univer. nomi. in i. col.¹⁵⁶

---

¹⁵¹ Speculum iudiciale, L. VI, Part. I, De treuga et pace, No. 4, p. 107: «Hoc quoque no. quod si haec fiant per procuratores, debent ad hoc speciale mandatum habere: de quo etiam in pacis instrumento fiat mentio specialis. ff. de procurat. mandato. ex^{tra} de arb. per tuas. et de transac. contingit ff. de pac. nam et nocere. et vide, quod notatur super pace infra de homi. ver. illud et seq.».

¹⁵² Dig. 5, 1, 29.   ¹⁵³ Dig. 29, 2, 26.

¹⁵⁴ Joannes Andreae ad X. 3, 35, 3, f. 176vb, No. 3: «[Hominia] i. homagia [...] & promittendo quod homo suus ligius erit deceterо, et ei fidelitatem servabit, et ipsum contra homines omnes adiuvabit: quam promissionem facit iurando, et osculando. et hoc potest facere secundo, salva tamen fidelitate primi. et tertio, salva fidelitate primi, et secundi. primum est licitum iuramentum, etiam secundum servandum est, de iureiuran. veniens, et c. eam te, in fi. [...]».

¹⁵⁵ L. F. 2, 7.

¹⁵⁶ Angelus de Ubaldis ad Dig. 3, 4, 1, f. 105vb: «Omne collegium regulariter est illicitum, nisi approbatum in iure inveniatur, aut auctoritate superioris instituatur aut confirmetur. h.d. [...] Collegia vero civitatis vel castri vel ville sunt approbata de iure gentium secundum Inn. in d. c. que ab ecclesiarum et infra de colleg. illi l. i quod intellige verum nisi fiant ad violentiam ut l. qu. cum castrorum C. de fun. limitro. li. xi. Et ideo fortilitia facta tempore guerre in limitibus territorii facientium guerram debent destrui pacis tempore, quum sunt emulativa pacis C. de edificiis priva. l. per provincias. Inn. de resti. spo. pisanis confederationes [...] et leges ad bonum et laudabilem finem intendentes licite sunt, Inn. in d. c. dilecto dicit quod non possunt esse ad bonum finem si sunt contra cesarem et

Quaestio. LXII.

¶ In confederata civitate potest puniri delinquens, secundum Ang. in auth. de rebus immobi.^(lllllll) alie.¹⁵⁷ vide Bar. in l. non dubito. ff. de cap.¹⁵⁸

Quaestio. LXIII.

¶ Si princeps promisit tractare aliquem sibi colligatum & confederatum, ut alios cives suos, faciendo legem specialem contra eum, dicitur princeps facere contra pactum. Bar.^(mmmmmmm) in l. quidam cum filium.^(nnnnnnn) in fi. ff. de verbo. obl.¹⁵⁹ Bal. in l. si praedium.^(ooooooo) C. de edil. acti.¹⁶⁰ ^(ppppppp) dicit, quod si promisit pro^(qqqqqqq) suis adhaerentibus, intelligitur promittere occasione guerrae, non

> papam, imo ille appellantur conspirationes que sunt interdicte, etiam contra prelatam inferiorem. Archi. xi. q. i. si quis et c. coniurationum ubi dicit quod omnis coniuratio presumitur ad malum finem factum [...]».
>
> ¹⁵⁷ Angelus de Ubaldis ad Coll. [2.1 (Nov. 7)] Coll. 5: De ecclesiasticarum immobilium rerum alienatione, f. 20ra: «Et circa rei immobilis alienatio et insolutum pro debito fiscali concesso permittitur de rebus ecclesiae, si ex mobilibus satisfieri non possit, nisi episcopi et clerici consensus accedat pro debito vero privati solum insolutum datio conceditur, exceptis rebus immobilibus ecclesiae Constantino, et aliarum sibi subditarum, vel recommendatarum, que nullatenus alienantur. hoc dicit iste titu. hodie vero indifferenter, si bona mobilia non sunt, possunt alienari immobilia ecclesiae, ut infra. de alie. et emphy. § etiam. unde sumitur authen. hoc ius porrectum C. de sacrosan. eccle. et de iure cano. servatur, quia authen. illa canonizata. an tunc ipse episcopus possit alienare, ex quo eius consensus requiritur, ut sibimet sic consentire possit. dic, quod non quia eius consensus per modum authoritatis requiritur, et ideo sibimet consentire non potest. de hoc est tex. in cle. i. de reb. eccle. non alie. facit l. i. de autho. tuto., ibi curam. no. curam. et sic ecclesiae erant sibi recommendatae, non autem subditae, ut apparet ex consequenti ver. dum de subditis facit mentionem, et sic apparet, quod civitas castelli recommendata civitati Perusii, non tamen dicitur subdita civitati Perusii facit iste tex. quod privilegia concessa civitatibus subditis et recommendatis per hunc tex. nam videmus, quod privilegia concessa ecclesiae Constantinopo. ut res eius immobiles non possint alienari, extenduntur ad ecclesias sibi subditas et recommendatas. An autem maleficium commissum in una civitate confederata? dic ut per Iaco. de Bel. in l. non dubito ff. de rap. Et ibi est tex. in l. fi.».
>
> ¹⁵⁸ Bartolus ad Dig. 49, 15, 7, f. 145ra (*cf. supra*, n. 35).
> ¹⁵⁹ Bartolus ad Dig. 45, 1, 132, No. 17, f. 55va: «[...] civitas promisit cuidam feneratori eum tractare ut civem demum fecerunt statutum quod illi feneratori non liceret petere debitum usque ad tres annos. querebatur an esset factum contra pactum. dixi per istam l. quod non: quia eum tractavit ut civem quia etiam contra cives suos consuevit concedi exceptio dilatoria: ut l. quotiens. C. de princi. impe. of. Sed quid si dixit eum tractare ut alios cives. certe tunc faciendo contra eum legem specialem faceret contra pactum. ita hic promisisset eum tractare ut alios... unde sis cautus quando talia pacta sunt».
> ¹⁶⁰ Baldus ad Cod. 4, 58, 4, ff. 130va–131rb, No. 27, f. 131rb: «facit ad quaestionem de eo, qui promisit pro suis adhaerentibus quia intelligitur promisisse de non offendendo occasione guerre, nec de aliis inimicitiis singularib. hominis ad hominem. Tene menti. Id .n. quod non subiicitur materia belli, non venit in natura pacti, vel pacis».

autem pro inimicis^rrrrrrr singularium personarum hominis ad hominem, quod no. pro capitulis pacis.

Corrections and other readings

Not all the variations in other editions or manuscripts are mentioned: abbreviations, smaller differences of the spelling, some obvious mistakes etc. have not been taken into account. The main text follows by and large the Venice 1584 edition, which is the most widely available version; emendations to that version are always mentioned. Not all the references to legal authorities have been identified, or identified with certainty. Identifications qualified by «cf». are doubtful, those followed by a question mark are most probably wrong.

    a. The text follows mainly the edition: *Tractatus illustrium in utraque tum pontificii, tum caesarei iuris facultate Iurisconsultorum, De Dignitate, & Potestate seculari* [...] Tomus XVI. (Venetiis, 1584); folio numbers in the main text refer to that edition.
    b. Sic L.1544; corr. a (V.1584): convetionibus.
    c. PBN: De confederationibus et conventionibus principum. MBS: De confederationibus. TUB: Sequitur alia Rubrica huius operis de confederationibus et conventionibus principum.
    d. PBN and TUB omit throughout the caption «Quaestio» and the number; this is also the case in MBS, but the questions are numbered in a (faint) red ink in the left margin.
    e. TUB: «non» deest.
    f. PBN om.: «privatorum».
    g. MBS: suaderetur contra.
    h. Sic L.1544; corr. a (V.1584): privare.
    i. TUB om.: «publica . . . l. utilitas».
    j. Sic TUB, PBN. L.1530, L.1544, V.1584: privile.
    k. TUB om.: «sui».
    l. PBN om.: « . . .vis fugi. . . . ff. de.».
    m. Questions 2 and 3 altogether omitted in PBN, MBS, TUB.
    n. TUB: subiecerit.
    o. MBS: preben.
    p. MBS, TUB: infringi.
    q. Sic PBN, MBS, TUB. V.1584: Bal.
    r. PBN, MBS, TUB: unum castrum.
    s. PBN om.: «suo».
    t. L.1544: donan.
    u. L.1544: in summa.
    v. PBN: Bar.

w. PBN: & pauca dixi in hoc opere feudali, sed dicam in opere incepto nudum tamen perfecto; MBS: & pauca dixi in hoc opere feudal[i], sed dicam in opere incepto nondum inperfecto; TUB: pauca dico in hoc opusculo de materia feudali quia tractabo plene in opere feudorum iam incepto sed nundum finito.
x. TUB: C. de pactis.
y. PBN, MBS: Nam [quando, PBN om.] Princeps vel communitas sunt confederati.
z. PBN, TUB: unus princeps.
aa. PBN, MBS, TUB add «de».
bb. TUB: alium Dominum quam Principem.
cc. PBN, MBS, TUB: et.
dd. PBN, MBS, TUB om.: «& an sit . . . de pace Constan.».
ee. MBS om.: «inter se»; TUB reads: inter eos.
ff. V.1584, MBS: Bal.
gg. PBN, MBS, TUB: Bal. L. 1530, L. 1544, V. 1584: Bar.
hh. PBN, MBS: «eo. ti.» instead of: C. de dona.
ii. TUB om.: «facit auth. . . . C. de dona.».
jj. PBN, MBS om.: «Dominis &.».
kk. L. 1530: defensio.
ll. Sic PBN, MBS, TUB. L.1530, V.1584: Bal.
mm. TUB om.: «inter civitates».
nn. PBN, MBS, TUB: Bal.
oo. PBN, MBS, TUB, L.1530: Francie.
pp. PBN: ne alii; MBS: ne aliquem; TUB: ne aliquando.
qq. PBN: et.
rr. MBS: nulli.
ss. PBN, MBS, TUB: ut licet tu frangas.
tt. PBN, MBS: duret.
uu. MBS, TUB: iurisdictioni.
vv. PBN: vult; MBS: vult ponere.
ww. PBN, MBS: tex.
xx. PBN. L.1530, V.1584: collaterales. TUB: cancellationes.
yy. TUB om.: «lib. 12».
zz. Sic L.1530, L.1544, PBN, MBS, TUB: accepto. V.1584: excepto.
aaa. PBN, MBS, L.1530: equidem. TUB: ex venditione, certe.
bbb. TUB: ut.
ccc. PBN, MBS, TUB: pe[nult].
ddd. PBN: C.
eee. PBN om.: quod cum . . . ducis.
fff. PBN, MBS: redd[i]endis.
ggg. MBS: «castri» instead of «& castris».

hhh. MBS: om. «habeant».
iii. MBS om.: «& faciunt ... transact.».
jjj. TUB: vel civitates.
kkk. TUB: Bal.
lll. TUB: in recollectis, non in lectura.
mmm. MBS: om. «& faciens ... .ff. de pact.».
nnn. Sic L.1544; corr. a (V.1584): Princepes pertinent.
ooo. PBN: quis neque.
ppp. TUB: de pace iura fir. The words «non servatur de consuetudine» are placed at the beginning of the sentence.
qqq. PBN, MBS om.: «in usib. feudorum».
rrr. Sic L.1544; V.1584: dicunt[ur?].
sss. PBN, MBS, TUB: miles, neque federatus (TUB: fede.).
ttt. TUB: apostolicus.
uuu. TUB: Bar.
vvv. PBN: capitulum; MBS, TUB: capitulis.
www. PBN, MBS: opinionis et intentionis.
xxx. L.1584, PBN, MBS: liberti.
yyy. TUB, L.1530: legibus.
zzz. L.1544: confederatis.
aaaa. PBN: instead of «plenius haec omnia»: plene hic ponit; MBS: plenius ponit.
bbbb. MBS, TUB: «circa princ.» instead of «§ etiam Principum».
cccc. TUB: dampnum.
dddd. L.1544: Bernarboe. PBN, L.1530: Bernaboe.
eeee. TUB om.: «ubi ... viceco.».
ffff. PBN: & fidelitas debent fieri veneri.
gggg. MBS om.: first «ff.» (n. 90), then «C.» (n. 91).
hhhh. PBN om.: in.
iiii. TUB: instead of «10.», reads: «c [blank]».
jjjj. TUB: probata.
kkkk. PBN om.: «not.».
llll. TUB adds: maxime.
mmmm. PBN, MBS om.: «de iureiur.».
nnnn. Sic PBN, MBS; L.1544. V.1584: paciscentur.
oooo. TUB: pacti.
pppp. PBN om.: «§ si qua vero».
qqqq. PBN: eligere.
rrrr. PBN, MBS om.: «pacem». TUB: pacem habuit.
ssss. PBN: Principes omnia debent. MBS: om. «debet».
tttt. PBN: spoliatus.
uuuu. Sic MBS. PBN, L.1530, L.1544, V.1584: postliminium.
vvvv. TUB: Venetis seu Florentinis.

wwww. MBS: federate. L.1530: considerate.
xxxx. Sic PBN; L.1544. Corr. a (V.1584): datur.
yyyy. PBN om.: «quia capite non». TUB om.: «non».
zzzz. MBS, TUB: cessare.
aaaaa. TUB: discernimus.
bbbbb. MBS: iudicanti.
ccccc. PBN om.: «est debitor».
ddddd. PBN om.: «debitum».
eeeee. TUB: civitates, and om.: «sub protectione».
fffff. TUB adds: eas.
ggggg. TUB adds: per tex. et.
hhhhh. MBS: omnis.
iiiii. PBN: non autem.MBS: nos.
jjjjj. Sic L.1530, L.1544; V.1584, TUB: comitatum.
kkkkk. PBN: maior.
lllll. PBN, MBS, TUB: rediguntur.
mmmmm. TUB om.: «qui est ... potentior».
nnnnn. MBS: potentior.
ooooo. PBN, MBS, TUB: colligatorum.
ppppp. MBS: «in principe» instead of: «si ... Principe».
qqqqq. TUB inserts here: «Confederatus non tenetur adiuvare socium nisi sit requisitus Bal. in c. ubi non est de for. fid.» (comp. *supra*, Qu. 28).
rrrrr. PBN om.: «dolo ... ff. de».
sssss. MBS: om. «hora».
ttttt. PBN, MBS, TUB: illis.
uuuuu. Sic PBN; L.1544. V.1584: sed.
vvvvv. PBN: dicuntur illi.
wwwww. MBS: intentioni & operibus illius. TUB: illi qui in operibus adherent.
xxxxx. PBN: opes.
yyyyy. TUB om.: «proditores ... dicantur».
zzzzz. PBN: Principes sive comites volentes. MBS: Principes sive communitates nolentes (!).
aaaaaa. PBN, TUB: in d[icto] consilio. MBS: in d. consi. 2 (!).
bbbbbb. TUB, L.1530: legibus.
cccccc. MBS: federationibus.
dddddd. PBN: ponit Ange. consilio 298. MBS, TUB: 298. L.1530, L.1544: 268.
eeeeee. PBN, MBS, TUB: anno.
ffffff. PBN, MBS: et confederationis. TUB: lege et confederatione.
gggggg. PBN: postposita et in gratia.
hhhhhh. PBN, MBS: tunc factum a maiori parte lige praeiudicat reliquis colligatis.

iiiiii. TUB reads: ... tunc factum a maiore parte preiudicat reliquis collegatis, no[ta.] in l. item si magister ff. de pac. ubi est casus: & Ang. probet [?] vide l. si cum patrono, fi. & ibi Bar. ff. de bonorum pos. servarem tamen in hoc consuetudinem, ar. c. cum dilectus. de fide instru.
jjjjjj. MBS: reprobare.
kkkkkk. PBN om.: «lega. i. ¶ Facta pace l. obsides ff. de».
llllll. PBN: tractandi pacem.
mmmmmm. MBS: stricte.
nnnnnn. PBN, MBS, TUB: Germanos (as in Cle. 2.9.1). Comp. *De principibus*, Qu. 22: « ... translatum est imperium a Grecis in Germanos ab Ecclesia ... ».
oooooo. MBS: citans.
pppppp. PBN: de appella. al. MBS, TUB: appel. alias de.
qqqqqq. PBN, MBS, TUB: «sub» instead of «sit in».
rrrrrr. MBS: de excusato. mune. lib. x.
ssssss. Sic PBN, MBS. V.1584, L.1544: Principes.
tttttt. PBN: si Princeps non exquisiverit.
uuuuuu. PBN: promissum.
vvvvvv. TUB: facienda.
wwwwww. PBN om.: «pro capitulis pacis. MBS om.: §. i. ... pacis».
xxxxxx. TUB: Genuensibus.
yyyyyy. MBS om.: confederationem.
zzzzzz. PBN, MBS, TUB: oritur.
aaaaaaa. TUB: actio.
bbbbbbb. L.1544: testa.
ccccccc. PBN, MBS: ligius duorum.
ddddddd. PBN: instead of «ligatus secundo»: ligius et confederatus secundi. MBS: instead of «est ... secundo»: [*waterstain: illegible word*] confederatorum secundi.
eeeeeee. PBN, MBS: ligius.
fffffff. PBN: infidelitatem aut.
ggggggg. PBN, MBS: instead of «confederatis & colligatis»: confederatus et ligius principis. (MBS: ... unius principis).
hhhhhhh. PBN adds: de prohi. feu. alie. per Fe. et c. i.
iiiiiii. TUB reads: ... ubi quando quis est l[ig]ius duorum solidum est ligius et confederatus secundi summo iure primi. Et ligius dicitur legalitatem servans in fidelitate et auxilii prestatione. Nam confederatus et ligius unus princeps potest aliam confederationem facere salvo iure primi c. i § fi. de prohi. alie. per Fede. et in c. i. de nova fide. for.
jjjjjjj. MBS: atque.
kkkkkkk. PBN, TUB: quisque.

lllllll. PBN: «eccle. rerum in mobi.» instead of «rebus immobi.». MBS: de eccle. rerum. TUB: de re. ecc. non alie.
mmmmmmm. PBN: Bal.
nnnnnnn. Corr. a (V.1584, L.1544): plurimum.
ooooooo. L.1544: presidium.
ppppppp. TUB: edic.
qqqqqqq. PBN: cum.
rrrrrrr. MBS, TUB: inimicitiis.

The references to Garratus' authorities have been checked in the following editions or manuscripts

Andreae, Ioannes: *Ioannis Andreae I.C. Bononiensis omnium canonici iuris interpretum facile principis, In secundum Decretalium librum Novella Commentaria* [...]. (Venetiis, Apud Franciscum Franciscium, Senensem, 1581 (reimp. anast. Turin 1963)).

Ioannis Andreae I.C. Bononiensis omnium canonici iuris interpretum facile principis, In tertium Decretalium librum Novella Commentaria [...]. (Venetiis, Apud Franciscum Franciscium, Senensem, 1581 (reimp. anast. Turin 1963)).

Barbatia, Andreas de: *Opus mirificum nuperrime in lucem datum eminentissimi iuris principis domini Andree Barbacie super clementinis* [...]. (Venetiis per Baptistam de Tortis, 1516).

Baysio, Guido de: *Archidiaconus super decretorum volumine.* (Impressa Mediolani opera industria et impendio Jo. Jacobi et fratrum de lignano, 1508).

Butrio, Antonius de: *Lectura super secunda parte Secundi Decretalium.* (Lugduni impressa in officina calcographica Joannis Crespin alias du Carre, 1532).

Lectura super Quinto Decretalium. (Lugduni impressa in officina calcographica Joannis Crespin alias du Carre, 1532).

Durantis, Guilelmus: *Gul. Durandi Episcopi Mimatensis I.U.D. Speculi Iuris* [...] Pars [...]. Basileae, Apud Ambrosium et Aurelium Frobenios fratres, 1574 (reimpr. anast. Aalen 1975).

Forlivio, Raynerius de: *Utilis ac secunda lectura domini Raynerii de Forlivio: in utroque iure doctoris luculentissimi: super Prima et secunda parte. ff. novi.* [...]. (Lugduni [Vincentius de Portonariis de Tridino de Monte Ferrato], 1523).

Garratus (Laudensis), Martinus: *Aurea ac perutilis lectura, clariss. ac iuris interpretis consummatiss. D. Martini de Caratiis, Laudensis, in lucrissimo, & prae caeteris practicabili Opere Feudorum* [...]. Basileae, per Thomam Guarinum, 1564.

Innocentius IV: *Apparatus preclarissimi iuris canonici illuminatoris d. Innocentii pape .iiii. super .v. li. decre. et super decretalibus per eundem d.* [...]. Lugduni in edibus Joannis Moylin alias de Cambray. Anno Virginei partus, 1525.

Lignano, Johannes de: [Commentary on the five books of the Decretals, *Liber extra*]. MBS Mss. CLM 8786 and 8787.

Pistoia, Cynus a: *Cyni Pistoriensis, iurisconsulti praestantissimi, In Codicem, et aliquot titulos primi Pandectorum Tomi, id est, Digesti veteris, doctissima Commentaria* [...]. Francoforti ad Moenum, Imprensis Sigismundi Feyerabendt, 1578 (reimp. anast. Turin 1964).

Pontanus (Romanus), Ludovicus: *Consilia sive responsa* [...]. Venetiis, 1568.

Rosate, Albericus de: *Alberici de Rosate Bergomensis* [...] *In Primam Codicis Partem Commentarii.* Venetiis, 1586 (reimp. anast. Opera iuridica rariora 27, 1979).

Alberici de Rosate Bergomensis [...] *In Secundam Codicis Part. Commentaria.* Venetiis, 1585 (reimp. anast. Opera iuridica rariora 28, 1979).

Saxoferrato, Bartolus a: *Bartolus super Secunda Infor* [...]. Venetiis per Baptistam de Tortis, 1526 (reimp. anast. Rome 1996–8).

Bar. Super Prima. ff. Novi [...]. Venetiis per Baptistam de Tortis, 1526 (reimp. anast. Rome 1996–8).

Bar. Super Secunda. ff. novi [...]. Venetiis per Baptistam de Tortis, 1526 (reimp. anast. Rome 1996–8).

Bartolus super prima Codicis [...]. Venetiis per Baptistam de Tortis 1526, (reimp. anast. Rome 1996–8).

Expolita commentaria Domini Bartoli de Saxoferrato omnium discipline legum viri exactissimi ac consultissimi in secunda parte Codicis [...]. Venetiis per Baptistam de Tortis, 1526 (reimp. anast. Rome 1996–8).

Consilia: Questiones: Et Tractatus [...]. Venetiis per Baptistam de Tortis, 1529 (reimp. anast. Rome 1996).

Bar. super tribus libris.C. Mediolani impressa per Joannem Angelum Scinzenzeler ad impensas Joannis Jacobi et fratrum de Lignanum, 1512 (reimp. anast. Rome 1996–8).

Segusio, Henricus de: *Egregii atque profundissime scientie viri inter omnes pontificii cesareique iurium professores nominatissimi: domini Henrici Cardinalis Hostiensis vulgariter nuncupati: insignis Ebredunensis ecclesie archipresulis. Iuris utriusque professoris: ac monarche clarissimi: eximia: copiosa atque admiranda lectura in quinque Decretalium Gregorianarum libros* [...] [Iehan Petit]. Venundantur Parisiis in vico divi Jacobi per Joannem Petit: sub intersignio floris lilii: et Thielmanum Kerver: sub intersignio craticule ferree [s.d.].

Ubaldis, Angelus de: *Lectura super Prima parte Digesti veteris* [...]. Lugduni, (impressa per Georgium Regnault) 1545.

Lectura super Prima Infortiati. Lugduni (Exarata per Georgium Regnault) 1545.

Lectura super Secunda Infortiati. Lugduni (Impressa Lugduni per Georgium Regnault) 1548.

Lectura super Codice. Lugduni (Impressum per Thomam Bertheau) 1545.

Angeli Ubaldi, Perusini, iuriscon. praeclarissimi, in authen. volumen commentaria [...]. Venetiis, 1580.

Excelsi ac eminentissimi J.U. doctoris domini Angelis de ubaldis de perusio responsa [. . .]. (Impressa Papie quam diligentissime per nobiles et accutissimos

Bernardinum et Ambrosium fratres de Novellis Papien. anno. domini MCC-
CCXCVIII die XXVI septembris).
Consilia seu responsa. (Joannes Moylin alias Cambray, Lugd.) 1539.
Ubaldis, Baldus de: *Baldi Ubaldi Perusini iurisconsulti Omnium concessu doctissimi pariter et acutissimi, Commentaria In primum, secundum et tertium Codicis lib.* [...]. Venetiis, Apud Iuntas, 1572.
Baldi Perusini ad tres priores libros Decretalium Commentaria [...]. Augustae, Taurinorum, Apud Haeredes Nicolai Beuilaquae, 1578 [col. i.f.: 1568].
Baldi Ubaldi Perusini, iuris utriusque consultissimi, in Feudorum Usus Commentaria [...]. Venetiis, Apud Iuntas, 1580. Includes ff. 96rb–104rb: *Commentariolum eiusdem Baldi, Super pace Constantiae.*
Zabarella, Franciscus: *Celeberrimi iurisconsulti Francisci Cardinalis Zabarelle Commentarii in Clementinarum volumen* [...]. (Impressum fuit Lugduni per Magistrum Nicolaum de Benedictis, 1511).

INDEX

Abelard, P. 166, 200–2
Abrams, I. 261
accession to treaty, third parties,
　inclusion as 35, 55–6
Accursius 154–5, 156, 212
adhaerentes/sequaces
　applicability of treaty provisions to
　　157
　implicit inclusion 195–6
　as partners 190
Adrianople, Treaty of (1713) 53, 354,
　355
Adrianople, Treaty of (1829) 360–1
　duration 360–1
　renewal of FCN treaties 373
Aelred of Rievaulx, St 169–70
Africa
　Arabs, dependence on Turkey 63
　Europe, relations with 63
　political savages 68–9
　sub-Saharan Africa 63
　unequal treaties 68
Aix-la-Chapelle, Peace of (1748) 52
　duration of Congress 52–3
　hostages as guarantee 48–9
Alexander III 152–3, 175, 177–81
Algeria 63
alliance, right of: *see ius foederis*
Allott, P. 288
Alsace-Lorraine 71, 90, 97
Althoff, G. 179 n. 66
ambassadors: *see also* diplomacy;
　negotiations
　absence of information on 186 n. 5
　precedence, Ottoman Empire 344,
　　348, 350

Russian ambassador to the Sublime
　Porte 355
amicitia
　15th-century Italian treaty practice
　　and 36
　18th-century developments 81–2
　19th-century practice 82–3
　alliance distinguished 81–2
　Ancient Rome: *see* Ancient Rome,
　　amicitia
　FNC treaties 64–5
　as indication of crisis in
　　international relations 37, 43,
　　406
　modern practice 36, 81–3
　Paris Peace Treaties (1919/20) 81, 83,
　　98
　rule of law and 36, 41
　stabilisation clauses and 41
　standardisation of clauses 36–7
　third parties, inclusion as
　　affirmation of 36–7
　trade provisions and 41
　treaties with non-European powers
　　83
Amiens, Treaty of (1475) (I)
　hostages as guarantee 28
　parties 17–18
Amiens, Treaty of (1475) (III)
　amicitia 41
　trade privileges 40–1
amnesty clauses: *see also* reparations
　activities within returned or ceded
　　territories 86
　applicability to subjects fighting for
　　the enemy 39

INDEX 449

conformity with laws of war and
  84–5
just war and 39
Ottoman Empire 356
personal amnesty 84, 86–7: *see also*
  war crimes, responsibility for
  advantages 87
  responsibility for the war and 40,
  84
  sovereign's monopolisation of
  warfare and 39
  standardisation/presumption of
  amnesty 39–40, 84
Ampala, Treaty of (1886), renewal of
  FCN treaty 372–3
analogies with private law 17, 136–9,
  157, 158, 159–60, 193–4, 224,
  226: *see also pacta sunt
  servanda; rebus sic stantibus*;
  restitution; treaty as private law
  contract; *uti possidetis*
private/international law, separation
  and 259
Ancenis, Treaty of (1468), princely
  word 25 n. 41
Ancient Greece, international law and
  113
  arbitration 126 n. 68
  contemporary commentators,
    usefulness as source 141 n. 110
  just war 128 n. 74
  treaties
    classification (Antiochus) 116
    epigraphic inscription 121 n. 52
Ancient Greece, legitimacy and 302
Ancient Rome, *amicitia* 154
  definition 120
  societas and 120
  as treaty element 114–16
Ancient Rome, dispute settlement
  arbitration 113, 126–8
  border disputes 126–7
    status quo ante/uti possidetis 127
    uti possidetis 230, 237
  recuperatio 116, 126 n. 68
Ancient Rome, international law in
  archaic formulas, retention 116
    n. 35, 128 n. 75

contemporary commentators:
  see also Caesar; Cicero; Gaius;
  Hermogenian; Justinian; Livy;
  Pomponius
  archives, influence 111 n. 21
  structure of texts 226
  usefulness as source 107–9,
    139–40, 141–6
dialectic, absence 113–14
existence: *see also ius gentium*
  enforcement machinery, absence
    107
  international relations between
    equals, absence 111–13, 131–2,
    136–9: loss of control and 112
  Greek experience, failure to exploit
    113, 129
  hospitium publicum 115, 117–18,
    120, 154
  hostis 117 n. 39
  interpretatio 114, 137–8
  interpretation, absence of theory
    113, 129
  koine 124–5
  natural law 204–5
  piracy 117 n. 39
  Principate, developments during
    112–13
  private law
    analogies 17, 136–9, 157, 158,
      159–60, 226
    relative sophistication 112–13,
      137–8
  religion and 109–11, 112, 119–21,
    137
    fetiales (priests), role: archives
    110–11; declaration of war 128;
    limited importance 119; oath as
    essential element in *foedus*
    120–1; travel abroad,
    prohibition 121
    politics, interrelationship 109–11,
    119–21, 124–5, 136–9: archives,
    priests' responsibility for
    110–11
    quasi-contract between gods and
    humans 110–11: religious
    oath 110–11, 120–1

Ancient Rome (*cont.*)
  sacer 110–11: signs,
    interpretation 110–11
  'state', emergence of concept 112
    n. 23
  as system 104–5
    codification distinguished 104–5
Ancient Rome, legitimacy and
  302–3
Ancient Rome, *pax*
  eirene compared 105 n. 7
  exception or rule? 105–6, 117,
    118–19, 122, 125 n. 38,
    244
  kiss of peace 167–9
  legal act/factual state (peace
    treaty/peace) distinguished 104,
    105–7, 115–16, 117–18, 122
  pax deorum 124–5
  postliminium in pace 105, 115,
    117–18
  as treaty objective 123, 140–1
Ancient Rome, treaties
  aequum foedus 114, 115–16
  agreement to agree, effect 157:
    see also sponsio *below*
  amicitia 115, 117–18
  authorisation, need for (*iussum
    populi*) 132–4
    agency law compared 133,
    140
  breach
    defectio 134–5
    foedifragi 128–9
    as generalised concept 126–7
    just war (*bellum justum*) and
    128
    loyalty principle (*fides/perfidia*)
    128–9, 138, 140 n. 102
    Punic Wars and 130–1
    war guilt and 130–1
  Cicero 135–6
  citizenship, restrictions on
    acquisition of 135–6
  commander's agreement,
    ratification, need for 132–4
  conceptualisation, absence 118
  content 121

content/form distinguished 121–2,
  125
control as objective 118–19, 137–8
conventio publica 114, 115–16, 122
  n. 54, 154
deditio 120
evocatio deorum and 122 n. 56
foederatus 119
foedus 117–18, 154
  decline in significance 119–20,
    137
  as general term 128
  oath as determining element
    120–1
foedus sociale 114, 115–16
formula iuris antiqui 114, 115, 116,
  128 n. 75
Greek classification and 116
hospitium publicum 115, 117–18,
  120, 154
impossibility of performance 135
indutiae 122, 154, 156
libertas and 128 n. 74
Livy 108–9, 114–17, 120–1, 122–3,
  129
pax distinguished 117–18
as political act 116–17, 127–8,
  131–2
Pomponius 115, 117–18
preventive purpose 124–5
prisoners of war 154
rerum repetitio 114, 115, 116 n. 34,
  128 n. 75
Rome–Carthage (509 BC) 121
societas 120
sponsio 122, 134: *see also* agreement
  to agree, effect *above*
Ulpian 122 n. 54
unequal/dictated treaties 114–16,
  154, 246
Anghie, A. 403
annexation of territory 89
Anselmus of Lucca 212–13
Antwerp, Treaty of (1609), duration 38
appetitus societatis 199, 203
  dualism and 219
  international law as independent
    system and 218–19

INDEX 451

ius voluntarium (voluntary law) 218–19
pacta sunt servanda and 218–19
Aquinas, T. 200–2, 212
arbitration: *see also* Permanent Court of Arbitration
Ancient Greece 126 n. 68
Ancient Rome 113, 126–8
Jay Treaty (1784) 258
pre-Hague Conferences (1899/1907) 258
uti possidetis as prelude to 230, 232, 233, 235–6
Aristides 303 n. 19
armistice/preliminary peace agreements: *see also* truce
agreement to agree, effect 157
as basis for eventual peace settlement 71, 72
by party
Egypt–Israel (1949) 378–9
Frederick 1–Lombardic League (1177) 151
Israel–Jordan (1949) 378–9
Israel–Lebanon (1949) 378–9
Israel–Syria (1949) 378–9
Israel–Syria (1974) 378–9
Paris Peace Agreement (1973) (Vietnam) 378–9
post-WWI agreements 71
by party Gulf War (1991) 378–9
Argentina–UK (1982) (Falklands: Instrument of Surrender) 379
indutiae 122, 154, 156
as interim arrangement 71, 154–5, 156
ratification, relevance 71, 72
sponsio 122, 134
termination of hostilities and 71, 72
treuga 156
Arras, Treaty of (1435)
zusammengesetzte Vertragsschliessungsverfahren 22
Arras, Treaty of (1482)
amnesty clauses 39
confirmation by oath 23
parties 17–18

princely word 25 n. 41
private person, breach by 42
ratification by estates 19
registration 19
restitution of private property 40
trade provisions 41
Asia, Europe, relations with
'civilised nations' concept and 67–9
European-dominated powers 62–3
independent states 62
unequal treaties 62–3, 67–8
Asser, T. M. C. 262
assistance, obligation
Ancient Rome 134–5
Garatus 195
Asti, Treaty of (1615), amnesty clauses 39 n. 80
Augustine, St 210–12
Austin, J. 200–2, 258–9
Austro-Hungarian Empire
break-up 61–2, 90
authenticated copies 81

Bagnolo, Treaty of (1484)
financial security against breach 28
papacy, obligation to defend 30–1
balance of power
18th-century treaties and 56–7
positivism as expression of 251–2, 408–9
as response to anarchy 293
Versailles, Treaty of (1919) and 399–402
Balkan states, aspirations to independence 89–90, 96–7
Barcelona, Treaty of (1493)
bona fides 158–9
oath 149–50
ratification documents 23 n. 37
as treaty of Holy Alliance 30
Barcelona, Treaty of (1529)
confirmation by oath 23
financial security against breach 28
Barkeley, R. 261 n. 17
basium: see kiss of peace
Baumgärtner, I. 184 n. 2
Bavaria: *see* Catholic League
Becket, Thomas 177–81

Bederman, D. 223
Bekker, E. I. 267–8
Belgium, independence 61
Belgrade, Peace of (1739) 356
  amnesty clauses 356
  duration 356
Bély, L. 54
Bergbohm, C. M. 267–8
Berlin, Act of (1878) 362–3
Berlin, Congress of (1878) 73
  territorial settlement 89–90
  third parties, inclusion 74
Berlin, Treaty of (1850) 73
  authenticated copies 81
  designation of plenipotentiaries 81
  object and purpose 80
Berlin, Treaty of (1866) (I)
  German Confederation (*Deutsche Bund*), dissolution 89
  parties 75
  reparations 85
Berlin, Treaty of (1866) (II)
  authenticated copies 81
  parties 75
  ratification 96 n. 129
  reparations 85
Berlin, Treaty of (1866) (III)
  parties 75
  reparations 85
Berlin, Treaty of (1866) (IV), ratification 96 n. 129
Berlin, Treaty of (1918), supplementing Treaty of Brest-Litovsk (1918) 90
Bernard of Clairvaux, St 169
Biel, G. 200–2
binding force: *see* implementation; *pacta sunt servanda*
Black Sea 94
Blackmore, S. 309 n. 26
Blois, Treaty of (1504) (I)
  confirmation by oath 23
  princely word 24–5
Bluntschli, J. C. 261–2, 263
Böckenförde, E.-W. 325–6
Bodin, J. 47, 243
Bohemian rebellion (1618) 320–1

Bologna, Treaty of (1529) 30–1
  emperor as head of Christianity 31
bona fides/good faith requirement 158–9: *see also* loyalty principle (*Reichstreue/fides/perfidia*)
  ambiguity and 242, 246, 249–51
  diplomacy 241–2, 244–52
  Fénelon 245
  quamdiu fides servetur 194–5
border disputes: *see also uti possidetis*
  in antiquity 126–7
  status quo ante/uti possidetis 127
Brabant (Wenceslas of Bohemia)–Holland (Albert, Duke of Bavaria) (1374), *bona fides* 158–9
Brassloff, S. 223 n. 7
Brazil, independence 62
breach of treaty: *see also* enforcement jurisdiction (pope); FCN treaties, termination by war
  Ancient Rome, generalised concept 126–7
  chivalry and 28–9
  compensation for damage caused 27–8
  excommunication for 150–1
  financial security against 28
  payment of dowry and 28 n. 50
  hostages as guarantee against 28–9
  just war and 27–8, 128
  loyalty principle (*fides/perfidia*) 128–9, 131–2, 138 n. 102, 140, 243
  pledge of goods and possessions 27–8, 160
  private person 42
  reprisal, right of 28
  war, as just cause 27–8
Breda, Treaty of (1667)
  Treaty of Commerce (1668) 369
  uti possidetis 234–5
Brest, Peace of (1435)
  bona fides 158–9
  oath 149–50
Brest-Litovsk, Treaty of (1918) (I)
  amicitia clause 83
  territorial settlement 90

Brest-Litovsk, Treaty of (1918) (II)
  amicitia clause 83
  reparations, renunciation 86
Brétigny, Peace of (1360),
  oath/ratification 149
Bretone, M. 124
Briand–Kellogg Pact (1928) 256,
  410
Brierly, J. 278 n. 58
British Association for the Promotion
  of Social Science 262
Bromsebrö, Treaty of (1645)
  amicitia 41
  prisoners of war 41
Bucharest, Treaty of (1812) 360
Bucharest, Treaty of (1913)
  amicitia clause 83
  parties 75
  prisoners of war 96
Buczacz, Treaty of (1672) 352
Bulmerincq, A. von 263, 266–7
Bureau International de la Paix 264
Burgundy–Austrasia *Pactio* (587)
  149
Burkhardt, J. 321
Burkina Faso/Mali, Frontier Dispute
  230
Buzan, B. 294, 299–300 n. 7
Byzantium
  decline and fall 339–40
  Ottoman rulers as successors 341

Caesar, J. 108 n. 13
Callistus II 171
Cambrai, Treaty of (1508) (I)
  confirmation by oath 23
  princely word 24–5
  prisoners of war 41
  registration 19
  respublica christiana and 29
  succession and
    ratification by heir apparent 21
    ratification by successor 21
  as treaty of Holy Alliance 30
Cambrai, Treaty of (1508) (II)
  papacy, obligation to defend 30–1
  reprisal, right of 42
  trade provisions 41

Cambrai, Treaty of (1517), ratification/
  oath distinction 25–6
Cambrai, Treaty of (1529)
  emperor as head of Christianity 31
  ratification/oath distinction 25–6
Cambrai, Treaty of (1529) (I)
  amicitia 41
  confirmation by oath 23
  dowry, guarantee 28 n. 50
  hostages as guarantee 28
Cambrai, Treaty of (1529) (II), *amicitia*
  41
Cambridge University, establishment
  of Whewell Chair 264
Candia, Treaty of (1669) 351–2
canon law: *see also* feudal law; *ius
    commune*; *ius gentium*; Roman
    law
  as basis of international
    relations/law of nations 11,
    26–7, 42–3, 404–5, 409
  glossators and 209–16
  Reformation and 12, 15, 24, 42–3,
    405–6
  Roman law inheritance 204–9, 404–5
  treaty law and 194 n. 32
capitulations: *see* Ottoman Empire,
  capitulations
Carthage: *see* Punic Wars
Catalano, P. 109
Câteau-Cambrésis, Treaty of
  (1559) (I)
  amnesty clauses 39
  confirmation by oath 23
  dowry, guarantee of 28 n. 50
  hostages as guarantee 28
  ratification by heir apparent 21
  registration 19
  reprisal, right of 42
  respublica christiana and 33
  third parties, inclusion 34–5
  trade provisions 41
  as treaty of Holy Alliance 30
Câteau-Cambrésis, Treaty of
  (1559) (II)
  amicitia 41
  private person, breach by 42
  respublica christiana and 33

Catholic League
  dissolution (Treaty of Pirna) 329–30
  imperial consent, need for 328–9
change, coping with 302–3: *see also* League of Nations; Versailles, Treaty of (1919); Westphalia Peace Treaties (1648)
  change and inertia in tension 308
  commonality of assumptions and 312–15
  consent, relevance 302–3
  globalisation 97–8: *see also* globalisation
  historiography and 291–2
  international system/law, reshaping 34, 42–3, 45–50, 60–1, 88
  ius gentium and 212, 225–9
  memetics and 308–9
  negotiating style 77
  publicists' role 272, 286–8
  social and economic causes of change 96–7, 99, 262
  subsumption of past and present 286–7, 292, 300–2, 304–7
  war, concept of 98, 310–11
  war crimes, responsibility for 86: *see also* war crimes
Charles V 12
  as *monarcha universalis* 31–2
Charles the Bold 15–17
China
  19th-century treaties 62–3
  as 'civilised nation' 69–70, 76–7
  Europe, relations with 62
  gunpowder and 310–11
  printing and 310
  sovereignty 62–3
chivalry, treaty practice and 28–9
Christianity: *see also respublica christiana*
  'civilised nations' concept and 69
Church
  institutionalisation 213–14
  as *universitas fidelium* 206–7, 312–13

Churruca, J. de 227
Cicero 135–6, 142–4
cities: *see civitates* (cities/city-states)
civil wars: *see also* Thirty Years War
  England (1642–49) 320
  Europe, cessation 10
  France (1563–98) 17
  Fronde 320
'civilised nations': *see ius gentium*, universality; unequal treaties
  Africa 68–9
  Americas, colonisation and 67
  Asia 67–9
  Christianity, as replacement for 69
  classification as 69–70
  common cultural and moral standards
    international law's dependence on 273
    loss post-WWI 271–2
  economic developments and 65, 66–9
  international law and 66–9
    subjects of, limitation to 69–70
  just war and 227
  League of Nations
    membership 276–7, 278
    as replacement for family of 275–6
  natural law and 67
  political savages 68–9
civitates (cities/city-states)
  rights, effect of peace treaty 193
  as treaty partners 190
co-ratification 19–20: *see also* ratification; succession to treaty obligations
  by estates 19, 47–8
  by heir apparent 21
    limitation to treaties of cession 21
  disappearance of practice 20, 43
  ratification by parliament distinguished 19–20
  registration by courts and exchequers 19–20
codification
  preliminaries to 286

INDEX

Roman law as system distinguished 104–5
treaty provisions as 242, 252
coercion, effect on treaty 194, 384–5
Vienna Convention on the Law of Treaties (1969) and 384–5
commerce: *see* economic developments; FCN treaties
Commission on Responsibility of Authors of the War (1920) 270, 284–5 n. 2
communications 94–5
compensation for breach of treaty 27–8: *see also* reparations; restitution
compliance with treaty, obligation: *see pacta sunt servanda*
composite monarchies 320–1
compulsory judicial settlement, need for 99
conclusion of treaties: *see* co-ratification; kiss of peace; negotiations; oath; ratification; signature; treaty practice
Conflans, Treaty of (1465)
  amnesty clauses 39
  parties 15–17
conflicting obligations under successive treaties 193
Congo Act (1885), unilateral nature 67, 90–1
congress: *see* peace congresses
consent: *see* law of nations (*ius gentium/Völkerrecht*), consent as basis
Constance, Treaty of (1183) 152, 156–7
  parties 151
  as source 155–6
Constantinople, Treaty of (1679) 352
Constantinople, Treaty of (1700) 353–4
Constantinople, Treaty of (1710) 354–5
Constantinople, Treaty of (1712) 354–5

Constantinople, Treaty of (1720), duration 355
Constantinople, Treaty of (1897)
  FCN treaty, agreement to conclude 374–5
  personal amnesty 86
  post and telegraph communications 94
  preliminary peace treaty 71–2
constitution of Europe, principles of law of nations as 242
constructivism: *see* historiography, constructivism and
Continental System 367–8
contracts: *see also* treaty as private law contract
  prince's obligation to observe 193–4
conventio: *see* Ancient Rome, treaties
corporate bodies/individual members, relationship 214–15
Corpus iuris civilis 148–9, 154, 205
Crépy, Treaty of (1544)
  amnesty clauses 39
  confirmation by oath 23
  papal enforcement jurisdiction and 27
  preservation of rights 232–3
  ratification by estates 19
  ratification/oath distinction 25–7
  registration 19
  respublica christiana and 33
  secret clauses 32 n. 63
  succession and 21
  as treaty of Holy Alliance 30
crusade
  peace as precondition 30–2
  treaties of Holy Alliance 30–1
custodia as objective criterion 215
customary international law, power to conclude treaties 133
Czechoslovakia, formation 90

Danube 94
Danube Commission 93
Dardenelles, Treaty of (1809) 359–60
Dawkins, R. 309

De Lapradelle, A. 283
Decretum Gratiani 147, 209–11
  ius gentium 227
  marriage 215–16
  natural/divine law, interrelationship 210–11, 212–13
  secular law, subordinate position 212 n. 33
deditio: *see* Ancient Rome, treaties
defectio 134–5
demilitarisation, as guarantee 91
Descartes, R. 203
Diceto, Ralph de 176–7
diplomacy: *see also* ambassadors; negotiations
  bona fides/good faith requirement 241–2
  as a civilising process 252–3
  as permanent institution 241
  as royal prerogative 241
diplomatic privileges and immunities, as international law issue 259
discoveries: *see* New World discoveries
dispute settlement: *see also* arbitration; League of Nations; Permanent Court of Arbitration; Permanent Court of International Justice
  Ancient Rome: *see* Ancient Rome, dispute settlement
  compulsory judicial settlement, need for 99, 277
  Münster, Treaty of (1648) 230
  Paris Peace Treaties (1919/20), absence of provision 91–2
dominium 215, 219–21
D'Ors, A. 227
dowry, guarantee 28 n. 50: *see also* marriage
droit d'aubaine 252
droit de souveraineté: *see ius foederis*
dualism: *see also* law of nations (*ius gentium*/*Völkerrecht*), as independent system
  appetitus societatis and 219
  depersonalisation of state and 13–14, 43
  essence of man 216–17
  individual, development of 214–16
  intentions/actions 214, 215
    signa voluntaria 220–1
  legal personality and 214–15
  legal subject/legal order 215–16
  liability and 215
  respublica christiana and 190
  subsistens/*subsistentia* 214, 214 n. 37
Duby, G. 297 n. 10
Duchhardt, H. 46
Dülffer, J. 257
Duns Scotus, J. 200–2, 215
Durantis, G. 157
duration
  peace congresses 52–5: *see also* peace congresses
  peace treaty as perpetual settlement 37–8, 47, 49–50, 386
    Ottoman Empire and 50, 355, 356, 357
  truce 37–8
duress: *see* coercion, effect on treaty
dux 190 n. 15

Ebro, Treaty of (226–225 BC) 130–1
ecclesiastical courts: *see also* enforcement jurisdiction (pope)
  papal/non-papal courts distinguished 23–4
economic developments: *see also* trade
  19th-century international law and 271–2, 371–5
  FCN treaties: *see* FCN treaties
  globalisation 299–300
  inequalities 65
  multilateral framework, effect 378
  social and political developments and 298–9
  war and 65, 257, 262
economic warfare 367–8
Edinburgh University 264
Edmunds, S. E. 271
Egypt 63
Eighty Years War (Spain–Netherlands) 322
eirene 105 n. 7

INDEX 457

Eisenstein, E. L. 310 n. 29
Elbe Commission 93
Electors
 non-imperial titles, dependence of status on 336
 rights, princes distinguished 332
emperor
 alternative capacities 332
 limitations on power (Westphalia) 332–4
 role (Garatus) 191–2
Encyclopédie méthodique 244
Encyclopédie raisonné (L. de Jaucourt) 242–4
 necessary/voluntary treaties distinguished 243–4
 succession to treaty obligations, presumption in favour of 244
 unequal treaties 244, 252
enforcement jurisdiction (pope) 182–3
 Becket and 182–3
 discontinuance 27, 34
 excommunication and 150–1
 express provision for 23–4
 Garatus 156
 Novet ille (Innocent III) 150, 155–6
 oath as basis 24, 25, 26–7, 34, 150–1
 rejection by Protestant rulers 24, 26–7
Enlightenment 202, 203–4
entry into force, date of 82–3, 350
Enzensberger, H. M. 223
equality of religion, Westphalia Peace Treaties (1648) 9–10
equality of states 67, 252: *see also* 'civilised nations'; sovereignty; unequal treaties
 droit d'aubaine and 252
 Oppenheim on 273–4
 victor/defeated relationship 386, 395
essence of man 199–200, 202, 203: *see also* natural law
 essence of society and 207
 secularisation of concept 207–8
Etaples, Treaty of (1492)
 amicitia 41
 confirmation by oath 23

excommunication and 150–1
prisoners of war 41
private person, breach by 42
reprisal, right of 42
succession and 21
third parties, inclusion 34–5
trade provisions 41
Ethiopia
 as 'civilised nation' 69–70
 independent status 63
exceptio non adimpleti contractus 224
extradition
 commanders negotiating treaty without authority 132–4
 defectors (*transfugae*) 134 n. 89
 hostages 28–9
 war crimes and 284
 Wilhelm II 283, 284, 393–4

facultas: *see ius*
Falklands Conflict (1982) 379
FCN treaties
 17th to 18th-century developments
 standardisation 367
 total war concept and 367–8
 19th-century developments 64–5, 370–5
 war as professional matter and 370–1
 20th-century developments 375–81
 absence from peacemaking process 370, 378–9
 Asia and 95
 by party (including economic provisions in peace treaties)
 Algiers–Sardinia (1816) 373–4
 Algiers–Two Sicilies (1816) 373–4
 Algiers–United States (1815) 373–4
 Argentina–France (1840) 374
 Argentina–Spain (1823) 374
 Bulgaria–Turkey (1913) (Constantinople) 373
 Burma–Japan (1954) 377–8
 Chile–Peru (1814) 373
 Chile–Spain (1883) 372–3

FCN treaties (cont.)
  China–Japan (1895)
    (Shimonoseki) 372
  Colombia–Ecuador (1864) 373
  Colombia–Peru (1829) 374–5
  Denmark–Prussia (1814)
    (Berlin) 373
  Denmark–Spain (1814) (London)
    373
  Ecuador–Peru (1860) (Guayaquil)
    373–4
  Egypt–Israel (1979) 380
  El Salvador–Honduras (1980)
    377–8
  El Salvador–Nicaragua (1886)
    (Amapala) 372–3
  Ethiopia–Italy (1896) (Addis
    Ababa) 374–5
  France–Austria (1859) (Zurich)
    372–3
  France–China (1885) 373–4
  France–Germany (1871)
    (Frankfurt) 372, 373–4
  France–Great Britain (1713)
    (Utrecht) 369
  France–Great Britain (1786) 369
  France–Mexico (1839) (Vera
    Cruz) 374
  France–Netherlands (1678)
    (Nijmegen) 369
  France–Netherlands (1697)
    (Ryswick) 369
  France–Netherlands (1713)
    (Utrecht) 369
  France–Spain (1659) (Pyrenees)
    368
  France–Spain (1814) 373
  Germany (Versailles 1919) 375–6
  Great Britain–Netherlands (1674)
    368, 369
  Great Britain–Spain (1630)
    (Madrid) 368
  Great Britain–Spain (1713)
    (Utrecht) 369–70
  Great Britain–United States
    (1814/15) (Ghent) 369
  Great Britain–Venezuela (1903)
    372
  Greece–Turkey (1897)
    (Constantinople) 374–5
  Greece–Turkey (1903) 374–5
  India–Pakistan (1966) (Tashkent)
    380
  Israel–Jordan (1994) 380
  Italy–Turkey (1912) (Lausanne)
    372–3
  Italy–Venezuela (1861) 373
  Japan–Allied Powers (1951) 377
  Kiva–Russia (1873) (Gandemian)
    373–4
  Peru–Spain (1865) 374–5
  Peru–Spain (1879) (Paris) 374
  Poland–Japan (1957) 377–8
  Russia–Turkey (1829)
    (Adrianople) 373
  medieval practice 366
  Ottoman Empire 94–5,
    349–51: *see also* Ottoman
    Empire, capitulations
  as parallel agreement 53–4, 94, 350,
    355, 368–70
  inclusion of provisions within
    peace treaty as alternative
    373–4
  Paris Peace Treaties (1919/20) and
    95
  as peace treaties 70–1
  renewal/revision options 369–70
    agreement to agree 374–5, 377–8,
    380
    interim grant of MFN status 374
    Lausanne (1923) 376
    post-WWII treaties 376–7:
      Japan–Allied Powers (1951)
      377; Japan–USSR (1956) 377
    reconclusion/reactivation
      distinguished 372–3
    selective renewal 373
    Versailles (1919) 376
  termination by war 368, 371–5
    Institut de Droit international 371
    multilateral framework and 378
    treaty provision: ad hoc approach
      371–2; confirming abrogation
      372; renewal of treaty 372–3; *see
      also* renewal/revision options

INDEX 459

Feldman, G. 392 n. 30
Fénelon 245
Ferdinand III 330, 332
fetiales: see Ancient Rome,
    international law in, religion
    and
feudal law, general rules and principles
    11: *see also* canon law; *ius
    commune*; legal system; Roman
    law
feudalism as anachronism 305–6
final provisions 96
Finland, independence 90
Finland–Germany, Treaty of Alliance
    (7 March 1918) 90
fiscal problems as cause/result of war
    320
Fisch, J. 38–9, 47
Fischer, F. 392
Fischer, M. 294 n. 7
foedus/foedera: see Ancient Rome,
    treaties
forms of address: see Ottoman Empire,
    peace treaties
formula iuris antiqui 114, 115, 116, 128
    n. 75
forum internum: *see also* loyalty
    principle (*Reichstreue/fides/
    perfidia*)
    Ancient Rome 131–2
    legitimisation of control of 206–7
Foucault, M. 206–7
Fourth Lateran Council (1215)
    213–14
France
    attitude towards Empire 332 n. 37
    co-ratification 19–20, 47–8
    international law as academic
        discipline 264
    ius resistendi 334–5
    Ottoman Empire, relations with
        342–4: *see also* Ottoman
        Empire, capitulations
        French ambassador, precedence
            344, 348, 350
        as mediator 347, 354, 356
        right of war against Ottoman
        ratification procedure 78

Francis I 12, 31–2
Frankfurt, Treaty of (1871)
    amicitia clause, absence 81
    bilateral nature 382
    equitable nature 387–8, 395
    historical background 382
    military resources, absence of
        reference to 392
    object and purpose, omission 80
        n. 58
    personal amnesty 86
    ratification 78, 96 n. 129
    reparations 85, 391
    rights of inhabitants 91
    states as parties 75
    termination of treaties 372
    terms, overview 382
Frederick I (Barbarossa) 155–6
freedom of navigation 94
freedom of worship in the Ottoman
    Empire 346, 353
French Revolution 207–8
Fried, A. H. 264
friendship: *see amicitia*
Friendship, Commerce and Navigation
    treaties: see FCN treaties

Gaignières, Cabinet de 54
Gaius 205
ius gentium 225
Garatus
    assistance, obligation 195
    impossibility of performance 195
    *Tractatus de confederatione, pace et
    conventionibus principium* and
    Rubrica De principibus 155–7,
    184–97
    ambassadors 186 n. 5
    emperor, role 191–2
    Italian sources 187, 189–90, 196–7
    ius foederis 189–92
    negotiation and conclusion of
        treaties 193
    overlap with civil and canon law
        187
    pope, role 191–2
    principes, as main theme 187,
        190–1

Garatus (cont.)
  self-standing work 186–7
  sovereignty 187 n. 9
  structure 187–9
  as treatise on international law 185–6
Garner, J. 284
Gattinara, Mecurino Arborio di 31–2
Geneva Convention for the Amelioration of the Condition of the Sick and Wounded of Armies in the Field (1864) 263
German colonies, reallocation 90
German Confederation (*Deutsche Bund*): see also North German Confederation (*Norddeutscher Bund*)
  applicable law 92
  dissolution 72, 89
  establishment 74, 88, 92
  institutional arrangements 92
  unity as nation-state, aspirations to 60–1, 96–7
German Empire: see also Holy Roman Empire
  establishment (1870) 61, 76
  nationalist approach to international law 255
  overseas ambitions 65
Germany
  international law
    as academic discipline 264
    approaches to 254
    sovereignty as key element 268
  Permanent Court of Arbitration, opposition to 266
Gerson, J.
Ghent, Treaty of (1814), FCN Treaty and 369
gifts of honour 345, 346
Gilpin, R. 298 n. 12
globalisation: see economic developments; international relations
Gratian: see Decretum Gratiani
Great Britain: see also England
  international law
    as academic discipline 264–5
  Realpolitik and 265

Ottoman Empire, relations with 344–5, 349
  as mediator 347, 352–3, 354, 358
  Permanent Court of Arbitration, support for 265
Greece: see Ancient Greece
Gregory VII 175, 212–14
Gregory IX 153
Grewe, W. G. 46, 66–7, 151 n. 27, 222, 271
Grotius, H.
  appetitus societatis 199, 217–19
  continuity with predecessors 10–11, 403–4
  De iure belli ac pacis
    as diplomatic primer 54
    hostages 48
  ius, definition 217–19
  ius voluntarium 209, 229
  pacta sunt servanda 409
  Roman law and 160–1
  subjective rights (*facultas*) 200–2
  war as state 367
Guayaquil, Treaty of (1860) 373–4
guilt: see war, responsibility for; war crimes, responsibility for
Guines, Treaties of (1520), zusammengesetzte Vertragsschliessungsverfahren 22
gunpowder, impact 310–11

Habsburgs
  co-ratification 19–20
  Ottoman Empire, relations with 341–2, 345–6, 351, 354
Hague Conferences (1899/1907) 64, 265–8
  ius in bello as objective 255–6
  Russian support for 265
Hague Treaties (1899/1907) 71
Hague, Treaty of Alliance (1596), *respublica christiana* and 33
Halliday, F. 294 n. 7, 301 n. 17
Hanseatic League
  ius foederis 48, 55–6
  sovereignty and 48

head of state
  development of concept 75–6
  war crimes, responsibility for, Treaty of Versailles (1919) 86–7, 274, 375, 393–4, 400
Heffter, A. W. 259 n. 12, 267–8
Heinemeyer, W. 22
Henniges, H. 335–6
Henry II of England 177–81
Hermogenianus 225–6
historiography
  Constructivism and 300–7
  Cox, R. 302
  disentanglement of past and present 306–7
  International Relations Realism and 293–300
  Busan, B. 294 n. 7
  Fischer, M. 294 n. 7
  Gilpin, R. 298 n. 12
  Little, R. 294 n. 7
  Osiander, A. 294 n. 7
  Schroeder, P. W. 294 n. 7
  dichotomy 289, 290–300:
    jurisprudence as bridge 290;
    timeframe 290–3
  Mann, M. 297–9
  Wallerstein, I. 291–2, 298–9
Hobbes, T. 14, 203, 367
Holthöfer, E. 233–4
Holtzendorff, F. von 263, 266–7
Holy Alliance, treaties of
  16th-century 30–1
  19th-century 263
  emperor as leader 31–2
  League of Rome (1571) 30
  papal status 30–1
Holy Roman Empire: *see also* German Empire; Habsburgs; *respublica christiana*; Thirty Years War
  collapse of authority 14
  as composite monarchy 320–1
  constitutional-military organisation (Peace of Prague) 330–1
  constitutional-religious settlement (Treaties of Westphalia) 10

monarchia universalis 31–2
Ottoman Empire, relations with 343
  as *Reichs-Staat* 323–5
  sovereignty and 337
  as *sytema plurium civitatem* 336
Holzendorff, F. von 263
homme de bouche et de main 171
Hong Kong 95
hospitium publicum 115, 117–18, 120, 154
hostages as guarantee against breach of treaty 28–9, 48–9, 164
  Ottoman Empire 352
  property rights 193 n. 24
Hostiensis 151 n. 27, 227
Hoyos, D. 2 n. 82
Hubertusburg, Peace of (1763) 52
humanity, law of 284–5
Hungary: *see* Habsburgs

Iceland (*Grágás*) 152
imperialism (19th-century) 60, 97, 257–8
  avoidance of war 257
impium foedus 339
implementation: *see also* breach of treaty; dispute settlement; reprisal, right of
  bona fides and 194–5
  conflicting obligations
    under successive treaties 193
  enemy, obligations to 195
  financial security 28
  guarantees
    demilitarisation 91
    hostages as 28–9, 48–9, 164, 193 n. 24
    kiss of peace 162–82: *see also* kiss of peace
    occupation 85, 91
    pledge of goods and possessions 27–8, 160
    third-state 34, 55, 361
  impossibility of performance 135, 195
  mixed commission 49
  obligation

impossibility of performance
  Ancient Rome 135
  Garatus 195
India
  amicitia clause 83
  Europe, relations with 62–3
  'civilised nations' concept and
    68–9
  MFN treatment 94
individual: *see also* subjective rights
    (*facultas*); war crimes,
    responsibility for
  dualism and 214–16
  law of nations (*ius gentium/
    Völkerrecht*) and 42, 410–11
  human rights and 400, 410–11
  responsibility for war crimes and
    282–3, 284, 400
  secularisation of theological
    framework and 214–16
  in society (*appetitus societatis*)
    216–17
Indonesia, Europe, relations with 62–3
indutiae: *see* Ancient Rome, treaties;
    armistice/preliminary peace
    agreements
Innocent III 150, 155–6
Innocent IV 213
Institut de Droit international
    261–4
  objectives
    status as permanent dispute
      resolution committee 261–2
    *Revue de Droit international et de
      législation comparée* 262–3
    treaties, effect of war on 371
Institut International de la Paix 264
institutional arrangements established
  by treaty
    German Confederation (Congress of
      Vienna (1815)) 61
    Holy Roman Empire (Westphalia
      Peace Treaties (1648)) 92
    International Labour Organisation
      93
    League of Nations (Treaty of
      Versailles (1919)) 92–3:
      see also League of Nations

Universal Postal Union (1878) 93
  n. 115
Waterway Commissions 93
international humanitarian law, initial
  steps 263
International Labour Organisation 93
International Law Association,
  establishment 263–4
international relations: *see also*
  diplomacy; historiography;
  negotiations
  globalisation 59–62, 63–4, 76–7,
    97–8, 299–300
  division into 'civilised nations'
    and dependent regions 65
  economic developments and
    Europe, role 63–4, 76–7, 97–8
  Realism school 293–300, 301
International Telegraph Convention
  (1875) 93 n. 115
interpretation
  international law, applicability 245
  natural law as basis 251–2
  precise language
    good faith and 242, 246, 249–51
    move to post-Westphalia 49–50,
      54–5
invocatio dei 79
  preamble as substitute 79–80
Isidore of Seville 147, 210, 212
Italy
  amicitia and 36
  pacification and unity as treaty
    objective 29–30
  prisoners of war, treaty practice 41
  unification 76, 89
  unity as nation-state, aspirations to
    60–1, 88–9, 96–7
iuramentum pacis 152
ius
  as *aptitudo* 217–18
  as *facultas* 217–18
  debitum/creditum 218
  dominium 218, 219–21
  libertas 220
  potestas 218, 219–21
  ius/lex distinction 218
  as justice 217–18

ius ad bellum, vassals 16
ius bellum, sovereignty and 325–7
ius commune 11: *see also* canon law;
    feudal law; Roman law
    breakdown 42–3, 405–6, 409
    peace treaties and 155–7, 404–5
ius contrahendi 16: *see also ius foederis*
ius foederis
    Garatus 189–92
    Hanseatic League 48, 55–6
    ius legationis and 47
    ius resistendi and 335–6, 337
    Peace of Prague (1635) 327–31
    princes of Holy Roman Empire 47,
        325–7
    principes 190–1: *see also principes*
    Protestant estates 335–6
    respublic christiana, limitation to 189
    sovereignty and 47, 325–7
    sovereign on own behalf 17–22, 47
    suzerain/vassal 151–2, 190–1
    Edict distinguished 16–17
    sovereign's monopolisation of
        warfare and 43
    Westphalia Peace Treaties (1648)
        325–7, 331–6
ius gentium: *see also* Ancient Rome,
    international law; 'civilised
    nations'; *ius voluntarium*
    (voluntary law); law of nations
    (*ius gentium/Völkerrecht*)
    Decretum Gratiani 227
    development of concept 225–9
    Gaius 225
    Hermogenian 225–6
    Isidore of Seville 226–7
    as link between ancient and modern
        international law 223–4
    as natural law 205, 208–9, 212,
        223–4, 225: *see also* natural law,
        rationality of nature (*naturalis
        ratio*) and
    universality 225–9
ius legationis 47
ius publicum Europaeum 403, 406:
    see also respublica christiana
    Westphalia Peace Treaties (1648) and
        406–9

ius resistendi 16, 332–6
    France 334–5
ius foederis and 335–6, 337
ius voluntarium (voluntary law): *see
    also ius gentium*; law of nations
    (*ius gentium/Völkerrecht*),
    consent as basis; natural law
    appetitus societatis and 218–19
    Encyclopédie raisonné 243–4
    Grotius 209, 229
    history of 200–2
    ius gentium necessarium
        distinguished 229
    natural law and 219
    secularisation of theological
        framework and 202, 215–16
    subjective nature of rights (*facultas*)
        and 199–200, 209
iussum populi 132–4
Ivo of Chartres 200–2, 216 n. 40

Japan
    as 'civilised nation' 69–70, 76–7
    Europe, relations with 62
    as global power 64
    gunpowder and 310–11
Jassy, Peace of (1792) 358–9
Jaucourt, L. de: *see Encyclopédie
    raisonné* (L. de Jaucourt)
Jellinek, G. 267–8, 279 n. 67
Johannes Teutonicus 212
jurisprudence, as empirical study
    290
just war
    amnesty clauses and 39
    Ancient Greece 128 n. 74
    Ancient Rome 128
    breach of treaty and 27–8, 128
    incompatibility with political
        realities 39
    rebellion and 151
    replacement by total war concept 367
    UN Charter and 410
    Versailles, Treaty of (1919) 98, 375,
        410
    war against non-Christians as 227
    war as law-enforcement mechanism
        366–7, 410

justice as basis for peace 98–9
Justinian 148–9, 154, 156–7

Kahlenburg, Battle of (1683) 50
Kaiser Wilhem II: *see* Wilhelm II
Kant, I. 98–9, 252–3, 386
Karlowitz, Peace of (1699) 50
Kaser, M. 226
Kaufmann, E. 267–8, 383–4
Keene, E. 403
Keylor, W. R. 391 n. 27
kiss of peace 162–82: *see also* implementation; oath; ratification; signature
Aelred of Rievaulx 169–70
Alexander III 175
Ancient Rome 167–9
  manumission and 168
baptismal peace 168
Becket, Thomas 177–81
Bernard of Clairvaux 169
Byzantium 174
Christian practice 168–70
  peace, significance 168–9
confirmation of contract/gift 170–1
Ermold Le Noir 173–5
as fixed formula 166–7
as greeting 171–2
Gregory VII 175
Henry II of England 177–81
homme de bouche et de main 171
Louis the Pious 173–5
loyalty (*Reichstreue/fides/perfidia*) and 171
papal feet 175
Paul, St 168
peace-making process and 177–81
rank and 169
as ritual 176–7
Rollo the Viking 174–5
as sign of Christian unity 176–7
Sillé, Robert de 178–9, 181–2 n. 64
Song of Songs 169
William the Conqueror 170–1
women and 172–3
Klüber, J. H. 259–61
Kohler, J. 266–7

koine 124–5
Korea, printing and 310
Koskenniemi, M. 138, 254 n. 1, 261 n. 18, 264 n. 26
Kücük Kainarci, Treaty of (1774) 357–8
  duration 357
  succession 357

Lahore, Treaty of (1846) 83
language of treaty: *see* Ottoman Empire, peace treaties
Lasson, A. 267–8
Latin American states, as 'civilised nations' 69–70
Laudensis: *see* Garatus, M.
Laurentius 212
Lausanne, Treaty of (1912)
  renewal of FCN treaty 372–3
Lausanne, Treaty of (1923) 364
  renewal/revision of treaties and 376
Lauterpacht, H. 224
law of nations (*ius gentium/ Völkerrecht*): *see also* analogies with private law; canon law; 'civilised nations'; compulsory judicial settlement, need for; dispute settlement; *ius gentium*; natural law
as academic discipline
  France 264
  Great Britain 264–5
Ancient Rome: *see* Ancient Rome
as applicable law 25, 26–7
outside Europe 12–13
breakdown of mediaeval system 10–13, 34, 42–3, 199, 405–6
Grotius' response to 204
New World discoveries and 12–13
canon law as basis 26–7, 182–3
'civilised nations' and: *see* 'civilised nations'
codification: *see* codification
consent as basis 14, 198–9, 409: *see also ius voluntarium* (voluntary law); unequal treaties

League of Nations and 279–80:
    changes to Covenant and 280
natural law, relevance 212
war crimes and 284–6
continuity 3–4, 222–4
    between 16th- and
    17th/18th-century writers
    10–11, 403–4
dualism: *see* dualism
enforcement machinery, relevance
    107, 273
formative phases
    18th-century peace congresses
    53
    1815–1914 257–8: expansion of
    treaty-making 257–8
    peace movements (19th-century)
    261–5
    post-WWI innovations 86–7, 90,
    97, 271–2: *see also* League of
    Nations; Versailles, Treaty of
    (1919): loss of common
    cultural and moral standards
    271–2
German approaches to 254
as independent system: *see also*
    dualism
    19th-century developments
    appetitus societatis and 218–19
    dominance of canon law and
    26–7, 42–3, 404–5
    treaty as contract and 15–16, 17
individual and 42, 282–3, 410–11:
    see also private person
ius publicum Europaeum 53, 403,
    406
as law between sovereign states 43–4,
    222, 271–2
legislative authority, relevance
    273
materials, availability 184–6
    Russian language treatise on
    international law 260
methodology
    codification: *see* codification
    reconciliation of new with old
    286–7
nationalism and 255

non-European relations, impact 3,
    66–9, 403
obligation to enforce 32–3
positivism: *see* positivism
private international law
    distinguished 259
professionalisation 153–4, 233–4,
    258–61
public law, overlap 185–6, 190–1,
    255, 260
publicists, role 286–8, 313–14
Realpolitik and 265
reform, pre-Hague Conference
    attempts at 258–65
religious wars, effect 13
retroactivity and 284–6
secularisation 79
as universal law 97–8
voluntary nature: *see* consent as basis
    above; *ius voluntarium*
    (voluntary law)
law-making treaties 252–3
Lawrence, T. E. 399
League of Nations
    as civilising process 271
    collective security and 64, 399–400,
    410
    Council as executive 275–6
    Covenant, scope for development
    276
    dispute settlement provisions,
    ineffectiveness 277
    dissolution, possibility of 278
    Great Power domination 277–8
    membership
        'civilised nations' and 276–7, 278
        exclusion of defeated states 92–3,
        276–7, 395–6
        universality 64, 97, 276–7,
        278
    Oppenheim and 274–81
    as replacement for family of civilised
        nations 275–6
    sovereign powers 279
    sovereignty of states and 274
    transparency, need for 278
    unanimity rule 280
    war crimes and 277

legal personality
  dualism and 214–15
  monasteries and 215 n. 38
legal system: *see* canon law; feudal law;
  ius commune; law of nations
  (*ius gentium/Völkerrecht*);
  Reformation; Roman law,
  Ancient Rome
legitimacy, relevance 302–3
Leipzig Trials 284
Leo X, Pope 12 n. 8
Lepanto, Battle of, papal role 30
letters of mark/countermark: *see*
  reprisal, right of
Leyser, K. 181–2
liability: *see also* war crimes,
    responsibility for
  custodia 215
  dualism and 215
  subjective failure, change to
    215
Liberia
  as 'civilised nation' 69–70
  independent status 63
libertas 128 n. 74, 220
Lima, Treaty of (1883) (I) 372–3
Linguet, S. N. H. 252–3
Liszt, F. von 266–8
Little, R. 294 n. 7, 299–300
Livy 108–9, 114–17, 120–1, 122–3,
    129
Locke, J. 200–2, 203, 207–8
Lodi, Treaty of (1454)
  parties 17–18
  prisoners of war 41
  restitution of trade privileges 40–1
London, Treaty of (1471), duration 38
London, Treaty of (1478), duration 38
London, Treaty of (1514)
  princely word 24–5
  ratification by estates 19
  reprisal, right of 42
  third parties, inclusion 30–1
London, Treaty of (1518)
  papacy, obligation to defend 30–1
  papal peacemaking and 12 n. 8
  succession and 21
  third parties, inclusion 35

London, Treaty of (1604)
  amicitia 41
  prisoners of war 41
  private person, breach by 42
  reprisal, right of 42
  respublica christiana and 33
  third parties, inclusion 30–1
Louis XI 15–17
Louis the Pious 173–5
loyalty principle
  (*Reichstreue/fides/perfidia*)
  128–9, 131–2, 138 n. 102, 140,
  243, 326–7, 332: *see also bona
  fides*/good faith requirement;
  forum internum
kiss of peace and 171
Lübeck, Treaty of (1629), succession
  and 21
Luhman, N. 123–4
Lutatius, Treaty of (241 BC) 130–1
Luther, M. 200–2
Luxemburg, independence 61
Lyons, Treaty of (1601), *respublica
  christiana* and 33

Mably, G. B. de 5, 242, 243
  career 247 n. 23
  structure of *Le droit public de
    l'Europe* 247
Machiavelli, n. , diplomacy, impact on
    241–53
Madrid, Treaty of (1526)
  amnesty clauses 39
  confirmation by oath 23
  dowry, guarantee 28 n. 50
  parties 17–18
  ransom 28–9
  ratification/oath distinction 25–6,
    27
  registration 19
  reprisal, right of 42
  respublica christiana and 29
    emperor as head 31
  restitution of trade privileges
    40–1
  succession and 21
    ratification by heir apparent 21
  third parties, inclusion 30–1

trade provisions 41
  as treaty of Holy Alliance 30
Madrid, Treaty of (1630)
  amicitia 41
  confirmation by oath 23
  restitution of trade privileges 40–1
  succession and 21
Mameluke Empire, collapse (1517) 12 n. 8
man as social animal: *see appetitus societatis*
Mandates system 90
Mangoldt, H. von 281 n. 81
Mann, M. 297–9
marriage: *see also* dowry, guarantee
  institutionalisation 208, 215–16
Martens, G. F. von 260
Martens clause 285
Martinus Gosia 208 n. 18
Marx, K. 309–10
Masinissa 127
Maximilian of Bavaria 322–3, 330
Maximus, Valerius 109 n. 15
mediators, use of 52, 73, 347, 352–3, 354, 356, 358
memetics as basis of social and political change 308–9
military resources, limitation on
  Frankfurt, Treaty of (1871) 392
  Versailles, Treaty of (1919) 392–3
Moghul Empire, gunpowder and 310–11
Mommsen, T. 118–19, 223, 267–8
Mommsen, W. J. 396 n. 35
monarchia universalis 31–2
monasteries, legal personality 215 n. 38
Monroe doctrine 62
Montesquieu 207–8, 245–6, 252–3
morality
  law and 284–6
  natural law and 205, 208, 209
Morocco 63
Muldoon, J. 213–14
Münster, Treaty of (30 January 1648)
  prisoners of war 41
  private person, breach by 42
  uti possidetis 230–1, 237
Muslims: *see* Ottoman Empire

Nanking, Treaty of Peace (1842)
  amicitia clause 83
  cession of Hong Kong 95
  reparations 85
  trading arrangements 95
Naples, Treaty of (1470)
  papacy, obligation to defend 30–1
  third parties, inclusion 34–5
nation-state: *see also*
  self-determination, right to;
  sovereignty; state; territorial settlement
  Balkans 89–90, 96–7
  German aspirations 96–7
  Grotius
  Italian aspirations 96–7
  universitas fidelium and 206–7
nationalism, international law and 255, 262
nationals, jurisdiction in respect of war crimes
  1870 Franco-German War and 281–2
  Peace Treaties (1919) and 274
natural law: *see also* essence of man; *ius voluntarium* (voluntary law); *iussum populi*
  Ancient Rome 204–5
  'civilised nations' and 67
  decline in role (19th-century) 259
  fundamental nature of 242
  God as lawgiver 205–6
  interpretation and 251–2
  ius gentium and 205, 212, 225
    moral/amoral concepts and 208–9
  ius voluntarium (voluntary law) and 219
  ius/fas distinction
  law prior to foundation of society/law before original sin distinguished 210–12
  as moral concept 205, 208, 213–14
  moral/amoral concepts, tension 208–9
  natural/divine law, interrelationship 210–15
  pacta sunt servanda 198, 409

natural law (cont.)
  as part of Enlightenment context
    203–4
  rationality of nature (naturalis ratio)
    and 205, 208, 225–9, 249–51
  structured society and 207–8
naturalism 203
navigation: see FCN treaties
negotiations: see also kiss of peace;
    mediators, use of; oath
  agency law compared 133, 140
  by plenipotentiaries 22, 73,
    78–9
  authority to commit head of state
    79, 157, 158
  customary international law 133
  designation in preamble 81
  full powers 157
  margin for negotiation 78–9
  verification of powers 81
  Vienna Convention on the Law of
    Treaties (1969) 133
congress: see peace congresses
exchange of signed texts by parties
    (unmittelbare
    Vertragsschliessungsverfahren)
    22
Frankfurt, Treaty of (1871) 387–8
full powers/negotiation/ratification
    (zusammengesetzte
    Vertragsschliessungsverfahren)
    22
Garatus 193
imposition of terms (Versailles
    (1919)) 77
materials relating to
  availability 54
  critical texts, need for 57–8
  value for understanding context 5,
    313–15
  professionalisation 51–2
  transparency, need for 241–2
  League of Nations 278
  Mably 248–51
  rhetorical wrapping, importance
    314–15
neighbourliness: see FCN treaties
Neitmann, K. 19 n. 27

Netherlands
  Ottoman Empire, relations with
    344–5, 349
  as mediator 347, 352–3, 354, 358
Netherlands, United Kingdom of the,
  break-up 61, 88–9
neutrality, rights 368
New World discoveries, legal system,
  effect on 12–13, 405–6
Nijmegen, Congress of (1676-78/9)
    52–3
  materials relating to, availability 54
Nijmegen, Peace of (1678)
  parallel treaties 369
  ratification/oath distinction 27
Nikolsburg, Treaty of (1866)
  preliminary peace treaty 71–2
  reparations 85
Nomos der Erde 87
Nördlingen, Battle of (1634) 329
Nörr, D. 223, 226
North German Confederation
  (Norddeutscher Bund): see also
    German Confederation
    (Deutsche Bund)
  establishment and dissolution
    89
Noyon, Treaty of (1516)
  confirmation by oath 23
  dowry, guarantee 28 n. 50
  ratification/oath distinction 25
  third-state guarantees 34
Numidia 127
Nussbaum, A. 222, 257

oath 164: see also implementation; kiss
    of peace; ratification
  in Ancient Rome 110–11, 120–1
  as basis of papal enforcement
    jurisdiction 24, 25, 26–7, 34,
    150–1
  discontinuance of practice 24, 26–7,
    42–3, 48, 96
  early Middle Ages 148–9
  late Middle Ages 149–50
  Muslim practice 338–9: see also
    Ottoman Empire, peace
    treaties, oath

as principal element of ratification process 22–3
ratification documents and 22–3, 25–7, 149
zusammengesetzte Vertragsschliesungsverfahren process and 23
occupation as guarantee 85, 91
Versailles, Treaty of (1919) 393
Oceana iuris, uti possidetis 233
Ockham, William of 200–2
Oder Commission 93
Olivi, J. P. 200–2, 219–21
openness: *see* negotiations, transparency, need for
Oppenheim, L.
  career 272
  WWI difficulties 283–4
  common cultural and moral standards, relevance 273
  compulsory judicial settlement, need for 99, 277
  equality of states 273–4
  existence of international law 273
  individual in international law 284
  law and morality 284–6
  League of Nations 274–81
    consent as basis of international law and: revisions to Covenant 280
    Council of Conciliation, need for 277
    Council as executive 275–6
    Covenant, scope for development 276
    dispute settlement provisions, ineffectiveness 277
    dissolution, possibility of 278
    Great Power domination 277–8
    membership 276–7, 278
    sovereign powers 279
    unanimity rule 280
    war crimes and 277
  legislative authority, relevance 273
  nullum crimen nulla poena sine lege 284–6

  Permanent Court of Arbitration 275
  Permanent International Court of Justice 275
  reconciliation of new with old 286–7
  sovereignty 273–4, 279
    divisibility 281
  success of *International Law* 272–3
  war crimes 281–6
oral agreements in modern treaty practice 163 n. 5
original sin 210–12
osculum: *see* kiss of peace
Osiander, A. 294 n. 7
Osnabrück, Treaty of (1648)
  hybrid character 10
  ius foederis 325 n. 15
  pledge of goods and possessions 160 n. 83
  reparations 85
  restitution 236–7
  third parties, inclusion 30–1
Ottoman Empire
  ambassadors, precedence 344, 348, 350
  amnesty clauses 356
  Arabs in Africa, dependence on 63
  Byzantium, as successor to 341
  capitulations
    continuation of system (18th-century) 349–50
    England (1583) 344–5
    England (1675) 344–5, 349, 359–60
    France (1535) 342
    France (20 May 1604) 343–4
    France (1673) 347–8
    France (1740) 349–50
    Netherlands (1680) 349
    Spain (1782) 351
    Venice (20 October 1540) 345
    Venice (24 June 1567) 345
  as 'civilised nation' 69–70, 76
  England, relations with 344–5, 347
  FCN treaties 94–5, 349–51

Ottoman Empire (cont.)
  France, relations with: see France,
    Ottoman Empire, relations with
  gunpowder and 310–11
  Habsburgs/Hungary, absence of
    treaty relations
    16th-century 345
    Middle Ages 341–2
  history 338
    break-up 61, 89–90
  Holy Rome Empire, relations with
    343
  Muslim perception of war and 338–9
  Netherlands, relations with 344–5,
    347
  peace treaties: see also capitulations
    above; truce below
    duration 50, 355, 356, 357
    equality of parties 340, 343
    as FCN treaties 349–51
    forms of address 340, 342, 343–4,
      345, 349–50, 351, 353, 354, 356,
      357–9
    freedom of worship 346, 353
    gifts of honour 345, 346
    Great Britain (1809)
      (Dardenelles) 359–60
    Habsburgs/Hungary (1615 et seq.)
      346
    hostages as guarantee against
      breach of treaty 352
    impium foedus 339
    language of treaty: Greek 340–1,
      342; Russian and Italian 358;
      Turkish 350–1; Turkish and
      French 358; Turkish with
      French translation 342–3;
      Turkish and Italian 350, 352,
      358; Turkish and Latin 353,
      355, 356
    Lausanne, Treaty of (1923) 364
    long-term truce as stepping-stone
      50, 338–9
    mediation, use of 347, 352–3, 354,
      356, 358
    Muslim attitude towards 338–9
    oath: examples (15th-century)
      340–1, 342, 344; examples

      (17th-century) 347–9; as
      general practice 338–9;
      invocation of God 338–9, 343;
      non-believer and 338–9; Quran
      and 338–9
    prisoners of war, release 352
    ratification, entry into force and
      350
    ratification, relevance 342
    reiteration of previous
      undertakings 340–1, 344
    San Stefano (1878) 89–90, 362–3
    Sèvres, Treaty of (1919)
      363–4
    succession 346, 350, 357
    as unilateral document 342–3,
      344–5
    uti possidetis 355
  printing and 310 n. 30
  truce
    Habsburgs/Hungary (1547) 345
    Habsburgs/Hungary (1562
      et seq.) 345
    Peace of Karlowitz (1699), 353
    as stepping stone to permanent
      peace treaties 50, 338–9
Ovid 109 n. 15
Oxford University, establishment of
  Chichele Chair 264

pacta sunt servanda
  appetitus societatis and 218–19
  as fundamental principle 198–9
  natural law 198, 409
  as obligation to peoples 245
  as obligation to society 243
  principes, obligation of compliance
    243–7
  private law analogy 224, 243
  reason of state and 243
  as religious concept 202
  subjective rights (*facultas*) and
    199
papal bull of 6 March 1517 (general
  truce between Christian
  Powers) 12 n. 8
Paris, Peace of (1515), third-state
  guarantees 34

INDEX 471

Paris, Peace of (1763) 52
Paris, Peace of (1783) 52
  FCN Treaty (1786) and 369
Paris, Peace of (1814)
  amicitia clause 82
  institutional arrangements 92
  object and purpose 80
  parallel treaties 73–4
  preliminary peace treaty 72–3
  rights of inhabitants 91
  territorial settlement 88
Paris, Peace of (1815)
  extension of MFN treatment
    to India 94
  reparations 85
  territorial settlement 88
Paris, Peace of (1856)
  amicitia clause 82
  freedom of navigation 94
  territorial settlements 89–90
  third parties, inclusion 74
Paris Peace Agreement (1973)
  (Vietnam) 378–9
Paris Peace Treaties (1919/20): *see also*
    Saint-Germain, Treaty of
    (1919); Sèvres, Treaty of (1919);
    Trianon, Treaty of (1919);
    Versailles, Treaty of (1919)
  amicitia clause, absence 81, 83
  designation of parties 75
  as fundamental turning point
    399–403
  institutional arrangements 92–3
  nationals, jurisdiction over 274
  parallel treaties 73–4
  renewal/revision of treaties 376
  renunciation of war and 64
  sovereignty 399–403
  territorial settlements 90
Paris, Treaty of (1325)
  bona fides 158–9
  pledge of goods and possessions
    160
  plenipotentiary powers 158
  succession and 160 n. 82
Paris, Treaty of (1515)
  ratification/oath distinction 25
  respublica christiana and 29, 33

Paris, Treaty of (1802) 359
Paris, Treaty of (1815), reparations,
    occupation as guarantee 91
Paris, Treaty of (1856) 361–2
Paris, Treaty of (1856) (II) 361–2
Paris, Treaty of (1857), *amicitia* clause
    83
Paris, Treaty of (1879) 374
Parker, G. 310–11
parties: *see ius foederis*; Ottoman
    Empire, peace treaties; third
    parties, inclusion
Passarowitz, Peace of (1718) 354–5
  parallel treaties 354–5
  uti possidetis 235–6, 355
Paulus 205
Pauw, A. 233–4
pax: *see* Ancient Rome, *pax*
pax Claudina (321 BC?) 134
peace clause: *see amicitia*
peace congresses: *see also individual*
    congresses
  discontinuance 97
  duration 52–5, 355
    global dimension, effect 53–4
    inchoate state of international law
      and 53
    logistical and tactical
      considerations 52–3
    termination, reasons for 54–5
  as negotiating medium 51–2, 76
  participation of non-European states
    76–7
peace movements
  19th-century 261–5
    Bureau International de la Paix
      264
    Institut International de la Paix
      264
  early 20th-century 255–6
    Hague Conferences (1899/1907)
      and 255–6
    Institut de Droit international 261–4
    international law and 261–5
Penn, W. 261
Pereira, J. de S. 213–14
perjury: *see* loyalty principle
    (*fides/perfidia*)

Permanent Court of Arbitration: *see also* arbitration
British support for 265
establishment 265–8
German opposition to 266
Oppenheim, L. 275
Permanent Court of International Justice, Oppenheim, L. 275
permanent peace treaties: *see* duration
Péronne, Treaty of (1199) 151, 158–9
Péronne, Treaty of (1468)
amnesty clauses 39
parties 15–17
ratification by estates 19
perpetual peace treaties: *see* duration
Persia
as 'civilised nation' 69–70, 76–7
Europe, relations with 62
Perusinus, R. 152–3
Petzold, K.-E. 128 n. 74
Philinus, Treaty of (306 BC) 129–30
piracy in Ancient Rome 117 n. 39
Pirna, Treaty of (1634) 329
alliances, prohibition 329
Poggi, G. 311 n. 33
Poland
Ottoman Empire, relations with
16th/17th-century 346–7, 352
18th-century 355
partition of 88
territory, acquisition 90
eastern territories 90
Polybius 109 n. 15, 128, 131 n. 74
Pomponius 115, 117–18
pope: *see also* enforcement jurisdiction (pope)
absolutism 213–14
as European leader 11
as head of Holy Alliance 30–1
obligation to defend 30–1
powers (Garatus) 191 n. 19
spiritual authority 11–12, 14, 23–4
loss of 33–4, 42–3, 46–7
Reformation and 12
as supreme authority 191–2
populus 190
Porretanus, G. 214 n. 37

Portsmouth, Treaty of (1905), territorial settlement 90–1
positivism
effect on historical interpretation 105–6, 107, 117 n. 38
as expression of balance of power 251–2
ius gentium, development of concept and 228
law, definition 107
secularisation of theological framework and 214
postliminium in pace 105, 115, 117–18
potestas
as *facultas* 218
sovereignty and 205–6
Prague, Peace of (1635)
amnesty clauses 39
ius foederis 327–32
organisation of war and 329–31
reparations 85
Prague, Treaty of (1866)
parties 75
personal amnesty 86
territorial settlements 89
preamble
attribution of blame (Paris Peace Treaties (1919/20)) 80
common intent, need for statement of 80–1
constitution of treaty as charter 81
intitulatio 79–80
object and purpose (*arenga*) 80
plenipotentiaries, designation 81
renewal of articles in previous treaties 242
as substitute for *invocatio dei* 79–80
preservation of rights
armistice/truce 37
Crépy, Treaty of (1544) 232–3
Preiser, W. 111, 222–3
princely word 24–5
principes
sovereignty (*superiore non recognoscentes*) 14, 17–19, 47, 190, 191, 192
emergence/precursor to sovereign state 39

obligation to enforce *ius gentium* 32–3
   as part of greater whole 13, 33–4, 46–7, 190–1
   totus orbis 32–3
treaty obligations, duty of compliance 193–4, 243–7
treaty partners
   adhaerentes/sequaces 190
   civitates (cities/city-states) 190
   populus 190
   vassals 190–1
printing, impact 310
prisoners of war: *see also postliminium in pace*
   personal rights of captors 41
   release clauses 41, 96
   Ancient Rome 154
   Italian treaty practice 41
   Ottoman Empire 352
private international law, public international law distinguished 259
private person
   breach of treaty 42
   public interest and 193
   reprisal, right of 42
privateers, démarches concerning 351
Protestant estates
   ius foederis 335–6
   right of cooperation
   Peace of Prague (1635) 329
   Treaty of Pirna 329
Prussia
   Ottoman Empire, relations with 350–1
   as mediator 358
   sovereignty, loss of 61
public law, international law and 255, 260
public opinion, war, attitudes towards 66
publica conventio: *see* Ancient Rome, treaties
Pufendorf, S. 68, 200–2
Punic Wars, war guilt and 130–1

punica fides: *see* loyalty principle (*Reichstreue/fides/perfidia*)
Pyrenees, Treaty of the (1659) 27

Quidde, L. 264

railways 94–5
ransom 28–9, 43
ratification: *see also* co-ratification; kiss of peace; oath; signature
   by successor 21
   commander's agreement (Ancient Rome) 132–4
   entry into force and 82–3, 350
   evolution of modern system 19–20, 27, 78–9, 96
   as matter for national constitutions 78, 96
   need for 78–9
   Ottoman Empire, treaties with 342
   pledge of goods and possessions 27–8, 160
   ratification documents, status 22–3, 25–7
   as secular law guarantee 27
   time required 49
real treaties: *see* succession to treaty obligations
rebellion, responsibility for war and 40
Rebuffus, P. 233
rebus sic stantibus 194–5, 224
recuperatio 116, 126 n. 68
Reformation
   canon law, effect on 12, 15, 24, 42–3
   legal system and 12, 42–3
   papal enforcement jurisdiction and 24, 26–7
respublica christiana and 33–4
rei vindicatio 230–1
Reichstreue: *see* loyalty principle (*Reichstreue/fides/perfidia*)
religion: *see* Ancient Rome, international law in, religion and; enforcement jurisdiction (pope); freedom of worship in the Ottoman Empire; natural law; pope
religious neutrality, Westphalia Peace Treaties (1648) 9–10

religious wars in Europe
 cessation 10, 408
 diplomacy/international law, effect
  on 13
renunciation of war: *see* Hague
  Conferences (1899/1907);
  Kellogg–Briand Pact (1928);
  League of Nations
reparations
 calculation 86
 costs and damages of war 40, 86,
  358
 as indemnity 85
 recuperatio 116, 126 n. 68
 rerum repetitio 114, 115, 116, 116
  n. 34, 128 n. 75
 for damages inflicted on civilian
  population 86
 Frankfurt, Treaty of (1871) 85, 391
 gifts of honour 345, 346
 guilt and 85–6, 391–2, 395
 occupation as guarantee 85, 91
 renunciation (Brest-Litovsk II) 86
 Versailles, Treaty of (1919) 391–2,
  395, 400
reprisal, right of
 for breach of treaty 28
 letters of mark/countermark 42
 for manifest denial of justice 42
 private person and 42
 sovereign's monopolisation of
  warfare and 42, 43
rerum repetitio 114, 115, 116 n. 34, 128
  n. 75
resistance theory: *see ius resistendi*
respublica christiana: *see also* Church;
  Holy Roman Empire; *ius
  commune*; pope
 16th-century attempts to revive
  10–13
 definition 11
 ius foederis, limitation to 189
 as juridical unity 11, 13, 14, 42–3,
  190–1, 212–13
 monarchia universalis 31–2
 obligation to maintain peace of 33–4
 obligation to uphold *ius gentium* and
  32–3

Reformation and 33–4, 405–6
 treaty references to 29–34
 Westphalia Peace Treaties (1648) and
  46–7
restitutio in integrum 236–7
restitution: *see also* reparations
 archives, documents and objets d'art
  96
 optional inclusion in treaty 157
 Osnabrück, Treaty of (1648) 236–7
 of private property occupied, looted
  or confiscated during war 40
 as Roman law remedy of *restitutio in
  integrum* 236–7
 of trade privileges 40–1, 94, 366–7,
  369–70
 see also FCN treaties,
  renewal/revision options
*Revue de Droit International et de
 Législation Comparée* 262–3
 nationalism and 262
Reynolds, S. 305–6, 307
Rheinbund 331
Rhine Commission 93
rights of inhabitants following
 territorial change 91
ritual, significance 164–7: *see also* kiss
 of peace
 definition 164–5
Rolin-Jacquemyns, G. 262
Rollo the Viking 174–5
Roman law: *see also* Ancient Rome
 as basis of international relations 11,
  409
 medieval peace treaties and 154–5,
  158–61
 natural law inheritance 204–9
 restitutio in integrum 236–7
 uti possidetis 230
Rome, League of (1571), papal role 30
Rome, Treaty of (1495), hostages as
 guarantee 28
Rome–Persia Treaty of Peace (562 AD),
 oath 148
Rousseau, J.-J. 207–8, 252–3
Rousset de Missy, J. 54
Roxburgh, R., *Oppenheim* 273,
 283–4

Rufinus of Bologna 172 n. 41, 211–12, 216 n. 40
Ruhr, occupation by France (1923) 393
rule of law
 amicitia and 36, 41
 trade and 41
Rüssbüldt, O. 264
Russia
 Ottoman Empire, relations with 353–4, 355–9, 360–3
 as protector
  Moldavia and Valachia 357
  Orthodox Christians 357
 support for Hague Conferences (1899/1907) 265
Russian Empire, break-up 61–2, 90
Russian language treatises on international law 260
Ryswick, Congress of (1697) 52–3
 materials relating to, availability 54
 parallel treaties 369

Sablé, Treaty of (1488)
 parties 16–17
 ratification by estates 19
 war, responsibility for 40
sacer 110–11
Sahr, status post-WWI 393
Saigon, Treaty of (1862), trading arrangements 95
St Petersburg, Declaration of (1868) 370–1
Saint-Germain, Treaty of (1919)
 renewal/revision of treaties 376
 territorial settlement 90
San Stefano, Treaty of (1878) 362–3
 territorial settlements 89–90
Sandornak, Treaty of (1879) 83
savium: see kiss of peace
Scheuner, U. 254–5, 268–9
Schleswig 90
Schmidt, G. 326–7
Schorn-Schütte, L. 304
Schreiner, K. 166 n. 17, 169 n. 26, 170–1, 180, 181

Schroeder, P. W. 294 n. 7
Schücking, W. 254–5, 266–8
secular law, subordinate position 212 n. 33
secularisation of theological framework
 essence of man and 207–8
 individual, development of 214–16
 ius voluntarium (voluntary law) and 215–16
 positivism and 214
security and tranquillity of Europe as treaty objective 57
self-determination, right to
 post-WWI 90, 97, 385–6
 territorial settlement under Treaty of Versailles (1919) 390–1, 402
Senlis, Treaty of (1493)
 amnesty clauses 39
 private person, breach by 42
 ratification by estates 19
 ratification/oath distinction 25–6
 registration 19
 restitution of private property 40
 third parties, inclusion 30–1
 zusammengesetzte Vertragsschliessungsverfahren 22
Sèvres, Treaty of (1919), as unequal treaty 363–4
Shimonoseki, Treaty of (1895)
 termination of treaties 372
 territorial settlement 90–1
Siam
 as 'civilised nation' 69–70, 76–7
 Europe, relations with 62
signa voluntaria 220–1
signature, significance 17–19, 22, 47–8, 71, 74 n. 35, 81, 163–4
Sillé, Robert de 178–9, 179 n. 64, 181–2
Simoda, Treaty of (1855), amicitia clause 83
Sistova, Peace of (1791) 358
social studies: see historiography, social studies and
societas 120
society: see appetitus societatis
Soleuvre, Treaty of (1475), duration 38
Soll, J. E. 328

sovereignty
  as abstract quality 273–4
  Americas 62
  China 62–3
  divisibility 281
  external 14, 406
  head of state as representative of 75–6
  Garatus 187 n. 9
  German states 60–1, 92
  as guarantee of order and legality 275, 279
  Hanseatic League 48
  internal 13–14
  international law and 43–4, 222, 268, 271–2, 400–1
  ius bellum and 325–7
  ius foederis and 17–22, 47, 325–7
  limitations on
    League of Nations 274–81
    post-WWI 271–2
    Oppenheim on 273–4
    Paris Peace Treaties (1919/20) and 399–403
  potestas and 205–6
  princes of Holy Roman Empire 325–7
  principes 190–1
  superiore non recognoscente 14, 190, 192
  Westphalia Peace Treaties (1648) and 9–10, 43–4, 337, 408–9
Soviet Union, legitimacy and 303
Spain: *see also* Habsburgs
  co-ratification 47–8
  Ottoman Empire, relations with 351
Spanish Empire
  17th-century provincial rebellions 320
  independence 62
  Spanish Netherlands, Eighty Years War 322
Spanish Succession, War of (1700–13) 336
Spinoza, B. 203, 218–19
sponsio: *see* Ancient Rome, treaties

Stadion, J. C. von (Grand Master of the Teutonic Order)
state: *see also* nation-state; sovereignty
  Ancient Rome 112 n. 23
  depersonalisation 13–14, 49, 75–6
  emergence of concept 13–14, 313–14
  monarch as external representative 75–6
  as shifting concept 302
  as unique subject of international law 13–14
status quo ante, restitution: *see also uti possidetis*
  Ancient Rome 127
  Sistova, Peace of (1791) 358
  Westphalia Peace Treaties (1648) 326–7
Steiger, H. 25–7, 35–6, 37
Stengel, K. von 266
Stevenson, D. 396 n. 35
Stoicism 225, 227, 229
Streseman, G. (German Foreign Minister) 396 n. 36
structure/event dichotomy 106–7, 140–1: *see also* treaty structure
Suarez, F. 10–11, 209, 219–21
subjective rights (*facultas*):
  see also individual
  appetitus societatis and 217–19
  development of concept 199
  dominium 215, 219–21
  pacta sunt servanda and 199
  voluntarism and 199–202
succession to treaty obligations 20–2, 43, 47, 160 n. 82, 245–46
  Ottoman Empire 346, 350, 357
  presumption in favour of (Jaucourt) 244
superior orders 282
Susa, Treaty of (1601), amnesty clauses 39
Suttner, B. 264

Tabula de Alcántara 103
Tashkent Declaration (1966) 380

technology, impact 310–11
termination of treaties: see breach of
  treaty; FCN treaties,
  termination by war
territorial settlement 87–91
  Frankfurt, Treaty of (1871) 387–8
  Nomos der Erde 87
  Paris Treaties (1919/20) 90, 97
  rights of inhabitants, provision for
    91
  self-determination and 90, 97, 385–6
  Versailles, Treaty of (1919) 90, 390–1
  Vienna, Congress of (1815) and 87–8
Teschen, Peace of (1779) 52
third parties, inclusion 34–7, 55–6: see
    also adhaerentes/sequaces
  as accession 35, 55–6
  as acknowledgment of new
    relationships between parties
    35, 74
  as affirmation of amicitia 36–7,
    55–6: see also amicitia
  confirmation by third party, need for
    34–5, 55–6
  as instrument of peace 35–6
  as reassurance to third party 35, 55–6
  Treaty of Paris (1856) 361
Thirty Years War
  as civil war 320–1
  fiscal problems caused by 320
  as state-building process 321
Tierney, B. 217, 220 n. 41
Tilly, C. 311 n. 33
totus orbis 32–3
trade
  Asia 95
  as contribution to peace 93
  non-discrimination 41
  overseas possessions and 94
  restitution of privileges 40–1,
    94
  rule of law and 41
transparency, need for: see
  negotiations, transparency,
  need for
treaty as charter 81
treaty objectives: see also amicitia;
  preamble

pacification and unity of Italy
    29–30
peace 123, 140–1
political control 113–14, 118–19,
    137–8: see also unequal treaties
prevention of war 124–5
reconciliation of interests 113–14
security and tranquillity of Europe
    57
treaty parties: see ius foederis; third
  parties, inclusion; treaty
  practice, personal nature of
  obligation
treaty practice: see also co-ratification;
  duration; implementation;
  interpretation; ius foederis; kiss
  of peace; negotiations; oath;
  ratification; signature
applicable law: see treaty as private
  law contract; enforcement
  jurisdiction (pope); law of
  nations (ius
  gentium/Völkerrecht)
authenticated copies 81
breach of treaty: see breach of treaty;
  enforcement jurisdiction
  (pope)
canon law of contract and 194 n. 32
chivalry and 28–9
dissimilarities pre-1648 15
enforcement jurisdiction: see
  enforcement jurisdiction
  (pope)
evolution in response to changes in
  social, economic and political
  attitudes 96–9
extra-European issues 53–4
full powers/negotiation/ratification
  (zusammengesetzte
  Vertragsschliessungsverfahren),
  confirmation by oath,
  stipulation for 23
identification of rules on limited
  evidence 106–7
internal/international practice,
  distinction 15–16, 20
oral agreements in modern practice
  163 n. 5

treaty practice (*cont.*)
  personal nature of obligations
    17–19, 28, 75–6
  princely word 24–5
  respublica christiana and 29–34:
    see also *respublica christiana*
  Roman law and 154–5, 158–61: *see
    also* Ancient Rome, treaties
  succession: *see* succession to treaty
    obligations
  treaty as political act 116–17,
    127–8
  treaty as private law contract 17, 21, 26,
    27, 224
  treaty structure 70–1: *see also amicitia*;
    final provisions; Ottoman
    Empire, peace treaties;
    preamble
  continuity of practice 404
  invocatio dei 79
  non-civilised nations and 71
  parallel treaties 73–4, 354–5,
    361
    FCN treaties 53–4, 94, 350, 355,
      368–70
  reiteration of previous undertakings
    252, 340–1, 344
treuga: *see* armistice/preliminary peace
  agreements
Trianon, Treaty of (1919), territorial
  settlement 90
Triepel, H. 267–8, 279 n. 67
Tripoli 63
truce 152–3
  duration 37–8, 153
  treugae/induciae distinguished
    154–5
  obligation to observe 195
  Ottoman Empire and 338–9,
    345
  preservation of parties' rights and
    claims 37
Truyol y Serra, A. 222
Tunisia 63
Turkey: *see* Ottoman Empire
Two Sicilies, Ottoman Empire,
  relations with 350
tyrannus 191

Ukraine, independence 90
Ullmann, W. 205–6
Ulpian 122 n. 54, 205, 208
unequal treaties: *see also* Ottoman
  Empire, peace treaties;
  Versailles, Treaty of (1919), as
  unequal treaty
  Ancient Rome 113–16, 154, 246
  Asia 67–8
  capitulations: *see* Ottoman Empire,
    capitulations
  China 62–3
  Encyclopédie raisonné 244, 252
  Paris Peace Treaties (1919/20) 77,
    80–1, 86–7, 92–3, 95, 98,
    375
  Treaty of Sèvres (1919) 363–4
unilateral acts
  Edicts 16–17
  Ottoman Empire 342–3, 344–5
United Kingdom: *see* Great Britain
United Nations Charter (1945)
  just war and 410
  war, legality 410
    as enforcement mechanism 410
United States of America
  Declaration of Independence (1776)
    62
  as global power 62, 63–4
  Monroe doctrine 62
  war crimes, responsibility for 283,
    284–6
  WWI peace conference,
    participation 76–7
Universal Postal Union (1878) 93
  n. 115
uti possidetis 127: *see also* preservation
  of rights; *status quo ante*,
  restitution
  arbitration, as prelude to 230, 232,
    233, 235–6
  Breda, Treaty of (1667) 234–5
  as conservatory measure 230
  decolonisation and 230
  Oceana iuris 233
  Passarowitz, Peace of (1718) 235–6,
    355
  Rebuffus, P. 233

rei vindicatio and 230–1
Roman law 230, 231–2
  re-emergence in 17th century 237
  Westphalia Peace Treaties (1648) 229–36, 237
Utrecht, Treaties of (1713)
  co-ratification 48
  materials relating to, availability
  mixed commissions 49
  negotiations 52
  parallel treaties 369–70
  ratification 49 n. 13
  third-state guarantees 55

validity, unfair or pernicious treaty 246–7
validity of treaty
  coercion and 194
  unfair or pernicious treaty 246–7
Vasquez, F. 200–2, 209
Vasvár, Treaty of (1664) 351
Vattel, E.
  good faith/perfidy 243, 246, 252–3
  pacta sunt servanda 243
  validity of treaty 246–7
Venice, Treaty of (1454)
  financial security against breach 28
  pacification and unity of Italy as objective 29–30
  third parties, inclusion 34–5
Venice, Treaty of Peace (1177) 151
Versailles, Treaty of (1871)
  preliminary peace treaty 71–2
  reparations 85–6
Versailles, Treaty of (1919)
  attribution of blame 80, 270–1, 375
  authenticated copies 81
  economic relations 375–6
  head of state responsibility for war crimes 270–1, 393–4, 400
  historical background 382–3
  just-war concept and 98, 375, 410
  as new law 86–7, 271–2, 284–6, 393–4, 395
  occupation as guarantee against renewal of war 91
  ratification 82–3, 96 n. 129
  reparations 391–2, 400

rights of inhabitants 91
territorial settlement 90, 390–1
  self-determination and 390–1, 402
as unequal treaty 80–1, 86–7, 92–3, 98, 375, 410
  common intent, absence 80–1
  exclusion from international community 395–6
  military resources, limitation on 392–3
  negotiating procedure 77, 388:
    alleged failure to respect previously agreed terms 389
  occupation as guarantee 393
  reparations 391–2
  territorial settlement 390–1
war crimes
  establishment of special tribunals 271–2
  responsibility for 86–7, 98, 395:
    Wilhelm II 86–7, 270–1, 274, 375, 393–4, 395
Vervins, Treaty of (1598)
  amicitia 41
  confirmation by oath 23
  hostages as guarantee 28
  papal enforcement jurisdiction and 27
  parties 17–18
  prisoners of war 41
  registration 19
  reprisal, right of 42
  respublica christiana and 33
  third parties, inclusion 34–5
  trade provisions 41
  as treaty of Holy Alliance 30
Verzijl 35
Vienna, Congress of (1736) 52
Vienna, Congress of (1815)
  institutional arrangements 92
  personal amnesty 86
  third parties, inclusion 74
Vienna Convention on the Law of Treaties (1969)
  coercion, effect on treaties 384–5
  oral agreements 163 n. 5
  power to conclude treaty 133
  war and 133 n. 87

Vienna, Treaty of (1866), territorial settlement 89
Villafranca, Treaty of (1859) (preliminary peace treaty) 71–2
Vitoria, F. de 10–11
ius as *facultas* 219–21
ius gentium
   non-European states 12–13, 68, 227–8
   rationality and 225–9
   moral/amoral concepts of law of nations 209
   positivism 212
   sovereignty 32–3
Völkerrecht: *see* law of nations (*ius gentium*/*Völkerrecht*)
voluntary law: *see ius voluntarium* (voluntary law)

Wallenstein, A. von 322–3
Wallerstein, I. 291–2, 298–9
war: *see also* just war; war, laws of
   changing concept 98, 310–11, 383
   fluidity 410–11
   as professional matter 370–1
   total war concept 367–8
   UN Charter and
   economic developments and existence of
   Arab–Israeli conflict 379
   armistice, relevance 379
   fiscal problems as cause/result 320
   Muslim concept 338–9
   as natural state
      Ancient Rome 105–6, 117, 118–19, 122, 125 n. 38, 244
      Hobbesian concept of society 14
   organisation of, Peace of Prague (1635) and 323
   public opinion and 66
   renunciation: *see* Hague Conferences (1899/1907); Kellogg–Briand Pact (1928); League of Nations; United Nations Charter (1945)
   responsibility for: *see also* Versailles, Treaty of (1919), as unequal treaty; war crimes, responsibility for
      in case of rebellion 40
      changing attitudes towards 383
   Punic Wars 130–1
   sovereign's monopolisation of 39, 42, 43, 410–11
   termination: *see* armistice/preliminary peace agreements; truce
   treaties, effect on: *see* FCN treaties, termination by war
   Vienna Convention on the Law of Treaties (1969) and 133 n. 87
war crimes
   consent and 284–6
   extradition and 283, 284
   jurisdiction
      head of state 270–1, 274
      League of Nations 277
      Leipzig Trials 284, 394–5
      over nationals 274, 281–2
      Oppenheim, L. 281–6
   responsibility for: *see also* amnesty; head of state, war crimes, responsibility for; liability
      Commission on Responsibility of Authors of the War (1920) 270, 284–5 n. 2
      individual as subject of international law and 282–3, 284, 400
   nullum crimen nulla poena sine lege 284–6, 393–4
   superior orders 282
   Versailles, Treaty of (1919) 86–7, 98, 274, 395, 400: establishment of special tribunals 271–2, 394–5
war guilt: *see* war, responsibility for; Versailles, Treaty of (1919), as unequal treaty; war crimes, responsibility for
war, laws of: *see also* amnesty clauses; just war; prisoners of war; reprisal, right of; restitution

Waterway Commissions 93
Watson, A. 109
Weber, M. 235–6
Wehberg, H. 266–8
Wendt, A. 310
Westlake, J. 262
Westminster, Treaty of (1474) (I)
  amicitia 36
  parties 17–18
  succession and 21
Westphalia Peace Treaties (1648): *see also* Münster, Treaty of (1648); Osnabrück, Treaty of (1648)
  full powers 157
  fundamental turning point, whether 4, 9–10, 43–4, 45–50
  institutional arrangements 92
  as internal constitutional-religious settlement 10, 323–5
  international relations, relevance to 9–10, 406–8
  ius foederis 325–7, 331–6
  ius publicum Europaeum and 406–9
  professionalism 233–4
  respublica christiana and 46–7
  as *restitutio status quo ante* 326–7
  restitution and 236–7
  sovereignty and 9–10, 43–4, 337, 408–9
  third-state guarantees 55
  uti possidetis 229–36, 237

Wilhelm II
  arraignment for offences against international morality and the sanctity of treaties 86–7, 270–1, 274
  Dutch refusal to extradite 283, 284, 393–4
  US opposition 283
Wilson, President W. 90, 385–6, 389, 402
Windelbrand, W. 291 n. 2
Winkel, L. 118–19
World War I: *see also* Paris, Peace Treaties (1919/20); Versailles, Treaty of (1919)
  armistice agreements (1918) 71

Yugoslavia (Kingdom of the Serbs, Croats and Slovenes), establishment 90

Ziegler, K.-H. 222, 223–4
Zorn, P. 266–8
Zsitvatorok, Treaty of (1606) 345–6
Zurich, Treaty of (1859) (I)
  object and purpose 80
  personal amnesty 86
  renewal of FCN treaty 372–3
  rights of inhabitants 91
  territorial settlement 89
Zurich, Treaty of (1859) (II), personal amnesty 86

For EU product safety concerns, contact us at Calle de José Abascal, 56-1°, 28003 Madrid, Spain or eugpsr@cambridge.org.